WITHDRAWN
HARVARD LIBRARY
WITHDRAWN

The Church & the Land

The National Catholic Rural Life Conference
and American Society, 1923–2007

David S. Bovée

The Catholic University of America Press Washington, D.C.

Copyright © 2010
The Catholic University of America Press
All rights reserved
The paper used in this publication meets the minimum requirements of American National Standards for Information Science—Permanence of Paper for Printed Library Materials, ANSI Z39.48-1984.
∞

Library of Congress Cataloging-in-Publication Data
Bovée, David S. (David Steven), 1952–
The church and the land : the National Catholic Rural Life Conference and American society, 1923–2007 / David S. Bovée.
p. cm.
Includes bibliographical references and index.
ISBN 978-0-8132-1720-8 (cloth : alk. paper)
1. Rural churches—United States. 2. Catholic Church—United States. 3. National Catholic Rural Life Conference (U.S.) I. National Catholic Rural Life Conference (U.S.) II. Title.
BX1407.R8B68 2010
282'.73091734—dc22   2009030756

For my mother and in memory of my father

Contents

	List of Tables	viii
	List of Illustrations	ix
	Preface	xi
1	Catholic Rural America to 1920	1
2	O'Hara and the Formation of the Conference	32
3	The Catholic Rural Population Problem	58
4	The Great Depression	85
5	Programs to Meet the Crisis	102
6	Inside the NCRLC	129
7	Ligutti Takes the Helm	152
8	The Conference Becomes International	176
9	Helping Developing Countries	192
10	The End of the Ligutti Era	224
11	Organizing for Social Involvement	231
12	For the Family Farm in the Age of Agribusiness	271
13	Fighting Poverty	313
14	Stewardship of the Planet	336
15	Catholic and American: The NCRLC over Eight Decades	358
	Bibliography	367
	Index	383

Tables

1	Catholic Rural Population in the United States, 1926	15
2	Catholic Rural Ethnic Groups in the United States, 1920	16
3	NCRLC Income and Expenses, 1942–60	174
4	Protestants and Catholics in the U.S. Population, 1920s to 1950s	360

Illustrations

Photographs are reprinted courtesy of Marquette University Archives unless noted otherwise

1	Edwin V. O'Hara	33
2	Religious vacation school, Forest Grove, Oregon, 1927	65
3	William Howard Bishop	80
4	Eleanor Roosevelt visiting Granger Homesteads, 1936	113
5	James Byrnes	135
6	Rural youth field Mass, St. Cloud, Minnesota, 1941	141
7	Luigi G. Ligutti speaking at Jefferson City convention, 1941	154
8	Edwin V. O'Hara with NCRLC officers and staff, about 1950	159
9	Symbols of rural life at the St. Cloud convention, 1957	164
10	Statuettes of St. Isidore and St. Maria della Cabeza Courtesy of National Catholic Rural Life Conference (NCRLC), *Rural Life Conference* (November 1957, p. 16)	168
11	International Rural Life Congress, Rome, 1962 Foto Attualita Giordani (official photographer of *Osservatore Romano*)	179
12	Monsignor Ligutti with Pope Pius XII Pontifica Fotographia	180
13	Hybrid seed corn donated by NCRLC Pressebild DCV, Frankfurt	195
14	Monsignor Ligutti as Vatican observer to the United Nations Food and Agriculture Organization Courtesy of NCRLC, *Catholic Rural Life* (January 1977, p. 22)	199

15	Bishop Edward W. O'Rourke at West Indies self-help project, 1973	205
16	James Vizzard, S.J., with other religious leaders	234
17	John McRaith	238
18	Pope John Paul II speaking at Living History Farms, Des Moines, Iowa, October 1979 Courtesy of NCRLC, *Catholic Rural Life* (October 1979, cover)	247
19	Gregory D. Cusack Courtesy of NCRLC, *Catholic Rural Life* (February 1985, p. 20)	250
20	Sandra La Blanc Courtesy of NCRLC, *Annual Report* (1995–1996, p. 3)	260
21	Bishop Maurice Dingman of Des Moines at family farm rally, Ames, Iowa, February 27, 1985 Courtesy of NCRLC, *Catholic Rural Life* (July 1985, p. 6)	293
22	Farm Unity Rally, Audubon, Iowa, June 3, 1985 Courtesy of NCRLC, *Catholic Rural Life* (July 1985, p. 10)	295
23	David Andrews Courtesy of NCRLC, *Rural Landscapes* (April 2000, p. 5)	311
24	Migrant farm workers	317
25	Black and white children at Glymount, Maryland, 1929 Courtesy of U.S. Conference of Catholic Bishops, *NCWC Bulletin* (July 1929, p. 7)	331

Preface

This book is a history of the National Catholic Rural Life Conference (NCRLC) and its relations to American society from its founding in 1923 to 2007. Previous work in American Catholic history has concentrated on the urban Church to the virtual exclusion of its rural component. This study gives due attention to this neglected rural component by providing the first scholarly history of the twentieth-century American Catholic rural movement, as embodied by the NCRLC.

The major thesis of this book is that the NCRLC maintained its basic principles throughout its history, but also changed the focus of its activities over the years in response to changes in American society as a whole. By these accumulated changes, the NCRLC "Americanized" or accommodated itself to its milieu, in much the same way as historian Philip Gleason described the assimilation of Catholics to American society over the course of the twentieth century. Yet the accommodation process was not all one way. For the NCRLC also tried to persuade American society to adopt its own principles concerning rural life. The Conference assumed the prophetic role of the Church and urged Americans to adopt rural life policies that it believed were called for by Christian values. It had success in certain areas, although in the main the powerful forces shaping rural America in the twentieth century proved impervious to the efforts of the tiny NCRLC. Thus the Conference was more changed than changer—a not unusual result for a small group trying to influence a complex society.

This work is an institutional and intellectual, not a social, study of twentieth-century rural Catholicism. It focuses on the ideas, purposes, and accomplishments of a comparatively small group of rural Catholic leaders, rather than on the masses of rural Catholics. It is history primarily "from the top down," not "from the bottom up." It could well be complemented by a "people's history" of the rural Catholic laity written "from the bottom up," like Jay P. Dolan's history of American Catholics, *The*

American Catholic Experience. My book is somewhat different from Jeffrey D. Marlett's recent work on twentieth-century American Catholic agrarianism, *Saving the Heartland.* Marlett's book takes a wider look at rural Catholicism than I do—beyond the NCRLC to include the Catholic Worker, literary figures, and related non-Catholic people, movements, and organizations—but over a shorter time span (1920–60).

Since my story concerns rural Catholics' "Americanization," it will be proper here to briefly explain what I presuppose that process to entail. I take the view that in becoming more "American" the NCRLC was conforming more and more to the dominant values of the United States. In the twentieth century, America was urbanizing and secularizing. Organization of interest groups was becoming the key to functioning successfully in a more diverse society. The United States became a world power in the twentieth century and claimed the mission of projecting its democratic and humane values, economic abundance, and technology to the rest of the globe along with its military might. Toward the end of the twentieth century, Americans developed a concern for the earth's environment, which they began to view in a more holistic way. The NCRLC was influenced by all of these trends.

The book is generally structured chronologically. The first chapter provides the background by discussing the settlement of Catholics in rural America up to 1920 and their characteristics. The next two chapters cover mainly the 1920s—the formation of the NCRLC and its preoccupation at that time with the Catholic rural population problem. Chapter 3, however, goes beyond the 1920s to complete the examination of the NCRLC's dwindling concern for the population problem. Chapters 4 through 6 are mostly on the 1930s—the impact of the Great Depression in turning the Conference's attention to the rural economy (with a flashback on the NCRLC's positions on economic issues during the 1920s), the Conference's programs to meet the crisis, and its internal workings during that decade. The next four chapters concentrate on the era of Monsignor Luigi G. Ligutti's leadership of the NCRLC from 1940 to 1960. Chapter 7 covers Ligutti's changes in the organization of the NCRLC. Chapters 8 and 9 chronicle the Conference's interest in international rural life that started under Ligutti and persisted into the twenty-first century. These two chapters somewhat violate chronological order by continuing the narrative of the Conference's international concerns beyond Ligutti's departure in 1960 all the way to the present. Chapter 10 recounts the troubled end of the Ligutti era. Chapter 11 is another organizational chapter on the NCRLC from 1960 to the pres-

Preface

ent. Chapters 12 through 14 discuss three major concerns of the Conference during this last period—the family farm, rural poverty, and the environment. The last chapter provides a summing up and conclusions regarding the NCRLC's history.

In researching and writing this book, I have received help along the way from many individuals and institutions. Professor Arthur Mann of the University of Chicago guided my work, and professors Kathleen Conzen and Neil Harris contributed many useful suggestions. Joan Allman was typist for an early version of the book. Charles B. Elston and Matthew Blessing, directors of the Marquette University Archives, archivist Philip Runkel, and other members of their staffs provided not only efficient access to the records of the NCRLC, but a friendly environment in which to work. I received similar courteous service from Anthony Zito and his staff at the Catholic University of America Archives, the Most Reverend George K. Fitzsimons and his staff at the Kansas City Archdiocesan Archives, Harvey Johnson and his staff at the Catholic Central Union of America Archives, H. Warren Willis at the United States Catholic Conference Archives, and Joyce Suellentrop at the Newman University Archives. The reverends Gerald Foley and John Zeitler and Gregory Cusack and their staffs provided hospitality and assistance during my visits to NCRLC headquarters in Des Moines. The most reverends Edward W. O'Rourke, John J. McRaith, and Maurice Dingman, and the reverends Leonard Kayser, Albert Ruschman, and Noel Hickie, past NCRLC officials, kindly consented to be interviewed. Professor Robert P. Hay of Marquette University read several chapters and contributed valuable suggestions. Monsignor George Higgins and Professor Clyde Crews read an earlier form of this manuscript and professors Margaret McGuinness and Jeffrey Marlett a later version; all made useful suggestions. The Reverend Francis Paul Prucha, S.J., and Gladys Bovee went meticulously through the entire manuscript and made numerous suggestions for improvement in both style and substance. Fort Hays State University generously supported the completion of the manuscript with a research grant. The staffs of the Department of History and the Forsyth Library at Fort Hays State University provided valuable assistance. David McGonagle, Theresa Walker, Elizabeth Benevides, and Susan Lantz of the Catholic University of America Press helped the manuscript through the press. My late father, Warren G. Bovee, and mother, Gladys Bovee, among all they have given me, always supported my pursuit of the academic life.

The Church & the Land

Chapter 1 Catholic Rural America to 1920

The Formation of the Catholic Rural Minority

The Catholic rural life movement in the United States was a response to the weakness of the Catholic Church in the American countryside. In 1920, when the movement began, only about one-fifth of American Catholics lived in the country, whereas the United States as a whole was about evenly divided between urban and rural dwellers.[1] The initial motive behind the Catholic rural life movement was the desire to redress this imbalance of Catholic residence. How did the numerical weakness of the Catholic Church in America's countryside come about?

At the time of American independence, most of the thirty-five thousand Catholics in the United States, like the vast majority of their fellow citizens, lived on the land. Most of them were Anglo-Catholics who lived on small farms either in the Calverts' Maryland or in Pennsylvania—to which they were attracted by the Quaker colony's tolerant attitude toward all religious faiths. In the nation's early years, these rural Catholics planted colonies in Kentucky and Ohio and linked up with French Catholic settlements and Indian missions in the Ohio and Mississippi river valleys. As late as 1820, the Catholic population of the United States was still found mainly on farms and in small villages.[2]

But the Catholic Church in America did not continue to be dominated by small groups of rural English, French, and Spanish Catholics. Instead, the Church was primarily shaped by the flood of immigrants that arrived in America from 1820 to 1920 and soon overwhelmed the old-stock Catholics in both numbers and influence. The vast majority of Catholic immi-

---

1. Raymond Philip Witte, *Twenty-five Years of Crusading: A History of the National Catholic Rural Life Conference* (Des Moines, Iowa: National Catholic Rural Life Conference, 1948), 1, 50, 57–58.

2. For the Catholic population in the new nation, see Gerald Shaughnessy, *Has the Immigrant Kept the Faith? A Study of Immigration and Catholic Growth in the United States, 1790–1920* (New York: Macmillan, 1925), 51–52.

grants, whether they were from Ireland, Germany, Italy, Poland, or any of the smaller nations of Europe, had lived on the land in the old country as small farmers or peasants. When they left their homes and migrated to the New World, most of them desired to be farmers there as well.[3] But only a minority succeeded in settling on the land.

Catholics were among the pioneers on the succession of American frontiers who often gave up church and community for the enticements of cheap land and an unfettered lifestyle. Some of these Catholic pioneers, along with others who came later, formed communities, built churches, and called upon pastors to come and serve them. These new parishes in turn attracted more Catholic settlers, many of them friends and relatives of those already a part of the community.[4]

The first Catholics to settle in rural New England were Irish immigrants who, between 1815 and 1845, landed at St. John, New Brunswick, and then traveled south by land or sea. Initially, most of the participants in this "second colonization of New England" worked as itinerant laborers on canals and railroads or in factories, but eventually a number of them found homes on the land. Of the diverse immigrants into New England later in the century, a small percentage, among whom French Canadians were prominent, also joined that region's always small Catholic rural population.[5]

In the middle Atlantic states, the original Anglo-Catholic settlers were overwhelmed by the new immigrants in the nineteenth century. There, Irish immigrants, like their countrymen in New England, bought farms after first working in country areas as road, canal, or railroad builders. A number of French Canadians, employed as miners and lumberjacks as well as farmers, populated the northern part of New York State. But Germans

---

3. Oscar Handlin, *The Uprooted: The Epic Story of the Great Migrations That Made the American People* (New York: Grosset & Dunlap, 1951), 7–36, 63–64; Kathleen Neils Conzen, "Peasant Pioneers: Generational Succession among German Farmers in Frontier Minnesota," in *The Countryside in the Age of Capitalist Transformations: Essays in the Social History of Rural America*, ed. Steven Hahn and Jonathan Prude (Chapel Hill: University of North Carolina Press, 1985), 259–92.

4. Dennis Clark, *Hibernia America: The Irish and Regional Cultures*, Contributions in Ethnic Studies 14 (Westport, Conn.: Greenwood Press, 1986), 1–12; Jon Gjerde, *The Minds of the West: Ethnocultural Evolution in the Rural Middle West, 1830–1917* (Chapel Hill: University of North Carolina Press, 1997), 92–100; Jeffrey D. Marlett, *Saving the Heartland: Catholic Missionaries in Rural America, 1920–1960* (De Kalb: Northern Illinois University Press, 2002), 93–96.

5. Robert H. Lord, John E. Sexton, and Edward T. Harrington, *History of the Archdiocese of Boston in the Various Stages of Its Development, 1604 to 1943*, 3 vols. (New York: Sheed & Ward, 1944), 2:110–40, 2:146–48, 2:275–77, 2:569–73, 3:189–238; Augustus J. Thebaud, *Forty Years in the United States of America (1839–1885)*, United States Catholic Historical Society Monograph Series 2 (New York: United States Catholic Historical Society, 1904), 132–33.

were by far the most numerous Catholic ethnic group to settle in the rural areas of the middle Atlantic states. In New York they settled in the fertile river valleys, such as the Mohawk, and in Pennsylvania they scattered to good farming areas all over the state.[6]

Very few Catholics settled in the rural South, except in Louisiana, where a culture that was the heritage of over a century of French and Spanish rule continued to attract large numbers of Catholic immigrants from many different lands. A large proportion of these immigrants lived on the state's plantations and farms. Most rural Irish in the southern states built the region's canals, levees, and railroads, but eventually gravitated to the cities. Some free blacks in the rural South and African American slaves owned by Catholic masters were converted to Catholicism. A small number of rural Italian colonies were planted in the southern states, in part because of the congenial climate.[7]

West of the Appalachians, the early Anglo-Catholic settlements in Kentucky were augmented by immigration. From Kentucky, the East Coast, and Europe, Catholics streamed into rural areas in Ohio, Indiana, and Illinois early in the nineteenth century. The new settlers of the Midwest came from almost every Catholic land. In addition to the old strains of Anglo-Americans, Irish, French Canadians, and Germans (who settled so heavily here that the Midwest became known as the "German Belt"), "new" immigrant nationalities such as French, Italians, Dutch, Belgians, Swiss, Poles, Czechs, Hungarians, and Lithuanians all formed Catholic rural communities of their own. These immigrants often purchased improved lands from American-born homesteaders who sold at a profit and moved on. The

---

6. Frederick J. Zwierlein, *The Life and Letters of Bishop McQuaid*, 3 vols. (Rochester, N.Y.: Art Print Shop, 1926), 1:1–290; Martin Joseph Becker, *A History of Catholic Life in the Diocese of Albany, 1609–1864*, United States Catholic Historical Society Monograph Series 31 (New York: United States Catholic Historical Society, 1975); Mary Christine Taylor, *A History of the Foundations of Catholicism in Northern New York*, United States Catholic Historical Society Monograph Series 32 (New York: United States Catholic Historical Society, 1976); Hugh J. Nolan, *The Most Reverend Francis Patrick Kenrick, Third Bishop of Philadelphia, 1830–1851* (Philadelphia: American Catholic Historical Society of Philadelphia, 1948); Joseph M. O'Hara, *Chester's Century of Catholicism, 1842–1942* (Philadelphia: Peter Reilly, 1942).

7. Randall M. Miller and Jon L. Wakelyn, eds., *Catholics in the Old South: Essays on Church and Culture* (Macon, Ga.: Mercer University Press, 1983); Roger Baudier, *The Catholic Church in Louisiana* (New Orleans: Roger Baudier, 1939); Rowland T. Berthoff, "Southern Attitudes toward Immigration, 1865–1914," *Journal of Southern History* 17 (August 1951): 332, 343–44; Andrew F. Rolle, *The Immigrant Upraised: Italian Adventures and Colonists in an Expanding America* (Norman: University of Oklahoma Press, 1968), 55–58, 73–90; Jean Anne Scarpaci, "Immigrants in the New South: Italians in Louisiana's Sugar Parishes, 1880–1910," in *Studies in Italian-American Social History: Essays in Honor of Leonard Covello*, ed. Francesco Cordasco (Totowa, N.J.: Rowman & Littlefield, 1975), 132–52; David T. Gleeson, *The Irish in the South, 1815–1877* (Chapel Hill: University of North Carolina Press, 2001), 33–35.

immigrant farmers, however, tended to stay on a plot of land once they settled there. Put together, the various immigrant nationalities made the Midwest the region with the nation's largest concentration of rural Catholics by 1920.[8]

In the Pacific Northwest and Rocky Mountain states, the Church followed in the wake of Catholic trappers, miners, and farmers. The relatively small number of rural Catholics in this region took advantage of cheap land and bountiful opportunity. One of the Church's most important preoccupations in the rural areas of this region was its care for Catholic Indians.[9]

The same was true for the Southwest, where Catholic Indian missions in the territory of the future United States dated from the Spanish conquistador Francisco Coronado's expedition of 1540 to 1542. By the time of the incorporation of this area into the United States following the Mexican War, some 108,000 Catholics lived in the states or future states of Texas, New Mexico, Arizona, and California. Most of these were rural Hispanic Americans and Indians, survivors from the old Spanish missions. Immigration into the area before 1920 greatly increased the urban and Anglo-American proportions of the population. In spite of that, the Southwest was still a fairly rural and Catholic region in 1920.[10]

Although many Catholic immigrants did settle in rural America, for most of them their original vision of a new life on the land became an unfulfilled dream. Many of the newcomers spent most of their meager savings on tickets and provisions for their crossing and could not afford to purchase a farm. They took employment in the cities, hoping to earn

---

8. The generalizations in this paragraph are based on numerous regional, ethnic, and diocesan histories. For immigrant land acquisition and tenure, see Joseph Schafer, *The Social History of American Agriculture* (New York: Macmillan, 1936), 30, 215–16.

9. Cyprian Bradley and Edward J. Kelly, *History of the Diocese of Boise, 1863–1952*, 2 vols. (Boise, Idaho: Diocese of Boise, 1953); Dominic O'Connor, *A Brief History of the Diocese of Baker City* (Baker City, Ore.: Diocesan Chancery, 1930); James P. Walsh, "The Irish in the New America: 'Way Out West,'" in *America and Ireland, 1776–1976: The American Identity and the Irish Connection*, The Proceedings of the United States Bicentennial Conference of Cumann Merriman, Ennis, August, 1976, ed. David Noel Doyle and Owen Dudley Edwards (Westport, Conn.: Greenwood Press, 1980), 165–66; Rolle, *Immigrant Upraised*.

10. See various regional and diocesan histories. The 108,000 figure was totaled from 25,000 in Texas from the Knights of Columbus of Texas, *Our Catholic Heritage in Texas, 1519–1936*, ed. James P. Gibbons and William H. Oberste, vol. 7: *The Church in Texas since Independence, 1836–1950, Supplement, 1936–1950*, by Carlos Castaneda, 109 (Austin, Tex.: Von Boeckman-Jones, 1936–1950); 68,000 in New Mexico and Arizona from Paul Horgan, *Lamy of Santa Fe: His Life and Times* (New York: Farrar, Straus & Giroux, 1975), 127; and 15,000 in California from Peter Thomas Conmy, "Catholicism along the Gold Dust Trails," in *Some California Catholic Reminiscences for the United States Bicentennial*, ed. Francis J. Weber: Published for the California Catholic Conference by the Knights of Columbus, 1976), 108.

the money needed to buy a homestead. In the majority of cases, however, they were never able to save enough to make this important purchase, and their "temporary" stay in the city lengthened to a permanent one. Catholic immigrants who arrived after the "closing of the frontier" in 1890 had particular difficulty in settling on the land. Good agricultural land became extremely scarce, and the land that was available often had to be reclaimed or irrigated. In addition, land prices were rising, and immigrants with their scanty savings were usually outbid for farms by American-born farmers with more capital.

Many Catholic immigrants found to their chagrin that their agricultural skills were unsuited to American farming conditions. The Irish peasants' techniques for growing small patches of potatoes were inapplicable to the large corn or wheat fields of the American Midwest. The use of farm machinery was unknown to Irish and Italian peasants alike. Many of the immigrants could not make the transition from the closely knit villages of Europe to the widely separated homesteads of the prairies, where, in the words of an Irishman who settled on a Missouri farm, "They calls them neighbors that live two or three miles off."[11]

Other immigrant peasants had no desire to return to the land. For many Catholic Irish, for instance, the land was a symbol of the poverty and oppression that they suffered in their English-dominated homeland. Such immigrants settled gladly in the cities.[12]

Finally, many Catholic immigrants stayed in the cities because churches, schools, and charitable institutions were concentrated there. The shortage of priests in the nineteenth-century United States demanded that facilities be clustered in centers where they would serve the largest number of communicants most efficiently. Therefore, Catholics who desired to receive the sacraments frequently and to live near a church usually had to settle in the cities. Similarly, urban centers attracted Catholic families who felt that the public schools were tainted with Protestant influence and wished their children to attend parochial schools. Needy immigrants often found the succor of Catholic orphanages, hospitals, and poorhouses in their ports of arrival. A pattern developed in which urban immigrants

---

11. Handlin, *Uprooted*, 63–93; Maldwyn Allen Jones, *American Immigration* (Chicago: University of Chicago Press, 1960), 118; Carl Wittke, *The Irish in America* (Baton Rouge: Louisiana State University Press, 1956), 62; Robert F. Foerster, *The Italian Immigration of Our Times* (Cambridge, Mass.: Harvard University Press, 1924), 371–72. The quotation is from William Forbes Adams, *Ireland and Irish Immigration to the New World from 1815 to the Famine* (New Haven, Conn.: Yale University Press, 1932), 342, quoting *Belfast News Letter*, April 17, 1821.

12. Gleeson, *Irish in the South*, 23–24; Jones, *American Immigration*, 121–22.

and Catholic institutions served as magnets mutually attracting each other to the cities. The whole process greatly accelerated the cityward trend of Catholic immigration.[13]

This pattern of urban settlement of immigrants near Catholic institutions was encouraged by many Church leaders, who feared that if Catholics settled in the country, they would be beyond the spiritual care of the Church and drift away to be converted by the numerous rural Protestants or simply slip into unbelief. Indeed, Protestant missionary societies competed with Catholics for souls in the Midwest, and a Protestant historian averred in 1888 that many immigrants deserted the Roman faith and that "this country is the biggest grave for popery ever dug on earth." Typical of the converts was a German Catholic farmer in Texas, "who, curious about a Methodist camp meeting held in his neighborhood, sneaked up to observe the affair from the concealment of some bushes. He became so caught up in the emotional goings on that he emerged from his hiding place and converted."[14]

Catholics in rural areas lacked many religious services in the nineteenth and early twentieth centuries. Priests doing mission work in rural areas sometimes discovered whole enclaves of unserved Catholics. Some communities waited years before obtaining a priest, and other scattered areas were served infrequently in "circuit rider" fashion. In western South Dakota, Catholics might have services only once a month, and that on a weeknight. In rural Michigan, some Catholics were unbaptized and uncatechized, or never received first communion. They had trouble attending Mass because of distance or poor roads. One pastor of a multiethnic parish had to import confessors who spoke German, French, Hungarian, and Polish. Some German Catholics there were members of proscribed secret societies or attended Christian Scientist services.[15]

---

13. Jones, *American Immigration*, 121–22; John Tracy Ellis, *American Catholicism* (Chicago: University of Chicago Press, 1956), 52–56.

14. Mark Wyman, *Immigrants in the Valley: Irish, Germans, and Americans in the Upper Mississippi Country, 1830–1860* (Chicago: Nelson-Hall, 1984), 107, 128; R. Laurence Moore, *Religious Outsiders and the Making of Americans* (New York: Oxford University Press, 1986), 11; Terry G. Jordan, "A Religious Geography of the Hill Country Germans of Texas," in *Ethnicity on the Great Plains*, ed. Frederick C. Luebke (Lincoln: University of Nebraska Press for the Center for Great Plains Studies, 1980), 113.

15. Marlett, *Saving the Heartland*, 92–95; Wyman, *Immigrants in the Valley*, 132–34; Paula M. Nelson, *After the West Was Won: Homesteaders and Town-builders in Western South Dakota, 1900–1917* (Iowa City: University of Iowa Press, 1986), 72; Leslie Woodcock Tentler, *Seasons of Grace: A History of the Catholic Archdiocese of Detroit* (Detroit: Wayne State University Press, 1990), 198–200, 406; Tentler, "'A Model Rural Parish': Priests and People in the Michigan 'Thumb,' 1923–1928," *Catholic Historical Review* 78 (1992): 418–19.

Catholic Rural America to 1920   7

The problem of loss of immigrants from the faith, which concerned the Catholic leadership until well into the twentieth century, became known as "leakage" from the Church. As early as 1836, Bishop John England of Charleston, South Carolina, estimated that of 5 million Catholics who had thus far entered the United States and their descendants, 3,750,000 had been lost to the faith. The Lucerne Memorial of 1891, which was presented to Pope Leo XIII by delegates of European emigrant aid societies, put the loss at 16 million. Two years later, Mary Theresa Elder, the fiery niece of Cincinnati's archbishop, upped the number of apostates to 20 million. She gave the following explanation: "Going into the country, there, far from priests and Sacraments those immigrants prosper materially perhaps, but spiritually they starve. It is most natural then that their descendants, fed only by Protestantism, become exemplary Baptists, Methodists, Campbellites, etc." Although these extravagant claims were questioned at the time, charges that millions were lost to the faith continued until well into the twentieth century.[16]

These charges inspired a strong missionary movement that aimed at reclaiming those souls lost by leakage. European missionary societies such as the Society for the Propagation of the Faith of Lyons and Paris, the Ludwig-Missionsverein of Bavaria, and the Leopoldine Stiftung of Vienna contributed millions of dollars during the nineteenth century to build churches, seminaries, and monasteries, educate and support immigrant priests, and even pay the normal expenses of missionary dioceses in the United States. By the early twentieth century, American Catholics joined in the effort, especially directing their attention to rural areas. The Catholic Missionary Union (founded by the Paulists in 1896) conducted much of its work in rural districts of the South and West, and the Catholic Church Extension Society (founded in 1905) proved phenomenally successful in building churches and chapels and providing other religious services in the countryside. In 1908 and 1913, two impressive missionary congresses held in Chicago and Boston gave a great boost to the movement and inspired the formation of new rural missionary communities, such as the Society of Missionary Catechists of Our Blessed Lady of Victory, founded in 1918 to serve the Spanish-speaking Catholics of the Southwest. Finally, in 1919,

---

16. Shaughnessy, *Has the Immigrant Kept the Faith?* 223–45; Roger Finke and Rodney Stark, *The Churching of America, 1776–1990: Winners and Losers in Our Religious Economy* (New Brunswick, N.J.: Rutgers University Press, 1992), 110–15; quotation of Mary Theresa Elder from "Our Twenty Millions Loss," *Boston Pilot*, September 30, 1893; responses to her charges, ibid., September 21, 30; October 21, 1893.

the American Board of Catholic Missions was formed, which funded a number of rural-related causes aimed at countering leakage, including, eventually, the National Catholic Rural Life Conference.[17]

Concern about leakage continued, and it was not until 1925 that the first statistical study of the subject, Bishop Gerald Shaughnessy's *Has the Immigrant Kept the Faith?* proved that the loss had been negligible. Subsequent studies of Protestant missionary efforts among Catholic immigrants exposed their expensive futility and confirmed Shaughnessy's findings.[18] But in the nineteenth century, the prevailing view, at least among the urban majority of Catholics, was that the cities were the only secure haven for the faith and that distribution of Catholics over rural areas carried an unacceptable risk.

For the Catholic leadership in the nineteenth century, the only permissible settlement of Catholics in rural areas was their concentration in colonies where their spiritual needs could be provided for. The idea of settling the ever more numerous boatloads of immigrants and the poverty-stricken masses of the cities in self-sufficient agricultural communities was a popular one among the American hierarchy—almost every bishop had a pet colonization scheme. The primary reason was the concern over loss of faith. Only if Catholic rural dwellers were concentrated in sizable communities, colonizers argued, could the Church afford to provide them with churches, schools, hospitals and other facilities. Only such all-Catholic settlements, well cared for by the Church, would be free from the danger of succumbing to the surrounding Protestants and unbelievers.[19]

In addition, Catholics, like most Americans of the time, believed in the moral superiority of the agrarian way of life. In the United States, this belief was associated with the Jeffersonian ideal of agrarian democracy, including its faith in the yeoman farmer as the most virtuous citizen of

---

17. Wyman, *Immigrants in the Valley*, 134–39; Aaron I. Abell, *American Catholicism and Social Action: A Search for Social Justice, 1865–1950* (Garden City, N.Y.: Hanover House, 1960), 119, 156; Francis C. Kelley, *The Story of Extension* (Chicago: Extension Press, 1922); Kelley, ed., *The First American Catholic Missionary Congress* (Chicago: J. S. Hyland., 1909); "Boston's Great Missionary Congress," *Boston Pilot*, October 25, 1913; J. J. Sigstein, "The Work of Rural Religious Communities," *Catholic Rural Life* 3 (April 1925): 1–2; *New Catholic Encyclopedia*, 1967 ed. s.v., "American Board of Catholic Missions," by R. Trisco.

18. Shaughnessy, *Has the Immigrant Kept the Faith?*; Theodore F. Abel, *Protestant Home Missions to Catholic Immigrants* (New York: Institute of Social and Religious Research, 1933); Lawrence B. Davis, *Immigrants, Baptists, and the Protestant Mind in America* (Urbana: University of Illinois Press, 1973), 71–76, 109–30; Leo Grebler et al., *The Mexican-American People: The Nation's Second Largest Minority* (New York: Free Press, 1970), 486–512.

19. Deirdre M. Moloney, *American Catholic Lay Groups and Transatlantic Social Reform in the Progressive Era* (Chapel Hill: University of North Carolina Press, 2002), 75–76.

the Republic. The deeper roots of agrarian idealism, however, go back to the birthplace of America's immigrant culture—the predominantly agricultural and deeply religious society of pre-industrial Europe. It was there that the rural and religious values of love of God, love of nature (particularly, love of the soil), family integrity, neighborly cooperation, and hard work were first instilled into the peoples that were to migrate to America. American Catholic leaders such as Bishop John Lancaster Spalding of Peoria and Archbishop John Ireland of St. Paul therefore tended to idealize rural life as a result of both their European and their American heritages.[20]

Colonization proponents were also appalled at the dismal living conditions of poor immigrants, particularly the Irish, in the cities. Poverty, slums, dangerous working conditions, low wages, unemployment, poor family life, saloons, corrupt politics—these conditions stimulated benevolent Catholics to provide new homes on the land for their poorer brethren. Similar ideas were popular with other philanthropic Americans in the nineteenth century: The Children's Aid Society (founded in 1853) settled ninety thousand street urchins from eastern cities in rural areas of the American West.[21]

A further incentive was nativism. From the 1830s through the 1850s, resentment against Catholics—as Papists, foreigners, and competitors for unskilled employment—swept through the cities of the eastern seaboard. Anti-Catholic periodicals and books were published, nativist societies were formed, bloody riots took place, churches and convents were burned. To secure the immigrants' lives and faith, Catholic leaders such as Bishop Benedict Fenwick of Boston and journalist Thomas D'Arcy McGee urged them to settle in secluded colonies away from the sources of nativist agitation.[22]

Finally, some Catholic leaders saw in the formation of colonies the fulfillment of racial, religious, or utopian ambitions. Several Irish colonizers dreamed of founding a "New Ireland" on the Great Plains, while German nationalism was an element in the formation of German-American Catholic

---

20. See A. Whitney Griswold, *Farming and Democracy* (New York: Harcourt, Brace, 1948); John Lancaster Spalding, *Essays and Reviews* (New York: Catholic Publication Society, 1877), 179–80; James H. Moynihan, *The Life of Archbishop John Ireland* (New York: Harper & Row, 1953), 21.

21. Mary Evangela Henthorne, *The Irish Catholic Colonization Association of the United States* (Champaign, Ill.: Twin City Publishing, 1932), 2–3, 11–30, 54; John Lancaster Spalding, *The Religious Mission of the Irish People and Catholic Colonization* (New York: Catholic Colonization Society, 1880), 87, quoted in Witte, *Twenty-five Years*, 25–26; Paul Boyer, *Urban Masses and Moral Order in America, 1820–1920* (Cambridge, Mass.: Harvard University Press, 1978), 98–100.

22. R. Billington, *The Protestant Crusade, 1800–1860* (New York: Macmillan, 1938); M. G. Kelly, *Catholic Immigrant Colonization Projects* (U.S. Catholic Historical Society, 1939), 34–37, 213–17, 270.

settlements in Wisconsin and Minnesota. Bishop Spalding and Bishop Mathias Loras of Dubuque fostered colonization with the hope of spreading Catholicism throughout America. Certain colonies were founded by Catholics who desired to live in the simple, idealistic ways of early Christianity.[23]

Rural Catholic colonies engendered widespread enthusiasm but also encountered determined opposition in certain quarters. The most fervent opponent was the influential Archbishop John Hughes of New York, who condemned colonization projects for their impracticality, their intention of forming exclusive "Irish towns," and, above all, putting the displaced faithful beyond the spiritual ministrations of the Church. Hughes's opposition was probably also influenced by his personal animosity to some of the promoters of the projects and by the tendency of all of the eastern bishops to oppose colonization projects because such projects depopulated their dioceses and threatened their material investments in churches and charitable institutions. Other Church leaders opposed Catholic colonies because they feared the formation of exclusive "national" communities that would delay the Americanization of Catholic immigrants. Many Irish Catholics in both the old country and in America opposed Irish colonization schemes because they thought that providing land for immigrants on easy terms encouraged emigration from Ireland.[24]

Catholic colonization up to 1920 had some successes but mostly failures—especially in the most grandiose projects. Attempts in the early 1800s to acquire federal grants of land for Catholic immigrants ended in failure.

23. Kelly, *Catholic Immigrant Colonization Projects*, 15–18, 23, 37–47, 119–32, 163–73, 190–92, 217–27; James P. Shannon, *Catholic Colonization on the Western Frontier*, Yale Publications in American Studies 1 (New Haven, Conn.: Yale University Press, 1957), 75–76; M. Claudia Duratschek, *The Beginnings of Catholicism in South Dakota* (Washington, D.C.: The Catholic University of America Press, 1943), 136–37; Robert Savage, "Irish Colonists on the Plains," in *The American Irish Revival: A Decade of The Recorder—1974–1983*, ed. Kevin M. Cahill (Port Washington, N.Y.: Associated Faculty Press, 1984), 371–81; John A. Hawgood, *The Tragedy of German-America: The Germans in the United States of America during the Nineteenth Century—And After* (New York: G. P. Putnam's Sons, 1940), 203–8; M. M. Hoffmann, *The Church Founders of the Northwest: Loras and Cretin and Other Captains of Christ* (Milwaukee: Bruce Publishing, 1937), 338–39, 353; Lord, Sexton, and Harrington, *History of the Archdiocese of Boston*, 2:279–80.

24. On opposition to Catholic colonies, see Henry J. Browne, "Archbishop Hughes and Western Colonization," *Catholic Historical Review* 26 (October 1950): 257–85; Kelly, *Catholic Immigrant Colonization Projects*, 251–52, 267–69; John R. G. Hassard, *Life of the Most Reverend John Hughes, D.D., First Archbishop of New York* (New York: D. Appleton, 1866; reprint ed., New York: Arno Press and New York Times, 1969), 214, 392–93; Theodore Maynard, *The Story of American Catholicism* (New York: Macmillan, 1941), 448–49; Witte, *Twenty-five Years*, 13–15; John Ireland, "Right Rev. Mathias Loras, First Bishop of Dubuque," *Catholic World* 68 (October 1898): 3–4; Richard M. Linkh, *American Catholicism and European Immigrants, 1900–1924* (Staten Island, N.Y.: Center for Migration Studies, 1975), 81; Colman J. Barry, *The Catholic Church and German Americans* (Milwaukee: Bruce Publishing, 1953), 95–97; Shannon, *Catholic Colonization*, 67–69, 70–74, 81, 156; Henthorne, *Irish Catholic Colonization Association*, 94–95.

Catholic Rural America to 1920

A proposal by several emigrant aid societies in 1818 that Congress set aside certain lands in the Illinois territory to be settled by Irish immigrants on easy terms was rejected, apparently because "the Representatives could see no reason why a man from Ireland should be permitted to buy land on easier terms than a person from any of the States of the union." In 1834, Congress granted public lands to Polish exiles from the unsuccessful rebellion of 1830. But they were never settled because of confusion and entanglement in legal technicalities on the part of both the Polish agent and the government.[25]

The first colonization proposal by a member of the American hierarchy was made by Bishop John England of Charleston in the columns of his magazine, the *United States Catholic Miscellany*, in 1822. England's plan, like so many of those proposed later in the century, contemplated aiding unemployed Irish immigrants languishing in eastern cities to settle in agricultural colonies in the interior of the country. After its publication in the *Miscellany*, nothing more was heard of the idea. It may have been dropped because of an inability to raise funds, a lack of priests to provide for the colonies, an unwillingness on the part of Catholic immigrants to settle in the South, or merely a suspension of interest on Bishop England's part.[26]

Bishop England's most immediate successors in the field of Catholic colonization, Bishop Mathias Loras of Dubuque and his protégé, Bishop Joseph Cretin of St. Paul, concentrated their efforts on the Upper Mississippi River Valley instead of the South. During his episcopate at Dubuque, from 1839 to 1858, Loras wrote frequent letters to eastern newspapers encouraging immigrants to come to his northwestern diocese and provided priests to care for their spiritual needs when they arrived. He obtained yearly grants from the Propagation of the Faith Society of Lyons and Paris, the Leopoldine Society of Vienna, and the Ludwig Mission Society of Munich to finance the upkeep of his priests and the building of new churches and schools. Cretin, Loras's vicar-general until he became bishop of St. Paul in 1851, adopted his mentor's colonization methods. Cretin in turn had an able assistant in the Reverend Francis Pierz, who promoted German settlement in the St. Paul diocese and was largely responsible for the German Catholic character of Stearns County, Minnesota, which persists to this day.[27]

---

25. Only illustrative examples of Catholic colonization projects are discussed here. On these Irish and Polish projects, see Kelly, *Catholic Immigrant Colonization Projects*, 9–12, 103–5; quotation, 12.
26. Ibid., 13.
27. Hoffmann, *Church Founders of the Northwest*, particularly 338–39, 352–57; Kelly, *Catholic Immigrant Colonization Projects*, 143–73.

Probably the most successful Catholic colonizer was Archbishop John Ireland of St. Paul. His success resulted mainly from following a more realistic and businesslike plan than the other colonizers. Instead of buying land as the other colonizers did and then being faced with the necessity of finding settlers for it, Ireland merely acted as the agent for railroads selling their lands. Between 1876 and 1880, Ireland signed eleven contracts with five railroads, giving him exclusive rights as agent for 379,000 acres of land in southwestern Minnesota. On these lands the archbishop created ten Catholic colonies, each with its own church and resident pastor. At first, Ireland, like most other colonizers, intended to settle poor Irish immigrants from eastern cities. But this proved unsuccessful, and he soon required all prospective colonists to have at least four hundred dollars in cash and some farming experience. With settlers of this type, the colonies soon flourished. Although Ireland's colonies were not successful as a benevolent measure, he did provide prosperous rural homes complete with the provision of religion for some four thousand families.[28]

Another relatively successful rural colonization venture was undertaken by Poles. From 1877 to 1884, the Polish Roman Catholic Union of America, headquartered in Chicago, employed John Barzynski as an agent to settle Polish Catholics in Nebraska. The Union believed that the colonists would both prosper materially and retain their faith, language, and customs better on the soil than in eastern industrial centers. Barzynski purchased land from the Burlington and Missouri Railroad in four counties in central Nebraska and settled several hundred Polish families around towns named New Posen, Warsaw, and Choynice.[29]

Between 1876 and 1891, the Irish Catholic Benevolent Union sponsored the formation of colonies at Keileyville, Virginia, and Butler City, Kansas, and the Irish Catholic Colonization Association of the United States planted colonies at Adrian, Minnesota, and Spalding and O'Connor, Nebraska. In the first decade of the twentieth century, Archbishop Sebastian G. Messmer of Milwaukee settled German Catholics in Wisconsin, the Association of Belgian and Holland Priests guided Flemish, Walloon, and Dutch immigrants to rural parishes, and Catholics in Minnesota, Missouri, and Louisiana formed colonization organizations to settle immigrants in their states.[30]

---

28. See Shannon, *Catholic Colonization;* Moynihan, *Ireland,* 20–32.

29. Henry W. Casper, *History of the Catholic Church in Nebraska,* vol. 3: *Catholic Chapters in Nebraska Immigration, 1870–1900* (Milwaukee: Bruce Publishing, 1966), 143–89; Meroe J. Owens, "John Barzynski, Land Agent," *Nebraska History* 36 (June 1955): 81–91.

30. Joan Marie Donohoe, *The Irish Catholic Benevolent Union* (Washington, D.C.: The Catholic

Because of dissatisfaction with such narrowly based colonization efforts, the Catholic Colonization Society of the United States was chartered in 1911. It offered help to city- as well as country-bound immigrants, but in practice it concentrated on settling Catholics in agricultural colonies. The society's services were open to members of all nationalities, and it pledged to settle each family in a colony of people with a similar language and nationality. The group worked with existing land companies, ten of which eventually cooperated. The land companies informed the society of tracts available for purchase, and in each case it sent out a team of expert inspectors to examine the land and determine its suitability for a colony. Besides certifying that the site had the appropriate agronomic, climatic, and commercial characteristics, the Society's inspectors also insisted that the land companies help provide for a Catholic church and school. The group also secured help from emigration agencies in Europe at the sources of immigration.

The Catholic Colonization Society succeeded in settling thousands of Catholics in more than a dozen old and new colonies throughout the United States. In 1913, it boasted that it had "colonies in operation from Washington to Florida, and from Minnesota to Arizona." As immigration to the United States slackened during World War I, so too did the work of the society. After the war, immigration restriction laws and urban prosperity further lessened the number of immigrants searching for rural homes. Much of the Catholic immigrant settlement work was taken over by the National Catholic Welfare Conference's Bureau of Immigration. The Catholic Colonization Society slipped into obscurity and was apparently dissolved around 1928.[31]

It is impossible to say exactly how many Catholics altogether settled in rural colonies before 1920. Certainly they must have numbered many thousands—forming a significant component of Catholic rural America—for there were scores of colonies in all, each with a few hundred to a few thousand souls. There were Catholic colonies—little, devout centers of

---

University of America Press, 1953), 102–54; Shannon, *Catholic Colonization*, 74–83, 214–44; Henthorne, *Irish Catholic Colonization Association;* Moloney, *American Catholic Lay Groups*, 84–91; Barry, *Catholic Church and German Americans*, 255; Linkh, *American Catholicism and European Immigrants*, 80; John Rothsteiner, *History of the Archdiocese of St. Louis in Its Various Stages of Development from A.D. 1673 to A.D. 1928*, 2 vols. (St. Louis: Blackwell Weilandy, 1928), 2:654–55; "Association of Belgian and Holland Priests," in Kelley, *First American Catholic Missionary Congress*, 472–76.

31. Kelley, *First American Catholic Missionary Congress*, 149–51, 407–8; Abell, *Social Action*, 158; Barry, *Catholic Church and German Americans*, 254–58; Linkh, *American Catholicism and European Immigrants*, 81–84; quote from "Catholic Colonization Activity," *Milwaukee Catholic Citizen*, January 18, 1913.

Catholicity—in almost every state outside of the South, and even there in several states.

The Catholic colonization movement was not able to alter the fundamentally urban orientation of the Church. In 1920, a year in which 51.2 percent of the American population lived in urban areas and 48.8 percent in rural, the Catholic percentages were 79.6 percent urban, 20.4 percent rural. Despite the best efforts of the colonizers, rural Catholics were firmly established as a minority within the American Church.

Catholic Rural America in 1920

By 1920, not only was the minority status of rural Catholicism well established, but its social characteristics were marked as well. Many of these characteristics remained basically unchanged throughout the remainder of the century. We may therefore choose that year as a point at which to take stock of the state of Catholic rural life in America on the eve of the formation of the National Catholic Rural Life Conference.

In 1920, the Catholic rural population of the United States was 3,795,708. Table 1 shows the distribution of this population in the various regions of the United States. The table shows that approximately 1.5 million rural Catholics—or about four out of ten of the 3.8 million rural Catholics in the United States in 1920—lived in the twelve states of the Midwest. This area was the Catholic rural heartland and formed the primary base of support for the National Catholic Rural Life Conference. Within this group of states rural Catholicism was especially strong in Wisconsin, Minnesota, Iowa, Nebraska, and the Dakotas. In addition, many rural Catholics lived in the Middle Atlantic states, especially New York, New Jersey, and Pennsylvania, though their proportion of the total population of these states was not large. Other special areas of Catholic rural concentration were Louisiana and the Southwest (especially New Mexico, where rural Catholics formed over a third of the state's total population). New England and the West had an average distribution of Catholics living on the land, while the South was the only region in which their numbers were exceptionally low.

Catholic rural America in 1920 was not dominated by any single ethnic group. No hard data are available because the U.S. Census did not report data by rural religious ethnic group. If one assumes, however, that Catholics were represented in the various ethnic groups in rural America in the same proportions as they were in their homelands, the distribution of Catholics would have looked like that presented in table 2. German Americans were probably the most numerous and were particularly concentrat-

Table 1. Catholic Rural Population in the United States, 1926

Region	Total U.S. population (1)	Total Catholics (2)	Urban Catholics (3)	Rural Catholics (4)
United States	105,710,620	18,605,003	14,809,295	3,795,708
New England[a]	7,400,909	2,922,509	2,533,965	388,544
Middle Atlantic[b]	24,371,379	6,633,817	5,915,609	718,208
Midwest[c]	34,019,792	5,946,319	4,390,212	1,556,107
South[d]	24,324,057	1,066,414	673,483	392,931
Southwest[e]	8,784,601	1,547,460	975,000	572,460
West[f]	6,809,882	488,484	321,026	167,458

Source: Sum of state populations from U.S. Department of Commerce, Bureau of the Census, *Abstract of the Fourteenth Census of the United States: 1920* (Washington, D.C.: Government Printing Office, 1923), 18. Sum of state Catholic populations from U.S. Department of Commerce, Bureau of the Census, *Religious Bodies: 1926* (Washington, D.C.: Government Printing Office, 1930), 2:1256.

a. Includes Maine, Vermont, New Hampshire, Massachusetts, Rhode Island, and Connecticut.
b. Includes New York, New Jersey, Pennsylvania, Maryland, Delaware, and the District of Columbia.
c. Includes Ohio, Indiana, Illinois, Michigan, Wisconsin, Minnesota, Iowa, Missouri, North Dakota, South Dakota, Nebraska, and Kansas.
d. Includes Virginia, West Virginia, North Carolina, South Carolina, Georgia, Florida, Kentucky, Tennessee, Alabama, Mississippi, Arkansas, and Louisiana.
e. Includes Texas, New Mexico, Arizona, and California.
f. Includes Oklahoma, Montana, Idaho, Wyoming, Colorado, Utah, Nevada, Oregon, and Washington.

ed in the Catholic rural heartland. "Austrians," among whom were many Czechs and Poles as well as German-speaking immigrants from the Dual Monarchy, most likely claimed second place. The Irish and Italians, two nationalities not usually associated with rural America, were only slightly less numerous than the Austrians. The Mexican Americans were the newest and fastest-growing Catholic rural ethnic group, concentrated in the Southwest but not yet drawing much attention from the Church at large. Many other ethnic groups, such as the French Canadians, Hungarians, French, Swiss, Dutch, and Belgians, gave rural Catholicism its character of a colorful ethnic mosaic. (Not included in the table are children of native-born Catholic rural dwellers, many of whom considered themselves members of their ancestral ethnic groups.)[32]

These rural Catholics still held on to many of their immigrant ways. In such characteristics as farming techniques, living conditions, education, organizational life, political participation, and religious practices, they were different in many ways from other rural Americans. These differences kept Catholics as a society apart and sometimes caused mistrust, animosity, and

---

32. For other estimates of ethnic groups in agriculture in the early twentieth century, see Robert P. Swierenga, "Ethnicity and American Agriculture," *Ohio History* 89 (Summer 1980): 323–44.

Table 2. Catholic Rural Ethnic Groups in the United States, 1920

Country of origin[a] (1)	Total rural U.S. population[b] (2)	Percentage of each ethnic group in its homeland that was Catholic[c] (3)	Estimated Catholic rural U.S. population[d] (4)
Austria	833,225	73	608,254
Belgium	48,903	95	46,458
Canada, French	196,841	90	177,157
Canada, other	571,432	18	102,858
England	700,554	5	35,028
France	99,296	90	89,366
Germany	2,583,498	37	955,894
Hungary	299,225	51	152,605
Ireland	702,491	74	519,843
Italy	516,961	97	501,422
Mexico	401,650	97	389,501
Netherlands	167,761	35	58,716
Portugal	38,151	97	37,006
Russia	553,824	8	44,246
Scotland	209,138	10	20,914
Switzerland	155,349	43	66,800
Wales	74,110	5	3,706
Other	103,809	10	10,381
Mixed foreign parentage	404,772	10	40,477

a. Pre–World War I boundaries.
b. Includes foreign-born, natives with both parents born abroad, and natives with one parent native and the other foreign-born. U.S. Department of Commerce, Bureau of the Census, *Fourteenth Census of the United States Taken in the Year 1920*, 11 vols. (Washington, D.C.: Government Printing Office, 1922), 2: 891, 959.
c. Gerald Shaughnessy, *Has the Immigrant Kept the Faith? A Study of Immigration and Catholic Growth in the United States, 1790–1920* (New York: Macmillan, 1925), 106–12.
d. Column 2 multiplied by the percentage in column 3. These figures are estimates only. Shaughnessy's percentages—themselves estimates—refer to the proportions of all Catholics of each ethnic group in their respective homelands rather than the proportions of rural Catholics of each ethnic group in the United States. Therefore, some of the resulting figures in column 4 may be quite inaccurate. They are offered merely as estimates in the absence of any more definite data. The U.S. Census did not report data by rural religious ethnic group.

conflict. Nevertheless, the assimilation process was at work, and Catholics were becoming more and more like other rural Americans.[33]

For example, assimilation was slowly influencing Catholics' agricultural practices. In the beginning, Catholic immigrants showed their difference from long-time settlers by their choice of land. Many immigrants chose to settle on land that reminded them of home: Thus, German Catholics

33. Gjerde, *Minds of the West*, 18–19, 226–31.

settled on wooded, well-watered land that reminded them of the forests of southern Germany, while an Italian looking for a site for a colony along the Mississippi River in Wisconsin, "struck with the resemblance of the country to his native Piedmont with its mountains, gorges, and narrow valleys," decided to settle there and called the place Genoa. Immigrants also tended to buy land secondhand because they were ignorant of land-clearing techniques and were otherwise disinclined to be pioneers. Immigrants usually purchased small plots of land, often of low quality, either because it was cheapest or because they were taken advantage of by land dealers. But what land they had they cultivated intensively, so that they got high yields out of it.[34]

Such yields were not obtained, at least at first, through modern farming techniques, because many Catholic immigrant farmers, such as the Irish and Italians, still employed hand tools such as the hoe, rake, and mattock. Many at first did not even use horses for farm labor. Farmers that settled in ethnic or religious colonies often kept distinctive agricultural methods for many decades. But by 1920, most were using farm machinery and scientific agricultural techniques, like other Americans. As historian Jeffrey Marlett noted, the shared experience of the rapid changes in agriculture in the early twentieth century helped to unify Catholic farmers with other rural Americans.[35]

Most Catholic rural groups—for example, Germans, Swiss, Czechs, and Poles—exhibited a pattern of long-lasting family continuity upon the land. Many of these groups, such as the Germans of Stearns County, Minnesota, formed closely knit communities that have persisted to the present day. Only a few small Catholic ethnic groups in rural areas—such as Italians and Portuguese—included a considerable number of "birds of passage," who stayed in America for only a short time and then returned to the mother country.[36]

---

34. Hawgood, *Tragedy of German-America*, 22–33; U.S., Immigration Commission, 1907–1910, William P. Dillingham, chairman, *Reports of the Immigration Commission*, Senate documents of 61st Cong., 2d and 3d sessions, 1911, 41 vols. (Washington, D.C.: Government Printing Office, 1911), 21:42, 88–93; quotation, 390; Terry G. Jordan, *German Seed in Texas Soil: Immigrant Farmers in Nineteenth-century Texas* (Austin: University of Texas Press, 1966), 103–7.

35. Edmund de S. Brunner, *Immigrant Farmers and Their Children* (Garden City, N.Y.: Doubleday, Doran, 1929), 48; *Reports of the Immigration Commission*, 21:41, 42–43, 68; Rolle, *Immigrant Upraised*, 68, 74–75, 83–84; Swierenga, "Ethnicity and American Agriculture," 330–40; Marlett, *Saving the Heartland*, 98.

36. On the Germans, Frederick C. Luebke, *Immigrants and Politics: The Germans of Nebraska, 1880–1900* (Lincoln: University of Nebraska Press, 1969), 29–31, 180; Sonya Salamon, *Prairie Patrimony: Family, Farming, and Community in the Midwest* (Chapel Hill: University of North Carolina Press, 1992), 31–32; Gjerde, *Minds of the West*, 166–67, 169; and Conzen, "Peasant Pioneers," 266; the Swiss,

By 1920, the vernacular architecture of rural Catholics showed considerable assimilation to American patterns. After building American-style log houses in the pioneer period, German Catholics reverted to half-timbered or stone houses, as in the home country. But by 1920, they were adopting the frame or brick houses of their American neighbors. Church architecture showed less rapid assimilation. Rural German Catholics in Iowa, Missouri, and Texas usually built solid stone churches rather than the frame structures characteristic of rural Protestants. The Catholic churches' richly decorated interiors contrasted with the simplicity of the Protestant buildings. Catholics also disdained the Protestant practice of scattered rural chapels, building most of their churches in the towns. Rural Catholics carried the practice of many crafts with them from the old country to their American homesteads. For example, the Germans of Missouri engaged in such traditional crafts as cabinetmaking, pottery, stonecutting, basketmaking, and the making of wooden shoes until well into the twentieth century. However, by 1920, these handicrafts were increasingly giving way to the purchase of factory-made articles. Many Catholic immigrants continued to wear their Old World clothes—Russian-German women their long black dresses and shawls and the men their caps and coats.[37]

Differences existed in the social life of rural Catholics and Protestants. Almost all Catholic ethnic groups were noted for a strong preference for community over individual life. Catholics sometimes initially clustered in farm villages reminiscent of Europe, although they usually quickly dispersed to typically American isolated farmsteads. The Protestant emphasis on temperance found little support among Catholic rural dwellers, who placed high value on the conviviality associated with German beer, Irish whiskey, and Italian and French wine. Most Catholics opposed Protestant-inspired Sunday "blue laws." Such laws were particularly objectionable in German areas, where Sunday was a favorite time for gatherings in beer

---

John Paul von Grueningen, *The Swiss in the United States* (Madison, Wisc.: Swiss-American Historical Society, 1940), 69–70; the Czechs, Thomas Čapek, *The Čechs (Bohemians) in America* (Boston: Houghton Mifflin, 1920), 69–70; the Poles, Merle E. Curti et al., *The Making of an American Community: A Case Study of Democracy in a Frontier County* (Stanford, Calif.: Stanford University Press, 1959), 74–75; the Italians, Rolle, *Immigrant Upraised*, 55–58, 68, 71–85; the Portuguese, *Reports of the Immigration Commission*, 22:491–92.

37. Charles Van Ravenswaay, *The Arts and Architecture of German Settlements in Missouri: A Survey of a Vanishing Culture* (Columbia: University of Missouri Press, 1977), 105–512; Jordan, "Religious Geography," 117–19, 125; Frederick C. Luebke, "Ethnic Group Settlement on the Great Plains," in *The American West: Interactions, Intersections, and Injunctions*, ed. Gordon Morris Bakken and Brenda Farrington, vol. 5: *The Urban West* (New York: Garland Publishing, 2000), 171; Gjerde, *Minds of the West*, 108.

gardens, and eventually they became dead letters through lack of enforcement.[38]

Fathers tended to have greater authority in Catholic rural families, especially those of immigrants, than in Protestant and native families. They worked their wives and children very hard, although they gave their farms to their children as entitlements, whereas "Yankee" sons usually had to buy them just like non–family members. Marriages had parental and even community involvement, whereas for Yankees they were considered a private affair between the couple. Catholic families tended to take care of elderly parents in the home, while Yankee families often left them on their own. The husbands' control over their wives and the economic benefits of children translated into higher birthrates for Catholic rural families than non-Catholics. In fourteen rural townships in Iowa and Wisconsin in 1900, there were eight or more children in 64 percent of German families, 46.7 percent of Irish, 44.3 percent of Norwegian, and 29.9 percent of "American." In a study of rural areas of six midwestern states in 1900 and 1910, immigrant families from Catholic areas (Ireland, Germany, and eastern Europe) averaged between 6.9 and 8.3 children, while immigrants from Protestant countries (England, Scotland, and Scandinavia) averaged between 4.6 and 7.2, and native-born families averaged between 4.6 and 6.5.[39]

The colorful religious life of rural Catholics clashed sharply with Protestant simplicity. Catholic homes were furnished with numerous crosses, statues, pictures, medallions, and other religious articles. Individual Catholics wore crucifixes or amulets. Devout Catholics said a wide variety of prayers: of particular importance to farmers were the Angelus and prayers blessing the crops. Most noticeable of all were the great and lavish religious festivals and processions, which included some superstitious practices dating back to pagan times. Such high points in the religious calendar included Easter, Christmas, Corpus Christi (for Czechs), Rogation Days (a rural festival at which fields and seeds were blessed—for Germans), and feasts of the Madonna and village patron saint days (for Italians).[40]

---

38. For community preference and eventual dispersion, see, for Germans, Hawgood, *Tragedy of German-America*, 32; and Jordan, "Religious Geography," 117; for the Irish, see Adams, *Ireland and Irish Immigration*, 342; for Italians, *Reports of the Immigration Commission*, 21:41. On opposition to liquor laws, see Hawgood, *Tragedy of German-America*, 34–37. However, for rural Catholic support of temperance, see John Mack Faragher, *Sugar Creek: Life on the Illinois Prairie* (New Haven, Conn.: Yale University Press, 1986), 195–96; Don Harrison Doyle, *The Social Order of a Frontier Community: Jacksonville, Illinois, 1825–70* (Urbana: University of Illinois Press, 1978), 137–42, 168–69; Curti et al., *Making of an American Community*, 131.

39. Gjerde, *Minds of the West*, 20, 159–62, 170–84, 191–95.

40. Joseph Cada, "The Pioneers. Czech-American Catholics after 1850," in *The Other Catholics*,

Catholic immigrant churches were initially different from Protestant churches in one very noticeable characteristic—language. As late as 1920, three-quarters of the Catholic rural churches in certain areas still used a foreign language. Many were bilingual—conducting services in both English and the mother tongue. In 1920, conservative factions within many Catholic ethnic groups were still fighting to retain foreign-language churches, but such churches were inevitably declining in favor of English-language ones.[41]

Foreign languages were also being used in many Catholic rural schools, especially among the Germans and other ethnic groups in the Midwest. However, as with foreign-language churches, the number of schools being taught in foreign languages was steadily declining. For example, in Nebraska, Germans were often mixed with other nationalities, so that the schools had to be taught in English. Even in mainly German parishes, the German language was commonly used only in religion classes as early as 1900.[42]

Up to one-half of Catholic children attending school went to public schools. Many of them attended public schools because they lived in rural or small-town areas where for economic or other reasons Catholic schools were not established. It was estimated that from one-fourth to one-third of the whole number of Catholic children lived in such areas.[43]

The conditions in Catholic rural schools were often primitive. Many schools had only one room and were under the charge of a pair of nuns who lived in a manner that "was all that the heart of an anchorite could desire." The curriculum was based on the "four Rs"—reading, writing,

---

selected and introduced by Keith P. Dyrud, Michael Novak, and Rudolph J. Vecoli (New York: Arno Press, 1978), 1–9; Rudolph J. Vecoli, "Prelates and Peasants. Italian Immigrants and the Catholic Church," in ibid., 227–33 (each article separately paginated); Gjerde, *Minds of the West*, 225, 229.

41. See Peter A. Speek, *A Stake in the Land* (New York: Harper and Bros., 1921), 182–83; and Brunner, *Immigrant Farmers*, 118. For conservatives fighting to retain foreign-language churches, see Barry, *Catholic Church and German Americans*, 101–2; and the essays (separately paginated) by Cada, "The Pioneers," 1–45; Stephen Torak, "Hungarian Catholics and Their Churches in America," 1–9; William Wolkovich-Volkavicius, "Lithuanian Immigrants and Their Irish Bishops in the Catholic Church of Connecticut, 1893–1915," 1–15; Daniel S. Buczek, "Polish-Americans and the Roman Catholic Church," 39–61; Victor R. Greene, "For God and Country: The Origins of Slavic Catholic Self-Consciousness in America," 446–60; M. J. Madaj, "The Polish Immigrant, the American Catholic Hierarchy, and Father Wencenslas Kruszka," 16–29; and Mark Stolarik, "Building Slovak Communities in America," 69–109, in Dyrud, Novak, and Vecoli, *Other Catholics*. For the decline of foreign-language churches, see Linkh, *American Catholicism and European Immigrants*, 103–10.

42. Speek, *Stake in the Land*, 156–75; J. A. Burns, *The Growth and Development of the Catholic School System in the United States* (New York: Benziger Bros., 1912), 294–337; Linkh, *American Catholicism and European Immigrants*, 110–15; Luebke, *Immigrants and Politics*, 46.

43. Burns, *Catholic School System*, 355–59.

arithmetic, and religion. Teaching methods, including much recitation of the catechism, were formal and unimaginative by later-twentieth-century standards. Instruction was seasoned, however, with a generous portion of the sisters' piety, gentleness, and love.[44]

Soon after arriving in this country, Catholic immigrants formed various societies and organizations. The earliest of these were naturally based on the societies, many Church-related, that they had known in the old country: Czech farmers and Mexican laborers in Nueces County, Texas, formed saint's societies of related families for mutual aid and religious practice. Some organizations were limited to a single parish, such as sodalities and rosary societies, and others, such as mutual-benefit or insurance societies and chapters of the Knights of Columbus, were not. These societies in turn often joined together, pyramiding into progressively larger organizations that became statewide or even national in scope. An example of such an organization was the German Catholic Central Verein, which began as a league of mutual-benefit societies, and by the twentieth century represented the interests of all German-American Catholics.[45]

At first, American Catholics, including rural dwellers, were prone to join societies authorized by the Church rather than other organizations because such popular American societies as the Masons, Odd Fellows, Grangers, Ancient Order of Hibernians, and Knights of Labor were considered suspect by the Church either because of their anti-Catholic programs or because they had secret oaths or rituals. Yet by 1920, rural Catholics were beginning to participate in a wide variety of organizations with non-Catholics. For example, in the Hill Country of Texas, German Catholics and Protestants shared membership in the numerous shooting, bowling, and singing clubs.[46]

In 1920, Catholic farmers also participated in rural economic organizations less often than did other American farmers. County agents polled

---

44. Ibid., 123–45; quotation, 134.
45. Handlin, *Uprooted*, 170–200; Brunner, *Immigrant Farmers*, 107–9; many of the essays in Dyrud, Novak, and Vecoli, *Other Catholics*, especially Stolarik, "Slovak Communities"; Linkh, *American Catholicism and European Immigrants*, 87–101; Josef J. Barton, "Land, Labor, and Community in Nueces: Czech Farmers and Mexican Laborers in South Texas, 1880–1930," in *European Immigrants in the American West: Community Histories*, ed. Frederick C. Luebke (Albuquerque: University of New Mexico Press, 1998), 156–58; and, on the Central Verein, Philip Gleason, *The Conservative Reformers: German-American Catholics and the Social Order* (Notre Dame: University of Notre Dame Press, 1968), esp. 5–29.
46. Fergus Macdonald, *The Catholic Church and the Secret Societies in the United States* (New York: United States Catholic Historical Society, 1946); Henry J. Browne, *The Catholic Church and the Knights of Labor* (Washington, D.C.: The Catholic University of America Press, 1949); Jordan, "Religious Geography," 114; Marlett, *Saving the Heartland*, 120–25.

in the 1920s believed that immigrant farmers in seventy heavily Catholic communities gave less support than native-born farmers to the Farm Bureau and cooperatives. In general, rural Catholics preferred the direct economic benefits of membership in marketing and purchasing cooperatives to the deferred returns from the new farming methods learned from educational agencies such as the Farm Bureau and agricultural colleges. Monsignor George Hildner of Claryville, Missouri, was a notable exception in using his parish as a soil conservation demonstration unit. As in the process of assimilation in other phases of life, Catholic immigrants increased their involvement with such agencies as they lengthened their stay in the country and had more contact with American society.[47]

Rural Catholics also gradually assimilated to political life. At first, political participation was retarded by the immigrants' lack of understanding of the American political process. Eventually, however, rural Catholics entered into the political arena, although in some cases not as quickly as Protestants.[48]

Politics first attracted rural Catholics when their own vital interests were affected. For example, nativism spasmodically provoked Catholic American response from the 1850s to the 1920s. In some cases, injustices at the hands of older Catholic immigrant nationalities roused newer ones to political action. Rural Catholics also showed interest in local office-holding and public works. Most of all, however, rural Catholics were interested in issues affecting religion and culture. They opposed such measures as dry laws, blue laws, and compulsory public school attendance laws (such as Wisconsin's Bennett Law and Illinois' Edwards Law in 1890)—which they saw as threats to parochial schools.[49]

Rural Catholics, like the majority in the Church, tended to vote for the Democratic Party. This was largely because the Republican Party was perceived as being against the immigrants, while the Democrats were seen as their protectors. However, Catholics did not always vote Democratic:

---

47. Brunner, *Immigrant Farmers*, 109–13; *Reports of the Immigration Commission*, vols. 21 and 22, esp. 21: 41–43, 48, 73–75, 87–88, 118–20; 22:158–61; Luebke, *Immigrants and Politics*, 44; Marlett, *Saving the Heartland*, 120.

48. Handlin, *Uprooted*, 201–26; Brunner, *Immigrant Farmers*, 235–37; Luebke, *Immigrants and Politics*, 67, 184–85.

49. Hawgood, *Tragedy of German-America*, 34–37, 47, 51; Brunner, *Immigrant Farmers*, 97–98, 203–6, 235–37; Curti, *Making of an American Community*, 325–26; Gjerde, *Minds of the West*, 283–308; *Reports of the Immigration Commission*, 21: 43, 86, 135, 239; 22: 250, 418; Donald L. Kinzer, *An Episode in Anti-Catholicism: The American Protective Association* (Seattle: University of Washington Press, 1964), 64–67; Luebke, *Immigrants and Politics*, esp. 5; Paul Kleppner, *The Cross of Culture: A Social Analysis of Midwestern Politics, 1850–1900*, 2d ed. (New York: Free Press, 1970), 76–79, 121–22, 158–71.

Catholic Rural America to 1920

There were many cases of even recently arrived immigrants voting quite independently. Moreover, prominent Catholics such as Archbishop John Ireland of St. Paul, Bishop Martin Marty of Sioux Falls, G.O.P. National Committeeman Richard C. Kerens of Missouri, and Monsignor Joseph Stephan of the Bureau of Catholic Indian Missions were outspoken Republican partisans.[50]

Sometimes the trend toward rural Catholic assimilation was reversed and native-born Americans adopted immigrant practices. For example, Americans in one community included German sauerkraut in their Thanksgiving feast. Protestants started to take additional vacation days around Christmas and New Year's Day in imitation of Catholics. American schools began teaching foreign languages. In one Catholic school the Irish children recited poems at school celebrations in German.[51]

Rural Catholic communities were sometimes divided by internal conflicts based on ethnic or regional differences. Irish settlers from County Cork quarreled with those from County Limerick over the naming of Garryowen, Iowa. When Catholics from northern Germany arrived a few years later, they formed their own parish, at which Bavarians, coming soon after that, were not allowed to worship. The latter had to form a third parish a mere six miles away. In another rural Iowa parish, Irish and German parishioners could not agree on a patron saint, and the bishop had to choose one for them. The church still had two sets of trustees, and the Germans and Irish were buried in separate parts of the cemetery. In Heron Lake, North Dakota, German settlers served by French-speaking nuns threatened to send their children to a public school if they did not get German sisters. A bitter dispute between a German priest and Irish parishioners over a site for a church in Sinsinawa Mound, Wisconsin, was eventually appealed all the way to Pope Leo XIII.[52]

Thus, there was considerable diversity not only between rural Catholics and non-Catholics, but within Catholic rural America itself. Overall,

---

50. Hawgood, *Tragedy of German-America*, 47; Humphrey J. Desmond, *The A.P.A. Movement* (Washington, D.C.: New Century Press, 1912; reprint ed., New York: Arno Press and *New York Times*, 1969); Kinzer, *Episode in Anti-Catholicism*, esp. 159, 224; John Higham, *Strangers in the Land: Patterns of American Nativism, 1860–1925* (New Brunswick, N.J.: Rutgers University Press, 1955), 28–29, 56, 98, 106–7; Brunner, *Immigrant Farmers*, 236–37; *Reports of the Immigration Commission*, 21:382; 22: 418, 538; Luebke, *Immigrants and Politics*, 65–66, 181; Kleppner, *Cross of Culture*, 38–40, 41–42, 55, 59, 66–69, 70; Doyle, *Frontier Community*, 143; Richard J. Jensen, *The Winning of the Midwest: Social and Political Conflict, 1888–1896* (Chicago: University of Chicago Press, 1971), 58–88.

51. Gjerde, *Minds of the West*, 230.

52. Ibid., 104–6, 111–12, 122–27; Anne M. Butler, Michael E. Engh, and Thomas W. Spalding, eds., *The Frontiers and Catholic Identities* (Maryknoll, N.Y.: Orbis Books, 1999), 94.

though, by 1920, Catholic rural communities had assimilated to American rural society in many ways. However, they had not disintegrated under the pressure of assimilation but had evolved and been transformed while still keeping their distinctive religious and often ethnic culture.[53]

Developing Ideas, 1891–1920

Rural Catholics were slow in developing an interest in social reform. Throughout most of the nineteenth century, the Catholic Church in America was an immigrant church struggling to maintain itself in a hostile Protestant society. Practically all Catholic social movements in America before the 1890s—consisting primarily of the rural colonies, mutual-benefit organizations, and charities of various kinds—were devoted to preserving the faith rather than to spreading Catholic social teaching to the rest of society. Furthermore, Catholic social action at this time was based on the idea that religion was mainly concerned with individual morality rather than with the structure of society. Thus, Catholic concern for social problems found its expression in charitable institutions that inevitably dealt only with the results of poverty rather than social reform that aimed at its causes. Such social action as existed was concentrated in the heavily Catholic cities, not in rural areas. These attitudes of defensiveness, concern with individual rather than social morality, and emphasis on the cities continued to limit American Catholic leaders' commitment to rural social action well into the twentieth century.[54]

At the same time, many American Catholics, especially immigrants, disapproved of individualistic American society, which they criticized from the point of view of a corporatist ideology derived from German and French romantic theories of an organic society, which stressed the importance of institutions such as church, community, and family as intermediaries between the individual and the state. Many rural Catholic spokesmen in the late nineteenth century lamented the immoral influence of urban, capitalist, secular America on Catholic immigrant families. This prefigured the National Catholic Rural Life Conference's cultural criticism of urban America.[55]

The decisive event in awakening the concern of Catholic Americans—

---

53. Gjerde, *Minds of the West*, 237, 240; Marlett, *Saving the Heartland*, 97–98, 120–25.
54. Joseph N. Moody, ed., *Church and Society: Catholic Social and Political Thought and Movements, 1789–1950* (New York: Arts, Inc., 1953), 849–52; Abell, *American Catholicism and Social Action*, 7–54, 139–40; Celestine J. Nuesse, *The Social Thought of American Catholics, 1634–1829* (Washington, D.C.: The Catholic University of America Press, 1945), 250–51, 286.
55. Gjerde, *Minds of the West*, 15–16, 164, 251–81, 311–16.

Catholic Rural America to 1920

indeed, of Catholics all over the world—to modern social problems was the appearance of Pope Leo XIII's encyclical *Rerum Novarum*, "On the Condition of Labor," on May 15, 1891. The encyclical's cardinal points were that the right of private property was inviolable (hence, the Church remained opposed to socialism), workingmen's organizations for the betterment of their conditions were justified, and all workers were entitled to a "living wage." Each of these three doctrines applied to rural as well as to urban labor.[56]

Four aspects of Leo's doctrine of private property were striking and of importance for the future of Catholic land policy in America. First, the principle of private property was held by Leo XIII to be so important that it approached an article of Catholic faith. He said that the right to private property was "sacred and inviolable," was "consecrated" by the practice of all ages, and derived from the "law of nature." Leo's commitment to private ownership was more absolute than the more flexible approach to the subject taken by St. Thomas Aquinas and Pope Clement XIII before him and Popes Pius XI and John Paul II later on. Some American Catholics at the time also thought Leo's position was too rigid, and these differences soon burst forth in the Henry George–Father McGlynn controversy.[57]

Second, from the principle of private property, Leo derived his call for the wider distribution of land. Since private property was so vital, governments should support its retention and try to encourage as many people as possible to be owners. This support for widely distributed land ownership was to form the basis for the future American Catholic rural movement's steadfast backing for a large class of family farmers.[58]

Third, the encyclical mentioned three "excellent results" that would follow from the spread of land ownership: the gulf between the rich and poor classes would be bridged, agricultural production would increase, and emigration because of rural poverty would come to an end. Conflicts

---

56. Aaron I. Abell, "The Reception of Leo XIII's Labor Encyclical in America, 1891–1919," *Review of Politics* 7 (October 1945): 464–95; see also Abell, *American Catholicism and Social Action*, 73–78.

57. Etienne Gilson, ed., *The Church Speaks to the Modern World: The Social Teachings of Leo XIII* (Garden City, N.Y.: Image Books, 1954), 210, 230–31. For more flexible ideas on private property, see Michael J. Schuck, *That They Be One: The Social Teaching of the Papal Encyclicals, 1740–1989* (Washington, D. C.: Georgetown University Press, 1991), 29, 81, 82, 101n45, 110n97; United States Catholic Conference, *Food Policy in a Hungry World: The Links That Bind Us Together* (Washington, D.C.: United States Catholic Conference, 1989), 9. In the United States, more flexible ideas were expressed by John A. Ryan, *Distributive Justice: The Right and Wrong of Our Present Distribution of Wealth* (New York: Macmillan 1927), 26; and George H. Speltz, *The Importance of Rural Life According to the Philosophy of St. Thomas Aquinas: A Study in Economic Philosophy* (Washington, D.C.: The Catholic University of America Press, 1945), 14–15.

58. Gilson, *Church Speaks*, 230–31.

eventually developed between Americans (Catholic and non-Catholic) who, like Leo, sought economic equality, increased agricultural production, or a "back-to-the-land" movement in conjunction with a commitment to widespread private property, and those who sought these goals for their own sakes.[59]

Fourth, Leo taught that governments should encourage private ownership. Thus, he did not say that the Church favored a totally laissez-faire economy. Although the Church opposed government ownership of property, it supported government intervention to assure a more equitable distribution of property. This support for a certain degree of government involvement in the economy would prove to be a controversial point in future Catholic rural policy.

In *Rerum Novarum,* Pope Leo gave the Church's sanction to labor unions and other workingmen's benevolent organizations, as long as they were formed under Catholic auspices. Although the encyclical did not specifically mention *rural* organizations, the principle applied to them. At other times during his pontificate, Leo voiced support for such rural organizations as cooperatives and credit unions and inspired the growth of vigorous rural organizations in Italy, Germany, Belgium, Holland, and other countries. In the United States, Leo's support of agricultural organizations was later to bear fruit in the development of the cooperative movement among Catholics.[60]

Another great influence of *Rerum Novarum* on Catholic rural policy was its argument in favor of the living wage. Leo XIII rejected the argument that there should be no limitation upon the right of "free contract" between employer and worker. According to him, a workman's wages should always "be sufficient to enable him comfortably to support himself, his wife, and his children," and "to put by some little savings and thus secure a modest source of income." Leo's call for a living wage was to be echoed by many American Catholics, particularly by John A. Ryan, on behalf of urban and rural laborers alike.[61]

In America, liberal Catholics greeted the appearance of *Rerum Novarum*

---

59. For this paragraph and the next paragraph, ibid., 230–38.

60. Ibid., 231–38. On Leo's support for rural cooperation in Europe, see Eduardo Soderini, *The Pontificate of Leo XIII,* trans. Barbara Barclay Carter (London: Burns, Oates & Washbourne, 1934), 1:116; and Edwin V. O'Hara, "Notes on the Catholic Rural Movement," in National Catholic Rural Life Conference, *Proceedings of the Twelfth Annual Convention* (St. Paul, Minn.: National Catholic Rural Life Conference, 1934), 56–57.

61. Quote from Gilson, *Church Speaks,* 229–30. See also John A. Ryan, *A Living Wage* (New York: Macmillan, 1906).

with great applause. However, conservatives in the hierarchy and elsewhere interpreted the encyclical mainly as a jeremiad against socialism, and they tried to prevent it from being used as the basis of a Catholic reform movement.[62]

The controversy over Henry George's single-tax doctrine exemplified these conflicting attitudes. The famous author of *Progress and Poverty* and proponent of a "single tax" on the "unearned increment" of land values found an avid supporter in the Reverend Edward McGlynn, a stormy New York pastor. McGlynn made a number of eloquent and well-publicized speeches in favor of the single tax. The Archbishop of New York charged that McGlynn, by voicing George's contention that the unearned increment was common property, had supported the condemned doctrine of socialism. McGlynn denied it, saying that the land itself would stay in private hands. Besides, he argued, the Church should leave the faithful free to disagree about social and economic questions that had no direct bearing on religion. The archbishop rejected these arguments and first suspended and then, in 1887, excommunicated McGlynn.[63]

The McGlynn controversy (coupled with the appearance of *Rerum Novarum* at the same time) sparked a discussion of the land issue among American Catholics that resulted in the evolution of a more social attitude toward property rights. Officially, the first step in this evolution was the apostolic delegate's reinstatement of McGlynn in 1892. Earlier, James Cardinal Gibbons had prevented *Progress and Poverty* from being placed on the Index of Forbidden Books. The controversy also exposed Catholics to land theories more flexible than the usual position that private property was absolute. While admitting the right of private property, more and more Catholics recognized that the state could regulate the exercise of that right for the common good. American Catholics were gradually advancing toward the concept of land "stewardship" that was so well elaborated by the National Catholic Rural Life Conference in the twentieth century.[64]

62. For positive reactions to *Rerum Novarum*, see Abell, *American Catholicism and Social Action*, 76–78; Abell, "Labor Encyclical," 467; and John Ireland, *The Church and Modern Society: Lectures and Addresses*, 2 vols. (New York: D. H. McBride, 1903), 1:412. For conservative responses, see Abell, "Labor Encyclical," 478–79, 480–83, 492–95; Gleason, *Conservative Reformers*, 125–26, 130.

63. For the McGlynn controversy, see Stephen Bell, *Rebel, Priest, and Prophet: A Biography of Dr. Edward McGlynn* (New York: Devin-Adair, 1937); Abell, *American Catholicism and Social Action*, 61–73; Abell, "Labor Encyclical," 470–72, 477–78.

64. For McGlynn's reinstatement, see Bell, *Rebel, Priest, and Prophet*, 294. For Gibbons and *Progress and Poverty*, see John Tracy Ellis, *The Life of James Cardinal Gibbons, 1834–1921*, 2 vols. (Milwaukee: Bruce Publishing, 1952), 1:574–85. For the continuing debate on property rights, see Abell, *American Catholicism and Social Action*, 63–64; Abell, "Labor Encyclical," 471; Arthur Preuss, *The*

Like the single tax, the radical proposals of the rural-based Populist Party of the 1890s attracted little official Catholic support. This was in part because Populism was often linked with anti-Catholicism; in 1896, when the Populists fused with the Democrats, many Catholics abandoned their longstanding loyalty to the Democratic Party and voted Republican. In some rural areas, nevertheless, Catholic nationalities such as the Irish, Poles, and Italians tended to side with the Populists for economic reasons.[65]

In the first two decades of the twentieth century, Populism gave way to the Progressive Era's milder version of rural reform, the Country Life Movement. This movement, inspired by a Commission on Country Life appointed by President Theodore Roosevelt in 1908, stressed betterment of social and cultural conditions by voluntaristic means. It was very popular among the Protestant churches, which formed denominational country life departments to promote the reforms, but the movement smacked too much of Protestantism and the secularism of rural sociologists to draw much Catholic support. Catholic backing was practically limited to the rural-minded Archbishop Sebastian Messmer of Milwaukee and several of his priests. Yet, when the Church began its own rural life movement in the 1920s, it borrowed many ideas from the Country Life Movement.[66]

When the United States entered World War I in April 1917, the government exercised its powers over the rural economy in unprecedented ways. In general, Catholics supported the government's wartime actions relating to rural and agricultural issues. They supported congressional legislation for price controls on agricultural products and President Wilson's appoint-

---

Fundamental Fallacy of Socialism: An Exposition of the Question of Land Ownership, Comprising an Authentic Account of the Famous McGlynn Case (St. Louis: B. Herder, 1908); and *The Catholic Encyclopedia*, 1913–14 ed., s.v. "Agrarianism," by Charles Stanton Devas (anti-George), and Ryan, *Distributive Justice*, 63–66 (pro-George).

65. For rural Catholics and Populism, see John A. Ryan, *Social Doctrine in Action: A Personal History* (New York: Harper Brothers, 1941), chap. 2; Luebke, *Immigrants and Politics*, chap. 5 and 58, 97, 103, 107; Kleppner, *Cross of Culture*, 248–49, 263, 318–21, 322–38, 345, 366–68; Clark, *Hibernia America*, 124; Rolle, *Immigrant Upraised*, 101–2.

66. On the Country Life Movement in general, see William L. Bowers, *The Country-Life Movement in America, 1900–1920* (Port Washington, N.Y.: Kennikat Press, 1974). For Catholic participation, see Rev. Joseph Heyde, "The Country Church and Community Life," *Second Wisconsin Country Life Conference, February, 1912*, Bulletin of the University of Wisconsin, Serial No. 509, General Series No. 342 (Madison, Wisc.: College of Agriculture, 1912), 25–28; and two articles in Charles Josiah Galpin, ed., *Rural Social Development: Being the Third Annual Report of the Wisconsin Country Life Conference, January, 1913*, Bulletin of the University of Wisconsin, Serial No. 591, General Series No. 413 (Madison, Wisc.: College of Agriculture, 1913), by Most Rev. Sebastian G. Messmer, "Some Moral Aspects of Country Life," 38–46, and Rev. A. Ph. Kremer, "The Genoa Parish, Walworth County," 46–48.

ment of Herbert Hoover as national food administrator. Some even favored stronger controls than the government envisioned. Industries that tried to get around the government price limitations were roundly castigated.[67]

In 1917, the American hierarchy formed the National Catholic War Council (NCWC) to coordinate the Church's war-related activities, and the NCWC soon became involved in rural affairs. It set up a rehabilitation school in Washington Grove, Maryland, for soldiers and sailors with tuberculosis, and prepared the servicemen mainly for rural employment. A farm next door was leased on which to teach general agriculture, poultry raising, dairy farming, truck farming, goat raising, and lighter industrial and commercial occupations. The NCWC also established thirty-nine employment offices for returning veterans in at least twenty-one states, many of which provided the men with rural employment. In all, NCWC employment bureaus placed 110,021 of more than 150,000 applicants.[68]

In 1919, the NCWC issued a comprehensive Catholic program of postwar "reconstruction." The statement, "Social Reconstruction: A General Review of the Problems and Survey of Remedies," became known as the classic exposition of Catholic social liberalism.[69] Although the "Bishops' Program," as it was called for short, dealt mainly with urban and industrial issues, the document did touch on rural issues on two points.

One of these was land colonization of returning veterans. The NCWC backed a plan to have the United States pay returning soldiers and sailors to prepare "arid, swamp, and cut-over timber lands" for cultivation, with government loans helping veterans to buy or lease the lands. The NCWC believed that not only would government colonization ease the postwar unemployment situation, but, if taken up by private enterprise, it would keep a strong middle class of family farmers on the soil. This would both

---

67. Frank O'Hara, "Organizing the Country for War," *Catholic World* 105 (July 1917): 517–26; "The Food Administrator," *America*, June 2, 1917, 192; Paul G. Rohr, "Some Problems of Government Control in Belligerent Countries," *Central-Blatt and Social Justice* 10 (May 1917): 39–41; 10 (June 1917): 68–70; 10 (July 1917): 97–99; 10 (August 1917): 127–29; 10 (September 1917): 158–60; 10 (October 1917): 198–200; "The Persistence of Greed," *Catholic Charities Review* 1 (November 1917): 259–61; "Extortion and Treason," ibid., 1 (June 1917): 163–64.

68. On the NCWC, see Elizabeth McKeown, "War and Welfare: A Study of American Catholic Leadership" (PhD diss., University of Chicago, 1972). For the council's rural activities, see notes on NCWC employment offices, *National Catholic War Council Bulletin* 1 (July 1919): 4, 5; 1 (August 1919): 23; 1 (September 1919): 31; "Unique Rehabilitation School," ibid., 1 (August 1919): 19; Agnes M. Geoghegan, "First Aid to the Discharged Service Men: Proud Record of the N.C.W.C. Employment Bureau," ibid., 1 (June–July 1920): 17–18.

69. "The Bishops' Program of Social Reconstruction," in *American Catholic Thought on Social Questions*, ed. Aaron I. Abell (Indianapolis: Bobbs-Merrill, 1968), 325–48; see Joseph M. McShane, *"Sufficiently Radical": Catholicism, Progressivism, and the Bishops' Program of 1919* (Washington, D.C.: The Catholic University of America Press, 1986).

form a buffer against socialism, and, if encouraged among Catholics by the Church, strengthen Catholicism in rural areas. The NCWC took up the refrain of Mary Theresa Elder and the nineteenth-century colonizers that "the future of the Nation belongs to the dwellers in the country." Although neither the government nor the Church acted on this proposal for colonization, the idea of using land settlement to strengthen the rural Church was to be carried on by the National Catholic Rural Life Conference in the coming decade.[70]

The second rural issue addressed by the Bishops' Program and the NCWC was cooperation. The NCWC used the example of guilds in the Middle Ages to refute the argument that all cooperation was necessarily socialistic. Therefore, American farmers should follow the examples in Denmark and Maine of producer cooperatives. These should be true cooperatives—set up on the British Rochdale model, with each member having an equal vote—not stock companies (with voting according to the number of shares owned, and profit, not marketing, as the main purpose). If state laws forbade this, they should be changed (and the NCWC composed a proposed state law for achieving this purpose). Consumer cooperatives, as in England, were favored as a way to reduce the middleman's share of food costs (reckoned at one-half). The NCWC endorsed the efforts of the Farmer-Labor Co-operative Congress, which met in Chicago on February 12–14, 1920, to bring farmers' and consumers' cooperatives together.[71]

In 1919, the Nonpartisan League, a political party consisting almost entirely of farmers, swept into power in North Dakota and enacted a state marketing association, a state bank, a state home-building association, a farmers' loan program, state lignite mines, and exemption of farm implements, marketing, and improvements from taxation. Many observers claimed the league and its program were socialistic, and indeed there was much truth behind their accusations. However, some Catholic responses were quite tolerant. While admitting that the Nonpartisan League's enactments were "revolutionary," one Catholic spokesman said that they were in conflict with neither "good morals" nor "sound economic practice."

70. John A. Ryan, *Social Reconstruction* (New York: Macmillan, 1920), 26–34; National Catholic War Council, Committee on Special War Activities, *Reconstruction Pamphlet No. 3, Unemployment* (May 1919), 15–16; idem, *Reconstruction Pamphlet No. 2, Land Colonization: A General Review of the Problems and Survey of Remedies* (March 1919), passim (quotation, 15).

71. "Bishops' Program," in Abell, *American Catholic Thought*, 339–40, 345–46; National Catholic War Council, Committee on Special War Activities, *Reconstruction Pamphlet No. 12, Co-operation among Farmers and Consumers* (April 1920); "The Cooperative Movement," *Catholic Charities Review* 3 (March 1919): 67–70.

The Nonpartisan League did not favor complete government ownership but only enough to provide competition with private enterprise, which could help prevent "monopolistic injustice." This benign reaction to the league showed that some American Catholics were able to tolerate considerable government control of the economy, short of socialism.[72]

By 1920, American Catholics, though living in an urban-oriented church, had begun to give attention to rural problems. In Leo XIII's social encyclical *Rerum Novarum,* as well as older Church teachings, they had the theoretical basis for a conception of rural life that favored economic and spiritual strength and a widespread distribution of small, owner-operated farms. Yet this conception had never been authoritatively and systematically articulated with specific reference to American conditions. Furthermore, in an age of ever-increasing special-interest-group organization, rural Catholicism had no single organization devoted to furthering its particular interests. Finally, the numerical weakness of the Catholic rural minority created in some a concern for the future welfare of the entire American Church. One American priest was conscious of all three of these problems, and in the coming decade he dedicated himself to their remediation.

72. On the Nonpartisan League in general, see Theodore Saloutos and John D. Hicks, *Agricultural Discontent in the Middle West, 1900–1939* (Madison: University of Wisconsin Press, 1951), chaps. 6 and 7. The Catholic reaction is in "Doctrines of the Non-Partisan League," *Catholic Charities Review* 3 (January 1919): 6–7 (quotation, 7); "The North Dakota Experiments," ibid., 3 (April 1919): 104 (with quotation); "Radical Laws in North Dakota," ibid., 3 (April 1919): 113–14.

Chapter 2 O'Hara and the Formation of the Conference

O'Hara and the Catholic Rural Population Problem, 1920

Edwin Vincent O'Hara, the founder of the National Catholic Rural Life Conference (NCRLC) and eventual bishop of Kansas City, was born on a farm near Lanesboro, Minnesota, on September 6, 1881.[1] His background prepared him well for his leadership of the Catholic rural life movement. O'Hara's parents, Owen and Margaret, ran a model Catholic farm. The family was to a large extent self-sufficient; they ate food grown in their own fields and garden and meat cured in their own smokehouse and wore clothes sewn by Mrs. O'Hara. The family said their prayers together every evening, and the few books in the simple household were on religious topics. The large family of eight children had two of their number embrace religious professions: Edwin, the youngest, and one of the girls, who became a nun.

The Lanesboro area had no Catholic parochial schools, so Edwin attended the local public elementary and high schools. In fact, for a period he even studied in Lutheran religious vacation (summer) schools. Later, O'Hara recognized that his personal educational experience was just one manifestation of the overall weakness of the Catholic educational system in rural areas.

In 1898, Edwin left the family farm to study at St. Thomas College in St. Paul. Besides providing him with a well-rounded Catholic liberal arts education, study at St. Thomas afforded young O'Hara the opportunity

---

1. My sketch of the life of Archbishop O'Hara is based on J. G. Shaw, *Edwin Vincent O'Hara, American Prelate* (New York: Farrar, Straus & Cudahy, 1957); Timothy Michael Dolan, *"Some Seed Fell on Good Ground": The Life of Edwin V. O'Hara* (Washington, D.C.: The Catholic University of America Press, 1992); and Joseph B. Collins, "Archbishop Edwin V. O'Hara, D.D., LL.D.: A Biographical Survey," in *The Confraternity Comes of Age: A Historical Symposium* (Patterson, N.J.: Confraternity Publications, 1956), 1–26.

Figure 1. Edwin V. O'Hara, founder of the Rural Life Bureau and National Catholic Rural Life Conference, about the time of his consecration as bishop of Great Falls, Montana, 1930.

to listen to Populist orators such as Ignatius Donnelly and William Jennings Bryan when they spoke in St. Paul. In 1900, O'Hara entered St. Paul Seminary in the same city, where his teacher in moral theology was the Reverend John A. Ryan, who was then at work on *A Living Wage.* O'Hara fell under his influence, and the two former Minnesota farm boys became fast friends and lifelong cooperators in the struggle for social justice.

O'Hara was ordained in 1905 and posted as assistant to the cathedral parish in Portland, Oregon, because of a priest shortage in that western diocese. Besides his usual pastoral duties, O'Hara engaged in a wide variety of activities that showed his social concern for the community. The young priest joined the Ancient Order of Hibernians and the Knights of Columbus, was appointed to the Portland Unemployment Commission, led a study group on Dante's philosophy, and defended the Church from charges of civil disloyalty. As archdiocesan superintendent of schools from the year of his arrival, O'Hara acquired valuable experience in the problems of urban and rural schools. In 1913, O'Hara served on the committee that recommended the Oregon Minimum Wage Law, largely wrote the law, and was the first chairman of the commission that put the law into operation. The law, guided by O'Hara at every stage, was a landmark in American social legislation—the first compulsory minimum-wage law to stand a Supreme Court test.[2]

Thus, O'Hara, building on his sound rural and religious upbringing, took upon himself the diverse roles of priest, educator, social activist, and Progressive reformer. In 1918, he topped off these experiences by serving his country as a Knights of Columbus chaplain in France during World War I, including work in a frontline hospital during the Argonne offensive.

On his return from Europe in 1919, O'Hara started his involvement in Catholic rural affairs. It began almost by accident. While still in the East, O'Hara, having expressed an interest in the subject, was requested by the National Catholic Educational Association (NCEA) to undertake a study of rural Catholic education.[3]

The study took a year to complete. O'Hara first did a statistical analysis of the current state of Catholic rural education. He confirmed by means of U.S. Census figures the well-known fact that America was rapidly chang-

---

2. See the Archbishop Edwin V. O'Hara Papers, Archdiocesan Chancellery, Kansas City, Missouri, Binder No. 4, for materials from this period. These papers will be hereafter cited as OH, followed by the binder number.

3. Shaw, *O'Hara*, 64–68; Witte, *Twenty-five Years*, 43–57. Two copies of the paper are in OH62; it was published in *Catholic Educational Association Bulletin* 17 (November 1920): 232–45.

ing from a predominantly rural to a mainly urban nation. For O'Hara, the causes of this urban growth were significant: the urban population was growing because of migration from the countryside and abroad—not because city people reproduced faster than rural dwellers. In fact, rural birthrates were much higher than urban ones. It was therefore the country that had the "fertile and prolific" population, and the city that demographically "tend[ed] to extinction."

Because American Catholics were heavily concentrated in the "unproductive" cities, this situation had "the gravest religious bearing" for the American Catholic Church. O'Hara calculated that the distribution of the American Catholic population was 81 percent urban and 19 percent rural. The implication was clear: the heavily urbanized Catholic Church was on the road to extinction in America unless it quickly moved to strengthen itself in rural areas.

The idea that the American Catholic Church had a rural population problem was not new. Mary Theresa Elder had issued a similar warning against rural weakness as early as 1893. Others had followed her in much the same vein. But there were several differences between O'Hara's jeremiad and theirs. First, and most simply, almost thirty years had passed, and the situation was clearer than before. The cityward trend, which some had thought reversible in the 1890s, was by 1920 conceded to be inevitable; the latest and greatest wave of immigration in the first two decades of the twentieth century had, despite colonization efforts, only further concentrated the Church in the cities. But O'Hara did more than just take advantage of the opportunity to see more clearly than his predecessors. He also bolstered his case, as they had not, with a bevy of impressive-looking statistics. In addition, O'Hara found a different cause of the Church's rural weakness. Elder and her followers had blamed leakage—Catholics converting to Protestantism because of a shortage of religious facilities in rural areas. O'Hara saw conversions as the negligible factor they in fact were, but held that the key factor was the migration of prolific rural Catholics to the cities. In the new age of ecumenism and social science, O'Hara hit upon a less religiously divisive, more "scientific" way to call attention to the old idea that the Catholic Church had a rural population problem.

As for the specific subject of his study, Catholic rural education, the situation reflected the weakness of rural Catholicism as a whole. O'Hara found that Catholic school attendance in the United States was even more concentrated in the cities than the Catholic population: 89 percent of Catholic school attendance was urban, 11 percent rural. This feeble educational effort was clearly part and parcel of the overall Catholic rural weakness and had to be reversed, he believed, to secure the future of the Church in America.

Having identified the problem in his own mind, O'Hara then tried to determine if others interested in Catholic rural education saw things in a similar light, and at the same time he cast about for solutions. To accomplish this dual purpose, O'Hara devised a twelve-point questionnaire and early in 1920 sent it off to one thousand rural pastors and other Church officials involved in rural life.[4]

The replies to the questionnaire showed that Catholic rural leaders shared O'Hara's concerns for the rural educational situation and for rural Catholicism as a whole. The respondents found a number of causes of this unsatisfactory situation. Many of them mentioned physical factors such as the distance to church, bad roads, and the weather. Lack of rural religious facilities—churches, parochial schools, religious literature, and priests—was seen as further aggravating the problem. But the most frequently mentioned reason was simple neglect: children neglected to attend their lessons. Parents neglected to send the children to their lessons or to provide guidance and instruction at home. Certain ethnic groups (Portuguese and Italians, as well as just "foreigners," were mentioned) were accused of neglecting religious education in general. Priests themselves were sometimes blamed—for being "lazy" and not making sufficient use of the time and resources at hand for religious instruction. The crowning culprits in the pattern of neglect, according to the respondents, were the authorities higher up, especially the diocesan authorities. Bishops were accused of not appreciating the work of country pastors, not exercising sufficient supervision over them, not rewarding or paying them enough, not seeing the necessity for lay catechists, allowing city parishes unnecessary "frills" while rural ones went without schools, and providing assistance which was "99 percent nil." Seminaries were criticized for not training priests for rural pastorates and religious communities for not working in rural areas.

The respondents had disappointingly little to say in answer to the questions about general rural social problems. This was perhaps not surprising, since hitherto Catholics had evidenced little social conscience concerning rural affairs. In answer to the question, "How far must the peculiar social problems of the country be considered in dealing with rural religious education?" one pastor responded "Very little," and another with a ques-

---

4. O'Hara apparently received about two hundred replies (Witte, *Twenty-five Years*, 43). However, only thirty-nine of them remain, thirty-seven in OH39 and one each in OH53 and OH62.

tion mark. A number of respondents thought that the question concerned only social get-togethers, and others answered the question by voicing concerns for proper standards in liquor, dances, and motion pictures. Anti-Catholic prejudice was the concern of several pastors. One of them felt that the "prejudices & passions of non-Catholics" would prevent Catholic children being taught religion after hours in public school buildings. Another urged that rural Catholics be kept in colonies, otherwise, "Better the slum than the bigoted-Protestant country." In some areas, particularly mining towns, ethnic diversity was a problem because of some groups' migratory habits, divisiveness between groups, and the difficulty of teaching in foreign languages.

Few respondents mentioned economic problems. Two of them wrote that city dwellers should help solve rural problems, while another maintained that "explanation of the Seventh Commandment ['You shall not steal'] would solve the whole matter." Two pastors mentioned rural poverty, one of them saying that a better distribution of wealth in Catholic parishes could do "estonishing [sic] things." A pastor from Colorado referred to the labor shortage and high prices as pressing economic problems. The president of the Catholic Church Extension Society pointed to priests on Prince Edward Island—who learned agriculture and joined agricultural societies—as worthy of imitation by American rural pastors.

Almost all of the respondents agreed with O'Hara that country children should be kept on the farm, but few of those who gave reasons for this preference saw the issue in the same terms that O'Hara did. Most of them favored keeping children on the farm because "morals" were better there: farming was "the best occupation for the whole man," and rural religious education should avoid producing "over-educated" youngsters, who would want to go to the cities, "where most social problems are caused." Only two of the respondents recognized, as O'Hara did, the potential religious significance of the rural-urban population shift and urged concentration on the rural districts to secure the Church's demographic future.

O'Hara received dozens of suggested solutions to the rural educational crisis—many of them directly opposed to one another. Some pastors favored massive assistance to rural areas by religious and secular authorities, while others felt that the individual rural pastor could handle the problems on his own if only he were willing to "sacrifice" and "return to the Spirit of Christ." Out of this welter of proposals, O'Hara focused on seven in his report to the NCEA.

First, O'Hara and his respondents called for a new recognition of the dignity and importance of rural religious leadership. Many of the pastors responding to O'Hara's questionnaire had requested such measures as increased pay, honors, or jurisdiction for rural pastors. O'Hara did not propose any such specific measures, but did call for a "new status" to be accorded the rural pastorate in light of its "critical importance" for the future of the Church as a whole.

Second, O'Hara and the pastors requested the multiplication of rural religious communities to bring religious instruction to rural children. They thought that such communities could teach Saturday or Sunday school, meet with children after public school on weekdays, manage sodalities, and do other work.

Third, religious vacation schools, held for a month to six weeks during the summer, were proposed to help make up the gap in the instruction of rural children. Some doubted that such instruction would be equal to a year-long parochial school program, but others felt that more could be accomplished during a concentrated summer session. The most convincing argument was that religious vacation schools had been tried by the Lutherans and, in isolated instances, by Catholics themselves, and they had worked.

Fourth, O'Hara proposed that lay catechists be used to instruct rural children. Some respondents thought that laypeople did not have the experience, perseverance, authoritativeness, or spirituality for the job. But again, others countered that they had already proved successful in a number of instances. Most impressively, the Pittsburgh Diocesan Confraternity of Christian Doctrine (CCD) had sent out almost five hundred teachers to catechize fifteen thousand children in the surrounding mining towns and rural districts over the past ten years.

Fifth, he proposed that religious correspondence courses be used to instruct children and adults in especially isolated areas. Some thought uneducated farmers would give a cool reception to correspondence courses, or that "the living voice" and face-to-face contact were needed for effective learning. Others defended the courses on pedagogical grounds, contending that "to write an answer one must really know it." It was proposed that religious communities could do the mailing and correcting of the courses.

Sixth, O'Hara proposed that the rural Catholic press be revitalized to help combat the rural exodus. He and his respondents did not feel that a specifically Catholic rural paper would be a success. But they did believe

O'Hara and the Formation of the Conference 39

that existing diocesan papers could include more rural material or that special pamphlets or leaflets could be distributed at churches or through the mails. Most importantly, this literature should be "rural-oriented"—it should "idealize" rural life to encourage rural Catholic youth to stay on the farm.

Seventh, and finally, O'Hara asked the National Catholic Educational Association to formulate a national rural educational policy "to replace the haphazard way in which this vast field is left to the initiative of individuals, enormously handicapped by rural poverty and lack of appreciation of the work on the part of Catholics." He did not suggest that a new nationwide organization be formed to oversee the Church's rural life or rural educational problem. The closest his respondents had come to that were a couple of proposals to extend the work of the Catholic Church Extension Society to include rural education.

O'Hara presented his study under the title "The Rural Problem in Its Bearing on Catholic Education" to the annual convention of the NCEA at New York City on June 30, 1920. The NCEA did not act on his proposal to formulate a national rural educational policy. But by that time he had already obtained something much more far-reaching: a rural life bureau within the National Catholic Welfare Council (NCWC).

The Early Rural Life Bureau, 1920–23

Before his NCEA study was completed—apparently sometime early in 1920—O'Hara sent two very similar memoranda to the Education and Social Action Departments of the NCWC. The six-point memoranda briefly outlined O'Hara's findings on the Catholic Church's rural weakness, the country's position as the source of city population, and his conclusion: "The future is with the Church that ministers to the country." To alleviate the situation, O'Hara proposed that the two departments organize rural sections "to study the rural Catholic problem, to suggest remedies and to enlist the active co-operation of all forces necessary to apply these remedies," as well as to cooperate with each other.[5]

The Education Department did not reply to O'Hara's proposal. But the Social Action Department was interested, and O'Hara was invited to a committee meeting of the department, under the chairmanship of Bishop Peter J. Muldoon of Rockford, during Easter week of 1920. Muldoon and his committee were favorable to the proposal, and O'Hara was appointed

---

5. Undated copies of these memoranda are in OH62.

director of the new Rural Life Bureau of the Social Action Department of the NCWC. On June 1, 1920, O'Hara was transferred from Portland to a rural parish in Eugene, Oregon, to take up his new duties.[6]

Although O'Hara started his rural life work immediately upon his arrival at Eugene, it was for a long time only a part-time job. In fact, the Rural Life Bureau was not officially established until October 1, 1921, when O'Hara first began to receive regular financial support from the Social Action Department of the NCWC.[7] Until that time O'Hara apparently derived his support from his position as a regular parish priest in the diocese of Portland. O'Hara became full-time director of the Bureau in 1928. Until then, the industrious priest also had to attend to his duties as pastor of his parish and as archdiocesan superintendent of schools, and to his work in connection with the local Catholic hospital, with the University of Oregon, and in Eugene civic activities.[8]

At first, the new organization was a one-man operation. Eventually, O'Hara was able to hire a part-time secretary-assistant, and from time to time he employed researchers and social workers for survey and study work. In addition, his brothers, journalist John and economist Frank, rendered him important unofficial assistance with various projects.[9]

The financial arrangements for the bureau show it to have been a shoestring enterprise. Hoped-for receipts from voluntary contributions and the sale of publications and periodicals proved to be negligible. That left the main burden of its support on the Social Action Department of the NCWC. For the first several years of its official existence, the bureau had a budget of $4,000 a year. Its expenses for the first nine months (October 1, 1921–July 1, 1922) ran as follows: salary—director, $1,800; salary—secretary, $835; office rent, $135; traveling expenses, $376.61; printing, $143.20; stamps, $37.75; office supplies, $170.48; total, $3,498.04. O'Hara was apparently a thrifty manager, and could "stretch a penny to do the work of a dollar." For example, he undertook to publish a monthly magazine without an increase in budget.[10]

---

6. Witte, *Twenty-five Years*, 58; Shaw, *O'Hara*, 68–71; O'Hara to Archbishop Christie of Portland, May 24, 1920, OH4, asking for transfer to rural parish; "Father O'Hara to Take up Study of Rural Problem," clipping from the *Oregon Sunday Journal*, n.d., in OH12.

7. See Witte, *Twenty-five Years*, 58; Bishop Peter J. Muldoon to O'Hara, September 24, 1921; [Muldoon] to O'Hara, n.d. [probably October 1921], both in OH62.

8. See Shaw, *O'Hara*, 80–81; O'Hara-Muldoon correspondence, OH62, also OH34 and OH50.

9. Shaw, *O'Hara*, 82–84.

10. "Constitution and By-Laws of the Rural Life Bureau, Social Action Department, National Catholic Welfare Council," attached to O'Hara to E. J. Ball, October 27, 1922, National Catholic Rural Life Conference Archives, Series 13, Box 1, Marquette University Archives, Milwaukee, Wis-

O'Hara ran the Rural Life Bureau with the guidance of Bishop Muldoon and the advice of the executive committee of the Social Action Department, a group of nine Catholic economists and sociologists from around the country. The bureau had a nominal "membership" of all the rural Catholic clergy in the United States, students and faculty of agricultural colleges, farmers whose names were forwarded by the clergy members, and others interested in the bureau's work. However, there was no membership list and no dues to pay; there were no regular meetings of "members;" and, at first, no regular publication kept them informed of the organization's activities.[11]

When Father O'Hara in June 1920 simultaneously entered upon the new duties of pastor of St. Mary's Parish in Eugene and director of the Rural Life Bureau, in his mind, these duties did not conflict. On the contrary, in the words one of his biographers, the direction of the bureau "was not so much accomplished in addition to running a parish or at the expense of that work as by running it and by giving intensive attention to that first work of a parish priest."[12] O'Hara planned to use his own rural parish as a model for what could be done in all of the rural parishes in the country. In good scientific fashion, O'Hara looked upon his parish as a laboratory in which he would experiment with solutions to Catholic rural problems. Ideas that worked in Eugene he would advocate, through the bureau, for adoption in rural Catholic parishes throughout the country.[13]

As the first step in solving the Catholic rural problems of his parish and, by extension, those of the rest of the country, O'Hara undertook a survey of Lane County, Oregon, whose boundaries were coextensive with those of his parish. The survey, with its attendant experiments in solutions to Catholic rural problems, lasted from O'Hara's arrival in Eugene in June 1920 until September 1921. The next year, with O'Hara's recommendations for strengthening Catholic rural life, it was published as a pamphlet, *A Program of Catholic Rural Action*.[14] The *Program* outlined the need for Catholic rural action based on the same birthrate theory O'Hara had expounded in

---

consin (these papers will be hereafter cited in the form NCRLC 13-1); section entitled "Expenses of the Early Rural Life Bureau," OH47; Muldoon to O'Hara, September 29, 1923, OH34; Muldoon to O'Hara, October 7, 1921; the Reverend Frederick Siedenburg to O'Hara, October 14, 1921; O'Hara to Muldoon, August 3, 1922; O'Hara to Muldoon, September 12, 1922, all in OH62; quote from Witte, *Twenty-five Years*, 60.

11. "Constitution and By-Laws of the Rural Life Bureau," NCRLC 13-1.

12. Shaw, *O'Hara*, 73–74.

13. See Witte, *Twenty-five Years*, 58; "The Lane County, Oregon, Experiment in the Catholic Rural Problem," *NCWC Bulletin* 2 (December 1920): 6; Shaw, *O'Hara*, 72, 75.

14. Edwin V. O'Hara, *A Program of Catholic Rural Action* (n.p.: Rural Life Bureau, Social Action Department, National Catholic Welfare Conference, 1922). Copy in OH46; photocopy in NCRLC 5-2.

his NCEA paper. It called for publicizing the importance of the Catholic rural problem, promoting cooperatives, making women's lives in the farm home more attractive, multiplying rural hospitals, creating social and recreational facilities, colonizing more Catholic families in rural areas, increasing rural religious literature, and developing means of religious instruction that were adapted to rural conditions. In covering all of the economic, social, cultural, and religious aspects of Catholic rural life, the *Program* went further than the NCEA paper of June 1920. It showed that the Church's moral concern extended beyond purely religious matters into every corner of rural life. It also attracted more attention than had the NCEA paper. The Catholic press praised O'Hara's conclusions and urged the implementation of his program.[15]

The thrust of O'Hara's *Program* was similar to the goals of Protestant rural reformers at the time. Scientific sociological surveys of the rural church were becoming characteristic of the Protestant country life movement in the 1910s and 1920s. These studies favored consolidating small rural congregations of competing denominations and using churches as community centers for social services—not just for religious purposes. These proposals were not put into effect because of continued denominational competition and rural churchgoers' lack of sympathy with the modernizing goals of the reformers. By World War II, most of the denominational rural life departments formed in the 1910s were moribund, whereas the NCRLC, which tried to represent its rural constituents rather than change them, continued to evolve in vital interaction with American society.[16]

O'Hara was assiduous in spreading the word of the Rural Life Bureau. The most important of his initiatives were the state rural life committees—also known as "advisory councils"—each formed around a nucleus of students and faculty from state agricultural colleges. O'Hara reasoned that these committees would easily spread the rural life message beyond the colleges to the farmers, because the Catholic faculty members were "in a position to reach the farmers whose boys come to the short term courses of the colleges." O'Hara himself organized the first state com-

---

15. See, for example, "Needs of Rural Parishes Set Forth by Fr. O'Hara After a Careful Survey," *NCWC News Sheet*, week of August 15, 1921; "Needs of Rural Catholic Parishes," *NCWC Bulletin* 3 (September 1921): 4–5; "Dr. O'Hara's Survey," ibid., 12; "The Need of Rural Hospitals," *NCWC Editorial Sheet*, Release for Month of September, 1921; "Let Us Discuss It," Milwaukee *Catholic Citizen*, May 27, 1922.

16. James H. Madison, "Reformers and the Rural Church, 1900–1950," *Journal of American History* 73 (December 1986): 645–68; Merwin Swanson, "The 'Country Life Movement' and the American Churches," *Church History* 45 (September 1977): 358–73; Finke and Stark, *Churching of America*, 199–236.

mittee at the Oregon Agricultural College at Corvallis by early 1922. After explaining the Catholic rural program to a large group of faculty and students, O'Hara formed an executive committee of five faculty members, two students, a rural newspaper editor, and the Corvallis pastor to coordinate the work in Oregon.[17]

At the same time, O'Hara wrote to a number of Catholic faculty members of agricultural colleges, inviting them to form similar state advisory committees. In April and May, he followed up these contacts by visiting ten of these schools and forming advisory committees at them. In January and February of 1923 he made another trip and organized more state committees. Eventually O'Hara organized committees in twenty-one states and the District of Columbia.[18]

These state advisory committees constituted the first sustained attempt by the Catholic rural life movement to reach out for a wider constituency. The committees secured a permanent representation of regional Catholic leaders in the movement. In various forms, such local committees have survived within the Catholic rural life movement to the present day. The state committees were also important in bringing into the movement many of its future leaders. Among these were the Reverend Joseph M. Campbell and Professor Paul C. Taff of Ames, Iowa; the Reverend Arthur J. Luckey of Manhattan, Kansas; Lucille Reynolds of the National Council of Catholic Women (NCCW); A. J. McGuire of St. Paul, Minnesota; the Right Reverend Victor Day of Helena, Montana; the Reverend Francis P. Leipzig of Corvallis, Oregon; and August Brockland and Frederick P. Kenkel of the Central Verein in St. Louis.[19]

But Father O'Hara was not uniformly successful in forming state Rural Life Bureau committees. Organization was difficult in areas with small numbers of rural Catholics or with an anti-Catholic tradition. In Georgia both problems were present. O'Hara received a letter from a horticulturist on the faculty of the University of Georgia that advised him that it would be "a waste of time" to try to organize a rural life committee in that state. Not only was the rural Catholic population extremely small, but the state's citizens were very suspicious of Catholics, as indicated by their election of the notorious Catholic-baiter Tom Watson as U.S. senator. The faculty

17. O'Hara to Muldoon, February 13, 1922, OH62 (quotation); "First Rural Life Bureau Advisory Council Formed," *NCWC News Sheet,* week of April 17, 1922.
18. O'Hara to A. H. Otis, February 14, 1922; List, Catholic Faculty members at Certain Non-Catholic Institutions (contains twenty-three names); A. C. Monahan to O'Hara, January 11, 1922; all in OH32; undated list of state advisory committee members, OH61.
19. These names are on the list of state advisory committee members in OH61.

member feared that if any Catholic rural organization were attempted, "a hue and cry [would] go up throughout the state that the Pope of Rome was trying to annex Georgia to the Vatican."[20]

Even in his home state of Oregon, O'Hara had trouble. Although he had been able to form a state advisory council for the Rural Life Bureau, he was unable to serve on any committee of any rural organization in Lane County because of the anti-Catholic prejudice of the Ku Klux Klan, which was very strong in Oregon in the early 1920s. The nationwide Klan resurgence of the same time must have hindered Catholic rural organization in other states as well.[21]

O'Hara used his trips for more than forming state advisory councils. He visited, in addition to agricultural colleges, Catholic colleges and seminaries, diocesan offices, agricultural and rural life conferences, and headquarters of any Catholic or secular organizations that might aid him in his rural life work. Sometimes the visits attracted publicity in the local press. O'Hara usually delivered an address on the Catholic rural life philosophy or program at his stops. Then he met with the local leaders to form an advisory committee, promote religious vacation schools, correspondence courses, cooperatives, agricultural courses at Catholic colleges and seminaries, and other aspects of his program.[22]

Much of O'Hara's work in the early Rural Life Bureau was establishing contacts with people and organizations interested in rural life, contacts that continued after the formation of the NCRLC in 1923. O'Hara naturally had ties with a number of Catholic organizations, among them the Catholic Church Extension Society of Chicago and the Catholic Association for International Peace. In the early 1920s, he briefly attempted to use state councils of the Knights of Columbus as a route to interest Catholic laymen in the rural life program. The Rural Life Bureau's parent NCWC was especially helpful in publicizing O'Hara's activities through the NCWC News Service.[23]

---

20. T. H. McHatton to O'Hara, March 1, 1922; O'Hara to McHatton, March 9, 1922; both in OH16.

21. O'Hara to Henry Israel, January 13, 1925, OH38. For more on the KKK in Oregon and throughout the nation in the 1920s, see Shaw, *O'Hara*, chap. 9, and Higham, *Strangers in the Land*, 265–70, 286–99, 327–28.

22. See, for example, "The Catholic Rural Problem," Milwaukee *Catholic Citizen*, May 13, 1922; "Duty of the Church towards Rural Life Problem," *NCWC News Service*, January 29, 1923; Shaw, *O'Hara*, 86–87, 91–92.

23. Kelley, *Story of Extension*, 119; O'Hara, *Program*, 21; O'Hara's correspondence with the state Knights of Columbus councils, OH 14 and 50; "Knights of Columbus in Rural Life Work," *St. Isidore's Plow* 2 (October 1923): 3; "Oregon K.-C.'s Interested," ibid., 2 (November 1923): 2; Francis J.

O'Hara and the Formation of the Conference 45

Perhaps the most important Catholic organization that O'Hara contacted was the German Catholic Central Verein, led by Frederick P. Kenkel, with headquarters in St. Louis. The Central Verein was one of the few Catholic organizations that had previous interest in rural life—having for years publicized a rural-oriented philosophy through its publication, *Central-Blatt and Social Justice*. St. Louis provided a convenient meeting place on some of O'Hara's trips around the country and, with Kenkel's help, served as the host city of the first meeting of the National Catholic Rural Life Conference. The Central Verein and O'Hara together provided the inspiration for an extensive program of rural lectures and activities sponsored by the Catholic Union of Missouri.[24]

Father O'Hara also established relations with numerous non-Catholic agencies interested in religion and rural life. These included the rural life departments of various Protestant denominations, Jewish rural agencies, farm organizations such as the Farm Bureau Federation, and many government agencies. He cooperated with Protestant and Jewish rural studies, but he also participated in a bitter controversy over Protestant "agricultural missions," whose major purpose, he contended, was not to teach agriculture in underdeveloped countries in Latin America and elsewhere, but to convert the (often Catholic) farmers to Protestantism.[25]

Among the non-Catholic agencies reached by O'Hara, his relationship with the American Country Life Association (ACLA) was probably the most important. The ACLA was founded in 1919 and promoted social and cultural, as well as economic, rural reform. O'Hara was the first Catholic member of the ACLA, which, although officially nonsectarian, was heavily influenced by the Protestant clergy. He soon became a prominent member of the organization, joining the editorial council of its house publication and its board of directors. Relations between O'Hara and the ACLA's

---

Haas, *American Agriculture and International Affairs* (Washington, D.C.: Catholic Association for International Peace, 1930), pamphlet—copy in "Agriculture," NCRLC 3-1; [Muldoon] to O'Hara, undated [probably October 1921], and memo or letter, presumably from O'Hara to Justin McGrath, both OH62; "Catholics in City and Country Eager to Study Social Needs," *NCWC News Service*, December 26, 1921.

24. See O'Hara-Kenkel correspondence, OH62; "Lectures in Rural Districts Planned by Catholic Union," *NCWC News Sheet*, week of September 18, 1922; "Missouri Catholics Inaugurate Rural Welfare Program," *NCWC News Service*, October 23, 1922.

25. See, for example, O'Hara's correspondence with Henry W. McLaughlin, director, Country Church Department, Presbyterian Church in the United States, OH53; and with Edmund de S. Brunner, Institute of Social and Religious Research, and Anna C. Brenner, director, Department of Farm and Rural Work, National Council of Jewish Women, OH61; "The American Farm Bureau Federation," *St. Isidore's Plow* 1 (October 1922): 1; letter, Edwin V. O'Hara to editor, *Rural America* 6 (April 1928): 13; "Agricultural Missions" (editorial), *Catholic Rural Life* 6 (June 1928): 4.

executive director, Henry Israel, were extremely cordial, and in 1923 the ACLA played an important part in the first meeting of the NCRLC.[26]

O'Hara was also eager to reach out to the rural life movement in foreign countries during the decade. He corresponded with many foreign rural life leaders and organizations to keep abreast of their developments. During the winter of 1925–26, he traveled to Europe to study Catholic rural life activities in Belgium, Holland, Germany, Italy, France, and the British Isles. In 1927, he renewed many of his foreign contacts and made new ones when the NCRLC convention in Lansing, Michigan, met in conjunction with the International Country Life Association.[27]

O'Hara's foreign contacts were extremely valuable to the American Catholic rural life movement. They brought the American movement out of its isolation and showed it that, despite its present weakness, there were possibilities for successful growth. The foreign movements encouraged the American movement and contributed many ideas to it. From Denmark and Ireland came examples of successful rural cooperatives. From Australia came news of a flourishing rural religious correspondence school. Belgium's League for Family Education provided the inspiration for the American "Parent Educator" movement, begun by O'Hara. Britain's Catholic Truth Society gave the NCRLC insight on how to deal with the problem of rural religious bigotry. The same country's Distributist philosophers provided the rural life movement with one of its most important ideological foundations. Saint Francis Xavier University of Antigonish, Nova Scotia, served as a model of Catholic agricultural extension education. Germany's "Raiffeisen" banks, which spread throughout Europe, were the precursors of the American credit unions. The International Institute of Agriculture at Rome provided O'Hara with examples of past papal concern for agriculture. Finally, foreign Catholic agricultural organizations such as the Boerenbond of Belgium, the Peasants League of the Netherlands, and the National Catholic Agrarian Confederation of Spain put the NCRLC to shame with their success in the mass organization of farmers.[28]

---

26. Witte, *Twenty-five Years*, 60–61; Shaw, *O'Hara*, 87–88; correspondence regarding the ACLA in OH38.

27. Shaw, *O'Hara*, 112–13; correspondence filed under "Foreign Contacts in Rural Life," OH45; NCRLC minutes binder (1923–32), NCRLC 8-1, 28–33; Edwin V. O'Hara, *Letters on Catholic Rural Action in Europe* (Eugene, Ore.: Rural Life Bureau, Social Action Department, NCWC, 1926), pamphlet, copy in National Catholic Welfare Conference Archives, The Catholic University of America Archives, Washington, D.C., transfile 29 (hereafter cited by folder title [if any], followed by "NCWC" and drawer or transfile number); O'Hara, *The Church and the Country Community* (New York: Macmillan, 1927), chap. 14.

28. O'Hara, *Church and Country Community*, chaps. 13–14; "A Business and a Life," *St. Isidore's*

In October 1922, Father O'Hara made good on the proposal in his rural education paper to increase the body of Catholic rural literature when he published the first issue of the Rural Life Bureau's official publication, *St. Isidore's Plow.* The publication was named after the thirteenth-century patron saint of farmers. *St. Isidore's Plow* was directed at the rural pastors and other agricultural leaders who made up the bulk of the members of the bureau. The original mailing list was the list of pastors who received O'Hara's questionnaire of 1920. As O'Hara informed Muldoon, the *Plow* was not intended to be a "farm journal": it was not supposed to reach out to the actual farmers. Besides O'Hara, who usually contributed several articles per issue, most of the writers were rural pastors, bishops, officials of Catholic organizations—especially those of the Central Verein—and agricultural college professors.[29]

O'Hara created further propaganda for the Rural Life Bureau by publishing pamphlets and articles. In its early years, the Bureau published a number of pamphlets outlining its program and philosophy. O'Hara also worked on a comprehensive "catechism of the rural problem," which was published in book form in 1927 as *The Church and the Country Community.* He also wrote numerous articles on rural life problems for Catholic periodicals such as *America, Catholic Charities Review,* and *Catholic World,* as well as secular magazines, farm papers, and newspapers. The message of the young Catholic rural life movement was well publicized during the 1920s.[30]

Establishing the National Catholic Rural Life Conference, 1923–30

In July 1923, Father O'Hara issued a call for a national meeting of American Catholics interested in rural life problems to be held at St. Louis, Missouri, on November 8, 9, and 10 that year. The meeting was held at the same time

---

Plow 1 (March 1923): 2; Edwin V. O'Hara, "The Thirty-fifth Anniversary of the 'Belgian Farmers' Union' ('Boerenbond Belge')," *Catholic Rural Life* 4 (June 1926): 5; "Adult Education in Denmark," ibid. (July 1926): 6; Roy F. Bergengren, "Cooperative Credit Unions," ibid. (August 1926): 2; Manuel Grana, "Poor Farmers in Spain Get 60,000 Acres in Gifts," ibid. 5 (June 1927): 3; "Religion by Post," ibid. (July 1927): 3; "News from Ireland," ibid., 5; "Training for Parenthood Urged by Paul de Vuyst, Director General of the Belgian Ministry of Agriculture," ibid. 6 (November 1927): 10; Msgr. Luytgaerens, "The Social Work of the Belgian Agricultural Federation," ibid., 10–11; L. H. Peters, "Catholic Rural Life Activities in the Netherlands," ibid., 11–12; John R. MacDonald, "The Rural Movement in Nova Scotia," ibid. (January 1928): 2; NCRLC minutes binder (1923–32), NCRLC 8-1, 33, 43, 48, 50, 55, 56.

29. Shaw, *O'Hara,* 91; O'Hara to Muldoon, August 31, 1922, OH62; O'Hara to Muldoon, January 14, 1924, OH27; O'Hara's correspondence with *St. Isidore's Plow* subscribers in OH26.

30. Report of the Rural Life Bureau from October 1, 1921 to July 1, 1922, enclosed in O'Hara to Muldoon, August 3, 1922; Report of the Rural Life Bureau from July 1, 1922 to July 1, 1923; O'Hara to Muldoon, May 11, 1923; all in OH62. Most of these publications are discussed elsewhere in this chapter or the next.

and in the same city as the sixth conference of the American Country Life Association. Organizers of the two meetings cooperated by planning interlocking programs and several joint sessions. The archbishop of St. Louis, John J. Glennon, was a rural life advocate who had founded a rural colony, Glennonville, in southeastern Missouri's bootheel.[31] And St. Louis happened to be the headquarters of the German Catholic Central Verein, whose director, Frederick P. Kenkel, an avid ruralist, took charge of the onsite arrangements for the conference.

The convention was heavily promoted by O'Hara and Kenkel. Together, they sent out over six thousand invitations to the hierarchy, rural pastors, and representatives of Catholic organizations.[32] In the light of this substantial promotional effort, the actual attendance of seventy-seven registered delegates seemed disappointingly small.[33] However, it was large enough and representative enough for their purposes. Among the seventy-seven, there were four bishops and forty-one parish priests. There were also ten heads or representatives of various Catholic organizations interested in rural life, two representatives of Benedictine abbeys, two teachers at Catholic colleges, five teachers or students from Kenrick Seminary in St. Louis, two apparent novices for the sisterhood, and eleven laymen or laywomen of unknown occupation, some of whom may have been farmers. The clerical emphasis was indicated by the fact that fifty-five of the delegates were clergy, while only twenty-two were laypeople. Among other reasons, St. Louis was chosen as the convention site because it was in the Midwest—the heartland of Catholic rural America. Accordingly, the meeting was dominated by delegates from that region—sixty-eight in all.

The attendance of the four midwestern prelates, John J. Glennon of St. Louis, Peter J. Muldoon of Rockford, Illinois, T. W. Drumm of Des Moines, and Vincent Wehrle of Bismarck, was important because bishops held most of the power to implement rural life work in the individual dioceses. The almost equally essential NCWC was of course represented by O'Hara, as well as by his supervisor for religious correspondence courses, Monsignor Victor Day, and Mary V. Bolton of the Social Action Department

---

31. Marlett, *Saving the Heartland*, 58–60.

32. Witte, *Twenty-five Years*, 64–65; correspondence in OH26, 34, 37, 38, 49, 50, and 62; microfilm reel "Clippings. Rural Catholic Action to R.L.C.N.C. (1938)," Central Bureau of the Catholic Central Union of America Archives, St. Louis, Mo. (hereafter "Clippings," CU); the 1923 NCRLC meetings and conventions file, NCRLC 8-1; Shaw, *O'Hara*, chap. 8.

33. I added several names from other sources to the seventy-three listed on the F. P. Leipzig document, "First Day Registration at National Catholic Rural Life Conference," 1923 NCRLC Meetings and Conventions file, NCRLC 8-1.

office in Chicago. Monsignor Francis C. Kelley personally represented his powerful Church Extension Society. Representation was also secured from the German Catholic Central Verein, the Knights of Columbus, the National Council of Catholic Women, the Catholic Union of Missouri, Conception and New Subiaco abbeys, the sodality magazine *The Queen's Work*, and, in addition to the Benedictines, five more religious orders—Jesuits, Servites, Basilians, Brothers of Mary, and Oblates of Mary Immaculate.

The conference itself did not generate any unusually new ideas. Archbishop Glennon, Father O'Hara, and Father Michael V. Kelly gave addresses on the familiar topics of respect for rural life and the Catholic rural population problem. Bishop Wehrle of North Dakota also decried the lack of respect shown rural life and claimed that it was the cause of the "rural exodus." He proposed aid to settle Catholics in rural areas. Addresses on rural mission houses, rural theater, and home planning covered topics new to the Rural Life Bureau, but they did not propose any significant new directions of Catholic rural policy.[34]

Nor did the resolutions adopted by the convention break new ground. O'Hara proposed "for the consideration of the Resolutions Committee of the National Catholic Rural Conference," such bold and Social Action Department–like topics as farm ownership, tenancy, farm labor, cooperatives, child labor, and colonization.[35] But the resolutions actually adopted by the convention harkened back to O'Hara's original proposals in his 1920 rural education paper. Of the six substantive resolutions, three recommended the major remedies to the Catholic rural problem proposed by O'Hara in 1920—religious correspondence courses, rural religious communities, and vacation schools. Of the other three resolutions, one recommended a "wider use of the facilities afforded by the agricultural colleges"—a project already being pushed by the Rural Life Bureau. The other two resolutions commended the work of the Church Extension Society in setting up a "rural extension station" at Lapeer, Michigan, and that of the Catholic Union of Missouri and the Central Verein in sending out rural lecturers and "setting standards of excellence."[36] This rather conservative program

---

34. Most of the addresses delivered at the 1923 convention were printed in *St. Isidore's Plow*, January, February, and April 1924, with excerpts in "First Rural Life Conference Is Great Success," *NCWC News Service*, November 12, 1923, and "First National Catholic Rural Life Conference," *NCWC Bulletin* 5 (December 1923): 16–17. Convention programs are in the folder on the 1923 convention, NCRLC 8-1.

35. [Edwin V. O'Hara], "Some Aspects of the Rural Problem," *St. Isidore's Plow* 2 (November 1923): 4.

36. The resolutions are printed in Witte, *Twenty-five Years*, 69–70; "First Rural Life Conference Is Great Success"; and "First National Catholic Rural Life Conference," 16.

seems to have been the work of the rural pastors and defensively minded Catholic leaders who made up the bulk of the participants at the convention. It revealed that the instincts of most rural Catholics were with defending the faith and that it would take considerable persuasion by the "social action" group led by O'Hara and others before they would venture into broader social and economic reforms.

The important work of the convention was establishing a permanent organization, the National Catholic Rural Life Conference. (From the beginning, the NCRLC's name engendered confusion. The sponsors usually called the first meeting "the first National Catholic Rural Life Conference." When the same title was adopted by the organization formed at that first meeting, subsequent annual meetings were usually called "conventions." These forms are used here, although various others appear in early sources relating to the Conference.) At a series of meetings closed to the public, a "general committee" of thirty-one members adopted a one-page "Constitution and By-Laws" of the Conference.[37] According to the constitution, the object of the NCRLC was to "promote the spiritual, social and economic welfare of the rural population." Unlike the Rural Life Bureau, which had rather arbitrarily conferred membership on all Catholic rural clergy and faculty and students at agricultural colleges, as well as any others interested in the Bureau's work, membership in the NCRLC was purely voluntary. It was "open" to "representatives of dioceses, parishes, societies and to individuals" who paid a one-dollar fee for dues and a subscription to *St. Isidore's Plow.*[38] The diocesan representatives were a new body created by the NCRLC and had rather the same function—to promote the rural life work locally—as the state committee members of the Rural Life Bureau. Together, the diocesan representatives were to form a "Diocesan Relations Committee," although in practice they never met as a committee. The Conference intended to secure a representative from every archdiocese and diocese in the United States; in the actual event, only the most interested rural dioceses ever selected one. They performed little local rural life work and after a few years dropped out of existence, until in the 1930s they were revived on a stronger basis.[39]

The NCRLC was organized to ensure that its officers were responsible

---

37. The thirty-one "general committee" members are listed in "First Rural Life Conference Is Great Success." Copies of the Constitution and By-Laws are in the NCRLC minutes binder (1923–32), NCRLC 8-1, 1, and in the "Constitution and By-Laws" folder, NCRLC 1-1.

38. Witte, *Twenty-five Years,* 69.

39. Ibid., 143–58.

O'Hara and the Formation of the Conference 51

to the members. The board of directors, originally of seven members,[40] was elected by the Conference members at the annual meetings. It dealt with the larger Conference matters and exercised supervision over the executive secretary, who handled the day-to-day operations. The executive secretary was defined as the person who held the position of director of the NCWC Rural Life Bureau—originally, of course, Father O'Hara. In 1924, O'Hara suggested that the Conference appoint a full-time executive secretary and separate that post from direction of the Rural Life Bureau. He was concerned that the NCWC, due to financial difficulties, might eliminate funding for the bureau, thus taking the NCRLC down with it. Accordingly, the Reverend Michael Schiltz of Des Moines was appointed NCRLC executive secretary. However, Schiltz was reassigned to parish work the next year, and O'Hara resumed holding both positions.[41]

Besides the executive secretaryship, the only other link between the NCRLC and the NCWC was the bishop chairman of the Social Action Department of the NCWC (at first, Bishop Muldoon), who was the exofficio honorary chairman of the board of the NCRLC. The Conference ensured widespread participation in its decision-making by provisions for resolutions voted on by the entire membership, annual conventions open to all, and amendment of the constitution by a majority vote of members at the annual meetings.

The makeup of the officers chosen at the first Conference reflected the preponderant influence of the clergy and "defensive" Catholicism. Every officer and every member of the board of directors was a clergyman, most of them rural pastors without knowledge of or experience in Catholic social action. The delegates, reputedly at a loss as to the selection of a president, took the suggestion of Monsignor Kelley of Extension and elected the Reverend Thomas R. Carey. Carey was the pastor in charge of Extension's "rural experimental station" at Lapeer, Michigan, where a team of four priests was revitalizing a dying parish by increasing the religious observance of the parishioners and allaying anti-Catholic bigotry in the surrounding populace.[42] Such a president and board of directors were representative of the rural Catholic clergy of the day. But the lack of lay

---

40. Membership in the board of directors was later raised to twelve, then fifteen, and counted as many as forty-seven by the 1940s.
41. Witte, *Twenty-five Years*, 71–73; Douglas J. Slawson, *The Foundation and First Decade of the National Catholic Welfare Council* (Washington, D.C.: The Catholic University of America Press, 1992), 234.
42. Witte, *Twenty-five Years*, 69, 189–90; Tentler, "'Model Rural Parish,'" 413–29.

representation left out that whole viewpoint on Catholic rural life, and the paucity of "social action" representatives made it unsurprising that the Conference was slow to tackle rural social and economic issues in the 1920s.

The formation of the National Catholic Rural Life Conference at St. Louis, important as it was for Catholic ruralists, was not a shot heard 'round the world. The secular press almost totally ignored it—not surprising in light of the "defensive" posture of the Conference.[43]

Catholic publications, on the other hand, usually gave considerable space to the conference, and their attitude toward it was positive—even enthusiastic. But their praise was vague. Like some of the rural pastors who attended the conference, they probably did not quite understand what it was all about. For example, the Milwaukee *Catholic Citizen* said the delegates pronounced the convention "a success in every detail" and that during it "numerous topics, beneficial to the country folk, [were] widely discussed and measures adopted towards the betterment of country life conditions, especially those affecting the Catholic rural people." Yet the "measures adopted" were not specified. Furthermore, the "conditions" needing "betterment" seemed but vaguely understood by the *Catholic Citizen*. The paper stated that the farmer "apparently seems to be overlooked . . . as to the conveniences, co-operation, living conditions, both religious and social, and his general welfare." *America* proclaimed that "Catholics at last are wide awake to the importance of not neglecting our great rural problems, both in the interest of the Church and the country," and the *Catholic Charities Review* was hopeful that "the meeting will result in real constructive efforts toward the improvement of the religious, social and economic conditions of the farmer." Other Catholic periodicals spoke in a similar vein, but none discussed specific issues, particularly the central issue of the conference, O'Hara's Catholic rural population problem. In fact, with the exception of the article distributed by the NCWC News Service, which contained quotations from conference addresses, very few of the articles gave any clear impression of the ostensible reasons for organizing the NCRLC.[44]

---

43. The only non-Catholic periodical to mention the conference was *Country Life Bulletin*, in untitled articles, 1 (October 1923): 1; and 1 (December 1923): 1.

44. "National Catholic Rural Conference," Milwaukee *Catholic Citizen*, November 24, 1923; "Note and Comment: First National Catholic Rural Life Conference," *America*, November 10, 1923, 95; "First Meeting National Catholic Rural Life Conference," *Catholic Charities Review* 7 (December 1923): 367; "Recent Events. National Catholic Rural Life Conference," *Catholic World* 118 (December 1923): 410; "First National Catholic Rural Life Conference," *NCWC Bulletin* 5 (December 1923):

But perhaps that was as it should have been. For the issues involved in the founding were not as important as the fact of that founding itself. The most prominent issue at the 1923 meeting, the Catholic rural population problem, was missing from the NCRLC's repertory eighty years later. But the organization still survived because there was still a Catholic rural interest for it to represent. In the language of sociology, the Conference's "latent function" of representing rural Catholics was more important than its "manifest function" of addressing certain issues peculiar to the time. It provided a sense of group identity for rural Catholics that they had lacked before. It can be said that the formation of the NCRLC marked the rise of rural Catholicism to "self-consciousness."[45]

But the Conference did also provide the manifest function of a vital new means for rural Catholics to make their needs felt in the larger society. The NCRLC was a natural extension of the work of the Rural Life Bureau, for the bureau represented rural Catholic interests but only from the point of view of the hierarchy and the Social Action Department of the NCWC. In a time of increasing special-interest organization in all areas of American life, the Catholic rural interest needed to constantly strengthen itself to deal with the complex issues involved in twentieth-century rural life.[46] The NCRLC broadened the input into the Catholic rural movement and extended its influence. It represented the Catholic viewpoint on rural issues in the same way that the Catholic Conference on Industrial Problems, which held its first meeting in June 1923, did on urban issues. In a broader sense, it can be seen as a part of the "Catholic Revival" of the 1920s and 1930s, during which numerous Catholic academic, literary, and cultural organizations were formed. Historian William M. Halsey has noted: "In the twentieth century, Catholics have developed parallel organizations in history, theology, education, journalism, philosophy, anthropology, sociology, librarianship, medicine, law, psychology, poetry, art, literature, and theatre. Many of these groups found their reason for being in the belief that the Catholic spontaneous response to life was different from, if not hostile to, those of non-Catholic associations." The formation of the

---

16–17; "First Rural Life Conference Is Great Success," *NCWC News Service,* November 12, 1923. The *NCWC News Service* article was picked up by the *Michigan Catholic* ("More Children in Country than Cities," November 15, 1923) and the St. Louis *Catholic Herald* ("First National Catholic Rural Life Conference," November 18, 1923; clipping in the 1923 convention file, NCRLC 8-1).

45. I am indebted to Gleason, *Conservative Reformers,* for providing a model for my discussion by making many of the same points regarding the German Catholic Central Verein. See vii, 1–13, 24.

46. Cf. Samuel P. Hays, *The Response to Industrialism, 1885–1914* (Chicago: University of Chicago Press, 1957). See particularly chap. 3, "Organize or Perish."

NCRLC alongside the American Country Life Association was analogous to the creation of these other Catholic organizations.[47]

The formation of the NCRLC also marked another stage in the assimilation of rural Catholics, and Catholics as a whole, into American society. By the very act of giving up their parochial isolation and forming an interest-group organization like so many other interest-group organizations in the United States, the Catholic rural pastors present at St. Louis in November 1923 became more American.

Following its initial conference, the NCRLC plunged into efforts to expand its membership and influence. As Father O'Hara observed, the Conference "met in increasing numbers" during the 1920s.[48] The inaugural St. Louis convention in 1923 had drawn seventy-seven delegates from seventeen dioceses. The next year, representatives from forty dioceses were present in Milwaukee, while the year after that more than ninety delegates from thirty dioceses came to St. Paul. In 1926, representatives from twenty-seven dioceses came to Cincinnati. A record attendance of five hundred was registered at the 1928 convention at Atchison, Kansas, a number equaled the next year at Des Moines.[49]

Throughout the decade, all of the conventions were held in midwestern cities and most of the delegates came from the Midwest: In 1925, of the thirty dioceses represented, only Baltimore, New York, and Oregon City were outside that region.[50] Thus, the national conventions—the most important organizational activities of the Conference—in themselves did little to spread the word of the NCRLC beyond the Catholic rural heartland. The Conference officials recognized this limitation of the national conventions and the additional drawbacks that they provided members with discontinuous contact with the rural life movement and imposed on some of them inconvenient distances to travel.

A solution to these problems was sought in diocesan rural life conferences. The first of these was held in Baltimore on October 28, 1925. It was apparently held on the initiative of Archbishop Curley and the local

---

47. William M. Halsey, *The Survival of American Innocence: American Catholicism in an Era of Disillusionment, 1920–1940* (Notre Dame, Ind.: University of Notre Dame Press, 1980), 56–57.

48. NCRLC minutes binder (1923–32), NCRLC 8-1, 31. Since no official tallies of NCRLC membership in the 1920s have survived, scattered convention attendance figures are the best numerical indicators of the conference's growing influence.

49. "First National Catholic Rural Life Conference," St. Louis *Catholic Herald*, November 18, 1923; NCRLC minutes binder (1923–32), NCRLC 8-1, 7, 23, 47; "Thirty Different Dioceses Represented," *Catholic Rural Life* 3 (November 1925): 8; "Bishop Lillis Opens C.R.L.C. Program," ibid. 7 (October 1928): 4.

50. "Thirty Dioceses Represented."

rural life leaders. Baltimore contributed more to the rural life movement than any other non-midwestern diocese in the twenties. The idea of diocesan conferences had apparently not occurred to the NCRLC before, but it quickly commended Baltimore's action and urged other dioceses to hold similar conferences. The Conference continued to endorse local rural life conferences throughout the rest of the decade.[51]

In 1926, besides a second Baltimore gathering, seven additional diocesan rural life conferences were held, all in the Midwest. At some of these, state or diocesan rural life conferences (organizations like the NCRLC) were formed. But, like O'Hara's early Rural Life Bureau state advisory committees, few lasted for long or accomplished much.[52]

More diocesan rural life conferences were held in 1927 and 1928, but the number dwindled toward the end of the decade. A local appearance by O'Hara was usually necessary to get them organized, and, as he became more involved in the activities of the CCD, he cut his traveling schedule and local organizing work. As a result, the local conferences withered until they were reorganized on a different basis in the 1930s.[53]

O'Hara turned over to the NCRLC his Rural Life Bureau publication *St. Isidore's Plow* in 1925, and its name was changed to *Catholic Rural Life*. It was then published under different editors in Des Moines, Iowa, Racine, Wisconsin, and Washington, D.C., until May 1930, when it ceased publication—thus ending the first series of NCRLC periodicals. By this time its circulation had risen to about three thousand. The magazine published mostly speeches given at the NCRLC conventions and the kind of article that had been published in *St. Isidore's Plow*.[54]

51. "First Diocesan Catholic Rural Life Conference to be Held in the Archdiocese of Baltimore, October 28, 1925," *Catholic Rural Life* 3 (October 1925): 1, 8; "The First Diocesan Catholic Rural Life Conference," ibid. (November 1925): 8; "A Diocesan Rural Life Conference," *Catholic Charities Review* 9 (November 1925): 345–47; John La Farge, S.J., "The Baltimore Rural Life Conference," *America*, November 21, 1925, 129–31; NCRLC minutes binder (1923–32), NCRLC 8-1, 19, 33, 36, 46; O'Hara, *Church and Country Community*, 58; "Diocesan Conferences," *Catholic Rural Life* 5 (February 1927): 4.

52. "Summer Course for Clergy at Agricultural Colleges," "The Kansas State Catholic Rural Life Conference," "The Iowa State Conference," all in *Catholic Rural Life* 4 (May 1926): 1; "The Growth of Catholic Rural Life Conferences," ibid. (June 1926): 1; Edwin V. O'Hara, "State Catholic Rural Life Conferences," ibid. (October 1926): 5; "Belleview [sic] Diocese Has Splendid Conference," ibid. 5 (November 1926): 2; Program, Diocesan Rural Life Conference of Belleville, Illinois, October 26, 1926, East St. Louis, Illinois, in OH34; Witte, *Twenty-five Years*, 144.

53. "Rural Life Problems in Concordia Diocese," *Catholic Rural Life* 5 (April–May 1927): 2; "The Maryland Conference," ibid. 6 (February 1928): 4; Francis Leipzig, "Oregon Conference Celebrates Centenary of Oregon Farming," ibid. 7 (November 1928): 10–11; NCRLC minutes binder (1923–32), NCRLC 8-1, 33; "Baltimore Rural Life Conference," *NCWC Bulletin* 9 (December 1927): 16. See Witte, *Twenty-five Years*, chap. 8, for later developments concerning the local conferences.

54. Witte, *Twenty-five Years*, 160–61; NCRLC minutes binder (1923–32), NCRLC 8-1, 31.

Reaching the rural Catholic laity remained an elusive goal for the NCRLC throughout the 1920s. Conference membership and leadership, the attendance as well as the speakers at the conventions, continued to be dominated by the clergy.[55] Yet throughout the decade, the NCRLC made continual efforts both to include laypeople in the organization of the Conference and to reach out to them through its activities. The Rural Life Bureau's unsuccessful advisory councils had been originally envisioned as means of reaching Catholic farmers. *Catholic Rural Life* made some effort to attract Catholic laypeople with fictional articles, rural humor, and "practical" articles on farming techniques, but circulation among the laity did not noticeably increase. Not until 1925 were laypersons elected to the NCRLC board of directors—Frederick P. Kenkel of the Central Verein, L. F. Graber of the Wisconsin College of Agriculture, and Margaret Lynch of the National Council of Catholic Women. At the 1928 convention, the board of directors instructed O'Hara and Lynch to work to expand the participation in the Conference of laymen and laywomen respectively.[56]

O'Hara had little success in inducing organizations of Catholic laymen to cooperate with the Conference. The Knights of Columbus rendered some aid to the vacation schools, rural boys' and girls' clubs, farmers' institutes, and other projects, but the major men's organization, the National Council of Catholic Men, was never a force in the NCRLC. Sessions for laymen did not generally succeed in attracting many farmers to the conventions.[57]

Lynch's NCCW was more active in its cooperation. In the 1920s, the organization played a major role in the growth of the religious vacation schools. At the 1928 and 1929 conventions, the NCCW organized sessions on the farm home and the farm woman. This attention to the needs of rural women increased noticeably the number of laywomen attending those conventions. The NCCW was involved in rural health and in other aspects of rural life as well.[58]

Rather shortsightedly, the Conference at first made no long-term fi-

---

55. Witte, *Twenty-five Years,* 73; convention programs and minutes in NCRLC 8-1; lists of conference officials on editorial pages of *Catholic Rural Life.*

56. O'Hara to Muldoon, November 20, 1924, "Correspondence, E. V. O'Hara," NCRLC 13-1, and OH15; NCRLC minutes binder (1923–32), NCRLC 8-1, 15.

57. "Rural Activities of the Knights of Columbus," *Catholic Rural Life* 3 (June 1925): 5; "The C.R.L.C. Convention," ibid. 7 (October 1928): 4; NCRLC minutes binder (1923–32), NCRLC 8-1, 2–3, 6, 14, 22, 28–29, 52–53.

58. NCRLC minutes binder (1923–32), NCRLC 8-1, 33–33A, 38, 47; "The C. R. L. C. Convention," *Catholic Rural Life* 7 (October 1928): 4. The *NCWC Bulletin* during the 1920s contained frequent notices of the activities of the NCCW.

nancial arrangements. A Conference treasurer was not elected until the 1924 convention, when the Reverend George J. Hildner of Claryville, Missouri, was chosen. The 1923 convention had been paid for by fifty-three of the registrants (who contributed one dollar each), the Central Verein (which paid for all of the convention's promotional expenses except for the final programs), and, mainly, the Rural Life Bureau.[59] Apparently, the NCRLC was at first viewed as consisting primarily of the annual conventions, for no funds were appropriated to sustain the organization between the meetings. It seems to have been assumed that the executive secretary's office would be provided for entirely by the Rural Life Bureau budget. This was soon found to be insufficient to cover the expenses of establishing a national office and publishing *Catholic Rural Life*. In 1925, a Founder's Club was formed of the more zealous NCRLC members, each of whom pledged one hundred dollars.[60] By 1928, the $4,015 raised by this method was practically exhausted, and the Conference assumed the additional expense of sponsoring religious vacation schools. At this point, it appealed to the American Board of Catholic Missions (ABCM), which by virtue of "the missionary nature of the work of the Conference in spreading the religious vacation school technique," granted the Conference five thousand dollars to be spent on the vacation schools in 1929. This generous grant made possible a dramatic jump in the number of vacation schools from two hundred in 1928 to seven hundred the next summer.[61] Once the Conference had its foot in the door of the ABCM, it clung to the board tenaciously as a means of regular financial support. In 1930 and subsequent years, the Conference reapplied for and was granted regular funds for religious vacation schools. By the mid-thirties, the ABCM money was spent for the NCRLC's office expenses and publications as well. Although the Conference continued to receive irregular amounts from voluntary contributions, convention receipts, magazine subscriptions, and the sale of publications, the ABCM was its financial mainstay.[62]

59. Witte, *Twenty-five Years*, 76; August Brockland to O'Hara, November 24, 1923; O'Hara to Brockland, December 1, 1923; both in OH37; Frederick P. Kenkel to O'Hara, December 14, 1923, folder on 1923 convention, NCRLC 8-1.
60. Witte, *Twenty-five Years*, 76, 231–32; "Catholic Rural Life Conference Treasurer's Record," NCRLC 22 unboxed, 1–16; NCRLC minutes binder (1923–32), NCRLC 8-1, 8.
61. Witte, *Twenty-five Years*, 77–78; NCRLC minutes binder (1923–32), NCRLC 8-1, 46, 48.
62. See Witte, *Twenty-five Years*, 76–78, 96–99, 120–23, 137–39; "Catholic Rural Life Conference Treasurer's Record."

Chapter 3 The Catholic Rural Population Problem

Publicizing the Problem

The main preoccupation of the Rural Life Bureau and the National Catholic Rural Life Conference during the 1920s was the relative weakness of the small rural sector of the Church and its implications for the overall American Catholic population. Since he began his work, Father O'Hara had warned that, because rural families had a higher birthrate than urban families, the heavily urbanized Catholic Church in the United States would inevitably decline in numbers relative to Protestants and other faiths unless it strengthened itself in the countryside. Throughout the 1920s, this theory provided the rationale behind all of the endeavors of the Catholic rural movement. This preoccupation with strengthening the rural Church put the NCRLC in harmony with the generally defensive stance of American Catholicism in the 1920s, when the Church considered itself under attack by immigration restriction aimed at Catholic nationalities, the resurgence of the Ku Klux Klan, Prohibition, and compulsory public school laws.[1]

As he had done during the early years of the Rural Life Bureau, O'Hara, after the foundation of the National Catholic Rural Life Conference in 1923, conducted numerous statistical studies of the Catholic rural population problem. These confirmed O'Hara's belief in the seriousness of the problem, for he found that the most recent federal census data once again demonstrated that the rural population was more prolific than the urban population. Studies by Dr. John Lapp of the NCWC showed that the number of immigrant Catholic farmers was decreasing, further weak-

---

1. Mary L. Schneider, "Visions of Land and Farmer: American Civil Religion and the National Catholic Rural Life Conference," in *An American Church: Essays in the Americanization of the Catholic Church*, ed. David J. Alvarez (Moraga, Calif.: Saint Mary's College of California, 1979), 108–9; Tentler, *Seasons of Grace*, 445–49.

The Catholic Rural Population Problem 59

ening the Church in the countryside. A study published in 1928 revealed that rural Catholics were still underserved. And Father Michael V. Kelly of St. Michael's College in Toronto demonstrated the superior religiosity of rural people and the trend of city populations toward extinction.[2]

These studies reinforced O'Hara's and the other Catholic leaders' convictions about the Catholic rural population problem. At the end of the decade of the 1920s, as at the beginning, they still believed that the rural Church supplied the devout migrants that maintained the urban Church and that therefore the key to Catholic prosperity in America was strengthening the rural Church. Some writers on the problem still believed that leakage to the Protestants was a major cause of Catholic rural weakness.[3] For many years, the Catholic rural movement labored under the assumption that the Church would inevitably decline as long as it was weak in the countryside—an assumption that proved incorrect as the Catholic Church more than held its own numerically in subsequent years.

Yet during the 1920s and later, the literature of the Rural Life Bureau and Conference was remarkably effective in convincing the people it reached of the accuracy of its representation of the problem. Most of the nationally circulated Catholic periodicals of the day either editorialized or carried articles on the subject—in all cases, they supported O'Hara's approach.[4] The Social Action Department of the NCWC and its top officials, such as Bishop Peter J. Muldoon and Father John A. Ryan, never questioned O'Hara's theory and sometimes specifically endorsed it. Nor did the rank-and-file clergy and laity of the Catholic rural movement ever question their leader's rationale for their endeavor.[5]

---

2. Edwin V. O'Hara, "Growth of the Church in the United States, 1906–1916," *America*, March 18, 1922, 515–16; O'Hara, "Slow Increase of the Catholic Population," ibid., March 25, 1922, 534–36; John A. Lapp, "The Immigrant and Agriculture," *Catholic Rural Life* 4 (May 1926): 3, 8; 4 (June 1926): 6; Lapp, "The Immigrant Farmer Offers a Grave Problem," ibid. 5 (December 1926): 5, 8; Gerald Shaughnessy, "Catholic Statistics for 1926," *NCWC Bulletin* 10 (November 1928): 21–23; Michael V. Kelly, *The Moral Danger of the City to the Youth of the Farm* (n.p.: n.p., n.d.), copy in "Catholic Church, General Information," NCRLC 3-5; Kelly, "Importance of Rural Parishes," *American Ecclesiastical Review* 67 (December 1922): 581–89.

3. William Schaefers, "The Farm Exodus and the Rural Church," *Homiletic and Pastoral Review* 26 (September 1926): 1286–90; W. Howard Bishop, "The Church and the Farm," *Catholic Mind* 28 (December 8, 1930): 478–84.

4. See, for example, "The Rural Life Conference," *America*, September 25, 1926, 558–59; "The Other Side of Nature," *Commonweal*, October 17, 1928, 593; Edwin V. O'Hara, "The Agricultural Profession," *Catholic World* 118 (December 1923): 333–41; Joseph Och, "Rural Problems of the United States Past and Present," *Central-Blatt and Social Justice* 16 (March 1924): 401–3.

5. See *NCWC Bulletin* throughout the 1920s and Ryan's introduction to O'Hara, *Church and Country Community*, 13–18. The NCWC Papers, The Catholic University of America, Washington, D.C., reveal no questioning by Social Action Department officials of O'Hara's theory. On the rural

Yet there were definite limits to the support of O'Hara's theory. The topic was not a priority of the highest prelates of the American Catholic Church nor of the NCWC as a whole. These people were more concerned with building facilities and solving the social problems of Catholics in urban areas.[6] Even most rural Catholic clergy and laypeople, isolated and concerned with day-to-day problems as they were, probably did not hear about the Catholic rural population problem. As a result, efforts to solve the problem did not get the support of the Church as a whole.

Nevertheless, the rural life movement itself remained preoccupied with the question. Although O'Hara himself, since his publication of *A Program of Catholic Rural Action* in 1922, had included broader social and economic goals among his priorities, the NCRLC, whose membership throughout the 1920s was predominantly conservative rural pastors, directed its attention much more narrowly toward solving the demographic problem alone.

This primary interest of the Conference was indicated by the types of clergymen it chose to represent it as its presidents. The first president, Thomas R. Carey of Lapeer, Michigan, was director of an experimental rural parish that had the goal of spreading the faith in the immediate area. Arthur Luckey of Manhattan, Kansas, president from 1926 to 1928, was best known as the pastor who lived in the pitiful "little 'shanty' in the West," whose chance meeting with Francis C. Kelley moved the latter to establish the Church Extension Society. William Howard Bishop of Clarksville, Maryland, the third president (1928–34), capped off his career as rural pastor and leader in the rural life movement by founding the Glenmary Home Mission Society in 1937. Thus, the presidents during the 1920s were more representative of the "defensive" than the "social action" type of clergyman and fit in well with the Conference's emphasis on alleviating Catholic rural weakness at that time.[7]

The rural population question dominated all of the Conference's official and unofficial statements and programs for action during the 1920s.

---

life movement response, see correspondence and survey responses in the O'Hara Papers, the letters column of *Catholic Rural Life*, and the NCRLC minutes in NCRLC 8-1.

6. The O'Hara Papers and NCRLC Archives reveal no contact between the rural life movement and leaders such as Cardinals O'Connell, Dougherty, Mundelein, and Hayes.

7. For a short biographical sketch of Carey, see "Leaders in the Catholic Rural Life Movement. The First President," *Catholic Rural Life* 7 (May 1929): 5. On Luckey, see Kelley, *Story of Extension*, 26–39; "Leaders in the Catholic Rural Life Movement: The Second President," *Catholic Rural Life* 7 (June 1929): 5. On Bishop, see Christopher J. Kauffman, *Mission to Rural America: The Story of W. Howard Bishop, Founder of Glenmary* (New York: Paulist Press, 1991) and "Leaders in the Catholic Rural Life Movement: The President," *Catholic Rural Life* 7 (April 1929): 5.

The Catholic Rural Population Problem

For example, the six resolutions of the first conference called for or praised religious vacation schools, correspondence courses, rural religious communities, rural missionary parishes, rural lectures and standards of excellence, and wider use of agricultural colleges, all of which were directly or indirectly related to attempts to retain rural Catholics. O'Hara's pamphlet, *The Agricultural Profession* (1923), discussed the problem and proposed a "twofold remedy": "first, to anchor the Catholic population already on the land; and second, to provide means for distributing our immigrants of farm experience where they may rent farms and ultimately become owners." In the 1924 and 1925 NCRLC resolutions, cooperative marketing and agricultural education were proposed as measures to promote the "stabilization of rural population," and seminary courses to prepare priests for rural service and the rural program of the Catholic Students Mission Crusade were recommended.[8]

The 1926 convention authorized the statement "Immediate Steps in Catholic Rural Life. The Problem and Some Remedies," which outlined the Catholic rural population problem and proposed as a long-term goal the "building up of ten thousand strong rural parishes." For the next year, 1926–27, the Conference proposed four "immediate steps": (1) spread "appreciation of the pivotal importance of the country parish" by means of diocesan and deanery rural life conferences and *Catholic Rural Life;* (2) increase rural religious instruction (vacation schools and correspondence courses); (3) train clergy for rural work (seminary courses and the Catholic Students Mission Crusade); and (4) promote "the economic and social conditions" of Catholic rural dwellers by means of agricultural colleges, boys' and girls' clubs, credit unions, and cooperatives. The fourth "step" marked the first time economic and social conditions were given separate recognition by the Conference, but they were still considered as only a factor in the overall solution of the rural demographic problem.[9] O'Hara's 1927 book, *The Church and the Country Community,* although it had a broad conception of the Catholic rural program, significantly began by discussing the narrower population issue that was its rationale.[10]

---

8. Witte, *Twenty-five Years,* 69–70; Edwin V. O'Hara, *The Agricultural Profession* (pamphlet, 1923, copy in Luigi G. Ligutti Papers, Marquette University Archives, Milwaukee, Wisconsin, file drawer E, folder entitled "General Correspondence—O'Hara, Edwin V., 1922–68;" these papers will hereafter be cited in the form LGL-E, with the folder title), 29; NCRLC minutes binder (1923–32), NCRLC 8-1, 12–13, 19–20.

9. NCRLC minutes binder (1923–32), NCRLC 8-1, 26–27A; "Immediate Steps in Catholic Rural Life," *Catholic Rural Life* 5 (December 1926): 1–2.

10. The preface and chapters 1–4 of the book are on the Catholic rural population problem.

The new topics mentioned in the 1927 NCRLC resolutions were religious instruction by family members (to be patterned after the Belgian League for Family Education), the Cardinal Gibbons Institute (for the agricultural education of African Americans), and training teachers for rural schools. At the 1928 convention, a "farm women's section" resulted in a resolution urging better farm living conditions. An article by O'Hara in the January 1929 issue of the *NCWC Bulletin* on the "Outstanding Needs of Catholic Rural America" outlined a four-point program of vacation schools (the "outstanding task" of the four), organization of farm women to improve home life, boys' and girls' clubs, and credit unions.[11]

In 1929, the Conference resolutions deemphasized the population issue, probably as a result of the influence of the "social action"–oriented priest, John La Farge, S.J. They began with the statement, "Our general objective is Rural Life," and then discussed health and economic problems. Only afterward did the resolutions address issues of the family, religious life, education, and community life—the usual areas of concern. The resolutions made a number of new departures in discussing relations with non-Catholics, rural African Americans, rural life problems of other countries, industrial labor problems, temperance, liturgy, and Rogation Days.[12]

But the 1930 convention went back to emphasizing the rural population problem. The four main resolutions of the convention concerned the Confraternity of Christian Doctrine, vacation schools, parent education, and credit unions (a credit union institute was held at the convention). W. Howard Bishop's presidential address recommended education for rural Catholics, anchoring Catholics on the land, and the conversion of rural non-Catholics. By the end of the decade, the Conference had become interested in other areas of rural life but was still mainly concerned with the population question.[13]

Combating the Problem through Education

For O'Hara, as for the NCRLC, the primary means of solving the population problem was education. "The rural problem can be stated in terms of education," O'Hara said flatly. "Education" was viewed in the broad, all-encompassing sense. It included both religious and secular education, the education of children, and various forms of adult education. The main activities

---

11. NCRLC minutes binder (1923–32), NCRLC 8-1, 33, 36–37; Edwin V. O'Hara, "Outstanding Needs of Catholic Rural America," *NCWC Bulletin* 10 (January 1929): 6.

12. NCRLC minutes binder (1923–32), NCRLC 8-1, 42–46.

13. Ibid., 56–57; W. Howard Bishop, "The Church and the Farm," *Catholic Mind* 28 (December 8, 1930): 478–84.

The Catholic Rural Population Problem

of the NCRLC in the 1920s were thus forms of education: religious vacation schools, correspondence courses, parent and family education, training of rural clergy, use of agricultural colleges and institutes, and rural-oriented education. The Conference's emphasis on education was a sign of O'Hara's affinity with the Protestant country life movement, which also used education in many forms as the primary means of furthering its program.[14]

The most prominent activity and accomplishment of the NCRLC in the 1920s was the religious vacation schools. *Catholic Rural Life* editorialized in 1926 that "this one project has justified [the Conference's] existence." To those who were not members, the NCRLC became most closely identified with the vacation schools. But the religious vacation school was seen only as a temporary solution to the problem of religious education in rural areas. Writing in 1927, O'Hara noted that of the 4 million Catholic schoolchildren in the United States, only 2 million received religious instruction in Catholic parochial schools. It would take some time for the Church to build parochial schools to care for those still untaught. In the meantime, some way was needed "to bring relief to the two million Catholic children who [were] spiritually starving for systematic religious instruction." Religious vacation schools (and correspondence courses to a lesser extent) provided this stopgap.[15]

Catholics had utilized religious vacation schools in isolated instances prior to 1920, but sustained development began with O'Hara's Rural Life Bureau in Lane County, Oregon. During his first year at Eugene (1920–21), O'Hara sent out three groups of sisters of the Holy Names of Jesus and Mary to conduct Sunday schools at his Lane County missions of Springfield, Junction City, and Cottage Grove. He inaugurated actual vacation schools in Lane County the next year. In June 1921 he sent out pairs of sisters to teach groups of between fifteen and twenty children at the three missions six days a week for a period of two weeks. The nuns divided the children into two grades and taught catechism, Bible history, lives of the saints, public and private prayer, the history of the Church, Catholic missions, and sacred music. Breaks in the academic routine were provided by games, "busy-work," and, for the girls, sewing.[16]

---

14. O'Hara, *Church and Country Community*, 51; David Danbom, *Born in the Country: A History of Rural America* (Baltimore: Johns Hopkins University Press, 1995), 169–75.
15. "The Cincinnati Conference," *Catholic Rural Life* 5 (November 1926): 4; Witte, *Twenty-five Years*, 181–86; material under "Religious Education of Special Groups," transfile 16, Confraternity of Christian Doctrine Archives, Catholic University of America Archives, Washington, D.C. (hereafter cited in the form CCD 16); O'Hara, *Church and Country Community*, 59–61.
16. O'Hara, *Program of Catholic Rural Action*, 22–23; Shaw, *O'Hara*, 77–78; Edwin V. O'Hara,

The Lane County vacation schools were deemed a success and were continued in the following years. In his visits around the country as Rural Life Bureau director, O'Hara promoted the idea along with his other proposals on rural life. In 1923, he published a pamphlet on vacation schools and correspondence courses, which described the Lane County schools and contained a detailed outline of how similar schools could be organized in other dioceses. When the first rural life convention met in St. Louis in 1923, vacation schools had been introduced into ten dioceses. Attendance at that meeting spurred some delegates to introduce the schools into their own dioceses.[17]

But the vacation school movement really took off after the National Council of Catholic Women got involved at the Milwaukee convention in 1924. Attending that convention, with Margaret Lynch of the national NCCW office, was Katherine Williams of the Milwaukee Council of Catholic Women, who immediately began preparations to hold vacation schools in the Milwaukee archdiocese the following summer; the Milwaukee schools flourished so rapidly that their program became a model for the rest of the country. Lynch's endeavors were even more instrumental in spreading the vacation school idea. From her national post she contacted the diocesan Councils of Catholic Women throughout the country and urged the vacation schools as a special project of their organizations. In 1927–28 she edited a vacation school column in *Catholic Rural Life*.[18]

Under the sponsorship of the NCCW, the religious vacation schools flourished. By 1926, they had been conducted in thirty dioceses and enrolled ten thousand children. In early 1929, O'Hara promoted vacation schools in southwestern and southern dioceses during a cross-country automobile trip from Oregon to Washington, D.C., resulting in the establish-

---

"Helping the Catholic Farmer," *Queen's Work* 13 (August 1921): 198, 219; "Vacation Schools Teach Religion in Rural Communities," *NCWC News Service*, June 18, 1923; materials on vacation schools in OH40 and 41.

17. O'Hara's report of the Rural Life Bureau from October 1, 1921 to July 1, 1922, attached to O'Hara to Muldoon, August 3, 1922, OH62; "Catholic Vacation Schools and Religious Correspondence Courses," OH41; Rural Life Bureau Report: July 1, 1923–July 1, 1924, 2, "General Correspondence—O'Hara, Edwin V., 1922–68," LGL-E; George J. Hildner, "Religious Vacation Schools: The St. Louis Experience," *Catholic Rural Life* 3 (January 1925): 3, 8; "Religious Vacation and Correspondence Schools are Promoted," ibid. 3 (March 1925): 2.

18. "Wisconsin Will Have Religious Vacation Work," *Catholic Rural Life* 3 (May 1925): 3; Katherine B. Williams, "Religious Vacation Schools in the Milwaukee Dioceses," ibid. (July 1925): 3; Williams, "Vacation Schools in the Archdiocese of Milwaukee," ibid. (January 1926): 1–2; Williams, "Religious Vacation Schools of the Milwaukee Archdiocese," ibid. 4 (February 1926): 3; "Archdiocese of Milwaukee Sponsors Elaborate Vacation School Program," ibid. 5 (June 1927): 2; Witte, *Twenty-five Years*, 78, 183–84.

Figure 2. Religious vacation school, Forest Grove, Oregon, 1927.

ment of fifty schools. By 1930, seventy-five thousand children attended one thousand vacation schools in one hundred dioceses. The vacation schools had thus shown astonishing growth in the seven years since the foundation of the NCRLC.[19]

The success of the vacation school movement created some new problems as well as new opportunities. Once O'Hara had convinced the local bishops, clergy, Knights of Columbus and NCCW leaders of the desirability of the vacation schools, they began to clamor for practical assistance in setting them up. One acute need was for teachers, and O'Hara and other rural life movement leaders spent considerable time arranging for teachers to go out to the schools. Sometimes the local parish priest conducted

19. Report of the Rural Life Bureau, September 1, 1925–September 1, 1926, 3, "General Correspondence—O'Hara, Edwin V., 1922–68," LGL-E; Shaw, *O'Hara*, 114; "Cross Country Trip of Father O'Hara Selling the Vacation School Idea" (five letters), OH41; and numerous articles in *Catholic Rural Life* and NCWC publications, particularly "Sixty New Religious Vacation Schools in the South and Southwest," *Catholic Rural Life* 7 (March 1929): 4; and "Bishop-Elect O'Hara's Findings Regarding Religious Vacation Schools," *NCWC Review* 12 (September 1930): 13.

the school, but more often religious communities (as in O'Hara's original schools), lay catechists, seminarians, or women from the NCCW had to be found to do the teaching.[20]

Another problem was the demand for advice on how to conduct the vacation schools. This O'Hara at first supplied through his personal appearances, articles in *Catholic Rural Life,* pamphlets, and his book *The Church and the Country Community.* However, by the end of the decade, a more thorough, systematic approach was found to be necessary. In 1929, the NCRLC appointed a committee to prepare a *Manual of Religious Vacation Schools.* This was ready by 1930, and new editions were prepared in subsequent years, until the task was turned over to the Confraternity of Christian Doctrine (CCD).[21]

The growth of the vacation schools also presented the rural life movement with the opportunity to use the schools to spread other aspects of the rural life program. The schools could be used for teaching more than religion. O'Hara urged that they be used to instruct the children in health as part of the Rural Life Bureau's overall health program. The programs of many vacation schools included recreational activities such as "[c]horus work, glee club work, plays, games, handwork, [and] playground activities." These "wholesome" activities would keep the children's minds off unsavory influences emanating from the city, and encourage them to stay on the farm and thus help solve the all-important Catholic rural population problem.[22]

O'Hara viewed religious correspondence courses as an important auxiliary to the vacation schools in solving the rural religious education problem. Although he judged correspondence courses inferior in quality to vacation schools, he considered them necessary to reach rural children either

---

20. Witte, *Twenty-five Years,* 185; numerous articles in *Catholic Rural Life;* material in OH41 on lay catechists; NCRLC minutes binder (1923–32), NCRLC 8-1, 36, 39, 61; material in "Seminaries and Seminarians, 1929–30," and "Seminaries and Seminarians—1931," NCWC 29.

21. Edwin V. O'Hara, "Rural Religious Vacation Schools," *Catholic Rural Life* 4 (March 1926): 5, 7; [O'Hara], "Catholic Vacation Schools and Religious Correspondence Courses" and "Religious Vacation Schools and the Diocesan Superintendent" (mimeographed bulletins), both in OH41; O'Hara, "Rural Vacation Schools" (folder), copy in NCWC 29; O'Hara, *Church and Country Community,* chap. 9. Copies of Leon A. McNeill, ed., *Manual of Religious Vacation Schools* (n.p.: Rural Life Bureau, NCWC, 1930, 1931, 1932) are in NCWC 29, and the 1932 and 1933 *Manuals* are in OH39. Correspondence and other documents regarding the manuals are in nine various folders of the Monsignor Leon A. McNeill Papers, Newman University Archives, Wichita, Kansas (hereafter cited by folder title, followed by McN).

22. Mary E. Spencer, "Progress in Child Health in Catholic Schools," *NCWC Bulletin* 9 (July 1927): 24, 27; O'Hara, *Church and Country Community,* 65; NCRLC minutes binder (1923–32), NCRLC 8-1, 61; M. B. Schiltz, "Boy and Girl Welfare Activities," *Catholic Rural Life* 6 (November 1927): 8–9.

The Catholic Rural Population Problem

too scattered or too distant to be given face-to-face instruction. During his first year as head of the Rural Life Bureau, O'Hara inaugurated a religious correspondence school to reach children and adults in outlying districts of the Portland diocese. Two courses were offered: the organization and public worship of the Church and the current history of the Church. They were continued weekly for six months, and one hundred and eighty families were enrolled, of which forty were in Lane County.[23]

In 1921, independently of O'Hara and the Rural Life Bureau, Bishop John P. Carroll of Helena, Montana, assigned Monsignor Victor Day of his diocese to prepare a First Communion correspondence course for use among the far-flung families of rural Montana. Day complied, basing his course on one he had used to teach his nieces and nephews in Alberta, Canada, around the turn of the century. Within three months, one thousand copies were printed. O'Hara heard of Day's work, and early in 1922 he secured Day's and Muldoon's permissions to have the Rural Life Bureau promote the use of Day's courses in dioceses other than Helena. At O'Hara's request, Day prepared a second course on the Creed, which was ready for distribution by the fall of 1923. New printings of both courses were soon asked for, and by April 1923 they were being used in twenty-eight states and three Canadian provinces. Like O'Hara's original courses, Day's were meant for use in the winter months, when the farm family spent the long nights at home. The courses took twenty weeks to complete, usually beginning in November and ending by spring planting time. The questions were based on the Baltimore catechism, and, according to Monsignor Day, were arranged in a "synthetical" manner that aided learning. The children's answers sometimes evoked their rural environment, as in young Emma Casagrande's response to the item, "Name some things man cannot do." She replied: "Man cannot make the sun and moon rise or set or make crops grow."[24]

Day nurtured the growth of the courses throughout the decade; by 1928 he had four different courses and had printed ten thousand cop-

23. Witte, *Twenty-five Years*, 187–89; O'Hara, *Church and Country Community*, 66–67; O'Hara, *Program*, 23–24; "Teaching Religion by Mail Being Tried in Oregon," *NCWC News Service*, December 15, 1920; "The Lane County, Oregon, Experiment in the Catholic Rural Program," *NCWC Bulletin* 3 (December 1920): 7; materials in OH32.

24. O'Hara, *Program*, 23–24; Shaw, *O'Hara*, 76–77, 92; Witte, *Twenty-five Years*, 187–89; Victor Day, "The Correspondence Course in Christian Doctrine," *St. Isidore's Plow* 2 (January 1924): 2; Day, "Catechism by Mail," *Catholic Rural Life* 3 (November 1925): 6; "Catholic Vacation Schools and Religious Correspondence Courses," OH41; correspondence relating to correspondence courses and Monsignor Victor Day and undated "Questions to First Chapter," in section entitled "Msgr. Victor Day," OH32.

ies of them, distributing nine thousand copies in the United States and Canada. But the use of the courses did not expand as rapidly as the vacation schools, and the former were overshadowed as a means of religious instruction by the latter. Moreover, Day was growing tired of the work and was losing money in his concern to keep the courses inexpensive. So in 1929 he turned responsibility for the courses over to the NCRLC. The project continued to decline in relative importance and was later transferred to the Confraternity of Christian Doctrine along with the vacation schools.[25]

For those in the Catholic rural life movement, secular education was as important as religious education in solving the rural population problem. For one thing, the rural exodus was to a great extent caused by a lack of Catholic educational facilities in the country. Thus, a high priority for the NCRLC was to increase the number of schools in the country in general. Catholics also believed that it was necessary to change the quality of rural education. Catholic rural leaders claimed that schools were educating students for the city by teaching from an urban point of view. A change from an urban- to a rural-oriented educational system was called for, they thought. A first step was to convince farmers that an education was desirable. According to O'Hara, "There are some who profess to be great friends of the farmer who think that no farmer should have more than a sixth-grade education." These Catholics feared that "book-larnin'" would seduce farmers' sons and daughters to leave the farms for the cities. However, O'Hara was convinced that it was not education in itself, but the wrong kind of education that led farm children to the cities. A properly rural-oriented education, far from leading them away, would actually keep more children on the farms.[26]

O'Hara and the NCRLC urged rural-oriented education at every possible level. They proposed changes in elementary and high school curricula, structure, teacher training, and physical conditions and held practical

---

25. Witte, *Twenty-five Years*, 187–88; "Why Should Pastors Worry?" *Catholic Rural Life* 7 (December 1928): 1; "Religious Correspondence Courses," ibid. (June 1929): 2–3; O'Hara to Day, March 8, 1929, "Correspondence. D," NCRLC 13-1; Day to O'Hara, March 14, 1929, and O'Hara to Day, March 20, 1929, "General Correspondence, O'Hara, Edwin V., 1922–68," LGL-E.

26. O'Hara, "The Rural Problem in Its Bearing on Catholic Education," in Witte, *Twenty-five Years*, 54–55; Shaughnessy, "Catholic Statistics for 1926," 22; O'Hara, *Church and Country Community*, 51–53; O'Hara, "Rural Education," *St. Isidore's Plow* 2 (March 1923): 3; O'Hara, "The Problem of the Rural School," ibid. 2 (November 1923): 3; NCRLC minutes binder (1923–32), NCRLC 8-1, 36; J. M. Wolfe, "Adapting the Curriculum to Rural Needs," *Catholic Rural Life* 7 (October 1928): 7–9, (November 1928): 7–9; O'Hara, "The Next Step in Rural Education," *Rural America* 4 (November 1926): 7; "Rural High School Advocated," *Catholic Rural Life* 8 (February 1930): 7–8.

demonstrations at the annual conventions.[27] The Conference also urged a change in higher education. It thought that more Catholic colleges should offer agricultural courses, and more Catholics should attend such courses. By 1928, colleges such as St. Benedict's in Atchison, Kansas, and the University of Notre Dame were offering such courses as agricultural economics and rural sociology. Notre Dame briefly operated an agricultural college, but it closed because of low enrollment in 1932. Some seminaries, such as St. Paul's in Minnesota and Kenrick in St. Louis, took steps to prepare their graduates for rural ministries. Finally, the NCRLC urged rural Catholics to take advantage of all kinds of rural-oriented adult education. The Conference itself sponsored institutes on such topics as farm women and credit unions. These changes, although they did not achieve a national reorientation of Catholic education toward rural life, did contribute to making Catholics more aware of rural America.[28]

Home Missionary Work and Colonization

If the NCRLC's primary means of solving the Catholic rural problem was education, an important secondary avenue was its connection with home missionary work. Considering that the origins of the Catholic rural life movement were bound up with the missions, it was only natural that this connection continued in the twenties, when the NCRLC was primarily concerned with increasing the number of Catholics in the countryside. The conversion of Protestants and the unchurched was believed to be an excellent way of providing the needed strengthening of the rural Church. Catholic rural life leaders complained that Catholics "talk of sending money and missionaries to China and we neglect our own cornland . . . The country is full of missionary opportunities." O'Hara said, "Among the

27. Wolfe, "Adapting the Curriculum to Rural Needs"; Leon A. McNeill, "Cooperation of Rural Life Workers and Educators," *Catholic Rural Life* 6 (December 1927): 1–2; McNeill, "The Catholic Rural Life Conference and the National Catholic Educational Association," ibid. (January 1928): 6–7; McNeill, "Rural Education," ibid. (February 1928): 3, 12–14; McNeill, "Rural Courses of Study," ibid. (March 1928): 6, 13–14, (April 1928): 3, 11, (May 1928): 3, 11–12; M. B. Schiltz, "Country Schools and Country Life," ibid., 1–2; [O'Hara], "The Secretary Looks at the Conference," 3, in NCRLC minutes binder (1923–32), NCRLC 8-1, 49; "School Exhibit at Rural Life Conference," printed description in "National Convention, Des Moines, Iowa, Oct. 15–17, 1929," NCRLC 8-1.

28. On the NCRLC urging rural-oriented higher education, see T. R. Daniels, "Agricultural Education Meets a Rural Need," *St. Isidore's Plow* 1 (May 1923): 2; NCRLC minutes binder (1923–32), NCRLC 8-1, 9, 13, 36. On courses at Catholic colleges, see Edgar Schmiedeler, "The Benedictines and Rural Life," *Catholic Rural Life* 6 (March 1928): 1, 11; "Rural Sociology," ibid. 6 (February 1928): 4; and Thomas J. Schlereth, *The University of Notre Dame: A Portrait of Its History and Campus* (Notre Dame, Ind.: University of Notre Dame Press, 1976), 149–54. On seminaries, see letter, The Mission Society, to the Editor, *Catholic Rural Life* 6 (April 1928): 5; NCRLC minutes binder (1923–32), NCRLC 8-1, 9. On conference institutes, see ibid., 33–33a, 53.

primary duties of the rural parish is that of bringing a knowledge of the Catholic religion to the non-Catholics who dwell within the parish borders." A correspondent from White Bear Lake, Minnesota, claimed that if "one hundred thousand lay apostles" were organized in America, they could gain hundreds of thousands of converts and make the United States "the shining Apostle of the Nations." Most Catholic rural life leaders were not this optimistic, but they did arrange for various forms of cooperation with the home missionary movement.[29]

The NCRLC's first president, Thomas R. Carey, was involved in the missionary movement by virtue of his directorship of the Catholic Church Extension Society's "rural experimental mission" at Lapeer, Michigan. The rural life movement rejoiced in the success of Carey's experiment, which in five years nearly doubled Mass attendance and tripled the number of communions. The mission was dissolved, however, in 1928, having "served its purpose." Despite the similarity in their goals, the Conference had little contact with the Extension Society after that.[30]

From the beginning, O'Hara's rural life writings encouraged religious communities to work in rural areas, usually with missionary goals in mind. Nuns were often used as religious vacation school instructors, and a number of religious communities were involved in other rural life activities. However, O'Hara, the Rural Life Bureau, and the NCRLC had little direct contact with religious orders regarding rural life work.[31]

Another connection between the NCRLC and the missionary movement was the Catholic Students Mission Crusade (CSMC), which was founded in 1918 to foster the awareness of Catholic students of all levels in both home and foreign missions. With the urging of O'Hara and the NCRLC, these enthusiastic students turned their energies to the rural problem. They discussed rural issues in study groups (guided by a spe-

29. H. F. Roney, "Missionaries for the Cornland," *Catholic Rural Life* 5 (April–May 1927): 4–5; Edwin V. O'Hara, "Missionary Aspects of the Rural Parish," ibid. 3 (March 1925): 5; "Why Not American Catechists?" (letter from W. F. Markoe), *America*, October 27, 1923, 36–37.

30. James P. Gaffey, *Francis Clement Kelley and the American Catholic Dream*, 2 vols. (Bensenville, Ill.: Heritage Foundation, 1980), 1:349–61, 2:119–23; [Thomas R. Carey], "First Annual Report, St. Philip Neri Mission," *Catholic Rural Life* 3 (May 1925): 2, 7; "St. Philip Neri Mission, Lapeer, Michigan," ibid. 6 (December 1927): 6, 14; Paul Ward, "What Concentrated Effort Will Do in a Missionary Parish," ibid. 6 (February 1928): 2–3; Ward, "Comparative Spiritual Tone," ibid. 6 (March 1928): 15; "Father Carey, First President of N.C.R.L.C., Transferred to Ann Arbor, Michigan," ibid. 7 (November 1928): 16.

31. O'Hara, *Church and Country Community*, 55–57; Witte, *Twenty-five Years*, 185; J. J. Sigstein, "The Work of Rural Religious Communities," *Catholic Rural Life* 3 (April 1925): 1–2; Sister Anna Mary, "The Work of a Rural Religious Community," ibid. 3 (July 1925): 1–2; Sister Josephine, O. Carm., "A Mission to Mexicans on the Ranch," ibid. 6 (January 1928): 1.

The Catholic Rural Population Problem

cial pamphlet written by O'Hara), contributed money to the missions, and served as catechists for vacation schools and as correctors for Monsignor Day's correspondence courses. The CSMC was organized in seminaries to interest the candidates in rural ministries.[32]

At the end of the decade, the NCRLC was drawn into involvement with the Catholic Missionary Union. In 1929, the Conference requested that the union provide funds to enable seminarians to teach in vacation schools. While this rather minor matter was under consideration, the editor of the Union's publication, the *Missionary*, proposed that his publication be consolidated with *Catholic Rural Life*, which was having its usual financial difficulties. At meetings later that year, the Conference decided against merging the publications, fearing that it would lose its identity of representing all aspects of Catholic rural life by so close a relationship with the missionary movement. Thus, the NCRLC rejected a more narrow identification with rural evangelization and left itself open to expand into many broader aspects of Catholic rural life, which it did in the next decade.[33]

In the 1920s, the NCRLC and the Rural Life Bureau returned to the idea of using colonization as a means by which to solve the Catholic rural population problem, despite the long and not very successful history of rural colonization in the American Catholic Church. While O'Hara was running the Rural Life Bureau in the early 1920s, he received numerous requests for colonization. Rural settlement was also urged by the Catholic press, although at least one publication, John A. Ryan's *Catholic Charities Review*, was skeptical. O'Hara himself did not favor a full-scale "back-to-the-land" movement of unknowledgeable city people moving to farms, for he believed that only families with previous agricultural experience could be successful in a farm settlement program.[34]

---

32. Joseph P. Donovan, C. M., "Catholic Students Mission Crusade and the Rural Problem in its Spiritual Aspect," *Catholic Rural Life* 4 (March 1926): 1–2; NCRLC minutes binder (1923–32), NCRLC 8-1, 13, 16, 20, 21; Report of the Rural Life Bureau, September 1, 1925–September 1, 1926, 3, "General Correspondence, O'Hara, Edwin V., 1922–68," LGL-E; *New Catholic Encyclopedia*, 1967 ed. s.v. "Catholic Students Mission Crusade," by M. McDonnell; Witte, *Twenty-five Years*, 183; Joseph P. Donovan, C. M., "A Movement That Will Catholicize Our Schools," *Ecclesiastical Review*, Seventh Series 5, no. 65 (December 1921): 562–70; Frank A. Thill, "The Catholic Students' Mission Crusade and Leadership," *NCWC Bulletin* 8 (August 1926): 18–20; Joseph P. Donovan, C.M., to O'Hara, March 30, 1924, OH40; "Week by Week," *Commonweal*, October 17, 1928, 590–91.

33. NCRLC minutes binder (1923–32), NCRLC 8-1, 39; Witte, *Twenty-five Years*, 75–76; F. P. Kenkel to O'Hara, November 5, 1929; O'Hara to Kenkel, November 9, 1929, OH30.

34. James H. Ryan, Executive Secretary, NCWC, to O'Hara, December 7, 1922, enclosing copy of William Hughes, Director, Bureau of Catholic Indian Missions, to NCWC, December 5, 1922; A. J. Millmann, President, Milwaukee County Council, National Council of Catholic Men, to O'Hara,

The colonization agitation came to a head soon after the founding of the NCRLC. Bishop Vincent Wehrle of Bismarck, North Dakota, spoke in favor of rural settlement of immigrants at the first NCRLC convention in November 1923. O'Hara endorsed the concept, and said that "the organization of a Catholic Agricultural Society . . . doing the work of . . . distributing Catholic immigrants and would-be farmers from the city throughout the United States" should be "the big, practical thing" that would come out of the Milwaukee NCRLC convention in October 1924. However, when O'Hara asked the National Catholic Welfare Conference to support the formation of a colonization agency, it turned him down, so the colonization session at the Milwaukee convention was an anticlimax. Eventually, O'Hara settled for a modest program of cooperation with the NCWC's Immigration Bureau in the settlement of a half dozen German farm families in Catholic parishes in Oregon.[35]

The Conference and the Rural Life Bureau made no further attempts at colonization in the 1920s. Although there were proposals for colonization from a number of sources and reports of some small-scale successes by private persons and individual dioceses, the rural life leaders gave up on colonization until the 1930s, when the Depression created more favorable circumstances.[36]

April 5, 1922, OH14; Stephen Good, S.J., to NCWC, March 2, 1923, OH16; P. H. Kiley to O'Hara, October 9, 1924, OH36; "Survey of the Immigrant Situation," *NCWC Bulletin* 2 (October 1920): 10, 30; "The Lane County, Oregon, Experiment in the Catholic Rural Program," ibid. (December 1920): 6–7, 13; "The Immigrant on the Farm," ibid. 5 (June 1923): 12; "Farms for Immigrants," *Catholic Charities Review* 5 (April 1921): 129; "The Agricultural Conference," ibid. 6 (March 1922): 89; "Rural Parish the Best Nursery of Faith, Says Father O'Hara," *Catholic Rural Life* 3 (November 1925): 5.

35. Vincent Wehrle, "How to Counteract the Exodus," *St. Isidore's Plow* 2 (February 1924): 1–2; O'Hara to Rev. William P. McDermott, April 8, 1924, OH38; "Rural Life Bureau Report: July 1, 1923–July 1, 1924," 3, "General Correspondence—O'Hara, Edwin V., 1922–68," LGL-E; Bishop Peter J. Muldoon to O'Hara, August 25, 1924, O'Hara to Muldoon, August 30, 1924, Muldoon to O'Hara, September 27, 1924, OH50; O'Hara's correspondence with Robert M. Patterson, OH49 and OH50, and with George F. X. Strassner, OH15 and OH36; NCRLC minutes binder (1923–32), NCRLC 8-1, 7; O'Hara to Muldoon, November 20, 1924, OH15, photocopy in "Correspondence, E. V. O'Hara, 1924, 1928," NCRLC 13-1; O'Hara to Bruce Mohler, Immigration Bureau, NCWC, January 30, 1925, O'Hara to Rev. Raymond McGowan, Social Action Department, NCWC, January 30, 1925, OH15; McGowan to O'Hara, February 10, 1925, O'Hara to McGowan, February 17, 1925, Mohler to O'Hara, February 12, 1925, O'Hara to Mohler, February 17, 1925, OH37.

36. Mark J. Thompson, "The Agricultural Specialist and Rural Life Improvement," *Catholic Rural Life* 4 (July 1926): 1–2, 8; [John A. Lapp], "The Immigrant Farmer Offers a Grave Problem," ibid. 5 (December 1926): 5, 8; [E. C. Meyers], "Settling Catholic Families on the Land," ibid. (February 1927): 1, 3; NCRLC minutes binder (1923–32), NCRLC 8-1, 22, 42; H. C. Kuthe, "Immigrants as Farmers," *Rural America* 3 (November 1925): 7–8; "Landsucher berathen!" *Central-Blatt and Social Justice* 21 (July–August 1928): 152; E. L. Chicanot, "Catholic Colonization in Canada," *America*, March 15, 1930, 549–51; "The New Population," *Commonweal*, June 9, 1926, 114–15; "Colonization in North Carolina," *NCWC Bulletin* 7 (April 1926): 17; "Holland Interested in Colonization Project," ibid. 10 (March 1929): 17.

The NCRLC and the Cultural Conflicts of the 1920s

The NCRLC's pursuit of a solution to the Catholic rural population problem was predicated on the traditional American belief in the prime value of rural culture. The 1920 census revealed that for the first time more Americans lived in urban than in rural areas. In the twenties the old attitude of "rural fundamentalism"—which asserted the superiority of agriculture to urban industry and of the rural to the urban way of life—began to die out, replaced by the attitude that the city was more "civilized" than the country and that agriculture was only one industry in an interdependent economic system. The programs of many urban social scientists, businessmen, and politicians for rural "reform" and "progress"—accompanied by professions of sympathy for the rural way of life—often actually expressed a desire to make agriculture more efficient in order to better serve the needs of urban America.[37]

Rural Americans did not take easily to this loss of prestige and preeminence. As the American society, culture, and economy became inexorably more urban-oriented, rural dwellers vented their frustration by fighting over peripheral issues that reflected the urban-rural tensions. Such well-known episodes or issues of the twenties were Prohibition, immigration restriction, the revival of the Ku Klux Klan, the Scopes trial, and the rural opposition to Al Smith in the 1928 presidential election.[38] American Catholics' involvement in these episodes usually resulted in bitter conflict with their Protestant countrymen, but the NCRLC's role in two of the most controversial social issues of the 1920s—Prohibition and religious prejudice—shows that its positions were not always hostile to those of rural Protestants.

Father O'Hara, the Rural Life Bureau, and the NCRLC never took a position on the Prohibition amendment itself. However, in the resolutions of the 1929 convention, at O'Hara's urging, the Conference "crie[d] out strongly against the evils of intemperance and its occasion, and urge[d] its members to make every effort to inform our rural people, and in particular our young men and women as to the evil effects of intemperance

---

37. Clifford B. Anderson, "The Metamorphosis of American Agrarian Idealism in the 1920s and 1930s," *Agricultural History* 35 (October 1961): 182–88; David B. Danbom, *The Resisted Revolution: Urban America and the Industrialization of Agriculture, 1900–1930* (Ames: Iowa State University Press, 1979), intro. and chap. 2.

38. James H. Shideler, "Flappers and Philosophers and Farmers: Rural-Urban Tensions of the Twenties," *Agricultural History* 47 (October 1973): 283–99; Don S. Kirschner, *City and Country: Rural Responses to Urbanization in the 1920s* (Westport, Conn.: Greenwood, 1970).

on the individual in undermining his health, demoralizing his character and destroying his freedom." It "recommend[ed] the ancient and laudable custom of inviting our boys and girls to abstain from intoxicating liquor in honor of the Sacred Thirst of Jesus Christ on the Cross, to a period extending to mature manhood and womanhood." The NCRLC's support for temperance in this resolution was closer to the Prohibitionist position of most rural Protestants than to the anti-Prohibition stand of the majority of American Catholics.[39]

In general, however, the decade of the 1920s was known for Catholic-Protestant conflict. Catholics responded to perceived prejudice by stressing the Church's compatibility with and contributions to American society, defending Catholic rights through political action, and forming organizations to assert their unity. But the tension came to a head when rural Protestant bigotry appeared to be a factor in Catholic Al Smith's defeat in the 1928 presidential election. That campaign left some Catholics more than ever pledged to bitter conflict with Protestants, but it gave others a desire to spread religious understanding to prevent such prejudice from emerging again. A number of organizations therefore initiated "campaigns against bigotry." Among them was the NCRLC.[40]

Many Conference members doubtless experienced anti-Catholic bigotry. O'Hara lived in Oregon, which had a strong Ku Klux Klan and in 1922 adopted a law (later nullified by the Supreme Court) imposing compulsory public education. During and after the 1928 campaign, leaders in the Catholic rural life movement and others showed their concern that most of the anti-Catholic prejudice was found in rural areas, and *Catholic Rural Life* announced that it would make its contribution to the anti-bigotry campaign by refuting anti-Catholic articles in the rural press.[41] In the fall

---

39. NCRLC minutes binder (1923–32), NCRLC 8-1, 39, 45. For another example of Catholic rural opposition to liquor, see B. W. Hilgenberg, "A Rural Catholic Program," *Rural America* 5 (March 1927): 4.

40. Kirschner, *City and Country*, 52–53; Michael Williams, *The Shadow of the Pope* (New York: Whittlesey House, 1932); Edmund A. Moore, *A Catholic Runs for President; the Campaign of 1928* (New York: Ronald Press, 1956); Oscar Handlin, *Al Smith and His America* (Boston: Little, Brown, 1958); Francis L. Broderick, *Right Reverend New Dealer, John A. Ryan* (New York: Macmillan, 1963), 170–87; Gaffey, *Francis Clement Kelley*, 2:172–74; Lynn Dumenil, "The Tribal Twenties: 'Assimilated' Catholics' Response to Anti-Catholicism in the 1920s," *Journal of American Ethnic History* 11 (Fall 1991): 21–49.

41. "Bishop Lillis Opens C.R.L.C. Program," *Catholic Rural Life* 7 (October 1928): 1; "Rural Religious Prejudice" (editorial), ibid. (November 1928): 4; Alice Avery, "My Program for Farm Relief," *America*, January 19, 1929, 354; "Rural Anti-Catholic Prejudice" (editorial), *Catholic Rural Life* 7 (June 1929): 4.

of 1929, the NCRLC's president, W. Howard Bishop, surveyed five hundred prominent Catholics for their recommendations on how to deal with anti-Catholic bigotry in rural areas. He presented the results at the 1929 annual convention in October, which included a special session on religious intolerance. At that convention, the NCRLC resolved to combat "religious antipathy" and charged a committee headed by Bishop to determine what role the Conference could play. Bishop initially favored forming a new bureau or agency to handle the bigotry problem. But O'Hara, after much discussion among Catholic rural life leaders, made his own proposal at the 1930 convention. In his mind, the growth of his new favorite project, the CCD, made it unnecessary to conduct the anti-bigotry campaign under the rather unsuitable auspices of the NCRLC. He proposed therefore that the CCD, whose general purpose was religious instruction, take over the anti-bigotry program. The Conference adopted his suggestion and thus relieved itself of an undertaking that was too vast for it to pursue and would only have diverted it from its primary mission of providing for the needs of rural Catholics.[42]

Continuing Concern for the Population Problem

In 1929, a period of transition began for the rural life movement's treatment of the problem of Catholic rural weakness. That year saw the start of a series of actions that gradually led to the transfer of the NCRLC's religious education activities to the CCD. Hitherto, religious education had been the Conference's primary means of attacking the issue and, indeed, the most important work of the Conference as a whole. Yet, as early as 1926, O'Hara allowed some of these activities, such as certain religious vacation schools, to be run by local units of the CCD, and his interest in the CCD began to compete seriously with his attention to the rural life movement.[43]

During 1929 he conducted a lengthy survey of Catholic apologetics in the United States, and in June of that year he announced the Home Mission Confraternity of Catholic Rural Life, which would take over the "religious vacation schools, religious correspondence courses, catechism classes, adult religious education based on the liturgy, and the dissolving

---

42. Bishop to F. P. Kenkel, September 5, 1929, "Clippings," CU; NCRLC minutes binder (1923–32), NCRLC 8-1, 38, 44, 50–51, 56, 58; Bishop, "Intolerance in Rural Communities. How to Meet It," *American Ecclesiastical Review* 81 (December 1929): 593–601; "Objectives of the Catholic Rural Life Conference," *Catholic Rural Life* 8 (December 1929): 6.

43. Shaw, *O'Hara*, 120.

of religious prejudices in rural communities"—in short, the Conference's entire religious education program. No specifics were mentioned, but they were provided in the spring of 1930, when the program changed its name to the Rural Life Confraternity. Announcements of the confraternity solicited membership contributions, which would pay for sending seminarians to conduct rural vacation schools. In return, members were promised an array of plenary and partial indulgences.[44]

But the Rural Life Confraternity was itself short-lived, for at the August 1930 NCRLC convention in Springfield, Illinois, the religious education part of the program was formally turned over to the CCD. For several years the NCRLC and the CCD operated in tandem, the CCD running the religious education section of the NCRLC conventions or, eventually, its own convention at the same site, but after the 1935 convention, the two organizations went their separate ways. The CCD took over the Conference's religious education program, and the Conference was left to concentrate more upon rural economic issues, which since the onset of the Depression had begun to occupy more and more of its attention.[45]

The early thirties showed considerable growth in the programs aimed at strengthening the Catholic rural population—largely because of the rapid expansion of the CCD. The religious vacation schools, which numbered 1,000, with 75,000 pupils, in 1930, instructed 250,000 children by the time the NCRLC and CCD formally separated in 1935 and numbered 6,112, with 547,000 pupils, in 1938. Catholics in many foreign countries considered the vacation school idea applicable to their own religious education problems and bombarded the Rural Life Bureau with requests for information. Vacation schools were set up in Jamaica and the western dioceses of Canada. The religious vacation school manuals, first published in 1930, expanded to an edition of ten thousand copies by 1933. The religious correspondence courses continued to be employed in the 1930s, but they became less necessary as the vacation schools and religious camp and boarding schools increased and took over the task of instructing the most scattered Catholic rural children.[46]

---

44. Ibid., 114–19; "The Home Mission Confraternity," *Catholic Rural Life* 7 (June 1929): 4; "Your Share," ibid. 8 (April 1930): 8; "Join the Rural Life Confraternity," ibid. (May 1930): 8; "The Catholic Church in City and Country," and "Rural Confraternity of Christian Doctrine" (leaflets), in "Catholic Rural Life Literature," NCWC 29; form letter, marked from "Editor, *Catholic Rural Life*" to "Seminarians on Lists, June 21, 1930," in "Seminaries and Seminarians, 1929–1930," NCWC 29.

45. Shaw, *O'Hara*, 121; Witte, *Twenty-five Years*, 90–96; Dolan, "Some Seed Fell," 129–30, and all of chap. 6 for O'Hara's involvement with the CCD as a whole.

46. "Annual Report of Social Action Department, National Catholic Welfare Conference,

The Catholic Rural Population Problem

In addition, the Conference continued to propose many of the same remedies to rural needs as it had offered in the 1920s. It continued to call for a more "rurally oriented" education for farm children. It wanted clergy and teachers to be specifically trained for rural work. The Conference proposed a variety of social, cultural, and recreational activities that would help keep rural folk on the land by adding spice to their lives. And it continued to urge the extension of Catholic charities into rural areas.[47]

In the early thirties the NCRLC was midwife to the birth of another movement that quickly separated from it—the "parent-educator" movement. This was another means of rural religious education promoted by O'Hara to keep rural Catholic families on the land. In the late 1920s, he had become convinced of the idea, promoted by popes and European societies since the late nineteenth century, that parents were a child's true and best educators in the religious life. O'Hara procured five speakers to contribute to a special session on family education at the 1930 rural life convention at Springfield, Illinois. At the convention, the speakers formed a Parent Educator Committee, with O'Hara acting as chairman. The committee undertook to promote the cause of religious education in the home through publications, speeches, and the formation of study groups. For a year, the committee was a part of the NCRLC, but since the parent-educator concept was not limited in its application to rural areas, direction of the movement soon passed to other hands. The National Council of Catholic Women took over sponsorship of the committee in 1931, and in 1936, a Parent-Educator Committee of the CCD was formed. The NCRLC, however, continued to hold sessions on family education at its conventions in 1931–33 and heard speeches on the topic at many subsequent meetings. Some of the talks were published in pamphlet form as volumes 1, 2, and 3 of *The Parent Educator*.[48]

July 1, 1933–July 1, 1934," (filed after folder "A-9"), NCWC 34, 19; William T. Mulloy, "Religious Vacation Schools and the National Catholic Rural Life Conference," in *Confraternity Comes of Age*, 34; "Religious Vacation Schools 1933. Latest Report from Rural Life Bureau, N.C.W.C.," *Landward* 1 (Autumn 1933): 5; "Report of Social Action Department, National Catholic Welfare Conference, July, 1931 to July 1932," (filed after folder "A-9"), NCWC 34, 8; "Report of Social Action Department, National Catholic Welfare Conference, July, 1932 to July, 1933," (filed after folder "A-9"), NCWC 34, 8–9; "New Religious Correspondence Courses under Way," *Rural Bureau Notes* 1 (February 1934): 4; "Religious Correspondence Courses," ibid. 2 (March 1935): 4; "Correspondence Courses in Catechism in the Diocese of Boise," *Catholic Action* 18 (June 1936): 4–5.

47. NCRLC minutes binder (1923–32), NCRLC 8-1, 58–59, 77; NCRLC minutes binder (1933–35), NCRLC 8-1, 94–95; National Catholic Rural Life Conference, *Manifesto on Rural Life* (Milwaukee: Bruce Publishing, 1939), 18–22, 26–28, 43–51; numerous articles in *Catholic Rural Life Bulletin*, 1938–39; Edgar Schmiedeler, *A Better Rural Life* (New York: J. F. Wagner, 1938), chaps. 12, 16, and 17.

48. Edgar Schmiedeler, "Catholic Rural Life Conference at Dubuque," (copy of article re-

The parent education movement was an example of a dilemma that characterized many of the causes championed by the NCRLC, and indeed, the organization itself. It was ironic that a movement that aimed at bypassing the church and the school and turning "right back to the foundation—the home" as the prime religious instructor would try to achieve its object by adding on another bureaucracy to teach the parents. The Reverend Edgar Schmiedeler tried to justify this apparent contradiction by claiming that the new complex conditions of the 1930s made it impossible for parents to undertake the task of religious instruction unaided by outside scientific expertise.[49] But by far the majority of the participants in the movement seemed to cherish the belief that the parent education movement would restore a simpler age in which the family, not the school, would be the prime religious educator. The Catholic rural life movement as a whole suffered from the same contradiction of trying to restore a decentralized, primitivistic way of life through centralized, modern, bureaucratic means.

In the 1930s, modern technology provided a new instrument for those Catholic missionaries attempting to build up the Catholic Church in the countryside—the "motor mission." Begun about 1935, motor missions involved priests driving automobiles or trucks equipped with loudspeakers into the center of small Protestant communities and holding one- to two-hour meetings. The meetings included recorded hymns, a question-and-answer period, a talk on a religious topic of interest to non-Catholics, and the distribution of apologetic literature. Sometimes follow-up missions visited the same communities, and interested persons or converts would be kept in touch by correspondence courses. Motor missions were eventually conducted in twenty-eight states, mostly in missionary dioceses of the South and West. Converts were few, each mission averaging one or two per year; a more modest goal was reducing anti-Catholic bigotry. Motor missions declined in the 1950s, when their novelty in isolated rural communities gave way to the convenience of television. The NCRLC promoted motor missions at its conventions, although it did not directly spon-

---

printed from *Ecclesiastical Review* 88 [May 1933]: 461–74), in "National Convention, Dubuque, Iowa, Oct. 19–21, 1932," NCRLC 8-1, 9–10; NCRLC minutes binder (1923–32), NCRLC 8-1, 31–32, 33, 52, 55, 56, 59–61; "Training for Parenthood Urged by Paul De Vuyst, Director General of the Belgian Ministry of Agriculture," *Catholic Rural Life* 6 (November 1927): 10; Mary Tinley Daly, "Parent Educator Program of the CCD," in *Confraternity Comes of Age*, 57–70; "Family Education Campaign Launched by National Committee," *NCWC Review* 13 (January 1931): 28; Edgar Schmiedeler, "The Parent Education Movement," ibid. 13 (August, 1931): 13–14; convention programs in NCRLC minutes binders, NCRLC 8-1, 8-2, and 8-3.

49. *Confraternity Comes of Age*, 57–58 (quotation, 57); NCRLC minutes binder (1923–32), NCRLC 8-1, 60; "Family Education Campaign Launched"; Schmiedeler, "Parent Education Movement."

The Catholic Rural Population Problem

sor any of them. A variation on the motor mission was the trailer-chapel, which allowed Mass to be said at any open space and was important for retrieving fallen-away Catholics.[50]

The formation of the Glenmary Home Mission Society in 1937 was inspired by the NCRLC, and it further relieved the Conference of responsibility for dealing with rural evangelization. In 1936, W. Howard Bishop, former president of the NCRLC, proposed the formation of a home missionary society dedicated to converting non-Catholics in the rural areas of the United States. One of his major arguments in favor of such a society was the same the-country-holds-the-future-of-the-city birthrate hypothesis so often repeated by the NCRLC. The following year Archbishop John T. McNicholas of Cincinnati agreed to sponsor the society with Bishop as its superior general. In 1940, the society established its motherhouse at Glendale, Ohio, near Cincinnati, took the title Glenmary Missioners, and began to send its missionaries into the rural Protestant areas of the South. Beginning with Bishop as its sole member, the Glenmary Missioners gradually expanded and worked at their patient plan of manning one-by-one the 1,022 "no-priest" counties that then existed in the United States. By 1962 the society numbered sixty-six priests, with one hundred more in training, and an associated group of sisters had more than one hundred members, novices, and postulants. By that time they had reduced the number of priestless counties to some seven hundred. In Appalachia, the missioners' work with the poor since the 1960s involved a new emphasis on social justice. Despite profound and sometimes disruptive changes in the men's and women's communities associated with the aftermath of Vatican II, Glenmary remained devoted to the evangelization of rural America at the turn of the millennium.[51]

---

50. Edgar Schmiedeler, "Motor Missions," *Ecclesiastical Review* 100 (February 1939): 132–42; Schmiedeler, "Motor Missions," *Homiletic and Pastoral Review* 38 (March 1938): 378–88; "Motor Missions Begin Summer's Work of Street Preaching in Rural Areas," and "Motor Missions Trailer Chapel," both in St. Louis *Register,* June 18, 1948, in "Clippings. Rural Life Meetings. 1935–1955," NCRLC 9-6; NCRLC, *Manifesto,* 41, 129–32; Marlett, *Saving the Heartland,* 131–61.

51. W. Howard Bishop, *A Plan for an American Society of Catholic Home Missions to Operate in Rural Sections of the United States* (Philadelphia: Dolphin Press, 1936), (reprinted from *Ecclesiastical Review* 94 [April 1936]: 337–47), in "Catholic Rural Life. The Farmer, Farm, Farm Home," NCRLC 3-5; "Our Mission Frontier," *Landward* 5 (Summer–Autumn 1937): 4; W. Howard Bishop, "The Home Missioners Find New Fields," *Catholic Rural Life Bulletin* 3 (August 20, 1940): 16–19; NCRLC minutes binder (1935–38), NCRLC 8-2, 186, 190, 215; Kauffman, *Mission to Rural America;* Herman W. Santen, *Father Bishop, Founder of the Glenmary Home Missioners* (Milwaukee: Bruce Publishing, 1961); Witte, *Twenty-five Years,* 195–98; *New Catholic Encyclopedia,* 1967 ed. s. v. "Glenmary Home Missioners" by R. P. O'Donnell, 509, and "Glenmary Home Mission Sisters," by J. Schmid, 507–9; Michael Glazier and Thomas J. Shelley, eds., *The Encyclopedia of American Catholic History,* s. v. "The Glenmary Home Missioners," by Christopher J. Kauffman, 591–93 (Collegeville, Minn.: The Liturgical Press, 1997).

Figure 3. William Howard Bishop, president, 1928–34, and founder of the Glenmary Missioners.

Although the NCRLC gradually participated in fewer activities devoted to solving the Catholic rural population problem in the 1930s, it continued to show considerable interest in the issue. Many Catholics still believed that there had been a great deal of leakage to Protestants in rural areas, despite the thorough studies by Shaughnessy and others disproving it. Instead of this popular leakage idea, the more scientific birthrate theory of rural Catholic weakness, originally proposed by Father O'Hara, was preferred by the Catholic ruralists connected with the NCRLC and the Rural Life Bureau, and in the thirties they updated it by new statistical studies. Most notably, the studies by O. E. Baker of the U.S. Department of Agriculture, who addressed the 1935 NCRLC convention, lent the prestige of a trained statistician to the birthrate theory. However, Baker, apparently a non-Catholic, was not concerned specifically with the threat to the Catholic Church because of its rural weakness. Instead, he warned that the population of the United States as a whole would begin to decline starting around 1950 if restrictions on immigration were not eased and/or the birthrate did not rise. For the latter to take place, Baker counseled, it was essential that the nation return to a rural-based society founded on the ideal of "the preservation of the family" and led by all the churches—Catholic, Protestant, and Jewish.[52]

Catholic ruralists tied their concern for the rural population problem into the more general Catholic crusade against birth control. To them, contraception was a product of the "paganism" and individualism of the cities. Not only was the practice itself immoral, they said, but if long continued it would inevitably lead to the extinction of the Catholic Church and of the nation. The basic cure was to reestablish the Catholic and rural values of respect for human life and the family. Federal legislation could help by paying a bonus to large families.[53]

In the 1940s, when the NCRLC's concern with the problems of the Depression and the "back-to-the-land" movement of the 1930s began to abate, the Conference revived somewhat its propaganda regarding the rural population issue. In 1940, the Conference expressed its continuing concern with the issue in a statement called "The Four Working Aims of the NCRLC":

1. To keep Catholics on the land.
2. To care for underprivileged Catholics on the land.
3. To settle Catholics on the land.
4. To convert non-Catholics now on the land.

---

52. "Leakage Out of Peter's Barque," *America*, November 14, 1936, 126–27; John A. O'Brien, "Causes of Catholic Leakage," *Ecclesiastical Review* 86 (April 1932): 412–21; Frank O'Hara, "The Lost Frontier," *Landward* 3 (Spring 1935): 1–2; L. G. Ligutti, "Cities Kill," *Commonweal*, August 2, 1940, 300–301; O. E. Baker, "The Church and the Rural Youth," in *Catholic Rural Life Objectives: A Series of Discussions on Some Elements of Major Importance in the Philosophy of Agrarianism* (St. Paul, Minn.: National Catholic Rural Life Conference, 1935), 7–29 (hereafter *Catholic Rural Life Objectives*, 1935); Baker, "Will More or Fewer People Live on the Land?" in *Catholic Rural Life Objectives: A Second Series of Discussions on Some Elements of Major Importance in the Philosophy of Agrarianism* (St. Paul, Minn.: National Catholic Rural Life Conference, 1936), 57–71 (hereafter *Catholic Rural Life Objectives*, 1936).

53. "Catholic Rural Life Conference Resolutions," *NCWC Review* 13 (December 1931): 22; "This Restriction Madness" (editorial), *Landward* 2 (Winter 1934–35): 4–5; "Looking Landward" (editorial), ibid. 3 (Summer 1935): 5; "Catholic Decline in Cities" (editorial), ibid. 3 (Autumn 1935): 4; "From the Spokane Resolutions," *Catholic Rural Life Bulletin* 2 (November 20, 1939): 17.

This set of slogans was used frequently in the 1940s. The Conference once more began to pass resolutions stressing the need "to balance the Catholic population in the United States," and it again made the population problem the basis of requests for financial contributions.[54]

In the 1940s and early 1950s, the NCRLC made the most extensive effort in its history to compile statistics on the actual state of the Catholic rural population and to study the demographic trends that affected it. It published many studies that showed that the rural population increased at a greater rate than the urban population. Most widely publicized were the findings of the Conference's semi-official statistician, O. E. Baker. The Conference frequently cited Baker's sensational calculation that in a "large city" the population would reproduce itself in a ratio from 10 children in the first generation to 7 in the second, to 5 in the third, to 3.5 in the fourth, whereas in a "rural region," the ratio would be from 10 to 13 to 17 to 22. In the NCRLC's silver anniversary history, published in 1948, Baker's statistics helped to provide the justification for the Conference's "Rural Crusade."[55]

In 1947, the NCRLC made a comprehensive study of the distribution of the Catholic Church's population and institutions in the United States and found, as expected, that "the Catholic Church is very weak in the countryside." Only 19.4 percent of Church members lived in rural areas, the survey found, compared to an average of 38.5 percent for Protestant denominations. This *Survey of Catholic Weakness,* as it was called, likewise revealed the paucity of Catholic church buildings, missions, and schools in rural areas. In 1955, the Conference, in bringing forth updated statistics, noted that "the basic findings are not much different today" from those of the *Survey of Catholic Weakness* and renewed the cry: *"Let's strengthen Catholicity in the rural districts of America."*[56]

To accomplish this, the Conference relied mainly on old methods. It called, as before, for Catholic farm youth to stay on the land and for the

---

54. Emerson Hynes, *"City Slickers" and "Dumb Farmers"* (St. Paul, Minn.: Wanderer Printing, 1940), 28–30, copy in "General Publications, 1940–1944," NCRLC 5-1; "The Working Aims of the NCRLC," *Christian Farmer* 1 (July 1948): 7; Witte, *Twenty-five Years,* 167–69; "We Resolve," December 1949, 1; "We Are Grateful," *Catholic Rural Life Bulletin* 4 (February 20, 1941): 14–15.

55. J. R. Pleasants, "Family Life and Catholic Life," *Catholic Rural Life Bulletin* 4 (August 20, 1941): 61–64; "Notes and Comments," *Land and Home* 9 (March 1946): 14–15; NCRLC, *A Study in Population Trends* (Des Moines, Iowa: National Catholic Rural Life Conference, ca. 1945), copy in "General Publications, 1944–46," NCRLC 5-1, 1; O. E. Baker, "The Debt of the City to the Country," *Catholic Rural Life Bulletin* 4 (August 20, 1941): 71–73; Witte, *Twenty-five Years,* chap. 1.

56. National Catholic Rural Life Conference, *A Survey of Catholic Weakness* (Des Moines, Iowa: National Catholic Rural Life Conference, 1948), copy in "General Publications, 1948–50," NCRLC 5-2, esp. 6, 11; [L. G.] Ligutti, "Catholicity in Rural America," *Rural Life Conference—Feet in the Furrow* 4 (September 1955): 6 (italics in original).

settlement of more Catholics on the land. Although religious vacation schools and correspondence courses were no longer under the Conference's direct control, it continued to propagandize for their use in solving the problem. In 1945, the twenty-fifth anniversary of Father O'Hara's first vacation schools in Oregon, the Conference proudly noted that there were eight thousand such schools, with more than seven hundred thousand students. It also continued to follow closely and support the progress of the Glenmary Missioners as they spread their missions over the non-Catholic areas of the United States.[57]

However, during these years, the Conference's concern with the rural population problem began increasingly to play second fiddle to its involvement with the economy and, beginning in the late 1940s, international affairs. The United States as a whole, and, within it, most Catholics, gradually began to accept the seemingly inevitable year-by-year decline in the rural population, which accelerated during and after World War II. As early as 1931, the editors of *America,* who were sympathetic to the NCRLC, admitted: "That we shall ever be a rural people is hardly probable. We must put up with the situation, utilizing what good it contains, and checking as far as possible what is evil." In May 1948 the Conference's executive secretary reported to the executive committee that the alarming facts of the *Survey of Catholic Weakness* had been received with "apathy . . . both by the Catholic Press and the overall Catholic group." Even within the Conference, officials began to downplay the importance of the issue, clearly feeling that it was no longer very important. In 1952, a prominent NCRLC official stated: "The matter of population was the most sensational part of rural life propaganda, but it was mainly used so that people would remain for the rest of the story." From the 1960s through the end of the century, an era of social justice and environmental concern, the population issue dropped out of NCRLC propaganda altogether.[58]

In the long run, the NCRLC's long-sustained concern for the rural pop-

57. Emerson Hynes, "Pastures for the Sheep," *Land and Home* 6 (December 1943): 106–7; "Notes and Comments," ibid. 8 (June 1945): 44–45; Sister M. Joanna, "The Aledo-Peoria Way," ibid. 6 (December 1943): 111–12; Olive M. Biddison, "A First-Born Grows Up," ibid. 8 (September 1945): 80–82; W. Howard Bishop, "The Home Missioners Find New Fields," *Catholic Rural Life Bulletin* 3 (August 20, 1940): 16–19; "Only 700 Counties to Go," *Catholic Rural Life* 9 (June 1960): 16–17.

58. "The Drift from the Farms" (editorial), *America,* September 19, 1931, 558; "Minutes of the Meeting of the Executive Committee, Council of Advisors, and La Crosse Convention Committee of the National Catholic Rural Life Conference, Tuesday and Wednesday, May 11–12, 1948, Headquarters of the NCRLC, Des Moines, Iowa," in "Exec. Committee Mtg., Des Moines, Ia., May 11–12, 1948," NCRLC 8-6, 2; Martin E. Schirber, "Catholic Rural Life," in *The American Apostolate,* ed. Leo R. Ward (Westminster, Md.: The Newman Press, 1952), 135.

ulation problem was successful, although not for the reasons the Catholic ruralists expected. The American Catholic Church, despite its small rural component, was successful in more than holding its own numerically both in that rural component and overall compared to Protestant churches right through the end of the century. The dire prediction of O'Hara and other Catholic rural life leaders that a rurally weak Catholic Church would inevitably decline in relation to other American churches was not borne out. However, the reasons for this success had less to do with rural dwellers becoming more important within the American Catholic Church than with some demographic trends that the NCRLC had not anticipated. American Protestants became much more urbanized in the mid- to late twentieth century, and thus lost any advantage they had over the rurally weak Catholics. And overall U.S. population growth was greatly slowed as the nation became more urbanized. As a result, the Catholic Church, with its small rural population, became more similar demographically to the Protestants and the nation as a whole. Although rural Catholics did not become a more important part of the Church, neither did this rural "weakness" lead to the decline of the Church as a whole in America. Thus, the fear of the threat posed by the rural population problem turned out to be unwarranted. This gradually became clear to the Conference itself as time went on. Thus, the NCRLC increasingly directed more and more of its attention to other aspects of rural life. The first of these areas, rural economics, attracted the Conference during the Depression of the 1930s.[59]

59. See the conclusion, chapter 15, for more on Catholic rural demographic trends into the twenty-first century.

Chapter 4 The Great Depression

In the 1930s, America's Great Depression propelled the National Catholic Rural Life Conference into a new era in its development. The severity of the Depression's impact upon Catholic farmers made it imperative that the Conference address economic issues in a serious and consistent way. In doing so, the Conference participated in the effort by the entire American Catholic Church to define its positions on the economic issues posed by the crisis of the day. As the Conference did this and as the economic crisis continued through the decade, the rural economy began to replace the rural population problem as the NCRLC's paramount concern.

Although the NCRLC did not officially trumpet the shift in emphasis, some Conference officials referred to it at the time. By 1933, Conference president W. Howard Bishop saw that the organization had evolved as a result of "the greatest agricultural depression in the history of our country" from devotion "primarily if not exclusively to missionary and educational problems in the small country parishes of America" to concern with "the economic and social phases of the rural problem."[1] Similarly, in 1939, the Conference's newly elected president, Vincent J. Ryan, declared that "a brief seventeen years ago, Bishop O'Hara of Kansas City called the Conference into existence as an instrumentality for the transfer of the advantages of religion to the spiritually underprivileged in rural America." Since then, however, "circumstances have forced an enlargement of the original sphere of Conference concern. While holding tenaciously to its essential purpose of serving the spiritual needs of the nation's agricultural population, it has taken to itself, as a matter of necessity, the task of interpreting the Christian principles of justice and charity to rural economists, governmental authorities, educators and social workers of every category."[2] The

---

1. [W. Howard Bishop], "Milwaukee 1924 and 1933," *Landward* 1 (Autumn 1933): 1.
2. Vincent J. Ryan, "A Statement by the President," *Catholic Rural Life Bulletin* 2 (November 20, 1939): 1.

NCRLC's concern with economic and social justice issues that thus began in earnest during the Depression years did not cease with the abatement of the crisis but carried on until the present.

The NCRLC and Rural Economics in the 1920s

Although the rural life movement had been primarily concerned with the rural demographic problem in the 1920s, it had given some attention to rural economic issues. The Rural Life Bureau and the NCRLC, like the rest of the Church, was only slowly developing a "social gospel" to justify branching out from purely spiritual concerns to tackle moral issues that existed in secular society.[3] The Social Action Department of the National Catholic Welfare Conference, led by John A. Ryan, was the spearhead of this movement, and the department's Rural Life Bureau, under O'Hara, to some extent shared in it. The NCRLC, with its backbone of old-fashioned rural pastors, was more reluctant in expressing interest in such rural "social action." In addition, some of the episcopal sponsors of the Conference were loath to let it branch out to consider social and economic topics.[4]

In the 1920s, the NCRLC—like most Catholics, and, indeed, most other Americans at the time—was committed to voluntarism in the economic sector. For many Catholics, government intervention in the economy was associated with dangerous "socialism," which meant, from a religious point of view, "atheism" as well.[5] The NCRLC followed this trend in its utterances on rural economic matters. Despite the severe economic depression that was afflicting American agriculture in the 1920s, neither the Conference nor the Rural Life Bureau formulated a short-term program aimed at mitigating it.

Insofar as Catholic rural leaders responded to economic problems, they thought in terms of long-range methods for improving farmers' economic lot. These would afford little immediate relief to the hard-pressed farmers, but they were the theoretically correct ways for gradually bringing about a better rural economic order. In keeping with the dictates of voluntarism, the three main means the Conference proposed were co-

---

3. David J. O'Brien, *American Catholics and Social Reform: The New Deal Years* (New York: Oxford University Press, 1968), chap. 2.

4. For example, Archbishop Glennon of St. Louis would not endorse statements on "Capital and Labor, State Ownership and Individualism, and similar subjects," at the first NCRLC convention. August F. Brockland to Frederick P. Kenkel, September 19, 1923, "Clippings," CU.

5. Abell, *American Catholicism and Social Action*, 204–5.

operative associations, agricultural education, and increasing ownership.

Cooperatives had been recommended in the Bishops' Program of Reconstruction (1919) and in O'Hara's *Program of Catholic Rural Action* (1922). The Conference and Rural Life Bureau strongly continued this support for cooperatives throughout the 1920s. Discussion of cooperatives formed a prominent part of both agencies' literature, and they were repeatedly recommended in the Conference's resolutions. Catholic social theorists and periodicals consistently supported cooperatives throughout the decade. Although Conference propaganda rarely distinguished between the various kinds of cooperatives, the less radical ones received the most favor. Marketing cooperatives were naturally of special interest to farmers and, since they were rapidly becoming an accepted part of the American mainstream, received the full approval of Catholic rural leaders. This was the kind probably thought of when the rural life movement mentioned "cooperatives." Consumer cooperatives and financial cooperatives (credit unions) received equal NCRLC sanction, however. Producer cooperatives, on the other hand, were seldom discussed by Catholics in the 1920s. This was probably because they were associated with the Soviet Union and therefore tainted with socialist implications. At any rate, Catholics in the 1920s seemed to assume that the only way for farmers to own the means of production was individually. At that time, many poor tenants, sharecroppers, and farm laborers could not afford the costs of individual land ownership.[6]

The Conference publicized the fact that Catholics like A. J. McGuire headed large associations such as the Co-operative Creameries of Minnesota, and they were probably influential in getting Catholics to join the cooperative movement. However, Catholic rural leaders had little success

---

6. O'Hara, *Church and Country Community,* chaps. 10, 12, 13; E. V. O'Hara, "The Church and the Rural Community," *Catholic Charities Review* 6 (April 1926): 115–16; J. V. Scheffer, "Co-operation: Festina Lente," *St. Isidore's Plow* 2 (May 1924): 3; Francis J. Haas, "The Ethics of Cooperation," *Catholic Rural Life* 3 (March 1925): 5; NCRLC minutes binder (1923–32), NCRLC 8-1, 12, 27A, 37, 42, 57; "Eliminating the Middleman" (editorial), *America,* October 8, 1927, 607; "Week by Week," *Commonweal,* July 22, 1925, 259–60; "Apathy vs. Enterprise in Cooperation," *Central-Blatt and Social Justice* 21 (February 1929): 361–62; "Farmer's Cooperative Experiment" (editorial), *NCWC Bulletin* 3 (September 1921): 12; "A Great Step Forward in Cooperation," *Catholic Charities Review* 4 (March 1920): 69–70; Aloysius J. Muench, "Credit Unions in the Parish," *Salesianum* 24 (April 1929): 15–21; Edwin V. O'Hara, *The Agricultural Profession* (pamphlet, 1923, copy in LGL-E), 17–18; Joseph G. Knapp, *The Rise of American Cooperative Enterprise, 1620–1920* (Danville, Ill.: Interstate Printers and Publishers, 1969), 438–39. The 1919 Bishops' Program and the NCWC Social Action Department specifically came out in favor of producer cooperatives (Abell, *American Catholicism and Social Action,* 202–3, 211–12), but the NCRLC and Rural Life Bureau never did so.

in inducing American Catholics to follow the example of Europeans in forming all-Catholic cooperatives.[7]

Most of the NCRLC's activity concerning cooperatives involved the parish credit union movement. American credit unions were growing rapidly in number during the 1920s. The Conference availed itself of this movement by inviting Roy Bergengren of the Credit Union National Extension Bureau of Boston to its 1926 convention to explain the principles of rural parish credit unions to the delegates. As a result, the Conference undertook to spread such credit unions as one of its "immediate steps" for the forthcoming year. Credit unions were quickly formed by parishes in Iowa and Missouri and showed promising growth in succeeding years. The 1929 convention had a special session on credit unions. In the same year, the NCWC Social Action Department formed the Parish Credit Union National Committee, under the chairmanship of O'Hara, to promote the movement nationwide. At the NCRLC convention the next year in Springfield, Illinois, the committee sponsored a Parish Credit Union Institute to provide practical information and advice to interested delegates, and the Conference urged the establishment of credit unions in every parish. That year, the number of Catholic parish credit unions more than doubled to forty-six. The promotion of parish credit unions continued to be the Conference's most important contribution to the cooperative movement for most of the next decade.[8]

The NCRLC's leaders believed that farmers would go a long way toward solving their economic problems by practicing more efficient production techniques. The Conference urged them to take advantage of the facilities of the agricultural colleges to learn how to produce more abundant harvests. In this, the NCRLC was only following the obsession with more efficient production that had captured all of rural America in the 1920s. Agricultural economists later realized that this concentration on production only yielded greater surpluses, lower prices, and ultimately more financial distress for American farmers.[9]

---

7. NCRLC minutes binder (1923–32), NCRLC 8-1, 6, 7, 22; A. J. McGuire, "Cooperation of Agriculture," *Catholic Rural Life* 3 (January 1925): 2; Edwin V. O'Hara, *Letters on Catholic Rural Action in Europe* (Eugene, Ore.: Rural Life Bureau, Social Action Department, NCWC, [1926]), (pamphlet), copy in NCWC 29.

8. NCRLC minutes binder (1923–32), NCRLC 8-1, 22, 23, 27A, 57, 58; Roy F. Bergengren, "Cooperative Credit Unions" (July 1926): 1, 3; ibid. (August 1926): 2, 8; Barney Barhorst, "Credit Unions in Missouri," *Catholic Rural Life* 8 (December 1929): 2, 7–8; "Credit Unions" (editorial), ibid., 4; J. M. Campbell, "The Parish Credit Union," ibid., 2, 5 and ibid. (January 1930): 2–3, 7–8; Joseph G. Knapp, *The Advance of American Cooperative Enterprise, 1920–1945* (Danville, Ill.: Interstate Printers and Publishers, 1973), 196.

9. O'Hara, *Agricultural Profession*, 13–16; NCRLC minutes binder (1923–32), NCRLC 8-1, 13, 20, 27A.

The third economic issue on which the NCRLC spoke out was widely distributed landownership—a traditional Catholic concern. The Conference appealed to the principles enunciated by Pope Leo XIII that called for widespread ownership because it would provide a large, stable, independent population that would be a bulwark against socialism. Moreover, individually owned farms were seen as the best setting for a wholesome family life. The Conference considered this social aspect of distributed ownership as more important than the economic aspect, because farming was "primarily a mode of life, and only secondarily a commercial business."[10]

The NCRLC urged all kinds of ways of increasing farm ownership. In 1929, it resolved on the "elimination of submarginal farming, by proper distribution of productive specialties, by scientific colonization (if or where possible), by expert guidance, governmental or otherwise." It was also concerned that farm tenants and laborers be provided with opportunities for moving up the "agricultural ladder" to ownership. However, the Conference was not involved in providing practical assistance to farmers for achieving more widely distributed farm ownership during the 1920s.[11]

The Impact of the Depression: The NCRLC Turns to Economics

When the stock market crash of October 1929 signaled the beginning of the great industrial depression of the 1930s, American farmers had already been suffering hard times for nearly a decade.[12] The American and worldwide depressions of the 1930s only made American agricultural conditions worse. Between 1929 and 1932, farm prices and agricultural income both declined by half. In addition, farmers' indebtedness became so burdensome that between 1930 and 1934 nearly 1 million farmers lost their farms.[13]

States with large Catholic rural populations suffered from the hard times as much as any of the others. In the Midwest the price for corn was so low that many farmers burned the grain as fuel, and many reacted to the crisis with various kinds of protest activity. In Wisconsin, one of the

---

10. NCRLC minutes binder (1923-32), NCRLC 8-1, 12, 42; O'Hara, *Agricultural Profession*, 19.

11. O'Hara, *Agricultural Profession*, 22–25; NCRLC minutes binder (1923-32), NCRLC 8-1, 42; A. J. Muench, "Farm Tenancy," *Catholic Rural Life* 3 (June 1925): 2.

12. James Shideler, *Farm Crisis, 1919–1923* (Berkeley: University of California Press, 1957), esp. 284–86; Danbom, *Resisted Revolution*, chap. 6. Danbom, *Born in the Country*, 188–89, says the agricultural depression of the 1920s may not have been very severe.

13. M. R. Benedict, *Farm Policies*, (Twentieth Century Fund, 1953), 246–47; Arthur M. Schlesinger Jr., *The Age of Roosevelt*, vol. 1: *The Crisis of the Old Order* (Boston: Houghton Mifflin, 1957), 174–75, 236–38; W. E. Leuchtenburg, *Franklin D. Roosevelt and the New Deal* (New York: Harper Brothers, 1963), 23–24.

strongest Catholic rural states, dairy farmers "went on strike" (refused to deliver their milk to market) three separate times in 1933. The Farmers' Holiday Association—which threatened to withhold farm produce from the cities unless farmers received "cost of production"—arose in Iowa, where some of the most prominent Catholic rural leaders lived. And all over the Midwest, crowds of farmers, some brandishing clubs and ropes, showed up at farm foreclosure sales and either prevented the proceedings altogether or forced sales at pittances, whereupon the properties were restored to their previous owners.[14]

Sometimes the Church was able to aid rural victims of the Depression. In three counties of northeastern Nebraska, drought and a grasshopper plague resulted in almost total crop failure for two consecutive years and left hundreds of Catholic families on the verge of destitution. To keep these families from losing their farms, the Omaha diocese collected "three carloads of grain, flour, and potatoes, and several truck loads of such supplies as beans, rice, canned goods, and clothes together with eight hundred dollars in cash," and shipped them to their stricken rural brethren.[15]

President Herbert Hoover's administration, hamstrung by its policy of voluntarism, did little to ease the hardship of the Depression in both urban and rural areas. Its creations, the Federal Farm Board and Reconstruction Finance Corporation, were too little or too late to deal with the crisis, and farmers refused to heed the administration's calls for voluntary crop reduction, waiting for their neighbors to join the program first.[16] Like Hoover, Catholics and the NCRLC responded slowly to the Depression crisis. They all shared a common belief in voluntarism and individualism, and the current economic order seemed to embody those principles. Thus Catholics, like the president, hoped that the American economy would be able to ride out the storms without any serious damage or the need for any drastic changes.

The NCRLC made no official statement in response to the Depression until 1931. W. Howard Bishop's presidential address at the Conference con-

14. Schlesinger, *Crisis of the Old Order*, 175, 266–69, 459–60; Leuchtenburg, *Roosevelt and the New Deal*, 23–24; A. William Hoglund, "Wisconsin Dairy Farmers on Strike," *Agricultural History* 35 (January 1961): 24–34; Saloutos and Hicks, *Agricultural Discontent*, 435–51; John L. Shover, *Cornbelt Rebellion: The Farmers' Holiday Association* (Urbana: University of Illinois Press, 1965).

15. Edgar Schmiedeler, "Catholic Rural Life Notes," *Catholic Action* 14 (February 1932): 30.

16. Benedict, *Farm Policies*, 239–41, 252–67; Gilbert C. Fite, *George N. Peek and the Fight for Farm Parity* (Norman: University of Oklahoma Press, 1954), 224–27; Schlesinger, *Crisis of the Old Order*, 236–40; David E. Hamilton, "Herbert Hoover and the Great Drought of 1930," *Journal of American History* 68 (March 1982): 850–75.

The Great Depression

vention that year reminded members that, even in the midst of a great agricultural depression, their primary concern should be for the spiritual side of rural life, not the economic side. The convention resolutions on economic problems were primarily affirmations of the general ideals espoused by Pope Pius XI's economic encyclical *Quadragesimo Anno,* which was issued earlier that year, not responses to the specific problems of the Depression.[17]

Catholics from outside the NCRLC actually gave more attention to the rural economic problems of the early Depression years than the Conference did. In 1930, the Catholic Conference on Industrial Problems discussed the effect of the industrial depression on farmers, and the next year, the U.S. bishops issued a call for local and federal appropriations for relief. A number of Catholic periodicals also spoke out, expressing little hope for the proposed remedies of the Hoover administration such as the Federal Farm Board. The German Catholic Central Verein went beyond disagreement with particular government policies to blame "finance-capital" for bringing on the Depression and to voice fears that the agricultural crisis would lead to the "extinction" of the nation's vital family farming class.[18]

The presidential election year of 1932 was crucial both for the United States and for the development of the NCRLC. The nation put in power a president—Franklin D. Roosevelt—and an administration committed to a new activist policy for solving the economic crisis. During the same year, the Conference spoke out for the first time on the rural economic issues of the day. Historian David J. O'Brien has argued that the Depression was the crucial force that impelled the American Catholic Church into supporting social reform. The history of the NCRLC provides a perfect illustration of his thesis.[19]

---

17. NCRLC minutes binder (1923–32), NCRLC 8-1, 71–72; [W. Howard Bishop], "Presidential Speech, C.R.L.C. 9th an. conv., Wichita, Kansas, Oct. 20, 1931," in "Ntn'l Convention, Wichita, Kansas, Oct. 20–22, 1931," NCRLC 8-1. Unfortunately, an assessment of the NCRLC's attitude during the early Depression years is hindered by the fact that the conference lacked an official publication from the demise of *Catholic Rural Life* in May 1930 until the first issue of *Landward* in spring 1933.

18. "Wages and Unemployment Subjects of Discussion at St. Paul Meeting," *NCWC Review* 12 (July 1931): 25–27, 29; "U.S. Bishops Issue Statement on Economic Crisis," ibid. 13 (December 1931): 8; "What the Farmer Needs," *Commonweal,* April 17, 1929, 669; "The Federal Farmhouse," *America,* July 18, 1931, 342–43; "Farm Mortgages," *Catholic Charities Review* 17 (February 1933): 35–36; "Where Would the Farmer Be?" *Central-Blatt and Social Justice* 22 (April 1929): 423; F. P. K[enkel], "'Farm Relief' According to the Chairman of the Federal Farm Board," ibid. (August 1929): 131; "Throttled by Industrialism," ibid. 24 (October 1931): 205–6; F. P. Kenkel, "The Farming Class Facing Destruction," ibid. 25 (May 1932): 39–41.

19. O'Brien, *American Catholics and Social Reform,* 47.

Pressure on the NCRLC for action regarding the rural depression built up over the course of the election year. Edgar Schmiedeler of the Rural Life Bureau believed that the farm situation was "very critical" and government action was needed. "Perhaps the forthcoming election will help to stir up matters a bit," he confided to a correspondent in August. Other Catholic spokesmen lamented the futility of the Hoover administration's agricultural programs and the vagueness of the major parties' farm platforms. They countered with a variety of proposals, ranging from the Central Verein's advocacy of participation in the cooperative movement and adherence to "the old fashioned virtues of thrift, industry, mutual help, justice and charity in fullest measure," to calls for the establishment of an occupational group system on the lines of *Quadragesimo Anno,* to proposals for reforms of the nation's monetary system and agricultural surplus disposal system.[20]

The NCRLC convention that met at Dubuque, Iowa, on October 19–21, 1932, was therefore in a frame of mind to speak out on the rural aspects of the Depression. Schmiedeler's publicity committee recommended that the Conference break its silence on such matters. Bishop, president of the Conference, agreed. In contrast to the previous year, he devoted most of his presidential address to a discussion of "the agricultural-economic side of the Conference's work." Bishop declared that submarginal and corporate farms senselessly added to the surplus without providing a decent living for a large number of farmers. The NCRLC's alternative of owner-operated family farms was not only the best spiritually but would also help to reduce the surplus:

More family-size farms mean fewer acres per farm, less power machinery, sold by high-pressure salesmen from the big business houses, eating up the cash income of the farm and consuming no farm crops. They mean more horses and mules that get their living from the soil and cut down costs at the same time that their feed needs reduce the marketing of crops now hopelessly overproduced. They mean more people enjoying the human blessing of wholesome life on the soil, more men, women and children and farm animals to be fed before any ex-

---

20. Edgar Schmiedeler to John Rausch, Lastrup, Minnesota, August 15, 1932, "General Correspondence—1932," NCWC 29; John La Farge, "The Party Agricultural Platforms of 1932," *America,* August 13, 1932, 443–45; "Resolutions Adopted by the 77th General Convention, C.C.V.A. Held at St. Louis, Mo., Aug. 19–24, 1932," *Central-Blatt and Social Justice* 25 (September 1932): 174–75; William F. Montavon, "Agricultural Relief Legislation," *Catholic Action* 14 (September 1932): 15; Charles R. Adair, "The Agriculture of Michigan," *Commonweal,* September 7, 1932, 447–48; "From Mr. Lippmann to Kansas," ibid., October 5, 1932, 521–22.

cess is sent to market, hence smaller quantities of produce offered for sale and higher prices for them as the surplus vanishes.

To spread the blessings of the family farm, particularly to American Catholics, Bishop called for "a Catholic Land Movement in America." He proposed that the Conference establish a "national advisory council" to coordinate the local efforts to get more Catholic families on the land. A Catholic land movement would be of particular benefit during the current depressed times by providing new homes and means of subsistence for some of the urban unemployed. As an additional help to the unemployed of the cities, Bishop recommended the establishment of urban garden projects. Thus, Bishop wanted the Conference to commit itself to full-fledged participation in a back-to-the-land movement.[21]

Bishop O'Hara—who as founder and (since his elevation to the episcopate in 1930) honorary president of the Conference was still its most influential person—urged the NCRLC to endorse the voluntary domestic allotment plan that had been widely publicized during the election year. The Conference responded by passing a resolution authorizing a message to be sent to the candidates of the two major parties calling for "immediate and effective support" for the plan. Franklin D. Roosevelt replied to the Conference's letter on November 1, 1932, commending the NCRLC's interest in agricultural legislation and reaffirming the pledge of his Topeka speech to "make the tariff effective for agriculture." This marked the Conference's first contact with an American president or presidential candidate; it was the beginning of ever-increasing involvement with the federal government.[22]

Other resolutions adopted at the Dubuque convention endorsed the social and economic principles of *Quadragesimo Anno,* approved "sane and honest" Catholic farm colonization ventures, recommended the establishment of home gardens for the unemployed, deplored industrial farming, and favored reduction of rural taxes. The Conference proposed the estab-

---

21. "Report of Publicity Committee," in NCRLC minutes binder (1923–32), NCRLC 8-1, 81b–81c; [W. Howard Bishop] "Presidential Address, Tenth Annual Convention, C.R.L.C., Dubuque, Iowa, October, 1932," in "Ntn'l Convention, Dubuque, Iowa, October 19–21, 1932," NCRLC 8-1.

22. NCRLC minutes binder (1923–32), NCRLC 8-1, 79, 83; *Sermon by Most Rev. Edwin V. O'Hara, Bishop of Great Falls, Montana, at the Tenth Annual Rural Life Conference, Dubuque, Iowa, October 19, 1932* (n.p.: Compliments of American Book Company, n.d.), in "Ntn'l Convention, Dubuque, Iowa, Oct. 19–21, 1932," NCRLC 8-1; Frank O'Hara, "The Voluntary Domestic Allotment Plan," *Catholic World* 136 (March 1933): 641–42; "Gov. Roosevelt Lauds Catholic Rural Life Conference Activity," *NCWC News Service,* November 28, 1932.

lishment of diocesan rural life bureaus, whose directors would guide the local development of Catholic rural life, particularly the Catholic landward movement. Finally, at the suggestion of Joseph Campbell, it authorized special meetings of the board of directors or the executive committee to be called at times between national conventions, particularly for the discussion of economic questions.[23]

Roosevelt's victory in November was accomplished with the help of the majority of both farmers and Catholics. FDR's electoral landslide included a sweep of all of the midwestern farm states. Catholics—urban and rural—formed an important part of the new political coalition that put the Democrats into power. After the election of Roosevelt, in the months leading up to his inauguration, Catholic support for governmental aid to agriculture continued to grow. Officials from the Conference and the NCWC, as well as periodicals such as *Central-Blatt and Social Justice* and *America*, called for debt relief for farmers and the enactment of the domestic allotment plan.[24]

Among the acts passed during the whirlwind Hundred Days at the beginning of the Roosevelt administration were the Agricultural Adjustment Act (AAA), which authorized the government to put into execution the domestic allotment and other surplus control plans, and the Farm Credit Act, which offered to refinance farm mortgages. American Catholics generally welcomed the new acts. At its October 1933 convention in Milwaukee, the NCRLC praised "the manifestly sincere efforts of President Roosevelt to come to the relief of the farm population of the land." Schmiedeler, noting that the AAA included many features of the NCRLC-endorsed domestic allotment plan, called the act "a charter of economic equality with the city." Catholics credited it with the increases in the prices

---

23. NCRLC minutes binder (1923–32), NCRLC 8-1, 79–83; Edgar Schmiedeler, "Catholic Rural Life Conference at Dubuque" (copy of article reprinted from *Ecclesiastical Review* 88 [May 1933]: 461–74), in "National Convention, Dubuque, Iowa, Oct. 19–21, 1932," NCRLC 8-1, 471–72.

24. Schlesinger, *Crisis of the Old Order*, 423–24; Benedict, *Farm Policies*, 273; Fite, *Peek*, 239–40; George Q. Flynn, *American Catholics and the Roosevelt Presidency, 1932–1936* (Lexington: University of Kentucky Press, 1968), 1–21; O'Brien, *American Catholics and Social Reform*, 47–51; Samuel Lubell, *The Future of American Politics*, 2d rev. ed. (Garden City, N.Y.: Doubleday, 1956), 29–43; memos, John J. Burke to Edgar Schmiedeler, December 23, 1932, and Schmiedeler to Burke, December 24, 1932, in "Inter-Offices (Gen'l), Requisitions, Statements, Etc.—1932," NCWC 40; Schmiedeler, *Why Rural Life* (n.p.: Rural Life Bureau, National Catholic Welfare Conference, 1933), 15, copy in NCWC 160; L. S. Herron, "Allotment Plan Poor Goal for Farmers," *Central-Blatt and Social Justice* 25 (January 1933): 302–4; "What Should the New Administration Do about Agriculture?" *Rural America* 11 (April 1933): 7 (reprinted as "What Should Be Done about Agriculture?" *Landward* 1 [Spring 1933]: 5, 8); "The Revolt in Iowa," *America*, May 13, 1933, 123.

of most farm commodities in ensuing years. The Conference also praised the Farm Credit Act and called for a moratorium on farm mortgage foreclosures until farmers could avail themselves of its benefits.[25]

However, practically from its beginning, many Catholics had serious reservations about the AAA. Father Bishop repeatedly bemoaned the "drastic and artificial" aspects of the act and saw it as only a temporary emergency device until an "ultimate permanent readjustment" could be devised and put into operation. As Edward S. Shapiro and other New Deal historians have noted, the AAA and other New Deal agricultural programs were intended primarily to provide immediate relief to hard-pressed commercial farmers by raising farm commodity prices. They did not promote any fundamental reforms in American rural society such as reducing farm tenancy, sharecropping, and hired labor or increasing owner-operated family farms, as the NCRLC wished. In fact, many New Deal officials believed, as Bishop feared, that "there were already too many farmers," and that agriculture would be better off if a smaller number of farmers had a higher average income. In the South, the AAA crop-reduction program resulted in many plantation owners throwing tenants off their land to receive benefit payments. Such policies, Bishop held, only benefited "a closed corporation" of large commercial farmers and excluded the possibility of a large property-owning class of middle-sized farmers enjoying both the material and spiritual blessings of farm life.[26]

Catholics were also apprehensive of the excessive government control involved in the New Deal agricultural programs. These fears of gov-

---

25. Leuchtenburg, *Roosevelt and the New Deal*, 48–52; Arthur M. Schlesinger Jr., *The Age of Roosevelt*, vol. 2: *The Coming of the New Deal* (Boston: Houghton Mifflin, 1959), 27–54; Edward S. Shapiro, "The Catholic Rural Life Movement and the New Deal Farm Program," *American Benedictine Review* 28 (September 1977): 307–32; Shapiro, "Catholic Agrarian Thought and the New Deal," *Catholic Historical Review* 65 (October 1979): 583–99; "Rural Life Conference Begins Second Decade of Rural Catholic Action," *Catholic Action* 15 (November 1933): 5; John A. Ryan, "Social Justice in the 1935 Congress," ibid. 17 (September 1935): 8–9; Edgar Schmiedeler, "Why Rural Life," in *Catholic Rural Life Conference: Proceedings of the Eleventh Annual Convention, October 16–19, 1933, Milwaukee, Wisconsin* (n.p.: n.p., n.d.), 8 [hereafter shortened as *NCRLC Proceedings, 1933*]; Schmiedeler, "The A.A.A. in Action," *Landward* 2 (Autumn 1933): 3; Schmiedeler, "Rescuing Agriculture," *Commonweal*, May 17, 1935, 69–71; NCRLC minutes binder (1933–35), NCRLC 8-1, 94.

26. W. Howard Bishop, "Presidential Address," *NCRLC Proceedings, 1933*, 11–12; [Bishop], "A Permanent Readjustment," *Landward* 1 (Summer 1933): 1; Bishop, "Presidential Address," *Proceedings of the Twelfth Annual Convention* (St. Paul, Minn.: National Catholic Rural Life Conference, 1934), 28–32 [hereafter shortened as *NCRLC Proceedings, 1934*]; Shapiro, "Catholic Rural Life Movement and New Deal Farm Program," 318–20; Shapiro, "Catholic Agrarian Thought and New Deal," 590, 593; Grant McConnell, *The Decline of Agrarian Democracy* (Berkeley: University of California Press, 1953); untitled editorial, *Catholic Charities Review* 18 (September 1934): 194.

ernment seemed realized when it was discovered that the government's schools for AAA administrators and other agricultural officials were teaching a "pagan," "materialistic," philosophy of rural life. Other Catholics believed that the New Deal was being controlled by the materialistic forces of finance capitalism. They argued that the Catholic position was the true "middle road" between the Scylla of socialism and the Charybdis of capitalism. NCRLC president Joseph Campbell took a slightly different tack: he argued that "national planning and regimentation in the economic order" was necessary under new conditions created by the Depression, but that this regimentation should take the form of cooperation among communities and occupational groups, not fascist or socialist coercion.[27]

One particular issue that concerned Catholics about the operations of the AAA was its policy of production restriction and crop and livestock destruction. Some within the NCRLC objected to the AAA's policy of crop restriction, holding that the real road to economic recovery lay in increasing both agricultural and industrial production. The Conference believed that the AAA's occasional resort to actual crop and livestock destruction was unwise, because the surplus might be needed at a later time, and even immoral, when so many people both at home and abroad were tragically deprived of the food and fiber necessary for life. However, some Conference officials defended the restriction policy as a purely emergency measure for dealing with the temporary surplus until a permanent program more in keeping with Christian principles could be implemented.[28]

In 1935–36, when questions arose over the constitutionality of the AAA, Catholics lined up on both sides of the issue. Some, such as John A. Ryan, held that, with all its flaws, the act overall was "in accord with social justice." Others, including a writer in *Commonweal*, believed that the act was too favorable toward commercial farmers. When, on January 6, 1936, the Supreme Court ruled the AAA's processing tax, and as a consequence the entire act, unconstitutional, many Catholics did not mourn its passing.

---

27. Aloysius J. Muench, "Religion and Agrarianism," *Catholic Mind* 38, no. 909 (November 8, 1940): 443–44; F. P. K[enkel], "Rural Economic Welfare in the Light of Present Conditions II," *Central-Blatt and Social Justice* 26 (December 1933): 275–77; Kenkel, "Shall the Farm Become a Public Utility?" ibid. (January 1934): 314; John La Farge, "The Farmers Are Taught How to Be Cultured Pagans," *America*, April 6, 1940, 706–7; John C. Rawe, "Agrarianism: The Basis for a Better Life," *American Review* 6 (December 1935): 176–92; J. M. Campbell, "Regimenting the Economic Order," *Landward* 2 (Autumn 1934): 2–3.

28. "Agricola," "A Way to Greater Production," *Landward* 3 (Summer 1935): 1, 11–12; Schlesinger, *Coming of the New Deal*, 39–64; Leuchtenburg, *Roosevelt and the New Deal*, 72–74; Schmiedeler, "A.A.A. in Action," 8; Bishop, "Presidential Address," *NCRLC Proceedings*, 1934, 27–28; "A Word for the AAA" (editorial), *Landward* 2 (Summer 1934): 4.

Others thought that suffering farmers needed assistance and that the AAA should be replaced by some program that would pass constitutional muster—perhaps the Roosevelt administration's proposal for benefit payments to farmers who practiced soil conservation.[29]

Historian Edward S. Shapiro has well stated that rural Catholics' "major criterion for evaluating the New Deal's nonagricultural programs was the degree to which they encouraged the widespread distribution of property and undermined the power of high finance and big business, while avoiding government paternalism."[30] For example, the NCRLC at first favored the National Recovery Administration (NRA) because of its similarity to the vocational group system outlined by Pope Pius XI in *Quadragesimo Anno*, but it soon came to believe that the NRA was controlled by the government and capitalists and did nothing to help farmers achieve parity with urban dwellers. Catholics favored the Roosevelt policy of reciprocal trade agreements because they believed the agreements increased the sale of American farm products. They also generally favored relief and social security programs but feared giving too much power to government relief or welfare agencies. As alternatives, they urged reliance on Catholic charities and programs that helped the indigent to help themselves. Catholic rural leaders argued that federal housing funds should be used to settle families on spacious rural lots, rather than "warehousing" them in cities.[31]

The Depression as a Moral and Social Crisis

Catholic rural leaders therefore gave qualified support to most of the rural and nonrural programs of the New Deal. They thought that these programs were justified as emergency measures to combat the Depression. But many of them began to think in more radical terms. They believed

---

29. Ryan, "Social Justice," 8–9; "One More Decision" ("Week By Week"), *Commonweal*, January 17, 1936, 311; Ernest F. Du Brul, "The Immorality of the AAA," ibid., January 24, 1936, 341–43; Charles Owen Rice, "In Defense of Farm Aid," ibid., August 21, 1936, 400–401; "The Agricultural Act," *America*, January 18, 1936, 343; "Dynamiting the Alphabet" (editorial), *Landward* 3 (Winter 1935–36): 4–5.

30. Shapiro, "Catholic Agrarian Thought and the New Deal," 593.

31. Ibid., 393–96; Abell, *American Catholicism and Social Action*, 248–51; O'Brien, *American Catholics and Social Reform*, 52–66; Flynn, *American Catholics and the Roosevelt Presidency*, chap. 5; "Agricola," "A Way to Greater Production," 1, 11; "Lower Prices and Prosperity" (editorial), *Landward* 3 (Autumn 1935): 4; Edgar Schmiedeler, *Agriculture and International Life*, Catholic Association for International Peace Pamphlet No. 24 (New York: Paulist Press, 1937), copy in "Agriculture," NCRLC 3-1, 42–61; Vincent J. Ryan, "The Fargo Plan," *Catholic Rural Life Objectives: A Third Series of Papers Dealing with Some of the Economic, Social and Spiritual Interests of the American Farmer* (n.p.: National Catholic Rural Life Conference, 1937), 133–36 (hereafter *Catholic Rural Life Objectives*, 1937); T. F. Doyle, "Catholic Action and the Slum Problem," *Catholic World* 152 (February 1941): 548–58.

that the New Deal programs were not capable of building a fundamentally sound rural society in the long run. These more profound theorists concluded that the problems that came to the surface during the Depression had such deep roots that the relatively mild reforms of the New Deal could do little to solve them. For them, the Depression was not only an economic collapse, but also—perhaps primarily—a moral one as well. Their solution was to radically reorient society more firmly on rural principles. Shapiro and other historians call these advocates Catholic "agrarians" or "ruralists." This group included most of the leaders of the NCRLC in the 1930s. But it was a wider assemblage that included many other Catholics who also favored a return to a primarily agricultural society during the Depression years.[32]

Like many other Americans, Catholic ruralists started with the observable facts of economic disaster and traced them back to deep-seated moral causes. It seemed to them that the phenomenon of want in the midst of plenty was caused by a flaw in the prevailing economic system. Liberalistic and capitalistic doctrines allowed speculation in land and commodities that brought about the farmers' financial crisis and the threat to the agricultural class. The bishops of the province of Cincinnati stated: "The radical evil of the economic situation . . . is that everything is judged from the standpoint of the market." Instead of "production for use," there was "production for sale." This put producers at the mercy of the vagaries of international trade and speculation. Liberalism and capitalism not only led to economic disaster for farmers, but they were immoral as well. They were basically "materialistic," Catholic agrarians claimed, based on a desire for money rather than on serving human needs. Thus, these theories were only a thin cover for "selfishness and greed." They agreed with Pius XI in *Quadragesimo Anno* that it was this simple greed that was the real root cause of the Depression.[33]

---

32. See Shapiro, "Catholic Agrarian Thought and the New Deal"; Shapiro, "Catholic Rural Life Movement and New Deal Farm Program." More will be said about the Catholic agrarians in the next chapter.

33. F. P. Kenkel, "The Influence of Liberalism and Capitalism on Agriculture," in "Addresses, Frederick P. Kenkel," NCRLC 10-1; Bishops of the Province of Cincinnati, "Problems of Agriculture," 1; NCRLC minutes binder (1935–38), NCRLC 8-2, 190; Luigi G. Ligutti and John C. Rawe, *Rural Roads to Security: America's Third Struggle for Freedom* (Milwaukee: Bruce Publishing, 1940), 9–10; Bishops of the Administrative Committee of the National Catholic Welfare Conference, *A Statement on the Present Crisis* (Washington, D.C.: National Catholic Welfare Conference, 1933), copy in "Bishops of U.S., Statements," NCRLC 3-2, 4–5, 7–9, 30. For the response of the Catholic Church in general to the Depression, see Franz H. Mueller, "The Church and the Social Question," in Joseph N. Moody and Justus George Lawler, eds., *The Challenge of Mater et Magistra* (New York: Herder & Herder, 1963), 112–26.

Catholic ruralists believed that the Depression was the natural result of some long-standing problems in American—and, in a broader context, Western—civilization. "Our recent civilization is out of tune with the laws of God," Father Bishop declared. Modern capitalistic culture, or "materialistic scientific mechanization," as one critic called it, was based in the cities. Catholic agrarians laid most of the evils of modern civilization at the door of urbanism and industrialism. To begin with, the cities were undesirable places in which to live. In the cities were the noisy, dirty, overcrowded, unhealthy slums, in which lived an underpaid or unemployed proletariat. The monotony of urban life resulted in the submergence of values into collectivism, the noise in a lack of contemplation, and the dependence of the whole economy on money in a gross materialism. Among the more prosperous urban dwellers, comfort was emphasized to an exaggerated degree, to the detriment of physically and mentally healthy work. Machinery dehumanized work and often needlessly displaced workers. In rural areas, farmers were often better off without machinery.[34]

Worst of all, they declared, were the effects of urban culture upon the family. Economist Goetz Briefs of Georgetown University argued that the debilitating effects of urban life on living conditions and the family made it increasingly difficult for the average city Christian to find his way to salvation. The NCRLC declared: "Industrial society works against the family and in favor of divorce, desertion, temporary unions, companionate marriage." Different workplaces for family members and commercialized amusements also tended toward the dissolution of urban families. City promotion of birth control and the lack of parental supervision of children at work and play worked against the "fundamental purpose of the family, namely the propagation and training of children."[35]

Unfortunately, Catholic ruralists pointed out with alarm, urban culture was not only ruining the cities, but its harmful effects were spreading to the countryside as well. Thus, farmers were accepting the urban economic value of production for profit, not for a living. Technology was needlessly upsetting the rhythms of agricultural work. And rural families

---

34. W. Howard Bishop, "Agrarianism, the Basis of the New Order," in "Convention Papers, 1940" (1st folder), NCRLC 8-3; Ralph Adams Cram, "Strength from the Good Earth," *Catholic Rural Life Bulletin* 3 (May 20, 1940): 1–3; Goetz Briefs, "The Back to the Land Idea," *Catholic Rural Life Objectives, 1937,* 93–98; Hynes, *"City Slickers" and "Dumb Farmers"*; Hynes, "The Dignity and Joy of Work," *Catholic Rural Life Bulletin* 1 (November 20, 1938): 16–18, 24–26; D. Marshall, "What about the Machine," *Commonweal,* June 21, 1935, 201–3; Irving T. McDonald, "Technocracy among the Agrarians," *America,* March 4, 1933, 524–25.

35. Briefs, "Back to the Land Idea;" NCRLC, *Manifesto,* 3–5.

were beginning to suffer from the debilitating effects of urban values. And now, with the Depression, the agrarians argued, rural people were beginning to pay the wages of sin for selling out to urban capitalism.[36]

Indeed, conditions were so bad that the agrarians thought that they had reached the proportions of a crisis. They saw the Depression as the natural worsening of the chronic diseases infecting the social order. Stopgap attempts like the New Deal to shore up capitalism would be futile in fending off "ultimate disaster." Some thought that the dispossession of farmers' land, with the consequent dissolution of the large propertyowning farming class, which had hitherto formed the basis of civilization, meant the end of an era and was "the darkest chapter of the Depression." As late as 1938, a prominent NCRLC leader still thought that the time was "an epochal moment in the life history of our democracy," more critical than any since the founding of the nation—including the Civil War era. He said that it was "the opinion of the experts" that America was at the "cross-roads" and that "what America thinks and does about her economic and social problems in the present critical hour will make or break her permanently as a power in the world."[37]

The Catholic agrarians looked at developments around the world and perceived that the social and economic crisis, particularly as it affected agriculture, was international in scope. The Most Reverend Ameleto Giovanni Cicognani, papal delegate to the United States, expressed it as follows at the NCRLC's 1937 convention at Richmond:

In the present world-wide disorder, brought about by the abuses of capitalism, by technological changes, and by dislocating relationships between rural and urban life, dangerous inequalities and disproportions have developed to the detriment and, in some places, to the degradation of the farm population. Those who live on the land form the larger proportion of the human family and their labor is the most important and indispensable for the livelihood of all.

Other Catholic ruralists said that they were "witnessing the collapse of a pseudo-civilization" and compared the period to the fall of the Roman Empire. Moreover, these Catholics claimed, the social and economic turmoil was having an effect on inter-state relations. The Jesuit John La Farge blamed the alarming international developments of the mid-thirties—the

---

36. Willis D. Nutting, "Foundations of a Rural Christian Culture," *Catholic Rural Life Bulletin* 2 (February 20, 1939): 1–2, 26–28; "My Kingdom for a Horse," ibid., 14–15.

37. Ralph Adams Cram, "Recovery or Regeneration?" *Commonweal*, November 2, 1934, 7–10; Joseph Matt, "The Darkest Chapter of the Depression," *NCRLC Proceedings, 1934*, 41–43; Luigi G. Ligutti, "A Statement by the President," *Catholic Rural Life Bulletin* 1 (May 20, 1938): 1.

failure of naval disarmament, the consolidation of Hitler's dictatorship in Germany, the Italian invasion of Ethiopia, and the Japanese invasion of China—on capitalism and its sanction of the *"unlimited* use of the means of material gain." As the decade drew to a close and the world seemed to be arming for another general war, James A. Byrnes claimed that the turmoil was caused by the imposition in many countries of "programs of social reconstruction . . . which . . . have, in some measure, failed in their purpose." Catholic agrarians thought that they saw the true solution—and it was the same for both the world and the American crises.[38]

38. "Comment," *America*, November 27, 1937, 170; Bishop, "Agrarianism"; Stanley B. James, "Catholic Colonies," *Catholic World* 135 (July 1932): 416–20; John La Farge, "The Crisis of Capitalism, 1935," *America*, January 4, 1936, 296–98 (italics in original); James A. Byrnes, "Foreword," *Catholic Rural Life Objectives*, 1937, 5–8.

Chapter 5 Programs to Meet the Crisis

The New Agrarian Order

Catholic rural leaders saw that the crisis of the Great Depression could also be a great opportunity, particularly for Catholic rural life. As Edgar Schmiedeler put it, when the heavy migration from farm to city took place during the 1920s, "Bishop O'Hara and his valiant and faithful crew kept rowing against the tide." But about 1930, "there came a change, a change that, by and large, has proved favorable to the Catholic rural life movement." For by means of the Depression, God, "in His Divine Providence . . . smote the city. He thereby stopped the drift of our population in its direction and then gradually turned it back toward the saner and more substantial things of life." W. Howard Bishop noticed the same developments and stated that it was therefore "an opportunity such as modern Catholicity has never before enjoyed" to reconstruct the social order on the principles of Leo XIII and Pius XI. "What better time is there," he added, "for us to foster the widespread distribution of property ownership that is the basis of the Church's economic ideal?" Ralph Adams Cram, an Anglican agrarian writing in *Commonweal,* claimed that Catholics were particularly well suited for leading a social reconstruction in an agrarian direction

> because they realize more clearly than any others the shortcomings of the old capitalist-industrial system . . . The system that has grown up during the last two centuries and is now in the process of dissolution was engendered in Protestant countries and by Protestants; Catholics never liked it much, at least they never surrendered to it except, sporadically, in this country. Leo XIII and Pius XI have stated the Catholic position and blazed the way. The road is open for Catholic advance.

On a more secular level as well, Catholic rural leaders such as Bishop Aloisius J. Muench of Fargo declared that a "new dawn has broken for agriculture." The Depression had made it clear that a "hands-off policy" for agriculture would not work and that the government must cooperate in achieving "a proper balance between industry and agriculture." The NCRLC would aid in this process by providing the spiritual underpinnings for the reformation of the American economy.[1]

In light of the decline of the American Country Life Association and the Protestant rural life departments by this time, the Conference believed that it now had a special mission, according to historian Jeffrey D. Marlett: "After 1930, the NCRLC members and other Catholic agrarians realized that they had emerged as the nation's premier church-affiliated agrarian movement. The salvation of rural America had become their responsibility. Therefore, improving Catholic rural life came to mean improving the rural life of other Americans as well."[2]

In striving to achieve a new rural order, the Catholic rural life leaders allied with a wider agrarian movement that also gained strength during the Depression years. American ruralists drew inspiration from British Catholic "Distributists" G. K. Chesterton and Hilaire Belloc, who preached a return to a society based on widespread family ownership of property such as small farms and businesses.[3] They also joined with a native secular agrarian movement, which included the twelve Nashville Agrarians, who in 1930 published the anti-modernist tract *I'll Take My Stand;* journalist Herbert Agar, whose books and periodical *Free America* publicized a return to Jeffersonian agrarianism; and New Yorker Ralph Borsodi, whose writings and "School for Living" taught subsistence farming and self-sufficient living techniques.[4] Most Catholic ruralists viewed the appearance of the secular

1. Edgar Schmiedeler, "Retrospect and Prospect," in *NCRLC Proceedings, 1933,* 74–81; [W. Howard Bishop], "Presidential Address, Tenth Annual Convention, C.R.L.C., Dubuque, Iowa, October, 1932," in "Ntn'l Convention, Dubuque, Iowa, October 19–21, 1932," NCRLC 8-1; Ralph Adams Cram, "Cities of Refuge," *Commonweal,* August 16, 1935, 380; A. J. Muench, "Address of Welcome at Solemn Civic Opening, Festival Hall, Fargo, N. Dak., October 11, 1936," in "Address, Muench, Most Rev. A. J.," NCRLC 10-4.

2. Marlett, *Saving the Heartland,* 27. On the decline of other church-based rural organizations, see ibid., 13, 15. For a perceptive analysis of the NCRLC's agrarian philosophy of the 1930s–1940s, see Christopher Hamlin and John T. McGreevy, "The Greening of America, Catholic Style, 1930–1950," *Environmental History* 11 (July 2006): 464–99.

3. See Jay P. Corrin, *G. K. Chesterton and Hilaire Belloc: The Battle against Modernity* (Athens: Ohio University Press, 1981); NCRLC minutes binder (1923–32), NCRLC 8-1, 82; Joseph H. Fichter, "A Comparative View of Agrarianism," *Catholic Rural Life Objectives, 1936,* 111–16.

4. See Paul K. Conkin, *Tomorrow a New World: The New Deal Community Program* (Ithaca, N.Y.: Cornell University Press, 1959), 24–27; Paul H. Johnstone and Dorothy C. Goodwin, "The Back-to-the-Land Movement," in *A Place on Earth: A Critical Appraisal of Subsistence Homesteads,* ed. Russell Lord and Paul H. Johnstone (Washington, D.C.: U.S. Bureau of Agricultural Economics, 1942), 14–18; L. G. Miller, "Some Agrarian Beginnings," *Catholic Rural Life Bulletin* 3 (November 20, 1940): 22–23; Edward S. Shapiro, "Decentralist Intellectuals and the New Deal," *Journal of American History* 58 (March 1972): 938–57; William H. Issel, "Ralph Borsodi and the Agrarian Response to Modern

agrarian movement as a vindication of their own position. They felt most akin to Agar, whose call for decentralization in farming and industry fit in well with Catholic rural thought. They were less enthusiastic about Borsodi and the Nashville Agrarians, viewing both as vaguely anti-religious.[5]

How did Catholic rural leaders propose that this change to a Christian agrarian order take place? To begin, they affirmed the teaching of Pope Pius XI's social encyclical *Quadragesimo Anno* (1931), which predicated any reform of the social order on a prior or concomitant spiritual renewal. Pius wrote, in words often quoted by Catholic ruralists: "This longed-for social reconstruction must be preceded by a profound renewal of the Christian spirit, from which multitudes engaged in industry in every country have unhappily departed." The NCRLC believed that conditions for such a spiritual renewal were most propitious in rural districts, from which it should grow into a movement for national and worldwide regeneration.[6]

The ruralists added particular ideas to this call for spiritual renewal. John La Farge thought that small groups "of intelligent, highly spiritual and self-sacrificing persons," guided and inspired by the Church, should act as mediators between the various groups in society and bring about "the rebuilding of our American culture." Others proposed rekindling Catholic spirituality by allying with the liturgical movement and reviving traditional Catholic rural rituals, ceremonies, and observances. Still others insisted that along with a general spiritual renewal, a return to specifically rural values and rural culture would have to take place. They thought that the Church should work to reinstill rural values into both rural and urban life. Values such as work for its own sake and production for the good of human beings should be cultivated. They advocated "throttling down the merely mechanical elements of efficiency and broadening its base to include the human, social values that are indispensable to the welfare of the nation at large because they benefit the largest number of individuals."[7]

America," *Agricultural History* 41 (April 1967): 155–66; Allan Carlson, *The New Agrarian Mind: The Movement toward Decentralist Thought in Twentieth-Century America* (New Brunswick, N.J.: Transaction Publishers, 2000); David Shi, *The Simple Life: Plain Living and High Thinking in American Culture* (New York: Oxford University Press, 1985), 223–47.

5. L. G. Ligutti, "Land Distribution a Social Necessity," *Landward* 4 (Autumn 1936): 6; Edgar Schmiedeler, "Herbert Agar's 'Land of the Free,'" ibid. (Spring 1936): 3, 11–12; W. Howard Bishop, "With or Without God?" ibid. (Autumn 1936): 1, 10; Fichter, "A Comparative View of Agrarianism."

6. Aloysius J. Muench, "The Farmer's Problem," *Landward* 4 (Summer 1936): 8; Byrnes, "Foreword," 5–8.

7. John La Farge, "Religion, the Groundwork of True American Culture," *Landward* 5 (Spring 1937): 1, 8–10; Paul B. Marx, *Virgil Michel and the Liturgical Movement* (Collegeville, Minn.: Liturgical Press, 1957), 298–337, 369–71; NCRLC minutes binder (1923–32), NCRLC 8-1, 82; numerous articles in NCRLC periodicals on the liturgical movement; Bishops of the Administrative Committee of

Reducing the role of machinery in rural labor was another objective. Some simply thought that farmers would live happier lives on the land if they did without complex machinery and its dependence on the outside forces of capitalism. But most proposed a compromise with modern technology by restricting machines to monotonous or "nonhuman" work, confining them to production for local, rather than national or international markets, and using them solely to ease the family's labor on the farm, not to displace workers.[8]

Some agrarians carried their revolt against modern technology so far that they embraced a return to a medieval-like society. Ralph Adams Cram most often spoke in those terms. He cited the philosopher Nicholas Berdyaeff, who predicted that the next era would be like the Middle Ages in spirit. To Cram, that meant a return to small, self-sufficient villages in which dedication to rural values was joined with the influence of religion. An English Catholic agrarian compared the times to the period after the fall of the Roman Empire and called for a movement like Benedictine monasticism to reconstruct a decaying society on a spiritual and agrarian basis.[9]

However, most Catholic ruralists wanted a rural culture that would combine the best of the old and the new. University of Notre Dame philosophy professor Willis Nutting believed that there was ample precedent in Catholic culture for an attempt to bring God into American rural ways and institutions as they were, and that this was the most practical method to rebuild American rural life. He argued for acceptance of the democracy, individualism, and family values of rural life in the United States, rather than trying to model it after the traditional village-centered rural society of Europe. Similarly, liturgical reformer Dom Virgil Michel, O.S.B., called for "modern agrarians" to move forward, not backward. He thought that society could be reconstructed on a modern rural basis by using the newly developed techniques of biodynamic farming, which would be more efficient than mechanized farming over the long run, and by taking control over the many new uses for farm products by "organizing these new

---

the National Catholic Welfare Conference, *A Statement on the Present Crisis* (Washington, D.C.: National Catholic Welfare Conference, 1933), copy in "Bishops of U.S., Statements," NCRLC 3-2, 31; Willis D. Nutting, "Pattern for a Native Rural Culture," *Catholic Rural Life Bulletin* 3 (May 20, 1940): 9–11, 28–29; Nutting, "Foundations of a Rural Christian Culture," 1–2, 26–28; Hynes, "Dignity and Joy of Work," 16–18, 24–26; "Efficiency versus Humanity" (editorial), *Landward* 4 (Spring 1936): 4.

8. Irving T. McDonald, "Technocracy among the Agrarians," *America*, March 4, 1933, 524–25; D. Marshall, "What about the Machine," 201–3; John La Farge, "Machines and Rural Life Need Not Be in Conflict," *America*, March 16, 1940, 620–21; Phillips Temple, "Is the Machine to Blame?" *Landward* 4 (Autumn 1936): 8–9.

9. Cram, "Strength from the Good Earth," 1–3; James, "Catholic Colonies," 416–20.

industries in neighborhood centers under neighborhood control and cooperation" rather than giving them over "to the present centralizing and monopolizing frankenstein."[10]

The Back-to-the-Land Movement

According to many Catholic rural leaders, the key socioeconomic reform necessary to establishing this rural culture was a radical redistribution of the population from the cities back to the land. A large-scale back-to-the-land movement, merely a dream to Catholic ruralists in the 1920s, seemed to be distinctly possible during the Depression. In 1934, Father Bishop declared that "a real landward movement is in the air." A year later, another Catholic agrarian claimed that "today the rural mind . . . begins to retake its place as the dominant American mind." In their enthusiasm, Catholic ruralists sometimes exaggerated the true extent of the back-to-the-land movement in the early Depression years. A number of articles in the early thirties cited statistics misleadingly to give the impression that the historic trend of cityward migration was being drastically, perhaps permanently, reversed.[11]

The truth was less dramatic, but it still indicated a significant, though temporary, shift in rural-urban migration patterns in the United States. From 1921 to 1929, the net migration to the cities varied between 400,000 and 1,137,000 people per year. During the early Depression years, the gains by the cities dwindled drastically. In one year—1932—for the only time in modern American history, the country actually outgained the city in population, by 266,000. The next year, however, urban areas regained the population lead, and they steadily increased their margin thereafter.[12]

The NCRLC began its involvement in the back-to-the-land movement by supporting government aid for subsistence farmers. With the severe urban unemployment of the early Depression years, thousands of city dwellers moved back to the country to raise crops for subsistence. Many of them called on the government for aid in doing so. As early as the Hoover administration, Father Schmiedeler of the Rural Life Bureau testified before Congress in favor of bills offering aid to subsistence farmers. The NCRLC joined in support of such legislation when it was proposed by

10. Nutting, "Pattern for a Native Rural Culture"; Virgil Michel, "Agriculture and Reconstruction," *Commonweal*, January 13, 1939, 317–18; "Making Men Peasants," *America*, June 30, 1934, 269.
11. W. Howard Bishop, "Significant Facts in Population Trends," *Landward* 2 (Spring 1934): 3; Charles Morrow Wilson, "Re-enter the Rural Mind," *America*, May 4, 1935, 81–83; [Bishop] "The Church and the Land Movement," *Landward* 1 (Spring 1933): 1; Edgar Schmiedeler, "Is a New Era Dawning?" ibid., 2.
12. Conkin, *Tomorrow a New World*, 23, 27–28.

Senator John H. Bankhead of Alabama during the Hundred Days. In May 1933 the efforts bore fruit when the Subsistence Homesteads Division was created, with an appropriation of $25 million "for making loans for and otherwise aiding in the purchase of subsistence homesteads." The Conference "hailed with joy" the passage of the legislation. Father Bishop expressed confidence that the Subsistence Homesteads Division would "help the farm-minded unemployed to get started on the land without adding to the farmer's surplus troubles." It might also aid "the farm tenant, the farm laborer and the farm boy who aspire to farm ownership but lack the means to gratify the desire," Bishop said. The Conference president also hoped that "diversification and high self-sufficiency may be inculcated into future farmers under the Subsistence Homestead plan." John A. Ryan of the NCWC quickly showed his support by joining Administrator M. L. Wilson's twenty-member National Advisory Committee on Subsistence Homesteads. The NCRLC voted resolutions in approval of the Subsistence Homesteads Division at its 1933 and 1934 conventions, and Schmiedeler proposed that a Catholic diocese take advantage of the plan by establishing a Catholic colony that would serve as an example for others. Although some Catholic leaders, such as the NCWC's John J. Burke, believed that subsistence homesteads would never be an important solution to the Depression, Conference officials such as Bishop thought only in terms of indefinitely expanding the program.[13]

During the early New Deal years, the federal subsistence homesteads program was indeed expanded. The Conference applauded the success of the Subsistence Homesteads Division, its successor Resettlement Administration, and the Federal Emergency Relief Administration in settling thousands of families in scores of different communities. After 1937, when the communities were administered by the Farm Security Administration—which was, however, prohibited from starting any new ones—the NCRLC voiced strong support of that agency.[14]

13. Ibid., 31–34, 87–130, 144; Sidney Baldwin, *Poverty and Politics: The Rise and Decline of the Farm Security Administration* (Chapel Hill: University of North Carolina Press, 1968), 69–76; [W. Howard Bishop] "A Missing Link Supplied," *Landward* 1 (Spring 1933): 6–7; Bishop to Edwin V. O'Hara, May 23, 1933, and O'Hara to Bishop, May 18, 1933, OH 47; Bishop, "Presidential Address," *NCRLC Proceedings, 1933*, 10–15; [Bishop], "A Permanent Readjustment," *Landward* 1 (Summer 1933): 1; [Bishop] "Subsistence Homesteads," ibid., 4; "Present Status of Subsistence Homesteads," ibid. (Autumn 1933): 8; NCRLC minutes binder (1933–35), NCRLC 8-1, 95–96; *NCRLC Proceedings, 1934*, 198; Edgar Schmiedeler, "Beyond the NRA," *Commonweal*, September 22, 1933, 485–87; John J. Burke to "Your Excellency," September 11, 1933, in "Granger Homesteads—Approvals of Project," LGL-A.

14. Conkin, *Tomorrow a New World*, 88–185; Baldwin, *Poverty and Politics*, 58–76 and chap. 4;

The subsistence homesteads projects under the Subsistence Homesteads Division, FERA, Resettlement Administration, and FSA constituted the New Deal's contribution to the back-to-the-land movement of the Depression years. But the New Deal was not committed to the back-to-the-land movement as a central aspect of its economic program. Other groups in the United States, including the NCRLC, saw the landward movement as much more vital to economic recovery and to the construction of a sound social and economic order.

The Conference was heartened by the many privately organized back-to-the-land efforts being tried across the United States. Father Bishop wrote approvingly of the "half-way-back-to-the-land movement" represented by subsistence gardens for the part-time employed and of philanthropist Hugh McRae's colonies in North Carolina. Father La Farge was in contact with Gabriel Davidson of the Jewish Agricultural Society, which sponsored a farm settlement program during the Depression years, and was impressed by the way the Jewish poultry farmers "bridged the gap between the city and the country."[15]

The American Catholic rural leaders were inspired by back-to-the-land activity abroad, especially that involving the Church. In Germany, the Church participated in a government program that resettled thousands of families from the south and west to farmlands in the east. The British back-to-the-land movement was guided by the radical ideas of the Distributists. The Conference admired Belgium's agricultural league, the Boerenbond, which combined religious and economic purposes. Conference officials studied firsthand the back-to-the-land movement in Canada, where Catholics cooperated with a large government program by running farmer-training sessions.[16]

Catholic rural leaders overwhelmingly endorsed the back-to-the-land

---

Bishop, "Presidential Address," *NCRLC Proceedings, 1934*, 29; NCRLC minutes binder (1935–38), NCRLC 8-2, 160; Lucile W. Reynolds, "Rehabilitating Farm Families," *Landward* 4 (Summer 1936): 7–8, 10–12.

15. "Back to the Land," *Rural Bureau Notes* 1 (December 1933): 2; W. Howard Bishop, "Colonization in North Carolina," *Landward* 2 (Autumn 1934): 7–8; [Bishop], "Milwaukee 1924 and 1933," ibid. 1 (Autumn 1933): 1; Bishop, "A Step toward Rural Colonization," *Catholic Action* 14 (September 1932): 19–20; John La Farge, *The Manner Is Ordinary* (New York: Harcourt, Brace, 1954), 237–38.

16. See, for example, Mae A. Schnurr, "Land Settlement Abroad," *Landward* 2 (Autumn 1934): 6, 8; Bishop, "Presidential Address," *NCRLC Proceedings, 1933*, 10–15; George Timpe, "Landward—At Home and Abroad," ibid., 47–51; Stanley B. James, "British Catholics Turn to the Land," *Catholic Action* 14 (March 1932): 13–14; Charles Leonard, "The 'Boerenbond,' Belgium's Cooperative Farm Association," *Landward* 2 (Summer 1934): 1–2; E. H. Gurton, "The Landward Movement in Canada," *NCRLC Proceedings, 1934*, 76–93.

movement. The NCRLC passed resolutions favoring the movement at its 1932 through 1935 conventions, and from 1933 to 1937, the title of the Conference's official publication, *Landward,* proclaimed the back-to-the-land emphasis of that period. The most prominent NCRLC officials, speaking out as individuals in favor of the movement, were able to cite the famous social encyclicals *Rerum Novarum* and *Quadragesimo Anno* and statements of the American bishops as evidence of papal and episcopal approval of the landward trend. These voices of authority were echoed by statements of the NCWC and editorials in the Catholic press.[17]

The reasons Catholics gave for their support of the back-to-the-land movement showed their religious, social, and economic concerns. When the religious welfare of the Church was the main focus of concern, they often stated that a Catholic back-to-the-land movement would solve the old Catholic rural population problem. Catholics also favored the landward movement because they believed that life on the land—especially on a subsistence farm—allowed individuals to live the most virtuous Christian lives. Allied with this was the idea that the landward movement would rescue Americans from the "crime and moral danger" of the cities. The movement would also promote the distributed ownership of property in a large middle class, which was urged in the social encyclicals. Finally, these Catholics argued that the back-to-the-land movement would solve the economic problems of the Depression by providing livings for millions of un- or underemployed industrial workers on subsistence farms. And, since these small farmers would consume what they produced and not add to the agricultural surplus, it would do no harm to the commercial farming sector.[18]

17. NCRLC minutes binder (1923–32), NCRLC 8-1, 82; NCRLC minutes binder (1933–35), NCRLC 8-1, 95; NCRLC minutes binder (1935–38), NCRLC 8-2, 160–61; *NCRLC Proceedings, 1934,* 198–99; J. M. Campbell, "Radio Broadcast. WLCO. Rural Life," in "Convention Papers, 1934" (2d folder), NCRLC 8-1; [W. Howard Bishop], "Presidential Address, Tenth Annual Convention," in "Ntn'l Convention. Dubuque, Iowa, October 19–21, 1932," NCRLC 8-1; Luigi Ligutti, "Paternal Acres," in "Convention Papers, 1936," NCRLC 8-2; Bishops of the Province of Cincinnati, "Problems of Agriculture from the Standpoint of Catholic Principles," 5; Bishops of the Administrative Committee, *A Statement on the Present Crisis,* 30–31; "Back to the Farm" (editorial), *America,* July 23, 1932, 368; untitled editorial, *Catholic Charities Review* 18 (September 1934): 194.

18. [Bishop], "The Church and the Land Movement," 1, 3; Margaret T. Lynch, "Living Standards and Christianity," *Landward* 1 (Winter 1934): 7; John F. Noll, "American Catholics in Agriculture," *Catholic Rural Life Objectives, 1936,* 7–11; John La Farge, "Humanity Uprooted," *America,* November 18, 1933, 153–54; NCRLC minutes binder (1923–32), NCRLC 8-1, 82; [Bishop], "A Missing Link Supplied;" Vincent J. Ryan, "Presidential Address," in "Ntn'l Convention, St. Cloud, Minn., September 29–30, October 1–2, 1940," NCRLC 8-3, 3. For an attempt to refute the "myth of urban irreligion" (based on the rather narrow, by NCRLC standards, measure of church membership), see Finke and Stark, *Churching of America,* 203–7.

The NCRLC made its first proposals for concrete aid to the back-to-the-land movement at its 1931 convention, where it proposed a credit agency to help beginning farmers. In the next year, the Conference laid plans for a full-scale program. It proposed a "national advisory council" on the Catholic landward movement, which would coordinate a nationwide system of diocesan rural life bureaus. Although the national council was never set up, many diocesan bureaus were established, which became enduring subsidiaries of the NCRLC. Originally conceived as aids to the back-to-the-land movement, the bureaus were to inform prospective settlers of available land and land prices, secure them from being taken advantage of, keep those who would not be successful farmers from going on the land, and make sure Catholic families settled where they could become part of a rural parish with a church and school. Diocesan rural life bureaus could also provide ancillary aid to the Catholic landward movement by encouraging cooperatives and credit unions, holding diocesan rural life conferences to spread back-to-the-land information among farmers, and aiding them in utilizing government credit agencies. In 1933, immediately after the establishment of the Subsistence Homesteads Division, Father Bishop wrote the hierarchy to urge the bishops to appoint diocesan directors of rural life so that they could participate in the federal homesteads program.[19]

Actual Catholic support for the back-to-the-land movement took two forms: aid to individual families and whole community projects. Most aid came from the diocesan rural life bureaus, several of which set up farm-finding services for prospective back-to-the-landers. The St. Louis Rural Life Conference, for example, distributed a survey to all of the rural pastors of the archdiocese requesting them to record all farms in their neighborhoods for sale or rent. These farms were then listed, with the sale or rent terms and proximity to Catholic church and school, in the St. Louis *Catholic Herald*.[20]

Families were also settled by individual Catholic back-to-the-land promoters. Most noteworthy of these was the Reverend George Timpe of Milwaukee, who settled families from the Midwest on farms in the north-

---

19. NCRLC minutes binder (1923–32), NCRLC 8-1, 73–74, 82, 83; "Suggested Projects for Diocesan Rural Bureaus," *Landward* 1 (Summer 1933): 4–5; "Bureau Directors' Meeting," *Rural Bureau Notes* 3 (November 1935): 1; Bishop to "Your Excellency," July 21, 1933, in "Correspondence, Bishop, W. Howard," NCRLC 13-1.

20. Clippings and correspondence, 1934, in "Archdiocese of St. Louis," NCRLC 3-2; "Bishop Winkelmann Sets up Bureau," *Landward* 2 (Spring 1934): 2, 8; "Catholic Rural Life Conference, Archdiocese of St. Louis," ibid. (Summer 1934): 9.

Programs to Meet the Crisis

ern Plains and Pacific Northwest. Other Catholic priests promoted rural settlement in the Red and Columbia river valleys.[21]

The Depression also spawned a number of Catholic farming colonies. By 1932, NCRLC President Bishop reported that "successful farm colonies" were already being conducted by Father Timpe in Minnesota, North Dakota, Montana, and Washington, Monsignor Victor Day in Montana, the Reverend Peter Schaeffer in Oklahoma, the Reverend Francis Gross in Louisiana, and a Mr. Beland in Florida. Little can be ascertained about most of these colonies. One about which some information was recorded was Schaeffer's colony at Tishomingo, Oklahoma, called Washita Farms. This colony was begun in the 1920s by the Chapman family, wealthy landowners in Texas and Oklahoma. Though non-Catholic, they wanted mainly Catholic farmers for their colony. In 1935, there were about fifty families there, living on eighty- to one-hundred-and-twenty-acre farms, raising grain, cotton, hogs, and poultry. The Chapmans were not, apparently, heavily influenced by Catholic agrarian thought, for they rented the farms on a share basis and made no provision for eventual ownership by the tenants.[22]

The best-known Catholic farming colony of the Depression era was that of the Reverend Luigi G. Ligutti at Granger, Iowa. Granger was the only Catholic homestead community formed with government aid. Ligutti applied to the Subsistence Homesteads Division for a loan in September 1933 for a project to settle fifty families of underemployed coal miners on two- to eight-acre subsistence plots. NCRLC and NCWC officials, especially Schmiedeler and Bishop, lobbied in Washington and helped secure the government's approval of the project on March 4, 1934. The Subsistence Homesteads Division loaned the project $100,000, later raised to $175,000. Ligutti originally formed a local homestead corporation to run the project, but in May 1934 the Subsistence Homesteads Division took over the project, although Ligutti still retained considerable influence. All houses in the project were occupied by December 15, 1935; all of the

---

21. George Timpe, "Landward—At Home and Abroad," 47–51; Memo, Bruce Mohler (NCWC Bureau of Immigration) to Rural Life Bureau, May 15, 1931, and attached extract of George Timpe to Mohler, May 12, 1931, NCWC 29; William Klinkhammer, "Opportunities for Catholic Farmers in the Red River Valley," *NCRLC Proceedings, 1934*, 65–67; C. M. O'Brien, "Economic and Sociological Aspects of the Columbia Basin Project," *Catholic Rural Life Bulletin* 2 (November 20, 1939): 4–6, 28–29.

22. [Bishop], "Presidential Address," in 1932 convention folder, NCRLC 8-1; "A Catholic Colony in Oklahoma," *Landward* 3 (Summer 1935): 7–8; Francis Mellen, "A Farm Colonization Experiment," *Catholic Charities Review* 16 (November 1932): 288.

families were off relief by 1935. The project was not entirely Catholic; only thirty-three of the fifty families were. In keeping with the Catholic agrarians' emphasis on cooperatives, Ligutti formed co-ops for buying, selling, and manufacturing and for ownership of heavy farm machinery, as well as a credit union. They were notably successful, although by the 1950s all but the credit union had been phased out. The Granger project, although modest in conception, was successful in providing the coal mining families with a subsistence livelihood; the circles of little houses were still occupied at the end of the century. As one of the most successful New Deal community projects, it was honored by a visit from Eleanor Roosevelt. It was extensively publicized by the Catholic press and helped to link the Catholic Church and the Catholic rural life movement to the New Deal.[23]

Several other significant Catholic back-to-the-land colonies were founded during or shortly after the Depression. Saint Teresa's Village in Bolling, Alabama, was started in 1937 by the Reverend A. W. Terminiello among black sharecroppers who were dropped as clients by the Resettlement Administration. As general director of Saint Teresa's, Terminiello built a successful, wholly cooperative community, including producer, consumer, and service (including a credit union) cooperatives. In 1940, the Benedictines of Saint John's Abbey of Collegeville, Minnesota, relied on Catholic rural thinking in forming a community in northwestern Pennsylvania. The monks settled fifteen families on the land "to provide the opportunity for converts from industrialism and urban, collectivized life, to find out if they can adapt themselves to the decentralized craft-agrarian way of life." Family Acres, a farming community located outside of South Bend, Indiana, was formed by a group of Notre Dame–educated men and their wives in 1947. The residents, including some connected with the NCRLC and the Catholic Worker movement, tried to integrate life and religion.[24]

The Catholic Worker movement formed several rural communities of its own during the Depression years. With its intensely anti-establishment, personalist emphasis, the famous movement founded in 1933 in New York City by Dorothy Day and Peter Maurin had little in common with the

23. Conkin, *Tomorrow a New World*, chap. 13; Ligutti's papers on Granger and correspondence in LGL-A, LGL-C, LGL-E, and LGL-F; Joseph O'Leary, "Father Ligutti's Project," *America*, March 31, 1934, 613–14; Edward Skillin Jr., "Granger Homesteads," *Commonweal*, May 24, 1940, 93–96; "Granger Homesteads," *Central-Blatt and Social Justice* 28 (March 1936): 386–87.

24. A. W. Terminiello, "St. Teresa's Village and the Negro Sharecropper," *Catholic Rural Life Bulletin* 3 (August 20, 1940): 20–21; Schmiedeler-Terminiello correspondence, 1937, NCWC 29; Ligutti and Rawe, *Rural Roads to Security*, 331–32; "Back to the Land," *Central-Blatt and Social Justice* 32 (March 1940): 384; Marlett, *Saving the Heartland*, 41, 67–68.

Programs to Meet the Crisis 113

Figure 4. Eleanor Roosevelt visiting Granger Homesteads (Monsignor Luigi G. Ligutti to her right), 1936.

more traditional and institutionalized NCRLC. However, the two movements did share a common passion for the idea of subsistence homesteads. The Catholic Workers referred to their subsistence homestead communities as "farming communes." "The House of Hospitality is the answer to the immediate needs of the poor; and the Farming Commune seemed the answer to the problem of providing human employment and independence for those poor who would take the step," a member of one of the communities wrote. Maurin, who prided himself on his French peasant background, especially emphasized the rural aspect of the Catholic Worker program. A Catholic Worker explained: "It was not part of Peter's social scheme that men should be dependent on a huge, interdependent economic machine which periodically broke down and gave Christians an opportunity to practice hospitality. His aim was the foundation of new

Christian communities which combined economic self-sufficiency with a new kind of community social life, communities which would be not only willing but able to take care of their own." The first Catholic Worker farming commune was begun at Easton, Pennsylvania, in 1936, and by 1941 there were nine of them across the country. Although many of these small communities disbanded soon thereafter, the Catholic Worker movement continued to foster farming communities in later years, and the idea of providing a simple Christian life by labor on the land continued to be strong in the movement. As late as 1988, there were seven Catholic Worker farms, but they were too urban-oriented and too small (two to five people) to effect much transformation of society.[25]

Ligutti met with Maurin at the 1938 NCRLC convention in Vincennes, Indiana, and soon thereafter wrote to Day with practical advice for the Easton farm. Later, he stayed overnight at the New York Catholic Worker house. The two organizations exchanged periodicals and other mailings, and Ligutti corresponded regularly with the Catholic Workers on the Easton farm. Despite their differences of approach, the monsignor believed the two groups "had much in common and would profit from close relations."[26]

After 1935, as America's industrial economy began to stabilize, Catholic calls for a back-to-the-land movement became less frequent. Although some declared that "Back to the Land" was still "a slogan full of promise for the blessings of economic and even spiritual freedom," most favored a more limited, practical program. For example, Bishop O'Hara favored a policy of "gradual penetration"—Catholic parishes adding a few new rural families at a time—and encouragement of rural Catholics to stay on the land.[27]

With the resumption of the farm-to-city population trend in the late 1930s, any real hope among Catholic rural leaders for a large-scale back-

25. William D. Miller, *A Harsh and Dreadful Love: Dorothy Day and the Catholic Worker Movement* (New York: Liveright, 1973), 100–101, 121–25, 195–96, 202–10, 237–38, 241, 312; Donald Powell, "An Open Letter to the Editor," *Landward* 3 (Autumn 1935): 2, 12; Powell, "What Can I Do?" ibid. 4 (Spring 1936): 7, 9–10; quotation from William Gauchat, "Cult, Culture, and Cultivation," in "Articles, Farming Commune, 1941," NCRLC 11-3; Julian Pleasants, "Personal Responsibility," in Ward, ed., *The American Apostolate*, 86 (quotation), 91–92; Marlett, *Saving the Heartland*, 68–88; John Zeitler, "Catholic Workers on the Land: Essays in Faith," *Catholic Rural Life* 37 (February 1988): 8–12.

26. Patrick Coy, "Two Views of the Community and the Land," *Catholic Rural Life* 37 (February 1987): 28.

27. A. J. Muench, "Youth's Road to Freedom," *Catholic Rural Life Bulletin* 2 (November 20, 1939): 4; Edwin V. O'Hara, "The Catholic Rural Problem in America," ibid. 1 (November 20, 1938): 1–2, 26–27.

to-the-land movement just about died out. Schmiedeler summarized the mood in his pamphlet, *Vanishing Homesteads,* published in 1941. "The welfare of the United States and its people calls for more, and not for fewer farm families," Schmiedeler stubbornly maintained. He acknowledged, however, that "economic efficiency has always been rated higher in the United States than human welfare, and is still so rated today." As a consequence of this attitude, he pessimistically predicted, "our farmsteads will continue to vanish."[28]

Proposed Agrarian Reforms

Besides the back-to-the-land movement, the NCRLC also supported various other socioeconomic reforms seen as necessary for bringing about its desired new agrarian order. Most of them, such as the establishment of an occupational group system, wide distribution and decentralization of productive property, and greater support for the family farm, were derived at least in part from *Quadragesimo Anno.* The proposal for the organization of economic "orders," which were also often referred to as "vocational" or "occupational groups," was the most important new contribution to Catholic social theory that Pius XI made in his social encyclical. In accordance with the Catholic conception of the organic nature of society and the principle of subsidiarity, Pius proposed that the workers and employers of each occupation freely organize themselves into an "order," which would serve as a link between the state and the individual. These orders would harmoniously cooperate with each other to regulate the economic life of a country. According to Pius, organization on the basis of occupation was the most "natural," would do away with class conflict by joining workers and employers and would lead people away from individualism and toward cooperation for the common welfare.[29]

American Catholic rural leaders had considerable trouble accommodating *Quadragesimo Anno*'s proposal for economic "orders" into their agricultural ideology, for the corporate idea was European in origin and uncongenial to individualistic American farmers. Frederick P. Kenkel of the Central Verein (whose organization *was* familiar with corporate philosophy) proposed that the Catholic agrarians publish a farm paper direct-

---

28. Edgar Schmiedeler, *Vanishing Homesteads,* NCWC Social Action Series No. 21 (New York: Paulist Press, 1941), 27. Copy in "Vanishing Homesteads," NCRLC 11-6.

29. The encyclical is printed as "Restoring the Christian Social Order (*Quadragesimo Anno*)," in *Social Wellsprings,* ed. Joseph Husslein, vol. 2: *Eighteen Encyclicals of Social Reconstruction by Pope Pius XI* (Milwaukee: Bruce Publishing, 1942), 178–234.

ed at actual farmers (unlike the NCRLC publications, which were aimed at leaders) to get them used to the idea. Without some such educational medium, the agrarians' vocational group proposals were bound to be ineffective. One rural priest favored the formation of "an American 'Boerenbond,'" which would be organized on the basis of parish units like the Belgian organization. Another thought the Farm Bureau would form the best foundation for an American occupational group system. Schmiedeler thought that the AAA's county agricultural conservation associations and county planning councils, with their provisions for referenda, recalls, and appeals, seemed to provide for the democratic control, with the aid of government, that Pius regarded as desirable. The 131 Catholic leaders who signed the 1936 statement *Organized Social Justice* thought that a constitutional amendment would probably be necessary to allow an occupational group system to be established in the United States.[30]

None of these schemes got beyond the drawing board. Father Ligutti probably expressed the feelings of the American Catholic farmer in his response to such theories. Reminiscing in the 1970s, he was critical of an attempt made by American Jesuits in 1939 to submit a proposed rural life encyclical on the lines of *Quadragesimo Anno*. "Corporatism . . . never appealed to me. Corporatism, which is a Fascist theory, was never my line," Ligutti said.[31]

The American institution which came nearest to the economic "orders" of *Quadragesimo Anno*, according to NCRLC leaders, was the cooperative. "In structure, cooperatives come as close to corporate groups, as envisaged by Pope Pius XI, as the grouping of any other profession or trade," Bishop Muench said. The NCRLC Cooperative Committee approved of producers' cooperatives because, "if properly regulated," they were "apt, by their very nature, to develop into vocational groups." Other rural Catholic leaders also made the connection between cooperatives and vocational groups.[32]

---

30. F. P. Kenkel to James Byrnes, March 5, 1936, in "General Correspondence—Byrnes, James," LGL-J; A. J. Martins, "The Encyclical '*Quadragesimo Anno*' and Rural Problems," (3-page typescript attached to Martins to Edgar Schmiedeler, February 3, 1932), in seventh (untitled) folder, NCWC 29; [George Nell], "Vocational Group Organization Applied to Agriculture as Proposed by Pope Pius XI in His Encyclical 'Reconstructing the Social Order,'" in "Articles, Agricultural Societies," NCRLC 11-1; Edgar Schmiedeler, *Pius XI's New Social Order and Agriculture* (Philadelphia: Ecclesiastical Review, 1940), (pamphlet, copy in USCC archives; published in *Ecclesiastical Review* 103 [October 1940]: 371–77); Social Action Department, National Catholic Welfare Conference, *Organized Social Justice* (New York: Paulist Press [1936]), 16 (copy in "Encyclicals, Pius XI," NCRLC 3-12).
31. "LGL—Transcription of tapes made with Monsignor Ligutti and extra documents used in writing his biography (Part I)," (interview with Vincent Yzermans), LGL-K, 139.
32. A. J. Muench, "Agrarianism in the Christian Social Order," *Catholic Rural Life Bulletin* 1

Programs to Meet the Crisis   117

Catholic rural leaders favored cooperatives not merely for their supposed compatibility with the visionary corporate order, but also for more immediate economic and spiritual reasons. In the economic sphere, they thought that cooperatives and credit unions allowed farmers and other working people to assume control over their economic lives. Farmers would never achieve economic security, they warned, unless they formed credit unions to take control over their credit from the banks, marketing cooperatives to assume control over their agricultural prices from the middlemen and boards of trade, and consumers' cooperatives to get control of the prices of the things they bought from the chain stores and agricultural implement companies. By the end of the 1930s, influenced by the success of the Rural Electrification Administration, Catholic rural leaders were also endorsing rural electrification cooperatives. They held that the voluntary and self-help features of cooperatives were far more conducive to economic independence than government attempts to intervene in the economy.[33]

Catholic rural leaders also thought that cooperatives and, especially, credit unions would help to solve the nation's economic crisis. Because of their sound basis, NCRLC officials believed that credit unions would contribute more toward leading the country out of the Depression than the old banking system. They thought that people had more confidence in financial cooperatives, which were under their own control, than in banks and loan sharks, which were not. They noted that whereas five thousand banks failed and four thousand required Reconstruction Finance Corporation (RFC) assistance in the first three years of the Depression, of over two thousand credit unions, only a handful in one state failed, and only three required RFC assistance. Credit unions also charged lower interest rates than banks and loan sharks, it was argued.[34]

According to NCRLC leaders, the Church added "super-natural reasons" to the existing natural reasons favoring cooperation. Cooperation was "a movement for greater material success to which the Church is glad

---

(May 20, 1938): 24; "Report of the Cooperative Committee of the National Catholic Rural Life Conference," in "Ntn'l Convention, Richmond, Va., November 7–10, 1937," NCRLC 8-2; Raymond J. Miller, "The '*Quadragesimo Anno*' and the Reconstruction of Agriculture," *Catholic Rural Life Objectives, 1936*, 53–56.

33. J. M. Campbell, "A Presidential Greeting," *Landward* 2 (Winter 1934–35): 1–2, 8; "Sidelights on Social Action," *Catholic Action* 22 (October 1940): 23, 31; "Catholic Farmers Speak Their Minds on the Condition of Agriculture," *Central-Blatt and Social Justice* 25 (June 1932): 93.

34. "Credit Unions vs. Depression: Roy F. Bergengren Tells of Marvellous Success," *Landward* 1 (Spring 1933): 5; Joseph M. Campbell, "The Credit Union the Instrument for Social Justice and Charity and Cooperation," *NCRLC Proceedings, 1934*, 184–88.

to give its hearty endorsement, because by its very nature it must tend to make better citizens and better men of those who resort to it." Cooperation "calls for honest dealing in its members and its leaders and best of all a spirit of mutual helpfulness that draws the farmer out of the intense individualism which is one of his greatest hindrances today," Bishop argued. "It takes away ruthless competition which is pagan and substitutes brotherly love which is Christian." For Catholic rural leaders, economic cooperation had its origin in the communal spiritual life of the Church. Virgil Michel linked the cooperative movement with the contemporaneous liturgical movement, of which he was the leader, by pointing out the former's basis in Catholics' common worship of the sacred mysteries. La Farge simply stated that the Catholic parish was "the most effective school of cooperation on the earth." For both, the common spiritual life of Catholics would naturally extend cooperation in a Christian spirit to all of their activities, including economic and financial.[35]

As a result of these arguments, most Catholics heartily supported the cooperative movement. The Catholic press frequently urged the advantages of cooperation on its readers. Books and pamphlets written by Catholics poured out during the thirties, supporting all kinds of cooperatives. Moreover, cooperatives were enjoying a period of popularity in the nation as a whole. The thirties, despite the Depression, witnessed a significant growth in the numbers of cooperatives and credit unions in the United States. The New Deal also gave considerable support to the cooperative movement. Almost every New Deal community project included some sort of local cooperative, and one rural industrial community and three farming communities were formed entirely on a cooperative basis.[36]

Despite the overall support for cooperatives, a few Catholics were not so positive. Some mocked consumers' cooperatives as merely "a better way to buy groceries" that would do little to accomplish the major reconstruction of society called for by *Quadragesimo Anno*. For this, they said, producers' cooperatives were necessary to bring about a more completely

---

35. John La Farge in "Report of the Cooperative Committee of the National Catholic Rural Life Conference," 3; W. H. Bishop, "Presidential Speech," in "Ntn'l Convention, Wichita, Kansas, Oct. 20–22, 1931," NCRLC 8-1, 5–6; Virgil Michel, "The Cooperative Movement and the Liturgical Movement," *Landward* 4 (Winter 1937): 2, 10–11; John La Farge, "Land the Hope of the Future," *NCRLC Proceedings, 1933*, 70–74.

36. T. J. Shaughnessy, "The Parish Credit Union," *America*, December 6, 1930, 213–14; Bertram B. Fowler, "Cooperation as a Technique," *Commonweal*, August 19, 1938, 422–24; Edgar Schmiedeler, "A Silent Revolution," *Catholic World* 143 (June, 1936): 279–84; Schmiedeler, *Cooperation: A Christian Mode of Industry* (Ozone Park, N.Y.: Catholic Literary Guild, 1941), chap. 5; Conkin, *Tomorrow a New World*, 202–11.

cooperative society. Other Catholics thought just the opposite, that the cooperative movement was going too far. They viewed cooperatives as undemocratic, controlled by a small group of managers or government officials sent from afar. To them, cooperatives worked against the Catholic goal of distributed private property by concentrating economic power in a few large centralized organizations. Bishop Muench warned that such big cooperatives tended to veer away from Christian principles and go the way of materialistic individualism, "lusting for power and putting themselves in warfare, one against the other in disregard of the common good." To such thinkers, cooperatives seemed like an opening wedge for the introduction of socialism or communism into American life. They feared that the vital Catholic principle of private property was threatened by the idea of a "cooperative commonwealth" touted by many, even some Catholics.[37]

Indeed, the NCRLC held up as a model a community that had an almost wholly cooperative economy. This was Antigonish, Nova Scotia, where the priests of St. Francis Xavier University used their extension program to stimulate cooperation among the farmers, miners, and fishermen of that maritime province. Antigonish cooperatives ran the whole gamut of credit unions, cooperative stores, marketing cooperatives, and even cooperative industries. NCRLC and St. Francis Xavier officials attended each other's conferences, maintaining a free flow of ideas on cooperation.[38]

During the 1930s, Catholics worked actively to promote cooperation in rural areas. Some Catholic priests helped to enact cooperative and credit union laws in their states. Others joined cooperative promotional organizations or helped form diocesan cooperative or credit union "conferences." The NCRLC held credit union institutes from 1929 to 1933 and sent out thousands of pieces of promotional literature to pastors urging their attendance. The Parish Credit Union National Committee, with Father Schmiedeler as secretary for "rural interests," continued its promotion of parish credit unions into the early 1940s. A number of Catholic pastors helped their parishioners to form cooperatives and credit unions. Among

37. Emerson Hynes, "Whither Cooperation?" *Free America* 1 (December 1937): 4–6; Ray Scott, "Cooperatives in the Parish," *Commonweal,* September 1, 1939, 431–32; Henry Blenker, "Let Is [sic] Be Careful," in "Convention Papers, 1940," NCRLC 8-3; "Report of the Cooperative Committee of the National Catholic Rural Life Conference," 2–3; Muench, "Agrarianism," 24; John Horton, "Are Cooperatives the Answer?" *Commonweal,* September 1, 1939, 429–31; Abell, *American Catholicism and Social Action,* 254–56.

38. "Canada's Rural Movement," *Landward* 2 (Summer 1934): 2, 7–8; Phillips Temple, "Why Not Co-operation?" ibid. 4 (Spring 1936): 5–7; M. M. Coady, "Cooperation in Nova Scotia," *NCRLC Proceedings, 1934,* 172–75; "Antigonish Holds Co-op Conference," *Pittsburgh Catholic,* August 25, 1938, in "Clippings, NCRLC, August, 1938," NCRLC 9-1.

the more famous Catholic rural cooperatives were those formed by Father Ligutti at Granger, Iowa, Father Terminiello at Bolling, Alabama, and the Reverend Hubert Duren at Westphalia, Iowa.[39]

However, rural Catholics were not always successful in forming cooperatives. One rural priest noted that pastors trying to induce their flocks to cooperate often struggled in vain against the farmers' isolation, individualism, and selfishness, their having been deceived by false promises before, and the propaganda of their exploiters. This limited success was illustrated by the case of credit unions. By 1938, there were seven thousand credit unions in the United States, but only 250 of them were organized on a religious or parish—rather than an occupational—basis. And of these few hundreds, most were in cities.[40]

The NCRLC connected its emphasis on occupational groups and cooperatives with a call for decentralization and distributism. It derived intellectual sustenance from the principles of the English Distributists G. K. Chesterton and Hilaire Belloc, which they pronounced "in full harmony with those of Christian solidarity." The ruralists wanted decentralized industries as well as numerous small family farms. Some agrarians favored accepting the prevailing American pattern of rather isolated individual homesteads, while others thought that gathering farmers into small, self-sufficient villages would better facilitate Christian cooperation and the formation of Pope Pius's intended agricultural vocational group. Those who especially feared the unsettled social conditions of the depressed times looked to self-sufficient rural villages as possible "cities of refuge" from social storms. The agrarians believed that a decentralized economy—contrary to common belief—could actually be more efficient than a centralized one, as well as allowing local people to retain control over their economic lives. Decentralization and an accompanying distribution of property would lessen the dangerous gap between rich and poor. Decentralization to small towns and rural areas would also ease city congestion, thus making possible a more comfortable family and home life.[41]

---

39. "Credit Unions in Oklahoma," *Rural Bureau Notes* 1 (November 1933): 4; Social Action Department Reports, folder "A-9," unfoldered after "A-9" and "Report, 1932–1939," NCWC 34; NCRLC minutes binder (1935–38), NCRLC 8-2, 167, 186, 190; Edgar Schmiedeler, "A Review of the Year," *NCRLC Proceedings*, 1934, 35; Schmiedeler, *Cooperation*, 42; Witte, *Twenty-five Years*, 107, 118–19, 215–18; Donald Hayne, "Westphalia: Pattern and Promise," *Catholic Rural Life Bulletin* 2 (August 20, 1939): 18–19, 28; Terminiello, "St. Teresa's Village," 20–21.

40. Urban Baer, *Farmers of Tomorrow* (Sparta, Wisc.: Monroe Publishing, 1939), chap. 1; "Department of Social Action, 1937–1938," in "Report, 1932–1939," NCWC 34, 13.

41. Virgil Michel, *Ideals of Reconstruction*, The Social Question—I (St. Paul, Minn.: Wanderer Printing, 1937), 52–55, in "Social Reconstruction," NCRLC 3-26; Michel, *Reconstruction Schemes*,

It was also for the purpose of promoting a better family and home life that the Catholic agrarians favored the family-owned and -operated farm. The NCRLC held that "no system of agricultural economy can be considered sound which does not rest upon the farm home and the family as the natural unit of rural social life." Only the family farm, Catholics insisted, could provide the proper environment for Christian family life, as well as a just and prosperous economic life. Moreover, to some Catholic ruralists, the times seemed especially propitious for a movement in favor of the family farm. Notre Dame English professor Leo L. Ward, C.S.C., claimed that the Depression had caused a disenchantment among farmers for commercial farming:

What the new farmer wants is security . . . The new farmer has rather definitely returned to an earlier point of view, . . . he has come to think of farming largely as a way of life, and not merely as a way of making money . . . For the moment it is pleasant, and just a bit exciting, to realize that we have met our grandfather again, and heard his voice talking very wisely back over the years.

Some of the Catholic agrarians argued that a back-to-the-land movement would only be successful if family subsistence farming replaced commercial farming: "There is only one way, however, that any mass movement to the soil can be inaugurated, and that is by featuring a revolution on the soil itself."[42]

Catholic rural leaders launched a number of different efforts in support of the family farm. One of them involved the publication of a great deal of practical information regarding family, and especially self-sufficient, farming. Among the techniques described in such literature were the use of small labor-saving machinery, canning, use of livestock and other farm products for a variety of purposes, efficient arrangement of the farm home, home crafts and industries, and "biodynamic farming."[43]

The Social Question—VII (St. Paul: Wanderer Printing, 1939), 21–24, in "Social Reconstruction," NCRLC 3-26; "Decentralization of Industry" (editorial), *Catholic Charities Review* 17 (March 1933): 67–68; Ligutti and Rawe, *Rural Roads to Security,* esp. chaps. 3, 18; Cram, "Recovery or Regeneration?"; Cram, "Recovery or Regeneration," *Commonweal,* November 9, 1934, 56–58; Cram, "Cities of Refuge"; La Farge, "Religion"; La Farge, "Decentralism and Rural Life," *Catholic Rural Life Bulletin* 3 (August 20, 1940): 1–3.

42. NCRLC minutes binder (1935–38), NCRLC 8-2, 159; Leo L. Ward, "Back on the Land," *Commonweal,* August 27, 1937, 419; "The Green Revolution," ibid., March 1, 1940, 395–96.

43. Jessie T. Dutton's articles in "Articles, Homesteads," NCRLC 11-3; Margaret T. Lynch, "Living Standards and Christianity," *Landward* 1 (Winter 1934): 7; Pauline M. Reynolds, "Lived Nobly and Well," *Catholic Rural Life Bulletin* 2 (February 20, 1939): 7–11; Ligutti and Rawe, *Rural Roads to Security,* chaps. 12, 13, appendices 2, 3; William Everett Cram, "Choosing Your Farm," *Commonweal,* March 16, 1934, 543–45.

Biodynamic farming involved treating the soil as a living organism and using natural processes to keep it healthy and fertile. Instead of commercial fertilizer, which only postponed the exhaustion of the soil, biodynamic farmers were to enrich their soil with animal manure, legumes, and earthworms. To provide the soil-enriching manure, proponents of biodynamic farming proposed the substitution of animal power for machinery for much farm work. This, incidentally, would also cut down on the farmers' outside costs and provide a more natural and self-contained life for farm families. Contrary to popular belief, NCRLC leaders such as John C. Rawe, S.J., argued, the small farm, lovingly and scientifically cultivated in the biodynamic manner, was actually more efficient than the large commercial farm to which the farmer could not give proper attention.[44]

The development of home arts and crafts would help, too. The NCRLC resolved that as many as possible of the arts and crafts that had been absorbed by the factory system be returned to the home, "in order that home life may be rendered more wholesome and satisfying to old and young while home necessities are produced with a minimum outlay of cash." The introduction of home crafts could revitalize economically depressed rural communities. Catholic ruralists looked with favor upon programs that were set up during the Depression years to teach handicraft techniques, such as those of Ralph Borsodi's School for Living and the Farm Security Administration.[45]

Rural Catholic leaders particularly condemned what they considered to be the utter antithesis of the family farm—corporate farming. They naturally deplored the effects of factory farming on family life, but they also declared that it was in the long run less efficient, especially since it would be less likely to take advantage of the new advances in biodynamic farming. Corporate farms would not be able to fit into the occupational group system, nor would they practice Christian cooperation.[46]

Catholic agrarians viewed with alarm the ten thousand companies already engaged in agriculture. They feared that a merging process of the largest of these companies might soon culminate in the formation of some

---

44. John C. Rawe, "Biological Technology on the Land," *Catholic Rural Life Bulletin* 2 (August 20, 1939): 1–3, 20–22; Rawe, "What, Where and Why of Bio-dynamics," *Land and Home* 6 (September 1943): 67–68. See Marlett, *Saving the Heartland*, 42–43, for the origins of the biodynamic farming movement.

45. NCRLC minutes binder (1935–38), NCRLC 8-2, 161; "Home-Craft for Rural Communities," *Central-Blatt and Social Justice* 24 (April 1931): 12; "Production for Use" (editorial), *Commonweal*, October 2, 1939, 526–27.

46. "Comment," *America*, September 9, 1939, 507; John La Farge, "Farm Ownership Linked with Trades Unions," ibid., December 4, 1937, 196–98.

Programs to Meet the Crisis   123

gigantic "General Farms Incorporated," comparable to the monopolistic industrial corporations. They reminded Americans that Marxists taught that the concentration of industry was the necessary prerequisite to the establishment of the communist state. The NCRLC applauded the decision of the Kansas Supreme Court revoking the charter of a huge Wheat Farming Corporation because it "constituted a public menace" to state and national policies favoring widespread property ownership.[47]

Rural Catholic leaders thought that the government could do much else to limit the growth of corporate farming and to aid family farms. Some of their proposals included limiting AAA benefits to family-sized economic units; raising agricultural prices; refinancing and scaling down farm mortgage debts; enlarging the FSA program, especially its tenant purchase program; including migratory families in social legislation; and establishing a farm placement service. Many of their proposals concerned taxation. Policies they favored included graduated taxes on land and on farmers who contributed to the surplus; the enactment of income rather than property or sales taxes; a tax exemption for all homes and all land used for family subsistence rather than for commercial purposes; and even the old "single tax" on unearned increment of land value. Other proposals to aid the family farm involved little or no governmental action: lengthening the term of tenant leases; encouraging the cooperative ownership and use of farm machinery; developing smaller and less costly farm machines; having farm families in a neighborhood bring pressure to bear on any who would try to start large-scale farms in their territory at the expense of small operators; and having rural education emphasize education for rural, not city, living, and further, for family-farm living, not commercial farming.[48]

In the late 1930s, however, rural Catholic leaders believed that American agricultural policy was diverging from their ideals. Despite an economic relapse in 1937, national income, farm income, and farm prices generally improved in the late thirties. Thus, the crisis atmosphere of the early thirties gradually dissolved, and the nation was less inclined toward the radical agrarian measures that the NCRLC favored.

In 1938, Congress passed the so-called second AAA, which replaced the

47. John C. Rawe, "Life, Liberty and the Pursuit of Happiness in Agriculture," *Catholic Rural Life Objectives*, 1936, 35–45.
48. Schmiedeler, *Vanishing Homesteads*, 22–27; "Efficiency versus Humanity"; NCRLC, *Manifesto*, 66–70, 188; John C. Rawe, "Some Problems in Modern Homesteading," in "Articles. Homesteads," NCRLC 11-3, 11–24; "Transcription of tapes made with Monsignor Ligutti and extra documents used in writing his biography (Part I)," (interview with Vincent Yzermans), LGL-K, 184–86.

hastily devised Soil Conservation Act of 1936 with a more comprehensive program of soil conservation, domestic allotment, intervention with respect to freight rates on agricultural commodities, loans, parity payments, consumer safeguards, marketing quotas, cotton pool participation trust certificates, and crop insurance. Among the new features of the second AAA was Agriculture Secretary Henry Wallace's plan for an "ever-normal granary." Inspired by the practice of the biblical Joseph in Egypt, the ever-normal granary would deal with the troublesome surplus by storing extra grain from bumper crop years for use in low production years.

Catholic rural opinion was generally favorable to the second AAA, so far as it went. Catholics wrote that the AAA and the ever-normal granary were practical and in accord with the principles of *Quadragesimo Anno*. Adverse comments, which came mainly from the conservative *Central-Blatt and Social Justice*, voiced fears of excessive government regulation or complained that the legislation did not go far enough to address more fundamental sources of the farmer's troubles such as the tariff and monopolies.[49]

However, Catholic rural leaders' major economic concern in the late 1930s was not agricultural adjustment but the welfare of the poorest of the rural poor—the tenant farmers, sharecroppers, and agricultural laborers. The rural poor had been forgotten by the American people and their government during the long Republican era prior to the Roosevelt administration—and even the first years of the New Deal had been preoccupied with restoring the prosperity of the agricultural sector as a whole. But by the mid-thirties, the recent experience of real poverty by so large a proportion of the American population, coupled with the revelations of books such as *Tobacco Road* and *The Grapes of Wrath*, called attention to a vast, hitherto-neglected rural underclass.

Catholics were among those beginning to take notice of the rural poor. Pope Pius XI had, indeed, urged them to look in that direction when he wrote in *Quadragesimo Anno* that "there is an immense army of hired rural laborers, whose condition is depressed in the extreme, and who have no hope of ever obtaining a share in the land." American Catholics deplored the wretched living and working conditions of the rural poor, the

---

49. John Michael Kennedy, "An Ever-Normal Granary," *Commonweal*, December 31, 1937, 257–59; "Reversing the AAA Decision," ibid., April 28, 1939, 1–2; Edgar Schmiedeler, "The New Farm Act" ("Current Rural Comments"), *Wanderer*, March 10, 1938, in "Clippings, Schmiedeler, Edgar," NCRLC 9-6; Lawrence Lucey, "Down on the Farm," *Catholic World* 149 (June 1939): 284–89; "Resolutions Adopted by the Catholic Central Verein of America at Its 83rd Annual Convention, Assembled in Bethlehem, Pa. (August 20–24, 1938)," *Central-Blatt and Social Justice* 31 (October 1938): 213–14; "Whither the New Farm Program," ibid. 31 (September 1938): 155–56.

Programs to Meet the Crisis 125

disruption of their family life, their insecurity of tenure, their exploitation by the large growers, and their degeneration into a seemingly permanent landless proletariat. Father Ligutti of Granger was among the Catholics moved by the plight of the dispossessed on the land. In 1937 and 1938, he served on an Iowa farm tenancy committee and took a leading role in writing its report.[50]

The NCRLC believed that AAA-type programs were insufficient in dealing with the problems of the rural poor. Policies directed at raising farm income tended to favor the large farmers, but they had little to offer poor tenants and sharecroppers—in fact, they often had the effect of forcing them off their land. As a starting point, the Conference urged, the rural poor needed direct help in improving their living and working conditions: camps for migrants should be stabilized and improved, and the federal government should intervene to end the "economic oppression and actual physical barbarities which local governments seem powerless or unwilling to redress." To aid in this improvement, Catholic ruralists encouraged the formation of unions of agricultural workers, such as the Southern Tenant Farmers Union. The best solution, because it was the only permanent one, the NCRLC claimed, was to make the rural tenants, sharecroppers, and laborers owners of their own small farms. Only this would end once and for all their dependence on their landlords or employers and allow them to join the great, independent middle class of family farmers. Government aid was a necessity to allow this hoped-for transformation to occur.[51]

In addition to their long-time support for subsistence homesteads and resettlement programs, Catholics, beginning in 1935, also put their weight behind a new series of legislative proposals aimed not merely at rural economic recovery, but at the eventual elimination of poverty on the land al-

50. Pius XI quoted in Raymond J. Miller, "Agriculture in the Industrial Encyclicals," *Catholic Rural Life Bulletin* 1 (August 20, 1938): 25–26; Frederick P. Kenkel, "The Economic Disfranchisement of the Sharecropper," *Catholic Rural Life Objectives, 1936*, 91–100; F. P. Kenkel, "Strangling the Cotton Growers," *Central-Blatt and Social Justice* 30 (February 1938): 342–43; Edgar Schmiedeler, "Current Rural Comment," *Wanderer*, January 28, 1937, in "Clippings, NCRLC, Jan., 1937," NCRLC 9-1; Iowa Farm Tenancy Committee, *Summary of Findings* (n.p.: Iowa State Planning Board, 1938), and correspondence in "LGL Outgoing Correspondence, 1936–1939," both in LGL-C; a number of folders on tenancy in LGL-E, LGL-G, and LGL-H; Vincent A. Yzermans, *The People I Love: A Biography of Luigi G. Ligutti* (Collegeville, Minn.: Liturgical Press, 1976), 40–43.

51. Percy A. Robert, "Farm Tenancy," *Landward* 4 (Spring 1936): 2, 4, 10; "Agricultural Laborers Meet in Washington," *Rural Bureau Notes* 3 (April 1936): 2–4; quotation from "Crime in the Cotton Belt" (editorial), *Landward* 4 (Summer 1936): 5, 12; NCRLC minutes binder (1935–38), NCRLC 8-2, 190, 215; Patrick T. Quinlan, "Rural Migrants on the March," *Catholic Rural Life Bulletin* 2 (May 20, 1939): 12–13, 25–28; NCRLC, *Manifesto*, 8–12, 52–54.

together. The Conference supported bills in Congress to provide loans for the purchase or improvement of farm homes, as well as "rehabilitation" loans for the purchase of supplies, equipment, and livestock. It applauded the formation of the Presidential Committee on Farm Tenancy and endorsed the committee's recommendations for loans and grants to tenants and other poor farm families, encouragement of cooperatives, services for migrant workers, and removal of farmers from submarginal land and their resettlement elsewhere. In August 1937 Congress created the Farm Security Administration (FSA) in accordance with these recommendations. Before its demise in the mid-1940s, the FSA made tens of thousands of loans to tenant purchasers and cooperative groups and hundreds of thousands of rural rehabilitation loans and relief grants.[52]

The NCRLC was generally very favorable toward the FSA. It was particularly supportive of the tenant purchase program, which would tend to break down the rural proletariat and increase the property-owning class on the land. The Conference repeatedly complained that the appropriation for this program was too small and called for it to be raised to $1 billion.[53]

When big farmers, businessmen, and lawmakers concerned with cutting the federal bureaucracy made a sustained and ultimately successful effort to dismantle the FSA, the NCRLC responded to the threat with its most intensive Congressional lobbying effort up to that time. In 1943, both the Reverend John O'Grady and Father Ligutti represented the NCRLC before Congress in defense of the FSA. They submitted a memorandum that praised three aspects of the FSA program: its promotion of ownership, its recognition of the importance of the family in agriculture, and its services—unique among government agencies—specifically aimed at the poorest of the nation's farmers. In one emotional session, O'Grady contended that the allegedly lavish amounts of money spent on the FSA's controversial homesteads projects at Coffee Farms, Alabama, and Terrebone, Louisiana, were worth it, for the areas were "revolutionized," and that any communistic aspects of the projects were merely transitional. He maintained that without the FSA, there would be no agency capable and willing to meet the needs of the lower third of the agricultural population. "What are you going to do about those further down the line?" O'Grady

---

52. Baldwin, *Poverty and Politics*, 126–54, 167–87, chap. 7; Conkin, *Tomorrow a New World*, 182–85; NCRLC minutes binder (1933–35), NCRLC 8-1, 138; NCRLC minutes binder (1935–38), NCRLC 8-2, 161; Byrnes, "Foreword," 3–6; L. G. Ligutti, "Farm Ownership and Land Tenancy," in "Articles, Land Ownership," NCRLC 11-3.

53. Edgar Schmiedeler, "A Review of Rural Insecurity," *Catholic Rural Life Objectives, 1937*, 43–52; Schmiedeler, *Vanishing Homesteads*, 23–25; minutes and resolutions throughout NCRLC 8-3 and 8-4.

Programs to Meet the Crisis 127

implored. "Are you going to leave them in filth, dirt, and degradation? What are you going to do about them?"[54]

Catholic rural leaders blamed the nation's commercial farming interests for the attempt to kill off the FSA. La Farge noted angrily that the major farm organizations had no conception of agriculture as a vocation and believed that farmers were too numerous already. Therefore, they opposed "any serious attempt to open agricultural opportunity for families who wish to return to the land." Ligutti accused some southern FSA opponents of wishing to perpetuate the system of "economic slavery for both white and black" that the FSA was combatting.[55]

Despite all of the Conference's efforts, the FSA was terminated by Congress in 1946.[56] The demise of the FSA was the culminating example of the frustration of practically all of the hopes that Catholic rural leaders had had for the agricultural economy at the end of the 1930s. The Central Verein spoke for the entire movement when it said that the agricultural programs of the last ten years, though "well intentioned . . . have not solved the problem or even approximated a solution." The AAA and Soil Conservation acts still had not raised farm income to parity with city income. Credit programs had not stemmed the steady abandonment of small, individually owned farms—whose former owners went to cities, while the farms themselves were added to large commercialized units. Relief and food-stamp programs for the urban unemployed were no substitute for payment of a living wage, or better yet, the settlement of such people on family-sized, self-sustaining farms. The materialistic view of farming as a business continued to gain ground against the Christian philosophy of farming as a way of life.[57]

---

54. Baldwin, *Poverty and Politics*, chaps. 11 and 12; Conkin, *Tomorrow a New World*, 214–30; McConnell, *Decline of Agrarian Democracy*; U.S. Congress, House, Hearings before the Subcommittee of the Committee on Appropriations on the Agriculture Department Appropriation Bill for 1943, 77th Cong., 2d Sess., Part II, 1942, 583–88; U.S. Congress, Senate, Hearings before the Subcommittee of the Committee on Appropriations, Agricultural Appropriations Bill for 1943, 77th Cong., 2d Sess., 1942, 519–35; U.S. Congress, House, Hearings before the Select Committee of the House Committee on Agriculture, to Investigate the Activities of the Farm Security Administration, 78th Cong., 1st Sess., Part II, 1943, 661–88.

55. "Conference Affairs," *Land and Home* 6 (June 1943): 56; John La Farge, "Agriculture and Vocation," *Commonweal*, July 1, 1938, 261; L. G. Ligutti to Editor, Des Moines *Register*, April 23, 1943, in "Correspondence, D," NCRLC 13-1.

56. Conkin, *Tomorrow a New World*, 214–30; Baldwin, *Poverty and Politics*, chap. 12; "Minutes of the Meeting of the Executive Committee of the National Catholic Rural Life Conference, May 16, 1944, Des Moines, Iowa," in "Board of Directors, Members, Executive Committee Meeting, Des Moines, Iowa, May 16, 1944," NCRLC 8-4.

57. "Resolutions of the Catholic Central Verein of America at its 84th Annual Convention, Assembled in San Francisco, Calif. (July 29–August 2, 1939)," *Central-Blatt and Social Justice* 32 (Oc-

The Conference's disappointment at its lack of influence on national agricultural policy was nevertheless a sign of its development. For during the Depression years, the Catholic rural life movement moved from a force primarily interested in the effects of rural life on the strength of the Catholic Church to one that was mainly concerned with the effects of Catholic social teachings on the rural life of the nation as a whole. David J. O'Brien and other historians have noted that it was during the Depression that Catholics began their move into the mainstream of American life. The NCRLC's activity in the 1930s was one example of this process.[58]

---

tober 1939): 212; [Vincent J. Ryan], "A Statement by the President," *Catholic Rural Life Bulletin* 3 (November 20, 1940): 1–2, 17–19; Emerson Hynes, "Agriculture in the Next Decade," ibid. (February 20, 1940): 3–5, 26–27; "Resolution of the National Catholic Rural Life Conference," in "St. Cloud Convention, September 29, 30, October 1–2, 1940," NCRLC 8-3, 2–3.

58. O'Brien, *American Catholics and Social Reform,* 47; Schneider, "Visions of Land," 103.

Chapter 6 Inside the NCRLC

Interlocking Conflicts

While the NCRLC grappled with the economic problems of the Great Depression in the 1930s, it suffered from a series of organizational difficulties and personal squabbles that interacted in a complex manner throughout the decade. These problems can be looked at from three major perspectives. First was the conflict between autonomy and higher direction of the Conference. The NCRLC and its "grass roots" of rural pastors were constantly involved in a struggle for control of the Catholic rural life movement with the bishops and "social action" priests of the NCWC. By the 1940s, when Luigi Ligutti became executive secretary, the NCRLC was, at least for a time, completely victorious in this struggle. Second, the thirties witnessed a constant tugging back and forth within the Conference between religious and economic concerns. In the 1920s, there was no question that the Conference had been more concerned with the Catholic rural population problem than with economic issues. But with the onset of the Depression, economic problems suddenly became so urgent that they threatened to sweep the NCRLC off its feet, to the detriment of religious concerns. A "mid-course correction" in 1935 involving the dropping of an economically oriented president established a fairly stable equilibrium between the two concerns that persisted in the following decades. Finally, unlike the 1920s, when Father O'Hara was the unchallenged head of the movement, and the 1940s and 1950s, when Ligutti gathered all of the reins into his hands, no single leader of the movement emerged in the 1930s. A number of strong personalities vied for the title, and their struggles created a third source of conflict.

The first precipitating event that broke the relatively tranquil state of the NCRLC leadership in the 1920s was O'Hara's appointment as bishop of Great Falls, Montana, in 1930. To take the episcopal post, O'Hara had to give up his dual positions of director of the NCWC Rural Life Bureau and executive secretary of the NCRLC. This left the Conference with the problems of filling these offices and also of coping with O'Hara's residual influence upon NCRLC direction. For after O'Hara's appointment as bishop, the Conference named him honorary president, and as such he continued to attend most NCRLC conventions. His prestige as founder tended to make the others defer to him when he cared to express an opinion. In the later thirties, O'Hara was chairman of the NCWC Social Action Department and thus became involved in the NCRLC–Rural Life Bureau controversy of that time. Some of the NCRLC's new leadership thought that O'Hara's continued involvement held the Conference back. In 1936, Executive Secretary James Byrnes wrote President William Mulloy that it would be in the interest of the Conference to "break away from the set-up of past years wherein Bishop O'Hara was the everything and all in the Conference." Byrnes said that "the organization is now proceeding under its own steam," and that O'Hara need not be involved in all decisions, but might be informed, "with all dignity and respect," of decisions the Conference had arrived at on its own.[1]

O'Hara's influence gradually declined as the decade went on and the NCRLC's new leaders became more experienced in directing the Conference. But no one of these new leaders emerged as the clear successor to O'Hara. Certainly O'Hara's immediate replacement as Rural Life Bureau director / NCRLC executive secretary, the Reverend Edgar Schmiedeler, O.S.B., did not meet with everyone's approval. Schmiedeler was a stockily built, square-faced man of middle age who had been teaching sociology at St. Benedict's College in Atchison, Kansas, since 1919. One reporter said that Schmiedeler's "personality evades analysis." He was described as a "cross between Mussolini and Mr. Milquetoast"; he exhibited a "dogged perseverance" but also a "well-informed, optimistic diffidence" that—according to the writer—impelled others to help him in his work.[2] Some colleagues in the rural life movement viewed him less positively as narrow-minded, self-righteous, and stubborn.

Schmiedeler officially took over as director and executive secretary on August 1, 1931. Thus there was a gap of a full year between O'Hara's departure for Great Falls and the installation of his successor. Enter a third per-

1. NCRLC minutes binder (1923–32), NCRLC 8-1, 79, 80, 81; NCRLC minutes binder (1933–35), NCRLC 8-1, 89–91, 129; NCRLC minutes binder (1935–38), NCRLC 8-2, 167, 169–71, 182, 185; O'Hara to W. Howard Bishop, December 13, 1932, in "General Correspondence, O'Hara, Edwin V.," in LGL-E; quotation from Byrnes to Mulloy, March 4, 1936, in "Ntn'l Convention, Fargo, N.D., October 11–14, 1936," NCRLC 8-2.

2. "Leaders Meet at Kansas Monastery," *Landward* 5 (Spring 1937): 11.

sonality, the NCRLC president from 1928 to 1934, the Reverend W. Howard Bishop. A rural pastor from Clarksville, Maryland, and future founder of the Glenmary Home Missioners, Bishop represented the "grass roots," decentralist desires of the Conference's rural pastors as against the centralizing tendencies of the Washington office of the Rural Life Bureau and the pietistic feelings of the rural missionaries as opposed to the logical programs of the "social science" priests. Thus, when Bishop, in the absence of any other authority in 1930 and 1931, began, as president, to take over direction of the Conference's affairs, he found a ready following among the Conference's rank and file. Bishop handled much of the Conference's substantive correspondence and paid for many of its expenses out of his own pocket. By the time Schmiedeler took over as executive secretary, there was already an embryo opposition to his authority, and this continued after Schmiedeler was established in his new post. It was Bishop, not Schmiedeler, who in 1932 injected the NCRLC into the economic problems of the Depression by calling at the Dubuque convention for a Catholic land movement as the solution for unemployment. A year later, Bishop put an end to the hiatus in Catholic rural periodicals by starting—with his own funds—*Landward*, which in 1934 was accepted as the official NCRLC organ. Bishop had become the Conference's real leader. In 1933, the board of directors, though not dissatisfied with Bishop's performance as president, decided that more rotation in office would be beneficial to the Conference. So he was continued as president for one more year (1933–34), and in 1934 a new president was elected. Although rural missionary work was his first love (he returned to it when he retired from the Conference presidency), Bishop combined the religious and economic objectives of the Conference with a sure balance, which earned him the trust and respect of the membership.[3]

Meanwhile, Schmiedeler was clashing with NCRLC officials over a variety of issues. One of the main causes of friction was the matter of control over the diocesan directors of rural life. At first, Schmiedeler attended the diocesan directors' meetings held at the annual conventions and received regular reports from them. Then, in 1934, the Conference wrote a revised constitution, which gave the diocesan directors the power to elect their own officers, without reference to the Rural Life Bureau director. Schmiedeler objected to this, and in 1935 met with the diocesan directors, who agreed that they would carry out the general policies of the NCRLC

---

3. NCRLC minutes binder (1933–35), NCRLC 8-1, 90, 124–25; testimonial to Bishop on his retirement from the presidency, in "1934 Conference Resolutions," *NCRLC Proceedings, 1934*, 196–97.

but that the Rural Life Bureau would direct their actual activities. Schmiedeler could continue to receive reports from the directors and provide direction at their meetings. The situation remained in this state of uneasy peace until the end of the Rural Life Bureau in the 1940s.[4]

The working committee for the 1934 constitutional revision included some of those who were most devoted to Conference autonomy and distrusted Schmiedeler, such as James Byrnes and Joseph Campbell. Schmiedeler was not on the committee, so he had no say in the future relationship between the Rural Life Bureau (of which he was director) and the NCRLC (of which he was executive secretary). The new constitution provided that the Rural Life Bureau director was merely a "liaison officer" between the bureau and the Conference and was not the ex officio executive secretary of the NCRLC. In 1934, Byrnes was appointed executive secretary; Schmiedeler was put on the board of directors, but not on the important executive committee, which in 1935 began to meet several times during the year—not only at the annual conventions, as before.[5]

Other conflicts and complaints soon began to further irritate the relationship between Schmiedeler and the NCRLC. Schmiedeler claimed that Bishop O'Hara removed the Rural Life Bureau papers when he vacated the office. Conference officials complained that Schmiedeler did not keep them informed on the Bankhead farm tenancy bill in Washington. In 1935, the Conference decided to stop subsidizing *Rural Bureau Notes,* and the next year Schmiedeler had to stop its publication. Schmiedeler complained to his superiors in the NCWC of his immense workload. Conference officials complained that Schmiedeler was "entirely impossible."[6]

In a series of meetings with the Conference leadership from 1935 to 1938, and in correspondence with his NCWC superiors, Schmiedeler tried to come to some understanding concerning his functions with the NCRLC. He sought some control over the Conference publications, the diocesan di-

---

4. Edgar Schmiedeler, "Catholic Rural Life Conference at Dubuque," (copy of article reprinted from *Ecclesiastical Review* 88 [May 1933]: 461–74), in "National Convention, Dubuque, Iowa, Oct. 19–21, 1932," NCRLC 8-1, 11–12; "Minutes of the Meeting of the Directors of Diocesan Rural Life Bureaus Held October 17, 1933," in "Minutes, Diocesan Directors, 1933–36," NCRLC 8-1, 4–5, 17; "Digest of the Minutes of the meeting of the Directors of Diocesan Rural Life Bureaus Held October 30, 1935," in ibid., 2–3; "Meeting of Diocesan Directors, October 30, 1935," NCRLC 8-2; "Constitution and By-Laws of the National Catholic Rural Life Conference," in *NCRLC Proceedings, 1934,* 17–19; John Heinz, "Who Shall Lead the Crusade," in "NCRLC History," NCRLC 11-4.

5. NCRLC minutes binder (1933–35), NCRLC 8-1, 91, 93, 121, 126.

6. Ibid., 138; NCRLC minutes binder (1935–38), NCRLC 8-2, 152, 158; "Rural and Family Report, 1938," NCWC 40; [Michael J. Ready], NCWC, to M. Lynch, Nov. 6, 1934, in "Social Action: Rural Life Bureau, 1931–1935," U.S. Catholic Conference Archives, Folder 56–N (hereafter USCC 56-N).

rectors, and the essay contest, and wanted the Rural Life Bureau raised to the status of a full department of the NCWC, but most of all he tried to gain back the executive secretaryship.[7] Schmiedeler justified his position on the latter crucial point as follows:

> Bishop O'Hara had closely linked the Rural Life Bureau and the Rural Life Conference, serving as Director of the former and Executive Secretary of the latter. When, after I had succeeded him, several in the Conference showed that they meant to separate the two organizations even to the extent of taking the Executive Secretaryship out of the Rural Life Bureau, I felt bound both in justice to the past work of Bishop O'Hara and to the Bishops who were supporting the Bureau at Washington to protest.[8]

On the other side of the fence, the Conference officials had little use for the Rural Life Bureau. They wanted it only as a liaison with the NCWC in Washington and as an information service (Schmiedeler to be "research secretary") to provide news of government and other rural life developments. They were confident that if the Rural Life Bureau was discontinued, some other official in the NCWC or a person authorized by the Conference could provide these services perfectly well.[9] Several factors were behind their desire to separate the executive secretaryship from the Rural Life Bureau. There is no doubt that most of the Conference leaders disliked Schmiedeler, and many had personally experienced frustration in dealing with him. There was also a natural urge to have control of Conference affairs in their own hands, rather than in those of the bishops and officials of the urban-oriented NCWC. And NCRLC leaders were strongly conscious of their rural and midwestern roots and were therefore reluctant, once they had set up a national office in the midst of their home territory, to give control back to an office in faraway Washington, D.C. For a rural organization, Washington, which existed primarily as a center for the federal government and had no rural hinterland, seemed an especially inappropriate center for their group. Far better, symbolically, to have the Conference headquarters at St. Paul, the center of the upper Midwest grain trade, or, as later, at Des Moines, the hub of the Corn Belt.

---

7. Heinz, "Who Shall Lead the Crusade;" NCRLC minutes binder (1935–38), NCRLC 8-2, 153, 167, 170, 175, 177, 178, 179–80, 181–83, 185–86, 194–97, 236; William Mulloy to Edwin V. O'Hara, February 28, 1938, and James A. Byrnes to Mulloy, March 4, 1936, in "Ntn'l Convention, Fargo, N.D., October 11–14, 1936," NCRLC 8-2; folders "Social Action: Rural Life Bureau, 1931–1935," and "Social Action: Rural Life Bureau, 1936–1940," USCC 56-N, copies in NCRLC Archives.

8. Schmiedeler to Muench, April 19, 1938, in "Inter-off.," NCWC 61.

9. NCRLC minutes binder (1935-38), NCRLC 8-2, 153.

These arguments eventually won over the NCWC. The breaking point, as far as Schmiedeler's throwing in the towel was concerned, came at a September 27, 1938, board of directors meeting. Bishop Aloisius Muench of Fargo—perhaps because Bishop O'Hara, chairman of the NCWC's Social Action Department, was absent—was called upon to explain to those present, including Schmiedeler, the relationship between the NCRLC and the Rural Life Bureau. Muench stated that the Rural Life Bureau was primarily a "research" organization; it would "provide the Conference with statistics, reports, government bulletins and other information," and "maintain contact with government officials and . . . watch federal legislation." The minutes noted that Schmiedeler, no doubt in a mood of resignation, "expressed satisfaction with the definition of his functions and offered to give the Conference any possible service." The Benedictine, who had meantime also become head of the NCWC's Family Life Bureau, continued to perform these duties until the Rural Life Bureau faded into an obscure end sometime early in the 1940s.[10]

Despite the conflict between Schmiedeler and the NCRLC, the two did cooperate in many useful projects during the 1930s, such as obtaining federal approval for the Granger homesteads and composing the Conference's important statement, the *Manifesto on Rural Life*. In early 1938, Schmiedeler confided to Muench: "Frankly, I do not feel that the situation in question [Rural Life Bureau–NCRLC strife] really affects our Catholic rural work in any substantial way."[11] Schmiedeler likely understated its effects; with a more harmonious relationship, more probably could have been accomplished.

The other Conference leaders were generally much more compatible with each other. The Reverend James A. Byrnes, the executive secretary from 1934 to 1940, had been superintendent of schools and rural life director of the St. Paul archdiocese. Byrnes was a dignified-looking man, "like a dean in a seminary," Ligutti said. Byrnes's two most important contributions to the Conference during his years at the helm were upholding NCRLC autonomy and guiding the formation of a Conference philosophy. For the latter task, he was suited by temperament; as Ligutti said,

10. NCRLC minutes binder (1935–38), NCRLC 8-2, 236. The last time the Rural Life Bureau was mentioned in an annual report of the NCWC Social Action Department was in 1940: National Catholic Welfare Conference, *Annual Reports, 1940, Department of Social Action* (Washington, D.C.: Administrative Board, n.d.), 9–11. National Catholic Welfare Conference, *Annual Reports, 1941, Department of Social Action* (Washington, D.C.: Administrative Board, n.d.), does not have a Rural Life Bureau report, nor do any of the subsequent *Annual Reports*.

11. Schmiedeler to Muench, April 19, 1938, "Inter-off.," NCWC 61.

Figure 5. Scholarly James Byrnes, executive secretary, 1934–40.

"Jimmy Byrnes was an intellectual." Others in the Conference remarked on Byrnes's perfectionism and on his sense of a need for "a solid philosophic basis for the [rural life] movement and the need of a long educational process before the work would be brought to fruition." He applied these instincts to his editorship of the NCRLC periodical *Catholic Rural Life Bulletin* and the *Catholic Rural Life Objectives* (a series of compilations of convention papers), and to his work on the *Manifesto on Rural Life,* and made them important sources for the intellectual underpinnings of the rural life movement.[12]

12. [William T. Mulloy] "Reverend James Anthony Byrnes," in "General Correspondence—Byrnes, Rev. James Anthony," in LGL-F, and the correspondence in that folder; "LGL—Transcription of tapes made with Monsignor Ligutti and extra documents used in writing his biography (Part I)," LGL-K, 21–22, 119; Vincent J. Ryan, "A Tribute to Father Byrnes," *Catholic Rural Life Bulletin* 4 (February 20, 1941): 14; Witte, *Twenty-five Years,* 163–67; "May He Rest in Peace," *Catholic Rural Life* 13 (May 1964): 1.

At the same time that Byrnes took over the executive secretaryship, a much more controversial figure succeeded to Father Bishop's long tenure as Conference president. The Reverend Joseph M. Campbell, a pastor from Ames, Iowa, was the archdiocesan rural life director for Dubuque before being elected president of the NCRLC in 1934. He fit in well with the new order in the Conference that was for autonomy; he had participated in the drafting of the 1934 constitution that had ousted Schmiedeler. Campbell was also known to be sympathetic to the new direction of involvement in national economic issues to which Bishop had turned the Conference two years earlier.

In fact, Campbell became preoccupied with the Church's response to rural economic issues to the virtual exclusion of the NCRLC's other concerns. Before his election as president, Campbell's participation in board of directors meetings was almost always to support the Conference's involvement in some economic matter: He called for meetings of NCRLC leaders more frequently than those at the annual conventions to consider economic issues and recommended giving official support to Ligutti's subsistence homesteads project. In an article in *Landward,* Campbell proposed that parish priests do more "as individuals for the prevention of poverty." As practical projects he recommended that priests personally "bring creditors and debtors together," inform the people of government relief measures, and foster the growth of the cooperative movement. In his first message as newly elected president of the NCRLC, Campbell, after giving his respects to the Conference's spiritual program, declared that "if we are to go forward, as we might, toward our goal of many thousands of strong rural parishes, it seems to me that we shall have to pay more attention to the economic aspects of our problem than we have in the past. Country life must be made inviting from an economic point of view before its spiritual advantages can have weight with people." He insisted that "our first concern must be economic rather than spiritual" and that "a sound economic order is essential to a thriving spiritual order."[13]

Campbell's actions as president further exhibited his economic preoccupation and aroused the concern of other NCRLC leaders. In January 1935, at a meeting of the NCRLC executive committee and midwestern diocesan directors at Des Moines, Campbell proposed that priests—whom farmers would trust more than paid managers—organize credit unions

13. NCRLC minutes binders (1923–32), NCRLC 8-1, 79–80; NCRLC minutes binder (1933–35), NCRLC 8-1, 91; Joseph M. Campbell, "The Priest and Community Leadership," *Landward* 1 (Winter 1934): 6, 8; Campbell, "A Presidential Greeting," ibid. 2 (Winter 1934–35): 1–2, 8.

with the purpose of providing farm credit under the farmers' own control. These credit unions would eventually "eliminate the necessity of any other banking service to farmers." Once the credit unions were established, they would form the basis for a "complete farm co-operative system" that would include purchasing and marketing cooperatives. The executive committee rejected Campbell's plan, and in the aftermath of the meeting, Conference officials such as Byrnes and Ligutti deplored the fact that Campbell, in his "enthusiasm for Credit Unionism," was giving rural priests and the press "the idea that the Conference is concerned primarily with the remaking of the nation's financial structure." Byrnes and Ligutti pledged to each other to try to "bring our worthy president to a more balanced attitude."[14]

The two leaders were apparently unsuccessful in persuading Campbell to change his course. At the convention in 1935, Campbell stated "that he was not in a position to accept reelection to the office of president, due to other work for which he can operate with greater freedom when he is not considered as an official representative of the Conference." He also resigned from the board of directors, and although he pledged further cooperation with the NCRLC upon his retirement from the presidency, he played no further part in its affairs. Following the rejection of his economic views by the Conference, Campbell went on to promote them on his own. In 1936, he became executive secretary of the National Cooperative Service Bureau, an organization he formed with Louis J. Willie, a former banker from Lincoln, Nebraska. The bureau's purpose was to propagandize for and organize credit unions—"people's banks"—throughout the United States.[15]

Campbell's successor as president, the Reverend William T. Mulloy (1935–37), was elected to restore the balance between religious and economic concerns. Mulloy, an energetic pastor from Grafton, North Dakota, profited more dramatically than anyone else from the "opening up" of the Conference's leadership in 1933. He suddenly appeared for the first time at the 1934 convention, where he gave a speech on "The Prospects for Agriculture in North Dakota." He also took part in the board of directors meetings at that convention, even though he was not an official member

14. NCRLC minutes binder (1933–35), NCRLC 8-1, 134–40; Ligutti to Byrnes, January 11, 1934 [actually 1935], Byrnes to Ligutti, January 14, 1935, and attached clipping, "Priests Study Farm Banks," Des Moines *Tribune*, n.d., in "General Correspondence—Byrnes, James," LGL-J; Byrnes to Bishop, January 17, 1935, in "Correspondence, Bishop, W. Howard," NCRLC 13-1; Witte, *Twenty-five Years*, 100–102.

15. NCRLC minutes binder (1935–38), NCRLC 8-2, 154, 156, 157-c; J. M. Campbell, "Structure of the Cooperative Credit Movement," in "Credit Unions," NCRLC 11-2.

of the board. Perhaps he took advantage of the provision, adopted at the 1933 convention, that diocesan directors were ex officio members of the board of directors, and attended the meetings as representative of the Fargo diocesan director, Vincent J. Ryan. At any rate, Mulloy then appeared at the even more exclusive executive committee meeting at the convention, dominated the meeting, and succeeded in getting himself appointed to the committee. He continued to take a full part in the executive committee meetings in the following year, becoming one of the biggest supporters of Conference autonomy vis-à-vis the Rural Life Bureau. At the 1935 convention, only Mulloy's second, he was elected president to succeed Campbell.[16]

As president, Mulloy was in the main line of NCRLC leadership by virtue of his balanced religious and economic program and his vigorous opposition to Schmiedeler. In 1944, he was made bishop of Covington, Kentucky, and he was reelected NCRLC president from 1946 to 1948. Mulloy was noted for his stentorian speaking voice and was described by Ligutti as a "doer." In later years, he became Ligutti's closest friend among the hierarchy. He died of a heart attack in June 1959.[17]

Mulloy's successor as NCRLC president was the most remarkable character in its history, the Reverend Luigi G. Ligutti.[18] Ligutti was born in 1895 in Romans, Italy. He migrated to America in 1912 and was ordained in 1917—at the time, the youngest priest in the United States. As a young priest, he exhibited a love for the classics, which his superiors allowed him to cultivate with graduate studies at the Catholic University of America, Columbia University, and the University of Chicago, and as a Latin teacher at the Des Moines Catholic high school. However, a shortage of rural pastors led to his appointment to a rural parish in 1920. After serving several years in Woodbine, Iowa, Ligutti was appointed in 1926 to Assumption Parish in Granger, fifteen miles northwest of Des Moines.

During the 1920s, Ligutti in many ways fit into the mold of the "isolated rural pastor." He devoted himself primarily to his parochial duties and seemed to have little use for John A. Ryan–style "social action." His most notable pastoral innovation was the introduction of tithing to his congregation. He spent his free time studying his beloved classics and coon hunt-

---

16. NCRLC minutes binder (1933–35), NCRLC 8-1, 117, 124, 127–29.

17. "Citation. Presentation of Distinguished Service Award," in "Biographical Sketches, Arcenaux—Wilmes," NCRLC 1-2; Yzermans, *The People I Love*, 54.

18. The major sources for this sketch are Yzermans, *The People I Love*, 1–58, and the Ligutti Papers.

ing in the woods with his three dogs. Yet Ligutti also wrote a constant stream of letters to the editors of the Des Moines *Register* and *Tribune* on topics ranging from the advantages of parochial education and the patriotism of American Catholics to Italian fascism. A man yearning for a larger field was striving to break through.

Ligutti's country pastorate exposed him to the various problems of Catholic rural life, and in 1924 he found an outlet for this growing interest when he joined the NCRLC. But until the 1930s, he was not a very active member. As the United States slid into the Depression, Ligutti's search for a meaning for the distress led him to read social and economic tracts ranging from the encyclicals of Leo XIII and Pius XI to radical socialist literature. Yet here also, his interest was not yet expressed in action.

The turning point in Ligutti's life came with the Granger homesteads project in 1933. Through efforts to provide a secure living for the unemployed coal miners of his parish, Ligutti emerged from an "isolated pastor" situation to a position in which, through "social action," he was actively involved in helping to solve the economic problems of the Depression. The success of the project gave him the notoriety to rise quickly to the top of the Catholic rural life movement. In 1934, Ligutti was appointed the Des Moines diocesan director of rural life and elected to the executive committee of the NCRLC. The next year, he was elected chairman of the diocesan directors section of the Conference, and in 1937 he was elected president.

Ligutti did not take an active part in the removal of Schmiedeler as executive secretary of the Conference in 1934, and in fact he preferred that the Conference have a strong connection with the bishops' conference. However, he defended the separation of the Conference and the Rural Life Bureau once it had been accomplished. As chairman of the diocesan directors' section and as president from 1937 to 1939, Ligutti, like other Conference officials, had occasion to suffer frustration in his dealings with the Benedictine, and he upheld the principle of Conference autonomy against Schmiedeler's intended encroachments. Ligutti became executive secretary in 1939; in that position he not only preserved the Conference's independence from the NCWC but centralized the NCRLC's operations in Des Moines and personalized its leadership in himself.

The last president of the decade, the Reverend Vincent J. Ryan, was not as controversial as some of his predecessors. He was born in 1884 on a family farm in Columbia County, Wisconsin. He volunteered to serve as a priest in a western diocese and was accepted for Fargo, North Dakota. For twenty-two years, he served as secretary to the bishop, chancellor of the diocese, and pastor of a church in Fargo.

In the 1930s, Ryan was appointed director of the Fargo diocesan charity bureau, which he built into a model rural charities program. With Mulloy and Muench, he was the third member of the "Fargo Trio," which hosted the very successful 1936 NCRLC convention and drafted the *Manifesto on Rural Life*. He served as president of the NCRLC from 1939 to 1941. In 1940, he was appointed bishop of Bismarck, North Dakota, and became the first episcopal president of the NCRLC. At the same time, he established a precedent: all but one of the future Conference presidents were bishops. Perhaps because he had already attained episcopal status, Ryan did not exhibit the ambition of some of the other NCRLC leaders. He did not engage in the infighting among the Conference leadership and was well liked and respected by his colleagues. A solid and unspectacular man, Ryan in his presidential messages still had an eloquent way of stating the NCRLC philosophy. Ryan died of heart failure in 1951.[19]

Organizational Expansion

Despite the internal turbulence and squabbling, the NCRLC in the 1930s expanded organizationally to reach a far greater number of people than it did in the 1920s. In fact, during the late 1930s and early 1940s, the NCRLC probably had a direct influence on more people than at any other time in its history, with the possible exception of the late 1950s. This popularity was manifested in the massive, enthusiastic annual conventions. The conventions around 1940 had the largest attendance of any in the Conference's history. After drawing only two to three hundred people to the conventions in the first half of the decade, the NCRLC attracted 4,800 to Fargo, North Dakota, in 1936; 7,000 to Richmond, Virginia, in 1937; 10,000 to Vincennes, Indiana, in 1938; 5,000 to Spokane, Washington, in 1939; 18,000 to St. Cloud, Minnesota, in 1940; more than 5,000 to Jefferson City, Missouri, in 1941; and 7,500 to Peoria, Illinois, in 1942. In addition, between 13,000 and 15,000 people attended rural Catholic action meetings in the diocese of Bismarck, North Dakota, in May and June 1941.[20]

---

19. "Bishop Ryan," *Catholic Rural Life Bulletin* 3 (May 20, 1940): 14; "Bismarck's New Bishop," ibid. (August 20, 1940): 22–23; Yzermans, *The People I Love*, 53.

20. Schmiedeler, "Catholic Rural Life Conference at Dubuque," 461; NCRLC minutes binder (1933–35), NCRLC 8-1, 99–106; "The Conference at Fargo," *Landward* 4 (Autumn 1936): 2; Witte, *Twenty-five Years*, 109, 125; "Away with Worry," *Catholic Rural Life Bulletin* 1 (November 20, 1938): 14; "Spokane in Retrospect," ibid. 2 (November 20, 1939): 14; "The St. Cloud Convention," ibid. 3 (November 20, 1940): 14; "The Convention," ibid. 4 (November 20, 1941): 118; "It Was Good for Us

Inside the NCRLC 141

Figure 6. Rural youth field Mass, St. Cloud, Minnesota, 1941.

The NCRLC made special efforts to attract these large numbers. Beginning with the Rochester, New York, convention in 1935, local meetings of the clergy in the convention area—sometimes attended by NCRLC officials such as the president or executive secretary—were held to build up enthusiasm and encourage a large attendance. The Conference made an effort to attract big-name speakers to the conventions: President Roosevelt was invited to the Rochester convention (he could not make it, and the Conference eventually settled for Assistant Secretary of Agriculture M. L. Wilson); and the popular Bishop Fulton Sheen spoke at the Richmond meeting. The "mass meeting" portion of the conventions at which the featured speakers appeared also included locally provided music on rural, religious, and patriotic themes. The president of the Conference usually delivered a

---

to Be There . . ." *Land and Home* 5 (December 1942): 1; "Rural Life in the Press," *Catholic Rural Life Bulletin* 4 (August 20, 1941): 87.

speech at these crowd-pleasing gatherings—just to ensure that the message of the NCRLC was not lost in all of the hubbub. The conventions of the late thirties made a special effort to be "practical" and of relevance to the average farmer and his family. To achieve this, subjects such as farming techniques and advice on taking advantage of government programs or on forming cooperatives and credit unions were included in the conventions. Special 4-H demonstrations and "Youth Days" proved successful in attracting thousands of rural young people to the gatherings. The 1940 convention in St. Cloud was especially geared to mass participation. It had only four formal speeches but a multitude of audience-participation panel discussions on topics such as religious instruction and missionary work, rural social welfare, rural education, the farm home, cooperatives, land acquisition, and farming methods.[21]

Another mass aspect of the NCRLC conventions in the thirties was the use of radio to spread the Conference message. Soon after the remarkable success of Detroit's "radio priest," Charles E. Coughlin, in the late twenties, the Conference began to promote its own message over the airwaves. The first NCRLC broadcasts were made at the 1931 Wichita, Kansas, convention by Bishop and Schmiedeler over local station KFH. In 1933, the Conference message was given national exposure when the same two officials broadcast from the Milwaukee convention over the National Broadcasting Company's "Farm Home Hour." Such coast-to-coast broadcasts over the Farm Home Hour were repeated at nearly every convention for the rest of the decade. The usual NCRLC broadcast included speeches by the president and executive secretary, a reading by a representative Catholic farmer, farm wife, or farm youngster, and rural-oriented musical selections—all moderated by an NBC announcer.[22]

Thus, the NCRLC, through gearing its conventions toward mass participation by dirt farmers and promotion by such means as radio, did much to increase its popularity in the 1930s. But other factors were also at work. That the Conference began to address the economic as well as the religious

21. Witte, *Twenty-five Years*, 106, chap. 6; NCRLC 8; "The St. Cloud Convention," *Catholic Rural Life Bulletin* 3 (August 20, 1940): 14.
22. NCRLC minutes binder (1923–32), NCRLC 8-1, 64; NCRLC minutes binder (1933–35), NCRLC 8-1, 86; *NCRLC Proceedings, 1933*, 5; *NCRLC Proceedings, 1934*, 10; NCRLC minutes binder (1935–38), NCRLC 8-2, 141, 174; "Richmond Radio Address," in "Ntn'l Convention, Richmond, Va., November 7–10, 1937," NCRLC 8-2; "The Conference Salutes the American Farmer," *Catholic Rural Life Bulletin* 1 (November 20, 1938): 11; "Catholic Rural Life Conference to Be Aired over NBC October 2," in "Ntn'l Convention, St. Cloud, Minn., September 29–30, October 1-2, 1940," NCRLC 8-3; "The National Farm and Hour [sic] Broadcast of the National Catholic Rural Life Conference, St. Cloud, Minn., Blue Network—11:30 to 12:00 a.m.," in "Convention Papers, 1940" (1st folder), NCRLC 8-3; Witte, *Twenty-five Years*, 106.

concerns of farmers doubtless attracted many new participants. There is also evidence that the Conference's views on agriculture as the nation's most basic industry, farming as a way of life, the family farm, the superiority of rural over urban life, and the need for religion in rural life closely paralleled the attitudes of grass-roots Catholic farmers.[23] Finally, the insecure social-psychological climate of the Depression years favored mass gatherings and made people more prone to become "joiners."[24] Many Americans followed demagogues such as Coughlin or Huey Long, and a large number of Catholic farmers apparently found their needs for security met by the religious and economic program of the NCRLC. The mass conventions gave rural Catholics a feeling of security in numbers from the dangers of low prices, foreclosure, and agnosticism from without, as well as an uplift from participation in a cause greater than themselves. In contrast, after World War II, attendance at NCRLC conventions dipped as Americans felt more secure in a revived economy, enjoyed higher status as the greatest power in the world, and could turn back to the individual pursuit of economic gain.

Another sign of the increased influence of the NCRLC in the late thirties was a rise in the number of members of the Conference and of subscribers to the periodicals. In 1929, there were 560 individual and 72 institutional memberships (seminaries and religious communities). By 1932, this had grown to approximately a thousand memberships.[25] In the mid-thirties, after Byrnes took over as executive secretary, the Conference began a series of membership drives intended both to raise money for the NCRLC and increase its influence.[26] Although membership fluctuated because of season of the year or type of membership, the numbers clearly increased considerably in the late thirties. Total memberships came to as many as 2,400 late in the decade, with 1,186 being the highest number recorded for "paid memberships." The first copy of *Catholic Rural Life Bulletin* was sent out to 4,940 individuals or institutions in May 1938.[27] Even these fairly modest increases

---

23. See Francis J. Gostomski, "Catholic Farmers," *Commonweal*, October 8, 1937, 545–46.

24. See, for example, Robert S. McElvaine, *The Great Depression: America, 1929–1941* (New York: Times Books, 1993), 237–38.

25. Margaret B. Hodges, Assistant to Editor, Social Work Yearbook, to Edgar Schmiedeler, November 14, 1932, and Schmiedeler to Hodges, November 26, 1932, in "General Correspondence—1932," NCWC 29.

26. NCRLC minutes binder (1935–38), NCRLC 8-2, 157, 171, 176, 179, 181, 189, 200, 205, 208–9, 224, 227; Byrnes to "Father" (circular letter), October 9, 1937, in "Ntn'l Convention, Richmond, Va., November 7–10, 1937," NCRLC 8-2; "Minutes, Ways and Means Committee, October 26, 1938," NCRLC 8-3.

27. "Exec. Committee Mtg., Dec. 27, 1939," NCRLC 8-3; "Board of Directors Mtg., Ntn'l Convention, St. Cloud, Minn., Sept. 29–30, Oct. 1–2, 1940," NCRLC 8-3; list headed "The following to receive first issue of C.R.L. BULLETIN:—" in "Membership—NCRLC," NCRLC 1-4.

in memberships did much to sink the roots of the NCRLC deep into the soil of rural Catholicism. The membership drives provided the Conference with a solid foundation of Catholic rural people imbued with its philosophy that it could draw on for strength in future years when mass conventions were no longer the rage.

The membership drives were also intended to bolster the NCRLC's chronically weak finances. In 1930, the Conference had to give up its publication *Catholic Rural Life* because of high costs. Schmiedeler, as the executive secretary in the early thirties, was cut off from the other administrators in the Conference and did nothing to aid its finances. On top of that, the Depression further reduced the NCRLC's income. Hitherto, the main source of the Conference's income had been the American Board of Catholic Missions (ABCM). The ABCM gave five thousand dollars in 1930 for religious vacation schools and the same amount in 1931 for the publication of the religious vacation school manual. But grants from the ABCM were slashed due to the Depression: to $3,333 in 1932; $2,500 in 1933; $2,250 in 1934 and 1935; $1,000 in 1936; $2,000 in 1937; and $3,000 in 1938 through 1940. No campaign for individual contributions, such as the Founders' Club of the 1920s, was initiated to take up the slack. Neither Schmiedeler nor Conference president Bishop was willing to solicit the membership for funds, probably because of the hard times. Eventually, Bishop himself generously paid for many expenses out of his own pocket. In 1933, he even began to publish *Landward* using his own funds. The first three issues were funded in this way, until the NCRLC accepted it as its official publication at the autumn 1933 convention. Meanwhile NCRLC support for outside programs languished. The ABCM grants—for several years in the early thirties the only source of income—had to be used to pay for the religious vacation school manuals and, eventually, the general operating expenses. This meant that direct support for religious vacation schools—the original use of the ABCM grants in the 1920s—was drastically reduced and finally, in 1935, dropped altogether.[28]

In the late thirties, as the Conference's conventions attracted ever-growing numbers and the NCRLC tried to expand its programs to keep pace, it felt the need for even more income. Byrnes, elected executive secretary in 1934, and Conference presidents Ligutti (1937–39) and Ryan (1939–41) tried numerous desperate expedients to raise more income, with the goal

---

28. Witte, *Twenty-five Years*, 99, 161; "Catholic Rural Life Conference Treasurer's Record," NCRLC 22; NCRLC minutes binder (1923–32), NCRLC 8-1, 55, 67, 80; NCRLC minutes binder (1933–35), NCRLC 8-1, 34, 89.

of eventually making the NCRLC financially self-sufficient. The Conference adopted a two dollar per year membership fee and a twenty-five cent convention registration fee. Attempts were made—some quite successful—to get attendees at the mass conventions to sign up for Conference memberships for at least one year. The Conference heavily promoted the sale of its periodicals and other publications. Donations to the Conference were solicited—and, indeed, income from this source began to pick up.[29]

None of these devices produced enough income. In 1938, the NCRLC budget committee decided that an annual income of ten thousand dollars was needed to meet the Conference's new demands; in fact, the budget never exceeded six thousand dollars per year during the thirties.[30] Nor did the Conference achieve financial self-sufficiency. By the end of the thirties, more than half of the Conference's expenses were still being paid for by the ABCM grants. In addition, Byrnes was beholden for his office to the good graces of his ordinary, Archbishop John G. Murray of St. Paul, who allowed the executive secretary to run the Conference from the same space he used as archdiocesan superintendent of schools. Murray also twice gave thousand-dollar donations to tide Byrnes over difficult times in the late thirties. In sum, then, the expenses of the Conference never came close to being paid for by its clientele—the rural pastors and people themselves. This condition of financial dependence—not unusual for organizations that promote the interests and viewpoints of a rather small minority—was a constant feature throughout the NCRLC's history.

Nevertheless, the NCRLC continued to mature organizationally, as illustrated by the development of a network of diocesan directors of rural life. The diocesan directors were the successors to O'Hara's state advisory committees, which flourished briefly and then died in the 1920s. In 1932, when the Conference was contemplating a colonization program, it felt the need to reinstitute a network of local operatives. Thus, at the 1932 convention, the NCRLC formally requested that all of the American bishops, especially those with rural dioceses, establish a diocesan rural life bureau with a diocesan director of rural life. The response from the approximately 120 American dioceses was encouraging, and by the autumn of 1933, 22 diocesan directors had been appointed. During the remainder of the de-

---

29. "Treasurer's Record"; NCRLC minutes binder (1935–38), NCRLC 8-2, 179, 181, 189, 200, 202, 205, 208–9, 226–27, 233, 234, 236–37; "Minutes, Ways and Means Committee, October 26, 1938," "Exec. Committee Meeting, December 27, 1939," and "Minutes, Finance Committee, January 23, 1940," all NCRLC 8-3; "Constitution and By-Laws of the National Catholic Rural Life Conference," in *NCRLC Proceedings, 1934*, 19; Witte, *Twenty-five Years*, 96–99, 121–23.

30. NCRLC minutes binder (1935–38), NCRLC 8-2, 234; "Treasurer's Record."

cade, the number of diocesan directors continued to grow: to thirty-one in 1934, forty-seven in 1935, and leveling off at around sixty-five in 1937.[31]

The diocesan directors performed all kinds of services in bringing the policy of the NCRLC to the local people. A prospectus was drawn up by Bishop:

> A few of the services such bureaus can perform are establishing and supervising religious vacation schools and correspondence courses in rural parishes that have no schools, fostering the spread of Confraternities of Christian Doctrine to boost religious education in rural parishes, making known the Church's attitude on all questions that affect the farmer and his life and work, aiding the spread of the co-operative movement among farmers in such a way that Christian ideals of justice and charity are upheld, co-operating in the back-to-the-land movement by helping Catholics to secure good, cheap land near their churches and schools or when possible, by developing Catholic colonies of farmers, encouraging and helping organize parish 4-H clubs and parish Agriculture and Home Arts Exhibits through co-operation with state extension departments, fostering the establishment of rural parish credit unions, soliciting and receiving funds from more fortunate parishes for distribution among the poor parishes of the country, conducting diocesan rural conferences and aiding farmers to avail themselves of the credit facilities offered by the Government to save their farms from foreclosure or to repossess foreclosed farms.[32]

By 1939, additional programs for diocesan rural life bureaus were being suggested: work with diocesan superintendents of schools to get the rural schools to develop a rural rather than an urban point of view; secure for rural Catholics the advantages of the Social Security Act; promote adult education through study clubs; encourage the beautification of the farm home and premises; assist governmental efforts to provide electrification to the countryside; promote rural parish recreational, dramatic, and social programs; provide retreats to rural laypeople; establish rural parish maternity guilds that would, among other things, combat birth control; develop diocesan rural libraries; and initiate diocesan rural research projects.[33]

The degree to which the individual diocese or diocesan director fulfilled this program varied considerably. Some diocesan directors did noth-

---

31. NCRLC minutes binder (1923–32), NCRLC 8-1, 83; NCRLC minutes binder (1935–38), NCRLC 8-2, 204, 207; Witte, *Twenty-five Years,* 144–46; [W. Howard Bishop], "Milwaukee 1924 and 1933," *Landward* 1 (Autumn 1933): 4; "News from the Field," *Rural Bureau Notes* 1 (March 1934): 1; "Rural Catholic Action Appointees," ibid. 2 (September 1935): 1; "Diocesan Directors Meeting, 1939," NCRLC 8-3.

32. [Bishop], "Milwaukee 1924 and 1933," 4.

33. "Diocesan Directors Meeting, 1939," NCRLC 8-3. See also Witte, *Twenty-five Years,* chap. 8.

ing more than receive the title from their bishop. Others, such as the directors of the St. Louis Rural Life Conference, developed a most varied and effective program. The St. Louis program included financial aid to rural schools and churches, transportation of students, vacation schools and correspondence courses, farm property listings for prospective Catholic settlers, essay contests, publication of Mass schedules, a girls' employment bureau, a young men's boarding home, a cemetery service, quarterly deanery meetings, and annual rural life conference meetings.[34]

The diocesan directors were the vital link in the Conference's attempt to provide an organization of American rural Catholics. They mediated between the Conference's central organization (executive secretary, board of directors, executive committee, national conventions, publications) and the individual parishes. The Conference recommended that diocesan directors gather committees of advisers that would meet several times a year to direct the rural activities of the diocese. The diocesan director and his committee might also reach out to the rest of the clergy and laity of the diocese through diocesan rural life conferences—annual meetings patterned on the national NCRLC conventions. Some diocesan rural life bureaus further amplified their organization by grouping several parishes into rural deaneries, with the deans serving as the representatives at the diocesan rural life bureaus.[35]

The diocesan directors were linked to the national Conference by meetings held at the annual conventions to discuss their experiences and form diocesan and national programs for rural action to carry out when they went back to their dioceses. By the mid-thirties, diocesan directors' meetings were sometimes held apart from the conventions, and regional diocesan directors meetings were held. Beginning in 1933, it was NCRLC policy that the diocesan directors were well represented on the Conference board of directors. Usually at least half of the board of directors were diocesan directors. *Rural Bureau Notes* (1933–36) was published primarily to provide information of use to the diocesan directors. It was edited by Schmiedeler of the Rural Life Bureau and thus provided a link between the diocesan directors and the NCWC.[36]

---

34. "St. Louis Points the Way," *Rural Bureau Notes* 2 (March 1935): 1–4; "A Demonstration Project," ibid. 3 (May 1936): 1–3; R. B. Schuler, "City and Country Cooperate in the Archdiocese of St. Louis," in "Addresses, Reverend R. B. Schuler," NCRLC 10-2; Schmiedeler, *A Better Rural Life*, 176–92.

35. "Recommendations for Plan of Organization and for Rural Bureau Activities," *Rural Bureau Notes* 1 (November 1933): 2–3; "Springfield, Illinois, Diocese Organizes," ibid. (February 1934): 1–2.

36. "Leaders Meet at Kansas Monastery," *Landward* 5 (Spring 1937): 6, 11; "First Institute for

Another index of the NCRLC's coming of age in the late 1930s was its development of a substantial body of propaganda. The Conference's periodical of the twenties, *Catholic Rural Life,* ceased publication in 1930. It was replaced by *Landward* (1933–37) and *Catholic Rural Life Bulletin* (1938–41). The latter, under the editorship of Byrnes, was an especially attractive and intellectually respectable vehicle of Catholic rural thought. Adding to the Conference's philosophical literature were the *Proceedings* of the 1933 and 1934 conventions and the *Catholic Rural Life Objectives* of 1935, 1936, 1937, and 1944, which also consisted of convention papers. From the Rural Life Bureau headquarters at the NCWC, Schmiedeler published the *Rural Bureau Notes* and turned out a stream of high-quality pamphlets and articles, as well as a rural life column for Catholic newspapers. Several books by Catholic ruralists also appeared in the late thirties—Schmiedeler's *A Better Rural Life* (1938), Ligutti and Rawe's *Rural Roads to Security* (1940), and the Reverend Urban Baer's *Farmers of Tomorrow* (1939), as well as the NCRLC *Manifesto on Rural Life* (1939).

The *Manifesto* was a particularly significant accomplishment: Coming at the height of the Conference's popularity, it was the lengthiest and most comprehensive statement of official NCRLC policy to date. It was also compiled by a broad spectrum of the NCRLC leadership: twenty-one Catholic agrarians worked on the first draft, while the final draft was written by the eminent "Fargo Trio" of Muench, Mulloy, and Ryan, with the scholarly "annotations" being compiled mainly by Schmiedeler. The final document, which covered every aspect of NCRLC policy from economic philosophy to means of rural religious enlightenment, became the primary source of American Catholic rural thought for years to come.[37]

The Conference used a number of other methods to spread its gospel. The NCRLC formed publicity committees to have articles on the Conference published in the Catholic and secular press and to get publicity over the radio. The NCRLC rejoiced in the appearance in 1934 of *The Catholic Farmer,* which was published as a biweekly supplement to the Milwaukee

---

Diocesan Directors," *Rural Bureau Notes* 4 (February 1936): 1–3; *NCRLC Proceedings, 1934,* 17; NCRLC minutes binder (1933–35), NCRLC 8-1, 90; NCRLC minutes binder (1935–38), NCRLC 8-2, 167, 169–70, 177, 179; "Constitution and By-Laws of the National Catholic Rural Life Conference," in "St. Cloud Convention, September 29, 30, October 1–2, 1940," NCRLC 8-3; "First Issue" and "Rural Life Bureaus and Directors," *Rural Bureau Notes* 1 (November 1933): 1.

37. Witte, *Twenty-five Years,* 177–80; "Manifesto on Rural Life, Author's Portfolio," "Notes on Manifesto on Rural Life," and "Background Questions on Rural Life from the Manifesto on Rural Life," all in NCRLC 5-1; "NCRLC History and Historical Reference," LGL-H; and "General Correspondence—Muench, Rev. Aloisius," LGL-J.

Catholic Herald and was the first newspaper for English-speaking Catholic farmers. In 1938, the Conference began a library loan service for rural priests. The NCRLC promoted study clubs for indoctrinating the laity in Catholic rural philosophy. Conference officials volunteered to join a speakers bureau to travel and give talks on the NCRLC's policy. They also offered courses or even whole "institutes" on Catholic rural life at several Catholic colleges.[38]

The logical extension of these occasional courses and institutes would be a department or whole college of Catholic rural studies, and the Conference made repeated calls for just such an institution throughout the 1930s. The model for such a rural college was the extension program of St. Francis Xavier University at Antigonish, Nova Scotia. Its program of lectures and study groups stimulated a cooperative economy among the farmers, miners, and fishermen of the maritime province. The leader of the program, the Reverend M. M. Coady, published several books and articles that were influential in the Conference and spoke at several conventions. Catholic agrarians hoped that an "American Antigonish" would be established, perhaps at St. Benedict's College in Atchison, Kansas, or St. John's University in Collegeville, Minnesota. Unfortunately, interest was never sufficient to fulfill that dream.[39]

In spite of the multitude of means used to spread its message, the Catholic rural life movement had very little impact on the larger Church's policies in the Depression years. For example, the Conference had hardly any effect upon the programs of the NCWC's Social Action Department. Schmiedeler, who had bad relations with both the NCRLC and the Social Action Department, never fulfilled his intended role of acting as a liaison between the two organizations, and the department's director John A. Ryan was never persuaded to alter its emphasis on urban industrial problems.[40]

The NCRLC also had little influence on policy statements by American Catholic groups during the Depression years. The Conference never joined with the Social Action Department or any other Catholic organiza-

---

38. NCRLC minutes binder (1923–32), NCRLC 8-1, 66, 81a–c; untitled editorial, *Landward* 2 (Summer 1934): 4; "Course on Rural Life at University," ibid. 1 (Spring 1933): 2; "Books for the Rural Priest," *Catholic Rural Life Bulletin* 1 (May 20, 1938): 8; Miriam Marks, "Study Clubs for Adults, High School and College Students," *NCRLC Proceedings, 1934*, 159–62; NCRLC minutes binder (1933–35), NCRLC 8-1, 127–28, 140, 195; NCRLC minutes binder (1935–38), NCRLC 8-2, 199–200, 204, 209; Witte, *Twenty-five Years*, 198–203, 207–9; Marlett, *Saving the Heartland*, 33–34.

39. "Canada's Rural Movement," *Landward* 2 (Summer 1934): 2, 7–8; Nora Bateson, "The Burning Bush in Nova Scotia," ibid. 4 (Autumn 1936): 3, 7, 10; "An American Antigonish?" *Rural Bureau Notes* 3 (February 1936): 3–4.

40. See Ryan, *Social Doctrine in Action*, and Broderick, *Right Reverend New Dealer*.

tions in statements. *Organized Social Justice,* a 1936 statement authored by 131 Catholic leaders, was signed by several of the Catholic agrarians only as individuals. Although rural life had a part in several of the bishops' statements of the Depression years, it was always in a subsidiary role. In particular, the urgent reasoning of the Catholic rural population problem and the back-to-the-land movement, which asserted the greater importance of rural over urban life, was always dropped (with the single exception of back-to-the-land in the American hierarchy's 1933 *Statement on the Present Crisis*) in national statements on Catholic action. The rural area was treated as just another area in need of "social justice," as part of a program that could easily be reconciled with the needs of the urban population.[41]

The NCRLC also had a limited impact on the United States as a whole. The high point was, again, the late 1930s conventions. The Conference believed that the widespread publicity given the St. Cloud convention (1940) of "an organization sponsoring a little known and less understood movement whose fundamental principles are in conflict with the generally accepted patterns of contemporary life" was "evidence that the movement in question is at least beginning to make an impression upon the consciousness, if not the thought, of the Nation." The convention was covered not only by many Catholic publications, but also by such secular publications as the *New York Times, Free America,* and cooperative journals. Representatives were also present from the United States Department of Agriculture, Canadian National Railways, the colonization departments of several American railways, several state agricultural colleges, and the Netherlands diplomatic legation in the United States. At the same time, the Conference was receiving increased publicity from the Catholic urban press and recognition of its ideas in academic textbooks. Indeed, many Catholic agrarians felt as did one who wrote to Ligutti that the NCRLC had "won recognition on the part of Bishops and priests and people" and had therefore passed beyond the "promotion stage," and should now emphasize "action" instead of promotion. Unfortunately, this period did not mark the "beginning" of Catholic rural life influence but was an early high point of it.[42]

The 1930s were marked by the Conference's dramatic entrance into

41. See, for example, O'Brien, *American Catholics and Social Reform.*
42. "The Conference Comes of Age," *Catholic Rural Life Bulletin* 3 (November 20, 1940): 13; F[rancis] J. G[illigan], review of *Social Problems* by Raymond Murray and Frank Flynn, ibid. 1 (November 20, 1938): 30; S.A.B., review of *Fundamental Sociology* by Eva J. Ross, ibid. 2 (November 20, 1939): 30; Catholic urban press clippings in NCRLC 9-1; George Nell to Ligutti, February 23, 1938, and March 10, 1938, in "General Correspondence—'N,'" LGL-E.

Inside the NCRLC

economic affairs in response to the crisis of the Depression and the emotional roller coaster of inflated hopes for a return to an agrarian order of society early in the 1930s, followed by the crushing disappointment of these hopes by 1940. The decade also witnessed disruptive personal squabbles within the Conference, which nevertheless did not prevent organizational growth. In the next period of the NCRLC's history, in the 1940s and 1950s, the Conference under the leadership of Ligutti finally attained stability of leadership and expanded its activities into yet another field.

Chapter 7 Ligutti Takes the Helm

The New Executive Secretary

In 1940, Monsignor Luigi G. Ligutti became executive secretary of the NCRLC. Remarkably, given the pervasive conflicts and multiplicity of leadership within the movement in the 1930s, Ligutti soon was able to centralize the movement under his own direction.

He had already begun to make contributions to the process in the years before he became executive secretary. First, as a member of the Conference's executive committee, he acquiesced in the election of James Byrnes as executive secretary in 1934—making the Conference independent of Edgar Schmiedeler and the NCWC. Then, as chairman of the diocesan directors section and president of the Conference, he fought along with other NCRLC officials to preserve its independence from Schmiedeler.

As executive secretary, Ligutti took even more definite (though perhaps uncalculated) steps that brought the movement further under his control. By becoming the NCRLC's first full-time executive secretary, he was able to devote all of his energies to the cause. In November 1940, he secured permission to move the Conference headquarters from St. Paul to his own diocese of Des Moines. Two years later, he purchased the large mansion at 3801 Grand Avenue in Des Moines for Conference headquarters. This house—which remained NCRLC headquarters until 1979—provided ample room for the expanded staff Ligutti envisioned as necessary to carry out his projects. In the same year, Ligutti brought the Conference's official periodical under his control by moving its editorial offices from St. Paul to his new building in Des Moines and softening its tone to accord more with his own "down-home" philosophy.[1]

In the course of his strong leadership of the NCRLC in the 1940s, Ligutti soon overshadowed all other possible rival centers of power. The

---

1. Witte, *Twenty-five Years*, 133, 166; Yzermans, *The People I Love*, 57–58.

Conference presidents, so influential during the 1930s, were soon reduced to mere figureheads. The defeated Schmiedeler soon lost interest in his Rural Life Bureau—to the point that by the end of the decade it ceased to function. Ligutti, by devoting himself entirely to the cause—like no other person in the history of the NCRLC—eventually became not only the most important spokesman for Catholic rural life but also the personal symbol of the Catholic rural life movement. No other person in the Conference's history came close to being the personal embodiment of the movement that Ligutti was. When Ligutti's biographer Monsignor Vincent Yzermans stated hyperbolically, "There would be no NCRLC without Luigi Ligutti and the considerable gifts he brought to the office," he was merely expressing a widely shared conviction among those who had witnessed his leadership.[2]

To further his personal achievement, after World War II, Ligutti brought the NCRLC into international rural life. Within a very few years, Ligutti and the NCRLC attained the leadership of all Catholic rural life in the world. This—the acme of his achievement—he continued to further after his retirement as NCRLC executive director in 1959, when he was appointed the Conference's director of international affairs. In his last active years—until the early 1970s—Ligutti was one of the foremost international Churchmen: the acquaintance of world leaders, confidant of popes, a participant in Vatican II, and a Vatican troubleshooter (as when in 1969–71 he was appointed to clear up the chaotic finances of the Church in Malta).

As Ligutti became the unquestioned leader of the Catholic rural life movement, his personal character became very important in determining the direction that the movement took and its general tone. One of Ligutti's most important contributions to the NCRLC was his remarkable energy. In the words of one of his biographers, "Ligutti was a 'driver.' Work for him was as important as the air he breathed. He rose early—about four-thirty—for prayers, meditation, and Mass. By seven o'clock he was prepared for the work of the day. He also retired early; by ten o'clock the day was done."[3]

In 1955, his assistant Michael P. Dineen wrote:

The Monsignor has a unique capacity for minute detail work as well as for the broad expansive activities.

. . . It is not unusual for him to spend an entire day writing as many as a

---

2. Yzermans, *The People I Love*, 51.
3. Ibid., x.

Figure 7. Charismatic Monsignor Luigi G. Ligutti speaking at Jefferson City convention, 1941.

hundred letters in his own hand, and yet there is time for the work outside—exercise, he calls it—snow removal at 4:00 a.m. or 3:00 p.m. as the need arises—and, of course, care of the garden and the lawn is a very special project.[4]

In fact, it soon became apparent to those around him—if not to Ligutti himself—that the monsignor tended to drive himself too hard. As early as October, 1941, NCRLC president Vincent Ryan warned Ligutti that he thought "the Executive Secretary was working entirely too hard and that a word of warning should be issued both on the health side and on the enthusiasm with which he throws himself into his work."[5] The warnings were repeated in future years; despite them, Ligutti continued to work with his great enthusiasm for the cause of the Catholic rural life movement. He suffered no serious collapse until 1958, when he was hospitalized for several weeks following a gall bladder operation.

Ligutti's energy could not be confined within the headquarters building in Des Moines. Practically from the beginning of his term as executive secretary, he traveled often, at first mainly within the United States—mostly by train—in a personal effort to spread the rural life philosophy. In the 1940s, he averaged only about fifty days a year at the national office. During 1948, a typical year, Ligutti delivered over two hundred lectures in the United States, Canada, and other parts of the world. Gradually, he be-

---

4. "From the National Headquarters," *Feet in the Furrow* 3 (January 1955): 2.
5. "Minutes, Board of Directors Mtg., Oct. 4, 1941," NCRLC 8-2.

Ligutti Takes the Helm

gan to devote more and more of his time to foreign travel, a development associated with the Conference's expansion into international rural life.[6]

On his many travels promoting the Conference, Ligutti dispensed his second unique contribution—his homespun, often humorous, philosophy. The monsignor had a talent for encapsulating Catholic agrarian beliefs into short, pithy, down-home sayings, which became known as "Ligutti-isms." Some of them were serious, such as the brief slogan in which he stated the goals of the NCRLC: "Christ to the Country—the Country to Christ." Others were frankly humorous, as when he advised an audience of farmers in Fargo, *"Ora et labora*—and use a lot of fertilizer!" Ligutti led an audience of three hundred nuns at a rural life summer school in reciting the following poem after him:

> A garden and a cow
> A smokehouse and a sow
> Twenty-four hens and a rooster
> And you'll have more than you usta'.

He could even put political philosophy into a simple, homely sentence. Conversing with Pope Pius XII on the international situation, Ligutti said, "When a poor family becomes the owner of a cow, then communism goes out the back door."[7]

Most of all, the Ligutti-isms expressed the monsignor's love and care for the simple family farmers around the world, whom he called the "little people." Ligutti said that "It takes many little people, in a lot of little places, doing a lot of little things, to accomplish great things in the world." While traveling in the Spanish countryside in 1951, Ligutti reflected on a barefoot farmhand carrying a sick child, "Most people don't want too much—some work, a little bread, a prayer and a smile. Why should not society arrange to satisfy such humble requests?"[8]

Growth in Conference Activities

During Ligutti's administration, the size and activities of the NCRLC central office grew by leaps and bounds. As the Conference expanded its activities, Ligutti required more and more staff to keep up. In 1941, he received

---

6. Witte, *Twenty-five Years*, 133; travel itineraries in various issues of *Catholic Rural Life Bulletin* and *Land and Home* in the 1940s; Yzermans, *The People I Love*, 63.

7. Yzermans, *The People I Love*, 58, 59; Luigi G. Ligutti, "Pope of Peace," *Catholic Rural Life* 7 (October 1958): 14.

8. Sandra LaBlanc, "A Man Ahead of His Time," *Catholic Rural Life* 34 (February 1984): 24; Yzermans, *The People I Love*, 106.

the help of an office manager and associate editor of the Conference periodical. As the monsignor began to devote much of his time to traveling, he felt the need of an assistant to take care of the office and carry on research on rural problems. Beginning in 1944, he acquired the services of a part-time—and the next year a full-time—assistant for this work. The year after that, this assistant also assumed responsibility for a year-round program of publicity. And so it went. On resigning the executive directorship in 1959, Ligutti remarked that "over the years [the NCRLC] grew up almost like topsy and it went through some of the wildest girations [sic]." By 1944, the NCRLC national office employed an executive secretary, assistant to the executive secretary, a combined part-time director of the Apostolate Library Service and the Rural Life Study Clubs, two stenographers, a bookkeeper, a mail clerk, and occasional temporary help. And it expanded even more in the 1950s. By the end of that decade, the NCRLC had eighteen full-time employees, including the executive director, executive secretary, Washington representative, four field representatives, and about ten secretaries and other office workers. Among their duties was the annual distribution of over three hundred thousand "devotional, liturgical, resource, study club, and policy statements books and booklets."[9]

After much urging by Ligutti, the board of directors finally agreed to find him a full-time priest-assistant, to be called the executive secretary (Ligutti's new title became executive director). In 1952, after a long search, the Reverend Daniel F. Dunn of the Boston archdiocese was acquired for the job. He ran the central office and edited the Conference periodical while Ligutti was off traveling on his national and international work. However, Dunn apparently did not suit the Conference's purposes, and he returned to Boston in April 1954.[10]

In November 1954 a replacement was found in the Reverend Michael P. Dineen of the Milwaukee archdiocese. The new executive secretary was only thirty years old and had held the Conference position of fourth vice president in charge of rural youth. Dineen made an energetic execu-

9. Witte, *Twenty-five Years*, 136–37; "Report of the Executive Director of the NCRLC," in "Board of Directors, Natn'l Convention, Aspen, Colo., Sept. 15–18, 1959," NCRLC 8-17; "To the Executive Committee and Advisory Board of the National Catholic Rural Life Conference, May 16, 1944," in "Board of Directors, Members, Executive Committee Mtg., Des Moines, Ia., May 16, 1944," NCRLC 8-4, 2; "Report of the Executive Secretary," in "Executive Committee Meeting, Fort Wayne, Indiana, June 17–18, 1958," NCRLC 8-16, 4; *1957: Serving Rural America 35 Years, National Catholic Rural Life Conference* (Des Moines, Iowa: NCRLC, 1957), in "General Publications, 1957," NCRLC 5-4, 7, 21.

10. Minutes for the late 1940s and early 1950s, NCRLC 8; "NCRLC Executive Officers," *Catholic Rural Life* 22 (November 1973): 10; *Feet in the Furrow* 1 (March 1952): 1, 4; ibid. 3 (April 1954): 10; ibid. (June 1954): 1.

tive secretary, full of bold, creative ideas that contributed to the NCRLC's great expansion—but also to its financial crisis—of the late 1950s.[11]

Ligutti's administration was notable for the inauguration of NCRLC representation in the nation's capital. In the early 1940s, Ligutti himself and other Catholic officials, such as Monsignor John O'Grady of the National Conference of Catholic Charities, occasionally made the trip to Washington to testify before congressional committees on issues such as the extension of the Farm Security Administration. In the late 1940s and early 1950s, the Reverend William J. Gibbons, S.J., and the Reverend Andrew Lawrence represented the NCRLC in Washington on a part-time basis. In September 1955 the NCRLC acquired its first full-time Washington representative when the Reverend James L. Vizzard, S.J., was transferred from California for the job. Vizzard became very active, frequently giving testimony before Congress and establishing connections with numerous government agencies and national Catholic and secular organizations concerned with agriculture. He wrote a regular column, "Washington Farm Front," for the Conference periodical, as well as many articles on rural life topics for other publications. Vizzard stayed on as Washington representative until ill health forced him to resign and return to California in April 1968.[12]

During the forties and fifties, the Conference under Ligutti made many efforts, intermittently successful, to extend its influence through propaganda, increased membership, and services. One way this was attempted was by trying to make more effective use of the Conference's periodicals.

The first step was taken in 1942, when Ligutti took over the editorship of the *Catholic Rural Life Bulletin,* changed its name to *Land and Home,* and moved its editorial offices to Des Moines. He remolded James Byrnes's "intellectual" periodical appealing mainly to the leaders of the movement to a more "popular" magazine aimed more at the rank-and-file dirt farmers. The number of articles on social justice and economic topics decreased, replaced by many fictional or "true-life" stories as well as nonfiction articles extolling the values of rural family life.

The next stage was the publication of a "Catholic farm journal" intended specifically for the average Catholic farmer, a step that had been contemplated as early as 1936. NCRLC officials believed that a new magazine was essential if the Conference were to realize its ambition of becoming a strong grass-roots organization based on the majority of Catholic

---

11. "NCRLC Executive Officers," 10; "From the National Headquarters," *Feet in the Furrow* 3 (December 1954): 2.
12. "NCRLC Washington Office," *Catholic Rural Life* 22 (November 1973): 11.

farmers. Accordingly, the *Christian Farmer News Letter* (later titled simply the *Christian Farmer*) debuted in October 1947.[13]

In a column in the first issue, Ligutti stated that the *Christian Farmer News Letter* was published for the five hundred thousand Catholic farm families who, until then, had "no Catholic magazine or paper especially written for them." The *Christian Farmer,* unlike earlier NCRLC publications, was intended primarily for those who were not NCRLC members—to bring the Conference's message to a group of readers who had not been exposed to it before. Ligutti vowed that the magazine would be written in a simple style "so the ordinary farmer won't need a dictionary to look up every other word." He hoped that it would become "a huge farmers' forum, wherein the expressions from the people on the soil will disclose truths greater than mere opinions formulated by theorists."[14]

The *Christian Farmer* included the same mix of informational and inspirational articles as *Land and Home,* and in addition contained much more practical information for farmers, such as crop forecasts and Susan Frawley Eisele's "My Fair Lady" column for farm women. The few long articles were on such topics as individual families' success in homesteading, co-operation, living self-sufficiently, and combining religion and rural life. In March 1948, having to choose because of printing costs between *Land and Home* and the *Christian Farmer,* the NCRLC discontinued the former and made the latter the Conference's official publication.[15]

The *Christian Farmer* at first seemed to show promise in reaching the average Catholic rural dweller. Early in 1948, the publication garnered seven thousand individual subscriptions, plus six thousand subscriptions that were distributed to parishes in bundles. In October 1948 total circulation reached fifteen thousand, the high-water mark. By January 1950 circulation dropped to 11,487, and by October of that year to 9,589, of which only 2,049 individual and 2,195 bundle subscriptions were paid. The paper never covered its costs. It was hoped that increased advertising would make the *Christian Farmer* self-sustaining, but the circulation was not enough to attract it. Rather than continue a losing proposition, the Conference discontinued the *Christian Farmer* in February 1951.[16]

13. "A Catholic Farm Journal," *Central-Blatt and Social Justice* 31 (February 1939): 353; NCRLC board of directors and executive committee minutes from 1940 to 1947, NCRLC 8-3, 8-4, and 8-5; Witte, *Twenty-five Years,* 165.
14. L. G. Ligutti, "The Monsignor Says;" anon., "Attention! N.C.R.L.C. Members;" and anon., "We Hope" (editorial), all in *Christian Farmer News Letter* 1 (October 1947): 1, 1, and 4.
15. "Announcement . . ." *Christian Farmer* 1 (March 1948): 1.
16. Meetings files for 1947–51, NCRLC 8; "We Hope," *Christian Farmer* 1 (January 1948): 2; "NCRLC Publications," *Catholic Rural Life* 22 (November 1973): 12.

Figure 8. Archbishop Edwin V. O'Hara (seated) with NCRLC officers and staff, about 1950 (Monsignor Luigi G. Ligutti behind O'Hara).

The demise of the *Christian Farmer* was a great disappointment to the NCRLC. Its publication came at a time when the Conference's influence was high and marked its most ambitious attempt to reach the rural grass roots with a publication. Such an attempt to publish a truly popular publication was never made again, and thereafter, with brief exceptions such as the late fifties, the Conference generally communicated with a steadily decreasing number of people.

Following the discontinuance of the *Christian Farmer*, the NCRLC used various other means to keep in touch with the rural laity. From 1950 to 1967, it published the Rural Pastor News Service, a weekly news release for insertion in small town newspapers and church bulletins. In 1951, the Conference began the *Catholic Rural Life Page*, a monthly mailing to diocesan newspapers. The typical *Rural Life Page* included editorial comments, a feature story, home economic suggestions, a liturgical column, a book review, and a question box. In the 1960s and 1970s, the materials became more issue-oriented. The majority of diocesan papers subscribed to the page, which continued as one of the means for spreading the NCRLC's message until 1988.[17]

For a time after the demise of the *Christian Farmer,* the NCRLC official publications suffered a decline in quality as the Conference strove to catch up financially. From 1952 to 1955, the monthly *Feet in the Furrow* was a mere four mimeographed pages. It was a folksy, informal publication edited by the Conference's executive secretary, Father Dunn. The quality of NCRLC publications improved markedly when Father Dineen took over as Conference executive secretary in November 1954. Dineen expanded *Feet in the Furrow* and successors *Rural Life Conference—Feet in the Furrow* and *Rural Life Conference* to eight and then sixteen glossy pages and included more substantial information on Conference domestic and foreign activities. By October 1958, the publication grew to thirty-two pages and adopted the name *Catholic Rural Life,* which, with a short break, has remained the title ever since. A new "field editor" was hired to collect stories and make *Catholic Rural Life* "a first class magazine." The publication also tried to greatly boost its advertising—Dineen claimed that the first issue of *Catholic Rural Life* contained 120,000 percent more advertisements than its predecessor. Despite the added advertising revenue, finances continued to be a problem. Unfortunately, the expense involved in the improved quality of the Conference publications played a role in the financial crisis that marked the end of Dineen's administration.[18]

The 1940s and 1950s saw the reinvigoration of the NCRLC's local leaders—the diocesan directors. In the late 1930s and early 1940s, these men as a group had lapsed into inactivity. Although some of them continued to be active in their local communities, no diocesan directors' meetings were held at the 1939, 1940, and 1941 conventions. However, at the 1942 convention at Peoria, NCRLC president Bishop Aloisius Muench met with the diocesan directors, appointed the Reverend Patrick Quinlan their chairman, and instructed him to prepare a monthly newsletter. At Milwaukee the next year, the diocesan directors decided to plan their own meetings and elect their own officers. The 1944 constitution of the NCRLC formal-

---

17. "NCRLC Publications," 12; file of Rural Pastor News Service, NCRLC 6-17 and 6-18; file of Catholic Rural Life Page, NCRLC 6-13 to 6-17; "Editorial Committee Meeting: January 23, 1988, Des Moines, Iowa," in "Editorial Committee Meeting 2/24/89," La Blanc Subject File, Box 4, NCRLC.

18. "NCRLC Publications," 12; "Bigger and Better," *Catholic Rural Life* 7 (October 1958): 2; files of publications, NCRLC 6-6 to 6-8.

ized these arrangements. The diocesan directors thus erected a network of mutual support that continued through the turn of the century. The number of diocesan directors also grew: from about 65 around 1940 to 83 in 1948, 99 in 1951, and 110 in 1961.[19]

The diocesan directors continued to expand the range of activities they performed in their local communities. In 1944, when the diocesan directors first submitted reports to the board of directors, some of their undertakings were these: street preaching by diocesan priests and Glenmary Missioners; vacation schools; formation of parish 4-H clubs; organization of the priests of the diocese under the diocesan director (sometimes into deaneries); study clubs for laypeople; "mileage funds" for priests with widespread missions; diocesan rural life "schools," "days," "institutes," and "conferences"; trips to study the Granger subsistence homesteads project; rural columns in diocesan newspapers; lectures by priests in coordination with federal agencies such as the Farm Security Administration and Rural Electrification Administration; and land location services—including some for returning soldiers. Diocesan directors also undertook the promotion of handicrafts, formation of credit unions, rural devotions and liturgical observances, correspondence courses, trailer chapels in missionary areas, promotion of cooperatives, Masses for migrant workers, radio programs, aid to the organization of locals of the Farmers' Union, essay contests, distribution of information on government services for farmers, aid for building churches and schools, and mobile medical clinics.[20]

During the Ligutti era, the NCRLC inaugurated a new program of rural life "institutes" to train and educate its more numerous leaders—not only the diocesan directors but also the other rural priests, sisters, seminarians, and laypeople on whom it was counting to help spread the rural life gospel. The first rural life institute was a two-week summer school attended by fifty-one priests, sisters, and laymen at St. John's University, Collegeville, Minnesota, in July 1939. Conference officials and local faculty members instructed the students in the Catholic perspective on rural life and in practical ideas to put into action in their rural communities. All future institutes had the same two theoretical and practical facets. The St. John's program was such a success that it was repeated the next summer. In 1941, a second school was held at the College of St. Benedict, Atchison, Kansas, and the next year two more were added at St. Louis University and St. Stanislaus

19. Witte, *Twenty-five Years*, 150–52, 157; "Conference Affairs," *Land and Home* 6 (December 1943): 114; NCRLC 8 for 1939–1961.
20. Witte, *Twenty-five Years*, 152–57.

College, Bay St. Louis, Mississippi. Schools for sisters were begun in 1943. The following year, the program was greatly expanded: forty-seven schools or institutes ranging from one to five days each were held in twenty-five dioceses. Total attendance was reckoned at twenty-five thousand. In 1945, fifty-five "institutes" and twenty-seven "schools" were held, with an attendance of seventeen hundred priests, 9,600 sisters, 9,900 lay people, and 775 seminarians in thirty-five dioceses and twenty states. From then on, however, the number of such schools decreased. In 1946, sixty-two schools of various kinds were held, and thirty-six in the next year. By the 1950s, the number of institutes leveled off to between four and ten annually. This rate continued into the early 1960s. As the Catholic rural population began to slowly decline, so did the need for trained leadership.[21]

The NCRLC also tried to foster rural leadership by cooperating with the Grail, an international organization of Catholic laywomen devoted to increasing the role of women in spreading Christian renewal. Grail women came to the United States from Holland in 1939 and established themselves on farms in Libertyville, Illinois, and later, with the help of Ligutti, in Loveland (near Cincinnati), Ohio. The latter farm, called Grailville, became a center for rural liturgy and the nurturing of rural culture. Young Catholic women came to Grailville from across the United States to take the Grail's course in rural leadership for laywomen, which centered not on book learning but on religious devotions, folk culture, and menial farm work. Many Grail women later became active in the NCRLC. "Ladies of the Grail" were also active at NCRLC conventions, particularly in demonstrating the folk dances, ballads, and songs they were dedicated to reviving.[22]

Trying to Reach the Grass Roots

Despite its considerable success in developing rural leadership, the NCRLC was concerned that its message was not reaching the grass roots—the average Catholic farmer and his family. Even at its most successful, the Conference had sensed that it was not very influential among the majority of

---

21. Ibid., 198–203; Yzermans, *The People I Love,* 67–68; untitled press release, June 14, 1945, in "Ntn'l Convention, Cincinnati, Ohio, Nov. 10–13, 1944," NCRLC 8-4; articles in nearly every issue of NCRLC periodicals, 1940–66, NCRLC 6.

22. Witte, *Twenty-five Years,* 126, 129; Yzermans, *The People I Love,* 74; Alden V. Brown, *The Grail Movement and American Catholicism, 1940–1975* (Notre Dame, Ind.: University of Notre Dame Press, 1989), 28–29, 43; *New Catholic Encyclopedia,* 1967 ed., s.v. "Grail, The," by D. Myers; James Shea, "To Be Saints and Apostles," *Land and Home* 10 (June 1947): 46–49; "Correspondence, The Grail, 1951–1968," NCRLC 13-1.

the nation's five hundred thousand Catholic farm families. A woman who attended the 1940 convention in St. Cloud, Minnesota, reflected: "If we were disappointed in anything about the Conference, it was the few farm people who were there. That is, in comparison to the hundreds of priests and Sisters attending. There should have been more farmers at St. Cloud, farmers and their wives and families." And this was at one of the largest conventions in NCRLC history—with an attendance estimated at eighteen thousand—one especially geared to farmers and farm wives. In 1950, in the wake of the great expansion of central and local leadership and influence in national and international affairs that marked the first decade of his administration, Ligutti likened the NCRLC to "a tree that spreads its branches far and wide but fails to build up its root system. Due to such a condition," he warned, "the magnificent growth at the outer perimeter may wither and die."[23]

To prevent such deterioration, the NCRLC made strenuous efforts in the 1940s and 1950s to increase lay participation in the Conference. The failed periodical *Christian Farmer* was one of the most important such efforts. The Conference also made a sustained attempt to include more laypeople in the leadership of the Conference. In 1943, in a symbolic move, the first farmer, Martin Salm of Chilton, Wisconsin, was elected to the board of directors. A more substantial step was taken the following year when the revised constitution provided for a special vice president whose job was to promote lay participation. The lay vice president was at first Paul Sacco, later Betsy Phelan. At the 1950 convention in Belleville, the Conference invited each diocese to send two official "lay delegates," who were to form an organization of "official lay representatives of rural life" to meet at each annual convention. The forty lay delegates from sixteen dioceses who attended the meeting adopted two rather unassertive sets of resolutions.[24]

More special meetings, sessions, and workshops for lay delegates and members were held at the conventions of 1952–58, but at the time they did not lead to a greater role by the laity. The laity as a group stayed within

23. Susan Frawley Eisele, "A Rural Pattern," *Catholic Rural Life Bulletin* 3 (November 20, 1940): 12; "Report of Executive Director," October 1950, in "Belleville Pre-Convention Mtg., 1950," NCRLC 8-7, 1.

24. Witte, *Twenty-five Years*, 139–40; materials in "Diocesan Directors Meetings, Names Appointed by Bishops, Ntn'l Convention, Belleville, Ill., Oct. 13–18, 1950," NCRLC 8-7; "Lay Delegates, Ntn'l Convention, Belleville, Ill., Oct. 13–18, 1950," NCRLC 8-8; "Minutes, Board of Directors Meeting, East St. Louis, Ill., Oct. 14, 1950," NCRLC 8-8, 3; "What Laymen Think on Christian Farming," *Christian Farmer* 4 (November 1950): 3.

Figure 9. Symbols of rural life added to the pomp and pageantry at the St. Cloud convention, 1957.

their particular section and did not try to exert a wider influence on the NCRLC. For example, only once in their meetings in the 1950s did the lay delegates discuss and pass resolutions on the farm economy, though this was obviously a great lay concern. In such matters, the lay members of the Conference appeared content merely to follow the direction of their clerical leaders. After 1958, the meetings of the lay delegates at the conventions were dropped.[25]

Besides the special lay delegates meetings, the NCRLC initiated many other convention activities calculated to attract laypeople. Beginning with the 1940 convention at St. Cloud, conventions included audience-participation formats such as panel discussions, question-and-answer periods, and workshops, instead of the unremitting speeches that had been characteristic of the conventions in the 1930s. Topics of discussion also shifted from

25. Materials on lay delegate sessions at NCRLC conventions, NCRLC 8, 1950–58.

Ligutti Takes the Helm

abstract consideration of "Catholic agrarianism" to the more practical concerns of farmers, farm wives, and farm youth. In 1957, in an attempt to boost grass-roots participation, the Conference held regional conventions in seven different states and multiple conventions in some of them: in Michigan, eight different locations were used. Despite the promising success of the regional convention system, it was not repeated in future years. These methods were successful in attracting large numbers to the midcentury NCRLC conventions. After a slump because of wartime restrictions, the "Victory Convention" in Green Bay, Wisconsin, in 1946 attracted over ten thousand people. Then came the blockbuster conventions at Lafayette, La Crosse (thirty thousand attendees), and Columbus (twenty thousand). Conventions in the 1950s were smaller: they averaged around five thousand, with no single convention attracting more than ten thousand except for the regional conventions of 1957, which brought out an estimated twenty thousand people. "Rural Life Days," utilizing many of the same techniques as the conventions, also attracted relatively large attendances in the 1940s and 1950s.[26]

As part of its attempt to interest the laity, the Conference inaugurated a number of programs directed at Catholic rural youth. The NCRLC's fourth vice president, appointed in the 1940s to be responsible for lay participation, promoted youth activities as part of his work. He had charge of the convention "Youth Days," a tradition from the 1930s that continued to be a fixture until 1968. The youth days featured special speakers, demonstrations, exhibits, entertainment, and small-group leadership sessions and sometimes drew thousands of participants. The fourth vice presidents drew up youth programs to be used by pastors in their local communities, and they chaired meetings of "youth delegates" to the annual conventions, similar to the meetings of lay delegates. At these meetings, the youth delegates elected their own officers and discussed issues of importance to rural youth such as getting started in farming, recreation, marriages between Catholics and non-Catholics, and "whether or not the rural youth should take a stand against the recent trend of Rock and Roll music." In 1957, Paul Taff, a longtime fourth vice president, developed the "God-Home-Country Award" for outstanding Catholic rural youths.[27]

---

26. "The National Catholic Rural Life Conference," *Catholic Rural Life* 22 (November 1973): 4–6; meetings and conventions files for the 1940s and 1950s, NCRLC 8; "What the NCRLC Is Doing," *Rural Life Conference* 6 (December 1957): 10; "Programs, 1942–82," NCRLC 8-25; "Programs, NCRLC, 1956–1971," and "Programs, NCRLC, 1956–1974," NCRLC 1-6.

27. "NCRLC Rural Youth," *Catholic Rural Life* 22 (November 1973): 15; NCRLC 6 (periodicals) and NCRLC 8 (meetings and conventions files); NCRLC, *A Program for Rural Youth* (Des Moines,

At one time, the Conference toyed with the idea of forming a separate youth organization, variously called "Catholic Action Farmers" or "Young Catholic Farmers." Inspired by the French and Belgian YCA (Young Christian Agriculturists), the Conference wrote several pamphlets and experimented with a few "cells" of youth in Stearns County, Minnesota. However, because of the competition from groups such as the Catholic Youth Organization and 4-H clubs, the Conference did not pursue the idea and urged Catholic youth to participate in these other organizations.[28]

Because of the potential impact on the laity, the NCRLC showed interest in two special endeavors to teach practical agriculture in accordance with Catholic principles. One was the Omar Research Farm at Elkhorn, Nebraska, directed by the Reverend John C. Rawe, S.J., which offered a one-year course in both "sound rural theory" and practical farming. The other was the first offerings of agriculture courses at a Catholic college—St. Ambrose in Davenport—by Paul Sacco. But the Omar school was short-lived, and the St. Ambrose courses remained an isolated example, not the beginning of a trend to link practical agriculture and the principles of the NCRLC.[29]

Perhaps the Conference's most successful method of reaching the rural laity was through its spiritual program of liturgical revival, retreats, and devotions. The years between 1920 and 1960 marked the high point of devotional Catholicism. This era witnessed peak Mass attendance, the popularity of Marian devotions such as May crownings and Sorrowful Mother novenas, St. Jude devotions, and liturgical weeks, and growth in sodalities, the Confraternity of Christian Doctrine, and Bible study. The NCRLC began its association with the liturgical movement, started at St. John's University in Minnesota by Virgil Michel, in the 1920s. At that time, the Conference urged greater attention to the rural meaning of the Church's rituals and advocated renewed emphasis on rural religious holidays such as Rogation Days. In the next decade, the Conference viewed the liturgical movement as providing the necessary spiritual glue for the hoped-for revived agrarian order.[30]

Iowa: NCRLC, 1953), copy in "Publications, N–P," NCRLC 5-6; quote from 1956 convention minutes of the youth section, "NCRLC, Youth Minutes, 1954–58," NCRLC 1-10.

28. Francis Lohmer, "Keeping Them up on the Farm," *Land and Home* 5 (September 1942): 21–22; "Youth Activities," *Feet in the Furrow* 3 (June 1954): 2.

29. "'An Invitation . . . and a Challenge,'" *Land and Home* 5 (March 1942): 15; Paul Sacco, "A Practical School of Agriculture," *Christian Farmer News Letter* 1 (November 1947): 1–3, 8; D. C. J[ennings], "AT LAST! Farm Courses in a Catholic College," *Catholic Rural Life* 9 (August 1960): 18, 29. On Rawe, see Peter McDonough, *Men Astutely Trained: A History of the Jesuits in the American Century* (New York: Free Press, 1992), 89–95, 120; and La Farge, *Manner Is Ordinary*, 235–37.

30. Jay P. Dolan, *In Search of an American Catholicism: A History of Religion and Culture in Tension*

The connection between the liturgical and rural life movements was continued and expanded in the 1940s and 1950s. NCRLC president J. H. Schlarman (bishop of Peoria) translated into English and published a collection of rural blessings and other rituals. The Reverend William Schimek of Rose Creek, Minnesota, was behind the Conference's request to the pope in 1945 for permission to use the vernacular for the special prayers on Rogation Days and for the blessings of the fields, livestock, and other objects of rural life. Despite the lack of action by Rome on this request, the NCRLC continued to publish a number of rural songs, prayers, and rituals in English. In 1958, this culminated in the publication of *The Rural Life Prayerbook*, edited by the Reverend Alban J. Dachauer, S.J.; its 410 pages contained rural prayers for the Mass and other occasions. The Conference also experimented with the use of dialogue Masses at their meetings. Thus, the NCRLC's attempt to attract more of the laity to its cause led it to pioneer in the use of some of the forms of lay involvement in the liturgy that became widespread after Vatican II.[31]

Rural retreats were another means of reaching the laity. The first was given by Father Schimek in Minnesota on January 3, 1945; the retreats spread quickly in the late 1940s, with many given by Monsignor Ligutti himself. At the end of the decade, rural retreats were being conducted in fifteen dioceses. The Conference also published a manual for the guidance of pastors giving rural retreats.[32]

The Conference attracted the laity by encouraging devotion to the Church's patron of agriculture, St. Isidore. Although Father O'Hara had used the name of the twelfth-century Spanish day laborer for his first NCRLC organ *St. Isidore's Plow*, actual devotion did not begin until Bishop Schlarman composed a prayer to the saint in the 1930s. This was followed by a commissioned painting of the saint and more hagiographical and devotional literature. In 1947, at the Conference's request, Pope Pius XII de-

---

(Oxford: Oxford University Press, 2002), 168–73, 183; NCRLC minutes binder (1923–32), NCRLC 8-1, 39, 43; folder "Rural Life Sunday—Liturgical Movement," NCWC 29; John La Farge, "Rural Environment As a Background for Religion," *Catholic Rural Life* 5 (February 1927): 7–8; a series of articles on the liturgy in ibid., 1929–30.

31. Witte, *Twenty-five Years*, 140–41, 174–77; J. H. Schlarman, trans., *With the Blessing of the Church* (n.p.: National Catholic Rural Life Conference, n.d.), in "General Publications, 1947," NCRLC 5-2; "Monsignor Ligutti Introduces the Rural Life Prayerbook," *Rural Life Conference* 7 (January 1958): 15; "NCRLC Holds Meeting at St. Cloud," ibid. 6 (June 1957): 3.

32. Witte, *Twenty-five Years*, 203–5; "Board of Directors Meeting, October 17, 1948," in "Ntn'l Convention, La Crosse, Wis., Oct. 15–20, 1948," NCRLC 8-6; three folders of retreat material in NCRLC 1-7; "Manual for Rural Retreats and Family Meditation" (Des Moines, Iowa: National Catholic Rural Life Conference, n.d.), 35-page typescript in "Manuals and Programs, 1954–1957," NCRLC 5-2.

Figure 10. Statuettes of St. Isidore and St. Maria della Cabeza sold by the NCRLC.

clared St. Isidore the patron saint of the NCRLC and granted permission for a more solemn celebration of his feast day (March 22, later May 15) in the United States. In the same year, work began on a shrine to St. Isidore in the NCRLC headquarters building in Des Moines. This Chapel of St. Isidore was finally dedicated on May 7, 1956.

Meanwhile, in 1950, the Company of St. Isidore was founded under the leadership of Bishop O'Hara to foster devotion to the NCRLC's patron saint. Members of the Company of St. Isidore were granted a number of special indulgences and given a membership card and medal, as well as the quarterly *Harvest of St. Isidore* and other prayer books and devotional material. The Conference sold statuettes of St. Isidore and his wife, St. Maria della Cabeza, as well as a "do-it-yourself" red cedar wood "outdoor shrine kit" to display them in. The Conference promoted an annual novena to St. Isidore on his feast day, and by 1956, more than a hundred thousand people participated. By 1959, a Conference official claimed that St. Isidore, who a decade ago was "unknown . . . except to a devout few," was honored on his feast day "in every church of the country—even in the cities." Rural Catholics carried their devotion to the saint over to Europe: in 1957, 1958, 1959, and 1962, the NCRLC sponsored pilgrimages to the shrine of St. Isidore in Madrid, and those Conference members who made frequent trips to Europe, such as Ligutti, made it a point to visit the shrine whenever they were there.[33]

33. Witte, *Twenty-five Years*, 212–15; "St. Isidore, The Farmer—NCRLC Patron," *Catholic Rural Life* 22 (November 1973): 16; Michael Dineen, "The '50s—Grass Roots Growth and Shared Lead-

Ligutti Takes the Helm

The attempts to increase lay involvement in the NCRLC were reflected in the membership rolls. In 1940, the total of 1,186 paid memberships was the highest thus far in NCRLC history. (The Conference also gave out annually anywhere from several hundred to several thousand complimentary memberships to bishops, convention attendees, and others.) The total gradually rose to 2,706 in 1945. The next recorded figure, 9,192 in 1948, was inflated by the enormously successful La Crosse convention of that year; the total for 1949 fell back to 3,105. The early 1950s were lean years, and when Ligutti and his assistant, Father Dineen, next looked at the membership rolls in 1955, there were only 446 paid members (230 priests, 216 lay). The two executives immediately decided upon a membership drive, as much to improve the Conference's financial situation through fees as to increase the NCRLC's influence on the laity. The drive was tremendously successful. In a year, the number of paid members rose to 1,198, and in another year, to 2,450. By January 1958 the membership totals had climbed to 7,500. NCRLC membership peaked in June of 1958 at "over 10,000." However, as so often in Conference history, this burst of enthusiasm was only temporary. In January 1959, membership was 8,052, and it declined steadily thereafter, leveling off in the mid-sixties at about three thousand. The drop coincided with the departure from the NCRLC of Dineen and his promotional ideas. Coupled with that, the laity seemed more attracted by the Conference's spiritual program, which crested in the late fifties, than by its rather self-sacrificing economic message. When the Church entered the era of Vatican II, with its emphasis on modernization and social justice rather than old-fashioned devotions, NCRLC membership rolls declined rapidly. By the mid-sixties, Conference membership once again consisted mainly of the solid core of leaders.[34]

Paying the Bills

All of Ligutti's expansion of the NCRLC during the 1940s and 1950s—the new building, expanded staff, new services of the central office, greater publicity, and Ligutti's own extensive traveling—required much more

---

ership," ibid. 33 (September 1983): 17; "St. Isidore Group Formed in Missouri," *Christian Farmer* 3 (August 1950): 6; "The Harvest of St. Isidore. Over 100,000 People to Participate in Novena," *Rural Life Conference—Feet in the Furrow* 4 (February 1956): 9; "The Company of St. Isidore . . . " *Rural Life Conference* 6 (March 1957): 6–7; "The McCartys Do-It Themselves: NCRLC Shrine Kit," ibid. 7 (April 1958): 6; J. L. V[izzard], "Devotion to Our Patron Growing," *Catholic Rural Life* 8 (February 1959): 2; devotional publications in NCRLC 6-21; four folders on NCRLC-sponsored pilgrimages in NCRLC 1-5; a number of folders of St. Isidore–related material in NCRLC 1-7 and 1-8.

34. Membership figures are from various documents in NCRLC 8-3 and following boxes.

money than had been available in the 1930s and would have been impossible but for a dramatic increase in the Conference's income during his term as executive director. In addition to being the energetic leader and symbolic father figure of the rural life movement, Ligutti was also a shrewd businessman and remarkably successful fundraiser. He was a careful manager of the resources at his disposal and an indefatigable hunter of new sources of revenue.

The reservoirs of funds that Ligutti eventually tapped were legion—which came to have the disadvantage that he was the only one who understood them all. To begin with, there were some of the traditional sources of revenue. In the 1930s the financial mainstay of the Conference had been annual grants from the American Board of Catholic Missions, which were gradually raised from three thousand to six thousand dollars during the 1940s, with the exception of 1946, when through an oversight no money was granted at all. This scare prompted the Conference to appoint a special Committee on Finance to plan more stable sources of income. As Ligutti's biographer noted, "Ligutti's philosophy of the NCRLC was built on the principle that it should be self-sufficient." Thus Ligutti tried in a number of ways to raise revenue from NCRLC members themselves.[35]

In 1941, the old idea of the Founders' Club of 1925 was revived under the name of the Hundred Dollar Club, or the Committee of One-Hundred. Conference members, especially diocesan directors, were asked to contribute a hundred dollars per year. Not all of the members gave the full amount every year, but the plan did raise several thousand dollars each year until it was dropped around 1950. Ligutti sometimes received honorariums for his speaking engagements, which paid for some of his traveling expenses. Sales of books and pamphlets raised two to four thousand dollars in the 1940s, but when the Conference began to publish more material in the 1950s, income from this source sometimes totaled over ten thousand dollars. Group subscriptions to the *Christian Farmer* were for a time an important source of income for the Conference, averaging about ten thousand dollars per year from 1946 to 1951. Later in the 1950s, the NCRLC raised a little money from the annual novenas to St. Isidore.[36]

The potentially most productive internal source of NCRLC income, however, was membership fees from the clientele the Conference served. The NCRLC became especially needy for a new source of income in the early 1950s, when the ABCM grants ended and certain other sources of

---

35. Witte, *Twenty-five Years*, 138–39; Yzermans, *The People I Love*, 78.
36. Witte, *Twenty-five Years*, 137–39; financial reports in NCRLC 8 and 22.

Ligutti Takes the Helm

income dried up. Conference officials believed that the NCRLC should have no financial difficulties if only a reasonable percentage of the more than four hundred thousand Catholic rural families in the United States became members. As a first step in increasing income from this source, the Conference raised the membership fee from two to five dollars, which it remained throughout the 1950s. But, since NCRLC membership in 1955 was only about four hundred, Ligutti and Dineen initiated the membership drive previously mentioned. They sent a brochure that explained NCRLC membership benefits to fifteen thousand rural people, increased promotion of devotions, and hired a young layman, Joseph C. Meisner, as full-time field representative. Throughout 1957 and 1958, Meisner and Dineen stumped across the rural countryside, contributing greatly to the large membership increases of those years. In April 1958, the Conference opened an "Every Member Get a Member" campaign, with a goal of twenty thousand members, and two months later NCRLC membership reached its highest level ever at more than ten thousand. But a severe financial crisis caused by over-expenditure of previous funds overtook the Conference at this point, and it had to cut down on the promotion. This inevitably led to a reduction in memberships and the income derived from them in the early sixties.[37]

The membership surge, temporary though it was, did add considerably to the NCRLC's income for that period. In 1954, the year before the membership drive, membership income was only a minor item in the NCRLC budget—$2,102. In succeeding years, it rose dramatically to a peak of $29,309 in 1959 and still was $20,695 in 1961. By 1967, membership income fell to $12,981. During this peak period, however, membership fees accounted for from a quarter to a third of the NCRLC's total income.[38]

There were two further important sources of income. For the years 1949–50 and 1950–51, the Conference received "refunds" of five thousand dollars per year from Catholic Relief Services for assistance in fundraising, which helped make up for the loss of ABCM funding that occurred at that time. A more enduring source of income was the "Bishops' Fund"—contributions from the bishops and archbishops of the United States solicited by the Conference president every year. The first response in 1942 netted

---

37. "From the National Headquarters," *Feet in the Furrow* 3 (February 1955): 2; Joseph Meisner, "Vital Need of Members Says Man in the Field," *Rural Life Conference* 6 (May 1957): 13; "United through NCRLC Membership," ibid. 7 (April 1958): 3; James L. Vizzard, "Editorial," *Catholic Rural Life* 8 (May 1959): 2; articles on Meisner's activity in almost every issue of *Catholic Rural Life* through May 1962.

38. Financial statements in NCRLC 22-2.

$3,890, and in subsequent years the fund raised anywhere from $1,000 to $16,000. The Bishops' Fund was discontinued when the NCRLC became an arm of the United States Catholic Conference (USCC) in 1968.[39]

Finally, the most important sources of NCRLC income—especially for its international activities—were donations and grants from individuals and foundations, which Ligutti seemed to have an almost magical ability to attract. Of the donations from wealthy individuals, an early example was the Mary Welsh Fund. Starting in 1942, Welsh gave a total of $15,500 to the Conference, which was used to establish an "Apostolate Library Service" that provided parishes with sets of pamphlets and periodicals to be lent to their children. In 1950, the Apostolate Library Service was terminated, and the Welsh money was apparently merged with the Conference's other funds.[40]

The most important individual contributor to the NCRLC, who indeed deserves to be called the Conference's "financial angel," was the Catholic convert Chauncey Stillman of New York. Stillman, who had acquired his fortune from his family's Texas oil wells and New York banks, bankrolled and was one of the editors of Herbert Agar's Distributist periodical *Free America*, as well as contributing to many Catholic charitable causes. He became interested in Ligutti's Granger project sometime in the late 1930s and arranged to meet the small-town pastor in New York City. "A deep and lasting friendship" sprang up between the gregarious Italian immigrant churchman and the elegant, rather reserved philanthropist, which incidentally served the NCRLC in good financial stead over four sometimes perilous decades.[41]

The first recorded grant made by Stillman to the Conference was in 1941, when he gave fifty dollars a month for the support of an assistant to Ligutti. Later in the decade, Stillman gave further occasional gifts of five hundred or a thousand dollars or so. Then he established the Homeland Foundation, with Ligutti a member of the board of directors. Louis Warren, treasurer of the foundation and Stillman's lawyer, became a close friend of Ligutti's and sought his advice on the foundation's grants. Many of them went to the NCRLC.

Stillman proved a true friend when he gave freely of his money during the Conference's precarious financial situation at the end of the 1950s.

---

39. Witte, *Twenty-five Years*, 139; financial statements in NCRLC 8 and 22.

40. Witte, *Twenty-five Years*, 137–38; NCRLC 8 and 22.

41. Yzermans, *The People I Love*, 291–92; Carlson, *New Agrarian Mind*, 136; Ligutti-Stillman correspondence in "Mr. Chauncey Stillman, Corres., 1954," NCRLC 13-4.

Ligutti Takes the Helm

About the middle of that decade, he purchased twenty-five thousand dollars worth of stock in the NCRLC's ill-fated York County farm settlement project, which he subsequently donated to the Conference. In 1958, he paid back a two hundred thousand dollar loan used to finance work in South America and gave a fifty thousand dollar matching grant to help pull the Conference out of its financial crisis. In 1960, after Ligutti left the central office to become director of international affairs, Stillman donated a house in New York for his residence. The following year, he donated 740 shares of stock in the Aluminum Company of America to the NCRLC. Finally, when Ligutti moved to Rome, Stillman built a house, called "Villa Stillman," for the monsignor to live in there.[42]

Another important financial angel for the Conference was Victor Emanuel, president of Avco Manufacturing Corporation in New York City. Emanuel helped raise funds for Ligutti's international activities—he was especially interested in halting the spread of communism. His fundraising helped to support Ligutti's Latin American rural life conferences of the 1950s. He had connections with New York City's wealthiest businessmen, such as the Rockefellers, and even secured a confidential contribution from President Eisenhower on the understanding that the Latin American rural life congresses were anti-communist in purpose.[43]

Ligutti was also remarkably successful in obtaining grants from charitable foundations. The most reliable source was naturally the Homeland Foundation founded by his friend Chauncey Stillman. In addition, from 1951 to 1960, he secured several grants from the Sears Foundation, first to support the 1951 annual convention, later to sponsor youth activities. The Ford Foundation picked up his travel expenses as Vatican observer to the UN Food and Agriculture Organization for four years, and the Ford and Rockefeller Foundations subsidized some of his Latin American rural life congresses. In 1957, grants were secured from the Crown-Zellerbach Foundation and Santa Clara University to support James Vizzard's NCRLC Washington, D.C., office. In 1960, the Merrill Trust gave sixty thousand dollars for three years for work with migrant farm workers. Two years later, the Ford Foundation granted over four hundred thousand dollars for a study of Third World missionary activity initiated by Ligutti.[44]

Beginning in the 1950s, money for Ligutti's international activities was

42. Yzermans, *The People I Love,* 206–8, 292; NCRLC 8; Mrs. A. P. Grane (Stillman's secretary) to J. G. Weber, January 10, 1961, in "Correspondence, R-S, 1961," NCRLC 13-18.
43. See "Victor Emanuel, Correspondence, Ligutti, 1954," NCRLC 13-2.
44. Yzermans, *The People I Love,* 158, 167–69, 252; NCRLC 8.

Table 3. NCRLC Income and Expenses, 1942–60

Year	Income ($)	Expenses ($)	Year	Income ($)	Expenses ($)
1942–43	18,456.16	18,223.42	1951–52	26,584.86	29,082.60
1943–44	32,953.34	26,694.37	1952–53	33,340.72	29,989.51
1944–45	38,520.33	30,650.58	1953–54	23,461.55	19,913.60
1945–46	25,747.23	25,072.52	1954–55	35,833.84	38,663.98
1946–47	32,841.17	31,716.30	1955–56	81,952.64	79,611.18
1947–48	47,183.02	46,997.34	1956–57	122,038.39	120,784.25
1948–49	36,486.06	39,802.29	1957–58	167,528.45	166,770.69
1949–50	41,115.80	35,501.21	1958–59	93,395.38	104,615.08
1950–51	28,704.06	32,755.93	1959–60	97,991.29	100,369.19

Source: Budget figures, NCRLC 22.

held in an "international fund," which was kept separate from the regular NCRLC "operating fund." The international fund consisted mainly of stocks, donations from Ligutti's wealthy friends, and grants from foundations. Thanks to the liberality of these contributors, by the mid-1950s the international fund was about as large as the NCRLC operating fund. Although Ligutti's management of the fund was very haphazard and careful records were not kept, the fund played no part in the Conference's financial crisis at the end of the 1950s, which took place entirely within the NCRLC operating fund.[45]

To summarize the sources of the NCRLC's funding during these years, during the 1940s, about a fifth to a third of the Conference's income came from memberships and subscriptions, one-fifth or so from the bishops' fund, one-fifth from the ABCM, anywhere from a fifth to a half from donations, and the remainder from sales of literature, speakers' fees, the Committee of One Hundred, and other sources. In the early 1950s, the sources of income shifted because the ABCM money was discontinued and income from memberships and subscriptions decreased. Income as a whole fell as the Conference depended mainly on emergency donations and refunds and the annual bishops' appeal. In the later fifties the Conference became much more self-sufficient financially. Sales of literature rose greatly with the popularity of devotions at that time, to make up about a third of the Conference's income. Membership income rose because of the membership drives from an almost insignificant amount to account

45. Financial statements in NCRLC 22.

Ligutti Takes the Helm

for another third. The bishops' fund contributed 10 to 20 percent, with sales, donations, and a few other sources accounting for the remainder.[46]

The most consistent large item of the Conference's expenditures was salaries, which tended to account for about one-third. Printing of publications varied from less than 10 percent in the early 1950s, when they were mimeographed, to over a third in the late 1950s when Dineen upgraded the quality and the Conference published much additional devotional literature. Other large items tended to be upkeep of the central office, travel expenses, mailing expenses, conventions, and promotion.[47]

All of this financial activity contributed to the great increases in the income of the NCRLC over the course of Ligutti's term—which then gave him the wherewithal to finance his expansion of the Conference's activities. The largest pre-Ligutti budget, in 1941, was about eight thousand dollars. From then on, it generally increased, as shown in table 3. This table shows perhaps as well as any description how the NCRLC rose to become a large-scale operation. Initially, there were few problems in the management of these large funds. The small deficits of the late 1940s and early 1950s were covered by the previous bank balance. However, the table does not show that the large expenses of the mid- and late 1950s, which threw the Conference into a financial crisis, were only covered by financial expedients resorted to by Dineen.[48]

46. Ibid.
47. Ibid.
48. Budget figures, ibid.

Chapter 8 The Conference Becomes International

Ligutti's Role

During the 1920s, the newborn NCRLC was most concerned with the Catholic rural population problem. Later, in response to the Great Depression, the Conference turned its attention to the economic aspects of rural life as well. During the 1940s, the NCRLC further expanded the scope of its activities by entering international affairs.

Before World War II, the NCRLC had little involvement with rural life outside of the United States. In the 1920s and 1930s, Father O'Hara and others in the Conference had studied rural life in Europe and exchanged information with people outside of the United States on how to deal with rural problems but had not undertaken any long-lasting commitments involving other nations. Starting with World War II, this began to change. The shift was in part a function of alterations in the NCRLC's environment. The United States became committed to the role of a great world power, and to some extent the activities of national organizations such as the NCRLC simply followed the flag.

The second cause of the Conference's growing involvement in international rural life was the personal influence of Monsignor Ligutti. The Italian-born immigrant was well suited to lead the NCRLC into concern for foreign lands. Ligutti perceived that after World War II the U.S. government, American rural life, and the American Catholic Church all became international: "The world looks to the Catholic Church for leadership in fighting for solutions to farm problems, especially as they affect farm families and all rural peoples. The United States came out of World War II the natural world leader. It naturally follows that the Catholic Church in America must assume leadership in solving these problems."[1] Ligutti brought an awareness to American farmers "that there is a Third World, a world of poverty and need where two-thirds of the people 'go to bed hungry at night'" and that the United States had a "responsibility for the needs of suffering mankind throughout the world." Ligutti's biographer went so far as to claim that the monsignor "almost single-handedly brought the conservative heartbelt of the United States into the mainstream of international life." He certainly did so for the NCRLC.[2]

While Ligutti was executive director of the NCRLC, he handled all of the international affairs of the Conference personally. He continued to deal with them from 1960 to the mid-1970s as director for international affairs. After Ligutti gradually faded out of the job in the mid-1970s, the Conference did not hire another international affairs director, even though the 1975 constitution provided for that possibility. Instead, international affairs were handled on an ad hoc basis by various NCRLC officials.[3]

Ligutti promoted the international role of the NCRLC in many ways. He collected news of international Catholic rural activities and shared it with the Conference membership through columns in the NCRLC periodicals such as "Other Lands" in *Land and Home* and "Around the World" in *Feet in the Furrow*. As he became a well-known international figure, his headquarters in Des Moines began to receive thousands of letters from around the world informing the Conference of rural developments in other lands and asking for advice. In addition, the headquarters became a popular stopping place for foreign Catholic priests, sisters, bishops, and laymen interested in rural life who were visiting the United States. It was not unusual for the headquarters to welcome with its famous hospitality a bishop from Tanganyika and a student from the Philippines at the same time.[4]

However, more important than other travelers' visits to Des Moines were Ligutti's own extensive travels to all parts of the world on behalf of rural life. Before Ligutti's time, Conference officials had traveled occasionally to Canada, Mexico, and Europe. But travel was a customary part of Ligutti's lifestyle, and he soon journeyed more than all of the others put to-

---

1. "Plan National Program," *Rural Life Conference* 7 (May 1958): 10.
2. Vincent A. Yzermans, "NCRLC's Work Discussed in Bicentennial Series," *Catholic Rural Life* 25 (April 1976): 11–13.
3. *Constitution of the National Catholic Rural Life Conference* (Des Moines, Iowa: NCRLC, 1975), in "Gen. Pubs., 1970–76," NCRLC 5-5, 7–8; issues of *Catholic Rural Life* since 1975.
4. See, for example, "Visitors at Headquarters," *Feet in the Furrow* 3 (February 1955): 2; "Spanish Rural Life Head Studies, Praises NCRLC," *Catholic Rural Life* 7 (December 1958): 24; "Visitors at Headquarters," ibid. 9 (November 1960): 20–21.

gether. As his biographer states: "One would need a computer to estimate the number of air miles he traveled within the United States and on international trips that carried him to every continent except the Antarctic and almost every nation except Russia." Most of Ligutti's trips were to study agricultural and religious conditions in the countries involved. But he also traveled to international rural life conferences, to Food and Agriculture Organization meetings, to areas involved in problems concerning displaced persons, relief, foreign aid, and migration, and to Rome for numerous purposes. Ligutti publicized his trips abroad from 1945 to 1965 in sixteen sets of delightful travel letters. These were mimeographed and sent to several score "close friends" of the monsignor; excerpts subsequently showed up in many publications.[5]

Ligutti used his foreign travels to arrange international rural life conferences and form international rural organizations. The NCRLC's first conference on international rural life, held at Blue Ridge Summit, Pennsylvania, in 1950, was attended by American Catholics only. Its purpose was to formulate a statement to update the Conference's *Manifesto on Rural Life* (1939) and broaden it to embrace all of the world. The next year, the Conference helped to form the International Catholic Rural Life Conference to promote the spiritual and material improvement of the world's rural population. This was basically a paper organization, without actual members, run by Ligutti as part of the NCRLC. The first truly international Catholic rural life conference was held in Rome the same year. Organized by Ligutti, it drew two hundred participants from twenty nations. In the next ten years, the monsignor organized four more international rural life congresses, all in Latin America (Manizales, Colombia, in 1953, Panama City, Panama, in 1955, Santiago, Chile, in 1957, and Caracas, Venezuela, in 1961), each larger than the one before and each issuing a statement on such international rural problems as hunger and land reform. In 1962 and 1967 international rural life congresses were again held in Rome, and in 1967 Ligutti helped plan a large Philippine rural life congress.[6]

At the 1962 Rome meeting, 124 rural organizations from forty-nine countries formed a more robust successor to the International Catholic Rural Life Conference called the International Catholic Rural Association (ICRA). ICRA opened an office in Rome and dedicated itself to fulfilling

---

5. Yzermans, *The People I Love*, 85; complete sets of travel letters in LGL-B.
6. L. G. Ligutti, "Attack on Hunger," *Rural Life Conference* 6 (June 1957): 11; Yzermans, *The People I Love*, 104–10, 158–65, 269–75; numerous articles in NCRLC publications on the international conferences; statements of the conferences in NCRLC 5.

The Conference Becomes International

Figure 11. International Rural Life Congress, Rome, 1962.

its purpose of exchanging information and organizing meetings among the participating groups. The NCRLC was represented on ICRA's executive committee from the beginning and at least until the 1980s contributed a thousand dollars annually to the organization. NCRLC representatives attended an ICRA conference in 1987, but ICRA then lapsed into oblivion for a long period. Concern for the effects of globalization and a desire to foster community-based agricultural development fueled the revitalization of ICRA around the turn of the millennium. Executive Director David Andrews and policy coordinator Robert Gronski attended conferences addressing these issues yearly starting in 2000 in Asia, Africa, Latin America, and Rome. About the same time, and for similar reasons, the NCRLC joined the International Federation of Rural Adult Catholic Movements (FIMARC), which had organizations in fifty-three countries and held meetings around the world.[7]

Ligutti brought his concern for the world's rural life to the highest lev-

7. "NCRLC International Work," *Catholic Rural Life* 22 (November 1973): 14; "International Activities," in "Diocesan Directors Meeting, San Antonio, Texas, March 4, 1975," NCRLC 8-24; "News from the Executive Director," *Common Ground* 6 (October 1987): 1–2; Robert Gronski, "Catholic Rural Associations to Gather in Rome," *Rural Landscapes* 8 (November 2000): 1; "Catholic Rural Organizations Meet in Rome," ibid. (May 2001): 7; "NCRLC Is Reaching out Internationally," ibid. 9 (June 2002): 1; "International Catholic Rural Association (ICRA)," ibid. 11 (January 2004): 3; "The Rising Call to Food Sovereignty," ibid. 11 (May 2004): 6; "Development Strategies Similar in Asia and United States," *Catholic Rural Life* (newsletter) 12 (February 2005): 1; David Andrews, "Dear Friends of NCRLC," *NCRLC Annual Report, 2005*, 3; Andrews, "Dear Friends of NCRLC," *National Catholic Rural Life Conference Annual Report, Fiscal Year 2005–2006*, 4–5.

Figure 12. Monsignor Ligutti had close relations with popes, such as Pius XII.

el of the Catholic Church—the Vatican. He developed personal friendships with Popes Pius XII, John XXIII, and Paul VI and used them to benefit rural life around the world. He was particularly close to Pius XII, whom he called "the Pope of Peace." Ligutti induced Pius to do much to further rural life: Pius named St. Isidore the NCRLC patron, appointed Ligutti permanent Vatican observer to the UN Food and Agriculture Organization (FAO), collaborated with Ligutti's hybrid seed corn project, and hosted the first international Catholic conference on rural life.[8]

Ligutti tried to use his influence in the Vatican to persuade the popes to make an unprecedented gesture in behalf of rural life by writing an encyclical on the topic. The NCRLC's agitation in this matter began in 1939, when

8. Raymond W. Miller, *Monsignor Ligutti: The Pope's County Agent* (Washington, D.C.: University Press of America, 1981), 96–98; Luigi G. Ligutti, "Pope of Peace," *Catholic Rural Life* 7 (October 1958): 14–15; "Policy Statement: Tribute to Holy Father," ibid. (November 1958): 6; "Pope Pius XII—Champion of Christian Rural Life," NCRLC 8A-2.

the board of directors instructed Ligutti, then Conference president, to prepare a brief for presentation to the pontiff requesting a rural life encyclical. Ligutti and Bishops Mulloy, Muench, and Ryan wrote a draft rural life encyclical during the 1940s and sent it to Pius XII with supporting documents such as NCRLC publications sometime after 1946. During the next decade, Ligutti continued to press the idea of the encyclical on Pius whenever they met, but the pontiff died in 1958 without taking action on it. Undaunted, the monsignor continued the campaign with Pius's successor, John XXIII, a fellow northern Italian of peasant background. Pope John did not write a rural life encyclical per se, but as Ligutti proudly reminisced later, "It all came out with [*Mater et Magistra*]," the pope's great encyclical on the broader topic of Christianity and social progress, issued in 1961. A long section of the encyclical, paragraphs 123–84, dealt with rural life or with economic development with specific reference to rural life. Delighted NCRLC officials said that "*Mater et Magistra* might appropriately be termed 'the agricultural encyclical'" and rejoiced that they found "in the Pope's words a reinforcement for the Conference's views and policy recommendations on farm problems." The Conference frequently reprinted extracts from *Mater et Magistra* as part of its campaign for rural social justice in the 1960s.[9]

Ligutti also used his clout inside the Vatican to have an impact in favor of rural life on the Second Vatican Council. He was named a consultant to Vatican II on the commission on the lay apostolate. In the pivotal document, the pastoral constitution on *The Church in the Modern World,* Ligutti influenced the section entitled "Certain Principles Governing Socio-Economic Life as a Whole," especially paragraphs 71 and 72, which "stressed the causes so close to his heart: ownership of private property, development of human dignity, land reform, cooperatives, conservation of resources, worldwide prosperity, and the promotion of peace." Ligutti also successfully worked for the passage of a statement on stewardship and tithing. In another Vatican-related matter, he was a founding father of the Pontifical Commission on Justice and Peace, established in 1967 to try to alleviate world poverty. Its first executive secretary was the Reverend Joseph Gremillion, who worked with Ligutti in the NCRLC and Catholic Relief Services.[10]

9. "Minutes Bd. of Directors, Oct. 16, 1939," NCRLC 8-3; "Exec. Committee Mtg., December 27, 1939," NCRLC 8-3; "Encyclical Material on Rural Life," LGL-H; "LGL—Transcription of tapes made with Monsignor Ligutti and extra documents used in writing his biography (Part I)," LGL-K, 139–40, 183; Yzermans, *The People I Love,* 82–83, 92–94; Edward W. O'Rourke, "The Encyclical and Agriculture," in Moody and Lawler, *Challenge of Mater et Magistra,* 238; James L. Vizzard, "Washington Farm Front," *Catholic Rural Life* 10 (September 1961): 22.

10. Yzermans, *The People I Love,* 206–30; folders in LGL-B, LGL-K, and LGL-O.

The Conference and World War II

The first international issue that confronted the NCRLC under Ligutti was World War II. During the 1930s, the Conference had blamed the Depression and the worsening international situation of those years on urban and capitalistic civilization. When World War II broke out in 1939, and the United States was drawn into the war in 1941, the catastrophe was ascribed to the same root causes. One country pastor wrote: "Wars are caused by the greed for exorbitant wealth, by the lust for ruthless power: vices born and nurtured more frequently in the cities . . . Because of all the allurements in the cities men's desires multiply, the urge to satisfy them becomes ever a stronger obsession, the race for the coveted prizes naturally limited to a few, becomes more frantic."[11] The Conference recalled that it had warned against the war: "We Catholic Agrarian Distributists have long been pointing to the evils that have caused this world-wide catastrophe—Industrialism, commercialism, urbanization, concentration of economic power. The results and consequences affect the family and human personality—hence organized society, state, church and international relationships."[12]

If urbanism caused the war, then ruralism was the solution to the war. The NCRLC believed the agrarian movement of which it was a part had a contribution to make not only to the cause of national economic and social reconstruction but to that of world peace as well. The Conference maintained that "democracy went to sleep" in the years preceding World War II "on few things more notably than the matter of rural life." But there was still time to try to adopt the NCRLC program of organizing the nation and the world on the basis of rural and family life. Through the Conference's plan of family farms, locally run cooperatives, and many decentralized communities, the United States and other nations could preserve both democracy and Christianity. "That means changes and perhaps an apparent breakdown of a few things we believe we cherish but why regret it if society can be established on secure footings?" The Conference held that "this is the only 'way to peace' if our analysis of 'Why the War' is correct."[13]

In the meantime, however, there was a war to win. Shunning the paci-

---

11. "I Am a Country Pastor . . ." *Land and Home* 5 (June 1942): 3.
12. "Why the War? How the Peace?" ibid. 5 (March 1942): 14.
13. Ibid., 14; John La Farge, "Decentralism and Rural Life," *Catholic Rural Life Bulletin* 3 (August 20, 1940): 1; editorial comment with Walter C. Lowdermilk, "'Lebensraum'—Agrarianism vs. War," ibid. 3 (November 20, 1940): 16.

fism of dissenting groups such as the Catholic Worker, the NCRLC joined most other American Catholics in putting itself wholly behind the war effort. At its first convention following America's entrance into the war, President Muench spoke for all of the Conference when he said, "To win the war is right now our chief concern . . . In this serious hour of need we pledge our whole-hearted loyalty to our country as well as our willingness to make whatever sacrifices are necessary to achieve victory." And indeed, the Conference viewed the rural family as "the first line of our national defense . . . The Catholic rural home that fosters worship of God, devotion to Church, appreciation of children, respect for authority, loyalty to country and practice of the moral virtues is, indeed, the bulwark of Christian civilization and the guardian of our national greatness."[14]

The NCRLC praised and supported U.S. agriculture policy during World War II. It applauded government efforts to raise agricultural production during the war. The Conference encouraged Catholic high school boys to cooperate in the government's plan to have youths work on farms during their summer vacations. The NCRLC lauded the wartime boom in "victory gardens," noting that they were "gardens for defense" (the war) as well as "gardens for self-defense" (self-sufficiency). It praised the government officials who ran the wartime programs—Secretary of Agriculture Claude Wickard, Extension Director M. L. Wilson, Food Administrator Chester Davis, and Colonel Jay Taylor of the Farm Labor Department—calling them "as social-minded as the Encyclicals." Conference officials also urged Catholic farmers to voluntarily do their part to help curb wartime inflation by using "their surplus income to retire farm indebtedness, to keep in repair the rural home and the operating facilities of the farm, and to purchase government bonds."[15]

Despite their eagerness to contribute to American victory in the war, some NCRLC officials believed that the war and some of the government's policies were having a bad effect on rural life. During the 1930s, the Conference believed it had started to reverse the cityward trend, but now the war was taking rural men for the armed forces and women for urban defense jobs. "All the good work that has been accomplished, so slowly,

---

14. A. J. Muench, "Presidential Address," *Land and Home* 5 (December 1942): 2; "Minutes of the Annual Meeting of the National Catholic Rural Life Conference, St. Cloud, Minn., October 2, 1940," in "St. Cloud Convention, Sept. 29, 30, Oct. 1–2, 1940," NCRLC 8-3, 292.

15. "Executive Committee" ("Conference Affairs"), *Land and Home* 6 (March 1943): 26; "Gardens in Self-Defense," ibid. 5 (March 1942): 15; "In Praise of Some," ibid. 6 (June 1943): 40; "Resolutions of the National Catholic Rural Life Conference Adopted at the Twentieth Annual Convention, October 3–6, 1942, Peoria, Illinois," ibid. 5 (December 1942): 23.

so painstakingly, seems to be impeded, if not entirely destroyed, just at the time when many were beginning to see the light," one country pastor lamented. The Conference was concerned that rural depopulation would result from the government's drafting of farmers into the armed forces. It was not consoled when the government decided to exempt farmers working on farms above a certain size, which were deemed "essential" for war production; it feared that this policy would destroy the small family farms. The NCRLC called on the government to desist from drafting farmers, and in 1943 was pleased when, in the interest of boosting agricultural production, the United States exempted farmers from military service and appealed to them to avoid defense jobs and stay on the farms.[16]

Postwar Reconstruction

Even before the Second World War was well under way, the NCRLC was already making plans for postwar reconstruction. The Conference predicted: "The end of the war will bring economic chaos, poverty, unemployment and social upheaval . . . No matter who wins the struggle, the old order is definitely finished." The NCRLC asserted: "We must play our part in reconstructing the social order. A world at war needs our program of rural life. Our democracy needs it to survive." Conference officials warned with Pope Pius XII that "to avoid the horror of a Third World War" certain conditions must be established, among them such long-time NCRLC goals as "distributed ownership of property, the abolition of large corporations and holding companies, the development of cooperatives and cooperative credit facilities," and above all, the fostering of family farming. As in their reaction to the Depression crisis of the previous decade, Catholic agrarians believed that the new postwar world would have to be established on the basis of a large class of family farmers. They were encouraged by evidence from Europe showing that even in the midst of invasion and devastation, peasants who lived on subsistence farms were relatively unaffected by the war. They were confident that such peasants would form the backbone of the society that would rebuild the world after the war.[17]

16. "I Am a Country Pastor . . . ," *Land and Home* 5 (September 1942): 12; "Essential Farms" (Quotation of an editorial from *Wallace's Farmer*), ibid. (December 1942): 19; "Resolutions of the National Catholic Rural Life Conference Adopted at the Twentieth Annual Convention, October 3–6, 1942, Peoria, Illinois," ibid., 22; "I Am a Country Pastor . . . " ibid. 6 (March 1943): 10.

17. "General Resolutions of the N.C.R.L.C.," *Catholic Rural Life Bulletin* 4 (November 20, 1941): 95; "We and the War," ibid. 4 (May 20, 1941): 45; John La Farge, "Post-War Problems in Relation to Rural Life," *Catholic Rural Life Objectives. A Fourth Series of Papers Dealing with Agrarianism with Special Emphasis on Post-War Planning* (Des Moines: National Catholic Rural Life Conference, 1944),

The NCRLC wanted to be part of an effort to ensure the existence of a large rural class in the United States after the war. To do this, the Conference returned to a favorite idea of the 1930s and proposed the large-scale settlement of families on farms. The Conference was fearful that returning veterans and defense workers released from their jobs might have to go on the dole or accept public service jobs. It proposed that they, along with war refugees from foreign countries, instead be settled as self-sufficient farmers. For veterans, the provision in the G. I. Bill for loans for the purchase or construction of homes could be used to acquire small farms. The NCRLC urged that the government similarly aid others who wished to go back to the land by granting long-term loans at reasonable rates of interest to any who wished to settle on family farms, by having mortgage limitations on family farmsteads, and by encouraging cooperatives. NCRLC president Ryan thought that the government might grant loans to "cooperative land settlement groups" and hoped that "the Government will not look with disfavor on the formation of religiously homogeneous cooperative groups." The Conference looked at Church support for back-to-the-land efforts made in other countries and believed that the Church in the United States could support postwar land settlement as well. Some Conference officials viewed rural settlement in the postwar period as an opportunity to work toward achieving Bishop O'Hara's old goal of ten thousand strong rural parishes—thus land settlement was combined with the old concern for Catholic rural weakness. The Conference solicited the opinions of a number of prominent agricultural experts, who all gave some hope that the postwar farm population was indeed capable of increasing.[18]

Yet there were many obstacles to a successful postwar back-to-the-land movement. One rural pastor noted the paucity of government assistance; the shortage of good farms; the high prices of land, stock, and machinery; the prospect of incurring debt; and the probability of a decline in the prices of agricultural products soon after the war.[19]

---

copy in "General Publications, 1940–1944," NCRLC 5-1, (hereafter *Catholic Rural Life Objectives*, 1944), 11; L. Bromfield, "The Happiest Man I Have Ever Known," *Land and Home* 7 (September 1944): 69–70; "Whole Wheat," from *New York Times*, ibid., 72.

18. Vincent J. Ryan, "Looking Ahead," *Catholic Rural Life Bulletin* 4 (November 20, 1941): 105; Muench, "Presidential Address," 3; "When Johnny Comes Marching Home" ("Notes and Comments"), *Land and Home* 5 (December 1942): 14; Elmer T. Peterson, "Rebuilding America from the Ground Up," ibid. 7 (September 1944): 68–69; Joseph V. Urbain, "Rural Communities of Tomorrow," ibid. 8 (March 1945): 2–4; Eugene S. Geissler, "GIs and the Bill of Rights," ibid., 6–8; "Is There Room on the Land for More Full-Time and Part-Time Farmers in Post-War America?" ("Notes and Comments"), ibid., 14–15.

19. "I Am a Country Pastor . . . " *Land and Home* 10 (March 1947): 25.

The Conference did what it could. It drew no response to its call for dioceses to establish agencies to provide financial aid to displaced workers and returning veterans wishing to settle on the land, but several of them did set up "land location services" to help Catholics find homesteads. Such farm placement services were located in the Springfield, Illinois; Evansville, Indiana; Fargo, North Dakota; and Madison and Green Bay, Wisconsin dioceses, and in many others individual pastors and diocesan newspapers gave assistance. In 1945, the NCRLC established a small fund for loans to farmers for purchase of livestock, tools, or other equipment. These services, in operation for ten to fifteen years after World War II, were probably successful in helping a few rural Catholic families, but they hardly effected the revolution in land settlement that the Conference hoped for. This effort to guide veterans and defense workers back to the land was soon overwhelmed by a problem and opportunity in land settlement that quickly occupied much more of the Conference's attention.[20]

This was the problem of "displaced persons." As World War II drew to a close, Americans became aware of a mass of homeless, helpless refugees in the war-torn areas of Europe. Estimates placed their numbers at between 12 and 15 million. Catholic officials claimed that over 50 percent of them were Catholic. They needed relief aid, and they also needed to be resettled, either in Europe or in other countries such as the United States.[21]

However, the United States did not enact a displaced persons program immediately after World War II. Many American legislators feared a postwar recession and were concerned that an influx of European refugees, coupled with returning veterans and an already worsening unemployment situation, would only aggravate the problem. In addition, patriotic societies wanted to limit the number of "hard-to-assimilate" foreigners admitted to the United States and feared that the new stream might include political subversives. As a result of this pressure, the only action taken was a presidential directive of December 1945 that gave war refugees priority under

---

20. "Resolutions Adopted at the 22nd Annual Convention, Cincinnati, Ohio, November 10–13, 1944," *Land and Home* 7 (December 1944): 92; "Summary of Resolutions Adopted at the 23rd Annual Convention, Des Moines, Iowa, October 23–25, 1945," ibid. 8 (December 1945): 93; "Diocesan Activities," ibid. 9 (September 1946): 69; "Farm Placement Service Established," *Rural Life Conference—Feet in the Furrow* 4 (January 1956): 10; "In the Dioceses," ibid. 5 (October 1956): 14; "Farm Listings Carried in Paper," ibid. (November 1956): 8; "We Salute the Diocese of Madison," *Catholic Rural Life* 7 (November 1958): 16–17; "Land Placement Service Really Works," ibid. 8 (September 1959): 17; "Diocesan Directors Reports, 1944–48," NCRLC 1-2; L. G. Ligutti to Diocesan Directors, June 26, 1945, in "Ntn'l Convention, Des Moines, Iowa, Oct. 16–18, 1945," NCRLC 8-5.

21. Yzermans, *The People I Love*, 118; L. G. Ligutti, "No Room for Others," *Land and Home* 8 (June 1945): 32–33; "The Monsignor Says," *Christian Farmer* 2 (October 1948): 1.

the existing immigration quotas but allowed only forty-one thousand war refugees to enter the country by 1948.[22]

The NCRLC deplored this miserly policy. Monsignor Ligutti felt shame for such governmental actions as the shipping of a trainload of Polish refugees from a port on the West Coast to a camp in Mexico: "We, generously, permitted them to see our country from a train window, but our policy is 'no room for others.'" The Conference attacked the economic arguments against accepting displaced persons, claiming that there was room in many sections of the country for experienced farmers and agricultural workers. It was actually the opponents of immigration who were pursuing the uneconomic policy: "These super-ultra-patriotic isolationists prefer to spend $800,000 per day ad infinitum to keep the Displaced Persons behind barbed wire fences." Ligutti believed that "the United States has an obligation commensurate with its resources . . . The United States has room both in the urban and rural field for more people, yes, for many homeless fellow beings." The Conference also denied the rumors that the displaced persons were "lazy" or "the scum of the earth," claiming they were "average human beings, dispossessed, and unfortunate through no fault of their own." They would surely make a worthwhile contribution to the country if allowed in. The Conference also urged that, in accepting immigrants, the United States revise its discriminatory immigration quotas, which tended to favor northern and western European newcomers over those from more Catholic southern and eastern Europe.[23]

Therefore, when Congress began to debate bills to admit displaced persons, the NCRLC threw itself strongly behind them. In 1947, William T. Mulloy, NCRLC president, and Monsignor John O'Grady of the National Conference of Catholic Charities testified in favor of the Stratton Bill, which proposed admitting displaced persons under the unfilled immigration quotas of the war years. When Congress finally passed the Displaced Persons Act in 1948, the Conference took some credit for its adoption. The legislation, as amended in 1950, provided for the admission of four hundred thousand refugees over a four-year period. Thirty percent of the

---

22. Jones, *American Immigration*, 32.
23. Ligutti, "No Room for Others," 33; "Resolutions of the National Catholic Rural Life Conference, Adopted at the Twenty-fourth Annual Convention, October 11–15, 1946, Green Bay, Wisconsin," *Land and Home* 9 (December 1946): 96; "Notes and Comments," ibid. 10 (September 1947): 75; "The Monsignor Says," 1; "Jubilee Convention Is Acclaimed Greatest," ibid. 1 (January 1948): 6; Executive Committee, National Catholic Rural Life Conference, *Statement on Displaced Persons* (Des Moines, Iowa: National Catholic Rural Life Conference, April 16, 1947), copy in "General Publications, 1948–1950," NCRLC 5-2.

newcomers were to be agricultural workers or farmers. The act avoided the old quota system, and the Conference rejoiced that "Catholics need not feel it is unduly discriminatory against them." Overall, the NCRLC was pleased that the "United States has gone officially on record as willing to take some responsibility for resettling those displaced by religious, political or racial persecution." After the Displaced Persons Act expired in June 1952, the Conference supported the Refugee Relief Act, which passed in 1953 and allowed for the admission of 214,000 persons until the end of 1956. It was unsuccessful, however, in its attempt to secure a two-year extension of the act.[24]

The NCRLC immediately made plans to cooperate in the settlement of displaced persons in rural areas both on its own and in cooperation with other Catholic agencies. In 1947, the Conference formed its own committee on the resettlement of displaced persons, and the next year joined with representatives of War Relief Services—NCWC (formed in 1943) and others to establish the National Catholic Resettlement Council, which lobbied for displaced persons legislation and coordinated Catholic efforts for their resettlement in the United States. In the summer of 1948, just after the Displaced Persons Act was enacted, Ligutti joined four other priests on a trip to Europe to study how American Catholics might aid displaced persons. The five visited displaced persons camps and talked to military, religious, and charitable officials in Germany, Austria, and Italy. The group advised Vatican, American Church, and U.S. government aid officials after their journey. They urged that in the settlement of displaced persons, families be kept together, programs be set up both to orientate the displaced persons in American life and to prepare Americans to accept the foreigners, and that special provisions be made for displaced priests, the sick, the aged, and the infirm.[25]

The NCRLC pledged "an all-out effort" to bring displaced persons into Catholic rural communities and to help them adjust. The Conference urged diocesan directors and priests to help coordinate the settlement of refugees in their communities and individual Catholic rural families to

---

24. "Notes and Comments," *Land and Home* 10 (September 1947): 75; W. J. Gibbons, "The Farm on the Potomac," *Christian Farmer* 1 (August 1948): 1; "People," *Feet in the Furrow* 4 (August 1955): 7; "Resolutions on Resettlement of Displaced Persons in Rural Areas, November 4, 1949," in "Ntn'l Convention, Columbus, Ohio, Nov. 4–9, 1949," NCRLC 8-6; Jones, *American Immigration*, 285–86.

25. "Minutes, Committee on Resettlement of Displaced Persons, Feb. 3, 1947," NCRLC 8-5; "Minutes of the Meeting of the Executive Committee of the National Catholic Rural Life Conference, January 8, 9, 1948, Morrison Hotel, Chicago, Illinois," in "Minutes, Exec. Committee Mtg., Chicago, Ill., Jan. 8, 9, 1948," NCRLC 8-6, 1; Yzermans, *The People I Love*, 96–100, 118.

sponsor displaced agricultural laborers or, preferably, whole farm families, in their homes for the necessary period of adjustment. Many of them did so. The Conference periodicals soon began publishing "success stories" about displaced persons who were now happily settled in the homes of Catholic farm families. Some dioceses were particularly successful in settling displaced persons: Paul Sacco, resettlement director in the Davenport, Iowa, diocese, claimed that he resettled 650 immigrants between 1949 and 1955. By 1949, forty thousand displaced persons had been settled in the United States through Catholic auspices, 32 percent of whom were given farm work. In all, Catholic Relief Services (the successor to War Relief Services—NCWC) brought 150,000 displaced persons to the United States after World War II. The number of these helped by NCRLC officials and members must have totaled many thousands.[26]

In addition to helping in the settlement of individuals, the NCRLC became involved in one community resettlement project. In 1955, the National Catholic Resettlement Council and Catholic Relief Services established the York County Farm Produce Company to bring landless farmers from Italy and settle them on abandoned South Carolina farmland. Ligutti was on the consulting board of the company, and the NCRLC acquired twenty-five thousand dollars of its stock through a donation from Chauncey Stillman. The project's director was Paul Sacco, who had made such a success of resettlement of displaced persons in the Davenport diocese. The plan was to eventually settle about seventy-five Italian families on small farms of thirty to forty acres each and to form a new Catholic parish of about five hundred souls in York County. Sacco intended production to center on fresh fruits and vegetables for sale in the immediate area. The first six immigrant families moved onto the York County land in January 1956. The project tried to dispel religious and racial prejudice, introduced new crops on the land, and gave a living to the Italian immigrants. However, despite strenuous fundraising efforts by Sacco and his sponsoring organizations, the York County Farm Produce Company soon ran into financial difficulties. Ligutti visited several times to try to encourage the immigrants, but

26. "Resolutions of the National Catholic Rural Life Conference, Executive Committee Meeting, Jan. 13, 1954, Milwaukee, Wisconsin," supplement to *Feet in the Furrow* 2 (February 1954); "Resolutions on Resettlement of Displaced Persons in Rural Areas, November 4, 1949," in "Ntn'l Convention, Columbus, Ohio, Nov. 4–9, 1949," NCRLC 8-6; "This DP Family Will Have a Merry Christmas," *Christian Farmer* 4 (December 1950): 4, 6, 8; Paul Sacco, "Nine Years in Review," *Feet in the Furrow* 4 (June 1955): 10; Aloysius J. Wycislo, "New Roots for the Homeless," mimeographed copy in "Ntn'l Convention, Columbus, Ohio, Nov. 6–9, 1949, Speeches," NCRLC 8-7, 2, 5; Eileen Egan, "With the World's Castoffs," reprint from *Sign*, November 1972, in "Catholic Relief Services—Post War Relief," LGL-P.

they all moved off the land to take better paying jobs in fabric mills in Charlotte. The NCRLC, entangled in a financial crisis of its own, could not bail out the project, and decided to dispose of it. The land was sold in February 1960, and the Conference and Catholic Relief Services lost most of their investments.[27]

During the 1950s, the NCRLC became involved in securing justice for immigrants in other ways, mainly through the efforts of Ligutti. The monsignor was involved in the formation of the International Catholic Migration Commission (ICMC) in 1951. The commission was founded to help deal with the chaotic worldwide migration situation in the years following World War II. Ligutti brought together the three Catholic officials who formed the organization. Headquartered in Geneva, the ICMC coordinated the work of Catholic and international migration agencies, promoted recognition of the spiritual and material rights of migrants, assisted migrants with social services, counseling, and loans, and held world conferences about every three years. Ligutti undertook a study tour for the ICMC and gave major addresses at two of its conferences.[28]

During the writing of federal legislation for displaced persons, the Conference tried to ensure that no immigrant groups, especially Catholics, were discriminated against. This struggle continued when Congress undertook the task of making a complete revision of American immigration laws. The resulting legislation, the McCarren-Walter Act of 1952, continued the discriminatory quota system that favored northern Europeans over eastern and southern Europeans (which included most of the Catholics). NCRLC representatives Ligutti and William J. Gibbons, S.J., testified against the legislation before the President's Commission on Immigration and Naturalization, calling it "undemocratic and un-Christian" and calling for a law that was both free of prejudice and provided for the reuniting of families. However, the law passed in 1952 over President Truman's veto.[29]

---

27. "Special Report. Rock Hill, South Carolina," *Feet in the Furrow* 4 (August 1955): 10; James L. Vizzard, "People without Land Find Land without People," ibid. 5 (April 1956): 5; Paul Sacco, "Barren Earth Lives Again," *Rural Life Conference* 6 (January 1957): 7–9; "Minutes of the Executive Committee Meeting of the National Catholic Rural Life Conference, Bruce Publishing Company, Milwaukee, Wisconsin, January 14–15, 1958," in "Executive Committee Meeting, Jan. 14–15, 1958, Milwaukee," NCRLC 8-16, 7; "Executive Committee Meeting, Des Moines, Iowa, June 15–16, 1959," NCRLC 8-17, 3; "South Carolina Farm, War Relief Services, 1956," NCRLC 1-9; Tom Cornell, "Monsignor Ligutti's South Carolina Project," *Catholic Rural Life* 36 (November 1986): 22–23.

28. Yzermans, *The People I Love*, 107, 111, 118–28; Yzermans, "NCRLC's Work," 11–13; *New Catholic Encyclopedia*, 1967 ed., s. v. "International Catholic Migration Commission," by J. J. Norris.

29. Yzermans, *The People I Love*, 129–43; "Statement of Rev. William J. Gibbons, S.J., to President's Commission on Immigration and Naturalization, October 1, 1952," in "Statements, Resolu-

Ligutti and the NCRLC did not give up after this defeat, and they continued to work for the abolition of the national origins quota system. In 1952, Ligutti aided in the formation of the American Committee on Italian Immigration, which tried to overturn the law that discriminated against Italian immigrants. Two years later, the NCRLC joined the American Immigration Conference, a nonsectarian group that similarly worked for nondiscriminatory immigration legislation. They were finally successful after many years. In 1965, Congress at last revoked the national origins quota system and replaced it with a single worldwide ceiling on immigration and a limit on the number of immigrants admissible from any single country.[30]

---

tions, Citations, Ntn'l Convention, Saginaw, Mich., Oct. 17–22, 1952," NCRLC 8-10; "We Resolve," *Christian Farmer* 2 (November 1948): 2; Jones, *American Immigration*, 286.

30. Yzermans, *The People I Love*, 143–48; "American Immigration Conference," *Feet in the Furrow* 3 (October 1954): 2; Charles B. Keely, "Current Status of U.S. Immigration and Relief Policy," in *U.S. Immigration and Refugee Policy: Global and Domestic Issues*, ed. Mary M. Kritz (Lexington, Mass.: Lexington Books, 1983), 339–40.

Chapter 9   Helping Developing Countries

Relieving Hunger

The NCRLC's involvement in international rural life started in response to World War II, but the Conference's primary foreign concern soon became developing countries. As Christians looking at the international arena, the Conference saw these countries as being the most in need of charity. The NCRLC helped them deal with the issues of hunger, self-help projects, land reform, and the overall structure of international economics. The Conference's help for developing countries started during the Ligutti years and continued through the end of the twentieth century.

The NCRLC's efforts to relieve hunger in the world started during World War II with aid to the battle-torn countries. In a major statement issued in 1943, the Conference predicted: "The first major task [after the war] will be to rush food to the starving people of war-stricken areas." Once the war was over, it noted that the average European adult consumed only 1,300 calories a day, compared to 4,000 for the average American. As a result, the average European adult weighed 27 to 30 pounds less than before the war. The situation called for the immediate shipment of the large American grain surpluses to Europe. Ligutti wrote: "Europe needs the grain now; USDA [U.S. Department of Agriculture] has it to spare now; USDA must jack up its allocations soon to the new, Truman-approved, 570 million bushel export goal."[1]

The NCRLC joined in a number of postwar relief programs—some of which have continued up to the present. The Conference had constant close relations with War Relief Services—NCWC, which after 1955 was called Catholic Relief Services. Originally, the NCRLC cooperated with

---

1. NCRLC, *Rural Life in a Peaceful World* (Des Moines, Iowa: National Catholic Rural Life Conference, 1944), in "General Publications, 1944–46," NCRLC 5-1, 19; "This Is Your News Letter," *Christian Farmer* 1 (December 1947): 1; Paul A. Sacco, "Europe's Food Needs," ibid. (February 1948): 1–2.

War Relief Services in food programs for Europe and in later years joined in land settlement and hybrid corn projects as well.[2]

In 1945, the NCRLC began to cooperate in the Heifer Project, a program started during the war years by the Church of the Brethren, which shipped live cattle to needy families overseas. The Conference appointed the Reverend H. J. Miller, diocesan director from Fort Wayne, Indiana, director of its participation in the project. He solicited "money, cattle, and sea-going cowboys from among Catholics in all parts of the United States." The program was soon expanded to include other farm animals and food and machinery. City people as well as farmers were urged to contribute money for the purchase of livestock to be sent overseas. One requirement for the receipt of an animal was that its first offspring had to be passed on to another needy family. NCRLC participation grew so much that by 1954 it had two members on the Heifer Project's board. The project also increased the amount of its aid: in 1955, it distributed 895 head of cattle, 231 goats, 150 pigs, 62,550 chicks, and 63,480 hatching eggs. By 1957, the Heifer Project had given about $3 million in aid, about $1 million of it to needy Catholics. In 1960, the NCRLC, still recovering from its financial crisis, dropped its participation in the Heifer Project, but it rejoined in 1970, attracted by the project's ecumenical character and its services to many poor Catholics in developing countries. The Conference continued its representation on the board of the organization renamed Heifer International into the new millennium, by which time it had provided livestock and training to more than 4 million families around the world.[3]

The NCRLC also participated in the Christian Rural Overseas Program (CROP), which was founded in 1948 by the NCRLC (as official representative of NCWC War Relief Services), Church World Services of the Division of Overseas Ministries of the National Council of Churches, and Lutheran World Relief to distribute nutritional food to underdeveloped countries. The Conference, of course, urged its members to contribute to the program, and by 1950, 2,100 priests in sixty dioceses were doing so, with $1 million a year collected through Catholic auspices. CROP was much larger

---

2. Yzermans, *The People I Love*, 128–29.

3. Witte, *Twenty-five Years*, 128–29; "Heifer Project," *Feet in the Furrow* 3 (December 1954): 10; "Heifer Project Reports 1955 Accomplishments," *Rural Life Conference—Feet in the Furrow* 4 (March 1956): 9; "NCRLC Aids Heifer Project," *Rural Life Conference* 6 (January 1957): 14–15; "Heifers, Inc., Sends Living Gifts to Poor of World," *Catholic Rural Life* 20 (March 1971): 1; six folders on Heifer Project, NCRLC 2-7; "Report of the Executive Director, November, 2001," in unprocessed mailings, NCRLC; "NCRLC Board Report, Brother David Andrews, CSC, Executive Director" [October 2006], in ibid., 2; Heifer International Gift Catalog, 2002, in author's possession, 3.

than the Heifer Project; in 1949 alone it distributed over 75 million pounds of food worth almost $6.6 million. However, by 1952, the NCRLC was no longer officially participating in CROP. Catholics were still allowed to contribute to the agency, but the Conference preferred to work in cooperation with its solely Catholic counterpart, Catholic Relief Services.[4]

Another relief project in which the NCRLC participated was the distribution of hybrid seed corn. In 1949, Ligutti noted that use of the hybrid corn allowed American corn production to greatly surpass that of Europe. "Make hybrid-corn possible for Southern Europe," the monsignor urged, "and a great part of the food problem will be solved." Other relief agencies planned to distribute the corn, and Ligutti predicted that it would increase yields from 25 to 150 percent. In 1950, the Conference distributed 350 tons of hybrid seed corn worth $70,000 to 25,000 small farmers mainly in Italy's Po Valley through War Relief Services—NCWC. Ligutti personally presented a sample of the corn to Pius XII in Rome. The next year, the Conference used $50,000 of CROP money to distribute hybrid corn to France, Italy, Spain, Portugal, Germany, and Austria. In 1952, the Conference announced the GROW ("Gifts . . . Returning . . . One World") program, in which it solicited five-dollar contributions to be used to purchase hybrid corn to be sent to a designated family farmer overseas. The first country chosen to benefit from the program was France, and it began to receive the hybrid corn in 1953. The modest program was gratefully accepted by France, but it was not continued beyond that first year.[5]

Ligutti was involved in the administration of CARE (Cooperative for American Remittances to Europe [later, Everywhere]), which was founded in 1945. He was on the CARE board of directors for eleven years (1954–65), where he worked to preserve the organization's cooperative character. He also helped to expedite CARE aid to Italy.[6]

The NCRLC continued to aid various relief programs for the develop-

---

4. Yzermans, *The People I Love*, 70; "We Resolve," *Christian Farmer* 2 (November 1948): 2; "What of C.R.O.P.," ibid. (June 1949): 3; "CROP" ("What's What?"), ibid. (August 1949): 5; "Catholic Dioceses CROP Cooperators," ibid. 3 (September 1950): 8; untitled article, *Feet in the Furrow* 1 (July 1952): 4; Kathlyn Gay, "FOOD—More than a Grocery List to 'CROP Women,'" *Catholic Rural Life* 12 (March 1963): 6; "Minutes of the Meeting of the Executive Committee, Council of Advisors, Past Presidents of the National Catholic Rural Life Conference, 7:30 P.M., November 3, 1949, Neil House, Columbus, Ohio," in "Exec. Committee, Council of Advisors Mtg., Columbus, Ohio, Nov. 3, 1949," NCRLC 8-6, 1–2.

5. "The Monsignor Says," *Christian Farmer* 2 (January 1949): 1-2; "25,000 Italian Farmers to Benefit by Hybrid Seed Corn," ibid. 3 (April 1950): 1; brochure *Gift Returning One World—Friend to Friend* (Des Moines, Iowa: NCRLC, n.d.), in "Publications, G–K," NCRLC 5-6; articles in *Feet in the Furrow*, November 1952 to May 1953.

6. Miller, *Monsignor Ligutti*, 190–94.

Figure 13. Hybrid seed corn donated by NCRLC after World War II aided this German farmer.

ing world from the 1960s into the 2000s. In 1964, 1965, and 1966, the Conference sponsored the "Tools for Freedom" program, in which the NCRLC served as the collection point for new and used farm tools that were donated to farmers in underdeveloped countries. In the first year, 9,328 pounds of tools were collected. Then, in 1970, NCRLC headquarters again served as a collection point for clothing, blankets, shoes, and medicine given for victims of the Peruvian earthquake, a program coordinated by the Iowa Partners of the Alliance Committee. In 1982, NCRLC official John Zeitler worked with World Vision, a nondenominational agency, to coordinate food relief to Poland. The NCRLC urged its members to contribute to the "Harvest of Hope"—the 1 million bushels of grain that were to be sent to Poland. In 1984, the La Crosse diocesan rural life committee initiated "Project Milk," which sent whole dry milk to the hungry poor of Central and South America. The committee, working in cooperation with farmers, consumers, and the government, solicited contributions of time and money and hoped to expand the program nationwide. In 1997, an NCRLC delegation, in a joint project with Catholic Relief Services called Harvest for Hope, gave two hundred metric tons of wheat donated by eastern Washington farmers and advice on terracing, soil conservation, and reforestation to the farmers of Bolivia's Tiraque region.[7]

The NCRLC's participation in post–World War II relief programs naturally drew it into a concern for the chronic problem of world hunger. Again, Ligutti was in the forefront of the Conference's participation in this area. He was very much interested in the United Nations' Food and Agriculture Organization, which was established by an original forty-two member-nations in 1945. The FAO was the fruition of an idea that had originated in the 1930s to coordinate the world's policies on food issues. The organization advised governments on food policies, assisted with technical development in agriculture, tried to promote stable world food prices, and coordinated emergency relief measures. Its headquarters were at first in Washington, D.C., then in 1950 moved to Rome. By the 1970s the organization had three thousand employees—two thousand of them in regional offices and field projects in most of the world's underdeveloped nations. In 1946, Ligutti was appointed Vatican observer to the FAO; in 1949 this ap-

---

7. "Aid to Poor at Home and Abroad," *Catholic Rural Life* 13 (October 1964): 4; "Good Response to NCRLC Appeal for Farm Tools," ibid. 14 (May 1965): 3; "Tools for Latin America," ibid. 15 (November 1966): 1; "Iowa Partners Aid Peruvian Quake Victims," ibid. 19 (October 1970): 1; John Zeitler, "Harvest of Hope," ibid. 32 (November 1982): 17–18; "Seeds of Compassion Yield a Harvest for Hope," ibid. 38 (Fall 1996): 36–38; "Conference News," *Common Ground* 2 (March 1984): 1; "Giving Hope to a World of Need," *Rural Landscapes* 5 (December 1997): inserted pages.

Helping Developing Countries

pointment was made permanent. In concert with his fellow Protestant observer, John Reisner, Ligutti pushed within the FAO for the Conference's main international objectives: uniting "people without land" with "land without people," bringing agricultural officials into cooperation with missionaries, supporting self-help projects, and increasing the levels of food aid and technical assistance for developing nations.[8]

In the years after World War II, the NCRLC gradually articulated its recommendations on the problem of hunger in the world. First and foremost was the principle that the United States, as the greatest agricultural producer in the world, should make available as much of its surplus production as was needed to feed those people anywhere in the world who for whatever reason did not have sufficient food. This postulate was stated most clearly in *A Program for Shared Abundance* (1955), in which the Conference laid down its belief that the United States should share its abundant food resources with the needy both at home and abroad. Ligutti believed that it was a scandal that the United States was hoarding food in warehouses while people were going hungry in foreign countries: "If the USDA is paying one million dollars rent per day for storage of surplus agricultural products [he stated in 1959], why worry about an undernourished world? . . . Just distribute the stuff and save the rent." The Conference received ample support for this simple principle from major statements of Popes John XXIII and Paul VI. In *Pacem in Terris,* Pope John called for emergency food aid to countries in need of it. Pope Paul similarly urged that "the superfluous wealth of rich countries should be placed at the service of poor nations" in *Populorum Progressio*. At the World Food Conference in Rome in 1974, he provided inspiration for the entire world effort to eliminate hunger when he adapted his famous United Nations statement "No more war, war never again!" to "No more hunger, hunger never again!"[9]

As a result of these convictions, the NCRLC threw itself strongly behind programs to distribute food surpluses to needy nations and to better manage that distribution. The Conference expressed repeated support for Public Law 480 (the Food for Peace program), begun by the American gov-

---

8. Yzermans, *The People I Love,* 231–60; "Other Lands," *Land and Home* 10 (December 1947): 99–100.

9. NCRLC, *A Program for Shared Abundance* (Des Moines, Iowa: NCRLC, 1955), copy in "General Publications, 1955," NCRLC 5-2; "Monsignor Ligutti Discusses Increasing World Population," *Catholic Rural Life* 8 (March–April 1959): 27; "'No More Hunger,'" ibid. 24 (January 1975): 4; "'No More Hunger,'" ibid. (February 1975): 6; Edward E. Y. Hales, *Pope John and His Revolution* (Garden City, N.Y.: Doubleday, 1965), 77; Joseph Gremillion, ed., *The Gospel of Peace and Justice: Catholic Social Teaching since Pope John* (Maryknoll, N.Y.: Orbis Books, 1976), 400–404.

ernment in 1954, which distributed agricultural surpluses abroad and often called for increases in the program. It also supported the smaller FAO food distribution program, the World Food Program, started in 1963. Ligutti and his successor as executive director, Monsignor Edward W. O'Rourke, served as advisers to the Food for Peace and World Food Program administrators. When these programs proved unable to deal with some emergencies, the NCRLC backed proposals made at the 1974 World Food Conference for a world food reserve—to include at least a 10 million–ton grain reserve for short-term, emergency famine relief. The Conference applauded Agriculture Secretary Robert Bergland's agreement in the International Food Aid Convention of 1980 to increase the U.S. contribution to the world grain reserve so as to bring the total up to 7.6 million tons. The NCRLC castigated Americans' wasteful tendency to eat large quantities of meat instead of the grains that went to feed the livestock that was slaughtered. The Conference noted that it took a little over one pound of grain to produce one pound of fish, three pounds of grain for one pound of poultry, five pounds for hogs, and seven pounds for beef. Conference officials therefore urged Americans to eat less meat, especially beef, and supported a bishop's call for two meatless days a week to save food for the world's hungry.[10]

The other pillar of the NCRLC's program to alleviate world hunger was technical assistance to aid developing countries in increasing their own food production. As the Conference put it in one statement, the developed countries should not only "share their abundance," but also share "the causes of their abundance with less developed nations." Thus, the NCRLC supported all kinds of programs to provide crop production advice, share technology, promote investment, guide self-help projects, and help self-sufficiency in developing nations. These began with the post–World War II Point IV program of the Truman administration and the United Nations, which gave technical aid and promoted investment in underdeveloped countries. The NCRLC enthusiastically claimed that Point IV would "raise productivity and improve living standards in backward areas," and Ligutti served on the program's committee of advisors. The Conference particularly favored pro-

---

10. NCRLC, *The Farmer and His Government* (Des Moines, Iowa: NCRLC, 1962), copy in "Publications, F," NCRLC 5-6, 2; E. W. O'Rourke, "War on Hunger," *Catholic Rural Life* 12 (August 1963): 2; "Sharing Abundance Takes on New Significance," ibid. (November 1963): 1; "NCRLC Urges Expansion of Food for Peace Program," ibid. 15 (April 1966): 7; Steve Bossi, "Food Reserve Proposals Face Strong Opposition," ibid. 24 (August 1975): 5–6; J. G. Weber, "Meatless Days," ibid. 23 (November 1974): 2; "An Answer to NCRLC's Call?" ibid. 29 (April–May 1980): 5–6; "Committee on Agriculture, Nutrition, and Forestry, United States Senate, Testimony by Most Reverend William Skylstad, Bishop of Spokane, Washington, on U.S. Food and Agriculture Policy and the 1995 Omnibus Farm Bill, August 2, 1995," in "Current Mailings, 1994–," NCRLC.

Figure 14. Monsignor Ligutti as Vatican observer to the United Nations Food and Agriculture Organization.

grams that combined food aid with technical assistance and development projects. Thus, O'Rourke commended the "food-for wage" aspects of Food for Peace and the World Food Program: "We especially approve the use of our food as payment for labor on projects which expand the industrial or agricultural production of these nations." Self-help agencies such as International Voluntary Services could work with the recipients of food aid on these projects to make sure they helped put the people of these developing areas on the road to self-sufficiency. Another program strongly supported by the NCRLC was the FAO's Freedom from Hunger Campaign, begun in 1960, which established foundations for a five-year program of aiding increased agricultural production and other phases of development in developing countries. The Conference urged Catholics to provide local participation and leadership for the campaign. Ligutti in Rome also lent his support to the program. The Conference favored proposals, such as the Humphrey foreign-aid reform bill of 1978, that would integrate all United States food and technical aid under a single agency devoted to relieving poverty and promoting development in the Third World.[11]

11. O'Rourke, "War on Hunger," 2; W. J. Gibbons, "The Farm on the Potomac," *Christian Farmer* 3 (May 1950): 2; Joseph Gremillion, "Sharing Our God-Given Abundance," *Catholic Rural Life* 10 (March 1961): 4–5, 27; L. G. Ligutti, "Freedom from Hunger Campaign," ibid. 11 (June 1962): 8; E. W. O'Rourke, "The Food Explosion," ibid. 12 (March 1963): 2; O'Rourke, "Thanksgiving in Southeast Asia," ibid. 15 (November 1966): 2; O'Rourke, "World Food Program," ibid. 19 (June 1970): 2; Stephen Bossi, "Humphrey Aid Reform Bill Bogged Down in Congress," ibid. 27 (June 1978): 3–5; Miller, *Monsignor Ligutti*, 68–76.

By the 1960s, the NCRLC believed that the continued application of such technical assistance in developing countries held the hope of eliminating world hunger once and for all. The Conference agreed with U.S. Agriculture Secretary Orville Freeman, who said that world food production could double by the year 2000, and Gaston Palewski of France, who maintained that only one-third to one-half of the arable land in the world was being cultivated. As Ligutti succinctly put it: "We are beggars sitting on a chair of gold." And, indeed, by 1970, the Conference joined the rest of the world in rejoicing that the technical aids to agriculture were effecting a veritable "Green Revolution" in many developing countries. Beginning about 1968, the introduction of new strains of rice, wheat, and corn increased production of these commodities two to four times in countries such as the Philippines, India, Iran, Japan, and Mexico. The "Green Revolution" made most of these nations, heretofore large food importing countries, self-sufficient in food, or close to it. O'Rourke thought that this agricultural revolution was particularly promising because "it is occurring in nations which have had serious imbalances between their population growth and food production."[12]

The NCRLC believed that the facts about the assured ability of the world to feed itself made senseless all of the talk of the dangers of a "population explosion." True, the world's population was increasing at an exponential rate, especially in developing countries, but the world's potential for food supplies was more than keeping pace. O'Rourke called all of the excitement over the "population explosion" "a myth." He was worried that the overpopulation panic was increasing the call for artificial birth control both at home and abroad. This was not only morally reprehensible, he believed, but, because of the sufficiency of space and food supplies for an increasing world population, quite unnecessary. He thought that such talk concerning the United States was particularly ridiculous, since the United States had a growth rate of only about 1 percent per year and a relatively low population density. He admitted that some developing nations with rapidly growing populations may need to reduce their population growth, but maintained that "even in these cases, proper care must be taken to employ only morally, medically and culturally acceptable means to limit conception." O'Rourke could draw support for this position from Pope

---

12. "Overflow Crowd of Priests and Seminarians Learns about FAO," *Catholic Rural Life* 9 (March 1960): 21; "World Food Congress Reports Growing Agricultural Potential," ibid. 12 (August 1963): 1; E. W. O'Rourke, "Agricultural Revolution in Asia," ibid. 19 (February 1970): 2; O'Rourke, "The Green Revolution," ibid. (November 1970): 2.

John XXIII, who in *Mater et Magistra* stated that the resources "which God in His goodness and wisdom has implanted in Nature are well-nigh inexhaustible." The way to meet the needs of the world's rising population, the pontiff said, was by using human "intelligence to discover ways and means of exploiting these resources," not by employing contraception.[13]

Despite the sufficiency of food resources compared to population, problems of hunger and malnutrition persisted after the 1970s. It gradually became apparent to the NCRLC that its previous formula of surplus food distribution and technical assistance was not sufficient to alleviate the world food crisis. A multitude of subtle problems prevented the world's abundant food supplies from reaching those most in need. As Ligutti realized, problems of production were now giving way to problems of distribution.[14]

Some of these problems involved the way that food and development aid was given from the United States and other wealthy nations. For example, it often seemed that some food distribution programs such as Food for Peace were being used more as convenient means of disposing of troublesome agricultural surpluses than as humanitarian hunger relief measures. It was charged that surplus American commodities were often "dumped" on underdeveloped nations without regard to those nations' needs. Not only were the commodities often nutritionally inappropriate to the particular countries' requirements, but such food aid also fostered dependence on the United States and contributed to a deterioration of the countries' own food production systems. To avoid such problems, the NCRLC urged that American food aid be given as payment for work on local development projects (the "food-for-wages" program) that would build eventual self-sufficiency in food production in developing countries. The Conference also urged that the Food for Peace program distribute "foods which are not now in surplus but which are the best and most economic means for meeting the nutritional needs of people in developing nations. This will prove that Food for Peace is a truly humanitarian work, not merely a surplus disposal operation."[15]

Another problem with U.S. humanitarian aid to developing countries was that it was often part of an overall foreign-aid package dictated by po-

---

13. Edward W. O'Rourke, *Population and Pollution in the United States* (Des Moines, Iowa: NCRLC, 1970), folder in "General Publications, 1970–76," NCRLC 5-5; Hales, *Pope John*, 79.

14. "Food Output Problems on Verge of Solution, NCRLC Priest Says," *Catholic Rural Life* 9 (December 1960): 15.

15. O'Rourke, "War on Hunger," 2; Jack A. Nelson, *Hunger for Justice: The Politics of Food and Faith* (Maryknoll, N.Y.: Orbis Books, 1980), 20–29.

litical and military priorities, not the food or development needs of the recipients. Thus, rather than going to where it was most needed, American aid went mostly to U.S. allies. The NCRLC castigated this heartless policy of using food as "a strategem of the cold war." Besides calling for an overall increase in developmental assistance as opposed to military aid in the foreign-aid equation, it also advocated separating military from humanitarian aid so that the latter could be given for its own sake, not just in accord with strategic priorities. The Conference praised a bill in 1975 that finally separated military from economic aid. It also supported the Hunger and Global Security Bill of 1981, a no-cost measure drafted in part by Bread for the World, an antihunger Christian citizens' group, which proclaimed that "the primary focus of US foreign policy concerning developing nations is the alleviation of hunger." In the meantime, the NCRLC urged that the food and development programs of private agencies and the FAO's World Food Program be supported because they were able to give help without political strings attached.[16]

The NCRLC eventually came to the conclusion that the global hunger dilemma could not be solved without major structural reforms of the world's food system. In this it was in agreement with such radical theorists as Frances Moore Lappe and Joseph Collins, who wrote their popular book *Food First* in 1977. The Conference came to believe that hunger was the result of "the distribution of power and resources in the food production/distribution system." This kind of thinking had an impact on the American hierarchy: In a statement on the world food situation issued in 1974, the National Conference of Catholic Bishops advocated not only increases in food and technical aid but also redistribution of food resources and limiting the impact of corporations on agriculture. A decade later, in their comprehensive statement *Economic Justice for All*, the bishops said that poverty and hunger in the developing world required "fundamental reform in the international economic order." The key to relieving such hunger, they said, "is the small farmers, most of whom are prevented from participating in the food system by the lack of a market incentive resulting from the poverty of the bulk of the populations and by the lack of access to productive agricultural inputs, especially land, resulting mainly from their own

---

16. James L. Vizzard, "Washington Farm Front," *Catholic Rural Life* 8 (January 1959): 30; J. G. Weber, "Our Foreign Aid Dilemma," ibid. 22 (July 1973): 2; Stephen Bossi, "Foreign Aid Bill Does Not Require Any U.S. Sacrifice," ibid. 24 (December 1975): 10–11; "Bill Would Reform Aid Programs," ibid. 29 (February 1981): 30–31; E. W. O'Rourke to George McGovern (Director, Food for Peace), June 30, 1961, in "Food for Peace, American Council, 1961–1964," NCRLC 2-6; Nelson, *Hunger for Justice*, 20–29.

poverty. In these poor, food-deficit countries, no less than in our own, the small family farm deserves support and protection." They agreed with the NCRLC that food aid should be provided to developing nations in a way that would not harm local food production.[17]

The NCRLC particularly pointed out the deleterious effects of multinational corporations on international rural life. By their control of land, capital, processing, and markets, the wealthy corporations controlled food production and squeezed out the small farmers. Moreover, most of the technical improvements of the "Green Revolution" were employed on the large corporation-owned farms, not on those of small, family farmers. Thus, across the world, the international agricultural corporations were disrupting the age-old farming patterns of traditional nations. Peasant farmers in many of these nations were being forced off their lands by the overwhelming competition of the corporations and were joining the masses of landless, utterly poverty-stricken, socially unstable people that grew so alarmingly starting in the 1970s. The NCRLC also exposed corporations' attempts to promote the use of processed foods and beverages such as Coca-Cola and infant formulas in developing nations. Such efforts aimed only at large profits for the corporations rather than the nutritional needs of the poor nations' populations, the Conference charged.[18]

Self-Help Projects

Self-help projects were one of the ways the NCRLC proposed to rectify the world food production and distribution system and to aid developing countries. The Conference's endorsement of self-help derived from its longstanding interest in cooperatives. But during the post–World War II years, it also grew out of a conviction that charitable aid alone would not be sufficient to rebuild the countries devastated by the war. As early as 1943, the NCRLC, in advocating emergency aid to war-stricken areas, warned that "our nation cannot be expected to be the free bread basket of

17. "Bishops Call for Action on World Food Situation," *Catholic Rural Life* 24 (August 1975): 21–22; Stephen Bossi, "Structural Problems Are the Critical Issue in Solving Hunger Dilemma," ibid. 25 (April 1976): 3–4; "Hunger Myths Attacked in Important New Book [*Food First*]," ibid. 26 (November 1977): 11–12; Sr. Amata Miller, IHM, "Food and Population: An Attainable Balance," ibid. 29 (February 1981): 10; Frances Moore Lappe, "Lessons from a Hungry World," ibid. 34 (November 1984): 21–23; National Conference of Catholic Bishops, *Economic Justice for All: Pastoral Letter on Catholic Social Teaching and the U.S. Economy* (Washington, D.C.: National Conference of Catholic Bishops, 1986), paragraphs 259, 283, and 284. Lappe was the featured speaker at the 1983 NCRLC convention attended by the author.

18. Bossi, "Structural Problems Are the Critical Issue"; Hank Frundt, "Agribusiness Giants Have Worldwide Farm Ventures," *Catholic Rural Life* 26 (November 1977): 7.

the world indefinitely . . . The interests of these nations will be best served if they are put on a self-help basis as quickly as possible." In 1947, Ligutti proposed that rather than giving charity, the United States should make "sound investments" in foreign countries that would eventually "pay back principal and interest." Such investments, not a nationalistic, self-seeking economic policy, would best serve America's long-term interests by helping to make the world economy as a whole strong.[19]

Ligutti also favored self-help because of its effects on the personalities of the recipients. Travels in European countries after World War II made him lament U.S. aid. While in Italy in 1950, Ligutti noted that unemployment and underemployment were high and that

artificial hiring, regulations against firing, and a whole chain of attempts to slow down unemployment [were] evident everywhere . . . The U.S. is blamed for everything or is expected to do everything. It is partially our fault, but chiefly their fault. Our paternalism and their child-like reliance does not build up independence or personality. When a person or a nation begins to place the responsibility and the blame on others, it's just impossible to make progress.

Ligutti claimed that food aid to Spain was creating "a whole group of paupers. We ruin characters when we merely feed stomachs." At that time he urged that food be given "as a reward for work done."[20]

Monsignor Edward W. O'Rourke, NCRLC executive director from 1960 to 1971, was an even stronger advocate of self-help than Ligutti. Like Ligutti, O'Rourke always emphasized self-help projects to aid the poor over handouts: "The food only lasts a day or two and hunger returns . . . The poor need and want an opportunity to earn for themselves. If they had the right kind of training, they would no longer have the humiliating need to accept the offerings of others." For this reason, O'Rourke argued that "self-help is, generally speaking, a much more appropriate manifestation of Christian love for the poor than those relief programs which destroy the respect and self sufficiency of the group we propose to help." Writing on American foreign-aid programs in 1977, O'Rourke maintained that the greatest contribution of the United States to the agriculture of developing countries was not agricultural technology or sophisticated marketing and finance systems but "refining the practices of self-help that a number of American organizations have developed over the past 20 years. Self-help

---

19. NCRLC, *Rural Life in a Peaceful World*, 20; [L. G. Ligutti], "For This We Stand," *Land and Home* 10 (March 1947): 15.

20. "The Monsignor Says," *Christian Farmer* 3 (May 1950): 2; Miller, *Monsignor Ligutti*, 179.

Figure 15. Bishop Edward W. O'Rourke (left) at West Indies self-help project, 1973.

programs improve agricultural production. More important, they restore dignity, self-esteem, and self-determination to people who are dehumanized and alienated." However, O'Rourke favored nongovernmental over governmental aid to self-help projects. He noted that governmental aid could end with a change in policy or the party in power. Nongovernmental agencies—especially such groups as missionaries—were able to provide the continuity necessary for the gradual growth of self-help projects. O'Rourke believed that ten years were often needed to firmly establish a self-help project. The NCRLC's self-help philosophy drew support from papal and Vatican II documents that urged self-help as a means of putting into practice the longstanding Catholic principle of subsidiarity, which held that social action should begin locally.[21]

Ligutti spoke for the NCRLC when he urged that "American Catholic groups should come into contact with small groups in developing countries and help them out." The Conference, especially under O'Rourke's

21. E. W. O'Rourke, "Christmas Baskets," *Catholic Rural Life* 15 (December 1966): 2; O'Rourke, "Self Help and Relief," ibid. 18 (July 1969): 2; O'Rourke, "U.S. Development Effort Should Stress Self-help," ibid. 26 (November 1977): 15–16; O'Rourke, *Self-help Works* (New York: Paulist Press, 1978), 1–16, 108–9; articles in "People to People Program, 1962–64," NCRLC 2-14; Hales, *Pope John*, 77; Gremillion, *Gospel of Peace and Justice*, 176–77, 226–27, 231, 322.

administration, practiced this precept by helping to establish a number of self-help projects in developing countries. Beginning in 1967, O'Rourke made several trips to the West Indian islands of Grenada and Carriacou to help the farmers, craftsmen, and fishermen there become more economically self-sufficient. He helped the islanders form several cooperatives, provided Carriacou a small corn sheller and the island's first tractor, and arranged for NCRLC financing of housing and resettlement projects and NCRLC support of two teachers sent there. A visit of O'Rourke to the Philippines in November 1968 resulted in the establishment of a hog cooperative. O'Rourke and NCRLC executive secretary John George Weber both participated in the Iowa-Yucatan Partners of the Alliance program, which sponsored cooperatives and medical and nutritional services and provided thirty thousand dollars worth of dairy and health equipment to the Mexican state.[22]

The NCRLC provided the impetus behind several larger-scale self-help endeavors. At the Panama international rural life congress in 1955, Ligutti assisted in the formation of the International Caribbean Cooperative Union. This fourteen-nation organization encouraged the formation of cooperatives and credit unions, worked for passage of legislation needed for the organization of cooperatives, and held training programs for cooperative leaders.[23] In 1970, Ligutti served as a papal envoy in presenting a gift of $1 million from Pope Paul VI's *Populorum Progressio* Fund to the Colombian Institute for Agrarian Reform to be distributed to three groups of farmers in the Cauca River Valley in southwestern Colombia. It was to be used for self-help through academic and technical courses, cooperatives, credit unions, and leadership-development institutes. Ligutti, who helped in the administration of the gift, estimated that ten to thirty thousand people would benefit directly from it.[24]

In 1969, the NCRLC joined with a group of private organizations to form Joint Venture Services (JVS), an agency that raised funds for and ad-

22. "World Food Congress Reports Growing Agricultural Potential," *Catholic Rural Life* 12 (August 1963): 1; E. W. O'Rourke, "Canadian Cod in the Caribbean," ibid. 16 (August 1967): 15; "Development Plan Launched in West Indies," ibid. (October 1967): 1; "NCRLC Launches Hog Cooperative in the Philippines," ibid. 18 (January 1969): 3; "1969 Report on NCRLC Achievements," ibid. 19 (February 1970): 4; "Achievements of NCRLC During 1970," ibid. 20 (March 1971): 3; "Ship $30,000 Worth of Equipment," ibid. 21 (February 1972): 3; O'Rourke, *Self-help Works*, chaps. 11 and 12; four folders on "Iowa-Yucatan Partners of the Alliance," NCRLC 2-9.

23. Yzermans, *The People I Love*, 161–62; "Around the World," *Feet in the Furrow* 4 (June 1955): 12; L. G. Ligutti, "Panama Postscript," *Rural Life Conference—Feet in the Furrow* 5 (December 1956): 4–5.

24. Yzermans, *The People I Love*, 170; "Holy See Gives $1 Million to Aid Columbian Peasants," *Catholic Rural Life* 18 (June 1969): 1; "Ligutti Reports Progress in Land Reform," ibid. 19 (December 1970): 1.

vised self-help projects in developing countries. O'Rourke was a trustee on JVS's board, and the Conference appropriated an annual contribution of three thousand dollars to the organization. JVS helped with the NCRLC-sponsored projects in the Caribbean and sent a volunteer to develop a milk plant project in India. O'Rourke resigned from the board of trustees when he became bishop of Peoria in 1971, and Stephen Bossi took the NCRLC's position on the board. JVS ran into financial difficulties and had to recall its volunteer from India in June 1972. The group apparently expired shortly thereafter.[25]

The NCRLC joined CODEL ("Coordination [sometimes "Cooperation"] in Development"), an interdenominational group of thirty-seven mission, relief, and development agencies, which supported self-help efforts in developing countries. The organization was formed in 1969 and was based in New York City. The NCRLC was represented on the CODEL board of directors and made a modest contribution to the organization until at least 1987.[26]

The NCRLC supported several agencies that provided volunteers for self-help projects and other development activities in developing countries. In 1961, the NCRLC seconded the NCWC's appeal to Catholics to join the newly formed Peace Corps. The Conference announced that it would handle applications at its headquarters from candidates with agricultural experience, who it said were "most in demand." The NCRLC urged Catholics to join Papal Volunteers for Latin America (PAVLA), an organization similar to the Peace Corps, but which provided catechists and other religious helpers as well as community and social leaders. "Volunteering for PAVLA or Peace Corps," O'Rourke wrote, "is among the ways to apply the spirit of St. Francis to our times."[27]

The NCRLC had a much closer relationship with the self-help agency International Voluntary Services (IVS), a nongovernmental body founded in 1953 that worked in close cooperation with the Agency for International Development (AID) and other United States and United Nations agencies.

25. Documents in "Joint Venture Services, Working Papers; 1969–71," NCRLC 2-9; "Joint Venture Services, Correspondence; 1969–71," NCRLC 2-10; "Executive Committee Studies Food Stamps, World Trade," *Catholic Rural Life* 18 (August 1969): 3.

26. Stephen Bossi, "How NCRLC's Development Effort Became Worldwide," *Catholic Rural Life* 26 (November 1977): 3–4; brochure *CODEL: Coordination in Development* (n.p.: n.p., 1978), in "Gen. Pubs., 1977, 78," NCRLC 5-5; "CODEL, Coordination in Development, Gen'l Material, 1969–73," NCRLC 2-4; "Organizations That NCRLC Is a Member or Board Member of," April 1987, in untitled folder, Fitzgerald Files, Box 1, NCRLC.

27. "Call for Catholics to Join Peace Corps," *Catholic Rural Life* 10 (September 1961): 2; "St. Francis, PAVLA and the Peace Corps," ibid. (October 1961): 2.

In the 1950s, Ligutti served on the board of directors of IVS, and from 1960 to 1970 O'Rourke held the same position. O'Rourke was the president of IVS from 1965 to 1968. During that time, he made three around-the-world trips, visiting IVS projects in India, Vietnam, Laos, Morocco, and other countries. One of his objectives was to try to coordinate IVS's self-help projects with the food relief programs of such agencies as Catholic Relief Services and Food for Peace, in accord with the NCRLC's philosophy that relief and development should go together.[28]

However, that goal was overshadowed in the later 1960s by IVS's controversial role in Vietnam and Laos. By the late 1960s, the organization had 220 volunteers working in the two countries, in the midst of the communist insurgency. O'Rourke, as IVS president, closely supervised their work during the height of the guerrilla war. Their accomplishments under such adverse circumstances were many. IVS volunteers introduced new strains of rice and initiated other agricultural improvements that greatly increased rice production. IVS teams helped over 1 million Vietnamese and 260,000 Laotian refugees readjust to their new surroundings near urban areas. They guided Vietnamese youth groups engaged in flood relief, village cleanup efforts, and refugee work. As later happened with the armed forces, O'Rourke helped plan the "Vietnamization" of IVS activities. He said that the Vietnamese youth leaders "demanded more of a front-line role in the activities of IVS and urged that eventually we should turn over entirely to them most of our activities. We agreed with them, for it is our purpose to work ourselves out of a job." O'Rourke refused to take a position for or against United States military involvement in Vietnam, stating that he did "not pretend to know the answers to the great political and military problems confronting South Vietnam." However, he affirmed that, whatever the desirability of the American military presence, "before, during and after the fighting in Vietnam, the self-help programs of IVS are indispensable." Despite their efforts to stay out of the politics of the region, the IVS volunteers were considered enemies by the communists in Southeast Asia, and ten were slain between 1966 and 1971. Likewise, Catholic priests were looked upon as foes by the guerrillas, and fifteen out of one hundred in Laos were killed in 1969. The IVS projects in Vietnam did not survive to face the eventual communist takeover in 1975. In 1971, all

---

28. "Msgr. O'Rourke Elected President of IVS Board," *Catholic Rural Life* 13 (July 1964): 1; O'Rourke, "Thanksgiving in Southeast Asia," 2; "Msgr. O'Rourke Tours Vietnam, Laos," ibid. 16 (January 1967): 1; John G. Weber and Edward W. O'Rourke, "Coalitions and Change in the 60's," ibid. 33 (September 1983): 19; O'Rourke, *Self-help Works,* chap. 10.

IVS volunteers were expelled from the country when they disagreed with the U.S. and Vietnamese governments on how the war was being run—with the consequent destruction of the projects and depopulation of the villages where they had worked.[29]

In 2005, the NCRLC started cooperating with the Sustainable Agriculture and Rural Development Initiative (SARD) of the United Nations' Food and Agriculture Organization. This program, which was government financed, grass roots led, and FAO facilitated, supported small farmers in overcoming hunger and poverty. It began operations in 2008.[30]

In all of the self-help projects that it sponsored or supported, the NCRLC was leery of trying to impose too much advanced technology on people used to simple, traditional lifestyles. The NCRLC favored what it called "intermediate technology" or "appropriate technology." This was "technology suited to the needs, education and resources of people at the grass-roots level." It was part of Ligutti's philosophy of putting human dignity above economic efficiency: "Modern technology in industry, commerce, or agriculture functions more efficiently and profitably in the production of goods and services when the human beings involved operate in keeping with their personal dignity, welfare of family, and the common good, and when they share in the ownership of the means of production and in its results." The Conference shared the concern of E. F. Schumacher, author of *Small Is Beautiful* (1973), for developing "technology with a human face." Thus, it looked favorably on such appropriate technologies as solar energy, biological agriculture, waterless toilets, handicrafts, bicycles, and recycling. The NCRLC joined with such groups as the London-based Intermediate Technology Development Group to hold symposiums publicizing the advantages of appropriate technology. It could point to a number of papal statements in favor of suiting technology to the needs of the people. Ligutti believed that the poor should be helped only by means of technology tailored to their particular needs and wishes. He held up as a model the Colombian project aided by Pope Paul VI that featured self-help projects and the participation of the poor in decision making.[31]

29. E. W. O'Rourke, "IVS in Vietnam," *Catholic Rural Life* 15 (April 1966): 2; "Msgr. O'Rourke Tours Vietnam, Laos," 1; E. W. O'Rourke, "Southeast Asia as Seen by Asians," ibid., 2; "Viet Cong Kill IVS Volunteer," ibid. 17 (March 1968): 8; E. W. O'Rourke, "Vietnam Revisited," ibid. 18 (January 1969): 2; O'Rourke, "Laos—Slaughter of the Innocents," ibid. 19 (January 1970): 2; O'Rourke, *Self-help Works*, chap. 10.

30. David Andrews, "Dear Friends of NCRLC," *National Catholic Rural Life Conference Annual Report, Fiscal Year 2005–2006*, 4; Andrews to Board of Directors, October 20, 2005, in unprocessed mailings, NCRLC.

31. Yzermans, *The People I Love*, 297; "Intermediate Technology Symposium Held in Rome,"

The NCRLC was concerned that self-help projects include attention to the religious needs of the people they were helping. For example, in 1954, the NCRLC noted that the one hundred thousand Catholic missionaries working in underdeveloped areas of the world, with their coworkers of other denominations, were willing to help implement FAO and Technical Cooperation Administration (TCA) programs and urged "the administrators of these programs to use more extensively these missionary resources." The Conference claimed that the missionaries' "familiarity with the language and culture of the native populations enable them to contribute most effectively to the projects pursued by FAO and TCA. Moreover, this policy would eliminate any danger of technological reforms being divorced from the dignity and spiritual development of man."[32]

In turn, the Conference urged that missionaries go beyond religion in their services to people in developing countries. While visiting Tanganyika in 1954, Ligutti wrote concerning missionaries:

It is my contention that the steps taken in making Christians ought to be broader than mere religious instruction. I consider as basic: Food production, distribution and marketing, housing, sanitation, health, diet, etc. I believe that a bit too much effort is put on formal education, especially the preparation of white collar workers . . . Certainly in these parts ninety-eight per cent of the people are farmers, so our missionaries are really rural missionaries. And yet our mission training institutes never prepare, even remotely, a missionary to deal with the bread-and-butter and starvation problems of his future flock. Of course, the missionaries have so many things to do, but I wonder why their view is not broadened in this day and age.

Similarly, O'Rourke urged the Church to practice "preevangelism"—"the creating of a necessary condition for the effective preaching of the gospel."[33]

Increasingly, Ligutti's international activity focused on fostering this involvement of missionaries in the social and economic betterment of people in developing countries. Many of Ligutti's travels to foreign countries involved visits to missions to provoke activity in this direction. In

---

Catholic Rural Life 18 (January 1969): 1; Rodolfo Katzenstein, "Monsignor Ligutti Jars Development Experts," ibid. 19 (July 1970): 1; special appropriate technology issue, ibid. 27 (March 1978), especially Stephen Bossi, "Technology Is Challenged by Low-Profile Movement," 5; documents in "Intermediate Technology Symposium, Oct. 11–16, 1968," NCRLC 2-8; Gremillion, *Gospel of Peace and Justice*, 171–72, 176–77, 226–27, 408–9; Hales, *Pope John*, 77–78.

32. "Resolutions of the National Catholic Rural Life Conference, Executive Committee Meeting, Jan. 13, 1954, Milwaukee, Wisconsin," supplement to *Feet in the Furrow* 2 (February 1954).

33. Yzermans, *The People I Love*, 192; O'Rourke, *Self-help Works*, 89.

Helping Developing Countries

1962, Ligutti secured funding from the Ford Foundation for a large-scale study, conducted by the International Federation of Catholic Institutes for Social and Socio-Religious Research (FERES) and the Protestant Institute of Social Studies, on Catholic and Protestant missionary activity in the developing world. The study included case studies of developing countries and information for aiding Christian missionaries "in their work of elevating the human person, teaching agricultural methods, and collaborating with other private and governmental agencies for improving the quality of life in the developing world." In 1968, Ligutti chaired a seminar in Rome of two hundred leaders of missionary societies which, based on the Ford study, examined how missionaries could bring about religious, social, and economic improvement in developing countries.[34]

Meanwhile, Ligutti was hard at work creating an organization devoted to helping Catholic missionaries promote agricultural development, which he called Agrimissio. In 1971, the organization began work at its headquarters in Rome, with the Reverend J. G. Brossard, O.M.I., a Canadian expert on cooperatives, as its first executive secretary. Ligutti was chairman and represented the NCRLC on the board of directors. The next year, Agrimissio established a Center for Social Research Training and Action (CESTA) in Rome to enable missionaries to be brought up to date on trends in agricultural and rural development. A few years later, Agrimissio began a program called SEDOS, a "development planning and consultation service," which funded a rural development expert who aided missionaries in such places as Ghana, South Africa, and the Philippines. The NCRLC provided some aid to Agrimissio. In 1970, the Conference created a corporation called the International Catholic Rural Life Conference to pursue the Conference's programs overseas and to help support Agrimissio. The next year, the Conference board voted to divide its International Fund, 80 percent going to Agrimissio, and 20 percent "to NCRLC International work for the purpose of helping underprivileged people help themselves."[35]

During the early 1980s, communication between the NCRLC and Agrimissio broke down, although the Conference continued to send its 80 percent contribution each year. Under the leadership of Sister Millicent

---

34. Yzermans, *The People I Love,* 167–69, 205; "Missionaries Study Development," *Catholic Rural Life* 17 (May 1968): 3.

35. Yzermans, *The People I Love,* 289–91; "Agrimissio Links FAO, Church, and Missionaries," *Catholic Rural Life* 26 (January 1977): 21–22; "Bishop Speltz Elected NCRLC President," ibid. 20 (January 1971): 3; Stephen Bossi, "International Activities of NCRLC," in "2nd Ntn'l Consultation of Rural Life Directors, Erlanger, Kentucky: 1977," NCRLC 8-25; "Resolution Adopted by NCRLC Board—June 22, 1971," in "Executive Committee Meeting, Colfax, Iowa, June 22–23, 1971," NCRLC 8-23.

Francis, R.S.C.J., Agrimissio published a bimonthly bulletin in English, French, and Spanish, providing practical instruction on basic processes in agriculture and developed a program providing small grants averaging five thousand dollars each to subsistence farmers for such things as hand tools, trees to plant, and training. In 1985–89, sixty grants went to nineteen countries in Africa, Asia, and South America. But by the end of the decade, the NCRLC was dissatisfied with the apportionment of the International Fund and began negotiations with Agrimissio to revise the relationship. Reluctantly, Sister Francis agreed to a severance of the relationship with the NCRLC and a fifty-fifty division of the principal of the International Fund between the two organizations. Agrimissio soon combined with the International Catholic Rural Association and limped along through the end of the millennium.[36]

Land Reform

Land reform was another important remedy that the NCRLC proposed to solve the world's agricultural problems. At first, the Conference thought principally in terms of bringing more land into cultivation or using it more efficiently to increase world food production. Ligutti, in his world travels in the 1940s and 1950s, repeatedly claimed that plenty of land was available for settlement and that its cultivation would cure the world's food problems. For example, on visiting Australia in 1947, he stated his conviction that the interior of Queensland could be colonized: "I believe there is plenty of good land for all Australians and many, many more, provided they are willing to work. The world is not too small—it's we men who are too small!" Similarly, the monsignor thought that land settlement in countries as widely scattered as Nyasaland, Turkey, Iran, and Brazil had great potential. He also believed that land already being cultivated could be much more efficiently utilized. Even the Japanese, who supported 6 million farm families on 13 million acres of cultivated land, were no exception: "I have said very often that no human being has yet gotten out of one acre of soil all that God has put into it. The Japanese are coming closer to it than anyone I have seen." Ligutti and the Conference proposed that all kinds of means, including irrigation, conservation, reclamation, and bet-

---

36. Millicent Francis to Joseph Fitzgerald, November 14, 1989, in "Official Files," "Files of Executive Director," Box 1, NCRLC; "National Catholic Rural Life Conference Board of Directors Meeting, Atchison, Kansas, June 9–10, 1995, Minutes," in "Current Mailings, 94–," NCRLC, 4; file "Agrimissio," Cusack Subject File, Box 16, NCRLC; Fitzgerald to NCRLC Board of Directors, December 11, 1992, in Fitzgerald Files, Box 1, NCRLC.

ter machinery, seeds, and fertilizers, in addition to disease and insect control, should be used to increase agricultural efficiency.[37]

One of the devices Ligutti proposed to unite "people without land" with "land without people" was called "agricultural concessions." Under this plan, a land-rich country would lease unused land to farmers from a land-poor country, who would send the produce to their country of origin to help relieve hunger there. Ligutti believed that the FAO could develop such a system "without undue complication or interference with national sovereignties, citizenship, etc." He stated: "By keeping separate the two elements we are not only going counter to God's evident purposes in creation, but we are causing human suffering." As an application of the "agricultural concessions" idea, the Conference publicized a proposal whereby Japan would lease land for landless workers in the United States and other countries.[38]

But this plan was not as practical as land reform implemented within each country. The encouragement of such land reform was a major theme of the international rural life congresses convened by Ligutti in the 1950s and 1960s. The congresses repeatedly urged that nations move in the direction of creating more medium-sized family farms. Ligutti regretted the presence in many developing countries of both large *latifundia* and the proliferation of many tiny *"minifundia."* "The one," he said, "creates a miserable proletariat, the other an inefficient land use." The meetings usually hesitated to call for forced expropriation of large estates and redistribution to family farmers. In cases where "partial expropriation" was justified, "just compensation is to be given to former owners. As a rule, there should be no total expropriation of large landholdings." The NCRLC totally rejected "collectivization of farms, . . . since it deprives [farmers] of property and reduces them to the status of landless farm workers, subject to the dictates of economic and political functionaries of an all-powerful state." However, Ligutti also castigated die-hard conservatives on the issue of land reform as "rightists who don't have much right in these days of revolution . . . By the unreasoning stupidity of their claims in favor of large land holdings they are actually paving the way for their own complete destruction." In 1944, he supported the land division law of Mexi-

37. Yzermans, *The People I Love*, 95, 152, 181, 182, 193, 199; "Exhuming Malthus," *Christian Farmer* 3 (December 1949): 3; NCRLC, *The Land: God's Gift to Man* (Des Moines, Iowa: NCRLC, 1952), copy in "General Publications, 1951–1954," NCRLC 5-2.
38. L. G. Ligutti, "Address to Plenary Session of FAO," *Rural Life Conference—Feet in the Furrow* 4 (January 1956): 9; William A. Kaschmitter, M.M., "19,000 Hungry in Japan—A Solution," ibid. (December 1955): 8–9; NCRLC, *Program for Shared Abundance*.

co's leftist government, calling it "plain Christian doctrine." Ligutti, the NCRLC, and the rural life congresses agreed that there was a "compelling necessity for some change" in the "agrarian structures" of Latin America. Ligutti believed that, through education and in conjunction with their traditionally strong religious faith, Latin Americans could develop a thriving system of individually owned farms, despite centuries of experience to the contrary. Changing times seemed to support his optimism. In a 1970 South American regional meeting of the FAO in Caracas, Ligutti reported that almost all of the delegates in attendance from twenty-five countries favored land reform, whereas most opposed it at the Latin American rural life congresses in the 1950s.[39]

Most of the time, Catholics called for limited forms of land redistribution. The second Vatican council, in a passage influenced by Ligutti, stated that "insufficiently cultivated estates should be distributed to those who can make these lands fruitful." The 1955 Panama congress called for Latin American countries to distribute nationally held land—which in many of these countries was extensive—to agricultural workers. Finally, Ligutti called on the Church to distribute its own land: "What a magnificent public relations impression would be made in Latin America if the Church would pull out from ownership of land at the present time. Some of it would be donated outright to settlers, the rest sold before confiscation and the receipts invested in anonymous stocks and bonds." The plea had some results: in 1962, the bishops of Chile offered to turn over for resettlement purposes the farmland owned by the Church. Ligutti quoted a bishop at the Manizales congress as warning: "The land reform will come with us, without us or against us."[40]

The need for land reform was one of the most important common denominators in the social unrest in developing countries in the twentieth century. The NCRLC, because of its rural perspective, tended to recognize and call attention to the issue earlier than most groups in the United States. As the United States tried to prevent communist takeovers in de-

---

39. Yzermans, *The People I Love*, 109, 152, 164–65, 197–98; NCRLC, *The Land: God's Gift to Man*, 16–17; L. G. Ligutti, "'Communism' Goes to Mass," *Land and Home* 7 (June 1944): 32; *Man and the Land: The Santiago Charter on Rural Life* (Des Moines, Iowa: NCRLC, 1957), in "General Publications, 1957," NCRLC 5-4, 7; "Ligutti Reports Progress in Land Reform," *Catholic Rural Life* 19 (December 1970): 1.

40. Yzermans, *The People I Love*, 165; Gremillion, *Gospel of Peace and Justice*, 307; L. G. Ligutti, "Sub Umbra Petra, Under the Shadow of Peter," *Catholic Rural Life* 11 (October 1962): 8; *Conclusiones de Panama, English Text* (Des Moines, Iowa: National Catholic Rural Life Conference, 1955), copy in "General Publications, 1955," NCRLC 5-2, 5-7.

Helping Developing Countries

veloping countries during the cold war, the NCRLC saw the part agrarian problems played in this unrest. "From Russia to China," Ligutti declared in 1955, "Communism has ridden to power on the shoulders of a dissatisfied peasantry." The Conference recognized that "the Communist lie, based on the promise of land and material, has a fatal appeal to the landless and dispossessed population of Portuguese and Spanish America." The Latin American rural life congresses convened by Ligutti called for the Church to join in land reform in Latin America in order to preempt communism. The congresses proposed Christian solutions to the problems of the poor in Latin America as alternatives to communism. Sometimes the unrest was very apparent to the congress participants: During the 1957 congress in Santiago, Chile, citizens rioted in the streets and martial law was declared. The Catholics pointed to the communist near-successes in Guatemala and British Guiana in the mid-1950s and the communist takeover in Cuba in 1959 as examples to be avoided.[41]

The solution involved the Latin American governments themselves initiating NCRLC-supported programs of reform including land reform and self-help projects. To prevent communist success, the "leaders, men of means, of influence, of position in their nation and community" must put themselves behind the reforms, the NCRLC maintained. It believed that "the mentality, the attitude, the social philosophy of the 'Elite group' have to be changed. They must lead in the social evolution taking place or they will be led to a very unpleasant and perhaps tragic end." The Catholic Church must be among these leaders of reform, Ligutti held: "The world is moving at a terrific rate. Christianity cannot lag behind. It must be dynamic, it cannot become fossilized. Bureaucracy must not be stabilized and consecrated. Christianity has the answer, but not the Christianity of word without deed, of form without substance." Such thinking was a precursor of the Latin American "liberation theology" of the 1970s and 1980s.[42]

Yet Ligutti and the NCRLC could also be rather conservative in their thinking on developing countries when the threat of communism was present. For example, Ligutti wrote the following during his 1956 Asian trip:

---

41. Yzermans, *The People I Love*, 163, 197; "World Leaders to Discuss Red Threat in Latin America," *Rural Life Conference* 6 (March 1957): 3; L. G. Ligutti, "Congress Held amid Chilean Strife," ibid. (May 1957): 4, 14; Ligutti, "Sub Umbra Petri, Under the Shadow of Peter," *Catholic Rural Life* 11 (October 1962): 8; Mariano Rosell y Arellano, Archbishop of Guatemala, *The Tactics and Works of Communism* (Des Moines, Iowa: NCRLC, 1956), in "General Publications, 1956," NCRLC 5-3.

42. Yzermans, *The People I Love*, 163–64; L. G. Ligutti, "Sub Umbra Petri, Under the Shadow of Peter," *Catholic Rural Life* 10 (October 1961): 23.

When visiting such places as New Guinea, the age-old question of colonialism comes to the fore. Is political independence possible or advisable for any and all colonies? What are the economic and social prerequisites? To my way of judging some strong ties with a real "mother" country are necessary. Also a considerable amount of regional unity is a must. A place like New Guinea is completely unready for any sort of self-rule. If the West abandons such spots either internal exploiters take over or Communist imperialism sweeps in.[43]

The Conference also appeared on the conservative side of developing world politics when the welfare of the Church was concerned. In the case of Mexico, several NCRLC-related clergymen opposed reforms (including land reform) in the 1920s, 1930s, and 1940s because they were implemented by anticlericals who persecuted the Catholic Church. Among these reform opponents were NCRLC executive secretary O'Hara, rural mission leader Bishop Francis C. Kelley, and NCRLC president Bishop Joseph H. Schlarman. In the 1940s, under the leadership of Schlarman and Ligutti, the NCRLC took steps to assist in alleviating both the religious and the rural problems of Mexico. The Conference helped sponsor rural courses at a seminary set up by the American hierarchy at Montezuma, New Mexico, for Mexican candidates for the priesthood who were prevented from studying in their own country. The NCRLC also arranged for farmer-training programs for Mexicans and for hybrid corn and fertilizer aid for Mexico.[44]

Despite the anticommunist quality of many of the NCRLC's activities, anticommunism was never the primary motivator of the Conference's international work. NCRLC leaders such as Ligutti and O'Rourke noted that the Conference was opposed to communism but that its principal emphasis was on improving living conditions in developing countries. Ligutti noted that American and Catholic charity to foreign countries was important in "stemming the advance of Communism" but added: "Even if Communism were to disappear tomorrow, we should do the same things and more. As stewards of God's abundance we must make available to others what we ourselves enjoy." O'Rourke said that the best way to oppose communism was not through a "reactionary" embrace of economic

---

43. Yzermans, *The People I Love*, 200.

44. Edwin V. O'Hara, *Letters from Mexico* (n.p.: n.p., 1928), copy in OH10; Francis Clement Kelley, *Blood-Drenched Altars* (Milwaukee: Bruce Publishing, 1935); Joseph H. Schlarman, *Mexico—A Land of Volcanoes* (Milwaukee: Bruce Publishing, 1950); Schlarman, "Presidential Address," in *Catholic Rural Life Objectives*, 1944, 69–70; "Conference Affairs," *Land and Home* 7 (June 1944): 55; L. G. Ligutti, "What the National Catholic Rural Life Conference Has Done in the Rural Field in Brazil and Mexico," in "Brazil and Mexico, NCRLC Activities There, n.d.," NCRLC 1-1.

individualism, but by encouraging family farms, cooperatives, unions, and government aid in social justice. A 1951 executive committee statement on "Communism—Methods of Combatting" urged emphasis on improving "the conditions of spiritual and material welfare" in countries threatened by communism, not military measures. The NCRLC was sometimes contacted by anticommunist individuals and organizations who wished to cooperate in various explicitly anticommunist programs, but the Conference always declined. It has been alleged (based on anecdotal evidence), that the CIA channeled money through a Philadelphia businessman to fund the Latin American rural life congresses.[45]

NCRLC officials like Ligutti recognized the intense anti-Americanism present in many developing countries, especially in Latin America. While visiting Singapore, Ligutti wrote: "United States capitalism in the minds of most people in these parts is really and truly a veritable devil . . . We are accused of everything under the sun. We are crooks, we are mistrusted, we want to subjugate people, to conquer them, make them pay through the nose." He believed that the often bitter "anti-Yankeeism" of Latin Americans was due to the folly of trying to make them think and act like North Americans:

No matter what we North Americans think or judge; no matter how other people may be wrong; the fact is, they are what they are. They think the way they think and we can't kid ourselves into believing they are going to accept us, our ways, our views, just because we have dollars. If we have failed in Latin America, it is chiefly because we have failed to interpret our aims, purposes, and even our U.S. existence to the Latin Americans.

Ligutti, in the words of his biographer, "became a crusader in both Church and State circles, pointing out the folly of ecclesiastical and governmental policies that fostered rather than diminished this bitterness of United States neo-imperialism." In 1961, Ligutti proposed that a "clinical examination, thoroughly objective and completely scientific," be made of the phenomenon of "anti-Yankeeism" in Latin America. His proposal formed the basis of a major study of that topic by FERES that was funded by the Homeland Foundation. The forty-two-volume report greatly helped gov-

---

45. L. G. Ligutti, "Attack on Hunger," *Rural Life Conference* 6 (June 1957): 10–11, 13; E. W. O'Rourke, "Farmer Fighting Communism," in "Communism and Agriculture, Articles; 1961–2," NCRLC 2-3; Executive Committee statement in "Communism—Methods of Combatting," NCRLC 8A-1; correspondence with Anthony J. Major, in "M Correspondence, 1954," NCRLC 13-3; Penny Lernoux, *Cry of the People: United States Involvement in the Rise of Fascism, Torture, and Murder and the Persecution of the Catholic Church in Latin America* (Garden City, N.Y.: Doubleday, 1980), 292.

ernments and religious groups to understand conditions in Latin American countries.[46]

After the Vietnam War, NCRLC leaders, like many other Americans, began to doubt the wisdom of U.S. interventions in the internal affairs of developing countries. Conference officials like O'Rourke believed American intervention in Southeast Asia had been "tragically unsuccessful" and had led to a "slaughter of the innocents" among the peaceful rural population of the region. At that time, O'Rourke urged the use of United Nations peacekeeping forces as an alternative to "unilateral" interventions by the great powers. He believed that both the United States and the Soviet Union might favor such an option and proposed a modification of the United Nations charter if necessary to make peacekeeping forces feasible.[47]

In the 1980s, the Conference denied the Reagan administration's reasoning that the revolutionary unrest in Central America was due to outside agitation by communists from Cuba or the USSR. Instead, it supported the United States Catholic Conference statement on Central America, which maintained that the main problems in the region were "the internal conditions of poverty and the denial of basic human rights which characterize many of these societies." The Conference particularly emphasized injustice on the land as the root of the difficulties in Central America. NCRLC officials Leonard Kayser and John Zeitler made trips to Nicaragua and other Central American countries in 1982 and 1983. They reported favorably on the revolution in Nicaragua that overthrew dictator Anastasio Somoza in 1979, especially on the new Sandinista government's land reform program which redistributed much of the land in small holdings to the *campesinos*. They did not seem to be very concerned about the growing tenseness of the Sandinistas' relationship with the Catholic Church. The NCRLC board passed a motion "that the NCRLC oppose extension of military aid to El Salvador until a genuine land reform program is reinstituted" and sent letters to the Senate Foreign Relations Committee endorsing its vote freezing aid until land reform was reinstituted. Many years later, in 1997, the NCRLC favored congressional legislation that would prevent tens of thousands of Central American war refugees from being deported from the United States.[48]

46. Yzermans, *The People I Love*, 149–50, 167, 202.
47. E. W. O'Rourke, "Open Door to Revolution, Communism," *Globe* [Sioux City, Iowa?], March 5, 1970, clipping in "Farm Page, from the Register, 1968–1971," NCRLC 2-5; O'Rourke, "Laos—Slaughter of the Innocents."
48. Sandra La Blanc, "Central America," *Catholic Rural Life* 32 (May 1982): 3; Leonard Kayser, "Central America: Is Its Present Our Future?" ibid. 33 (February 1983): 8–10; John Zeitler, "From Fr.

Helping Developing Countries 219

The Conference allowed two opponents of the Ferdinand Marcos government of the Philippines to address the 1983 NCRLC consultation in Des Moines, although no official statement supporting them was made. After the revolution led by Corazon Aquino overthrew Marcos in 1986, the Conference published a series of special reports that sympathized with land reform for Filipino peasants.[49]

The NCRLC gave only lukewarm support to the "liberation theology" that underlay much of the revolutionary agitation in the developing world. Executive director Gregory Cusack warned that "liberation theology . . . can be a slippery term." He said that the NCRLC opposed violence, but that

> not all liberation theology advocates violence, nor draws easy political lines between the United States and other countries.
>
> When I read liberation theology, I try to recognize that it is a voice of a people long oppressed . . .
>
> It is the nuggets of truth in that "voice of the oppressed" that I think has much to teach those of us who live in a land of "winners" . . . I think it is very important, however, not to read off entirely such a theological approach because of the violence embraced by some of its advocates.[50]

The Structure of the World Economy

The NCRLC favored modifications of the world economy that would aid developing nations and help make wars and revolutions in those areas unnecessary. In the years immediately following World War II, the Conference called for lifting protectionist restrictions to ensure "a reasonably free flow of agricultural products in international trade." It believed that such a free trade policy would benefit both American farmers, who would be able to sell more of their surpluses abroad, and developing countries, most of which "rely upon the export of agricultural products as a source of capital with which to improve their standard of living and to strengthen their economies." By the 1970s, however, the NCRLC began to doubt the wisdom of a totally free trade policy. Taking its lead from Pope Paul's encyclical *Populorum Progressio* (1967), the Conference noted that wealthy nations

---

John's Desk," *Common Ground* 2 (July 1983): 3; "Minutes, NCRLC Board of Directors, May 26–28, 1982," in Cusack Subject File, Box 19, NCRLC, 7; "A Bird's Eye View," *Rural Landscapes* 5 (October 1997): 2, 4.

49. Author's observations at 1983 NCRLC consultation; Ken Meter, "Behind the Revolution. A Quest for the Land," *Catholic Rural Life* 36 (April 1986): 4–25; Meter, "Filipino Farmworkers Initiate Their Own Land Reform," ibid. 37 (February 1987): 32, 31; Meter, "Filipinos Struggle over Land Reform Policy," ibid. (April 1987): 12–15.

50. Gregory Cusack to Jerome V. Bambenek, June 16, 1983, in "Correspondence 1983," La Blanc Subject File, Box 3, NCRLC.

tended to benefit from free trade at the expense of developing nations. Their greater resources allowed their large corporations to dominate certain markets. To alleviate this situation, the NCRLC called for the United States to give trade preferences to some developing nations to help their new industries. The Conference supported implementation of the United Nations Declarations on a New International Economic Order (NIEO), adopted in 1974 and 1975, which proposed reform of trade policy, international monetary policy, development assistance, multinational corporation influence, agricultural development, food reserves, industrial investment, research and technology, and the United Nations structure.[51]

By the turn of the millennium, the NCRLC was concerned about the increasing economic integration of the world by trade and technology—the phenomenon known as "globalization." It quoted Pope John Paul II: "The church in America is called . . . to cooperate with every legitimate means in reducing the negative effects of globalization, such as the domination of the powerful over the weak, especially in the economic sphere, and the loss of the values of local cultures in favor of a misconstrued homogenization." NCRLC officials David Andrews and Robert Gronski predicted that the United States–China trade agreement of 1999 would help multinational corporations but would hurt American farmers by giving them lower prices and would hurt Chinese farmers by eventually forcing 10 million of them off the land.[52]

The Conference criticized the World Trade Organization (WTO) for favoring large corporations. Gronski noted that when, for example, four large agribusiness corporations controlled over 80 percent of the world cereals trade, the WTO's "free trade" language was misleading. Globalization's search for a "level playing field" in trade hurt the half of the world that was poor. Rich countries like the United States and the European Union could subsidize their farmers and dominate poor countries' farmers in a free trade environment. Therefore, special preferences should be given to poor nations, Gronski said. The NCRLC supported the call for "food sovereignty," a term coined at the World Food Summit +5 at Rome

---

51. "Resolutions of the National Catholic Rural Life Conference Adopted at the Twenty-fourth Annual Convention, October 11–15, 1946, Green Bay, Wisconsin," *Land and Home* 9 (December 1946): 96; E. W. O'Rourke, "Washington Farm Front," *Catholic Rural Life* 20 (June 1971): 8; Stephen E. Bossi, "NIEO: International Issue with Justice Implications," ibid. 27 (December 1978): 6–8; NCRLC, *World Trade, Farm Income and the Future of Developing Nations* (Des Moines, Iowa: NCRLC, 1969), copy in "General Publications, 1963–69," NCRLC 5-5.

52. David Andrews, "Globalization, Rural Life, and the WTO," *Catholic Rural Life* 42 (Spring 2000): 34–37; "U.S.–China Trade Deal May Not Help Farmers," *Catholic Messenger*, December 2, 1999, copy in "Current Mailings, 94–," NCRLC.

in 2002 to refer to developing countries' desire to resist control by the forces of globalization in agricultural matters.[53]

Gronski and Andrews attended the 1999 Seattle WTO meeting that was marked by violent protests, and they generally agreed with the protesters that the WTO needed to be broadened to include "civil society" organizations that were more favorable to non–large corporate interests and the environment. The two were also at the 2003 Cancun WTO meeting, which Andrews called a "mixed blessing" when it ended without an agreement, because the United States and the European Union had proposed eliminating their agricultural subsidies but in return for greater access to markets in Third World countries. When the pair attended the 2005 WTO meeting in Hong Kong, the poor countries at least had a voice, with the NCRLC being among the accredited nongovernmental organizations at the gathering.[54]

In 2002, the NCRLC, along with the Center for Concern, formed the Agribusiness Accountability Initiative (AAI), a global forum that documented the degree of corporate influence in the international food system. It investigated developments such as the "revolving door" appointments of food industry executives in government regulatory positions affecting agriculture. Starting in 2006, the AAI was headquartered at the NCRLC, when Judith Pojda was appointed coordinator. Under Pojda, the AAI developed a network of regional steering committees for each of the five major continents of North America, South America, Asia, Europe, and Africa.[55]

The NCRLC came out against food-rich nations using their food as an economic "weapon" against food-poor nations. In a major statement in 1980, the rural midwestern bishops stated: "We forcefully affirm the principle that food should never be used as a weapon against any nation or people as a tool of oppression to starve them into submission." In light of the U.S. surpluses and the Conference's principle against "withhold-

53. Robert Gronski, "The Aftermath of World Summits," *Rural Landscapes* 10 (December 2002): 3, 6; Gronski, "Agriculture, Trade and the Common Good," ibid. 11 (December 2003): 3–4; "The Rising Call to Food Sovereignty," ibid. (May 2004): 6.

54. Robert Gronski, "World Trade and Civil Society," *Rural Landscapes* 7 (January 2000): 3, 6; "On the Road," *Catholic Rural Life* (newsletter) 13 (December 2005): 5; Shirley Ragsdale, "All Small Farmers Want Trade Access," Des Moines *Register*, September 20, 2003, clipping in unprocessed mailings, NCRLC.

55. Peter O'Driscoll, "Agribusiness Accountability Initiative Growing," *Rural Landscapes* 11 (March 2004): 1; "AAI Secretariat to NCRLC," *Catholic Rural Life* (newsletter) 13 (July 2006): 1; "National Catholic Rural Life Conference, Semi-Annual Board Report, November 2006, Judith Pojda, Agribusiness Accountability Initiative Coordinator," in unprocessed mailings, NCRLC.

ing food from hungry people regardless of the nation in which they live," the Conference in 1963 sent a resolution to President Kennedy urging the United States to consider "selling wheat to Russia's satellites and perhaps even to Russia herself." Similarly, during President Carter's Soviet grain embargo of 1980, NCRLC president Bishop Lawrence McNamara urged Carter to set up a task force to study the moral effects of grain embargoes on both U.S. farmers and the recipients of the grain.[56]

The problem of huge debts owed by developing countries drew the NCRLC's attention. To get a better balance of payments and repay the debts, farmers in these countries tried to grow more for export with less imported fertilizer, Conference board member Leonard Weber noted. He said that International Monetary Fund (IMF) guidelines forced developing countries to devalue their currencies and cut back public spending, resulting in higher prices for necessities such as food, medicine, and clothing for the poor. He criticized the George H. W. Bush administration for urging banks to forgive a portion of the debts while encouraging "reforms" similar to the counterproductive IMF policies. The Conference noted that the American hierarchy and Pope John Paul II urged scaling down or even a moratorium on these debt payments as the Jubilee year of 2000 approached.[57]

As the new century neared, the NCRLC became convinced that as the rest of the world modernized, its farmers confronted problems similar to those of American farmers. European farmers experienced the most similarities, including the industrialization of agriculture, environmental degradation, and young people wanting to leave the farms for the cities. In postcommunist Poland, for example, Smithfield Foods, the world's largest pork processor, acquired a major interest in Poland's biggest packing company. Small farms and the environment were suffering in Latin America. The Conference worried that China's impending membership in the World Trade Organization would result in the uprooting of 10 million farmers. Even in the African Sahel, nomadic animal herders were forced to sell off their herds and become employees, similar to many American livestock farmers.[58]

---

56. *Strangers and Guests: Toward Community in the Heartland* (Sioux Falls, S.D.: Heartland Project, 1980), in NCRLC, Gen. Pubs., 1979–, NCRLC 5-5, 24; "Sell Wheat to Russia?" *Catholic Rural Life* 12 (November 1963): 1; "Carter Urged to Look into Embargo Morality Question," ibid. 29 (January 1980): 12; whole issue on "Food as a Weapon," ibid. 33 (July 1983).

57. Leonard Weber, "Third World Debt and Justice," *Earth Matters* 38 (Summer 1989): 30; National Conference of Catholic Bishops, *Economic Justice for All,* paragraphs 273–77; Dan Misleh, "Catholics Weave the Web of Life at Home and Abroad," *Catholic Rural Life* 40 (Spring 1998): 40.

58. Filippo Cortesi, "Identity and Universality," *Catholic Rural Life* 35 (July 1985): 19; Patrick G.

Helping Developing Countries   223

In response, the Conference began to reemphasize international rural life around the turn of the millennium, after a long period of relative disinterest that started with the departure of Ligutti as international affairs director in the 1970s. As already mentioned, the Conference gave increasing attention to problems such as globalization. Under the leadership of executive director David Andrews, the NCRLC revived its old cooperation with agencies such as the Heifer Project and ICRA. It also engaged in some new projects. Andrews participated in a study tour of Belize with the Protestant organization Agricultural Missions, and the Conference considered collaboration with Catholic Relief Services on a study of the North American Free Trade Agreement's impact on Mexican and American small farmers. Conference officials also attended meetings in Rome of the Pontifical Council for Justice and Peace and the United Nations Food and Agriculture Organization's World Food Summit. In a more globalized world, the NCRLC was rediscovering the connection between the planet's largest economy and international rural life.[59]

Coy, "Russian Rural Life Facing a New Freedom," ibid. 37 (February 1988): 4–7; "Rural Life Connected throughout the World," *Rural Landscapes* 5 (December 1997): 1; "Polish Officials Visit Mid-Atlantic Region, Midwest . . . ," ibid. 7 (October 1999): 4; "U. S.–China Trade Deal May Not Help Farmers," *Catholic Messenger*, December 2, 1999, copy in "Current Mailings, 1994–," NCRLC; David Andrews, *The Vatican and USDA Call for Agrarian Reform* (brochure, 1998), copy in ibid.

59. "Report of Executive Director, November, 2001," in unprocessed mailings, NCRLC, 3; "NCRLC's International Work," [2002], in ibid.; "NCRLC Is Reaching out Internationally," *Rural Landscapes* 9 (June 2002): 1.

Chapter 10 The End of the Ligutti Era

Along with Monsignor Ligutti's many accomplishments in bringing the NCRLC into international rural life came new tensions within the organization. Ligutti's biographer, Vincent A. Yzermans, called the 1950s the "time of trouble" for his subject. "No decade in his life caused Monsignor Ligutti as many headaches and heartaches as the 1950s," Yzermans wrote. At the crux of the trouble was the conflict between the expanding NCRLC's need for new leaders to share the increasing duties with Ligutti and the latter's personal style of leadership. As Yzermans put it:

One of Ligutti's problems was his inability to manage a national office and at the same time carry out his international commitments. This problem he was forced to face in this decade. It was, perhaps, the greatest cross he carried throughout his life. He was a one-man team, which had both its virtues and its shortcomings, and this he was forced to reckon with in many dramatic and heart-rending events.

The Reverend Michael P. Dineen, who played a major part in these events, described the same process more from the viewpoint of the Conference:

The fifties was a time of sharing leadership. The pain of sharing was in the beginning insufferable to Ligutti. He loved the Conference; he wanted it to progress in the mold which he envisioned and possessed. He wanted no tampering with it. Through Dunn and Dineen, the courageous and indomitable [Reverend Edward] Ramacher, the steadfast and determined Vizzard, the patient and persistent [Reverend John George] Weber and the wise and spiritual O'Rourke—supported by hundreds more who loved Ligutti and who wanted this giant he inherited and developed preserved—the Conference was wrestled from one leader and shared with others.[1]

Though it was Ligutti's tendency to personalize his leadership of the NCRLC, he was alive to the long-term dangers of the process. In 1949, he

1. Yzermans, *The People I Love*, 76; Michael Dineen, "The '50s," 16.

The End of the Ligutti Era

told the board of directors: "I resent and regret that my name and personality are considered by the public and even by some superiors as one and the same with the N.C.R.L.C. The cause certainly suffers if it is merely considered a pet personal hobby of mine. If that's the case it will be most wise for me to step out of the picture." In 1957, he apologized for his personalization of the Conference's international work, and expressed the hope that it would not remain so in the future:

> It is a joy to see the NCRLC develop soundly and rapidly. I would like to see our international work develop more than on a personal basis. If, thus far, it has been rather personal, such procedure was prompted by a desire of not implicating the NCRLC in a possible failure. Now that there is a tradition and that perhaps independent financial support is possible, I feel that I should fade away like a good soldier provided that the work is continued and developed in accordance with the wishes of our Superiors.[2]

According to Yzermans, Ligutti "knew his abilities in the realm of ideas and planning, just as he knew his weakness in the area of management and office structure." Thus, the monsignor "was constantly searching for someone to help direct the office." Ligutti asked the board of directors for help throughout the 1940s and finally obtained it in the Reverend Daniel F. Dunn of Boston, who joined Ligutti as executive secretary in 1952. When Dunn proved unsatisfactory, he was replaced two years later by Dineen. Ligutti rejoiced: "The coming of Father Dineen as a co-worker at the Headquarters of the NCRLC indicates the beginning of a new era, most welcome by me, and I pray most effective for the NCRLC."[3]

For a while, it seemed that Ligutti's prayers were being answered. With Dineen in the national office, the NCRLC grew in membership and expanded in services as never before, and Ligutti felt free to devote more and more of his time to international affairs.

However, he was already ignoring danger signs. Archbishop Albert Meyer of Milwaukee, Dineen's superior, had opposed his appointment, warning, "Dineen is not the man suited as executive secretary of the Conference." Even Dineen's supporters—such as NCRLC president Bishop Ralph Hayes of Davenport, Iowa, and Bishop William Mulloy of Covington, Kentucky—advised Ligutti, "Don't go off traveling too often and

---

2. "Report of the Executive Secretary," in "Ntn'l Convention, Columbus, Ohio, Nov. 4–9, 1949," NCRLC 8-6, 1; "Report of the Executive Director, N.C.R.L.C.," in "Executive Committee Meeting, Jan. 14–15, 1957, Milwaukee, Wis.," NCRLC 8-14, 4.
3. Yzermans, *The People I Love*, 59; "Report of the Executive Director," in "Executive Committee Meeting, Jan. 11–12, 1955," NCRLC 8-11, 1.

don't stay away too long." The monsignor later said, "I think they were right, but I did not follow their advice."[4]

In Ligutti's absence, Dineen greatly increased the Conference's domestic expenses. He spent a lot of money on his new projects such as the Company of St. Isidore and upgrading the quality of the Conference publication. He also incurred many personal expenses: he did a great amount of traveling to promote the Conference and had a personal telephone installed at NCRLC headquarters, particularly angering Ligutti.[5]

Much of the trouble between Ligutti and Dineen, as Yzermans saw it, was a result of their different philosophies of the nature of the Conference:

Ligutti firmly believed in small beginnings and build from there. On the other hand, Dineen believed in starting with major concepts and building from them ... Monsignor Ligutti was becoming more and more an international churchman ... On the other hand, Father Dineen was striving to build up the NCRLC. His ideas and plans, to be sure, were different from Ligutti's. The latter lived through the years of the Great Depression; the former was accustomed to the years of wealth following the Great War. Their economic sense of values, each so different from the other, were bound to clash. More than that, Ligutti felt that the NCRLC would be built on the shoulders of the poor and struggling farmers. Dineen felt it would be more practical to reach the leaders of agriculture-business in helping the small farmer ... It was Ligutti's conviction that Dineen was spending too much money; it was Dineen's resolve to make the Conference better known to the general public through a massive public relations program ... Ligutti's philosophy of the NCRLC was built on the principle that it should be self-sufficient. Other leaders of the Conference felt that money should be secured anywhere, anyplace, as long as it promoted the Conference.[6]

Ligutti later admitted that his "lack of interest" in the Conference's finances and domestic operations were partly to blame for the difficulties. He conceded that because of his absorption in his international activities he was "not at all active for 5 years" in his position as executive director. He charged that Dineen meanwhile was "using funds for purposes not intended by the donors, ... issuing false reports to the Board, kiting checks—and particularly ... using funds held in escrow" for his "ill-fated operations." Ligutti was particularly outraged that Dineen had dipped into his so-called Santa Claus Fund, which contained about eighty thousand dollars and had been formed in 1954 out of bequests Ligutti secured from individuals and foundations. According to Ligutti, Dineen used the money "for national

---

4. Yzermans, *The People I Love*, 76.   5. Ibid., 77
6. Ibid., 77–78.

The End of the Ligutti Era

promotion—the funds were to be used only for international work." By 1957, the Santa Claus Fund was expended, there were no new sources of revenue, and the Conference was "virtually bankrupt."[7]

Soon, the deplorable financial state of the NCRLC was known to Ligutti's and Dineen's superiors. In June 1958, while Ligutti was away on one of his trips, Bishop Edward Daly of Des Moines peremptorily ordered Dineen out of the diocese. Dineen returned to Milwaukee and on October 1, 1958, submitted a letter of resignation to the board of directors. It was unanimously accepted at the annual meeting at Fort Wayne on October 16, 1958.[8]

Thus Dineen was sacrificed as the supposed cause of the NCRLC's financial crisis. It would take the skills of a certified public accountant to determine whether he had seriously mismanaged the funds entrusted to him. Without affixing any blame, the financial crisis can perhaps be best understood, as Yzermans did, as a consequence of the different goals and perceptions of the newcomer Dineen and the Conference's older leaders. Up until Dineen, the NCRLC's leaders had always been very fiscally conservative. When they (and especially Ligutti, Dineen's nominal superior) left control of the Conference's finances in Dineen's hands, they assumed he would be the same way. They liked his new promotional ideas, without at first inquiring closely into his means of financing them. Dineen was an optimist. His projects were predicated upon ever-increasing growth in the membership of the Conference. When membership did not increase as fast as Dineen hoped, the Conference was left with the alternatives of either cutting its losses or going further into the red in the hope of eventually stimulating enough growth to pay for the debts already incurred. When it came to this pass, the old-guard leaders of the Conference would not take the risk of placing their bets on further expansion and opted to cut back. They simply were not prepared to follow where Dineen wanted to lead them.

The story of *Country Beautiful* magazine may serve as a kind of postlude to an account of the NCRLC's financial crisis. This was one of the biggest projects Dineen planned during his tenure as executive secretary.

---

7. "Report of the Executive Director of the NCRLC," in "Board of Directors, Ntn'l Convention, Aspen, Colo., Sept. 15–18, 1959," NCRLC 8-17, 3; "Report of the Executive Director: Msgr. L. G. Ligutti," in "Executive Committee, Milwaukee, Wis., Jan. 12–13, 1959," NCRLC 8-17; Yzermans, *The People I Love*, 76–77, 78; L. G. Ligutti, memorandum "To: Interested parties in N.C.R.L.C., Re: History and practical work of the International Affairs Dept. of NCRLC," November 18, 1975, in "Correspondence and Memos. N.C.R.L.C.—Agrimissio, U.S.A, 1974–1975–1976," LGL—unprocessed files acquired February 9, 1984, 2; NCRLC 8 for 1957–58.

8. Yzermans, *The People I Love*, 80–81; Dineen to Executive Committee of the NCRLC, October 1, 1958, in "Bd. of Directors, Ntn'l Convention, Ft. Wayne, Indiana, Oct. 16–17, 1958," NCRLC 8-17.

In 1957, he conceived the idea for a high-quality, popular, monthly rural magazine to be patterned after *Arizona Highways*. Dineen planned *Country Beautiful* as a "national medium of Christian rural philosophy for families living on, or interested in the land. Its prose, poetry, art and color printing will be of the highest quality." Ligutti opposed the project, demanding a "scientific market study" to test its feasibility. However, after Dineen left the NCRLC, starting in August 1958 he devoted himself full-time to *Country Beautiful*. The NCRLC did not take direct responsibility for its development. Instead, it was published by a separate Country Beautiful Foundation, which, however, did have many NCRLC officials on its board. Dineen was the magazine's publisher and editorial director.[9]

The glossy, colorful publication, with large illustrations and original articles on rural philosophy as well as reprints of stories by popular authors, finally made its debut in November 1961. By an agreement with the NCRLC, it was published each month in tandem with a scaled down (eight page, newsletter format) *Catholic Rural Life*—NCRLC members receiving both periodicals. However, *Country Beautiful* also reached many outside the NCRLC—by 1964, circulation was 146,000. In the following years, the Country Beautiful Foundation also published fourteen illustrated books on American heroes—especially John F. Kennedy—and the beauties of the American landscape. Some of these books were big sellers. The publishers hoped that the books, along with the revenue from advertising, would bring *Country Beautiful* to financial solvency. But the lavish magazine continued to be a big money loser. As the years went by, its publication schedule was increasingly cut down. After the first two issues in November and December of 1961, *Country Beautiful* was published ten times in 1962, seven times in 1963, and only twice each in 1964, 1965, and 1966. According to Ligutti's records, when the last issue was published in November 1966, the magazine had a $750,000 deficit.

While Dineen began to devote himself to *Country Beautiful*, the NCRLC started to work its way back to financial solvency. In 1958, the Reverends James Vizzard, S.J., and Edward Ramacher were brought into the national office. They expanded the revenue from novena contributions and advertising in *Catholic Rural Life*, but the prospects from such sources were not encouraging. Nor were memberships a promising avenue, since the Con-

---

9. For this paragraph and the next, Yzermans, *The People I Love*, 78–79; "Country Beautiful Organized; Father Dineen Trades Posts," *Catholic Rural Life* 7 (November 1958): 26; "COUNTRY BEAUTIFUL—the new NCRLC magazine for all rural America," ibid. 8 (November 1959): 6–7; "Country Beautiful for NCRLC Members," ibid. 11 (March 1962): 1; NCRLC 8.

ference spent six dollars for every five-dollar membership it received. In the end, as Vizzard admitted, the NCRLC was "able to continue operating only because of extra contributions from generous members and friends." Chauncey Stillman offered a fifty-thousand-dollar matching grant, and Vizzard and Ramacher pleaded with bishops, diocesan directors, *Our Sunday Visitor* magazine, and others to equal it. In the end, $94,000 was raised, which sufficed to pay off all outstanding debts by September 1959. To stay solvent, the NCRLC drastically cut down on expenses. From a high of $166,000 during Dineen's last year, the NCRLC budget dropped steadily until it leveled off at about $50,000 a year in the mid 1960s.[10]

Dineen was not the only casualty in the NCRLC leadership in the fall of 1958. Ligutti had been incurring the displeasure of some of his superiors for various reasons throughout the 1950s. His relations with his ordinary, Bishop Daly, had been strained since at least 1952, when Daly formally "severed all connection" with the NCRLC over Ligutti's alleged criticism of bishops and archbishops who supported immigration quotas. From that time on, Ligutti was persistently troubled by Daly's "lack of interest" in the organization with headquarters in his diocese. Certain members of the NCRLC executive committee, including Conference president Bishop Stephen Woznicki of Saginaw, Michigan, criticized Ligutti for his alleged partisanship toward Italian immigrants. They were also concerned that he spent too much time on his international activities, to the detriment of his duties as executive director. The secrecy of many of the monsignor's fundraising activities—especially the highly personalized international finances—also came under attack. The financial crisis of 1958 came as the last straw: it seemed the natural result of Ligutti's neglect of the national office and unorthodox financial practices.[11]

In the autumn of 1958, Ligutti had a gall-bladder operation in which a gallstone "nearly as big as a hen's egg" was removed. The subsequent recuperation period caused him to miss the Fort Wayne board of directors meeting in October. "He was distressed spiritually and physically depressed, but not beaten." Meanwhile, the other NCRLC officials discussed the future of the Conference in the wake of the financial crisis. Besides accepting Dineen's resignation, the board also discussed the charges that

---

10. Yzermans, *The People I Love*, 79; J. L. Vizzard, "Editorial," *Catholic Rural Life* 8 (May 1959): 2; Vizzard, "Editorial," ibid. (September 1959): 2; financial report in "Exec. Committee, Ntn'l Convention, Aspen, Colo., Sept. 15–18, 1959," NCRLC 8-17; documents throughout NCRLC 8.

11. Yzermans, *The People I Love*, 80–81, 139–40; "Addenda (Part 5) of Executive Director's Report," in binder "Executive Committee Minutes, October, 1956, Sioux Falls, South Dakota," in "Executive Committee Mtg., Sioux Falls, S.D., Oct. 19–23, 1956," NCRLC 8-13.

Ligutti was over-involved in international activities. As a solution, Vizzard proposed that the position of "director of international affairs" be created for Ligutti and that the Conference hire both a new executive director and a new executive secretary. The board accepted the proposals and notified Ligutti. The monsignor was deeply hurt and angrily charged that during his illness investigators of the Conference's financial difficulties had accused him "of financial self-interest at the expense of the N.C.R.L.C. . . . My personal files have been pried into, some materials have been removed, my daily personal diary searched and quoted . . . even blackmailing threats have been made." He blamed the financial mess on Dineen while admitting that he was "not faultless or sinless." He did not apologize for the secrecy of many of his international activities, and stated—probably correctly—that "the Conference has not suffered either financially or otherwise because of this situation." Even three years later, Ligutti was writing to Vizzard: "The wound within me has been too deep and to the quick—it just has not healed as yet—I hope it shall before I face God in judgement. Persons whom I esteem—I trust almost ad absurdum—you can finish the sentence." But he accepted the position of NCRLC director of international affairs. He stayed on as executive director for over a year while the Conference searched for his replacements. Finally, at the end of 1959, the Reverend Edward O'Rourke of Peoria, Illinois, was found for the post of executive director, and the Reverend John George Weber of Salina, Kansas, accepted the position of executive secretary, both to begin in January 1960. The next month, Ligutti moved out of the Grand Avenue house, boarded a plane, and flew to Rome, where he rented an apartment and began work as the director of international affairs. He was by now more than reconciled to the end of his two decades of Conference leadership: "Perhaps I should—and do—thank you [Vizzard] and a few more in the N.C.R.L.C. who pushed me into making a decision for which I thank God every moment. I enjoy my work, I believe it is effective—and I hope the Lord will give me just a few more years to enjoy it and perfect it." The monsignor continued to manage the Conference's international concerns until he gradually faded out of the job in the mid-1970s. The grand old man of the NCRLC died on December 28, 1983, in Rome.[12]

12. Yzermans, *The People I Love*, 79–83; "Executive Director Recovering from Major Operation," *Catholic Rural Life* 7 (October 1958): 13; Sandra A. La Blanc, "A Man ahead of His Time," ibid. 34 (February 1984): 24; "Report of the Executive Director: Msgr. L. G. Ligutti," in "Executive Committee, Milwaukee, Wis., Jan. 12–13, 1959," NCRLC 8-17; Ligutti to Vizzard, November 12, 1961, in "Correspondence, General, A–L, 1961," NCRLC 13-25.

Chapter 11 Organizing for Social Involvement

The O'Rourke Years

In the latest phase of its history, from 1960 through the beginning of the twenty-first century, the NCRLC focused on new issues of the times, most prominently social justice and the environment. At the same time, the Conference's organization opened up in harmony with the era of Vatican II in the Church and modernized in response to the emerging computer age in American society. The executives of the NCRLC set the tone for these changes.

When the NCRLC board of directors began their search for the successor to Luigi G. Ligutti as executive director in 1959, it looked upon the Reverend Edward W. O'Rourke as the "logical choice." His background fit him perfectly for the post. O'Rourke was born on October 31, 1917, on a farm near Downs in McLean County, Illinois. He went to the seminary in 1938, where, O'Rourke reminisced later, his bishop, NCRLC president Joseph Schlarman of Peoria, "apparently began even at that time to groom me for involvement in the work of the Catholic rural life movement." O'Rourke was ordained in 1944 and assigned to the Newman Center at the University of Illinois, where Schlarman asked him to "learn everything that the College of Agriculture at that university might be able to teach" him. From April to June 1944, he served at NCRLC headquarters as a temporary substitute for Ligutti's assistant when the latter was ill and absent. Then O'Rourke became the diocesan director of rural life, in which position he attended NCRLC conferences and edited a monthly farm page in the diocesan newspaper. As diocesan resettlement director for the Peoria diocese, O'Rourke effected the resettlement of 1,400 displaced persons and refugees from 1949 to 1958. His appointment as NCRLC executive director was effective starting in 1960. A priest of great inner strength, O'Rourke fully lived up to Michael Dineen's description of him as "wise and spiritual," but he was also shrewd and realistic and knew the issues like few others. His solid qualities were given recognition when he was named a domestic prelate in 1963. He left the Conference when he was appointed bishop of his old diocese of Peoria in 1971.[1]

For executive secretary, the Conference chose a priest of the Salina, Kansas, diocese, the Reverend John George Weber. Weber grew up on a farm near Park, Kansas. He was ordained at the Josephinum Seminary in Ohio in 1943. He then served as a priest in the Salina diocese for seventeen years, finally becoming a pastor in Aurora, Kansas, and diocesan director of rural life. On becoming NCRLC executive secretary in 1960, Weber directed the staff at the Des Moines headquarters. He was chiefly responsible for the Conference's financial affairs and edited *Catholic Rural Life* and the *Rural Life Page* press service. Though his duties were mainly administrative, he also handled the NCRLC's participation in soil conservation matters—a particular interest of his—and the Conference's long, often frustrating effort to bring about a coalition of the major American farm organizations. O'Rourke called Weber "a fine person to work with," and, with the various lines of responsibility very clearly drawn between them, the tandem worked together very effectively, without the friction that often bedeviled the relations between Ligutti and his executive secretaries. Like his cohort O'Rourke, Weber was created a monsignor ("papal chamberlain") in 1963. He continued to serve as executive secretary for several years after O'Rourke's departure, alongside new executive director the Reverend John J. McRaith. In 1976, he was reassigned by his bishop to a parish in Hoxie, Kansas. Since Weber's departure, the NCRLC has not had another executive secretary.[2]

O'Rourke and Weber's first task was to preside over cutbacks in the national office made necessary by the financial crisis at the end of the 1950s. From a high of eighteen full-time workers in 1958, the office was already down to twelve when the two took over in 1960. Ligutti on his departure admitted that the office could do with even fewer, and indeed, O'Rourke

---

1. "Rev. E. W. O'Rourke, Biographical Sketch, 1971," NCRLC 1-5; minutes in "Steering Committee, Des Moines, Iowa, March 2, 1959," NCRLC 8-17, 1; transcript of tape, "Bishop Edward W. O'Rourke, Interviewed by David S. Bovee, Sheraton Inn in Des Moines, Iowa, 4 October, 1983," in "NCRLC, Oral History," NCRLC, 1; Dineen, "The '50s," 16; "NCRLC Executive Director Named Domestic Prelate,"*Catholic Rural Life* 12 (July 1963): 1.

2. Transcript of tape, "Bishop Edward W. O'Rourke, Interviewed by David S. Bovee," 4; "NCRLC Executive Secretary Becomes Monsignor," *Catholic Rural Life* 12 (March 1963): 1; "NCRLC Executive Officers," ibid. 22 (November 1973): 10; "Msgr. Weber Reassigned," ibid. 25 (February 1976): 7.

Organizing for Social Involvement 233

and Weber did economize on personnel over the following years. By 1962, there were only three full-time employees supporting the work of the two executives.[3]

At the same time, the Conference continued to operate its office in Washington, D. C. Its director from 1955 to 1968 was the Reverend James L. Vizzard, S.J. Vizzard was born in San Francisco in 1916. He had masters' degrees in philosophy and theology and was teaching English at Santa Clara University in 1940 when he read *The Grapes of Wrath* and was converted to the cause of working for the rural poor. Vizzard studied agricultural economics at Georgetown before returning to Santa Clara to teach. When offered the job as NCRLC Washington representative, he was chairman of the economics department at Santa Clara, a corresponding editor of *America,* and a regular contributor to various other Catholic publications. From 1958 to 1960, he went to Des Moines temporarily to help sort out the Conference's financial mess, but he much preferred his work in Washington. O'Rourke recalled that Vizzard was "a brilliant man, and wrote very effectively, and just loved his involvement in the political arenas in Washington. He was the man for that—except for his health. His health did not hold up." Vizzard had a bad back, suffered through several back operations in the 1960s, and often performed his very strenuous job in considerable pain.[4]

Vizzard was sometimes a hard personality to deal with. He got into a number of scrapes with his superiors over such things as his assignments and his zealous support of the migrant farm workers. He wrote to an associate: "A few have bluntly reminded me that my training as a Jesuit Priest should render me a little more docile. My only retort, I guess, must be that the 'brain washing' process wasn't quite complete." One complaint made of Vizzard was that he was using his position in Washington to speak out on issues peripheral to the central concerns of the NCRLC. For example, Vizzard's extensive lobbying on behalf of migrant farm workers did nothing

---

3. "Report of the Executive Secretary," in "Executive Committee Meeting, Fort Wayne, Indiana, June 17–18, 1958," NCRLC 8-16, 4; John George Weber, "Report of the Executive Secretary," in "Executive Committee Meeting, Chicago, Ill., June 15, 1960," NCRLC 8-18, 1; "Some Thoughts and Suggestions for the Executive Committee Meeting of January, 1961, from Monsignor L. G. Ligutti, Director of International Affairs, N.C.R.L.C.," January 3, 1961, in "Executive Committee Meeting, Milwaukee, Wis., Jan. 16–17, 1961," NCRLC 8-18, Exhibit H; "Exec. Committee Meeting, Des Moines, Iowa, June 18, 1962," NCRLC 8-19, 2.

4. Julie Sly, "James Vizzard, S.J.: Champion of the Migrant Laborer," unpublished article, 1983, notes on interview of Sly with Vizzard, Santa Clara, California, April 27, 1982, notes by Sly on James L. Vizzard Papers, Stanford University, Stanford, California, all in possession of Julie Sly; transcript of tape, "Bishop Edward W. O'Rourke, Interviewed by David S. Bovee," NCRLC, 11; "NCRLC Washington Office," *Catholic Rural Life* 22 (November 1973): 11.

Figure 16. NCRLC Washington, D.C., representative James Vizzard, S.J., with other religious leaders presenting an open letter in support of the Mutual Security program.

to benefit the main financial backers of the Conference—midwestern family farmers. In 1958, NCRLC president Bishop Stephen Woznicki therefore asked Vizzard to "rather circumscribe your expanding activities," and concentrate more on "services needed to maintain the resources of NCRLC." Vizzard defended himself, maintaining:

> One of the strongest selling points now being used by the Conference is the fact that we do have a Washington office . . . Willy-nilly, we have become not only the Conference's but also the Church's chief spokesman on some of these issues [such as migrant labor] and we do have considerable influence. Maybe that's the "penalty" for doing too good a job. The question is, shall we abdicate this conceded competence and responsibility—which, according to Monsignor Ligutti as well as the authorities of the NCWC is of great value to the Church as well as to the Conference—particularly in the absence of any other effective voice.

As the NCRLC joined in the antipoverty crusade of the 1960s under O'Rourke, Vizzard's view of the Conference's purpose gradually began to prevail over Woznicki's. Like Ligutti in international affairs, Vizzard helped turn the Conference from mainly serving the needs of its financial contributors to a wider concern for social justice in all of rural America. Perhaps his independence was aided somewhat by the fact that throughout the 1960s about half of the Washington office's funding was provided by an outside source—*Our Sunday Visitor* magazine. (The other half came from general NCRLC funds.)[5]

In April 1968, Vizzard resigned as NCRLC Washington representative because he "was totally burned out and desperately overcommitted to too many things." He returned to Santa Clara but came to Washington again in 1972, this time as a lobbyist for the United Farm Workers. He stayed until 1977, when he again retired to Santa Clara. Following Vizzard's departure, Monsignor O'Rourke shuttled back and forth between Des Moines and Washington to represent the Conference in the nation's capital, until 1970, when Stephen E. Bossi became Washington representative. Bossi, a political science graduate of Seattle University, had spent two years in the Peace Corps in India and one year as assistant to the director of the Division for Poverty of the United States Catholic Conference before coming to the NCRLC. Bossi continued to write the "Washington Farm Front" column for *Catholic Rural Life* and also edited the *Washington Memorandum*, a monthly report on congressional legislation and national programs distributed to diocesan rural life directors and others interested in rural issues. Bossi left the Washington office to become NCRLC director of research and policy development in 1975; he left that post in 1977. Bossi was the last NCRLC-employed official to represent the Conference in Washington. After 1975, a USCC coordinator for rural issues lobbied in Washington and provided liaison with the NCRLC. From 1975–78, the coordinator for rural issues was Kathleen White; from 1978–80, David Byers; from 1980–91, Walt Grazer; from 1992–95, Ron Jackson; from 1995–2001, Dan Misleh; and starting in 2001, Andrew Rivas. Their duties included attending NCRLC board meetings, consulting on a regular basis with the Conference staff, coordinating advocacy efforts in Washington, sending out action alerts to interested persons and organizations, and writing a column for *Catholic Rural Life*.[6]

As usual, finances were a big problem for the NCRLC in the 1960s. For most of the decade, O'Rourke and Weber had an annual budget of only about fifty thousand dollars to work with. Up until 1967, they were not able to come up with any new sources of income. They had to rely on the old established sources. The bishops' fund and memberships each contributed about a third of the Conference's income, and the rest was accounted for

5. Vizzard to Rabbi Marc H. Tanenbaum, January 8, 1960, in "Clergy, T–, 1960," NCRLC 13-17; Stephen Woznicki to Vizzard, June 20, 1958, and Vizzard to Woznicki, June 24, 1958, in "Correspondence: Vizzard, M-, 1956–58," NCRLC 13-12; financial statements in NCRLC 8.
6. Sly, "James Vizzard"; "NCRLC Washington Office," 11; "NCRLC Activities Report—1978," in "Annual Board Meeting, Hartington, Neb., Nov. 6–7, 1978," NCRLC 8-25, 5; untitled article, *Rural Landscapes* 3 (June 1996): 4; Andrew Rivas, "Capitol Update," ibid. 9 (January 2002): 2.

by donations, speakers' stipends, the 100-League of St. Isidore (members who donated a hundred dollars per year), and sales of literature. However, O'Rourke and Weber believed that, in view of the NCRLC's services to the American Catholic Church as a whole, they were justified in asking the National Catholic Welfare Conference for a supporting contribution. As early as 1961, they considered asking the NCWC for thirty-five thousand dollars. They did not actually do so for several years out of fears that the NCWC would make the Conference relocate to Washington, D.C., or submit to their dictates in policy matters. The financial straits of the Conference were such, however, that in 1964 the NCRLC board finally did vote in favor of affiliating with the NCWC. By the time it did so, the NCWC itself underwent a reorganization. At its 1966 meeting, the American hierarchy decided to divide the NCWC into two organizations—the National Conference of Catholic Bishops (NCCB) to deal with ecclesiastical affairs and the United States Catholic Conference (USCC) to carry on the Church's civic and social relations. This organization took force as of January 1, 1967, and immediately the NCRLC began negotiating to acquire the status of "representing rural interests within the new structure of USCC." The USCC proved agreeable, and beginning January 1, 1968, the NCRLC—while retaining its old title—also became the Division for Rural Life of the USCC's Department of Social Development and World Peace. The Conference was allowed to keep its headquarters in Des Moines, and the affiliation was "financially . . . a God-send." The USCC gave the Conference a half-year contribution of fifteen thousand dollars in 1967 and thirty thousand dollars in 1968. In succeeding years, the USCC contribution steadily increased until it reached $71,035 in 1974. Its proportion of the NCRLC budget increased from about one-half in 1968 to three-quarters in 1974. The USCC contributions allowed the total NCRLC budget to increase from less than sixty thousand dollars in the first year to ninety-five thousand in the latter year. The tie with the USCC helped the Conference financially—without affecting its self-determination in policy-making—until it again became an independent organization in 1975.[7]

The issue-oriented (and financially weak) O'Rourke years de-emphasized some of the traditional aspects of NCRLC organization. For example, the

7. "The National Catholic Rural Life Conference," *Catholic Rural Life* 22 (November 1973): 7; minutes and financial statements in NCRLC 8-18 to 8-25, especially "Executive Committee Meeting, Milwaukee, Wis., Jan. 16–17, 1961," NCRLC 8-18, 8-9, and "National Catholic Rural Life Conference, Minutes of Board of Directors" Meeting, Statler-Hilton Hotel, St. Louis, Mo.—Aug. 27, 1964," NCRLC 8-20; five folders on "United States Catholic Conference," NCRLC 2-17.

Conference began gradually to phase out the expensive annual conventions. No convention was held in the year of the financial crisis, 1959, and biennial conventions were started in 1960 and continued in every even-numbered year until 1968. These were much smaller than the conventions of the 1950s and usually drew only a few hundred delegates, with the exception of the last one in ever-enthusiastic St. Cloud, Minnesota, which attracted 1,500 participants. After 1968, to partially substitute for the conventions, the NCRLC concentrated more on regional workshops and rural life days.[8]

The O'Rourke years witnessed a general deterioration in NCRLC membership. After a high of more than ten thousand members in 1958, the rolls had already declined to about six thousand when O'Rourke and Weber took over in 1960. The numbers continued to decline until they reached a low for the O'Rourke years of 2,800 paid members in 1969. Membership drives were few and far between and were not given the massive promotion that Dineen had been able to muster. For example, in a drive in O'Rourke's last year, 1971, the Conference merely put advertisements in a few Catholic weekly newspapers and mainly relied on diocesan directors to recruit new members. Despite this weakness in membership, the NCRLC claimed to have "1,600 rural life chairmen in various Catholic organizations" in 1964. During the 1960s the NCRLC was especially strong in women's organizations such as the National Conference of Catholic Women, the Catholic Daughters of America, and the Daughters of Isabella.[9]

McRaith and Rural Ministry

The NCRLC underwent a change of emphasis under O'Rourke's successor, the Reverend John J. McRaith, who joined Weber as codirector on January 1, 1972. McRaith was born on a farm in Hutchinson, Minnesota, in 1934. He was ordained for the New Ulm, Minnesota, diocese in 1960, and until his appointment as codirector served as assistant and pastor for several small town parishes in Minnesota, the last at Sleepy Eye. As codirector, McRaith basically took over O'Rourke's job as executive director, while Weber continued his mainly administrative duties. When Weber left the Conference in 1975, McRaith became sole executive director. He retired from that post in 1978, when he returned to New Ulm as chancellor and

---

8. See articles in *Catholic Rural Life* and minutes in NCRLC 8.
9. "Announcing Membership Campaign," *Catholic Rural Life* 10 (October 1961): 24; "NCRLC Aim—More Members, More Involvement," ibid. 20 (April 1971): 1; *New Catholic Encyclopedia*, 1967 ed., s.v. "National Catholic Rural Life Conference," by E. W. O'Rourke; NCRLC 8-20 through 8-24; folder "Committee on Rural Life, 1955–1958," NCRLC 1-1.

Figure 17. Laidback John McRaith, executive director, 1972–78.

vicar general. Four years later, McRaith joined his predecessors O'Hara and O'Rourke in being raised to the hierarchy as bishop of Owensboro, Kentucky.[10]

McRaith came to the codirectorship with very little experience in the NCRLC. His only role had been as diocesan director for the New Ulm diocese from 1965 to 1968. Unlike most of his predecessors, McRaith had been neither an officer nor a board member of the NCRLC before his appointment, and his early actions reveal an understandable unfamiliarity with procedures and policies. Unlike O'Rourke, McRaith was not an "issues" person, and it took most of his tenure as director before he was able to establish continuity with the social-justice policies of his predecessor. The title of McRaith's column in *Catholic Rural Life*, "Climbing a Mountain," symbolized his concern that leading the Conference would be an uphill task. Many of these early columns reflected his concern at the immensity of the challenge before him and the difficulty of changing the tide running against the Conference's principles. In 1972 he wrote, "The more one walks around [the mountain] the larger it becomes and the more aware

10. Tape, "Interview, Bishop John McRaith of Owensboro, Ky. w/ David S. Bovee (over telephone, Owensboro and Milwaukee, Wisc.), Dec. 19, 1983," in "NCRLC, Oral History," NCRLC; "NCRLC Executive Officers," *Catholic Rural Life* 22 (November 1973): 10; "Rev. John McRaith Named Co-director," ibid. 20 (November 1971): 3; "Bishop Dingman Announces Two NCRLC Staff Changes," ibid. 27 (April 1978): 20; "McRaith, Former NCRLC Director Ordained Bishop of Owensboro, Ky.," ibid. 33 (February 1983): 17.

Organizing for Social Involvement

one becomes that there are not very many people interested in doing anything about the problems the mountain represents."[11]

McRaith believed that the NCRLC's role should be that of "people changer," not "problem solver." Thus, he turned away from O'Rourke's emphasis on social and economic issues and self-help projects to focus on bringing the Christian gospel to rural people. After the social justice emphasis of the O'Rourke years, in which the NCRLC served especially the rural poor in the United States and abroad, the Conference under McRaith went back to ministering mainly to the Catholic rural communities that had always been its mainstay. This expressed itself in his attempt to build up the NCRLC's organization. McRaith tried to get more active diocesan directors with a wider geographical distribution. He also tried to increase the Conference's membership—although he never succeeded in having it reach even the four thousand mark.[12]

McRaith himself looked at his change of emphasis as most of all a new focus on the "rural ministry"—providing services for rural priests. McRaith initiated a number of new services for rural pastors to help them in ministering to their flocks. For example, in 1976, the Conference published an *Idea Book for Small Town Churches,* a compendium of 151 parish ministry ideas contributed by Catholics from across the country. The ideas were for programs related to Catholics, other religions, the unchurched, community and social service, the worldwide mission of the Church, and administration and fundraising.[13]

The NCRLC began to offer the Rural Parish Service to pastors in 1975. For fifty dollars, the rural pastor received a monthly packet containing a homily outline relating Sunday readings to rural issues, items on rural topics for parish bulletins, liturgical and prayer material suited to rural needs, NCRLC publications, and other resources. The service was offered in response to a call from pastors for rural ministry materials "that directly address the values and concerns of the rural people they are serving." Despite this apparent need, there were only 185 subscribers to the Rural Parish Service in 1977. The service consequently became a big money loser, and in 1980 the board of directors voted to issue it according to liturgical seasons rather than once a month and cut the number of copies of

---

11. "Rev. John J. McRaith, Co-director's Report," in "Executive Committee Meeting, Colfax, Iowa, June 20–21, 1972," NCRLC 8-24.
12. John J. McRaith, "Let's Take a Look at Ourselves!!" in "Diocesan Directors Meeting, Lincoln, Nebraska, Sept., 1972," NCRLC 8-24; reports in NCRLC 8-24.
13. Tape, "Interview, Bishop John McRaith;" NCRLC, *Idea Book for Small Town Churches* (Washington, D.C.: Glenmary Research Center, 1976), copy in "Gen. Pubs., 1970–76," NCRLC 5-5.

Catholic Rural Life included from ten to two. This did not help, and the service was discontinued the next year. It was revived in 1993, offering a yearly packet of similar materials, especially special prayers for rural feasts and the seasons of the year.[14]

In 1976, the Conference began issuing the R.U.R.A.L. Education Service (Religious Understanding of Resources in American Lifestyles), developed by Sister Annette Fernholz of the NCRLC staff. This consisted of packets of educational resources for use by elementary-age children in the school and the home. The thirty-five subscribers in 1977 grew to eighty-eight the next year. At the same time, Fernholz was reportedly swamped with requests for workshops on presenting the materials. The service was very much Fernholz's personal project, and it was discontinued when she left the Conference in 1980.[15]

In general, the 1970s was the era of the workshop for the NCRLC. The Conference found workshops a much more effective means for educating local Catholic leaders for rural social action than the more elaborate and expensive conventions. They were tailored to local needs and sometimes to specific groups such as priests or sisters. The NCRLC cooperated with a number of other groups—universities, the Great Plains Church Leadership School, the Appalachian Regional School for Church Leaders, the National Federation of Priests Councils, and the Glenmary Missioners—in conducting its workshops. In particular, McRaith, along with the Reverend Bernard Quinn, director of the Glenmary Research Center in Washington, D.C., held a number of workshops for rural priests. One series of workshops organized by the two priests addressed such issues as farm policy, strip mining, Native Americans, absentee landownership, and natural resources.[16]

McRaith and other priests who were giving rural ministry workshops found that they could not fill all requests. Thus, in 1978, McRaith and three

---

14. NCRLC News Release, "New Service to Rural Parishes Announced," in "Diocesan Directors Meeting, Cincinnati, Ohio, Nov. 4, 1975, NCRLC 8-24; NCRLC Staff, "Building a Presence: In the Church, in the Nation, in the World; NCRLC Activities Report—1977," in "2nd Ntn'l Consultation of Rural Life Directors, Erlanger, Kentucky, 1977," NCRLC 8-25, 1; Minutes, "Ntn'l Board Meeting, Techny, Illinois, November 18–21, 1980," NCRLC 8-25, 6; Gregory Cusack and Bart Pollock to Rural Parish Service Subscribers, n. d., in "Misc. Correspondence," Cusack Subject File, Box 16; copies of 1993–2000 Rural Parish Services in boxes "NCRLC Pubs. ca. 1990–1994 Rec'd.: 4/21/94" and "Current Mailings, 1994–," NCRLC.

15. NCRLC Staff, "Building a Presence," 1, 5; "NCRLC Activities Report—1978," 1–2; file "Sr. Annette Fernholz," Cusack Subject File, Box 17, NCRLC.

16. "The National Catholic Rural Life Conference," *Catholic Rural Life* 22 (November 1973): 6–7; "Rural Ministry Workshop Planned," ibid. 24 (February 1975): 4; and many other articles in *Catholic Rural Life* in the 1970s.

Organizing for Social Involvement   241

other priests founded the Edwin V. O'Hara Institute for Rural Ministry Education, which was intended to "work with dioceses, religious orders, seminaries, and other groups in providing education for those who are entering rural ministry or are already involved in it." Nine organizations, including the NCRLC, the Glenmary Missioners, religious orders, seminaries, and theological schools, established a council to guide the institute and provided financial support. Monsignor Charles Fortier from the Diocese of Lafayette, Louisiana, was the first director of the O'Hara Institute, which was housed initially at NCRLC headquarters. However, this presented conflicts in the workloads of the NCRLC staff, so in 1981 the institute was moved to Washington, D.C., where it gained by association with the Washington Theological Union. At that time, Brother David Andrews, C.S.C., became director of the institute. He brought the institute to the height of its activity, inaugurating a series of four national rural ministry conferences and publishing a journal on rural ministry education, *Rural Roots*, in addition to giving numerous workshops and presentations and consulting with many Catholic rural-related organizations. For a time the institute was envisioned as taking over the NCRLC's rural evangelistic endeavors, allowing the Conference to concentrate on political and economic matters. But the organization declined after Andrews left in 1986, because its services were increasingly available from local offices of rural life, educational institutions, or regional ecumenical endeavors. After an attempt to link the languishing institute with the NCRLC—rejected by the Conference—it was dissolved in 1991.[17]

During the McRaith years, the NCRLC had an unusually active president in Archbishop Ignatius J. Strecker of Kansas City, Kansas. Strecker was president from 1972 to 1976 and again from 1983 to 1986. He broke the mold of the mainly unassertive figurehead presidents of the earlier decades who usually had let Ligutti and O'Rourke run things. Strecker personally lobbied for specific rural legislation. He supported McRaith's new emphases on increasing NCRLC membership and serving the rural ministry. His

17. "Msgr. Charles Fortier Heads New Rural Ministry Institute," ibid. 27 (April 1978): 7; Gerald Foley, "New Institute Supports Rural Parish Ministry," ibid. (May 1978): 5–6; David Andrews, C.S.C., "Changing Rural Communities Affect Faith, Ministry," ibid. 31 (April–May 1981): 26–27; Minutes, in "Executive Committee Meeting, Des Moines, Dec. 11–12, 1978," NCRLC 8-25, 1–2; The Edwin Vincent O'Hara Institute for Rural Ministry Education, *Rural Ministry Institute Report, 1984*, in Box 23, "Publications Acq'd: 6/30/94," NCRLC; ten folders on O'Hara Institute in Cusack Subject File, Box 16; Gregory Cusack to Andrews, December 22, 1981, and minutes of O'Hara Institute executive committee, June 25, 1982, Atchison, Kansas, both in "EVO," ibid., Box 17; three unboxed folders on the institute, NCRLC; "Council Meeting, Oct. 14–15, 1988, Minutes," in "EVO, October 1988 Board Meeting," in NCRLC Minutes of Meetings, 1985–89, Box 3.

most significant contribution was in restructuring the NCRLC to loosen its dependence on the USCC and make it more financially self-sufficient.[18]

Shortly after McRaith took over as director of the Conference and Strecker became its president, negotiations began with the USCC to redefine the NCRLC–USCC relationship. As with the NCWC in the 1930s, the problem was reconciling the independent-minded NCRLC with the centralized USCC, especially now that the USCC provided most of the funding for the Conference. The USCC was undergoing a reorganization, and it asked the NCRLC to restructure itself so as to resume greater responsibility for both its policy direction and its financial support. The NCRLC did so in a revised constitution, written mainly by Strecker, which was adopted in 1975. Under this constitution, the NCRLC executives, McRaith and Weber, were continued, but the Washington office was terminated, the Washington liaison to be handled by a USCC coordinator for rural issues. The NCRLC was no longer considered the Division of Rural Life of the USCC, but, after less than a decade as part of the USCC resumed its independence. It was now considered as providing services to individuals, parishes, dioceses, and the USCC. Under the "purchase of service agreement" negotiated by Strecker, the USCC compensated the NCRLC for these services by paying it, to begin with, thirty thousand dollars a year. This arrangement reestablished the NCRLC's independence while continuing the financial aid that was needed from the USCC. The USCC increased its payment to the conference to thirty-five thousand dollars in 1978 and continued the purchase of service agreement through 1980.[19]

On the same principle as the purchase of service agreement with the USCC, the Conference in 1975 tried to promote financial self-sufficiency by establishing membership fees for services rendered to individuals, parishes, and dioceses. In addition to the $5 individual ($10 supporting) membership, the Conference instituted $50 parish and $250 diocesan memberships. In ensuing years, the income from diocesan memberships was larger than expected, but the number of parish memberships was disappointing, and the NCRLC continued to rely on outside financial support from the USCC and ABCM. After 1975, these outside sources still accounted for about a third of the Conference's income, about half was from individual, parish,

18. Ignatius Strecker, "A Message from Our President," *Catholic Rural Life* 24 (January 1975): 2.
19. *Constitution of the National Catholic Rural Life Conference, Revised and Adopted Nov. 6, 1975* (Des Moines Iowa: NCRLC, 1975), copies in box "NCRLC Current/Incoming Pubs. to be Filed," NCRLC Archives; Strecker, "A Message from Our President," 2; documents in folders "Board of Directors Meeting, Columbia, Missouri, October 23–24, 1974," "Diocesan Directors Meeting, Columbia, Missouri, October 22, 1974," and "Loose Meeting Material, Late 70's," all NCRLC 8-24.

Organizing for Social Involvement 243

and diocesan memberships, and the rest was from sale of publications, the speakers' bureau, workshops, Period of Prayer donations, and unrestricted contributions.[20]

Strecker's constitutional revision in 1975 affected the way the Conference handled its international funds. After Dineen's unauthorized use of his "Santa Claus Fund" between 1954 and 1958, Ligutti set up a special "International Account" of money solely for international uses. Most of the fund consisted of contributions from Chauncey Stillman and the Homeland Foundation. In 1974, the international fund contained $359,675; it earned in interest $22,809 in 1972 and $18,899 in 1973. At that time, the fund was administered by a committee consisting of Ligutti, Weber, and the NCRLC attorney.[21]

The Conference decided in 1971 to divide the fund so as to give 80 percent to Ligutti's Agrimissio organization and 20 percent to the NCRLC for its own international work. However, the 1975 constitutional revision proposed by Strecker provided that the international funds be distributed by the NCRLC board of directors. Ligutti, from Rome, protested the change, which was made without his consultation. He feared that the NCRLC board could decide to allocate the international funds for general purposes, which was against the wishes of the donors and would destroy Agrimissio. In the course of a long correspondence extending to April 1976, Strecker assured Ligutti that the funds would be spent for Agrimissio, and the latter eventually accepted the change.[22]

At the end of Strecker's first term as president, the NCRLC took a sort of half step back toward national conventions when it instituted annual "diocesan directors' consultations." The consultations, which were held in conjunction with the fall board of directors meeting, were scaled-down versions of the old conventions that met needs for community and support that NCRLC members still felt. They were attended by at most a few hundred people and consisted of a few speakers, workshops, and board of directors and diocesan directors meetings extending over three to five days. The sixtieth anniversary consultation in 1983 was planned as a more

20. Documents in NCRLC 8-24 and 8-25, especially documents in "Ntn'l Board Meeting, Techny, Illinois, November 18–21, 1980," NCRLC 8-25.
21. "General Correspondence—Warren, Mr. Louis, 1956–61," LGL-E; Louis B. Warren-John George Weber correspondence in "Laymen, M–Z, 1968," NCRLC 13-25; "Trust Funds and Savings Accounts," in "Diocesan Directors Meeting, Columbia, Missouri, October 22, 1974," NCRLC 8-24; documents in "Correspondence and Memos, N.C.R.L.C.-Agrimissio, U.S.A., 1974–1975–1976," LGL—unprocessed files acquired February 7, 1984.
22. Documents in "Correspondence and Memos, N.C.R.L.C.-Agrimissio, U.S.A."

elaborate gathering that would generate much publicity and more memberships, but it proved disappointing. After that, the consultations became less elaborate, with fewer speakers and workshops, and concentrated on the meeting of the diocesan directors (later called "rural life directors") themselves. Briefly in the late 1980s, during an interregnum in NCRLC executive leadership, the diocesan directors issued resolutions on major topics in lieu of the national office.[23]

Strecker's successor as NCRLC president, Bishop Maurice J. Dingman of Des Moines, also had a substantial impact on the Conference. Dingman was born in 1914 on a family farm near St. Paul in southeast Iowa. He studied at St. Ambrose College in Davenport and at the North American College and the Pontifical Gregorian University in Rome, where he showed an interest in Catholic rural life by writing a term paper on the topic. He was ordained in 1939 and served as chancellor of the Davenport diocese from 1953 to 1968. He developed close friendships with Strecker and Ligutti, and the latter at one time asked him to become NCRLC executive director. He was consecrated bishop of Des Moines in 1968.[24]

Dingman served as NCRLC president from 1976 to 1979. Like Strecker, he was open in speaking out on issues of importance to rural Catholics. In the early 1980s, he appeared on many national news telecasts when he carried a white cross at several Iowa rallies demonstrating in favor of federal aid to debt-ridden farmers. When he called for a "new Moses or Martin Luther King" to be a prophet for the abandoned people of the land, many thought that Dingman himself was that prophet. But he suffered a stroke in 1986 in the midst of the farm crisis and was forced to retire as bishop. He never recovered enough to resume even a limited role in the fight for rural justice, and he died in 1992.[25]

Dingman provided the leadership that brought about the widespread

23. "Consultation Scheduled for Diocesan Directors," *Catholic Rural Life* 25 (September 1976): 16; "Minutes, NCRLC Board of Directors, October 6–7, 1983, Sheraton Hotel, Des Moines, Iowa," in "Board Communications," Cusack Subject File, Box 19; "Rural Life Directors Business Meeting," *Common Ground* 5 (March 1987): 3; other articles in *Catholic Rural Life* and *Common Ground*; meetings files, NCRLC 8-25; author's observations at 1983 consultation in Des Moines, Iowa.

24. Shirley Crisler and Mira Mosle, *In the Midst of His People: The Authorized Biography of Bishop Maurice J. Dingman* (Iowa City, Iowa: Rudi Publishing, 1995), 27, 63, 77; Tape, "Interview of Bishop Maurice J. Dingman of Des Moines with David S. Bovee, Sheraton Inn, Des Moines, Iowa, October 5, 1983," in "NCRLC, Oral History," NCRLC; "NCRLC's New President Is Bishop Maurice Dingman," *Catholic Rural Life* 25 (December 1976): 5–6; Maurice J. Dingman, "Bishop Dingman Discusses NCRLC's Strong Commitment to Rural Justice," ibid. 26 (January 1977): 2, 23.

25. Crisler and Mosle, *In the Midst of His People*, 227–28, 231, 233, 235; Norm White, "Farewell to Maurice Dingman: Friend and Bishop," *Common Ground* 11 (March/April 1992): 2; Gregory Cusack-Dingman correspondence, 1986, in "Bishop Dingman," Cusack Subject File, Box 19, NCRLC.

Organizing for Social Involvement 245

participation of both leaders and rural people in formulating the 1980 Midwest Catholic land statement, *Strangers and Guests*. Dingman began planning for the statement in 1978. The statement encompassed forty-four dioceses in a twelve-state area (Indiana, Michigan, Wisconsin, Minnesota, Illinois, North Dakota, South Dakota, Iowa, Kansas, Nebraska, Colorado, and Wyoming). Hearings on the statement were held throughout 1979. More than twelve thousand persons participated in four hundred "Strangers and Guests" hearings—by far the largest input into any Catholic rural statement. That made *Strangers and Guests* a true "people's statement" when it was released on May 1, 1980.[26]

With the aim of following up the principles of *Strangers and Guests* with action, the Midwest bishops sponsored a second phase called the "Heartland Project." The NCRLC took over the Heartland Project in 1981 and continued its development of educational materials such as half-hour and ten-minute films, three slide-tape presentations, and a five-session study guide, all based on *Strangers and Guests*. The Heartland Project also sponsored a Land Stewardship Project in 1983–84—a series of county meetings held in midwestern states on land stewardship issues such as urban sprawl onto farmland and soil conservation.[27]

The electronic promotion of *Strangers and Guests* by films, slides, and tapes was characteristic of the trend in NCRLC promotion from the late 1970s onward. Similar to the methods of Father Dineen in the 1950s, the Conference again utilized modern promotional techniques. These began under media consultant Roger Blobaum (1975–80) and continued under two women, Sandra A. La Blanc (editorial director, 1982–99), and Patricia Prijatel Kucera (*Catholic Rural Life* editor, 1982–87). During this period, the NCRLC planned films of Monsignor Ligutti in retirement in Rome and of Pope John Paul II's visit to Iowa in 1979 (only the former film was completed), and videocassette programs on rural issues. La Blanc and Kucera also converted *Catholic Rural Life* into a slick magazine published only five times a year, filling in the other months with *Common Ground,* a no-frills newsletter. The former, featuring thematic issues, incisive articles, and ar-

26. *Strangers and Guests*; "Participation Urged in Land Statement Hearings," *Catholic Rural Life* 27 (November 1978): 2; "Plan 'Listening Process' on Regional Land Document," ibid., 22–23; Helen Vinton, "Land Statement Hearings Reflect Uncertain Future," ibid. 28 (February 1979): 5–7; "Witnesses Tear into Land Use and Ownership Issues," ibid. (November 1979): 15–16.
27. *Strangers and Guests: A Study Program* (Des Moines, Iowa: NCRLC, 1981), and *Scripts for Land Issues Slide Programs* (Des Moines, Iowa: NCRLC, 1981), both in "NCRLC, Gen. Pubs., 1979–," NCRLC 5-5; John Hart, "Strangers and Guests: A Statement on God's Land," *Catholic Rural Life* 29 (April–May 1980): 3–6; "Conference Takes over Heartland Project," ibid. 31 (September 1981): 43; "Heartland Happenings," *Common Ground* 2 (March 1984): 2–3.

resting original photography, won thirty national journalism awards in the 1980s. Although it sometimes seemed at odds with the Conference's simple traditions, the NCRLC had entered the modern media age.[28]

Interregnum

After McRaith resigned as director in 1978, the executive leadership of the NCRLC underwent a kind of interregnum. It had three executive directors in three years. The first was the Reverend Gerald Foley, who had been serving as associate director since July 1977. Prior to that, Foley had been a rural pastor and director of Catholic social services for the diocese of Crookston, Minnesota. He had a strong commitment to social justice. While executive director, he made a controversial visit to the migrant farm workers in California, which portended that he would become a leader of the Conference on the lines of O'Rourke. However, the board of directors asked him to resign after only a year, in March 1979. It was satisfied with Foley as an "outside presence" but disappointed in his ability to "inspire and lead the staff." He went on to pursue his interest in Catholic Engaged Encounter, with which he was on the National Executive Team.[29]

Foley's successor as executive director was most notable for being the first layman to hold the NCRLC leadership post. He was William J. Schaefer, a forty-year-old native of Minot, North Dakota. Before his appointment, Schaefer had been a teacher at Minot State College and director of a national project for farm couples. But he was relatively new to the Conference, having been a member of the board of directors only since 1977. He felt great pressure in the job and disliked the heavy travel (he was married with two children). The NCRLC treasurer questioned his attempt to borrow money and raise staff salaries. Administrative differences came to a head in spring 1980 when Schaefer fired one staff member and another quit shortly thereafter. In June he resigned to take a position teaching communications at Grand View College in Des Moines.[30]

28. Reports, etc., on promotion in NCRLC 8-24 and 8-25; files of *Catholic Rural Life* and *Common Ground* in NCRLC 6, especially "Conference News," *Common Ground* 2 (March 1984): 2; Joseph Fitzgerald to members, friends, and coworkers of NCRLC, February 7, 1990, in "Press for Spring '90 EM," La Blanc Subject File, Box 4, NCRLC.
29. "Father Gerald Foley Appointed NCRLC's New Associate Director," *Catholic Rural Life* 26 (June 1977): 8; "Bishop Dingman Announces Two NCRLC Staff Changes," ibid. 27 (April 1978): 20; "Father Foley Resigns as NCRLC Executive Director," ibid. 28 (March 1979): 5; Fr. Gerald Foley, "Autobiography," in "Form Letters, Memorandums, to Members and Officers, 1973-81," NCRLC 13-28; author's discussions with Foley, NCRLC headquarters, Des Moines, Iowa, September 20-22, 1978; William Schaefer to NCRLC Executive Board, March 1, 1979, in "Edwin V. O'Hara Institute," Cusack Subject File, Box 16, NCRLC.
30. "Bill Schaefer Is Appointed NCRLC Executive Director," *Catholic Rural Life* 28 (June 1979):

Organizing for Social Involvement

Figure 18. Pope John Paul II speaking at Living History Farms, Des Moines, Iowa, October 1979.

Schaefer was replaced on an interim basis by the Reverend Leonard Kayser, who was NCRLC vice president and Sioux Falls, South Dakota, diocesan director at the time of his appointment. Like Foley, Kayser was a social-action oriented priest. The Conference committee searching for a permanent executive director was happy with Kayser's initial months of work and offered him the job. However, Kayser declined because the committee would not increase his staff. He did not have time to establish a long-range policy before he returned to South Dakota and was succeeded by a new director in September 1981.[31]

The NCRLC got a big boost in prestige when Pope John Paul II visited Des Moines in October 1979. His sojourn in Iowa was the result of a letter from an Iowa farmer. The pontiff's appearance at Living History Farms near Des Moines, where 350,000 people attended the Mass, symbolized his

---

16; "Layman Named to Head Rural Life Conference," *Catholic Mirror,* June 28, 1979, unfoldered clipping in "NCRLC Minutes of Meetings 1980–1985," Box 2; Stephen Bossi-Schaefer correspondence, 1979, in "Bossi, Steve," Cusack Subject File, Box 16, NCRLC; Schaefer to Dan Florea, May 12, 1980, in "Florea/Baxter," ibid., Box 17; folder "Loan Application, NCRLC," ibid.; folder "McNamara, Bishop," ibid.; folder "Memos to Staff from WJS," ibid.

31. "Rev. Leonard Kayser Named NCRLC Interim Director," *Catholic Rural Life* 29 (June 1980): 28; tape, "Interview of Rev. Leonard Kayser, with David S. Bovee, Living History Farms, Des Moines, Iowa, October 5, 1983," "NCRLC, Oral History," NCRLC; Duane Pribula to Diocesan Director, May 22, 1981, in "EVO-1981," Cusack Subject File, Box 16; Adelaide Paradise, "A Man of the Land and God," *Earth Matters* 37 (Winter 1988): 11.

commitment to rural life. At the ceremony, John Paul accepted the gift of a basket containing soil from each of the forty-four dioceses participating in the "Strangers and Guests" statement and preached a homily on rural stewardship.[32]

Starting in the late 1970s, the NCRLC aimed to stimulate participation among the grass roots and respond to needs in certain areas of the United States by gradually developing a network of regions. The Conference had made attempts to interpose a layer of organization between the national office and the diocesan directors in the 1940s and again in the 1950s, but they were short-lived. This latest process of regionalization was more enduring than the earlier attempts because the regions grew organically in conjunction with favorable circumstances in each area, rather than being imposed as a single uniform nationwide structure all at once. Thus the Appalachia region was based on the Catholic Committee of Appalachia, the Midwest on the "Strangers and Guests" process, and the Northwest and Southwest on coordinators (Stephen Bossi and Teresa Nira) who were able to devote a considerable amount of time to organizing their regions. Meanwhile, in a region such as the Southeast, where few rural Catholics lived, the Conference at first made no attempt to establish a regional organization. By the mid-1980s, regional organizations were in place for the Pacific Northwest, Appalachia, the Southwest, and several regions of shifting groups of states in the Midwest, and regional statements had been published for the Midwest *(Strangers and Guests)* and Appalachia *(This Land Is Home to Me)*. The Midwest regions were by far the most active. They held meetings with up to one hundred participants, issued resolutions, and initiated NCRLC statements on tax reform and the 1985 farm bill. Regional activity declined in the 1990s, with new regions being added, others dropping out, but most meeting only sporadically. The bishops of Appalachia updated *This Land Is Home to Me* in 1995, with *At Home in the Web of Life*, and southeastern bishops issued a statement on the poultry industry. In 2001, the NCRLC hired a coordinator for the hitherto neglected Northeast region, but he was succeeded the next year by an organizer who went out to various areas throughout the United States. This national organizer left without replacement in 2005. Given the Conference's financial limitations and the regions' dependence on local interest, the NCRLC had to be content with this steadily declining level of regional activity.[33]

32. Articles in *Catholic Rural Life*, September and October, 1979.
33. Witte, *Twenty-five Years*, 134–36; "Directors Appointed in 17 Rural Life Regions," *Rural Life Conference—Feet in the Furrow* 5 (May 1956): 7; "Special NCRLC Committee Studies Regional

Cusack and Controversy

In 1981, the Conference finally reestablished some continuity in the position of executive director. In September of that year, the NCRLC named its second layman to that post, thirty-eight-year-old Gregory D. Cusack. Cusack had been a Democratic representative in the Iowa state legislature for eight years; his appointment demonstrated an awareness of a growing need for political savvy in the Conference.[34]

Cusack and the NCRLC made an important contribution to the United States bishops' landmark pastoral letter *Economic Justice for All* (1986). The bishops originally planned that the document not include a separate rural chapter but were convinced otherwise by former NCRLC president George Speltz and other rural bishops. Cusack and others wrote the first draft of the rural chapter, other Conference members responded to several of the drafts, and Cusack and Bishops Strecker, Dingman, O'Rourke, and Speltz testified before the bishops' committee that was writing the pastoral. The final result echoed NCRLC concerns on the 1980s farm crisis, the concentration of farm ownership, the loss of minority farms, the conditions of farm workers, the preservation of family farms, and the stewardship of natural resources. Much work was done on a NCRLC study guide for the pastoral, but after Cusack left the Conference it was never completed.[35]

Growth," *Catholic Rural Life* 28 (December 1979): 15–16; "Notice to NCRLC Members," ibid. 31 (October–November 1981): 3; Minutes, "Board of Directors Meeting, Des Moines, Iowa, November 7–8, 1979," NCRLC 8-25, 3–4; "Central Heartland Plans Annual Meeting," *Common Ground* 5 (March 1987): 2; "Regional News," ibid. (June 1987): 2–3; "New Rural Partnerships Are Created in Amarillo," ibid. 12 (February 1993): 3; "Building Community," *Rural Landscapes* 2 (October 1994): 3; "Southern Bishops Examine Poultry Industry," ibid. 8 (January 2001): 7; files in Cusack Subject Files, Box 19, on several regions; Leonard Kayser to Al Fritsch, S.J., August 28, 1980, in "Fritsch, Al—S.J.," ibid., Box 17; "Report to the Board of Directors, National Catholic Rural Life Conference, May 6, 2002, Northeast Regional Coordinator, William P. Jordan (Bill)," in unprocessed mailings, NCRLC; "National Catholic Rural Life Conference, NCRLC Board Report, November 2004, Report from Toby Pearson, National Organizer," in ibid.

34. "NCRLC Names New Executive Director," *Catholic Rural Life* 31 (September 1981): 41–42; Cusack to Leonard Kayser, June 24, 1981, with resume, in "Cusack, Gregory," in Cusack Subject File, Box 16, NCRLC.

35. "Diocesan Rural Life Directors Meet in Kansas City," *Catholic Rural Life* 35 (February 1985): 22; "Regional News," *Common Ground* 4 (July 1985): 2–3; "Conference News," ibid. (May 1986): 1; George H. Speltz, "Ministry to Rural People and Society," *Earth Matters* 38 (Summer 1989): 31–34; "Minutes of the Meeting of the Board of Directors of the National Catholic Rural Life Conference, May 13–15, 1985, St. Joseph Retreat House, Des Plaines, Illinois," in "NCRLC: Board Meeting," in "Fitzgerald Files: Board Related, ca. 1986–89," Box 1, 3; "Statement of the Board of Directors of the National Catholic Rural Life Conference on the Second Draft of the U. S. Catholic Bishops Pastoral Catholic Social Teaching and the U. S. Economy, January, 1986," ibid.; "A Report to the Membership of the National Catholic Rural Life Conference by Greg Cusack, NCRLC Executive Director" [November 1985], in "Correspondence with Archbishop Strecker," Cusack Sub-

Figure 19. Gregory D. Cusack, executive director, 1981–87.

Cusack initiated a controversial series of four Theology of Land conferences sponsored by the NCRLC and St. John's University in Minnesota in 1985, 1986, 1987, and 1989. By this time, the Conference's helplessness in the face of the ominous decline of the family farm led it to try to influence the broader and deeper ideas behind humans' relationship to the land. It hoped that the conferences would have a long-range impact on the Catholic theological community, perhaps through publication of the addresses in theological journals. The conferences, held at St. John's, featured from two to five speakers with national reputations (or, in the case of Archbishop Dom Helder Camara of Brazil, who addressed the 1987 conference, an international one) and drew from 60 to 120 participants. The theme of the first conference was the ethical framework for a theology of land; that of the second, forms of community on the land; the third, land reform; and the fourth, rights and responsibilities of ownership. The conferences were publicized by books, videos, and audiotapes of the proceedings.[36]

However, they did not have the intended influence on the Catholic

---

ject File, Box 19, 2; drafts of NCRLC study guide in "Economic Pastoral, Periods of Prayer, 1987 Spring," La Blanc Subject File, Box 4; National Conference of Catholic Bishops, *Economic Justice for All*, paragraphs 216–50.

36. "Conference News," *Common Ground* 4 (October 1985): 1–3; "1986 Theology of Land Conference," ibid. 5 (August 1986): 2; "1987 Theology of Land Conference," ibid. 6 (August 1987): 1–2;

Organizing for Social Involvement 251

theological community. In fact, they created much dissension within the NCRLC itself. Cusack and the liberals wanted speakers representing the ecumenical, feminist, liberation theology, and radical ecology points of view. Other members of the board warned that these needed to be balanced by more traditional voices. Although some mainstream theologians were invited, most attention was attracted by the radicals, who made a number of controversial statements. One said that Creation should not be viewed as "a hierarchy where one life form has greater value than another"—a position that opposed the traditional Catholic emphasis on "the primacy of the person." Another similarly praised the Native American perspective in which "humanity is not seen as superior to other life forms." A new constitutional amendment that would grant legal protection to "species of life, singular natural features, and the functioning of major life systems" was proposed by a third speaker. A fourth, in drawing parallels between the abuses of both women and the land throughout history, said that "the problem is 'basically male machismo.'" The mere presence of pro-choice feminist theologian Rosemary Radford Ruether at the 1986 conference induced several conservatives—including NCRLC president Strecker—to boycott the meeting. For his part, Cusack seethed, "I . . . have had it up to my gills with 'official' Catholicity and the new wave of censorship." After he left the Conference, the Theology of Land project gradually petered out and in 1993 was renamed Rural Faith and Justice to merge with the NCRLC's traditional rural policy development concerns.[37]

"NCRLC Materials," ibid. 8 (July 1989): 4; "Order Tapes Today!" ibid. 8 (Fall 1989): 3; "Minutes of the Spring Meeting of the Board of Directors of the National Catholic Rural Life Conference, April 30–May 2, 1986, Our Savior of the World Seminary, Kansas City, Kansas," in "NCRLC: Board Meeting," "Fitzgerald Files: Board Related, ca. 1986–89," Box 1, 6, 9; "Program/Project Description," in "Theo. Land—Media Grant Appl.," ibid., Box 1; "Minutes, NCRLC Board of Directors Meeting, November 30–December 1, 1988, Bloomington, MN," in "Fall 1988 Board Meeting," La Blanc Subject File, Box 1, 3, 5.

37. "1986 Theology of Land Conference," 3; "Association of Diocesan Directors' Meeting, January 9–11, 1985, St. John's Pastoral Center, Kansas City, Missouri," in "NCRLC: Board Meeting," "Fitzgerald Files: Board Related, ca. 1986–89," Box 1, 3; Martha Mary McGraw, "If We Exploit People, We Will Exploit the Land," *Sooner Catholic*, October 6, 1985, copy in "Theology of Land Conference 1985 Follow up Material," Cusack Subject File, Box 20; James R. Cunningham to Cusack and Bernard F. Evans, June 12, 1986, ibid.; Cusack to Evans, June 17, 1986, ibid.; Ignatius Strecker to Cusack, August 7, 1986, in "Correspondence with Archbishop Strecker," ibid., Box 19; John Hart, "Land, Theology, and the Future," in *Theology of the Land*, ed. Bernard F. Evans and Gregory Cusack (Collegeville, Minn.: Liturgical Press, 1987), 90; Richard Cartwright Austin, "Rights for Life: Rebuilding Human Relationships with the Land," in ibid., 122; Lynn Hayes to Program and Planning Committee, April 7, 1993, in "May 93 Bd. Mtg.," Executive Director File, Box 2, NCRLC.

Under Cusack's leadership, the NCRLC continued to suffer from its longstanding internal problems. Membership declined from 2,793 in 1979 to 1,256 in 1986. The customary small-scale membership drives (one in 1982 had a goal of adding a thousand members) did little to alleviate the situation. Cusack attributed some of the membership decline to the lethargy of the diocesan directors of rural life, whom he called "our weakest organizational link" and of whom he claimed only thirty or forty out of 116 were active. He complained that many diocesan directors were not even members of the NCRLC, yet they were supposed to be "our frontline troops in selling and promoting the Conference, including memberships."[38]

In 1981, the NCRLC made an effort to strengthen diocesan rural life programs by instituting a "shared membership" policy (whereby 20 percent of each member's annual membership fee was returned to the diocesan rural life program), providing diocesan directors with regularly updated lists of the Conference members in their dioceses, and allowing NCRLC staff to delegate authority to local members to represent the Conference on appropriate occasions. The results were disappointing. Cusack lamented that except in Minnesota and Kayser's diocese in South Dakota, new members from the policy were "virtually zilch!"[39]

Finances were also a problem. The NCRLC received a short-term financial boost in 1979 when it sold its large old headquarters in Des Moines for $232,000 and purchased a much smaller building at 4625 Beaver Drive for $68,000, with the balance going into a "building fund." In 1981, the purchase of service agreement with the USCC was terminated, and for two and a half years the Conference received approximately equal grants from its old supporter, the American Board of Catholic Missions. But when these were not renewed, the Conference entered a period of prolonged fiscal crisis. In 1982, the NCRLC budget ran a twenty-six thousand dollar deficit, which had to be covered by a drawdown on the building fund. Deficits continued through most of the rest of the Cusack years. The Confer-

---

38. "Minutes, NCRLC Board of Directors Meeting, Des Moines, Iowa, Nov. 7–8, 1979," in "Board of Directors Meeting, Des Moines, Iowa, November 7–8, 1979," NCRLC 8-25, 5; untitled sheet in "Board Meeting 11/29–30/89," La Blanc Subject File, Box 1, NCRLC; "A Product of the Times," *Catholic Rural Life* 31 (February 1982): 5; "NCRLC Board Approves Regional Thrust," ibid., 22; "Report of the Executive Director Greg Cusack to the Board of Directors of the National Catholic Rural Life Conference on the occasion of the Spring Board Meeting of the Board of Directors, Kansas City, Kansas, Apr. 30–May 2, 1986," in "NCRLC: Board Meeting," in "Fitzgerald Files: Board Related, ca. 1986–87," Box 1, 4; Cusack to Officers of the Diocesan Directors' Association, December 8, 1982, in "Diocesan Directors' Association," Cusack Subject File, Box 19.

39. Bart Pollock, "Notice to NCRLC Members," *Catholic Rural Life* 31 (October–November 1981): 3–5; Cusack to Officers of the Diocesan Directors' Association, December 8, 1982.

Organizing for Social Involvement 253

ence's expenses increased by about ten thousand dollars a year, but no stable source emerged to replace the lost USCC or ABCM grants. The USCC refused requests by NCRLC presidents Bishop Lawrence McNamara and Strecker to reinstate the purchase of service agreement between the two organizations. Despite increasingly desperate appeals, contributions from the bishops—the most important source of income—leveled off at about sixty thousand dollars per year. Raising the cost of membership and pursuing grants gained little additional income. A fundraiser hired for $12,800 raised only $24,625. The NCRLC was in the black for only one full year of Cusack's administration—when Bishop Dingman gave it over fifty thousand dollars left over from money contributed by the Heartland region to pay for the pope's visit.[40]

As a result of the "financial tightrope" walked by the NCRLC, Cusack adopted a number of cost-cutting measures. Staff was laid off and salary increases were few and far between. *Catholic Rural Life* was cut from eleven issues a year to five, other programs were cut, and no new programs started that would have required additional staff. At one point, besides freezing all unnecessary expenditures, Cusack suggested that all staff go without paychecks for a month.[41]

Problems with the bishops and the USCC were related to the Conference's financial troubles during the Cusack years. Archbishop Strecker, who resumed the presidency of the NCRLC in 1983, believed that the Conference did not get much financial support from the bishops because it was too midwestern in orientation and insufficiently included the bishops in its governance. At the time, two-thirds of the NCRLC board of directors was from the Midwest, with no bishops besides the president. Strecker proposed that more bishops representative of the entire nation be appointed to the board and that NCRLC headquarters join the other bishops' offices in Washington, D.C. Conference officials opposed a move to Washington, though they supported including more nationally diverse bishops on the

40. "Report on Sale of NCRLC Property—3801 Grand Avenue, DM, Ia.," in "Brd. Meeting 79," Cusack Subject File, Box 16; "Minutes, NCRLC Board of Directors, May 26–28, 1982," in box "NCRLC Current/Incoming Pubs. to Be Filed," NCRLC, 3-4; John Zeitler, "Wednesday, October 5; Thursday, October 6," *Common Ground* 2 (October 1983): 4; budget figures in Cusack Subject File, Box 18; file "Correspondence with Bishop McNamara," ibid., Box 17; Gregory Cusack to Maurice Dingman, October 8, 1984, and attached correspondence in "Misc. Correspondence," ibid., Box 16; file "Correspondence with Archbishop Strecker," ibid., Box 19; "Report of the Executive Director Greg Cusack to the Board of Directors of the National Catholic Rural Life Conference on the Occasion of the Spring Board Meeting of the Board of Directors, Kansas City, Kansas, April 30–May 2, 1986," in "NCRLC: Board Meeting," "Fitzgerald Files: Board Related, ca. 1986–89," Box 1, NCRLC, 5-6.
41. "Report of the Executive Director Greg Cusack"; Cusack to All Staff, April 12, 1984, in "Staff Memos," La Blanc Subject File, Box 8.

board. In 1985, Strecker convened two "bishops' rural caucuses" at the biannual meetings of the hierarchy to discuss the relationship between the NCRLC and the bishops, as well as the family farm crisis. The forty to fifty bishops from rural dioceses at the meetings agreed with Strecker that more bishops from a wider area of the nation should be put on the NCRLC board. But nothing was accomplished in this area during Cusack's administration except the creation of hard feelings between NCRLC officials on the one hand and Strecker and other bishops on the other.[42]

Although Cusack lasted longer as director than his three predecessors, he still had many personal troubles in the role. As early as his second year in the position, he was having difficulties with the internal "politics" of the NCRLC and the personalities of the staff. Cusack had particular problems with Strecker when he resumed the presidency in 1983. Besides his refusal to attend the Theology of Land conference because of Ruether, the archbishop was angered by Cusack's public criticism of the bishops' financial support of the Conference. The board of directors was concerned about Cusack's lack of fundraising activity, his handling of the staff, and his not including the bishops or Catholic spirituality sufficiently in the Conference's work. In August 1986 Cusack was so concerned about the poor financial state of the NCRLC that he contemplated closing it down. The next month he fired three of the staff's six employees, prompting an emergency visit by the executive committee. It concluded that the terminations were unjustified and, along with the other problems, constituted cause to ask for Cusack's resignation. He left at the end of the year to take a position in the Iowa Department of Agriculture.[43]

---

42. "Minutes of the Meeting of the Board of Directors of the National Catholic Rural Life Conference, November 6–8, 1985, Our Savior of the World Seminary, Kansas City, Kansas," in "NCRLC: Board Meeting," "Fitzgerald Files: Board Related, ca. 1986–89," Box 1, NCRLC, 2; "National Catholic Rural Life Conference Board of Directors, Jan., 1985," ibid.; "Rural Life Directors Association, National Meeting, Bergamo Center, Dayton, Ohio, January 24, 1986," ibid.; Gregory Cusack to NCRLC Board of Directors, April 18, 1986, ibid.; Cusack to Board Members Attending Board Meeting of November 6–8, 1985, November 17, 1985, ibid.; Cusack to NCRLC Board of Directors, July 12, 1985, in "NCRLC Budget," ibid., 2–3; [Ignatius Strecker], "The National Catholic Rural Life Conference," in "NCRLC—Bishops' Task Force," ibid.; Charles Isenhart, "Rural Life Conference Could Face a Shutdown," *National Catholic Register*, July 27, 1986, in "N.C.R.L.C.," Fitzgerald Files, Box 1, 1, 8; Cusack to Strecker, October 31, 1985, in "Correspondence with Archbishop Strecker," Cusack Subject File, Box 19.

43. Cusack-David Andrews correspondence, 1982, in "EVO," Cusack Subject File, Box 17, NCRLC; file "Correspondence with Archbishop Strecker," ibid., Box 19; "Report, On-Site Study of National Catholic Rural Life Conference by Team for the NCRLC Board of Directors, Des Moines, Iowa, October 6–7, 1986," in "NCRLC Budget," in "Fitzgerald Files: Board Related, ca. 1986–89," Box 1, NCRLC; Cusack to Members of the Board of Directors of the NCRLC, December 18, 1986, in untitled folder in "Fitzgerald Files," Box 1, NCRLC.

Stabilization under Fitzgerald

Cusack was replaced effective September 1987 by another layman, Joseph K. Fitzgerald, diocesan director of rural life of the archdiocese of Louisville, president of the diocesan directors association, and a member of the NCRLC board of directors. Fitzgerald had been raised on a diversified farm in Iowa, earned degrees in humanities and theology, and then taught high school before becoming a diocesan director.[44]

Fitzgerald was successful in stabilizing the NCRLC's finances and the relations among the staff. The budget ran a surplus as often as a deficit. Diocesan contributions were increased to about one hundred thousand dollars a year and grants from twenty-five thousand to ninety-seven thousand dollars a year. But it was still a struggle. Special grants from the USCC and the ABCM tided the Conference over two difficult years. Suspending publication of the Conference periodical and canceling one of the semiannual board of directors meetings saved money in another year. Fitzgerald also negotiated the agreement that divided the international fund fifty-fifty instead of giving 80 percent of the income to Agrimissio. The $308,000 together with $68,000 from the St. Isidore fund was invested with Franklin Research and Development Corporation, a socially responsible investor, and used for broadly international purposes. This proved to be a considerable source of income for the NCRLC.[45]

Fitzgerald attempted to increase the NCRLC's membership and the income from that source. Certain dioceses (first Owensboro, Kentucky, and Omaha, later Bismarck, Lubbock, Texas, and St. Paul / Minneapolis) were targeted using diocesan adaptations of *Common Ground*. Membership income increased in the first year from twenty-one thousand to thirty-one thousand dollars but fell back to the original figure after two more years. Memberships also temporarily increased but declined overall to 927 by 1993. Members were also older: in a *Catholic Rural Life* readership survey, 68.4 percent of the respondents were age 55 and over.[46]

---

44. "NCRLC Names New Executive Director," *Common Ground* 6 (October 1987): 1; "Joseph Kvale Fitzgerald" (résumé, 1987), in "Press Release for New Executive Director," La Blanc Subject File, Box 4, NCRLC; "Joseph K. Fitzgerald Resigns as Executive Director of the National Catholic Rural Life Conference," NCRLC Press Release, January 14, 1994, in box "NCRLC Pubs. ca. 1990–1994 Rec'd: 4/21/94," NCRLC.

45. Financial documents in "Fitzgerald Files: Board Related, ca. 1986–89," and "Fitzgerald Files: Budget, 1989–93; Board Meetings," NCRLC.

46. Board of directors meeting minutes in Fitzgerald Files, Box 2; Fitzgerald to Joe Chrastl, March 16, 1993, unfoldered in Executive Director Files, Box 1; Dianne Avgerinos, untitled paper

The NCRLC's periodicals were reshaped at this time. The Conference board thought that "the 'Catholic' in *Catholic Rural Life* may have the effect of limiting the appeal of an excellent publication" and adopted the more ecumenical and environmental title of *Earth Matters*. The change lasted for only two years, and in 1990 the periodical was suspended for financial reasons. At the same time the newsletter *Common Ground* was made a monthly and sent not primarily to NCRLC members but to "a broad network of people who are concerned about rural, food, agricultural and environmental issues"—an increase in circulation from 1,800 to 12,000. This experiment also did not last, and in 1994 *Common Ground* was succeeded by *Rural Landscapes,* a newsletter circulated to Conference members and a few others as before.[47]

During Fitzgerald's administration, the NCRLC strengthened its relationship with the bishops. Relations between Cusack and Conference president Strecker and the bishops in general had been strained. In 1986 Archbishop John R. Roach of Minneapolis / St. Paul, a former president of the National Conference of Catholic Bishops (NCCB), replaced Strecker as president of the NCRLC. Immediately following publication that same fall of the bishops' economic pastoral, NCCB president Bishop James Malone asked Roach to form a special task force to study rural and food issues. The task force consisted of bishops and non-bishops, including some NCRLC board members, and its report received unanimous approval by the NCCB in 1988. It said that "the issues of land control, hunger, rural poverty, and natural resource use need to be addressed with a sense of greater urgency and visibility" and set up a new rural subcommittee of the USCC which included Fitzgerald. It urged the NCRLC to expand its efforts at pastoral ministry and education (policy analysis and advocacy were to remain the province of the USCC), though it offered no new financial resources. Three to five bishops should be added to the NCRLC board.[48]

---

attached to Avgerinos to Sandra La Blanc, May 5, 1984, in "CRL Readership Survey 1985," La Blanc Subject File, Box 6, Table XII of Appendix D.

47. "A Preview of Fall Fashions," *Catholic Rural Life* 38 (June 1988): 3; Sandra A. La Blanc, "Another New Beginning," *Earth Matters* 37 (Fall 1988): 3; "National Catholic Rural Life Conference," ibid. (Spring 1990): 28; "Minutes, NCRLC Board of Directors, December 7–8, 1987, Bloomington, MN," in "NCRLC: Board Mtg. (Minutes)," in Fitzgerald Files, Box 2, 5; "Diocesan Relations Committee, May 9, 1994," in "NCRLC Incoming Minutes, 1994–," in "NCRLC Current Mailings, 1994–."

48. "Archbishop John R. Roach Unanimously Elected President of NCRLC" (NCRLC news release), in untitled folder in "Fitzgerald Files," Box 1; "Minutes, NCRLC Board of Directors Meeting, November 30–December 1, 1988, Bloomington, MN," in "NCRLC: Board Mtg. (Minutes)" in ibid., Box 2; Joseph K. Fitzgerald, "Report on the Food and Agriculture Task Force," *Common Ground* 7 (January 1989): 1; Walt Grazer, "An Invitation to Education," *Earth Matters* 38 (Summer 1989): 36; National Conference of Catholic Bishops [and] United States Catholic Conference, *Re-*

Organizing for Social Involvement 257

The NCRLC complied with the last recommendation by electing three bishops to the board, but they failed to attend meetings, and by 1991 the board was again down to two bishops. After that, the Conference seemed satisfied with one or two bishops on the board (usually two, including the president). In 1991, when the Reverend William J. Wood, S.J., replaced Roach as president, Bishop William Skylstad of Spokane was chosen "bishop liaison" to represent NCRLC interests to the NCCB. Wood, the first non-bishop president since Ligutti in the late 1930s, was the executive director of the California bishops' conference, an official in Food First and Bread for the World, and a dedicated environmentalist. Skylstad, son of an apple grower and noted for his concern for Hispanics and farm laborers in Washington's Yakima Valley, replaced Wood in 1993, ending the bishop liaison experiment and restoring the presidency to bishops.[49]

The NCRLC complied with the bishops' recommendation to expand their efforts in the areas of rural ministry and education by forming the Grassroots Rural Ministry Program (GRMP) in 1990. GRMP utilized a program director in Des Moines and several field representatives who covered multistate regions in the Midwest. They held meetings attracting up to one hundred diocesan directors and other local rural leaders to train and educate them on agricultural, rural lifestyle, environmental, and liturgical issues. GRMP published three booklets that advised local rural advocates on how to hold rural life day celebrations, community support groups, and listening sessions. However, the program had little discernible effect in broadening the base for the NCRLC's work, and such regional outreach was folded back into the executive director's duties in 1995.[50]

About the same time as the dissolution of GRMP, the rural life directors' association was dissolved and their consultations ceased. This still left

---

port of the Ad Hoc Task Force on Food, Agriculture, and Rural Concerns, November 15, 1988 (Washington, D.C.: United States Catholic Conference, 1989), in "Publications Acq'd: 6/30/94, Box 23, NCRLC, quotation, 24.

49. Board of directors meeting minutes, 1988–93, in "NCRLC: Board Mtg. (Minutes)," in Fitzgerald Files, Box 2, NCRLC; "California Jesuit Named NCRLC President," *Common Ground* 10 (February 1991): 2; "National Catholic Rural Life Conference Board Profile," ibid. (May 1991): 4; Mark Pattison, "Sowing the Seeds of a New Farm Policy," Superior *Catholic Herald*, February 4, 1993, copy in "NCRLC Board Meeting: May 6–7, 1993," Fitzgerald Files, Box 2.

50. "Grassroots Rural Ministry Program Begins Outreach," *Common Ground* 10 (September 1990): 3; "NCRLC Offers New Resources for Rural Ministry Programs," ibid. (May 1991): 2; "NCRLC Conferences Offered Insight and Challenge," ibid. 11 (March/April 1992): 3; "Minutes, Board of Directors Meeting, National Catholic Rural Life Conference, Airport Sheraton, Bloomington, Minnesota, November 9–10, 1992," in "NCRLC: Board Mtg. (Minutes)" in Fitzgerald Files, Box 2; "The National Catholic Rural Life Conference Board of Directors Meeting, December 1 and 2, 1995, The Mount Conference Center, Atchison, KS, Executive Director's Report," in "Current Mailings, 94–."

the diocesan rural life directors as the vital link between the national office and the grass-roots members for the NCRLC, as they had been throughout the Conference's history. Officially, there were an impressive 172 rural life directors in the 188 dioceses in the United States, but 106 of them combined their rural duties with other ministries, and only about a dozen of the others were full-time. A Conference official said, "It is the exception that anything significant happens in a diocese where the position of rural life director is not full time." Such full-time directors as Sister Christine Pratt of the diocese of Toledo were mainstays in bringing the message of the NCRLC to local areas into the new millennium despite the lack of a formal rural life director network.[51]

In addition to ending the rural life directors consultations, by the time Fitzgerald became executive director the NCRLC had stopped holding annual conventions. As a partial substitute, the Conference started in 1988 to participate in the USCC's "social ministry gathering" held every year in January or February in Washington, D.C. There Conference leaders networked with USCC (which in 2001 became the United States Conference of Catholic Bishops—USCCB) staff, bishops, representatives from Catholic organizations such as Catholic Charities and the Campaign for Human Development as well as non-Catholic groups, officials from government agencies like the Department of Agriculture, and congresspeople. They listened to nationally prominent speakers such as legal scholar Mary Anne Glendon and journalists Mark Shields and Paul Gigot. The NCRLC held its own "wrap-around session," which included the top leaders such as the executive director, president, and diocesan rural life directors, but to which all Conference members were invited. A session in 1997 attended by forty people was called "a BIG success." In this way, the NCRLC, while retaining its headquarters in the heartland, maintained a regular presence at the center of national Catholic and governmental affairs.[52]

Under Fitzgerald the NCRLC put a renewed emphasis on prayer and worship materials, which had slacked off under Cusack's administration.

---

51. "Minutes, Board Meeting, National Catholic Rural Life Conference, December 2–3, 1993, Days Inn Civic Center, St. Paul, Minnesota," in Executive Director Files, Box 2, NCRLC, 1; [David Andrews?], "Towards an Official Definition of a Rural Life Director" [1995], in "Current Mailings, 1994–," NCRLC, 4; "Background and Justification for the Grassroots Rural Ministry Program" [1990] in "Official Files" in Executive Director Files, Box 1, 1; "Report from Sr. Christine Pratt, Diocese of Toledo" [November, 2006], in unprocessed mailings, NCRLC.

52. Folders "RLDA Mtg. Feb. '88" and "February 1989 RLD Mtg.," in La Blanc Subject File, Box 6, NCRLC; documents in "Current Mailings, 1994–," NCRLC; "Building Community," *Rural Landscapes* 4 (April 1997): 3.

Organizing for Social Involvement 259

In 1989, the Conference published *Rural Life Prayers, Blessings and Liturgies*, a comprehensive rural prayer book edited by Victoria M. Tufano. It offered Advent and Lenten Period of Prayer materials and briefly reinstituted the Rural Parish Service, which Cusack had discontinued. Such materials—including prayers in Spanish, a reprint of the 1949 "classic" *Cooking for Christ*, and a rural-oriented Way of the Cross prayer book—continued to be offered under Fitzgerald's successor in future years.[53]

Fitzgerald's strengths were in administration; he was not very assertive in policy formation. The board of directors appointed a task force to advise the young director on public policy issues, although it did not seem to exert its will on him forcefully. The board chided him for being tentative with it and not showing enough initiative or coming forth with his own proposals.[54]

The NCRLC board of directors was very pleased overall with Fitzgerald's performance as executive director, and it reappointed him to additional three-year terms in 1990 and 1993. He did not complete his third term, resigning in 1994 to become director of farm operations for New Melleray Abbey in Dubuque, Iowa.[55]

Fitzgerald's replacement on an interim basis, Sandra A. La Blanc, broke new ground as the first woman to serve as executive director. She had edited the NCRLC's publications since 1981 and in many ways held the Conference together through numerous changes in staff as she continued as director of communications until 1999. A Lutheran, she was also a symbol of the Conference's ecumenism. She left the NCRLC to become the director of the Evangelical Lutheran Church's rural ministry office.[56]

---

53. "Period of Prayer Planned," *Earth Matters* 37 (Fall 1988): 24; "New Prayerbook Published by NCRLC," *Common Ground* 7 (April 1989): 5; "NCRLC Announces New Lenten Period of Prayer," ibid. 12 (January 1993): 4; "Introducing the 1994 Rural Parish Service," ibid. 13 (Fall 1994): 3; flyers "New and Updated Rural Life Prayers, Blessings and Liturgies—both English and Spanish Editions—Are Available!" and "Cooking for Christ" in "Current Mailings, 94–," NCRLC; Sr. Pegge Boehm, P.B.V.M., *The Way of the Cross: The Seasons of Rural Life* (Des Moines, Iowa: National Catholic Rural Life Conference, 2000), in unprocessed mailings, NCRLC; David Andrews, "Dear Friends of NCRLC," *National Catholic Rural Life Conference Annual Report, Fiscal Year 2005–2006*, in ibid., 5.

54. "Minutes, NCRLC Board of Directors Meeting, November 30–December 1, 1988, Bloomington, MN," in "NCRLC: Board Mtg. (Minutes)," in "Fitzgerald Files," Box 2, NCRLC, 5; "Executive Director Review" (April 1993) in "May 93 Bd Mtg.," in "Exec. Dir.," Box 2, NCRLC.

55. "Executive Director Review"; William S. Skylstad, "A Message from the President of the Board," *NCRLC Annual Report, 1993–94*, unfoldered in "NCRLC Current Mailings, 1994–," 2.

56. "Minutes, Board Meeting, National Catholic Rural Life Conference, December 2–3, Days Inn Civic Center, St. Paul, Minnesota," unfoldered in "Exec. Dir.," Box 2, NCRLC, 3; Sandra A. La Blanc, "Farewell My Friends," *Catholic Rural Life* 41 (Spring 1999): 35.

Figure 20. Sandra La Blanc, editor of NCRLC publications and director of communications, 1981–99; interim executive director, 1993–94.

Andrews and a New Century

In 1994, a new executive director was found in Brother David Andrews, C.S.C. He grew up in the small village of Myricks, Massachusetts, joined the Congregation of the Holy Cross after high school, and then taught high school for ten years in the brothers' schools. After directing a retreat center for several years, he acquired his first connection with the NCRLC when he became director of the O'Hara Institute for Rural Ministry in 1981. He was provincial director of his order's schools when he became executive director of the NCRLC. Andrews, who was described as "looking and sounding a little like Nebraska's famous orator and rural advocate, William Jennings Bryan," had an enthusiasm and charisma that had not been seen in the Conference since the time of Ligutti. He eventually acquired something of Ligutti's international influence as well, being picked to serve as a consultant to the Vatican on social justice issues. He resigned in 2007 to become the "coordinator of peace and justice" for the Congregation of the Holy Cross. Andrews was replaced on an interim basis by Tim Kautza, the Conference's science and environmental education specialist. In 2008, James F. Ennis, former director of Food Alliance Midwest, a sustainable-agriculture certification program for farms, ranches, and other food-related businesses, became the new executive director.[57]

57. "National Catholic Rural Life Conference Board of Directors Meeting, St. Paul, Minnesota, November 11–12, 1994, Minutes," unfoldered in "Fitzgerald Files: Board Related, ca. 1986–89," Box 1, NCRLC, 1–2; David Andrews, "A Message from the Executive Director," NCRLC Annual

Organizing for Social Involvement

As usual, the Conference's finances had their ups and downs during the Andrews years. After a couple of rough early years in which he had to draw on the reserve fund, the executive director was able to achieve mostly balanced budgets through 2002. The overall financial resources available to the NCRLC swelled from between one hundred thousand dollars and two hundred thousand dollars in the 1980s to two or three times that during Andrews's tenure, spiking at $685,000 in 2002. Diocesan memberships remained the most steady and usually the largest source of income at about $110,000 a year. But Andrews also worked hard at raising money from religious orders and especially in winning grants from foundations and other groups. Over the years, he acquired grants for hundreds of thousands of dollars each from the Beldon Foundation, Oxfam—Holland, Community Food Security, and the Catholic Campaign for Human Development, and smaller ones from sources such as the Knights of Columbus, the Nathan Cummings Foundation, the Midwest Sustainable Agriculture Coalition, the Kellogg Foundation, the Leopold Center, the United States Conference of Catholic Bishops, the Iowa Foundation for the Environment, the Clean Water Network, the Presbyterian Church, Higher Plain, and the Wellmark Foundation.[58]

The NCRLC received an appropriate addition to its financial resources when the Joyce family farm was given to it. The Reverend John and Edith Joyce, brother and sister from Henderson, Minnesota, donated their eleven-hundred-acre farm to the NCRLC in 1993, with the provisions that they be allowed to live on it the rest of their lives and that some of the land be used to educate the rural youth of the area. After the Joyces died in 2001, the NCRLC sold the land for $2,124,691, mostly to local farmers. The Conference paid $554,000 to the New Ulm diocese and St. Paul / Minneapolis archdiocese to fulfill the rural youth education provision and placed the

---

Report, 1994–95, in "Current Mailings, 1994–," NCRLC, 2-3; Curt Arens, "Voting with Your Fork," *Cedar County News* (Huntington, Nebraska), October 8, 2003, copy in unprocessed mailings, NCRLC; Renato Raffaele Cardinal Martino, President of the Pontifical Council for Justice and Peace, to Andrews, September 19, 2005, in ibid.; Martino and Norberto Cardinal Rivera Carrera, Archbishop Primate of Mexico, to Andrews, September 21, 2005, in ibid.; "Br. David Andrews, CSC, to step down as NCRLC executive director," www.ncrlc.com/BDA_resignation.html, accessed June 11, 2009; Ronald Gilmore, "Call to Stewardship," *Catholic Rural Life* (newsletter) 14 (July 2007): 1, untitled article, www.ncrlc.com/NCRLC_Executive_Director.html, accessed August 30, 2008.

58. Financial statements in "NCRLC Current Mailings, 1994–," NCRLC; "National Catholic Rural Life Financials for 2001," *NCRLC Annual Report, 2000–2001,* 10; "National Catholic Rural Life Conference Board of Directors Meeting, St. Paul, Minnesota, November 11–12, 1994, Minutes," unfoldered in "Fitzgerald Files: Board Related, ca. 1986–89," Box 1; Andrews to NCRLC Budget and Finance Committee, October 20, 1994 and April 10, 1995, in "NCRLC Current Mailings, 1994–"; grant reports and financial documents in unprocessed mailings, NCRLC.

rest of the proceeds with Christian Brothers Investment Services, which by this time was handling their investments. Along with the international and reserve funds, the Joyce property fund swelled the amount of the Conference's money in the hands of Christian Brothers to $2,528,259.[59]

It was just in time, because the periodic nemesis of financial crisis soon returned to strike the NCRLC. A great weakness of the Conference's finances was its heavy dependence on grants, which were usually for one to three years and were renewed at the caprice of the grantor. In 2002, the NCRLC received $362,535 in grants; the next year, despite numerous applications by Andrews, it was given only $41,887. The next two years were similarly lean, and the Conference had to sell off hundreds of thousands of dollars of its investments each year to make ends meet. In 2006, grant income rebounded to $485,280, but $255,000 of investments still had to be sold to balance the budget. By 2007, the Christian Brothers investments were down to $1,049,000. In response, the Conference hired a fundraising consultant, who proposed initiatives such as a new annual appeal, sought more stable sources of income, and considered cutbacks at the NCRLC headquarters.[60]

The changing fortunes of the Conference's finances had consequences for the NCRLC staff. In the 1990s Andrews made do with the same five or six people at the Des Moines headquarters who had served Cusack and Fitzgerald—the executive director, a communications director, one or two other professional staff, and two office workers. By 2000 and 2001, improved finances allowed him to hire an environmental specialist and two staff for the Ligutti Rural Community Support Program, raising the number of staff to eight. However, in 2007, the financial crisis caused the Conference to eliminate three staff positions, the codirectors of the Ligutti program and an office manager.[61]

Andrews had the aid of a very strong president, Bishop Raymond L. Burke of La Crosse, Wisconsin. Burke was raised as the youngest of six

---

59. "The Joyce Farm, Board update 11/9/01"; "The Joyce Farm Closing"; David Andrews to John C. Nienstedt, Bishop of New Ulm, Minnesota, January 30, 2003; and "National Catholic Rural Life Conference, Total Relationship, Participant Summary, Periods Ending June 30, 2002"; all in unprocessed mailings, NCRLC.

60. Financial documents in unprocessed mailings, NCRLC; "NCRLC Board Meeting, Nov. 5–6, 2004," in ibid., 4; "NCRLC Board of Directors Meeting, November 10, 2006, Sheraton Overland Park Conference Center, Kansas City, Kansas," in ibid., 4–5; David Andrews, "Dear Friends of NCRLC," *National Catholic Rural Life Conference Annual Report, Fiscal Year 2005–2006*, 4.

61. NCRLC files and publications, 1990s–2000s; Gilmore, "Call to Stewardship"; "Call to Stewardship Difficult, NCRLC President," www.ncrlc.com/e-bulletins/July%206%202007.html, accessed August 7, 2007.

children on a small family farm in southwestern Wisconsin. After ordination he studied church law and worked in Rome before being consecrated bishop in 1995. The NCRLC elected him president the next year. Pope John Paul II had greeted the new bishop by saying he came from the "good farm country," and Burke made the phrase a kind of motto for his work both in his diocese and for the NCRLC. He was an eloquent and forceful proponent of the Conference's positions, especially support for the family farm. Succeeding Burke as president were Bishop David Ricken of Cheyenne, Wyoming, (2001–5) and Bishop Ronald M. Gilmore of Dodge City, Kansas (starting in 2005).[62]

Under Andrews, the NCRLC went back to holding annual conventions—more modestly called "gatherings," "conferences," or "meetings." The Conference apparently felt it necessary to offer a get-together for the grass roots now that the leadership was participating in the USCC social ministry meeting in Washington, D.C., each year. In 1991 a "celebrating rural life" event had drawn about one hundred people to Des Moines, and Andrews made such gatherings annual affairs. They were held in Midwest cities and included guest speakers, workshops, worship services, and entertainment. They usually drew about one hundred participants, except for the seventy-fifth anniversary celebration in 1998, which attracted double that number. The previous year, the Conference varied the pattern with seven smaller regional conferences held in scattered locations—from New Hampshire to Texas, but again mostly in the Midwest. However, by 2006, the NCRLC's old concerns reappeared about the lack of a "national character" and the low attendance at the annual conferences.[63]

These factors also affected the Conference as a whole. "Memberships" in ever-changing categories declined from 1,256 in 1986 to 1,162 in 1990 to 927 in 1993 to 586 in 1996. In 2006, they had increased slightly to 705, but this continued low number caused the Conference to plan a strategy to work toward five hundred to one thousand "consumer-based" members with appeals focused on the "food security issue." This was reasonable considering only 12 percent of NCRLC members were full-time farmers,

62. "NCRLC Board of Directors Meeting, December 13, 1996, Atchison, KS," in "Current Mailings, 94–," NCRLC; Raymond L. Burke, "Homily" (September 16, 1998), ibid.; "A New Year Begins at the Conference," *Rural Landscapes* 9 (January 2002): 1; "Bishop Gilmore Elected to Lead NCRLC," *Catholic Rural Life* (newsletter) 13 (July 2005): 2.

63. "Date Set for NCRLC's First Annual 'Celebrating Rural Life' Event," *Common Ground* 10 (March 1991): 3; "Bergland Becomes Newest NCRLC Member," ibid. (June/July 1991): 3; articles in *Rural Landscapes* and *Catholic Rural Life* (newsletter), 1997 to present; documents in "NCRLC Current Mailings, 1994–"; "NCRLC Board of Directors Meeting, November 10, 2006, Sheraton Overland Park Conference Center, Kansas City, Kansas," in unprocessed mailings, NCRLC, 5.

and only 14 percent were part-time. Conference president Gilmore "raised his desire to see NCRLC more effective with people at the local level in the parishes." He suggested a pilot program to help spark interest in priests.[64]

The Conference's longstanding problem of maintaining its national focus also recurred after 2000. The NCRLC had always been anchored in the Midwest, but a significant amount of its attention became even more narrowly focused on Iowa. This had started noticeably with Cusack, the native son who developed networks with a number of local groups during the family farm crisis of the 1980s. About 2000, the Iowa emphasis again became prominent when the two full-time staff members of the Ligutti Rural Community Support Project cultivated projects situated exclusively in Iowa. Other staff members, especially the environmental education specialist, devoted much of their time to coordinating local groups such as Rural Advocacy (a coalition of Iowa nongovernmental organizations interested in rural issues), the Iowa Interfaith Climate and Energy Campaign (which educated about climate change), and Iowa Interfaith Power and Light (which helped congregations improve energy efficiency). Some of these activities had the virtue of connecting the Conference directly and effectively with grass roots rural people, which it had accomplished only sporadically in its history, but the NCRLC's limited resources did not allow this connection to extend beyond Iowa.[65]

Andrews mixed the old with the new in his methods of communication. In 1996, he brought back the traditional Conference magazine *Catholic Rural Life* in the slick format characteristic of the 1980s—although only twice a year. In 2004, the bimonthly newsletter was renamed *Catholic Rural Life* as well. But he also charged full speed ahead into the computer and Internet age. Under Andrews, the NCRLC inaugurated an official website, a weekly e-mail information service, desktop publishing of most of its publications, and presentations by compact disc and PowerPoint. By

64. Membership figures compiled in an attempt to provide comparable totals from untitled sheet in "Board Meeting 11/29–30/89," La Blanc Subject File, Box 1, NCRLC, and NCRLC annual reports; "NCRLC Board of Directors Meeting Minutes, November 4, 2005, Holiday Inn Downtown, Des Moines, Iowa," in unprocessed mailings, NCRLC, 3; "NCRLC Board of Directors Meeting, November 10, 2006, Sheraton Overland Park Conference Center, Kansas City, Kansas," in unprocessed mailings, NCRLC, 5; "Membership Survey 2004," *NCRLC Annual Report, 2005,* 5.

65. "Report of the Science and Environmental Education Specialist, Tim Kautza, May 20, 2004," in unprocessed mailings, NCRLC, 4–5; "Report of the Science and Environmental Specialist, Tim Kautza, November 2005," in unprocessed mailings, NCRLC, 1; "Report of the Science and Environmental Education Specialist, Tim Kautza, November 2006," in unprocessed mailings, NCRLC, 1. For criticisms of the midwestern emphasis of the NCRLC, see Marlett, *Saving the Heartland,* 99; Thomas More Bertels, *In Pursuit of Agri-Power: The One Thing North American Farmers and Ranchers Can't Produce* (Manitowoc, Wisc.: Silver Lake College Press, 1988), 176–88.

Organizing for Social Involvement   265

2006, the NCRLC website was contacted six thousand times a day, and the "e-bulletin" went out to three thousand leaders, who in turn circulated it to their own lists, reaching an estimated fifteen thousand people each week. Still, the Conference showed its simple rural roots in having doubts about these new technologies. In 1995, the board of directors had an extended discussion "about the meaning and value of striving for 'efficiency' through technology" and "whether we had truly explored the 'evil' nature of some similar and related efforts throughout the economy ... Are we assuming that because the technology is there we 'ought' to use it and that using it is really 'good'?"[66]

The Age of Vatican II

From the 1960s into the 2000s, the NCRLC was affected by the era of the Second Vatican Council (1962–65). Vatican II was followed by an open atmosphere that encouraged activities such as Catholic participation in the ecumenical movement and greater participation by bishops, clergy, and laypeople in the government and apostolate of the Church. The NCRLC illustrated some of the changes in American Catholic institutions that occurred during the era of Vatican II.

After Vatican II, a movement toward independence from authority arose within the American Church. This was exemplified by assertions of autonomy from Rome, turmoil in religious communities, and the activities of individuals such as the pacifist Jesuits Daniel and Philip Berrigan.[67] In this area, the Conference had been a precursor of the era of Vatican II. It had been involved in conflicts of authority since the 1930s—first in the persistent struggle to retain its independence from the NCWC in Washington and later in the actions of strong-willed individuals such as Father Vizzard. This continued with the Conference's difficult adjustment with the USCC from the 1960s through the rest of the century.

The NCRLC urged rural Catholics to heed Pope John's call in *Mater et Magistra* to "observe, judge, and act." Members of the Conference were

---

66. "Tool Kit," *Rural Landscapes* 5 (October 1997): 2; "Resources," ibid. 9 (January 2002): 8; National Catholic Rural Life Conference Annual Report, 1995–96, in "Current Mailings, 94–," NCRLC, 1; "Computer Phases," attached to Andrews to Board of Directors of NCRLC, December 6, 1995, in ibid.; "Minutes, The National Catholic Rural Life Conference Board of Directors, December 1 and 2, 1995, the Conference Center at Mount Saint Scholastica, Atchison, KS," in ibid., 5; Sandra La Blanc to Chuck Elston, January 15, 1997, unfoldered recent acquisition, NCRLC; David Andrews, "Dear Friends of NCRLC," *National Catholic Rural Life Conference Annual Report, Fiscal Year 2005–2006*, 5.

67. John Tracy Ellis, *American Catholicism*, 2d ed. (Chicago: University of Chicago Press, 1969), 210–22, 224–36.

encouraged to participate in rural apostolates such as Rural Area Development Committees, cooperative marketing, sharing abundance, "people-to-people" programs, participation in the liturgy, cursillos, and the Christian family movement.[68]

This applied especially to the laity. O'Rourke quoted the "Decree on the Apostolate of the Laity" published during Vatican II on the duty of laypeople to "take up the renewal of the temporal order as their own special obligation." O'Rourke believed that rural laypeople ought to participate in education, politics, farmers' groups, and antipoverty programs. One application of this idea was the activity of FOCIS (Federation of Communities in Service), which was formed in 1967. This was an organization of ex-Glenmary sisters who abandoned convent life and an emphasis on evangelization to live individually among the people of Appalachia and promote social justice.[69]

After Vatican II, the laity acquired a much more important role within the NCRLC. This followed the national trend in which by 1999 seven out of ten parish ministers were laypeople. In 1979, the Conference had the first of its four lay executive directors. The next year, the NCRLC elected a Native American educator, a female Hispanic migrant farm-worker organizer, a family farmer, an African American organizer, and a Hispanic farmer to the board of directors in an attempt to increase lay representation in its decision-making process. This did not work out well because these laypeople rarely attended meetings and did not connect the Conference to significant constituencies. The NCRLC discontinued the plan to have so many laypeople on the board, but it usually tried to include at least one farmer.[70]

The laity also acquired increased influence among the diocesan directors. By the late 1970s, more and more of the approximately 120 diocesan directors were laypeople, and the directors had their first lay president. The diocesan directors were also more active. A survey of diocesan direc-

---

68. "Opportunities for Social Action" (1963), in "Christian Social Principles—Application to Issues of Early 60's," NCRLC 8A-1.

69. E. W. O'Rourke, "Vatican Council II to Laymen," *Catholic Rural Life* 15 (February 1966): 2; Mary Beth Dakoske Duffey, "Fidelity to a Promise of Service," ibid. 31 (April–May 1981): 16–25.

70. Jay P. Dolan, *In Search of an American Catholicism*, 229; whole issue of *Catholic Rural Life* 27 (October 1978); NCRLC News Release, "Election Brings Diversity to NCRLC Board," in "Bd. of Directors Meeting, Techny, Illinois, November 18–21, 1980," NCRLC 8-25; Gregory Cusack to Jim Krile and Larry Nawrocki, July 26, 1983, in "Nominations Committee," Cusack Subject File, Box 19; "Report of the Executive Director Greg Cusack on the occasion of the Spring Board Meeting, April 30–May 2, 1986," 2; "NCRLC Board Development Committee, Conference Call Meeting Minutes, October 3, 1990," unfoldered in Fitzgerald Files, Box 2; "Dear Sisters," n.d., in "NCRLC Board Meeting: May 6–7, 1993," ibid.

tors in 1979 showed that more of them took the position by choice rather than appointment by their bishop. Most of them organized rural life committees, which involved more people in the planning of rural life activities, and more cooperated with other offices in the diocese such as social concerns or diocesan charities. In 1981, Dingman hired the first full-time diocesan director, and five years later there were six of them. Because of the family farm crisis, directors increased their involvement in rural issues through personal assistance and education.[71]

The NCRLC mirrored the post–Vatican II trend of increased women's involvement in the Church. By 1999, 82 percent of parish ministers nationwide were women. In the Conference, women such as Sandra La Blanc served vital roles in the central office. A deliberate policy increased gender balance on the board of directors, which eventually became about one-third to one-half women. Some of the most active diocesan directors were women, such as Sister Christine Pratt of Ohio, who repeatedly had to answer the question, "What does a nun know about farming?" Women were prominent in the Farmers' Legal Action Group, which gave legal assistance to family farmers. In rural America, the percentage of female farm operators increased while more women ran for state office, mayors, county government, and school boards. At the same time, rural women were exploited as low-wage service workers, earning forty-four cents to every dollar earned by men. The Conference tried to compensate in some measure by drawing upon "the powerful and illuminating contemporary visions of feminist theology" in its Theology of Land conferences.[72]

The NCRLC also paid attention to the clergy during the era of Vatican II, when the Church suffered from a crisis in religious vocations. It asserted that this was another reason to support the family farm, since an estimated one-third of vocations came from rural areas. Dingman said that "more religious vocations come from family farms proportionately than from any other similar group . . . The more family farms, the more

71. "NCRLC Diocesan Directors," *Catholic Rural Life* 22 (November 1973): 13; "Emerging Lay Involvement In Rural Ministry Is Cited," ibid. 27 (October 1978): 2; "Trends: Diocesan Rural Life," ibid. 28 (May 1979): 19; "Report of the Executive Director Greg Cusack on the Occasion of the Spring Board Meeting, April 30–May 2, 1986," 5; Crisler and Mosle, *In the Midst of His People*, 205.

72. Dolan, *In Search of an American Catholicism*, 229; Gregory Cusack to Members of NCRLC Nominating Committee, July 29, 1985, in "Nominations Committee," Cusack Subject File, Box 19; whole issue on rural women, *Earth Matters* 38 (Spring 1989), particularly Joseph K. Fitzgerald, "What If Food and Agriculture Were Influenced by Women?" 4, Tom Kelly, "Service and Solidarity," 5, Cornelia Butler Flora, "Women Find New Options, Forge New Roles in Rural America," 11, A. V. Krebs, "Agribusiness and Sexism," 16, and James T. Massey, "Women Lead FLAG's Legal Education Efforts in Farm Community," 17–20; "The 1986 Theology of Land Conference," *Common Ground* 4 (June 1986): 3.

vocations; the fewer the family farms, the fewer the vocations." To try to take advantage of this supposed propensity of rural men and women for vocations, the NCRLC publicized the National Religious Vocation Conference's handbook "Vocations in the Rural Church," which guided pastors, vocation directors, and families in encouraging vocations.[73]

The NCRLC eagerly supported the liturgical changes of Vatican II aimed at more lay participation, such as celebrating the Mass in the vernacular and the lay administration of sacraments. The Conference changed its own popular devotional literature to accommodate the new liturgy. O'Rourke wrote in supporting the changes: "A renewed liturgy should make us renewed Christians." By the 1990s, however, the NCRLC was concerned that most of the liturgical changes had "a decidedly urban or suburban bias." It thought that liturgy in rural parishes should reflect the unique characteristics of rural communities and suggested that the rural aspects of liturgical feasts, prayers of petition, church environment, and art be emphasized.[74]

Ecumenism was another area in which NCRLC activity preceded Vatican II. Early NCRLC leaders had cooperated with members of other faiths, and under Ligutti, ecumenism became an important part of NCRLC policy. As Ligutti's biographer wrote:

> He was ... practicing ecumenism long before most American Catholics even knew how to spell or pronounce the word. He was speaking in Methodist and Lutheran churches; he was addressing Protestant students on university campuses; he was inviting Protestant clergymen and their wives to the national conventions of the NCRLC. At a luncheon given in honor of Protestant clergymen during the 1942 NCRLC convention in Peoria, he brought down the house by opening his remarks, "My dear fellow heretics!"

Such stories of Ligutti's shocking (for the day) relations with members of other faiths abounded. The monsignor cooperated with Protestant and Jewish rural life departments in such endeavors as overseas relief, soil conservation, and the FAO. He helped to bring scores of Catholic, Protestant, and Jewish leaders together to publish two major statements on rural life,

---

73. Maurice Dingman, "Why Save the Family Farm?" *Catholic Rural Life* 35 (November 1985): 24–25; Jenada Fanetti, SDS, and Steve Pawlek, GLMY, "Nurture Vocations from and for the Rural Church," ibid. 38 (Fall 1996): 27–31; "Vocations in the Rural Church," *Rural Landscapes* 9 (October 2001): 7.

74. Joseph V. Urbain's "Living the Liturgy" column, *Catholic Rural Life*, e.g., 14 (February 1965): 5; E. W. O'Rourke, "The New Liturgy," ibid. 14 (August 1965): 2; Victoria M. Tufano, "An Inheritance from Generations: Liturgy Feeds the Faithful," ibid. 38 (Fall 1996): 14–17.

Man's Relation to the Land (1947) and *God's Bounty and Human Hunger* (1956). He also had a strong influence on Protestant rural life statements, which often sounded as if they were written by the NCRLC itself.[75]

For a while, the NCRLC made an attempt to join with Protestants in a common propaganda organization. From 1952 to 1955, the NCRLC and the Rural Life Association, which was led by Stanley Hamilton and headquartered in Richmond, Indiana, cosponsored the National Committee on Religion and Rural Life. The new organization's purpose was to sponsor "educational activities emphasizing the value of rural living and the religious basis for the conservation and development of spiritual, human and natural resources in rural areas." Its board of directors, composed entirely of laypeople, consisted of five Catholics and five Protestants. However, the committee apparently could do little that the component organizations could not do separately, and it eventually failed through lack of financial support.[76]

The NCRLC's commitment to ecumenism continued in the post-Ligutti years. O'Rourke stated: "Perhaps there is no other area of life in which there is so much ecumenical cooperation as in rural life." During his administration, the NCRLC stated that it would contribute to ecumenism "chiefly through social action programs jointly supported by Catholic and non-Catholic." Such cooperation continued in later years. The Conference worked with the Rural Church Network, a group of sixteen religious organizations active in rural areas, on issues such as the family farm crisis, rural ministry, and seminary education. Executive directors Cusack and Andrews served on the board of Agricultural Missions, an ecumenical organization dedicated to improving agriculture throughout the world, especially through cooperation among missionaries. Cusack joined with representatives of four other rural religious organizations in issuing "A Call to Justice and Action by the People of the Land" (1983), which urged public

---

75. Yzermans, *The People I Love*, 69; Edward W. O'Rourke, "Catholic-Protestant Cooperation," in "Article, Catholic-Protestant Cooperation, O'Rourke, Edward, 1960," NCRLC 11-1; *Man's Relation to the Land* (Des Moines, Iowa: National Catholic Rural Life Conference, n.d.), in "General Publications, 1947," NCRLC 5-2; *God's Bounty and Human Hunger* (n.p.: Committee on American Abundance and World Need, 1956), in "General Publications, 1956," NCRLC 5-3; Mark A. Dawber, "The Protestant Point of View," in "Religion and Agriculture. Papers Presented Before the Christian Rural Fellowship," *Rural America* 16 (September 1938): 7–9; Council for Social Action of the Congregational Christian Churches, "Federal Farm Policy" (1948), with note from Shirley E. Greene to Ligutti, in "Federal Farm Policy," NCRLC 8A-1.

76. "Articles of Incorporation of National Committee on Religion and Rural Life, Inc.," in "Ntn'l Committee on Religion and Rural Life, Description, Program, Articles of Inc., etc, 1952–1955," NCRLC 1-5, 1.

policies to alleviate the family farm crisis. The statement was adopted by the National Council of the Churches of Christ, but an attempt to act on it through a group of ten denominations did not get far. Andrews cooperated with the National Religious Partnership for the Environment, which helped to fund several Conference projects. He and NCRLC science and environmental specialist Tim Kautza joined an ecumenical group of religious leaders who met with the White House Office of Faith-Based and Community Initiatives to urge protection of the environment based on their religious beliefs. Sandra La Blanc, a Lutheran, brought religious diversity to NCRLC headquarters, and the Conference always made sure to have a Protestant to "represent the ecumenical community" on the board of directors.[77]

In 2005, the NCRLC joined Jewish, Muslim, and other Christian groups in starting the Sacred Foods Project. They developed an "eight-dimension" program of food and farm principles aimed at improving "food production, processing and accessibility" through common measures. In the post–September 11, 2001, era, the Conference seemed to instinctively reach out to participate for the first time in a project with Muslims. The NCRLC's participation in the Sacred Foods Project exemplified its growing ecumenical involvement during the age of Vatican II.[78]

---

77. Miller, *Monsignor Ligutti*, 34; NCRLC executive committee resolution, "Our Contribution to Ecumenism," in "Exec. Committee Meeting, June 21–22, 1966, Des Moines, Iowa," NCRLC 8-21; file "Agricultural Missions," in Cusack Subject File, Box 16; Agricultural Missions brochure in ibid., Box 20; Gregory Cusack to Members of the NCRLC Board of Directors, August 1, 1984, in "Board Communications," ibid., Box 19; *Rural Crisis: A Call for Justice and Action, Message adopted by the Governing Board of the National Council of the Churches of Christ in the U.S.A., May 17, 1984*, unfoldered in ibid., Box 20; "Building Community," *Rural Landscapes* 3 (April 1996): 3; "Building Community," ibid. (June 1996): 3; "NCRLC Welcomes New Board Members," ibid. 7 (January 2000): 4; "Ecumenical Partnerships," ibid. 9 (April 2002): 3; "Religious Coalition Meets with White House Staff," ibid. 9 (June 2002): 3; "Executive Director's Report, December 4/5, 1998," in "Current Mailings, 94–," NCRLC, 2; "Report of the Executive Director, November, 2001," in unprocessed mailings, ibid., 3; "Report of the Science and Environmental Education Specialist, Tim Kautza, May 20, 2004," in ibid., 5.

78. "Interfaith Sacred Foods Project Underway," *Catholic Rural Life* (newsletter) 13 (October 2005): 2; David Andrews, "Sacred Food," *Catholic Rural Life* 49 (Winter 2006): 4–5.

Chapter 12 For the Family Farm in the Age of Agribusiness

The Post–World War II Context

From World War II to the end of the century, the NCRLC continued to hold up the family farm as an ideal and to promote policies that supported it, despite an increasingly unfavorable economic and social environment. American society as a whole tended more and more to accept large-scale agribusiness rather than the family farm as the nation's primary agricultural institution. This evolution began during the agriculturally prosperous World War II years.

During World War II, with food production a high national priority, American farmers demanded, and were able to receive, very favorable supporting legislation. Because of the efforts of farm lobbyists—especially the Farm Bureau and the Grange—farmers received 100 percent, and even 110 percent, of parity in federal legislation. As a result of these price supports, high demand, and high production, American farmers prospered during World War II. Prices soared from a 1939 average of 80 percent of parity to 105 percent of parity in 1942, and 123 percent in 1946. Farmers still earned less than nonfarming workers, but the percentage went up from 36.7 in 1940 to 56.9 in 1945.[1]

After the war was over, the demand for farm products dropped off, and American farmers' prospects for continued prosperity became less favorable. They thus became even more dependent than before on federal support payments, which were therefore lobbied for with unprecedented intensity by farmers and their representatives in Washington. The lobbyists used all of the arguments at their command, especially appeals about the necessity of agriculture to the national economy and the moral supe-

---

1. Gilbert C. Fite, *American Farmers* (Bloomington: Indiana University Press, 1981), 65, 83, 86, 87, and 101, and chap. 5.

riority of the family farm, and they were successful in winning favorable legislation. According to historian Gilbert C. Fite, the high rigid price supports written into the World War II acts set the precedent for the favorable farm legislation received by farmers throughout the postwar era.[2]

Proponents of these programs maintained that their ultimate goal was the preservation of the American family farm system. Presidents such as Eisenhower and Kennedy and farm organizations such as the Farm Bureau, the Grange and the Farmers Union repeatedly expressed their faith in the value of family farming.[3] Postwar federal farm legislation was presented as benefiting the farming sector as a whole, especially family farms. But, according to many historians, it only benefited the better-off farmers. One of them, Louis H. Douglas, said:

After World War II it became increasingly clear that the federal farm policy was contributing to the cleavage between large-scale commercial agriculture which received substantial subsidies and small-scale farming for which no satisfactory program had been developed. In the latter sector insecurity, poverty-level income, migration, and poor public facilities for human development were characteristic. Carelessly characterized as "surplus," some of these rural families drifted into cities where they added to the problems of slums, unemployment, and delinquency.[4]

Historians have claimed that all of the postwar farm subsidy programs, from Eisenhower's "soil bank" to the George W. Bush programs after 2001, tended to favor the large-scale commercial farmers. There was no ceiling on support payments, which sometimes amounted to hundreds of thousands of dollars for single operations, until a fifty-five thousand dollar per crop ceiling was enacted in 1970. (Under Reagan's Payment in Kind [PIK] program, this ceiling was suspended on the grounds that such a monetary limitation should not apply to payments in kind.) With the size of support payments thus dependent on the size of their farms, it was no wonder that from the 1940s to the 1980s, American farmers, in Fite's words, made ever-increasing efforts to "expand their operations and to increase their efficiency. They saw no other avenue by which they could raise their income and standard of living. The slogan 'get bigger, get better, or get out,' was accepted by more and more farmers." In the years after the end

---

2. Ibid., chap. 5.
3. Ibid., 130–33.
4. Louis H. Douglas, ed., *Agrarianism in American History* (Lexington, Mass.: D. C. Heath, 1969), 138. Cf. Fite, *American Farmers,* chap. 7, esp. 121.

of World War II, the vast majority of American farmers "got out." The 1940 farm population of 30,547,000 (23.1 percent of the total U.S. population) dropped to 15,635,000 (8.7 percent) in 1960, 6,051,000 (2.7 percent) in 1980, and 4,400,000 (a minuscule 1.6 percent) in 2000. At the same time, the number of American farms declined from 6,350,000 in 1940 to 3,963,000 in 1960, 2,428,000 in 1980, and 2,172,000 in 2000. A small group of only 16.7 percent of these farms produced 80 percent of all agricultural products in the United States in 2000. The application of such innovations as more complex machinery, herbicides, pesticides, and computers to farming, of course, made this phenomenal production possible. Fite commented: "As far as the production of food and fiber was concerned, the United States would hardly have missed the complete disappearance of the other 1.2 million commercial farmers . . . [This] change had taken place with frightening speed, within a single generation."[5]

As commentators such as A. Whitney Griswold pointed out as early as 1948, the Jeffersonian ideal of the family farm was fast becoming an anachronism in late-twentieth-century America. The family farming way of life was threatened from both the top and the bottom. From the top, the family farms were becoming so large and efficient that their "business" aspects tended to overwhelm their "way of life" aspects. Plus, of course, the ever more numerous very large operations were not family-run at all, but corporate businesses managed according to the principles of the factory. From the bottom, the small farmers who could not compete in the race toward bigness and efficiency were either wallowing in the poverty of subsistence farming or getting out and moving to the towns and cities. From 1945 to 1970, the number of farms larger than five hundred acres increased by 28 percent, while the number of farms between one hundred and five hundred acres declined by over 40 percent. As historian David Danbom explained, "The middle-sized farmer—large enough not to have time to hold a second job but too small to achieve economies of scale—was most likely to be squeezed out."[6]

This was the context in which the NCRLC formulated its position on American domestic farm policy after World War II. The three basic pillars to that policy were preserving the family farm, improving the conditions of the rural disadvantaged, and conserving natural and agricultural

---

5. Fite, *American Farmers*, 101, 176, 180, 181–86, 240; R. Douglas Hurt, *Problems of Plenty: The American Farmer in the Twentieth Century*, The American Ways Series (Chicago: Ivan R. Dee, 2002), 155–56.

6. Griswold, *Farming and Democracy*; Danbom, *Born in the Country*, 243.

resources. The family farm had been a priority of NCRLC policy from its beginning. Helping the disadvantaged had been added to the agenda during the Depression years, and conserving resources emerged as an important plank only after World War II.[7]

Foremost among these priorities was preserving the family farm. The NCRLC deplored the postwar agricultural trends and said that it could not "sit idly by and watch over the dismemberment and death of one of civilization's prime institutions—agriculture organized on a family basis." It defined the family farm as "a socio-economic institution in which the capital, labor, and management of the family is organized toward production of food and fiber for the benefit of the family and society." Die-hard support for the family farm was of course to be expected from the mainstream NCRLC members and officials who hailed from the family farm belt in the Midwest, but even James Vizzard, an untypical Conference official in that he came from California and was most concerned with migrant workers, affirmed that the key aim in farm legislation "must be the strengthening of the family farm . . . Government farm policy should be family farm policy." The NCRLC continued to defend the family farm right through the end of the century in much the same terms that it always had. In 1989, veteran Conference official Bishop George Speltz insisted that the family farm embodied the values of

a wider distribution of private ownership of the land giving a greater measure of freedom, independence, security; preserves a way of life, maintains a culture that for 150 years has given strength to our national character; acts as a checks-and-balances system of political and economic power; efficient; realizes the essential economics of scale; permits good conservation practices; can provide specialty foods, less contaminated, better quality; food security, less dependence on large capital, less danger of monopolies; valuable form of work on the land and in rural communities.

In 1998, to emphasize the continuity of this policy, Executive Director David Andrews published a long compilation of NCRLC and Catholic statements supporting the family farm from the 1930s to date.[8]

---

7. For statements of NCRLC domestic farm policy priorities, see John J. McRaith, "The Six Principles That Apply to All Farm Bills," *Catholic Rural Life* 26 (March 1977): 3–4; "Fair Return to Producers Urged in NCRLC Testimony," ibid. (April 1977): 15–16.

8. NCRLC, *Corporate Agriculture vs. Family Farming* (Des Moines, Iowa: NCRLC 1968), leaflet in "General Publications, 1963–69," NCRLC 5-5; NCRLC, *A Program for the Family Farm* (Des Moines, Iowa: NCRLC, 1956), in "General Publications, 1956," NCRLC 5-3, 2; James L. Vizzard, "Washington Farm Front," *Catholic Rural Life* 8 (February 1959): 30; George H. Speltz, "Ministry to Rural People and Society," *Earth Matters* 38 (Summer 1989): 34; David G. Andrews, *The Catholic*

For the Family Farm in the Age of Agribusiness					275

The American Catholic Church as a whole was lukewarm in supporting the Conference's fight for the family farm for much of this period. After a long silence, the USCC's "Policy Statement on Family Farms" (1979) endorsed NCRLC positions and offered recommendations for action by Church leaders, farmers, and the government that would strengthen the family farm. However, the American hierarchy's important 1986 economic pastoral merely defended the "right" to productive property such as small- and medium-sized farms and declared that family farms should be "preserved" and their economic viability "protected." A few years later a group of mostly rural bishops more enthusiastically "favored" family farms "as the primary structural component of a just food system." In 2005, Pope Benedict XVI called for "safeguarding small family farms" and "recognizing the essential role of the rural family as a guardian of values and a natural agent of solidarity in relationships between the generations."[9]

The most prominent part of federal farm policy in the postwar years was price-control or income-support programs—the various successors to the Agricultural Adjustment Act (AAA)—which were maintained in one way or another through most of this period. A typical NCRLC resolution stating the policy on these programs was passed in 1949: "National and international action taken to bring about fair prices should be such as to protect and foster the family-type, owner-operated farm."[10] In other words, the NCRLC maintained that ensuring fair (or high) prices or income for farmers was important, but it should be subordinated as a goal to preserving the family farm. A look at NCRLC positions on certain of the income-maintenance programs of the government from the 1940s to the end of the century will show how this principle worked itself out in practice.

The NCRLC and Federal Farm Programs

During World War II, NCRLC president Aloisius J. Muench supported the prevailing system of 100 percent parity prices for farmers—and even supported 110 percent, as demanded by some farmers, so that the average over the year would be over 100 percent. He declared that the parity prin-

---

Rural Ethic: Past and Present (Des Moines, Iowa: National Catholic Rural Life Conference, 1998), in "Current Mailings, 1994–," NCRLC.

9. "Document Urges Action to Save Family Farm System," *Catholic Rural Life* 28 (February 1979): 21–23; "The Agrarian Vision of the Holy See: Catholic Social Teachings and Rural Life," ibid. 48 (Spring 2006): 23; National Conference of Catholic Bishops, *Economic Justice for All,* sections 114, 233; National Conference of Catholic Bishops [and] United States Catholic Conference, *Report of the Ad Hoc Task Force on Food, Agriculture, and Rural Concerns, November 15, 1988* (Washington, D.C.: United States Catholic Conference, 1989), in "NCRLC Archives, Publications Acq'd: 6/30/94," Box 23, 15.

10. "We Resolve," *Christian Farmer* 3 (December 1949): 3.

ciple was "sound" and "in full consonance with Catholic ethics." Executive Secretary Ligutti less enthusiastically stated that there was not "anything better to offer" than the parity price system "at the present time." He cautioned NCRLC members to "not freeze our thinking on the parity price implement." Conference resolutions of the time paralleled Ligutti's thinking in supporting parity and flexible price supports calculated so as to maintain the income of family farmers, not give an undue advantage to large-scale farmers.[11]

While the NCRLC generally supported price-support programs, it opposed restricting production as a means for obtaining higher prices. The Conference believed that the United States had a moral duty to engage in full agricultural production in order to feed the hungry at home and abroad. It used this reasoning throughout the postwar decades, despite the popularity of the notion of production control as a means for raising prices.[12]

After the war, the NCRLC supported the farm program proposed by the new Agriculture Secretary Charles F. Brannan, which was cowritten by James Patton, president of the Farmers Union. What the NCRLC liked about the Brannan Plan, which was in most respects a rather typical farm subsidy program, was its proposal for a limit of $25,700 worth of products on which farmers could receive support payments. Ligutti hailed this as a "proposal to limit price protection to the 98% of the family-type farmers." He claimed that the other 2 percent were the big operators who were "the employers of the Grapes of Wrath migrants" and who had been "powerful enough to exclude farm labor from the minimum wage and social security legislation." However, another NCRLC official predicted that, due to the opposition of the "big growers, . . . such a proposal is not likely to be accepted in the immediate future." And indeed, the Brannan Plan was vigorously resisted by the Farm Bureau and defeated in Congress.[13]

From 1953 to 1955, the NCRLC went beyond commenting on others' farm proposals to propose a "new farm policy" of its own. The Conference claimed that the present "price support system with its inevitable acreage and marketing controls is wasteful, ineffective, and in its broad applications,

---

11. A. J. Muench, "Justice for the Farmer," *Land and Home* 5 (June 1942): 1–2; Muench, "Presidential Address," 2; [L. G. Ligutti], "Equality versus Parity" ("Notes and Comments"), ibid. (September 1942): 15; 1944 resolution "A Just Price for the Farmer" and 1949 resolution "Parity Income for Farmers," both in "The Farmer and Economics," NCRLC 8A-1.

12. National Catholic Rural Life Conference, *Rural Life in a Peaceful World* (Des Moines, Iowa: National Catholic Rural Life Conference, 1944), in "General Publications, 1944–46," NCRLC 5-1, 22; "Just Target Prices," *Catholic Rural Life* 24 (April 1975): 1.

13. Fite, *American Farmers*, 96–98; [L. G. Ligutti], "An Editorial Opinion," *Christian Farmer* 2 (May 1949): 1; [W. J. Gibbons] "The Farm on the Potomac," ibid. (November 1949): 3.

For the Family Farm in the Age of Agribusiness 277

un-Christian." The "un-Christian" aspects were its favoritism for the largest farmers over small family farmers and farm laborers and its callousness toward the hungry of the world. The key feature of the new plan would be direct payments to farmers in times of need (to take the place of price supports—the price of the products themselves would be subject to a free market). President Eisenhower had proposed such a direct-payment-plus-free-market plan for the wool crop, which the Conference supported. The Conference also proposed that the direct payments be limited to family-size farms: "It seems unnecessary to use government funds to perpetuate corporation farms, absentee landlordism, suitcase farmers, and speculators." This proposal drew some support from Catholic publications such as *America*, but it failed to make an impact on the national scene.[14]

The NCRLC was critical of the Eisenhower administration's "soil bank" program, which paid benefits to farmers in return for their practicing conservation by taking their croplands out of production. Conference officials stated that "its objectives are praiseworthy enough: to stop erosion and soil depletion, to increase farm income and to eliminate 'surpluses.'" However, they thought that there were better ways to save soil and that the "soil bank" was effective neither in controlling surpluses nor in raising the income of the smaller farmers who needed it most. In order to favor low-income farmers, the NCRLC supported proposals for an income limit below which small farmers would not be required to reduce acreage for the soil bank and a limit to the amount of payments made to farmers cooperating in the program.[15]

The Kennedy administration's farm program found more favor with the NCRLC because it proclaimed as its major objective the preservation of the family farm. However, the Kennedy farm program was often modified by Congress, and the Conference often differed with some of the resulting details. For example, NCRLC officials questioned the program's mandatory controls and disagreed with its method of acreage reduction allotments. Father O'Rourke urged that the Kennedy administration adopt a lower percentage of acreage reduction for smaller farms in order to help preserve the family farm.[16]

---

14. Martin E. Schirber and Emerson Hynes, "A New Farm Policy," *Commonweal*, November 27, 1953, 191–94; "Resolutions of the National Catholic Rural Life Conference, Executive Committee Meeting, Jan. 13, 1954, Milwaukee, Wisconsin," supplement to *Feet in the Furrow* 2 (February 1954); Benjamin L. Masse, "Farm Program for Abundance," *America*, February 5, 1955, 475–77, reprinted in *Feet in the Furrow* 4 (April 1955): 13–16.

15. James L. Vizzard, "Washington Farm Front," *Rural Life Conference—Feet in the Furrow* 5 (September 1956): 15; "NCRLC Executive Committee Meeting," ibid. 4 (February 1956): 4–5.

16. James L. Vizzard, "Washington Farm Front," *Catholic Rural Life* 10 (August 1961): 23; Edward W. O'Rourke, "The Missing Ingredient," ibid. 11 (March 1962): 2; O'Rourke, reply to letter

The Conference found more to disagree with in the Johnson farm policy. O'Rourke supported Johnson's pledge to help the small farmer but asserted that more needed to be done. He was worried about the administration's intention to cut the cost of farm programs, which he believed would result in lower subsidies to farmers. Above all, O'Rourke was outraged at Johnson's and Agriculture Secretary Orville Freeman's efforts to keep down the prices of farm commodities, charging the administration with pursuing a "cheap food policy" and pandering to urban consumers.[17]

The Conference's crusade for limitations to farm subsidy payments came to a head during the Johnson and early Nixon administrations, when the idea finally became popular in Congress. The Conference supported an amendment to limit subsidy payments to twenty thousand dollars per individual, and O'Rourke called it "shameful" when the proposal was defeated. He testified to Congress that "the payment of many hundreds of thousands of dollars to wealthy individuals, while we curtail aid to the poor, is very bad public policy." He argued against the claims of opponents of benefit limitations that the huge payments to big farmers were needed to get them to participate in production-control programs: "Large operators who refuse to join the farm program would soon find that it is not profitable." Finally, a limitation of fifty-five thousand dollars in benefits for any one crop was enacted. However, O'Rourke maintained that "to be meaningful, this limitation should have been set at a much lower figure," and he continued to press for a twenty thousand dollar limit.[18]

The NCRLC was not especially favorable toward production-control legislation. But during the Nixon administration, it was faced with programs, supported by the administration and the Farm Bureau, that tended toward a free market in the farm economy, with no definite provisions for income support for small farmers. At this time, in the absence of any politically practical alternative, the Conference supported commodity programs as they already existed.[19]

The most important development affecting government farm policy

from Orville L. Freeman, ibid. (May 1962): 7; NCRLC, *The Farmer and His Government* (Des Moines, Iowa: NCRLC, 1962), in "Publications, F," NCRLC 5-6.

17. Edward W. O'Rourke, "Squeeze on Small Farmers," *Catholic Rural Life* 14 (March 1965): 2; O'Rourke, "Cheap Food Means Hungry People," ibid. 16 (September 1967): 2.

18. O'Rourke, "Washington Farm Front," ibid. 17 (September 1968): 8; O'Rourke, "Washington Farm Front," ibid. (November 1968): 9; O'Rourke, "Washington Farm Front," ibid. 18 (August 1969): 12; O'Rourke, "Washington Farm Front," ibid. 19 (November 1970): 3; O'Rourke, "Washington Farm Front," ibid. 20 (June 1971): 8.

19. O'Rourke, "Washington Farm Front," ibid. 19 (June 1970): 8.

during the Carter administration was the formation of the American Agriculture Movement (AAM). AAM was a nationwide organization of farmers that was formed in the summer of 1977 and threatened to "strike" (neither grow or sell crops nor buy from dealers or merchants) unless the government guaranteed 100 percent parity. Although the AAM "strike," held in December 1977, had little effect, the movement did hold two dramatic "tractorcades" to Washington in 1978 and 1979, which pressured Congress into passing some emergency legislation for farmers—although not 100 percent parity. A few NCRLC members, such as the Reverend Andrew Gottschalk, diocesan rural life director of Denver, gave the strikers direct support. But most, such as Executive Director McRaith, gave only general support for higher prices, coupled with proposals for special aid for family farms. The NCRLC board declared itself to be "in sympathy with your cause in seeking a just price for your products," adding, "preservation of family farm agriculture through parity prices has been a goal of our organization for many years."[20]

The Conference was very critical of the Reagan administration's farm policies. An NCRLC spokesman agreed with Representative Tom Harkin of Iowa, who referred to the 1981 farm bill, which stabilized prices at only 57 percent of parity, as "the family farm liquidation act of 1981." He maintained that the only way to make money farming under the current conditions was "by writing it off as a tax loss" and concluded that "we must expect that the declining trend in family farm numbers will continue unabated." The Conference found a multitude of faults with the Reagan administration's later PIK program: The program added to the federal budget deficit by its huge cost (it was the most expensive farm program to date); it reduced the Gross National Product—resulting in layoffs and job elimination in agriculture-related industries affecting some fifty thousand workers; it benefited mainly larger farmers by virtue of the USDA's unilateral (without congressional authorization) waiving of the traditional fifty thousand dollar per farmer price support limitation—fifty farms in California received over a million dollars in PIK cotton, including an enterprise part-owned by the chief USDA administrator of the PIK program;

---

20. Fite, *American Farmers*, 209–17; John J. McRaith, "Public Interest in Farm Strike Is a Hopeful Sign," *Catholic Rural Life* 27 (February 1978): 3–4; Rev. Andrew Gottschalk, "Tractors to Washington: A Participant's Report," ibid. 28 (February 1979): 17–19; "Business Meeting of Rural Life Directors Minutes," in "2nd Ntn'l Consultation of Rural Life Directors, Erlanger, Kentucky, 1977," NCRLC 8-25, 2; NCRLC, "Press Release," in "2nd National Consultation of Rural Life Directors; Erlanger, Kentucky: 1977" (second folder), NCRLC 8-25.

and it was only partially successful in reducing the surplus. Moreover, PIK did not help the farm economy—after it had been in operation for some time, parity was still only 58 percent.[21]

For the 1985 and 1990 farm bills, the Conference supported targeting benefits to middle-sized farmers, but Congress passed bills that refused to grant any special favors to aid family farms and economized on farm programs. In 1990, the George H. W. Bush administration's bill cut farm programs by 25 percent in order to help reduce massive federal budget deficits and planned a 75 percent reduction over the next ten years aimed at getting the "government out of the farming business." The Conference charged that such cuts constituted a "pronounced break with the social contract this society has historically had with its farmers. In exchange for stable supplies of quality food at affordable prices, society has been willing to offer government support to farmers." The NCRLC's Walt Grazer bewailed the programs' emphasis on increasing agricultural exports and free trade, which he said would hurt farmers in developing countries and depress prices for American farmers.[22]

The North American Free Trade Agreement (NAFTA) of 1993, which lifted restraints on trade among the United States, Canada, and Mexico, aroused concerns on the part of the NCRLC on several levels. The Conference thought negotiation of the treaty should have included more citizen participation, and it opposed the "fast-track" consideration of it in Congress. It thought that the treaty would benefit corporate agriculture, especially in Mexico, and create from half a million to one-and-a-half million landless laborers there. The agreement would probably not help American agricultural exports to Mexico, because Mexican production would itself increase. Finally, NAFTA did not do enough to address the environmental and health problems that would probably result from the increased industrialization of agriculture. Ten years later, the NCRLC charged, many of these predictions had come true. The Conference hosted a forum at which Mexican farm leaders said NAFTA led to lower farm-worker wages, reduced

---

21. Bart Pollock, "A Farm Bill by Any Other Name," *Catholic Rural Life* 31 (December 1981): 29–31; Walt Grazer, "PIK Update" ("Washington Watch"), ibid. 33 (September 1983): 24.

22. Walt Grazer, "Assessing the Farm Bill," *Catholic Rural Life* 36 (February 1986): 28; [Grazer] "Department of Social Development and World Peace, Office of Domestic Social Development," in "Spring 1986 Board Meeting," in Cusack Subject File, Box 20, NCRLC, 2; "Committee on Agriculture, Nutrition and Forestry, United States Senate, Testimony by Most Rev. Ignatius J. Strecker, Archbishop of Kansas City, Kansas, on U.S. Food and Agricultural Policy and the 1985 Omnibus Farm Bill, April 25, 1985," in "NCRLC—Bishop's Task Force," in "Fitzgerald Files: Board Related, ca. 1986–89," Box 1, NCRLC; "Budget Cuts Jeopardize Farm Programs, Food Security," *Common Ground* 10 (November 1990): 1.

exports, lower prices for corn, and farmers leaving farms—many coming to the United States to seek work. Andrews said NAFTA also hurt the United States, because Mexicans who lost farms often crossed the northern border as illegal immigrants. In Iowa, they took dangerous, lower-paid jobs in packing plants and doing seasonal fieldwork. "The effect of opening up agricultural trade has been huge and devastating in the countryside here and in Mexico," Andrews said. In 2005, when the Central American Free Trade Agreement (CAFTA) was proposed, the NCRLC opposed it for similar reasons: it would result in lower farm prices, reduced workers' wages, and increased migration to urban centers and the United States.[23]

The Conference was hopeful that agricultural policies would improve under the Democratic administration of Bill Clinton beginning in 1993. Indeed, according to the NCRLC, the 1995 farm bill "turned out better than many family farm advocates thought it would," with some "small but significant victories." This attitude changed abruptly with the passage in 1996 of the Freedom to Farm Act, which was intended to revolutionize the government's relationship with agriculture and save huge amounts of federal money by eliminating the crop-control payments that had formed the major component of farm programs since the New Deal years. The Conference called the legislation "a boon to industrialized agriculture" and predicted it would "strengthen access to credit for larger investment enterprises, foster the consolidation of food production in the hands of a few multinational corporations, result in higher prices and poor quality food for consumers. It will, however, create havoc for small farmers and rural communities." The Freedom to Farm Act resulted in a wave of farm foreclosures, which prompted the government to backtrack and give farmers a new safety net in the form of billions of dollars in disaster assistance in place of the old crop-control payments.[24]

The Department of Agriculture finally sponsored a study on small

---

23. "Faith Concerns for NAFTA Pose Solutions," *Common Ground* 12 (January 1993): 1–2; "Trading for the Common Good," ibid. (March/April 1993): 1–2; "Vote No on NAFTA!" ibid. 13 (Fall 1993): 4; Jerry Perkins, "Mexican Farmers in Iowa Criticize NAFTA," Des Moines *Register*, October 14, 2003, copy in unprocessed mailings, NCRLC; Elizabeth Becker, "Farmers and Labor Press Global Trade as a Campaign Issue," *New York Times*, October 21, 2003, copy in ibid.; "NCRLC Visits Capitol Hill," *Catholic Rural Life* (newsletter) 12 (April 2005): 2.

24. Mark Pattison, "Sowing the Seeds of a New Farm Policy," Superior *Catholic Herald*, February 4, 1993, copy in "NCRLC Board Meeting: May 6–7, 1993," in Fitzgerald Files, Box 2, NCRLC; "A Bird's Eye View," *Rural Landscapes* 3 (April 1996): 2; David Andrews, "Globalization, the Rural Life Conference, the Family Farm and Agrarianism," *Catholic Rural Life* 38 (Fall 1996): 39; Dan Misleh, "Fluctuating Commodity Prices Has Definite Impact on Rural Communities," ibid. 41 (Spring 1999): 36; Misleh, "Prospects of Major Changes in Farm Policy Unlikely in Election Year," ibid. 42 (Fall 1999): 32.

farms called *A Time to Act* (1998), which recommended ten issues to work on and which was supported by the NCRLC. However, a year later family farm advocates gave Agriculture Secretary Dan Glickman poor marks in implementing the recommendations. The most prominent issue at this time was the control of commodity markets by large corporations, which depressed prices. The NCRLC joined the Organization for Competitive Markets (OCM), which called for mandatory price reporting to make markets more transparent. It called legislation that required meat packers to regularly report prices for cattle, swine, and lambs "a step in the right direction" but it was disappointed in overall progress in market reform.[25]

When Republican George W. Bush became president in 2001, the Conference noted hopefully that he was in favor of reforms, but it called the farm bill adopted the next year "bittersweet." The bill provided huge farm payments of $190 billion over ten years without placing an effective cap on the amount offered to large farms. The Conference praised increased funding for conservation, rural development, nutrition, and food stamp programs. For the 2007 farm bill, the NCRLC favored a five-point program of supporting family farmers and ranchers (it wanted a $250,000 limit on commodity payments to a single operation), reducing hunger and improving nutrition, building rural businesses and promoting entrepreneurship, conservation programs, and equal opportunity for black, Native American, Asian, and Hispanic farmers.[26]

Other Programs to Aid the Family Farm

Besides the year-to-year farm programs, the NCRLC supported a variety of other proposals intended to aid the family farm. It pushed for more credit and other financial aid for farmers, particularly requesting increased lending authority for the Farmers Home Administration (FmHA), the government's principal lender to family farmers. Because of the rising prices of land, young farmers found it especially hard to get started in farming; the NCRLC supported a number of bills over the years to give special financial aid to beginning farmers. It was successful when Congress passed

---

25. "Executive Director's Report, December 4/5, 1998," in "Current Mailings, 94–," NCRLC; "Report Card Gives USDA Poor Marks on the Hog Issue" (Time to Act Campaign Press Release), February 9, 1999, in ibid.; Misleh, "Prospects of Major Changes in Farm Policy Unlikely in Election Year."

26. Robert Gronski, "2002 Farm Bill: Next Steps," *Rural Landscapes* 9 (June 2002): 2; "NCRLC Visits Capitol Hill," *Catholic Rural Life* (newsletter) 12 (April 2005): 2; "Seeking Balance in U.S. Farm and Food Policy," *Catholic Rural Life* 49 (Spring 2007): 9–16.

the Agricultural Credit Improvement Act of 1992, which targeted a portion of FmHA loan funds specifically to beginning farmers.[27]

The family farm could also be aided by reforming the tax structure, the NCRLC believed. Of the three major types of state taxes, the Conference opposed property taxes because they placed an unfair burden on family farmers and discouraged property ownership, and sales taxes because they hurt low-income groups. It concluded that income taxes were the most just kind. If there must be a property tax, the NCRLC said, it should be graduated to tax large landholdings more than small ones. It also proposed the elimination of farm loss tax write-offs and other tax subsidies that encouraged nonfarmers to speculate in farmland and called for increased property and severance taxes on mineral extractive industries.[28]

Government-aided research could also do its part in supporting the family farm. The Conference reiterated the charges of Jim Hightower in *Hard Tomatoes, Hard Times* (1972) that research in the Department of Agriculture and the agricultural colleges was mainly directed toward finding ways to increase production—which mostly helped large farmers. Instead, it proposed, research should be specifically directed toward helping family farmers to continue to make a living.[29]

One of the Conference's hardest-fought battles on behalf of the family farm was its effort to maintain the 160-acre limitation on landholdings irrigated under the Reclamation Law of 1902. The NCRLC first entered the fray in 1947, when it joined its San Francisco archdiocesan director of rural life Charles Philipps in opposing an attempt to repeal the acreage limitation in legislation governing the Central Valley of California. The issue came up again in 1958, when Vizzard testified against a bill that would have exempted the Seedskadee Project in Wyoming from the acreage provision. In the mid-sixties, the Conference lobbied against the granting of contracts

---

27. Edward W. O'Rourke, "Washington Farm Front," *Catholic Rural Life* 18 (February 1969): 15; "Washington Watch," ibid. 31 (April–May 1981): 37–38; "New Legislation Assists Beginning Farmers," *Common Ground* 12 (November 1992): 1–2.

28. "New Policy Statement Champions Family Farm," *Catholic Rural Life* 8 (February 1958): 10; Marty Strange, edited by Sandra Pollard, "Taking Back Control of American Agriculture," ibid. 33 (February 1983): 4–7; "Seeking Just Tax Policies in Agriculture: Proposals for Reforming U.S. Tax Policy. A Major Policy Statement by the National Catholic Rural Life Conference, May, 1985," ibid. 35 (July 1985): 4–10; NCRLC, *Taxes and the Land* (Des Moines, Iowa: NCRLC, 1975), in "Genl. Pubs., 1970–76," NCRLC 5-5.

29. Fite, *American Farmers*, 186–87; NCRLC, *Toward a Sound Family Farm Policy* (Des Moines, Iowa: NCRLC, 1967), in "Publications, T–Y," NCRLC 5-7; John George Weber, "USDA Hit for Refusing to Help Small Farmers," *Catholic Rural Life* 24 (November 1975): 6–7; "A Bird's Eye View," *Rural Landscapes* 3 (December 1995): 2.

by the Bureau of Reclamation to large corporate farmers in California's Westlands Project. The large farmers claimed that they could be supplied water as the "unavoidable result" of furnishing water to lands within the 160-acre limit, but Vizzard was successful in persuading Interior Secretary Stewart Udall to maintain the limit. Instead of allowing corporate farms to take over, the NCRLC called for a "bold new" Interior Department program to "recreate family farming and family-based rural communities in the irrigated areas of the West" by subsidizing sales of reclaimed land to family farmers by means of a $1 billion revolving fund. However, the corporate farms continued to try to circumvent the Reclamation Law by siphoning off federal water. In the late 1970s and early 1980s, they made another attempt to repeal the law by proposing to raise the acreage limit to 3,360 acres and eliminating residency requirements. The NCRLC said of one such bill, the Reclamation Reform Act of 1979: "Actually there is no 'reform' in the bill. It merely legitimizes virtually every past and present violation of the current reclamation law." The NCRLC supported a USCC statement that listed four goals to be used in modernizing the reclamation law: "encouraging the widespread ownership of land, establishing resident owner-operators as the norm in water districts, making it easier for new and small farmers to own land, and fostering responsible stewardship of our water supplies."[30]

The NCRLC supported a number of government proposals that sought to deal in a comprehensive way with the family farm problem. In 1959, Vizzard supported a bill in Congress for a new Country Life Commission, similar to Theodore Roosevelt's fifty-one years before, which would have focused on "protecting and promoting the family farm as the dominant unit in American agriculture." However, it was never established. In 1972, Congress enacted the Rural Development Act, a wide-ranging piece of legislation providing for grants and loans for rural industrialization, community facilities, environmental protection, research and extension, planning, farm ownership and operation, and home ownership. The NCRLC praised the

---

30. "Executive Committee, Wednesday, April 16th, Des Moines, Iowa," in "Exec. Committee, Mtg., Des Moines, Iowa, April 15, 1947," NCRLC 8-5, 1–2; Gerald F. Cox, *The Radical Peasant* (Victoria, B.C.: Trafford Publishing, 2006), 109–11; Vizzard testimony in "Reclamation Law, May 1958 Hearings," NCRLC 1-6; Vizzard to O'Rourke, August 14, 1964, and attached documents, "Correspondence, V, 1964," NCRLC 13-21; Vizzard, "Washington Farm Front," *Catholic Rural Life* 13 (July 1964): 8; "Strengthening Family Farms through Reclamation Program," ibid. 15 (April 1966): 8; "Acreage Limits: A Look at Misconception and Reality," ibid. 28 (September 1979): 15–16; "Land Reclamation Statement Given," ibid. 29 (April–May 1980): 31; "Washington Watch: Action Alert," ibid. (July–August 1980): 31; Walter Grazer, "Reclamation Act Revision: S. 1867 and H.R. 5539," ibid. 32 (March 1982): 28–30.

For the Family Farm in the Age of Agribusiness   285

act, in which it thought "Congress commit[ted] itself to a sound balance between rural and urban America." However, it believed that the appropriation of only $500 million constituted "promises, promises" and called for a much more "aggressive" rural development program. By 1975, the Conference thought that the act was not going to have much effect, as there had been long delays in issuing guidelines, and the funds spent fell well short of the amount Congress had authorized. Three years later, the Conference supported the Family Farm Development Act, a bill that included a variety of economic and other proposals to aid the family farm. It was sponsored by the National Family Farm Coalition, which was formed to support the bill. Despite NCRLC support, the bill did not get far in Congress. The NCRLC viewed authorization of the Fund for Rural America in 1996 as "a significant victory in a time of severe budget cuts." Executive Director Andrews was chosen as a reviewer for rural development grants offered by the fund.[31]

As a last hurrah to the tradition of NCRLC support for family farm land settlement projects, the Conference in 1968–69 made an ill-fated decision to back an agricultural development project in Florida. Two development corporations proposed to start a project to clear two hundred thousand acres of timbered land in western Florida and lease it to experienced farmers. The NCRLC, "convinced that new lands such as these can and should be tilled by family-type farmers," agreed to help recruit prospective tenants for the Florida land. In March 1969, 550 people met with NCRLC officials and the developers in Des Moines to learn about the project. Hopes were high, with over two hundred applicants for farms on the Florida land. However, an investigation by a member of the NCRLC board soon burst the bubble and revealed a boondoggle for corporate agriculture. It turned out that the developers had no plans to eventually sell the lands to the tenant families. Instead, they planned to have the land "farmed for a few years by small farmers and brought into top condition" and then drop the leases and bring in corporate agriculture. The NCRLC realized it had been deceived and advised its members against participating in the project.[32]

31. James L. Vizzard, "Washington Farm Front—Bill in House for Country Life Commission," *Catholic Rural Life* 8 (May 1959): 34; John J. McRaith, "It's a Start!!" ibid. 22 (January 1973): 3; Stephen E. Bossi, "What Can You Do under the Rural Development Act of 1972?" ibid. (February 1973): 8–10; Bossi, "Washington Farm Front," ibid. (May 1973): 16; "Big Promises, Not Much Performance, in Rural Act," ibid. 24 (July 1975): 21–22; Joe Belden, "Farm Bill Would Reverse USDA Emphasis on Bigness," ibid. 27 (March 1978): 11–12; "A Bird's Eye View," *Rural Landscapes* 3 (April 1996): 2; David Andrews to Chuck Elston [Board of Directors], August 27, 1997, in "Current Mailings, 94–," NCRLC.

32. "New Farm Lands Available in Florida," *Catholic Rural Life* 17 (November 1968): 8–9; "Keen

This threat of corporate agriculture to the NCRLC's ideal rural society of family farms was a constant concern from the 1940s through the end of the century. Corporate farms were few in the 1940s, and they had not yet attracted much attention. By 1968, there were 13,300 farming corporations in the United States; this 1 percent of American commercial farms operated 7 percent of the farmland and had 8 percent of all farm sales. Only six years later, the nation already had twenty-eight thousand farming and ranching corporations.[33]

The NCRLC was alarmed at the rapid growth of corporate farms primarily because it believed that it was impossible to duplicate the moral values of life on an owner-operated family farm on a corporate farm. But faced with a society that was fast losing its faith in the value of farming for a living, the Conference brought forth many more practical objections to corporate farms. For example, it denied the oft-stated claim that larger operations run on purely business principles were always more efficient and produced less expensive agricultural products than family farms. It asserted that most of the methods used to make corporate farms more efficient could be scaled down for use on family farms. A family farmer also tended to take better care of his land and thus avoided wasteful land-use practices that were inefficient in the long run. O'Rourke contended that the profits of many big "factories-in-the-fields" were due in large part to their exploitation of the migrant workers they employed. Another NCRLC writer used the failure of Red River Valley bonanza farms in the late nineteenth century as an example of how large-scale farming had been doomed throughout history:

But in view of the history of ancient empires which rose on the production of their agricultural families and fell when these families were destroyed; in view of our contemporary observations of the failure of Chinese and Russian Communist communes; in view of world history, which shows the large collectivized farm, whether communal or capitalistic, produces more famine than food; in view of these historically recent bonanza experiences here in our own country, why do we permit the present hell-bent race toward corporate collective farms which have never, ever worked?[34]

Interest in Leasing Florida Land," ibid. 18 (April 1969): 1; Eugene Miller, "Report on Florida Land Development," ibid. (May 1969): 6.

33. Fite, *American Farmers*, 194, 196.

34. Edward W. O'Rourke, "Farm Question Box," *Christian Farmer* 4 (February 1951): 2; Dana C. Jennings, "Why the Bonanza Busted," *Catholic Rural Life* 16 (March 1967): 5; *Policy Statement on Vertical Integration, Immigration Legislation, Surplus Distribution, American Country Life Commission, Inefficiency of Large Scale Farming, Low-Income Farmer, Migratory Labor* (Des Moines, Iowa: National Catholic Rural Life Conference, 1958), in "General Publications, 1958," NCRLC 5-4, 4–5.

For the Family Farm in the Age of Agribusiness 287

The NCRLC also argued that corporate farms not only forced out family farmers but also rural small businessmen, because the large farms bought nationally rather than locally. Thus corporate farms were causing the decay of the small-community-based society throughout rural America. NCRLC official Robert Gronski asserted that they went against the Catholic principle of subsidiarity—"the natural right for local groups to associate and organize without a larger organization intervening and stripping a community of local capabilities." Corporate farms endangered farmers' control over their lives by the vertical integration of all the processes of food production. The Conference believed that the dangerous rise of corporate farming ultimately affected not just farmers but all Americans, because "control over our destinies falls into the hands of corporate decision-makers who are not accountable to the American people." Finally, the Conference charged that corporate agriculture threatened the health and survival of the planet, because highly specialized farms were the chief causes of air and water pollution from animal wastes, fertilizers, and pesticides.[35]

The apathy of government when it came to the corporate farming danger concerned the NCRLC. In 1968, O'Rourke lamented that in the Democratic and Republican platforms, neither party pledged to take significant steps to inhibit the entrance of large corporations into agriculture. Government tax and credit policies, the Federal Reserve system, farm programs, and international trade negotiations all favored "mega-farms." Neither Congress nor any presidential administration was willing to place any restrictions on corporate farming. By the end of the century only a few midwestern states such as Iowa, Minnesota, Kansas, Nebraska, and North Dakota had done so.[36]

The role of corporations in American agriculture could be limited in a number of ways. The Conference recommended a graduated land tax and a ban on tax write-offs for losses in farming against nonfarm income. It also supported a more direct approach—legislation prohibiting nonfarm businesses from owning agricultural land. It strongly backed the Family Farm Antitrust Act bills proposed from 1972 to 1975 by Senator Gaylord

35. Stephen E. Bossi, "Washington Farm Front," *Catholic Rural Life* 21 (June 1972): 8; Edward W. O'Rourke, "Needed: Diversified Family Farms," ibid. 20 (January 1971): 2; Robert Gronski, "Rural Roads to Security," ibid. 43 (Fall 2000): 24; "Mid-Winter Executive Board Meeting Attacks Vertical Integration," *Rural Life Conference* 7 (March 1958): 15.

36. Edward W. O'Rourke, "Washington Farm Front," *Catholic Rural Life* 17 (October 1968): 8; Mary Mark Tacheny, "Legislative Action," *Common Ground* 7 (July 1988): 6–7; Joseph K. Fitzgerald, "If Not Mega-Farms, What?" *Earth Matters* 37 (Spring 1990): 4–5; Fite, *American Farmers*, 197; David Andrews to Alan Greenspan, April 18, 2000, in "Current Mailings, 1994–," NCRLC.

Nelson and Representative James Abourezk, which would have prohibited some or all nonfarming corporations from engaging in agriculture. These bills were not successful, but the Conference was victorious on a small scale in Nebraska. In 1982, diocesan rural life director Neal P. Nollette of Grand Island organized Catholic support that aided the passage of Initiative 300, which prohibited non–family farm corporations from owning farmland in the state.[37]

The NCRLC urged that the states require all corporations engaging in agriculture to register with the secretary of state as a first step toward regulating them and their impact on agriculture. In 1977, the Conference joined other groups in protesting the planned formation in Chicago of Ag-Land Fund I—a $50 million trust fund to buy up agricultural land—and helped cause the abandonment of the project. The NCRLC participated in the Food Action Campaign and the Agribusiness Accountability Initiative, which studied concentration in the farm industry and tried to restore competition. It joined the National Catholic Coalition for Responsible Investment and the Interfaith Center on Corporate Responsibility to assess the moral impact of its own investments and be a part of stockholder initiatives to make changes in corporate policies.[38]

Starting in the 1990s, the NCRLC campaigned against the explosive growth in the number of "confined animal feeding operations"—large factory-like hog or poultry farms. It organized a petition drive and a legal defense fund collection for Lincoln Township, Missouri, a community of 146 people that was sued by Premium Standard Farms for $7.9 million for passing a zoning ordinance that excluded its planned corporate hog farm. In 1997, the Conference made an influential call for a moratorium on the expansion and building of such farms until the effects on the environment from waste and on the economy in local communities were studied. Many midwestern bishops—even urban ones like Cardinal Francis George of Chicago—supported the campaign. The NCRLC, in cooperation with

---

37. Edward W. O'Rourke, "Washington Farm Front," *Catholic Rural Life* 18 (February 1969): 15; John George Weber, "Family Farm Antitrust Act of 1973," ibid. 22 (June 1973): 2; Neal P. Nollette, "Initiative 300," ibid. 33 (February 1983): 11–13; NCRLC, *Corporate Agriculture vs. Family Farming* (Des Moines, Iowa: NCRLC, 1968), in "General Publications, 1963–69," NCRLC 5-5.

38. John George Weber, "Regulating Agricultural Corporations," *Catholic Rural Life* 22 (March 1973): 2; "NCRLC Supports Food Action Campaign," ibid. 23 (February 1974): 3; "Absentee Investment, Not Bank Funds Is the Issue," ibid. 26 (March 1977): 2; "Bank's Land Buying Plan Runs into Hornet's Nest," ibid., 19–20; "Magazine Plans Special Issue on Ag-Land Fund I," ibid. (June 1977): 2; "Responsible Investment Coalition," ibid. 28 (December 1979): 12; Donald J. Kirby, S.J., "Farmers, Investors Share Responsibility of Ownership," ibid. 30 (October 1980): 16–18; "Agribusiness Accountability Initiative, Project Narrative," and attached documents [February 2002], in unprocessed mailings, NCRLC.

For the Family Farm in the Age of Agribusiness 289

other rural advocacy groups, achieved the passage of legislation regulating large feeding operations in states such as Iowa, South Dakota, and Colorado. Later, as the construction of such farms continued to divide many rural communities, the Conference developed a resource guide called "Who Is My Neighbor?" for holding parish meetings on the issue. In 2004, it helped form the National Poultry Justice Alliance of growers, workers, and environmental and faith-based groups to work for better wages and conditions for poultry industry workers and a cleaner and safer environment near poultry processing facilities. Andrews and NCRLC board member Bishop Richard Garcia of Sacramento were appointed to the National Commission on Industrial Farm Animal Production, funded by the Pew Charitable Trusts, to make a definitive study of the issue. The Conference called for the 2007 farm bill to have eight provisions to create competition among agricultural commodities such as meat and poultry that were controlled by a few corporations.[39]

The NCRLC believed that farmers themselves could act to check the growth of corporate control over agriculture. For example, farmers could prevent corporate control of food production through vertical integration, forming cooperatives to carry out their own food processing.[40]

The NCRLC's support for cooperatives was one part of its policy of encouraging more widespread ownership of property among all Americans. In the postwar decades, the Conference still believed, as it had throughout its history, that ownership of property was the way to keep control of one's economic life. Individual, rather than corporate, ownership of farms was of course the most commonly cited means to attain widespread distribution of property. Cooperatives were another such means. O'Rourke wrote that cooperatives helped "make ownership of income-producing property more widespread." Another NCRLC spokesman pointed to Canada, "where cooperatives control the economy in a manner the corpora-

39. Robert Gronski, "The Impact of Industrial Production on Food Quality," *Rural Landscapes* 8 (May 2001): 3, 6; "Rural Advocates Gain Successes in Iowa," ibid. 9 (June 2002): 3; "Justice Alliance Created for Poultry Industry," ibid. 11 (June 2004): 3; "New Alliance to Address Poultry Justice Issues," *Catholic Rural Life* (newsletter) 12 (June 2005): 2; "Swine Production: Who Is My Neighbor?" ibid. 13 (October 2005): 6; "Call for a Competition Title in the Farm Bill," *Catholic Rural Life* 49 (Spring 2007): 20; "Are Corporations above the Law?" in *In the Field News* 2 (March 1995) and other documents in "Current Mailings, 1994–," NCRLC; "An Immediate Moratorium on Large-Scale Livestock and Poultry Animal Confinement Facilities" (A Statement from the Board of Directors of the National Catholic Rural Life Conference, December 18, 1997), in ibid.; "Executive Director's Report, December 4/5, 1998," in ibid., 2–3; Andrews, *Catholic Rural Ethic*, 4–5; Perry Beeman, "Pew Bankrolls Study of Large Livestock Farms," Des Moines *Sunday Register*, June 25, 2006, copy in unprocessed mailings, NCRLC.

40. "Various Views on Vertical Integration," *Catholic Rural Life* 7 (December 1958): 10.

tions control the U.S.," as an example to emulate. O'Rourke also thought that cooperatives were a good way for poor minority groups such as African Americans to gain a share of economic power. In the late 1950s, Vizzard thought that farmers were turning to cooperatives for self-help and bargaining power in exasperation at ineffective "political" farm programs from Washington such as the soil bank.[41]

The NCRLC, carrying on from earlier decades, continued to do what it could to promote cooperatives. It urged Catholic pastors to help form cooperatives in their parishes, citing successful examples such as the cooperative economy of Westphalia, Iowa, organized by the Reverend Hubert Duren, and the cooperative processing and health services set up by the Reverend J. Fridolin Frommherz in Assumption, Ohio. Paul Sacco of the NCRLC was agricultural adviser to the Catholic Institutional Cooperative Association of Philadelphia in the 1940s; the association ran producer, marketing, and consumer cooperatives for the Catholic institutions of the city. The NCRLC continued to act with the Credit Union National Association in promoting parish credit unions. The 1950s were a time of particular growth in parish credit unions; from 1953 to 1960, they increased from 738 to 1,224.[42]

The NCRLC retained close ties with the Antigonish, Nova Scotia, cooperative movement: In 1959, the Coady Institute was established there, which brought people to Antigonish and conducted seminars throughout the world—especially teaching people from developing countries. The NCRLC supported legislation favorable to cooperatives, such as the National Consumer Cooperative Bank Act of 1978, which provided for grants, loans, and advice to low-income cooperatives. Twenty years later, the Conference favored amending the Agricultural Fair Practices Act of 1967 to enable farmers who contracted with processors to form cooperatives. This would give them more bargaining power than the current arrangement considering them "partners" with processors. In 1973, the NCRLC cosponsored an ecumenical conference on church-supported cooperatives in Washington, D.C. It also made occasional efforts to promote community land trusts and small farm-worker cooperatives.[43]

41. Edward W. O'Rourke, "Coop Month in a Coop Year," ibid. 17 (October 1968): 2; Joe Meisner, "Can Cooperatives Cooperate?" ibid. 21 (October 1972): 3, 6; Edward W. O'Rourke, "From Riots to Cooperatives," n.d., in "Cooperatives, Articles, Proposals, 1961–67," NCRLC 2-3; James L. Vizzard, "Washington Farm Front," *Rural Life Conference* 6 (September 1957): 14, and (November 1957): 15.

42. Witte, *Twenty-five Years*, 209–18; "Credit Unions—Important for Farm Ownership," *Feet in the Furrow* 3 (February 1955): 18; "86 New Parish Credit Unions," *Catholic Rural Life* 9 (July 1960): 23.

43. Gerard McMahon, "Consumer Co-op Bank Bill Is Landmark Legislation," *Catholic Rural*

But by the end of the century, cooperatives were not as important a part of the NCRLC philosophy as they had been in the 1930s or even the 1950s. In part, this was because of changes in cooperatives themselves. Andrews charged that "some of them have become investment enterprises for a globalized economy, ignoring their past honor as stalwarts of local community control." A friend of the NCRLC said that "they are interested mainly in expansion and turning in a good record for the management, regardless of whether this helps the farmer or not." For example, the big farm cooperatives pushed fertilizer, pesticides, and chemicals even though recklessly pursuing greater production did not benefit farmers.[44]

O'Rourke found it "ironic that in the United States, where we so loudly defend capitalism, only about five percent of our citizens own significant amounts of income-earning property." He supported profit-sharing plans and economist Louis Kelso's "second-income plan," whereby workers would own stock in the companies they worked for. Although the NCRLC throughout its history consistently upheld the right of private property and opposed socialism, in the 1980 *Strangers and Guests* statement the Midwest bishops held that under certain circumstances ("economic conditions, local or national needs, soil quality, climate, personal commitment or other factors") social ownership might be advisable.[45]

As another means to increase the economic vitality of rural areas, the NCRLC supported the moving of industry into rural communities. This concern derived from the decentralist movement, which was very influential within the NCRLC in the 1930s and still somewhat in the 1940s. The Conference's interest in rural industry resurfaced around 1960, when it issued a statement supporting agriculture-related industries, manufactured goods designed by local craftsmen, expanding existing rural industries, and incentives to attract outside industries. The Conference argued that rural industries would both ease rural underemployment and give industrial workers who moved from the cities a better way of life. It joined the Coalition for Rural America, a group composed largely of ex-governors

---

Life 27 (November 1978): 19–20; Gerald Foley, "Antigonish Movement for Building Co-ops Lives On," ibid. (December 1978): 17–19; Kathleen White, "Keeping up with the 70s," ibid. 33 (September 1983): 21; Dan Misleh, "A Bird's Eye View," *Rural Landscapes* 5 (March 1998): 2.

44. David Andrews, "Building Community," ibid. 4 (October 1996): 3; Lauren Soth (columnist of Des Moines *Register and Tribune*) to John George Weber, August 28, 1972, in "Annual Meeting of the Board of Directors and Diocesan Directors, Good Counsel Retreat House, Waverly, Neb., Sept. 25, 26, 27—1972," in "NCRLC Minutes of Meetings, 1972–1980," Box 1, NCRLC.

45. O'Rourke, *Self-help Works*, 33; *Strangers and Guests*, 35n31; NCRLC, *Ownership and Income* (Des Moines, Iowa: NCRLC, 1968), in "General Publications, 1963–69," NCRLC 5-5.

that formed in 1971 to encourage development in rural America and supported legislation such as the Rural Development Act of 1972, which aided industries in locating in rural areas.[46]

The Family Farm Crisis

None of these policies was able to prevent the family farm crisis of the 1980s. Historians disagree over whether the crisis was caused by farmers' reckless expansion during the good times of the 1970s or the inflation policies of the federal government. In any case, American farm debt increased from $54 billion in 1971 to $212 billion in 1985, while farmers' average net income in the hardest hit state, Iowa, fell from $17,680 in 1981 to a loss of $1,891 in 1983. As a result, an estimated two hundred thousand to three hundred thousand commercial farmers were forced to default on their loans, most of them in Iowa, Minnesota, and Wisconsin. In Iowa alone, twenty-six thousand farmers, 20 percent of the total, went out of business. Farmers' troubles had a ripple effect on all of rural America, where poverty increased from 13.8 percent in 1979 to 18.3 percent in 1983. In one twelve-month period in 1985 and 1986, rural America lost 632,000 people—the largest one-year loss in fifty years.[47]

The NCRLC responded to the crisis on many levels. On a grass-roots basis, diocesan rural life directors stood with farmers facing foreclosure in farmyards and courthouses, counseled them at their kitchen tables and in seminars on financial problems and stress management, formed support groups and crisis hotlines for farmers, and buried those who died by heart attack or suicide. The Reverend Norm White of Dubuque, who received the Conference's first Amos Award for excellence and commitment in rural ministry for his fight against "soul erosion" during the crisis, said that he felt "like a professional mourner at the death of so many family farms." Under Project Isidore, the diocese of Springfield, Illinois, and the archdiocese of Milwaukee provided interest-free loans of up to two thousand dollars to farmers.[48]

---

46. "Minutes, Bd. of Trustees of School of Living, March 29, 1941," NCRLC 8-3, 14; NCRLC, *Developing Rural Industry* (Des Moines, Iowa: NCRLC, 1960), in "Publications, D–E," NCRLC 5-6; "Rural Coalition Formed," *Catholic Rural Life* 20 (November 1971): 4; "NCRLC Co-Director Testifies," ibid., 5.

47. Mark Friedberger, *Shake-out: Iowa Farm Families in the 1980s* (Lexington: University Press of Kentucky, 1989), 17–80; Neil E. Harl, *The Farm Debt Crisis of the 1980s* (Ames: Iowa State University Press, 1990), xvii, 13–17; Osha Gray Davidson, *Broken Heartland: The Rise of America's Rural Ghetto* (Iowa City: University of Iowa Press, 1996), 16–17, 59–60, 75; Kathryn Marie Dudley, *Debt and Dispossession: Farm Loss in America's Heartland* (Chicago: University of Chicago Press, 2000), 13.

48. "Diocesan Rural Life Directors Meet in Kansas City," *Catholic Rural Life* 35 (February 1985): 20; whole issue, ibid. 36 (July 1986); "Rural Happenings across the US," *Common Ground* 6 (April

For the Family Farm in the Age of Agribusiness 293

Figure 21. Bishop Maurice Dingman of Des Moines at family farm rally, Ames, Iowa, February 27, 1985.

Conference members participated in many protests calling attention to the plight of farmers. They spoke at emotional farm rallies, most dramatically when past NCRLC president Dingman addressed an estimated fifteen to twenty thousand farmers in Ames, Iowa, on February 27, 1985. He held up a large white cross symbolizing the death of a farm through foreclosure and said: "Today I am planting it in your midst as a living sign of contradiction. It is up to you to decide: Does it mark the burial place of the American dream?" The Conference initiated a nationwide tolling of church bells on Ash Wednesday, 1985, which was observed by Protestant as well as Catholic churches. Diocesan directors in Iowa and Minnesota

---

1988): 2; "Rural Life Happenings across the United States," ibid. 7 (January 1989): 2; "In Farm Crisis, Church Fights 'Soul Erosion,'" *Courier,* February 1986, clipping in "RLD Activities," La Blanc Subject File, Box 6, NCRLC; "Fast Start for Wisconsin Project . . . " *Catholic Post,* February 9, 1986, clipping in ibid.; "Fr. Norm White Receives Rural Ministry Amos Award," *Witness,* August 23, 1987, clipping in ibid.

were arrested for acts of civil disobedience in opposing foreclosure sales of family farms. The NCRLC, fearing that the stress of the crisis threatened violence, warned against domestic abuse and suicide in farm families and rejected retaliation against loan officers or responses based on bigotry.[49]

The NCRLC led calls for government action in response to the crisis. Dingman represented the Conference in testimony before Congress in favor of emergency credit for farmers. For once the broader church reinforced the NCRLC. The Reverend J. Bryan Hehir, secretary of the USCC's Department of Social Development and World Peace, appealed to Congress for debt restructuring, reduced interest rates, and resale of farmland held by the FmHA and Farm Credit System to family farmers. The whole American hierarchy supported similar proposals in their major economic statement *Economic Justice for All*. The NCRLC was lukewarm toward statewide farm foreclosure moratoria such as that adopted by Minnesota. The Conference thought moratoria could raise interest rates, and it noted that only 11 percent of farmers lost farms through foreclosure. On the positive side, the NCRLC believed that moratoria could help some farmers to continue operating. The Conference did work with other organizations in the Iowa Farm Unity Coalition, which supported a moratorium as a stopgap until other credit remedies could take effect.[50]

President Reagan vetoed the emergency farm credit bill as budget busting, but eventually the NCRLC helped to get some remedial legislation passed. Iowa, Minnesota, and South Dakota adopted mandatory mediation laws that were successful in encouraging farmers and lenders to negotiate rather than go through the legal system. The new Chapter 12 bankruptcy category established by the federal government also helped owners to stay on their farms. The federal Farm Credit System was bailed out with $4 bil-

---

49. Crisler and Mosle, *In the Midst of His People*, 209; "Conference News," *Common Ground* 3 (January 1985): 2–3; "The First Trial for Civil Disobedience during the Rural Life Crisis," ibid. 5 (May 1987): 1–3; special issue on "Violence in Rural America," *Catholic Rural Life* 35 (November 1985); Gregory Cusack to NCRLC Board of Directors, March 20, 1985, in "National Catholic Rural Life Conference (N.C.R.L.C.)," in Fitzgerald Files, Box 1, NCRLC; "Statement on the Threat of Violence in Rural America by the Board of Directors of the National Catholic Rural Life Conference," in "NCRLC: Board Meeting," in "Fitzgerald Files: Board Related, ca. 1986–89," Box 1, NCRLC; "Farmers, COACT Members Opposed Threatened Foreclosure," copy of clipping from *Paynesville Press* [Minnesota], n.d., in "Conference Mailings," La Blanc Subject File, Box 3, NCRLC.

50. "The National Catholic Rural Life Conference Annual Report to Members—1985," *Catholic Rural Life* 36 (February 1986): 22; "An Appeal to Congress," ibid. 37 (September 1987): 28; National Conference of Catholic Bishops, *Economic Justice for All*, section 242; Nancy Thompson, *Farm Foreclosure Moratorium* (Des Moines, Iowa: National Catholic Rural Life Conference, [1983]), brochure in "Interns," Cusack Subject File, Box 19, NCRLC; Mark Friedberger, *Farm Families and Change in 20th Century America* (Lexington: University Press of Kentucky, 1988), 195–96.

For the Family Farm in the Age of Agribusiness 295

Figure 22. Farm Unity Rally, Audubon, Iowa, June 3, 1985.

lion and reformed by many provisions pushed for by the Iowa Farm Unity Coalition—a fair review process, the right of a previous owner to purchase or rent land that was lost to the system, the disclosure of interest rates, and the establishment of mediation.[51]

Although the family farm crisis did not get much attention after the 1980s, it continued. In the 1990s, 32,500 farmers were still leaving the land every year. In the late 1990s, low commodity prices coupled with the Freedom to Farm Act's removal of government support programs resulted in a new wave of farm foreclosures around the country. The NCRLC tried to call attention to the crisis with the Green Ribbon Campaign. The wearing of green ribbons started with a North Dakota parishioner, was officially adopted by the NCRLC, and spread to Protestants and secular farm organizations throughout the United States and in Canada and England. The Conference published Green Ribbon Campaign packets containing prayers (including a "Prayer Service for Loss of the Farm"), suggestions for responses to the rural crisis, and instructions on forming rural community support groups. Green Ribbon Churches engaged in various activities to call attention to the crisis and received materials from the NCRLC. The

---

51. Friedberger, *Shake-out*, 88–90, 103, 160–61; Harl, *Farm Debt Crisis*, 102–47, 161–209, 275–77; Walt Grazer, "Legislative Action," *Common Ground* 6 (January 1988): 5–6; Grazer, "A Victory for All" ("Washington Watch"), *Catholic Rural Life* 37 (February 1988): 32.

hierarchy responded by forming a new Ad Hoc Committee on Agricultural Issues, which included former NCRLC presidents Skylstad and Burke.[52]

The family farm crisis engendered a kind of revival of the NCRLC as an organization. It gave the Conference an immediate reason for existing, and the NCRLC responded with a surge of activity. The NCRLC was relevant to the needs of actual farmers in a way it had not been for a long time. Historian Mark Friedberger claimed that as a result of the farm crisis the rural church underwent "something of a renaissance" during these years. He added that the Catholic Church was "one of the most powerful and best organized denominations," with the Catholic clergy being "more outspoken" than those of other denominations early in the crisis. The NCRLC and other family farm advocates "won the battle over electronic media coverage with their skillful courting of television and the press early in the farm crisis." At first, Friedberger claimed, the crisis discredited the "establishment" of the Farm Bureau, the Extension Service, commodity organizations, agribusiness, and the state agricultural bureaucracy. But he said that the family farm advocates exaggerated the severity of the crisis, were unable to achieve their goals in the 1985 farm bill, and eventually lost the support of the conservative majority of farmers back to the "establishment" and its safety net of government programs.[53]

However, Friedberger claimed that the values of the "frugal farmer" championed by the NCRLC were successful during the farm crisis. The crisis discredited the "entrepreneurial" style of farming based on risk taking, specialization, and capital favored by agribusiness and the land grant colleges and showed the durability of the traditional practices of diversification and limitation of expansion to family needs. Many farmers responded to the crisis by forms of diversification such as raising different crops or livestock, growing organic foods, taking off-farm jobs, or going into food processing. As a result, despite the crisis, many family farmers were able to "recycle" and stay on the land.[54]

---

52. "A Bird's Eye View," *Rural Landscapes* 2 (February 1995): 2; "We Need YOUR Help!" ibid. 6 (January 1999): 1; Dan Misleh, "Capitol Update," ibid. 7 (March 2000): 2; Misleh, "Fluctuating Commodity Prices Has Definite Impact on Rural Communities," *Catholic Rural Life* 41 (Spring 1999): 36; David Andrews, "The Green Ribbon Campaign, the Jubilee, the Work of the NCRLC," *National Catholic Rural Life Conference Annual Report, 1998–1999*, 1; "Green Ribbon Campaign" and Margaret Mary O'Gorman, "Prayer Service for Loss of the Farm" (both 1999), and David Andrews, "Joining the Struggle for Rural America," *Word and World* 20 (Spring 2000): 140, copy, all in "Current Mailings, 1994–," NCRLC; "Green Ribbon Churches" [2002], in unprocessed mailings, NCRLC.

53. Friedberger, *Shake-out*, 82, 95, 145–46.

54. Ibid., 127–43, 146, 166; Danbom, *Born in the Country*, 267–68.

National Politics, Farm Organizations, and Advocacy Groups

The NCRLC's efforts to support the family farm naturally involved it in governmental politics and the more specialized politics of the various farm organizations. The Conference's role in these two levels of politics was ambivalent. While professing the neutrality that a church organization must under the American system of the separation of church and state, the NCRLC actually tended to favor (or disfavor) certain sides in both the national two-party and farm organization political arenas.

The NCRLC's official policy on the two kinds of politics was expressed in a 1943 statement. It said that the Conference "should never engage in politics, but that its policy should be to support all farm organizations, political or non-political, wherever they merited help. On the other hand, support should be denied whenever such organizations fostered views contrary to those of the Conference." In national partisan politics, the Conference tried to adhere to this evenhanded standard as much as possible. For example, in 1960, NCRLC officials gave testimony before both the Democratic and Republican platform committees. In an analysis of the two parties' 1968 platforms, O'Rourke gave the pros and cons of each without expressing a preference for either of them. NCRLC official Dan Misleh described the platform positions of the Democratic, Republican, Reform, and Green parties on rural issues in 2000 without specifically endorsing any. In 2004, the Conference stated that it "does not endorse candidates," and pointed to a United States Conference of Catholic Bishops guide and the NCRLC website for Catholic positions on issues to compare to the candidates' stands.[55]

In a large number of cases, nevertheless, the NCRLC came down on the side of the Democrats alone. On the various family farm issues, it supported Democratic positions much more often than Republican ones. The Eisenhower, Nixon, and Reagan farm policies came in for particularly sharp criticism from NCRLC officials, while the Kennedy, Carter, and Clinton policies were treated quite favorably. Vizzard, who admitted in a letter to a newspaper that he was a "life-long Democrat," made much more use of Democratic contacts in his work in Washington than Republi-

---

55. Witte, *Twenty-five Years*, 128; James L. Vizzard, "Editorial," *Catholic Rural Life* 9 (June 1960): 2, 28–29; Joe Ryan, "Musings of the Managing Editor," ibid. (August 1960): 4; Dan Misleh, "Faithful Citizenship," ibid. 43 (Fall 2000): 42–43, 44; "Guides to Inform Your Vote," *Catholic Rural Life* (newsletter) 12 (October 2004): 1; Edward W. O'Rourke, "The Party Platforms," *Register, Diocese of Peoria Edition*, October 6, 1968, clipping in "Farm Page, From the Register, 1968–1971," NCRLC 2-5.

can ones. Among the Democratic politicians Vizzard had frequent contact with were Hubert H. Humphrey, Paul H. Douglas, Wayne Morse, Gaylord Nelson, Eugene McCarthy, and George McGovern. The only Republican with whom he worked to an equal extent was Senator George Aiken of Vermont. Later the Conference worked closely with Democrats such as Agriculture Secretaries Bob Bergland and Dan Glickman and Senator Tom Harkin of Iowa.[56]

This was the time when farmers' political power was being substantially weakened. Legislative reapportionment, which, based on the one-person, one-vote principle, did away with the overrepresentation of sparsely populated rural districts as opposed to crowded urban constituencies in state legislative bodies, disappointed the NCRLC. So did the trend toward regional governments, in which cities sought to link adjoining rural territory to metropolitan areas to help pay for expensive urban services. Food stamp programs, limitations on farm support programs, and food embargoes such as the Russian grain embargoes of 1975 and 1980 showed that unions and consumer groups had more clout in Washington than farmers.[57]

To make up for this lost political power, the NCRLC urged farmers to try to attain their goals by working through the major farmers' organizations. In a general policy statement issued in 1955, it urged "farmers to join at least one general farm organization and to participate intelligently in its programs and deliberations." It recommended no particular farm organization but urged farmers to scrutinize "organizations' stands on issues of social justice" and reserved the right to "criticize those organizations which take a stand contradictory to the social teachings of the Church."[58]

Of the major farm organizations—the Farm Bureau, the Farmers Union,

56. James L. Vizzard to the Editor, Des Moines *Sunday Register*, May 19, 1960, in "Lay, Da–Dl, 1960," NCRLC 13-15; "Senators Agree on Government's Role," *Catholic Rural Life* 7 (November 1958): 7; "What Do National Leaders Think of NCRLC?" ibid. (October 1958): 10–11; James L. Vizzard, "Washington Farm Front," ibid. 10 (December 1961): 6; Vizzard, "Washington Farm Front," ibid. 12 (March 1963): 8; John George Weber, "New Directions for U.S. Agricultural Policy," ibid. 21 (August 1972): 2; Kathleen White, "Carter Choices Appear to Be Good on Rural Issues," ibid. 26 (March 1977): 8–10; "Bergland Becomes Newest NCRLC Member," *Common Ground* 10 (June/July 1991): 3; "Clinton Focuses on Rural America," *Rural Landscapes* 2 (May 1995): 1; David Andrews, "National Catholic Rural Life Conference's 76th Anniversary Gives Hope to Rural America," ibid. 7 (January 2000): 1; Vizzard to Eugene J. McCarthy, May 26, 1958, in "Correspondence: Vizzard, M–, 1956–1958," NCRLC 13-12; Vizzard–George S. McGovern correspondence in "Lay, Mc, 1960," NCRLC 13-16; "Overview Exclusive: John Deedy Interviews Brother David Andrews, C.S.C." (1998), in "Current Mailings, 1994–," NCRLC.

57. Fite, *American Farmers*, 138, 150–52, 172–73, 199, 205–7, 227–28; Edward W. O'Rourke's articles in "Regional Governments and Planning, 1970, '71," NCRLC 2-14.

58. "N.C.R.L.C. Resolution on Farm Groups Quoted," *Rural Life Conference—Feet in the Furrow* 4 (October 1955): 9.

the Grange, and, later, the National Farmers Organization (NFO)—the one that received by far the most criticism from the NCRLC was the Farm Bureau. The feud with the Farm Bureau dated from at least the 1940s, when the two groups disagreed fiercely over the Farm Security Administration. In the 1950s they were pitted against each other over the Farm Bureau's organizational tie-in to the federal government through the Extension Service; accusations circulated by agents of the Farm Bureau, among others, that the Farmers Union was a communist front organization; and the Conference's *Program for Shared Abundance* statement of 1955 (which the Farm Bureau was practically the only organization to comment unfavorably upon).[59]

In 1960, the Conference published a detailed comparison of NCRLC and Farm Bureau policies, pointing out the "gross conflict" between the two organizations on such issues as food stamps, direct payments to farmers, limitations on payments to farmers in conservation reserve programs, extension of minimum wage and hours laws to farm workers, federal regulation of farm labor camps and licensing of farm labor contractors, unionization of farm workers, distribution of surplus food by Public Law 480, and U.S. financial contributions to the Mutual Security program of aid to developing countries. The editorial provoked an intense reaction from NCRLC members and others; Vizzard stated that "nothing else the NCRLC has published in recent years ever aroused such a massive response." He boasted that "the affair received terrific coverage in the press, both diocesan and secular, and the response has been overwhelmingly favorable with the exception, of course, of Farm Bureau officials."[60] The feud between the two organizations continued on many issues in the 1960s and 1970s. In particular, the NCRLC stoutly defended its right to speak out on secular agricultural policy issues against Farm Bureau charges that it was violating the separation of church and state. After that, although policy differences continued, they did not result in public controversies.[61]

---

59. W. J. Gibbons, "The Farm on the Potomac," *Christian Farmer* 3 (September 1950): 2; correspondence in "National Farmers Union, Correspondence, Program, Report, 1954–57, 60," NCRLC 1-5; E. Howard Hill to Michael Dineen, December 21, 1955, in "Resolutions Acknowledged (Program for Shared Abundance), Ntn'l Convention, Lexington, Ky., Oct. 22–26, 1955," NCRLC 8-12.

60. James L. Vizzard, "Editorial," *Catholic Rural Life* 9 (February 1960): 2; "NCRLC and AFBF Policies Compared," ibid., 12–13; [Vizzard], "Editorial," ibid. (April 1960): 2, 22–23; Vizzard to Harold F. Hall, February 12, 1960, in "Lay, Ca–Ce, 1960," NCRLC 13-15; approximately 80 letters in "Fr. Vizzard, Letters on his Farm Bureau Editorial, 1960," NCRLC 13-17.

61. "Excerpt from 1968 Resolutions of the American Farm Bureau Federation, Rural Living—Religious Life," in "Rural Living—Religious Life," NCRLC 8A-2; NCRLC executive committee, "Our Right to Defend Rights," in "Exec. Committee Mtg., Lincoln, Nebr., Jan. 23–24, 1968," NCRLC 8-22; "Dingman Answers Attack on Churches by Farm Bureau," *Catholic Rural Life* 28 (January 1979): 21–22.

Because of the decline in farmers' political power, the NCRLC believed that the only way to get their just needs met would be by joining together—in collective bargaining and in a coalition of the major farm organizations. Beginning in the 1950s, but most notably in a series of statements in the 1960s and early 1970s, the Conference called on the major farm organizations or farmers themselves to "jointly create new, neutral marketing associations for the chief commodities." These bargaining associations would enter into contracts with wholesalers and processors to assure just prices. Only through such neutral bargaining groups that included the majority of producers in each commodity would farmers have the bargaining power they needed to ensure receiving just prices. Therefore, for the good of all farmers, the farm groups should end their "narrow organizational feuding" and join together. During the farm crisis of the 1980s the Conference again stressed the "moral obligation" of collective bargaining for farmers.[62]

The NCRLC favored a number of proposals in Congress aimed at making it easier for farmers to bargain collectively. From 1968 to 1971, it supported a series of bills introduced by Senator Walter Mondale to provide for bargaining at the marketplace. O'Rourke came out in favor of strengthening the Agricultural Fair Practices Act to require processors and others to negotiate with producer groups. About the same time, the Conference urged the liberalizing of the 1937 Agricultural Marketing Agreement Act (which legalized marketing orders—an order to buy or sell at the price prevailing in the market when the order is executed—agreed to by the government and farmers) to make it easier to agree to marketing orders and to allow their extension to such commodities as poultry, hogs, eggs, and possibly cattle.[63]

Although the NCRLC's ideal was for all four of the major farm organizations to end their feuding and bargain together, it particularly supported the individual efforts of the one farm organization—the NFO—formed specifically for the purpose of working for collective bargaining. The NFO was begun in 1955 in Corning, Iowa, to help farmers achieve collective

62. *Cooperation at the Marketplace* (Des Moines, Iowa: NCRLC, n.d.), in "General Publications, 1963–69," NCRLC 5-5; "Minutes, NCRLC Board of Directors, June 22–23, 1983, Savior of the World Seminary, Kansas City, Kansas," in "Board Communications," Cusack Subject File, Box 19, NCRLC, 11.

63. Edward W. O'Rourke, "Washington Farm Front," *Catholic Rural Life* 18 (February 1969): 15; "Co-Director's Report, Msgr. J. G. Weber," in "Board and Diocesan Directors Meeting, Evansville, Ind., Oct. 26–27, 1971," NCRLC 8-23, 1; Edward W. O'Rourke, "Washington Farm Front," *Catholic Rural Life* 20 (March 1971): 8; O'Rourke, "Marketing Orders," ibid., 2.

bargaining in any or all commodities. Under President Oren Lee Staley, it proposed to act as the agent for farmers and negotiate contracts with processors that would guarantee them cost of production plus a profit. In the 1960s, it used a number of militant tactics, including economic pressure on competing cooperatives, holding actions (keeping a commodity off of the market), "strikes," pouring out milk on roadsides, destruction of livestock, tractor marches, and—some charged—coercion and violence to get farmers to join in their actions.[64]

Despite the controversial nature of the NFO's tactics, the NCRLC gave it strong support. In response to a flood of letters from anxious Catholic farmers, it issued a statement in 1960 asserting that "the NFO's basic objectives are sound: to organize farmers and achieve economic justice for themselves," and that its "means" also "seem to be legitimate." It urged Catholic NFO members to be "active, responsible members of their organization," as with all farm organizations, and condemned farm organizations motivated by "organizational competition and jealousy" that attacked the NFO. O'Rourke worked vigorously behind the scenes to urge nonviolence on NFO leaders and to heal dangerous splits in the organization's leadership. He gave speeches at NFO conventions urging nonviolence, cooperation with other farm organizations, and the observance of the principles of "majority rule and minority rights" within the NFO.[65]

The NCRLC generally supported the NFO strikes and holding actions and their accompanying dramatizing actions, but it always counseled moderation—negotiation and cooperation rather than confrontation. In 1963, when Minnesota farmers poured out milk in a dispute over whether the NFO should be the bargaining agent for dairy cooperatives, O'Rourke refused to take sides but urged all parties to "work together toward commodity-wide bargaining." The next year, the diocesan directors reasoned that the NFO's current holding action lived up to the five general principles that would morally justify such a strike: It was for a just cause (raising farmers' income, which was currently based on only 63 percent of parity); other means of obtaining the objective had failed; the good outweighed the evil of the action; there was a reasonable hope of success; and it was carried out by lawful means. When the Justice Department

---

64. Fite, *American Farmers*, chap. 9.
65. Dana C. Jennings, "Farmers Subsidizing America, NFO Speaker Says," *Catholic Rural Life* 9 (March 1960): 18-19; James L. Vizzard, "Washington Farm Front," ibid. 13 (May 1964): 7; letters throughout NCRLC 13 for the 1950s and 1960s; folder "Ntn'l Farmers Organization; Correspondence, By-Laws, Articles, 1962–64, 1969, 1972–74," NCRLC 2-11.

threatened to declare an NFO holding action in violation of the Sherman Anti-Trust Act, O'Rourke asked that farmers be given "more extensive exemption from the Sherman Act similar to that enjoyed by the labor unions." Later, Weber served as arbitrator in a dispute between the NFO and two dairy cooperatives but was unsuccessful, the conflict ending in litigation.[66]

The one time the NCRLC officially opposed an NFO action, a storm of protest was aroused among its members who were sympathetic toward the organization. This was O'Rourke's condemnation of the "hog kill" of 1968, in which the NFO dramatized a holding action by slaughtering ten thousand hogs. O'Rourke met with NCRLC and NFO officials, including President Oren Lee Staley, but not with the Conference executive committee, before penning a controversial editorial in which he stated: "I object vigorously to the destruction of meat in a world suffering from protein deficiency." He wished that instead of destroying the hogs, NFO members had donated them to the hungry. He noted that CROP had offered to ship hogs to the needy overseas, and he approved a project of NFO members of a parish in Ohio who donated one thousand hogs to needy ghetto dwellers in Cleveland. When the NCRLC executive committee next met, O'Rourke had to defend his editorial in "one of the liveliest sessions . . . ever conducted." Some lay members of the committee supported the morality of the hog kill, contending that "the plight of the farmers is so great that even distasteful actions such as the hog kill are needed." But, based on the longstanding Conference policy of supporting bargaining by farmers in principle but never any particular farm organization, a vote to endorse NFO policies and programs was defeated.[67]

Later, the NCRLC cooperated to a certain extent with the National Farmers Union, which favored small farmers more than the Farm Bureau did. The two organizations worked together on public policies affecting family farms. In the 2000s, the Farmers Union helped with the Confer-

66. Edward W. O'Rourke, "Spilt Milk in Minnesota," *Catholic Rural Life* 12 (May 1963): 2; O'Rourke, "NFO Milk Holding," ibid. 16 (May 1967): 2; "National Catholic Rural Life Conference Diocesan Directors Resolution, St. Louis, Mo.—August 28, 1964," in "The Farmer and Economics," NCRLC 8A-1; documents in "Ntn'l Farmers Organization; Correspondence, By-Laws, Articles, 1962–64, 1969, 1972–74," NCRLC 2-11.

67. Edward W. O'Rourke, "A Protest against NFO Hog Burials," *Register, Diocese of Peoria Edition*, May 5, 1968, clipping in "Farm Page, from the Register, 1968–1971," NCRLC 2-5; letters in "Ntn'l Farmers Organization, Hog Burials, 1968," NCRLC 2-12; Edward W. O'Rourke to Rev. Clarence L. Diegelman, May 3, 1968, Diegelman and Leo Buehler to O'Rourke, May 7, 1968, and O'Rourke to Buehler, May 24, 1968, in "Laymen, A–F, 1968," NCRLC 13-25; O'Rourke's report in "Executive Committee Mtg., Des Moines, Iowa, June 18–19, 1968," NCRLC 8-22; "Farmer Discontent Reflected in Torrid NCRLC Session," *Catholic Rural Life* 17 (August 1968): 3.

ence's Green Ribbon Campaign, distributing packets of NCRLC literature through its state unions.⁶⁸

NCRLC support for collective bargaining was one of the reasons it sought a coalition of the major farm organizations. It believed that unless the different farm organizations worked together, the fortunes of America's farmers would continue to decline. It did not think it was desirable for the individual farm organizations to lose their identities, because each had its own useful functions. However, conflict and a "survival of the fittest" philosophy among farm organizations only weakened American agriculture as a whole.⁶⁹

In 1943, the Conference set a precedent for trying to arrange a farm organization coalition when it sponsored a Farm Organization Unity Program, at which high officials from the Farm Bureau, Farmers Union, and Grange participated in a forum. No attempt was made, however, to bring the three organizations to any kind of agreement at that meeting.⁷⁰

Under O'Rourke and Weber in the 1960s, the NCRLC made a more sustained effort to bring the farm organizations together. The 1964 convention in St. Louis was devoted to trying to forge a farm unity coalition, and it adopted a resolution calling for an "American Federation of Agriculture" that would give "agriculture a united and effective voice in the councils of the nation, without destroying the identity of the participating organizations." Weber chaired a panel discussion of representatives of the four major farm organizations (now including the NFO). The four representatives made little effort to compromise their positions, although they did carry unanimous resolutions to "come together in a bona fide manner to cooperate and find a meeting of minds" and to try to set up a "National American Farm Federation."⁷¹

The remainder of the decade was filled with efforts to follow up on the beginning made at St. Louis. O'Rourke and Weber, together with other religious representatives, met repeatedly with officials of the major farm

---

68. Harold D. Guither, *The Food Lobbyists: Behind the Scenes of Food and Agri-Politics* (Lexington, Mass.: Lexington Books, 1980), 294; "National Catholic Rural Life Conference, NCRLC Board Report, June 2004, Report From Toby Pearson, National Organizer," in unprocessed mailings, NCRLC, 1.

69. Weber and O'Rourke, "Coalitions and Change," 19; O'Rourke, "Appraising Farm Organizations," *Catholic Rural Life* 11 (October 1962): 2.

70. Witte, *Twenty-five Years*, 127–28; "Conference Affairs," *Land and Home* 6 (September 1943): 86; "Conference Affairs," ibid. (December 1943): 114.

71. "American Federation of Agriculture Urged," *Catholic Rural Life* 13 (October 1964): 1; "The Farm Organization Panel," in "40th Anniversary, St. Louis, Mo., Aug. 27–30, 1964," NCRLC 8-20 (third folder).

organizations, including three times with their presidents in Washington, D.C. They urged the organizations both to work together on individual issues and to form a unity coalition. Unfortunately, their efforts were continually frustrated by the jealousies of the farm organization leaders and their uncompromising stands on issues. Most recalcitrant was the Farm Bureau, which "would not change its policy regarding government involvement in farm programs." The NCRLC effort to create farm unity peaked in 1969, when Sister Thomas More Bertels, O.S.F., a history professor at Holy Family College in Manitowoc, Wisconsin, aided the Conference by giving eighty lectures to groups of farmers promoting "farm unity agencies" at both the federal and local levels. In the same year, the Conference managed to bring about the formation of the Coalition of 22—which included all of the major farm organizations except the Farm Bureau. The coalition stayed together for several years and had some success in influencing farm legislation in Washington. However, as O'Rourke and Weber lamented, "without the Farm Bureau, . . . it lacked the basic ingredient of unity which could have made it a powerful influence."[72]

Although it was unsuccessful in forming a lasting coalition of national farm organizations, on a much smaller scale the NCRLC was instrumental in forming a coalition of Iowa farm organizations called the Iowa Farm and Commodity Organizations (IFCO). For several years, Weber served as chairman of IFCO, which met monthly to exchange information and ideas and, by 1971, issued fifteen policy statements on rural issues.[73]

Starting in the late 1970s, the NCRLC no longer sought to bring together the major farm organizations but instead joined in coalitions with like-minded advocacy groups. Father McRaith was instrumental in the formation at a meeting in Washington, D.C., of Rural America, a membership organization that sought, "through research, technical assistance, education, and advocacy, to ensure rural people equity in the formation and implementation of public policies and programs." McRaith was elected to the board of the new organization, which he claimed "allowed individuals and organizations like the National Catholic Rural Life Conference to

---

72. "Nun Urges Creation of Farmer Power," *Catholic Rural Life* 18 (February 1969): 14; "Varied Activities Reported at NCRLC Meeting," ibid. (September 1969): 1; Edward W. O'Rourke, "Washington Farm Front," ibid. 19 (January 1970): 8; Weber and O'Rourke, "Coalitions and Change," 19; "Farm Unity Agencies. A Report of Progress by the National Catholic Rural Life Conference, December 1, 1969," in "Executive Committee Meeting, Sioux City, Iowa, Jan. 20–21, 1970," NCRLC 8-23; Bertels, *In Pursuit of Agri-Power*, esp. 37.

73. Weber and O'Rourke, "Coalitions and Change," 19; Edward W. O'Rourke, "Rural Middle Class and Rural Poor," *Catholic Rural Life* 20 (June 1971): 2.

For the Family Farm in the Age of Agribusiness

participate in a rural movement without being co-opted." Rural America, which had 2,315 members in 1979, was formed mainly by rural electric cooperatives, labor unions, and church groups, and had a reputation as a "poverty lobby." It networked with other liberal rural public-interest organizations such as the NCRLC, the National Farmers Union, National Land for People, the Agribusiness Accountability Project, the Family Farm Coalition, and the National Center for Appropriate Technology—but not with the Farm Bureau, Grange, or NFO. It helped bring federal funding and assistance to the rural poor, who otherwise might have been ignored. In 1979, the NCRLC helped form a Religion and Rural Life Council as a division of Rural America, but it did not accomplish much. Rural America itself died out from lack of philanthropic patronage contributions in the mid-1980s.[74]

However, Executive Director Cusack had been working closely on the farm crisis with David Ostendorf, director of the Midwest office of Rural America, headquartered in Des Moines, and preserved this cooperation when Ostendorf continued to run his office under the name Prairiefire after the demise of Rural America. The Conference under Cusack worked with Prairiefire on a number of projects, but the connection lapsed when he left the NCRLC.[75]

The NCRLC was a charter member of Rural Coalition, an association of public interest groups concerned with the rural poor and community development. It was the only "faith-related group" in the organization, which by 1984 consisted of over one hundred groups. Cusack attended Rural Coalition meetings in Washington, D.C., where the NCRLC influenced the organization to emphasize tax reform and the needs of family farmers. Rural Coalition helped achieve greater funding for Native American reservations and local government public works programs and construction opportunities for rural builders and contractors. However, Cusack complained that it lacked focus and vision, and it ran into financial difficulties and dissolved by the end of the 1980s.[76]

---

74. "Members Elect McRaith to Rural America Board," ibid. 24 (December 1975): 8; John J. McRaith, "Huge Turnout Shows Rural Commitment," ibid. 27 (January 1978): 7–9; "Religion and Rural Life Council Proposal Pushed," ibid. 28 (April 1979): 23; Guither, *Food Lobbyists*, 118–20, 167, 294, 319–24; William P. Browne, *The Failure of National Rural Policy: Institutions and Interests* (Washington, D.C.: Georgetown University Press, 2001), 79, 82; Patrick J. Ronan to Gregory Cusack, December 7, 1981, in "CCA," Cusack Subject File, Box 19, NCRLC.

75. "Prairiefire Rural Action Board of Directors," file "Mr. Greg Cusack, Rural Crisis Consultation," and other documents in Cusack Subject File, Box 20, NCRLC.

76. Greg Cusack, "Conference News," *Common Ground* 2 (May 1984): 1; Guither, *Food Lobbyists*, 295, 324; Browne, *Failure of National Rural Policy*, 79; Cusack to Staff, January 18, 1984, in "Staff Memos," La Blanc Subject File, Box 8, NCRLC.

Cusack cooperated with Farm Aid, which originally held concerts and rallies to raise funds for emergency relief for farmers during the 1980s crisis. He claimed that he helped move Farm Aid beyond providing emergency relief to address changing national policies to deal with the underlying causes of the farm crisis. Farm Aid indeed endured beyond the farm crisis, and Andrews collaborated with it in the 1990s.[77]

Starting in 1988, the Conference cooperated with the Sustainable Agriculture Working Group (SAWG), a network of over thirty farm, religious, conservation, environmental, food, and rural advocacy groups. The wider focus of this network coincided with the NCRLC's more holistic view of rural life at the end of the century. SAWG was the main group through which the Conference worked to influence farm legislation in the 1990s and 2000s. In all, the NCRLC collaborated with at least seventeen rural, environmental, and religious organizations on the 2007 farm bill.[78]

From "Farm" to "Food"

But fighting to save the family farm was a losing battle. The Conference was opposed not only by the trend toward efficiency, which encouraged the "get big or get out" philosophy, but also by politicians, economists, businessmen, and big farmers, who sent out the cry that there were "too many farmers." These opponents, led by Agriculture Secretary Ezra T. Benson in the 1950s and the Committee for Economic Development (CED) in the 1960s, believed there were too many small, inefficient, economically unjustified farmers in the United States. They proposed (in proposals such as the CED's "An Adaptive Program for Agriculture," published in 1962) that the government create programs to get these "unnecessary" farmers off the land and help them gain nonagricultural employment.[79]

The NCRLC, along with others who believed there was a value for individuals and society beyond the economic in farming, opposed these proposals. For example, in 1958, Vizzard rebutted the argument that forcing small farmers off the land would automatically cut down the bothersome surpluses and mean more income for the farmers who were left. Leaving aside the problem of "where the refugees go or what they do, what they

---

77. Folder "Farm Aid," Cusack Subject File, Box 19, NCRLC; "Church Land and Community Program, Board Report: December 4, 1998, Joan Allsup," in "Current Mailings, 1994–," NCRLC, 2; "Calendar," *Rural Landscapes* 7 (October 1999): 2.

78. Untitled article, *Earth Matters* 38 (Winter 1989): 3; *Midwest Sustainable Agriculture Working Group,* folder in "Publications Acq'd: 6/30/94," Box 23, NCRLC; "NCRLC Launches Campaign for a New Farm Bill," *Catholic Rural Life* (newsletter) 13 (April 2006): 1.

79. Fite, *American Farmers,* chap. 7, especially 122–26.

gain or lose by abandoning the land," Vizzard pointed out that even if all of the 1.2 million farmers with sales of less than $2,500 a year were forced off their farms, it would only reduce production seven percent. Furthermore, the land they left would probably be acquired by nearby large farm operators who would produce more efficiently and abundantly, resulting in even greater surpluses. O'Rourke denied the family farm was doomed to decline: "The family farm is a very hardy institution. It will survive and grow stronger unless it is burdened with unwarranted disadvantages."[80]

The NCRLC made a number of efforts to oppose this movement to push small farmers off the land. O'Rourke secured appointment to a Kennedy administration committee that studied the effects of government policies on family farms. In the late 1960s, the Conference propagandized against the "Adaptive Program for Agriculture" and the Farm Bureau–sponsored whole-farm land retirement proposal that would provide federal assistance to help small farmers get out of agriculture. In 1972, the Conference secured the support of the American hierarchy, whose statement *Where Shall the People Live?* called for measures to stop the migration from rural America and the decline of the family farming system. The next year, McRaith joined a Coalition for Land Reform, which studied ways to keep family farmers on the land. During the foreclosure epidemic of the 1980s, the NCRLC deprecated America's complacent attitude toward so many farmers being forced out of agriculture, denying that such "farm exiles" got better city jobs.[81]

In the last decades of the twentieth century, the Conference made one concession to changing times by giving up its support for the small subsistence farm. As early as 1952, a priest connected with the NCRLC wrote that the glorification of the subsistence farm as portrayed in Ligutti and Rawe's *Rural Roads to Security* or Willis Nutting's *Reclamation of Independence* "lacks realism" under modern conditions. He wrote that the small farmer "must have a sizable cash income from the sale of farm products or from employment off the farm if he wishes to have electricity, decent

---

80. James L. Vizzard, "Washington Farm Front," *Rural Life Conference* 7 (February 1958): 15; Edward W. O'Rourke, "Family Farm Policy Review," *Catholic Rural Life* 11 (September 1962): 2; NCRLC, *Toward a Greater Rural America* (Des Moines, Iowa: NCRLC, 1968), in "General Publications, 1963–69," NCRLC 5-5, 5, 10n3.

81. O'Rourke, "Family Farm Policy Review;" O'Rourke, "Washington Farm Front," *Catholic Rural Life* 18 (May 1969): 10; "Land Reform Conference Attended," ibid. 22 (July 1973): 1; whole issue on "The Embattled Farmer," ibid. 34 (September 1984); Bill Smith, "The Equation and Farm Exiles," ibid. 35 (April 1985): 15; NCRLC, *Toward a Greater Rural America*, 5, 10n3; United States Catholic Conference, *Where Shall the People Live?* (Des Moines, Iowa: NCRLC, 1972), in "Gen. Pubs., 1970–76," NCRLC 5-5.

housing and simple conveniences, buy insurance, keep the family car running and remove the tonsils of [the] children. These products and services do not grow in gardens." In the 1960s and 1970s, Vizzard and O'Rourke similarly withdrew their support from the "marginal and subsistence farms" that have "been by passed by progress" and "never will provide the members of the family with a satisfactory way of life." Instead, they favored "diversified family farms," which sold enough produce to support the family.[82]

Despite this concession, at the end of the century the NCRLC continued to insist on the economic viability as well as the moral value of the family farm system of agriculture as a whole. It cited a Missouri study that claimed that small farms "fooled the experts" in the amount of unreported income they were able to generate. And it paid tribute to end-of-century Christian rural communities as a "remnant"—like "the people of Israel in the Old Testament—a remnant people kept faithful in difficult times to a vision and way of life."[83]

Indeed, secular studies confirmed the NCRLC's contention that there was still a place for the family farm in the agricultural system of the United States at the turn of the millennium. A study of Iowa and the Central Valley of California concluded that well-managed, diversified farms survived the crisis of the 1980s as they had earlier farm crises. Another author reported that after decades of decline, the number of farms actually increased slightly in the 1990s. The average farmer's net income of seventy thousand dollars in 1999 was substantially more than the average American household income—a dramatic reversal of a long period of sub-par incomes for farmers. The key factor was a rise in off-farm income—seen by some as a sign of farmers' desperation, by others as a way to enjoy the amenities of rural living despite the meager economic returns of farming alone.[84]

Although the number of farmers declined tremendously during the existence of the NCRLC, they did not lose as much influence as they might

---

82. Martin E. Schirber, "Catholic Rural Life," in Word, ed., *The American Apostolate*, 136–40; Edward W. O'Rourke, "Needed: Diversified Family Farms," *Catholic Rural Life* 20 (January 1971): 2; James L. Vizzard, "Statement on H.R. 6400, 'The Agricultural Act of 1961,' presented to the House Agriculture Committee, May 5, 1961," in "Vizzard, James L., Statements before House and Senate Committees, 1961–64, '66," NCRLC 2-17, 2–3.

83. "Small Farms—Fool the Experts," *Common Ground* 8 (Fall 1989): 5; Robert Gronski, "Rural Roads to Security," *Catholic Rural Life* 43 (Fall 2000): 19.

84. Friedberger, *Farm Families and Change*, especially 246–51; Hurt, *Problems of Plenty*, 150–51, 156, 172–73; Bruce Gardner, review of *Problems of Plenty: The American Farmer in the Twentieth Century*, by R. Douglas Hurt, *American Historical Review* 108 (June 2003): 856.

For the Family Farm in the Age of Agribusiness 309

have because of the United States' transition to an interest-group society sensitive to the protection of the rights of minorities. If simple majority rule had been in effect, farmers' decline from the majority to less than 2 percent of the population would have been catastrophic. As it was, special legislation protected them as a class into the twenty-first century. The NCRLC's perspective on this was not quite the same as American society's as a whole. To most Americans, farmers were an economic minority; the Conference, while recognizing the economic aspect of farming, also defined it as a way of life. This fit in with the valuing of diversity in American society that developed in the late twentieth century. Thus, the NCRLC still had some prospects of success in its dedication to the protection of the right of this minority group to exist in twenty-first-century diversified American society.

As the family farm became a less important part of the total American agricultural system, the NCRLC modified its mission from an emphasis on the family farm to promoting a "just food system." Beginning in 1984 under Cusack's leadership, the Conference planned to issue a series of statements dealing with some of the major problems in the American and worldwide food system from a Christian ethical perspective. The statements would deal with new, consumer-oriented issues such as the increase in nonnutritious processed food and the impact of international food embargoes as well as traditional NCRLC concerns like the family farm, chemical use on farms, and world hunger. In conjunction with the Theology of Land conferences, these statements would "help NCRLC make a very significant contribution to the building of an intellectual construct for the kind of alternative future we wish for rural America," Cusack hoped. Although none of the statements were completed before Cusack was let go in 1986, the just food system concept was adopted as a unifying theme by the Conference and used in testimony before Congress on the 1985 farm bill and before the bishops' committee drafting the pastoral on the American economy.[85]

The emphasis on a just food system not only altered NCRLC policy objectives but seemed to offer a new basis for the Conference's membership and identity. As the president of the Diocesan Directors Association

85. Greg Cusack, "Food!" *Catholic Rural Life* 34 (February 1984): 3, 10; Cusack, "Food Policy: Change Is Coming," ibid. (July 1984): 3; "Report from the Executive Director, Greg Cusack," *Common Ground* 3 (March 1985): 1; "Conference News," ibid. 4 (May 1986): 1; "Report of Greg Cusack, NCRLC Executive Director, to the Board of Directors of the National Catholic Rural Life Conference, Kansas City, Kansas, November 6–8, 1985," in "NCRLC: Board Meeting," in "Fitzgerald Files: Board Related, ca. 1986–89," Box 1, NCRLC, 1–2.

wrote: "The word 'food' ... draws everyone into the issue: farmers, city folk, rural, urban, suburban, food producers, packagers, handlers, transporters, local, national and international people. This linking word will help broaden the base of support for the N.C.R.L.C. in the future." With the new emphasis on a just food system the NCRLC hoped for a larger and more diverse constituency—both urban and rural, both consumer and producer—in the future. Thus, while the decline of the family farm might have seemed to portend the gradual extinction of the Conference, it saw it as an opportunity for redefinition and renewal.[86]

The concept of a just food system eventually took hold in the NCRLC after Cusack left the Conference. The new broader thinking seemed to be gaining acceptance in the nation as a whole, as evidenced by Congress's 1990 omnibus food and farm bill being officially dubbed the "1990 Food Security Act." At the turn of the millennium, Andrews modified Cusack's vision slightly when he tried to show how intimately each individual was affected by the NCRLC's concerns by using the key word "eating" rather than "food." "We all need to eat," he said. "We believe eating should be a moral act ... Eating involves a wide web of relationships. It brings in environmental, social, cultural and economic factors." At a rally he held up a small American flag and a fork and called for an "eaters' revolt." What one ate affected the social structure: "Think before you eat," Andrews said. "Evaluate how your food was raised before you ask a blessing over it. Does it come from a family farm ... or does it come from factories? ... The fork you use is a lever by which you shape your world." The Conference stated that "the right to food is guaranteed by international law. The right to food includes a right to safe, healthy, nutritional food and a system which will protect health." It applied seven basic Catholic principles—human dignity, the integrity of creation, the common good, the universal destination of goods, subsidiarity, option for the poor, and solidarity—to a wide range of issues related to eating, such as working conditions of farm workers and food workers, providing nutritious food for the hungry, purchasing food from local family farms, and the growing global obesity epidemic.[87]

One concern was for healthy food. The NCRLC cited the United States

---

86. "Report by Fr. Larry Nawrocki—President of Diocesan Directors Association," *Common Ground* 2 (June 1984): 1.

87. Sandra A. La Blanc, "Join a Vision for Rural America," *Earth Matters* 38 (Winter 1989): 3; "Rally for Rural America 2000," *Rural Landscapes* 7 (April 2000): 5; David Andrews, "Dear Friends ..." ibid. (June 2000): 1; Curt Arens, "Voting with Your Fork," *Cedar County News* (Hartington, Nebraska), October 8, 2003, copy in unprocessed mailings, NCRLC, 1–2; "Eating Is a Moral Act" and "Values for Eaters" (both 2003), cards in ibid.

Figure 23. Brother David Andrews with flag and fork proclaiming "eating as a moral act," 2000.

surgeon general's prediction that the children of the current generation may be the first to be less healthy and have a shorter life span than their parents. In light of the obesity crisis among American children, Andrews called for Catholic schools to set a good example by serving healthier food. Expressing shock that 24 percent of pediatric hospitals in the country had a fast food outlet, he urged healthier food in Catholic hospitals as well. The Conference opposed the practice of irradiating meat, which killed bacteria and increased shelf life but depleted vitamins and nutrients, posed cancer risks, and tended to aid agribusinesses that shipped meat over long distances at the expense of locally produced food.[88]

In 2000, the NCRLC started an "Eating as a Moral Act" campaign. It published eight "ethics of eating" cards, which highlighted the moral connections between producers and consumers of food. Thousands of the cards were distributed, and the campaign was picked up by dioceses and the media and featured in five Catholic and agricultural magazines. The University of New Hampshire held a weeklong symposium on "Eating as

---

88. "Call for a Just Farm Bill," *Catholic Rural Life* (newsletter) 14 (February 2007): 3; "Irradiation, School Lunches, Catholic Thought," ibid. 12 (December 2004): 7; David Andrews, "Food in Catholic Schools," *Catholic Rural Life* 48 (Spring 2006): 11–14; Andrews, "Food in Catholic Hospitals," ibid., 16–17.

a Moral Act," with Andrews as keynote speaker, and he conducted workshops on the topic. Although the NCRLC was still loyal to the family farm, its new focus on food and eating was a more inclusive way to look at agriculture and its impact that drew in urban and rural people alike.[89]

89. "Resources," *Rural Landscapes* 7 (June 2000): 4; "Report of the Executive Director, November, 2001," in unprocessed mailings, NCRLC, 1–2; "Report of the Executive Director," June 11, 2004, in ibid., 1.

Chapter 13 Fighting Poverty

Besides trying to save the family farm, the NCRLC made efforts to aid the least fortunate of those living on the land. The United States had pockets of rural poverty in areas such as Appalachia as well as poor farmers who did not own land—the migrant farm workers. Rural minorities such as African Americans and Native Americans were also suffering. The Conference began to focus on these problems in the 1960s under Father O'Rourke. It continued its concern for alleviating poverty through the end of the century, following the American bishops who in the economic pastoral *Economic Justice for All* (1986) spoke of a "fundamental option for the poor."[1]

When O'Rourke became executive director in 1960, the United States and the Catholic Church were entering into a decade of change and reform. As he reminisced more than two decades later, "Those were very interesting days. See, you have a combination of ideas, which are powerful, and circumstances. This was the decade of hope: We had Pope John XXIII talking on hope and the Church, we had John Kennedy talking about hope and the civil society, and we believed it—we totally believed it right away." O'Rourke led the NCRLC into full participation in the reform movements of the 1960s. Early in his administration, he proposed that the Conference promote "a vigorous program for Christian social action in rural affairs."[2]

Joining the War on Poverty

The aspect of O'Rourke's program most in tune with the spirit of the 1960s was its participation in rural antipoverty programs. When President Lyndon Johnson declared an "unconditional war on poverty" in his 1964 State of the Union address, the NCRLC pledged its "vigorous cooperation." It

---

1. National Conference of Catholic Bishops, *Economic Justice for All*, section 87.
2. Transcript of tape, "Bishop Edward W. O'Rourke, Interviewed by David S. Bovee," 9; "Report of the Executive Director—Edward W. O'Rourke," in "Executive Committee Meeting, Milwaukee, Wis., Jan. 16–17, 1961," NCRLC 8-18, Exhibit C.

supported such War on Poverty programs as rural areas development, vocational training for rural youth, stabilizing migrant farm workers, fostering cooperatives, and promoting the civil rights of minority groups. It gave especially strong support to basic War on Poverty programs like food stamps and welfare. In urging support for food stamps, Monsignor Ligutti wrote in 1959: "Hunger and dietary inadequacies among so many U.S. citizens are a scandal on a nation blessed with abundance such as ours." And in the 1970s, the Conference supported welfare programs that guaranteed a minimum income and improved health conditions.[3]

But NCRLC officials—especially O'Rourke—were skeptical about poverty programs imposed from above. For example, in 1965, O'Rourke emphasized the need for individual solutions to the unique local circumstances of poverty. And five years later, he criticized current welfare programs for encouraging dependence on government and the breakup of families. He urged support for President Nixon's welfare reform package, which would provide incentives for poor families to work rather than receive welfare and encourage families to stay together.[4]

The Conference always favored antipoverty programs in which aid was provided by private groups or individuals suited to the local circumstances of the poor or in which the poor were helped to help themselves. It supported the formation of the VISTA program of volunteers to serve the poor in the United States—Father Vizzard thought it would provide needed aid on Indian reservations and to migrant workers as well as in city slums. It urged its members to join antipoverty programs in their own rural communities.[5]

The NCRLC cooperated with various other groups in promoting antipoverty programs. In 1964, it joined about five hundred other organizations in the Crusade Against Poverty, which proposed to work with the government in the War on Poverty and civil rights arenas. At the same time Vizzard worked within the National Association of Manufacturers (NAM) to prepare the STEP program—Solutions to Employment Problems. Vizzard was chairman of NAM's Clerical Advisory Council, which,

3. Executive Committee Resolution, "War on Poverty" (1964), in "Poverty—The War Against," NCRLC 8A-1; "Telegram to Congress," *Catholic Rural Life* 8 (September 1959): 23; Stephen E. Bossi, "Washington Farm Front," ibid. 20 (May 1971): 10.
4. Edward W. O'Rourke, "Causes and Cures of Poverty," *Catholic Rural Life* 14 (April 1965): 2; O'Rourke, "Washington Farm Front," ibid. 19 (May 1970): 3.
5. James L. Vizzard, "Washington Farm Front," *Catholic Rural Life* 11 (January 1963): 8; Edward W. O'Rourke, "A Rainbow Division for the War on Poverty," ibid. 13 (October 1964): 2; NCRLC, *Enlist Now in the War on Poverty* (Des Moines, Iowa: NCRLC, 1967), in "General Publications, 1963–69," NCRLC 5-5.

Fighting Poverty

with the NAM Clergy–Industry Relations Committee, prepared this plan for research, information sharing, and encouragement of local action programs aimed at creating new employment opportunities.[6]

The Conference continued to support the War on Poverty and its component parts even when the program fell on hard times beginning in the late 1960s. In 1967, budget cuts for War on Poverty programs, in large part due to increased defense spending because of the Vietnam War, caused O'Rourke to warn that the War on Poverty was "lagging." He castigated Americans for putting the war in Vietnam above the War on Poverty. He believed they were "penalizing the poor twice," because the poor constituted the bulk of the armed forces and also suffered cuts in programs intended to help them. In order to win the War on Poverty, the Conference called for increased appropriations for poverty programs, especially to rural areas, which it charged were "receiving less than their full share of funds."[7]

In the 1970s and 1980s, the NCRLC opposed cuts in the food stamp program proposed by the Ford and Reagan administrations. It called the Hunger Prevention Act of 1988 "a landmark piece of legislation" for providing increases in food commodities for food banks and increased eligibility of the poor in the United States for food assistance. In the 1990s, the Conference opposed proposed federal block grants to states that might result in overall decreases in food stamp and other food programs. It charged that the 1996 welfare reform legislation that devolved welfare to the states would result in significant cuts in food stamps that would "push more children and families into poverty." The rural poor would get left out of the generally urban-centered welfare programs, it feared. It urged President Clinton to add $13 billion in food stamps that was cut in the welfare reform, but was only successful in getting $818 million in food stamps for legal immigrants restored. The Conference still considered food stamps and other supporting programs "a critical source of food" after the turn of the millennium and thought they should be strengthened in the 2007 farm bill.[8]

---

6. "Crusade against Poverty Launched," *Catholic Rural Life* 13 (September 1964): 1; "NAM Launches Plan to Improve Employment," ibid. (December 1964): 1.

7. Edward W. O'Rourke, "S.O.S. for the War on Poverty," *Catholic Rural Life* 16 (February 1967): 2; John George Weber, "Chaff and Wheat," ibid. 17 (March 1968): 8; "Supporting the War on Poverty," in "Poverty—The War Against," NCRLC 8A-1.

8. Stephen E. Bossi, "Washington Farm Front," *Catholic Rural Life* 24 (March 1975): 8; Leonard Kayser, "Let Them Eat Bombs," ibid. 31 (June, 1981): 39; Walt Grazer, "Do People Have a Basic Right to Eat?" ibid. 32 (June 1982): 30–31; "Seeking Balance in U.S. Farm and Food Policy," ibid. 49 (Spring 2007): 11; "More Legislative Items of Interest," *Common Ground* 7 (January 1989): 6; "A Bird's Eye View," *Rural Landscapes* 3 (December 1995): 2; Dan Misleh, "A Bird's Eye View," ibid. 4 (October 1996): 2; "A Bird's Eye View," ibid. (February 1997): 2; Dan Misleh, "A Bird's Eye View," ibid. 5 (June 1998): 2.

O'Rourke tied the NCRLC's increasing emphasis on the rural poor as opposed to middle-class family farmers in the 1960s to the sources of the Conference's funding. Writing in 1971, O'Rourke said that in the 1950s,

> NCRLC was supported chiefly by membership fees from middle class rural Americans and by the generous contributions of Bishops of the rural dioceses of the Midwest. We felt, therefore, that it was right for us to utilize these limited resources primarily . . . to strengthen the family farm, to improve farm income and to promote the economic growth of rural communities.
>
> During recent years [starting in 1967] NCRLC has become a part of the U.S. Catholic Conference and is deriving approximately two-thirds of its financial support from the National Conference of Catholic Bishops. Membership fees represent a relatively small part of our total income. Meanwhile, the needs of the poor in rural America have become more acute and more apparent. Consequently, we are devoting a very substantial part of our time now to help the rural poor help themselves.[9]

Besides supporting the government's main antipoverty programs, the NCRLC directed its efforts in this area in three specific directions: migrant farm workers, self-help projects, and minorities.

Migrant Farm Workers

The concern for migrant workers began even before World War II. During the Depression of the 1930s, the Reverend Charles "Pop" Philipps, San Francisco archdiocesan director of rural life, promoted credit unions, cooperatives, and family farms among Hispanic migrant workers. During the war, the number of "our Spanish-speaking brothers and other migrant workers" on America's farms greatly increased to help with the country's need to produce more food. Public Law 78—the *bracero* program—permitted the importation of Mexican farm workers on a seasonal basis. This program, which proved advantageous to the large growers, was continued after the war. During the war, migrant labor was part of the responsibilities of the Farm Security Administration, whose program the NCRLC commended. When responsibility for migrant workers was transferred from the FSA to the Farm Bureau–controlled Extension Service in 1943, the Conference protested and several years later reported that conditions of migrants had worsened.[10]

---

9. Edward W. O'Rourke, "Rural Middle Class and Rural Poor," *Catholic Rural Life* 20 (June 1971): 2.

10. NCRLC, *Manifesto*, 52–54; Jeffrey M. Burns, "The Mexican Catholic Community in California," in *Mexican Americans and the Catholic Church, 1900–1965*, ed. Jay P. Dolan and Gilberto M.

Fighting Poverty 317

Figure 24. The NCRLC was concerned about the living and working conditions of migrant farm workers.

The overall circumstances of migrant laborers were indeed deplorable. The migrants were worked overly hard, for excessive hours, and for substandard wages. After the demise of the FSA, migrant labor camps were either nonexistent or inadequately supervised, which led to their being crowded, dilapidated, and unsanitary. Transportation of migrants was often unsafe. Migrants were often discriminated against by social service agencies. The bracero system made things even worse. The competition of Mexican workers depressed wages for domestic workers. The program disrupted the family life of the Mexicans who participated. In the 1960s and 1970s, the migrants suffered additional evils: if they participated in unionization, they were harassed or even killed. And increasing applications of pesticides were often sprayed on the fields regardless of their serious effects on the health of the migrants.[11]

Hinojosa (Notre Dame, Ind.: University of Notre Dame Press, 1994), 214; Baldwin, *Poverty and Politics*, 380; "Resolutions of the National Catholic Rural Life Conference Adopted at the Twentieth Annual Convention, October 3–6, 1942, Peoria, Illinois," *Land and Home* 5 (December 1942): 23; "Notes and Comments," ibid. 10 (September 1947): 74–75; Gerald F. Cox, *The Radical Peasant* (Victoria, B.C.: Trafford Publishing, 2006).

11. "What We've Been up to," *Rural Life Conference* 7 (September 1958): 6; Cyrus Karraker, "Discrimination against Migrant Children," *Catholic Rural Life* 9 (May 1960): 12–13, 24; Kim Larsen, "Chavez Describes Workers' Fear of 'Walking Death,'" ibid. 18 (December 1969): 1; John J. McRaith, "Is That Fair?" ibid. 22 (September 1973): 3.

In trying to help the conditions of migrant workers, the Conference cooperated with other concerned Catholic agencies such as the Social Action Department of the NCWC and the Bishops' Committees for the Spanish Speaking and for Catholic Migrants. In 1963, Vizzard was elected the first chairman of the National Council on Agricultural Life and Labor, a group of forty-one unions, church groups, and public interest organizations, which, among other things, promoted the interests of migrant workers.[12]

In the 1940s and 1950s, the NCRLC lobbied for improving conditions in the migrant labor camps set up by the federal government and under the bracero program. The Conference cited calls for protecting migrants under the Fair Labor Standards Act. In the 1950s, the NCRLC backed Labor Secretary James P. Mitchell in his efforts to provide federal protection for migrants in the areas of minimum wage, maximum hours, housing, and transportation against the opposition of Agriculture Secretary Ezra T. Benson. Also in the 1950s, the Conference pressed for Social Security benefits for migrant laborers, which was achieved to some extent.[13]

During the 1960s, Vizzard—a Californian by birth, and intensely dedicated to the farm workers there—performed his zealous work. Never one to shun controversy, he made a number of dramatic gestures on behalf of the migrants. For example, in 1963, just days before John F. Kennedy's assassination, he charged that the president, in rescinding the ninety-five-cent-per-hour minimum wage for Florida's migrant workers, was "snatching pennies from the hands of the poor" and making the "shoddiest kind of political deal" with a senator representing Florida fruit-growing associations. In the less flamboyant but more lasting area of legislation, Vizzard's persistent lobbying contributed to the passage of the Migrant Health Act (1962), the Labor-Contractor Crew Leader Registration Act (1964), the Omnibus Housing Act for farm workers (1965), and the inclusion of farm workers under minimum wage (1966).[14]

In the 1970s, the NCRLC pressed in Washington for protection for mi-

---

12. "Aid for Migrant Workers . . . ," *Rural Life Conference* 6 (February 1957): 15; James L. Vizzard, "Washington Farm Front," *Catholic Rural Life* 12 (March 1967): 8.

13. W. J. Gibbons' statement and other materials in "Farm Labor Controversy, 1947," NCRLC 1-2; "Migratory Workers ('Rural Life in the Press')," *Land and Home* 9 (March 1946): 28; W. J. Gibbons, "The Farm on the Potomac," *Christian Farmer* 4 (October 1950): 2; William M. Blair, "Catholics Score Farm Federation," *New York Times*, January 31, 1960, clipping attached to Harold F. Hall to James L. Vizzard, February 3, 1960, in "Lay, Ca–Ce, 1960," NCRLC 13-15.

14. Julie Sly, "James Vizzard, S. J.: Champion of the Migrant Laborer," unpublished article, 1983, in possession of Julie Sly, 1, 3.

Fighting Poverty 319

grants in the areas of unemployment compensation, additional minimum-wage legislation, educational guarantees (including Spanish-speaking education), pesticide regulation, and housing.[15]

In keeping with the NCRLC's longstanding family farm ideology, the Conference was not satisfied with improving the migrants' conditions under the current system but hoped that eventually they might be able to own farms of their own. In 1942, Monsignor Ligutti wrote: "Should we have a union label on every apple or frozen strawberry? Perhaps so, but what is better and more practical—we should have more families raising their own vegetables." In its major statement on migrant workers, *A Program for Migratory Farm Labor* (1961), the Conference declared that the "industrialized" type of farm work then performed by migrant laborers could and should "be conducted on a family basis as is almost all other farming in the United States." As late as 1978, NCRLC executive director Gerald Foley urged: "Instead of trying to ease [farm workers'] condition in the farm labor system, we should consider helping them get land and become self-sufficient." Foley paid visits to some small vegetable farms in California where former migrant workers were trying to accomplish just that. However, the Conference was practically alone in urging a family farm solution to the migrant worker problem, and it was beyond its resources to give more than moral support for such a movement.[16]

The NCRLC opposed the bracero program of importing Mexican farm workers both because of the effects on the Mexicans themselves and because their cheap labor depressed the conditions of domestic American workers. It called for an end to the program as early as 1947. Lobbying in Congress to achieve that goal was one of Vizzard's greatest struggles in the late 1950s and early 1960s. After many partial victories early in the 1960s, Congress finally voted to end the program in 1964. The Conference still had to fight off attempts to revive the program in later years. It was concerned about the effects of the termination on the Mexicans, for whom the program had been an outlet for their unemployment problem. To compensate for this, the NCRLC urged that the United States increase

---

15. Stephen E. Bossi, "Washington Farm Front," *Catholic Rural Life* 19 (October 1970): 3; ibid. 20 (August 1971): 16; ibid. 21 (December 1972): 8; ibid. 22 (February 1973): 16.

16. L. G. L[igutti], review of *Ill Fares the Land*, by Carey McWilliams, *Land and Home* 5 (June 1942): 29; National Catholic Rural Life Conference; the Social Action Department, National Catholic Welfare Conference; the Bishops' Committee for the Spanish Speaking; the Bishops' Committee for Migrant Workers, *A Program for Migratory Farm Labor* (Des Moines, Iowa: NCRLC, 1961), in "General Publications, 1960–62," NCRLC 5-4, 21; Gerald Foley, "Suggests Strategy Change for Helping Farmworkers," *Catholic Rural Life* 27 (October 1978): 12–13.

its foreign aid to Mexico so that that country could raise the standard of living of its people.[17]

The Conference's proclivity toward self-help led it to support the farm workers' right to organize into unions as early as 1945, and it continued to urge unionization right through the 1950s. Finally, in the late 1950s, the National Agricultural Workers Union of the AFL-CIO began an organizing drive among California farm workers. Vizzard offered the support of the NCRLC and its diocesan directors to the union's president. Two priests of the Archdiocese of San Francisco, diocesan rural life director Donald McDonnell and Thomas McCullough, helped the organizing effort in the San Diego diocese, but the growers in the area protested to the bishop of San Diego, Charles F. Buddy, a bracero supporter, who ordered them to stay out of the diocese unless they limited their aid to spiritual ministry. In a correspondence with Buddy, O'Rourke denied he had sent the two priests into his diocese but defended their work on behalf of the farm workers. In the 1960s, the NCRLC, hitherto weak in California, acquired diocesan directors in all eight dioceses in the state, and all actively concerned themselves with the migrant problem. O'Rourke himself met with the California growers in Stockton to persuade them to agree to negotiate with the farm workers. He later reminisced:

Bishop Donohue, then Bishop of Stockton, and I met with a group of growers who were the growers of almost all of the asparagus crop, and I was invited as the outsider to make a few preliminary remarks. So I began to talk about this: Have harmony and understanding, and dialogue, and justice between yourself and your workers. And one big fellow stood up and said: "Look, Father. We have the power to do it the way we're doing it, and if you guys ever have the power to do it otherwise, let us know." And he walked out. So that was the atmosphere that created a need for what Cesar Chavez did.[18]

In the 1950s, McDonnell, Philipps' successor as San Francisco archdiocesan director of rural life, helped organize a Spanish Mission Band (a

---

17. "Resolutions Adopted at Silver Jubilee Convention, National Catholic Rural Life Conference, La Fayette, Louisiana," in "Silver Jubilee Convention, Lafayette, La., Nov. 23–26, 1947," NCRLC 8-5; numerous articles in NCRLC publications in 1950s and 1960s; Stephen E. Bossi, "Washington Farm Front," *Catholic Rural Life* 22 (October 1973): 8; copies of Vizzard's testimony in "Vizzard, James L., Statements before House and Senate Committees, 1961–64, '66," NCRLC 2-17.

18. "Summary of Resolutions Adopted at the 23rd Annual Convention, Des Moines, Iowa, October 23–25, 1945," *Land and Home* 8 (December 1945): 93; minutes in "Executive Committee Meeting, June 21–22, 1966, Des Moines, Iowa," NCRLC 8-21; James L. Vizzard—H. L. Mitchell (President, National Agricultural Workers Union) correspondence in "Correspondence, Me–Mi, 1959," NCRLC 13-11; O'Rourke—Buddy correspondence in "Correspondence, A–B, 1961," NCRLC 13-18; transcript, "Bishop Edward W. O'Rourke, Interviewed by David S. Bovee," 5–6.

Fighting Poverty 321

group of missionaries) to improve migrant farm workers' conditions and met Chavez. McDonnell developed a teacher-to-student relationship with the young Hispanic leader, taught him Catholic social doctrine, and urged him to organize the farm workers. As a result, Chavez joined the Community Service Organization and became its national director. O'Rourke had his first contact with Chavez in 1960. Two years later, Chavez founded the National Farm Workers Association, the predecessor of the United Farm Workers (UFW). Beyond its support for the principle of collective bargaining by farm workers, the NCRLC supported Chavez's union because of its Catholic character. Chavez was a devout Catholic who frequently had Masses said at UFW meetings and on picket lines. He insisted that the UFW employ only nonviolent tactics, even when its opponents used violence against it. At critical points in his union's struggle, Chavez fasted for weeks in the manner of a saint, and he broke the fasts by taking Holy Communion. His Easter march to Sacramento in 1966 was like a religious pilgrimage. In 1974, he even received papal sanction for his work when he was personally blessed in a meeting with Paul VI.[19]

After several years of organizing, Chavez and his union felt strong enough to begin their first large-scale strike in September 1965, when they struck the grape growers in the area of Delano, California. Vizzard immediately wrote privately to Chavez, expressing his support and saying: "So convinced am I that your cause is right that if I could I'd be on the picket line myself . . . Particularly praiseworthy is the acceptance and practice of the principles of non-violence in pursuing your legitimate ends." However, O'Rourke and the NCRLC, as well as the California bishops, were tardy in giving official support to the strike, so the impatient Vizzard, against O'Rourke's wishes, took it upon himself to join in a tour of the strike area in December 1965, along with ten other religious leaders. The Jesuit's action drew rebukes from both O'Rourke and Bishop Aloysius Willinger of Monterey-Fresno, who called it "an act of unadulterated disobedience, insubordination and breach of office." The NCRLC Executive Committee, when it next met on January 26, 1966, was more indulgent. In a statement that was not published, it expressed its fullest "respect and appreciation" for Vizzard and declared that his Delano visit manifested "no errors of fact or doctrine," though it did call it "ill advised" and asked Vizzard to "exercise greater prudence and restraint in the future." More importantly, the committee finally stated its support for the UFW strike, calling its requests

---

19. O'Rourke, *Self-help Works*, 42; Burns, "Mexican Catholic Community," 214–17, 230; Jacques E. Levy, *Cesar Chavez: Autobiography of La Causa* (New York: W. W. Norton, 1975).

for higher wages and collective bargaining "in keeping with their basic rights." The committee condemned the growers' refusal to negotiate with the union, their harassment of the strikers, and their bringing in of strikebreakers. It pledged that the Conference would "go out to these workers" and try to bring the strikers and their employers together at the bargaining table, help see to their education, training, housing, and medical needs, assist the formation of community action committees, and work for social legislation to benefit the farm workers.[20]

The Delano strike went on for five years—the longest strike in American history. Throughout it, the NCRLC continued to support the farm workers. The Conference held frequent meetings with the strikers and repeatedly urged the growers to negotiate with them. In 1965 and 1966, the eight California diocesan directors met six times on the strike crisis, sometimes with O'Rourke, Vizzard, bishops, and representatives of the growers, and drafted a comprehensive statement on "Agriculture in California," which supported the farm workers' collective bargaining rights. In order to secure these bargaining rights, the NCRLC urged that Congress pass legislation to include the farm workers under the National Labor Relations Act. In 1968, when the UFW initiated a boycott of nonunion grapes, O'Rourke judged that it was "justified by reason of the long record of refusal to bargain in good faith on the part of the grape growers." The Conference rejoiced when finally in July 1970 the majority of the California grape growers signed contracts with the UFW.[21]

After the O'Rourke era and the dramatic grape strike, the NCRLC had less direct contact with the UFW, but it continued to work for migrant workers' rights. It persisted in urging that farm workers be included under the National Labor Relations Act and supported the formation in 1975 of the California Agriculture Labor Relations Board. In 1973 and 1974 farm workers received the support of the American Catholic bishops, who is-

20. Sly, "James Vizzard," 4; notes by Sly on James L. Vizzard Papers, Stanford University, Stanford, California, in possession of Sly; "NCRLC Defends Right of Striking Grape Workers," *Catholic Rural Life* 15 (March 1966): 4; NCRLC Executive Committee resolution, "Rights of Agricultural Workers," January 26, 1966, NCRLC 8A-2; documents in folder "Delano, Calif. Strike and Willinger—Vizzard—O'Rourke Debate, 1965–66," NCRLC 2-5.

21. Edward W. O'Rourke, "The Grape Boycott," *Catholic Rural Life* 17 (June 1968): 2; O'Rourke, "Union Labels on Grapes," ibid. 19 (September 1970): 2; resolution on "Agricultural Workers and the National Labor Relations Act," from "National Catholic Rural Life Conference—Executive Committee, Policy Resolutions Adopted—Covington, Ky.—January 19, 1967," in "Poverty—The War Against," NCRLC 8A-1, 4; John T. Dwyer, "Report on the Activities of the Catholic Rural Life Directors of California," in "Minutes, Diocesan Directors Mtg., Manhattan, Kansas, Oct. 14, 1966," NCRLC 8-21; Levy, *Chavez*, 182–94, 201–325.

Fighting Poverty 323

sued statements backing their right to organize and boycotts of grapes and lettuce.[22]

Not all Catholics supported the UFW boycotts. Sister Thomas More Bertels, a history professor who had worked with the Conference on farm organization in the 1960s, claimed that the UFW exaggerated the plight of the farm workers in its propaganda. Seventy-five percent of the people surveyed in heavily Catholic Stearns County, Minnesota, also opposed the boycotts. A scholar who studied the county wrote: "Few of the rural people understood that the church was boycotting some of the largest corporate farms in the United States. The local farmers tended to identify with the 'farmer' rather than the 'farm worker.'"[23]

In 1981, the NCRLC supported a strike in Ohio tomato fields of the Farm Labor Organizing Committee (FLOC) against the Campbell's and Libby's companies for just wages, adequate housing, safe working conditions, elimination of child labor, and protection from dangerous pesticides. It also supported a boycott of Campbell's and Libby's products. The Conference action again generated controversy, in part because the board of directors had not consulted with the diocesan directors (especially the Toledo diocesan director) before voting to support the strike. Bertels opposed the boycott because she believed that "they don't work," and she urged reconciliation between farmers and farm workers. A rural pastor from Wisconsin, in opposing the boycott, objected to the northern Ohio family farmers who employed the farm workers being referred to as "growers" who exhibited "greed" and "independence."[24]

In the later 1980s, the NCRLC influenced the American bishops to take a strong stand in support of farm workers in their pastoral *Economic Justice for All*. The bishops said that farm workers had the right to organize in unions and that they should get minimum wages, benefits, and unemployment compensation like other workers, as well as improvement in

---

22. O'Rourke, *Self-help Works*, 46; "Farm Labor Resolution," *Catholic Rural Life* 24 (January 1975): 3; whole issue on farm workers, ibid. 31 (March 1981).

23. Bertels, *In Pursuit of Agri-Power*, 252–310; Paul Folsom, "Rural Ministry—A Response to Change. What Has Happened to the Church on Main Street, U.S.A.?" (Doctorate of Ministry Pastoral Project, Aquinas Institute of Theology, Dubuque, Iowa, May 1976), 2:217.

24. "Minutes, NCRLC Board of Directors, November 5–6, 1981, Techny, Illinois," in "NCRLC: Board Mtg. (Minutes)," in "Fitzgerald Files," Box 2, NCRLC, 7; Rev. Larry Nowrocki to Gregory Cusack, December 10, 1981, and Cusack to Nowrocki, December 15, 1981, in "Board Communications," Cusack Subject File, Box 19, NCRLC; folder "FLOC Boycott," La Blanc Subject File, Box 5, NCRLC; folder "FLOC," in "NCRLC Acq'd 10/17/89," Box 3; "Growers 'Battle' Church, Laborers on Farm Issues," *National Catholic Reporter*, August 1, 1980, clipping in "S and G Articles in Press," in ibid., Box 8; "Readers Respond to CRL Issues" (letter by Father Charles D. Loehr, Theresa, Wisconsin), *Catholic Rural Life* 38 (June 1988): 27; Bertels, *In Pursuit of Agri-Power*, 311–17.

housing, health care, and education. At about the same time, the rural life directors called on American dioceses to refuse to serve California table grapes at church gatherings and functions in support of the UFW campaign against pesticides. The Conference opposed the Reagan administration's plan to set up a new "guest worker" program that would allow up to 350,000 foreign migrant agricultural workers into the United States because it feared poor conditions for the workers.[25]

The NCRLC also opposed a guest worker program proposed in Congress during the Clinton administration. At about the same time, Bishop Skylstad joined in a letter to Congress that helped save a legal-services program for migrant workers that was in danger of being cut. In 1998, the Conference called for people to fast the day after Thanksgiving and donate the amount they would have spent on food to the farm worker organization of their choice. A little later, it protested the poor working conditions, low wages and benefits, and Immigration and Naturalization Service raids to expel undocumented workers at fruit and meatpacking plants. In 2004, the NCRLC supported the Agricultural Job Opportunity, Benefits and Security Act, which would have legalized the status of more than 7 million undocumented farm workers by the end of the decade. The next year, the NCRLC worked to help farm workers in the tomato fields of Florida. The Conference visited with the Imokolee Farmworkers, an organization of Florida farm workers, to try to help them gain just conditions, and it participated in a conference on the Florida tomato field problem.[26]

The NCRLC was involved in a few programs to provide direct aid to migrants. In the 1940s and 1950s, the Conference participated in several spiritual, educational, and recreational programs for farm workers, which were mainly provided by certain dioceses. Beginning in the 1950s, the Conference printed some of its rural literature, including prayers and liturgical rites, in Spanish for use among the Hispanic migrant workers of the Southwest. From 1983 to 1985, the NCRLC funded a southwestern representative who worked with farm workers in Texas, New Mexico, and Arizona, where a union was still in the process of organizing and legislation was still needed

25. National Conference of Catholic Bishops, *Economic Justice for All*, sections 247 and 249; "Rural Life Directors Business Meeting," *Common Ground* 5 (March 1987): 3; Rural Coalition to Peter W. Rodino Jr., November 18, 1985, in "NCRLC Sign-ons," in Cusack Subject File, Box 18, NCRLC.
26. David Andrews, "The Green Ribbon Campaign," *Catholic Rural Life* 41 (Spring 1999): 3; Lourdes Gouveia, "From Aliens to Neighbors," ibid. 43 (Fall 2000): 27–34; Dan Misleh, "Faithful Citizenship," ibid., 44, 42–43; Dan Misleh to NCRLC Board Members, June 14, 1996, in "Current Mailings, 1994–," NCRLC; "Join the Fast for America's Farmworkers, November 27, 1998" (fax alert from NCRLC), in ibid.; "NCRLC Emphases Highlighted at Social Ministry Gathering," *Rural Landscapes* 11 (May 2004): 1; David Andrews, "Dear Friends of NCRLC," *NCRLC Annual Report, 2005*, 3.

Fighting Poverty

to assure migrants better wages, housing, medical care, and education. In 2004, Conference scientist Tim Kautza led a project to educate farm workers in the Yakima, Washington, area about pesticide safety.[27]

The most important NCRLC program for migrants was funded by an eighty thousand dollar grant from the Charles E. Merrill Trust of Ithaca, New York, from 1960 to 1966. This wide-ranging program aimed at integrating migrants into communities in the Midwest, California, and Texas. O'Rourke directly oversaw the programs established in six different centers in the Midwest and advised the other programs run by the Bishops' Committee for the Spanish-Speaking in San Antonio and the Bishops' Committee for Migrant Workers in Stockton. The various programs included retraining in skilled industrial crafts; employment services; religious services; legal counseling; leadership training; help in forming cooperatives, credit unions, and neighborhood councils; educational programs; and studies of the migrants. By 1963, it was estimated that the Merrill Trust project had retrained several hundred migrants and found jobs for over three thousand.[28]

Self-Help Projects

Self-help projects were a major part of the NCRLC's domestic and international policies, especially during the 1960s when under O'Rourke it emphasized antipoverty programs. The Conference believed that self-help projects would be a particularly important means for raising the poor to economic self-sufficiency. In 1965, it declared: "As we enter the second year of the War on Poverty, it becomes increasingly evident that cooperatives and credit unions are a most important tool for uplifting the economic, educational and cultural welfare of poorer citizens, particularly those of minority racial and ethnic groups." It therefore urged government loan assistance for low-income cooperatives, government funds for salaries of cooperative managers, and the dissemination of information on cooperatives to low-income

27. "Migrant Apostolate" ("Gleanings"), *Land and Home* 10 (December 1947): 111; untitled note, *Feet in the Furrow* 2 (September 1953): 4; "In the Dioceses," ibid. 4 (August 1955): 9; "NCRLC Assists New Girl Scout Program," *Rural Life Conference—Feet in the Furrow* 4 (November 1955): 8; Teresa Nira, "Report from the Southwest," *Common Ground* 3 (October 1984): 2; two folders on "Southwest Project," Cusack Subject File, Box 19, NCRLC; "Protegiendo Nuestro Futuro Underway," *Rural Landscapes* 11 (June 2004): 1.

28. "Vocational Training for Ex-Migrants," *Catholic Rural Life* 11 (September 1962): 6; "Serving California's Migrant Workers," ibid. (December 1962): 3; Edward W. O'Rourke, "Minority Rights—Everybody's Responsibility," ibid. 12 (July 1963): 2; "Merrill Trust Helps Farm Workers," ibid. (December 1963): 1; "Private War on Poverty among Mexican Migrants," ibid. 14 (March 1965): 14–15; folder "Merrill Trust—Disbursement," NCRLC 2-11; reports on Merrill Trust program in meetings file, NCRLC 8-18 through 8-22.

people. For a time, it supported bills in Congress in 1968–69 to create government-aided community development corporations for the poor, but it eventually turned against them because it believed they involved too much government involvement in private industry.[29]

O'Rourke devoted a great amount of effort to promoting self-help projects among the poor in the 1960s and early 1970s. He traveled extensively to promote the self-help idea and personally helped to form several hundred cooperatives. Notably, he assisted Albert McKnight, an African American priest who established the Southern Consumers' Cooperative of Lafayette, Louisiana, in 1962. McKnight went on to organize the Federation of Southern Cooperatives, which by the 1980s included 130 largely African American low-income cooperatives in fourteen states. In 1970–71, the NCRLC participated in self-help institutes held in Texas. When the Campaign for Human Development—a nationwide collection in Catholic parishes for aid to self-help projects—was established in 1970, O'Rourke was chosen to evaluate all of its rural development projects.[30]

O'Rourke and the NCRLC were strong supporters of the U.S. Department of Agriculture's Rural Areas Development (RAD) program, which was begun in 1961. Under the RAD program, people in rural communities formed committees that worked out overall economic development plans, the projects of which were given aid by the Department of Agriculture. The NCRLC praised the RAD program for giving "unity and direction to many divergent efforts to improve rural areas" and for providing a "proper division of responsibility between local leaders and governmental agencies." Instead of just allowing rural people to migrate to cities, the program provided a positive approach to rural problems. The NCRLC liked the program's insistence on local action and its dedication to helping those most in need—"low income farm families and the underemployed villagers."[31]

In 1962, O'Rourke was appointed to the National Advisory Committee

29. "Resolutions of Policy—National Catholic Rural Life Conference—Adopted at the Board of Directors Meeting—Santa Clara, Calif.—August 19, 1965," in "Alien Farm Workers," NCRLC 8A-1, 4–6; Edward W. O'Rourke, "Washington Farm Front," *Catholic Rural Life* 17 (November 1968): 9; O'Rourke, "Washington Farm Front," ibid. 18 (January 1969): 8.

30. "New Role Predicted for Coops in the South," ibid. 14 (September 1965): 1; Edward W. O'Rourke, "Cooperatives Can Reduce Poverty," ibid. 19 (July 1970): 2; "Self Help Institutes Planned at San Juan, Texas," ibid. (November 1970): 3; "Rio Grande Farmers and Workers Plan Discussions," ibid. 20 (January 1971): 1; "Co-op Federation Crippled by FBI Harassment," ibid. 29 (February 1981): 28–29; Weber and O'Rourke, "Coalitions and Change," 19; "Spotlight on Organizations," *Common Ground* 7 (November 1988): 8; O'Rourke, *Self-help Works*, chaps. 2 and 8.

31. "The National Catholic Rural Life Conference," *Catholic Rural Life* 22 (November 1973): 6; Weber and O'Rourke, "Coalitions and Change," 19; NCRLC, *Developing Rural Resources* (Des Moines, Iowa: NCRLC, 1962), in "General Publications, 1960–62," NCRLC 5-4.

Fighting Poverty 327

on Rural Areas Development and to that committee's standing committee for "Area Planning and Rural Renewal." As a member of those committees, he asserted his belief that the main cause of poverty was the "failure to utilize fully the human and natural resources of the area." He believed that the most promising activities RAD could promote to make use of those resources were bringing industry into rural areas and developing outdoor recreational facilities. As a member of the RAD National Advisory Committee, O'Rourke helped write a report on strengthening the family farm, which proposed most of the measures consistently supported over the years by the NCRLC.[32]

O'Rourke and other NCRLC officials and individual pastors went out into the field to help the people in rural communities form and utilize RAD committees. A two thousand dollar grant from the Sears-Roebuck Foundation was spent for travel for O'Rourke to give lectures to RAD committees and to publish leaflets on RAD. O'Rourke estimated that the NCRLC helped form nearly one thousand RAD committees during the 1960s.[33]

O'Rourke and the NCRLC played a similar role with the Office of Economic Opportunity (OEO). The Economic Opportunity Act, passed with the help of Vizzard's lobbying in 1964, provided aid to local development projects proposed by community action committees, which were similar to RAD committees. The OEO program concentrated on the War on Poverty as a whole, whereas RAD had been limited to rural development. From 1965 to 1968, O'Rourke worked as a paid consultant for OEO in setting up rural community action committees. Often using the personnel and planning from previously established RAD committees, he helped form nearly one hundred community action committees. Other NCRLC members aided additional OEO projects. The NCRLC lobbied extensively but unsuccessfully against the Nixon administration's effort to terminate the OEO in the early 1970s.[34]

---

32. "Rural Areas Development Moves Ahead," *Catholic Rural Life* 11 (February 1962): 1; "Church Leaders Assist in Rural Areas Development," ibid. (April 1962): 1; Edward W. O'Rourke, "Want in the Midst of Plenty," ibid. (August 1962): 2; "New Laws and USDA Policy Urged to Save Family Farm," ibid. 12 (February 1963): 1; O'Rourke, "Rainbow Division for War on Poverty," 2.

33. "Planning Rural Areas Development in Nebraska," *Catholic Rural Life* 11 (June 1962): 1; "Clergy Prominent in Linn Co., Mo. RAD Association," ibid. 12 (June 1963): 1; Edward W. O'Rourke, "A Decade with NCRLC," ibid. 19 (August 1970): 2; O'Rourke, *Self-help Works,* chap. 5; Edward W. O'Rourke, "Report on RAD and the Sears Foundation Grant," in "Executive Committee Mtg., Omaha, Neb., Jan. 21–22, 1963," Exhibit H-a, NCRLC 8-19.

34. "Monsignor O'Rourke Named Consultant by Anti-Poverty Office," *Catholic Rural Life* 14 (June 1965): 1; "Fr. Keleher Vice-President Of Development Corporation," ibid.; Stephen E. Bossi,

In his role as OEO consultant, O'Rourke confronted a revealing conflict between his self-help and his civil rights principles. While fighting the War on Poverty, the OEO was also charged with obeying the Civil Rights Act provisions for representation by the poor and minority groups on community action committees. O'Rourke feared that excessive interference by OEO authorities in Washington in the internal activities of local community action committees would harm the self-help character of the committees, "demoralize" them, and ultimately render them ineffective. In this conflict of principles, O'Rourke ultimately came down on the side of self-help: he urged that the Washington OEO office "not over-ride the decisions of the local CAP committee on any matter except those which are clearly contained in the Economic Opportunity or Civil Rights Acts." He believed that the OEO should concentrate on the War on Poverty, not "be used as a means to establish integration," though "as in any other federal program, discrimination is out of place and should not be tolerated."[35]

Self-help projects were a part of the NCRLC's program for alleviating poverty in rural Appalachia. In 1966, the NCRLC joined the Commission on Religion in Appalachia (CORA), a group of representatives of Catholic and Protestant churches that dealt with religious, moral, and spiritual issues in Appalachia by consultation, research, study, education, and the coordination of projects. Two years later, Catholic bishops and priests formed their own Catholic Committee of Appalachia, with which the NCRLC cooperated closely. Finally, after two years of meetings, dialogue sessions, and drafting, the Catholic Committee of Appalachia (CCA) in 1975 issued the eloquent statement "This Land Is Home to Me," signed by twenty-six bishops, on the problems of the land in Appalachia.[36]

Self-help projects were needed in Appalachia, the Conference believed, because of the complete ineffectiveness of government programs. In 1969, O'Rourke blasted the use of the $1.5 billion appropriated for the federal Appalachian Development Program since the Kennedy administration, saying the money was mostly spent building "magnificent highways used

---

"Washington Farm Front," ibid. 20 (April 1971): 8; Weber and O'Rourke, "Coalitions and Change," 19; Sly, "James Vizzard," 1.

35. Edward W. O'Rourke to Theodore Barry (Director, Community Action Programs, Office of Economic Opportunity), April 16, 1965, in "Lay and Clergy—Pink, A–G, 1965," NCRLC 13-22; O'Rourke to Richard Hausler (Director, Rural Task Force, Office of Economic Opportunity), March 27, 1965, in "Lay and Clergy—Pink, H–M, 1965," NCRLC 13-22.

36. "NCRLC to Participate in Appalachian Commission," *Catholic Rural Life* 15 (August 1966): 1; "Appalachian Bishops and Priests Form Committee," ibid. 17 (December 1968): 1; "'This Land Is Home to Me,'" ibid. 24 (May 1975): 1; "Appalachian Pastoral Is Still a Popular Document," ibid. 29 (February 1980): 19–20.

Fighting Poverty

chiefly by outsiders" or funneled to "cities and towns which are already relatively prosperous and in which live many of the industrialists, bankers and politicians who have perennially exploited the poor of the region." He urged that "anti-poverty programs should serve the poor."[37]

As chairman of CORA's Self-Help Task Force, O'Rourke personally visited projects, gave advice, held cooperative training seminars, and arranged for grants and loans. In 1970, the NCRLC collaborated with CORA in raising $1 million to support self-help projects among low-income people in Appalachia. In 1974, CORA helped form the Human Economic Appalachian Development (HEAD) Corporation, which provided training, technical, and direct assistance to community development groups in the mountain regions of Kentucky, Virginia, and Tennessee. One of the HEAD Corporation's projects was Operation MATCH—Marketing Appalachia through the Church. The NCRLC cooperated with several Protestant denominations in this effort to advertise the wares of about twenty-five low-income Appalachian handicraft cooperatives. It coordinated the efforts of Appalachian community land trusts to control the ill effects energy companies had on the lives of rural families in that mountain region—effects such as strip mining, water pollution by acidic mine drainage, and the displacement of families. The Conference continued to cooperate with CORA and the CCA in the 1980s and 1990s.[38]

Aid to Rural Minorities

The third concentration of NCRLC antipoverty activities—after aid to migrant workers and self-help projects—was its effort to improve the conditions of rural minorities, especially African Americans and American Indians. When the NCRLC was founded in the 1920s, about two hundred thousand African American Catholics lived in the United States. Over half lived in Louisiana and Maryland, the descendants of slaves held by Catholic masters in those two most Catholic of the Southern states. Most of the African American Catholics in those states were still rural, since the great

---

37. Edward W. O'Rourke, "Opening the Door of the Inn," *Catholic Rural Life* 18 (December 1969): 2.
38. "Coop Institute Held in W. Va.," *Catholic Rural Life* 18 (April 1969): 1; "Achievements of NCRLC During 1970," ibid. 20 (March 1971): 3; "NCRLC Joins Operation Match," ibid. 23 (October 1974): 1; "Self-help in Appalachia," ibid. 24 (January 1975): 6; Sr. Mary Margaret Pignone, "Land Reform Pushed at Meeting in Appalachia," ibid. 25 (April 1976): 21–22; O'Rourke, *Self-help Works*, chap. 3; "1969 Report on NCRLC Achievements," in "General Publications, 1963–69," NCRLC 5-5; file "CCA," in "NCRLC Acq'd 10/17/89," Box 3; "NCRLC Places and Faces," *Rural Landscapes* 6 (June 1999): 2.

black migration to the cities and the North, which began during World War I, was barely under way.[39]

Concern on the part of American Catholics for rural African Americans, where it existed, had been largely from a missionary viewpoint. That such a large body of people should be suffered to remain Protestant or unchurched was not in keeping with the ideal of the "universal Church," some Catholics thought. Not to evangelize among African Americans would be a sign of "spiritual lethargy." Hence, a number of male and female religious orders, such as the Josephites, the Divine Word Fathers, the Oblate Sisters of Providence, the Sisters of the Blessed Sacrament, and the Sisters of the Holy Family, were formed to work among African Americans in the United States. The orders, however, were not well supported by the hierarchy and made few converts.[40]

Despite that failure, the growing social action movement in the Church started to be concerned with the welfare of minorities from the social and economic point of view. During the 1920s, the first Catholic organizations designed to fight prejudice and discrimination against African Americans—the Committee against the Extension of Race Prejudice in the Church, the Federated Colored Catholics of the United States, the Clergy Conference on Negro Welfare, and the Catholic Layman's Union—became active. At the same time, Catholic "social action" groups began to work for the alleviation of African Americans' economic problems, including agricultural ones.[41]

The interest displayed by the NCRLC in African Americans took a more "social action" than missionary approach. During the 1920s, the Conference expressed concern for the social and economic conditions of African Americans and endorsed the work of the Cardinal Gibbons Institute. The institute, which opened in 1924 and was located at Ridge, Maryland, in the heart of that state's black Catholic region, was the NCRLC's primary link to rural African Americans. John La Farge, S.J., editor of the Jesuit magazine *America*, a founder of the Clergy Conference on Negro Welfare

---

39. William A. Osborne, *The Segregated Covenant: Race Relations and American Catholics* (New York: Herder & Herder, 1967), 20, 32; John T. Gillard, S.S.J., *The Catholic Church and the American Negro* (Baltimore: St. Joseph Society Press, 1929 [New York: Johnson Reprint Corporation, 1968]), 46–57, 94–133; Gillard, *Colored Catholics in the United States* (Baltimore: Josephite Press, 1941), 14–59, 152–79.

40. Lawrence Landrigan, "Catholic Activity on Negro Missions," *America*, March 11, 1922, 492–93; Osborne, *Segregated Covenant*, 22–32; Gillard, *Catholic Church*, 79–93; Gillard, *Colored Catholics*, 127–37.

41. Osborne, *Segregated Covenant*, 35–37; "Welfare of Negro Workers Aim of Baltimore Conference," *NCWC Bulletin* 11 (October 1929): 33–34.

Figure 25. Black and white children at a religious vacation school at Glymount, Maryland, 1929.

and NCRLC board member, was one of those who urged that the institute be founded and served as its chaplain. Under the leadership of Victor Daniel, the privately funded institute carried on a "social action"–type of agricultural education for the area's African American Catholics. Daniel stated that the institute's objective was "the development of a more productive, more complete, healthier and happier farm life, for every member of the colored rural population." To achieve this objective, the institute offered courses on agricultural techniques and farm management and extension activities such as farmer conferences, health campaigns, and dental clinics. For a time, its practical, self-help approach had a revitalizing influence on Maryland's African American Catholic farmers. However, financial support from Catholic donors withered, the institute acquired a large debt, and it was forced to close in 1933.[42]

In the 1920s, the NCRLC, along with the Church as a whole, failed to vigorously press for full equality for African Americans. According to W. E. B. Du Bois, the Catholic Church was the most prejudiced of the churches, and Catholic church buildings, schools, and hospitals were usually segregated. This was true in rural as well as urban areas. For example,

42. NCRLC minutes binder (1923–32), NCRLC 8-1, 33, 37, 45, 54; section "Cardinal Gibbons Institute," OH46; "Negro Institute Site Purchased," *NCWC News Sheet*, week of September 18, 1922; "Field Day to Aid Gibbons' Institute," *NCWC News Service*, September 22, 1922; "K. of C. to Aid Card. Gibbons Negro Institute," *NCWC News Sheet*, week of September 24, 1923; "Gibbons Institute Celebrates George Washington's Birthday," *Catholic Rural Life* 5 (April–May 1927): 5; V. H. Daniel, "Agricultural Education of Negroes in Maryland," ibid. 6 (January 1928): 3, 14–15; Daniel, "A Busy Day at Cardinal Gibbons Institute," ibid. (April 1928): 2; David W. Southern, *John La Farge and the Limits of Catholic Interracialism, 1911–1963* (Baton Rouge: Louisiana State University Press, 1996), 34–44, 152–73.

the whites in one rural Maryland Catholic community, "who were determined not to allow the negro to get ahead of them," spent three times as much for their white elementary school as they did for their black one—for an approximately equal number of students—and provided a white high school but none for African Americans. Discrimination was probably also practiced in NCRLC projects such as the religious vacation schools, as indicated by a photograph of a rural Maryland class that shows the seven white children lined up next to the white pastor, while the more numerous black children are standing around in no particular order or crowded into a truck.[43]

In the 1930s and 1940s, the NCRLC favored black participation in its favorite proposal, the back-to-the-land movement. It believed that, as with whites, "the real freedom and independence for the Colored people is the ownership of family farms." La Farge wrote in 1944 that he favored rural life for blacks for the same reasons that he favored it for whites. Rural African Americans had the same problem as rural whites in maintaining family farms in the midst of an industrial economy; but in addition, they suffered racial prejudice. Thus they were discriminated against doubly both as African Americans and as small farmers. La Farge believed that "the greatest challenge that exists as to the home-mission work of the American Church is the establishment by heroic Catholic missionaries of rural parishes where there will be a complete union and cooperation in all matters that pertain to the common good between families of all races regardless of color or national origin."[44]

O'Rourke had a deep concern for racial justice well before his appointment as NCRLC director, as evidenced by a strongly worded statement against segregation he wrote in the 1950s. As director, he lobbied for the Civil Rights Act of 1964, and after its passage secured appointment by President Johnson to the National Citizens Committee for Community Relations, a body intended to create a climate for equal treatment and equal opportunity for all Americans under the new legislation.[45]

---

43. Gustave B. Aldrich, "The Church and the Negro," *Commonweal*, June 27, 1926, 326–27; Osborne, *Segregated Covenant*, 29, 33–35; Patrick E. Conroy, "The Church and the Rural School," *Catholic Educational Association Bulletin* 23 (November 1926): 353–55; Edwin V. O'Hara, "Sixty Hours of Religious Education," *NCWC Bulletin* 11 (July 1929): 7.

44. "General Resolutions of the N.C.R.L.C.," *Catholic Rural Life Bulletin* 4 (November 20, 1941): 96; John La Farge, "Rural Racial Problems," *Land and Home* 7 (September 1944): 66–67.

45. Edward W. O'Rourke, "Racial Segregation and the Christian Conscience," and letters in "Civil Rights, Statements, Articles, Correspondence, ca. 1964," NCRLC 2-2; "Msgr. O'Rourke Serves Civil Rights Committee," *Catholic Rural Life* 13 (September 1964): 1.

Fighting Poverty

O'Rourke and the NCRLC believed that the best way they could help rural African Americans attain equal rights was by ensuring their participation in antipoverty and self-help programs. In 1965, O'Rourke stated that "new civil rights legislation and recent economic development in the South demands a shift from protests to cooperation among the races, especially in anti-poverty programs." The NCRLC pledged to promote interracial justice by helping minorities participate in the liturgy, the War on Poverty, the RAD program, cooperatives and credit unions, education, and programs for stabilizing migrant workers. As already mentioned, O'Rourke did especially notable work in giving assistance to black self-help projects in the South.[46]

In the 1980s and 1990s, the NCRLC, along with the hierarchy and the USCC, drew attention to the low level of farmland ownership by minorities. Despite the strong agricultural traditions of African Americans and Hispanics, few of them owned farms any longer. Farm ownership by African Americans fell from 14 percent of American farms in the 1920s to 1 percent in the 1990s. A writer in *Catholic Rural Life* charged that much of the land was taken illegally by "unscrupulous land speculators" and for water transportation or recreational development such as at Hilton Head, South Carolina. In 1987, the Conference helped sponsor a conference on African Americans' land loss that called for a moratorium on all foreclosures of farms owned by African Americans, access to more farm credit, research and extension programs targeted to small minority farms, more representation by racial minorities in the Department of Agriculture and other agencies, and educational and legal assistance for minority farmers to help them gain clear title to their land. One of these proposals was realized the next year when a reform of the Farmers Home Administration targeted credit to minorities.[47]

In the 1990s, the Conference charged that the Department of Agriculture discriminated against racial minority employees and that it tried to acquire minority farmers' land and transfer it to wealthy owners. It was pleased when the department acted with "uncharacteristic speed" on ninety-two recommendations to remedy the discrimination, such as federalizing

---

46. "Catholic Leaders of the South Discuss Changing Racial Issues," *Catholic Rural Life* 14 (September 1965): 3; Executive Committee statement "Interracial Justice" (1964), NCRLC 8A-1.

47. National Conference of Catholic Bishops, *Economic Justice for All,* section 229; Jerry Pennick, "Black Land Loss: An American Crisis," *Catholic Rural Life* 37 (July 1987): 4–7; John Bookser-Feister, "Putting Heads Together to Battle Crisis," ibid., 8–9; Walt Grazer, "Legislative Action," *Common Ground* 6 (January 1988): 6; Dan Misleh, "A Bird's Eye View," *Rural Landscapes* 6 (January 1999): 2.

all county positions. The department also agreed to settle discrimination claims by five thousand African American farmers.[48]

Native Americans received little attention from the NCRLC before 1960. When the Conference did notice them, Indians were viewed as people in need of missionary activity. Its only work among them had been a few vacation schools.[49] But in the 1960s, the NCRLC under O'Rourke viewed Native Americans as another rural minority group in need of assistance. O'Rourke claimed that American Indians should, "in reparation for past injustices," get "first consideration in the war on poverty," and urged the OEO to aid Indian antipoverty projects. He helped with the Southwest Indian Foundation, which was established by Franciscans among Navajos at Gallup, New Mexico, to assist in manufacturing prefabricated houses, rehabilitating Indian "hogans," building schools, and constructing bridges. He also aided the Chippewas in North Dakota initiate a Head Start program, build a retirement center, and train for new jobs, and became involved in the formation of Menominee Enterprises, Inc., a self-help organization on the Menominee reservation in Wisconsin.[50]

The Conference favored bills giving improved health care and housing, increased capital, and extension of federal responsibility for Native Americans. It supported a 1977 USCC statement for social justice for Indians, especially urging the "speedy and equitable resolution of treaty and statute questions," and "protection of Indian land and resource rights." It was sympathetic to Indian land claims against the United States government in Alaska, in the Black Hills, and on the Navajo reservation—especially lands considered sacred to Indian religions and used for religious ceremonies. On the difficult question of whether Indians should continue to live on reservations, the Conference urged that they be given the freedom to choose. Finally, the NCRLC began to see that Native Americans had long held many of the same attitudes toward the land that it had been trying to spread among Americans. In *Strangers and Guests,* the Midwest bishops noted that "people of the heartland might learn from American Indian

---

48. Ibid.; Misleh, "A Bird's Eye View," ibid. 4 (April 1997): 2, 4; David G. Andrews, "Economic Injustice Often Accompanies Racial Injustice," *Catholic Rural Life* 38 (Spring 1997): 39.

49. A Corpus Christi Sister, "With the Indian," *Catholic Rural Life* 7 (November 1928): 6-7; Arnold J. Barker, "Sunday in Temagami," ibid. (February 1929): 8; "Sixty New Religious Vacation Schools in the South and Southwest," ibid. (March 1929): 4.

50. Edward W. O'Rourke, "The First Americans," *Catholic Rural Life* 14 (June 1965): 2; O'Rourke, *Self-help Works,* chap. 7; Executive Committee resolution, "Opportunity for American Indians," in "Exec. Committee Meeting, Oklahoma City, Okla., Jan. 25–26, 1966," NCRLC 8-21.

Fighting Poverty 335

ways of living in harmony with the land, and thus of fulfilling their own responsibility to be its stewards."[51]

NCRLC president William Wood was reported to have said in 1991 that the Conference's greatest challenge would be to "extend active participation and leadership to the poor, to farm workers as well as farmers, to new immigrants, and to people of color. 'It's not just a matter of what we may give to such people, but what we have to receive from them and learn from them.'" The NCRLC always maintained its original midwestern white ethnic orientation and therefore did not give leadership to disadvantaged groups. However, Wood's statement did express the NCRLC's turn toward social justice and its great concern for minorities by the end of the century.[52]

51. Kathy White, "Washington Farm Front," *Catholic Rural Life* 23 (August 1974): 16; *Strangers and Guests*, 27; Executive Committee resolution, "Opportunity for American Indians"; whole issue on "The Earth Is Our Mother: A Native American Perspective," *Earth Matters* 37 (Fall 1988).

52. "Newly Elected President Redefines Our Mission for the '90s," *Common Ground* 10 (March 1991): 1.

Chapter 14 Stewardship of the Planet

In the late twentieth century, the meaning of rural life in the United States changed significantly. As the number of family farms decreased greatly, the rural area was seen less as connected to the family farming lifestyle than as an environment that affected urban and rural people alike. The NCRLC adapted its priorities to address the new issues arising out of this altered view of late twentieth-century rural life.

Addressing Problems of Modern Rural Life
As early as the 1930s, the NCRLC perceived that many of the psychosocial problems of modern life were connected to the transition from a predominantly rural to a mainly urban lifestyle. In commenting on these problems, the Conference at first—from the 1930s through the 1950s—usually viewed them as favorable rural traits being replaced by unhealthy urban ways of living. In 1938, Catholic ruralist Emerson Hynes contrasted the conviction of urban society that work was "evil" and that people must seek happiness in their leisure activities with the traditional rural attitude that people found happiness and fulfillment through their work. Another NCRLC member put it this way: the rural attitude was that "work was a part of life," whereas in the modern "leisure state," "the reason one worked was only in order not to work." Another writer commented on the transition from rural forms of recreation based on community participation to the urban modes of mass entertainment that caused people to suffer from "spectatoritis." Extensive travel and other stressful kinds of leisure activities led many modern people to being not recreated but "wreck-reated." A nun lamented the modern tendency of schools to perform educational functions that could be done better within the family. In 1956, an article by NCRLC president Bishop Peter W. Bartholome of St. Cloud listed education among other modern institutions that weakened the family:

Stewardship of the Planet 337

government, which legalized divorce; industry, which employed mothers and children; social welfare, which made families dependent upon relief; and even the Church, which, "for very laudable purposes," established organizations that took the place of family functions. This urban vs. rural attitude even persisted to some extent into the O'Rourke era: O'Rourke claimed that the lack of a stable, natural life on the land caused much of the restlessness of "The Under-25 Generation," and the Conference lamented that mechanization had taken modern culture away from nature and proposed to bring it back to nature through rural arts.[1]

In more recent years, the NCRLC seemed to accept the changes of modern society more on their own terms and recommended coping with them rather than trying to totally reverse them. Instead of proposing a back-to-the-land movement, the Conference said that the recent increase in the rural nonfarm population might be encouraged as providing a better living environment for urban workers. By the 1990s, the rural population as a whole was increasing, due to an influx of commuters, retirees, and people in the recreation and service industries. Executive Director David Andrews said hopefully, "People prefer living in small towns. That's why they're moving to rural areas." The rural population just was not "predominantly tied to agriculture" anymore.[2]

Instead of solely championing rural producers, the NCRLC supported establishing the U.S. Consumer Product Safety Commission. It accepted the feminist movement, consistently supporting a greater role for women in the leadership of rural communities. It urged dealing with the new problems of drug abuse, stress among farmers, and the rural elderly. Rural America had a number of health concerns: affordability of health insurance; the trend toward managed-care plans harming access to health care; closings of rural hospitals; a high percentage of elderly; toxic chemical use, waste dumps, and water pollution; and work accidents (farming was

---

1. Hynes, "Dignity and Joy of Work," 16–18, 24–26; Joseph Hufner, "Youth and Recreation," ibid. 4 (February 20, 1941): 20–21; Sister Anne, O.S.B., "What's Wrong with Education Today?" ibid. 4 (May 20, 1941): 31–34; "Chores and Delinquency" ("Notes and Comments"), *Land and Home* 7 (March 1944): 14; "I Am a Country Pastor . . . " ibid. 8 (March 1945): 12; Peter W. Bartholome, "First the Family," insert in *Rural Life Conference* 5 (December 1956); "Art Culture and the Rural Community—A Policy Statement of the National Catholic Rural Life Conference—First Draft," in "Art, Culture and the Rural Community, 1963," NCRLC 8A-1; "The Under-25 Generation," in "Youth and the Farm," NCRLC 8A-2.

2. "Rural Living for Non-Farm Families," *Rural Life Conference—Feet in the Furrow* 4 (January 1956): 3; Ray Mueller, "Demographic Trends in Rural Population Reveal Huge Changes in Recent Decades," *Wisconsin State Farmer*, June 7, 1996, copy in "Current Mailings, 1994–," NCRLC.

the nation's most dangerous job). The Conference urged remedies such as parish nurses, intermediate medical facilities between clinics and hospitals for rural areas, and rotating medical residents to rural areas.[3]

In light of changes in rural life, the NCRLC recommended that the Church adopt new pastoral methods. Because of declining numbers of priests, parishes might have to be consolidated or priests be assigned multi-parish "circuit-riding" duties. Communicating by e-mail or the Internet might be needed in rural dioceses in the future. Rural areas would also have to plan for new immigrants, such as Hispanics.[4]

This adaptation was threatened by a continued urban bias on the part of the American Catholic Church, many in the Conference believed. In the 1980s, David Andrews complained that the University of Notre Dame Study of Catholic Parish Life followed the ideas of scholars such as Andrew Greeley and Jay Dolan to find more evidence of "community" in urban parishes than rural ones based on "activist" definitions that favored large urban parishes. Another Conference member who worked with the Notre Dame study said that without her urging it might not have included rural parishes at all. Executive Director Joseph Fitzgerald said that although the study found that about one-third of Catholics lived in small towns or rural areas, this huge field was overlooked by the Church. Raising concerns remarkably similar to those revealed by Edwin O'Hara in his original study of the rural Church in 1920, Fitzgerald charged that "young priests are assigned to rural parishes for 'training,'" and "stressed-out, burned-out, or 'problem' priests are assigned to a pastorate that 'anyone can manage,'" leading to an excessive turnover rate of rural pastors. A diocesan director of rural life said that professional social workers tended to lack understanding of the problems of farm families, and she met with them to make them more familiar with rural circumstances.[5]

---

3. Edward W. O'Rourke, "Washington Farm Front," *Catholic Rural Life* 20 (March 1971): 8; special issues on rural elderly, ibid. 26 (February 1977) and 33 (November 1983); special issue on rural women, ibid. 31 (October–November 1981); Ted L. Napier, "Rural Drugs," ibid. 32 (September 1982): 10–11; Arlene Shako, "Rural Life: Romance vs. Reality," ibid. 34 (September 1984): 18–20; Ken Meter, "Church Faces Treatment of Chemical Dependency," ibid. 37 (February 1988): 25–26; special issue on rural health, *Earth Matters* 38 (Fall 1989); "Conference News," *Common Ground* 3 (January 1985): 2–3.

4. Gary Burkart, "Pastoral Planning: Needs for the Contemporary Rural Church Are Unique," *Catholic Rural Life* 38 (Fall 1996): 8–13; Burkart, "When Does Rural Make a Difference?" ibid. 39 (Fall 1997): 5–9.

5. David Andrews, "Parish Life Studies Reflect Urban Bias," *Catholic Rural Life* 37 (September 1987): 18–23; Susan R. Raftery to Sandra La Blanc, November 3, 1987, in "Correspondence 1987," La Blanc Subject File, Box 3, NCRLC; Joseph K. Fitzgerald, "New Study Reveals Huge Rural Catholic Church," *Common Ground* 7 (November 1988): 1; "Rural Happenings across the United States," ibid., 3.

In the late 1990s, Andrews warned that rural communities were threatened by the worldwide trend toward globalization and by the enduring conflict between the Catholic principles of the common good and subsidiarity. For example, an Iowa Supreme Court decision overruling a county ordinance prohibiting hog farms favored large corporations and a perceived "common good" over subsidiarity and local home rule. Andrews cited thinkers such as Edmund Burke, Thomas Jefferson, Alexis de Tocqueville, and Wendell Berry in calling for "a thousand webs of life"—"sustainable communities" based on local, face-to-face relationships rather than the impersonal globalization characteristic of the modern social and economic system.[6]

In this vein, the Conference backed the "community-supported agriculture" movement, in which consumers bought food directly from farmers in their area rather than from big supermarkets controlled by agribusiness. Besides supporting local family farmers, this would also reduce dependence on oil for transportation of the food. The NCRLC lauded Catholic institutions such as a Sisters of St. Joseph community in Pennsylvania and schools in the Archdiocese of Chicago that bought their food locally. It worked with the University of Portland and the Upper Midwest Sustainable Campus Association to promote "campus sustainability" among Catholic higher education institutions. By 2004, the movement achieved some success: Iowa had three times as many farmers markets as seven years earlier, and among NCRLC members, 61 percent sometimes bought locally grown foods when possible, 28 percent always.[7]

In 2001, the NCRLC started a significant effort to help rural communities make the transition to modernity by establishing the Luigi Ligutti Rural Community Support Program. Two codirectors guided the program: Cecilia Arnold led Passages, the mental health component, and Carol Richardson Smith was in charge of Directions, its socioeconomic transition dimension. All of the work took place in Iowa in the first few years, though it was hoped that the activity there would provide a model for its spread throughout rural America. As part of Passages, Arnold trained fifty

---

6. David Andrews, "A Spirituality for Subsidiarity and the Common Good: Ways to Live within Community," ibid. 37 (Spring 1996): 9–13; Andrews, "The Principle of Subsidiarity and Home Rule," ibid. 40 (Spring 1998): 19–23; Andrews, "Globalization and Local Communities," in [National Catholic Rural Life Conference], *Justice in the Global Food System: A Faith Perspective on Food Security* (Des Moines, Iowa: National Catholic Rural Life Conference, 1997), 11–19.

7. "Free Trade and Food Security—Compatible?" *Rural Landscapes* 11 (May 2004): 3; David Andrews, "Food Procurement and Other Items," *Catholic Rural Life* 48 (Spring 2006): 4; "Membership Survey 2004," *NCRLC Annual Report, 2005*, 7; "NCRLC Report, June 2006, Brother David Andrews, CSC, Executive Director," in unprocessed mailings, NCRLC, 3.

"rural life associates" who provided mental health education and referrals. She worked with Everywhere Iowa and the Uncommon Network, two groups that linked people in need with services, and she provided education on depression and human trafficking in rural areas. Smith directed the Growing Food and Profit program, which set up local networks linking farmers and consumers in four Iowa counties. She started a program for immigrant farmers to grow culturally appropriate food for themselves and their communities. Over nine hundred Iowa women in fifteen counties participated in her "Women, Land, and Legacy" meetings, in which they shared their views on rural life; findings were presented at a Rural Sociology Society conference. The NCRLC published "Work of Our Hands," a guide to help people "turn their hobbies, avocations, enterprises, and dreams into the beginnings of a small business."[8]

Environmental Stewardship

In addition to noticing the social consequences of modernization, the NCRLC pointed out its effects on the land—and eventually on the physical environment as a whole. From its early days, the Conference approached this issue through the concept of stewardship: Biblical passages such as "The Lord took Adam and placed him in the garden of Eden to cultivate and care for it" (Gen. 2:15) and "The earth is the Lord's and the fullness thereof" (Ps. 24:1) implied that human beings only acted as stewards of the land, which properly belonged to God, and owed Him the duty to care for it responsibly and preserve it to be fruitful for future generations. In 1983, one NCRLC official wrote that more recently,

the experience of strains on the earth's capacity to produce food, clean water, energy or needed minerals has led the Church to universalize its concept of stewardship. It now sees that responsibility for the care of the earth must be borne by all, not just those on the land, and that global systems of land conservation, water purification, and other resource preservation give better expression to the just claims of all human beings on the resources of the earth.[9]

---

8. "NCRLC Unveils Luigi Ligutti Rural Community Support Program," *Rural Landscapes* 8 (January 2001): 1; board of directors meeting minutes and reports of Arnold and Smith, 2000–2006, in unprocessed mailings, NCRLC; "Building a Neighborly Economy," *Catholic Rural Life* (newsletter) 13 (July 2005): 4; "Ligutti Rural Community Support Program," *National Catholic Rural Life Conference Annual Report, Fiscal Year 2005–2006*, 10–12.

9. J. A. Higgins, "The Stewardship of Property," *Central-Blatt and Social Justice* 31 (October 1938): 187–89, (November 1938): 231–33, (December 1938): 266–68, (January 1939): 304–6; Weber and O'Rourke, "Coalitions and Change," 19; Stephen Bossi, "Catholic Theology and the Work of the NCRLC," ibid., 7.

Stewardship of the Planet   341

The NCRLC was sympathetic to the theorists who starting in the 1960s pointed out that the world's resources were finite and would run out if not carefully conserved. The limited resources theory popularized by the Club of Rome's *The Limits to Growth* (1972) was taken up in papal encyclicals such as *Mater et Magistra, Populorum Progressio,* and *Octogesima Adveniens,* and in the Vatican II document *Gaudium et Spes*—all of which called for stewardship of the environment. For example, in *Octogesima Adveniens,* Pope Paul VI wrote: "Man is suddenly becoming aware that by an ill-considered exploitation of nature he risks destroying it and becoming in his turn the victim of this degradation." John Paul II spoke of the "serious obligation to care for all of creation" in the first papal message focused entirely on "the ecological crisis" in 1990.[10]

The NCRLC joined wholeheartedly in the environmental movement that began in the late 1960s. O'Rourke tied the nationwide Earth Day celebration in May 1970 to the Conference's traditional observation at the same time of year of Soil Stewardship Week. He spoke at several Earth Day functions, demonstrating the NCRLC's new concern for the whole environment.[11]

In its enthusiasm for and consistent support of the environmental movement, the NCRLC was generally ahead of most American Catholics. As historian Patrick Allitt noted, at first, many Catholics had definite objections concerning environmentalism: its tendency to favor restricting economic growth conflicted with attempts to alleviate poverty; its attempt to restrict population went against the Catholic prohibition of birth control; and its view of all species being equally valuable denied the Church's insistence on the unique dignity of humanity. Not until the 1990s did environmentalism become a mainstream belief of American Catholics. The Conference, on the other hand, from the beginning of its concern around 1970, had few of the reservations and hesitations of other American Catholics.[12]

In the 1980s, the Theology of Land project, with four conferences held under Cusack's direction, attempted to steer NCRLC policy toward an environmental awareness. In 1990, the NCRLC chose a president who was especially devoted to the environmental cause in William Wood, S.J.,

---

10. Gremillion, *Gospel of Peace and Justice,* 91–110, 495–96; "NCRLC Board of Directors Makes Statement on Creation," *Common Ground* 10 (May 1991): 1; Marjorie Keenan, *From Stockholm to Johannesburg: An Historical Overview of the Concern of the Holy See for the Environment, 1972–2002* (Vatican City: Pontifical Council for Justice and Peace, 2002), 39, 122.

11. Edward W. O'Rourke, "The Environmental Crisis," *Catholic Rural Life* 19 (May 1970): 2.

12. Patrick Allitt, "American Catholics and the Environment, 1960–1995," *Catholic Historical Review* 84 (April 1998): 263–81.

who said: "The programs of the National Catholic Rural Life Conference endeavor to bring the gospel to bear on the ecological crisis." In 1991, the NCRLC board of directors stated: "At the heart of the National Catholic Rural Life Conference's mission is its commitment to build support for '*the integrity of God's creation.*'" They claimed that "NCRLC puts more emphasis on protection of the environment than any other Catholic organization in the United States." Charging that "Catholic theology has neglected theological reflection on the environment," they hoped that the Theology of Land project would fill that void. "It will be the advancement, communication, and application of this new American ecological ethic that will form the core of the mission of the National Catholic Rural Life Conference." A draft of this statement was sent to the USCC and influenced its 1992 statement *Renewing the Earth: An Invitation to Reflection and Action on the Environment and Catholic Social Teaching.* The NCRLC published study guides for children, teens, and adults on this statement and called for it to be publicized from the pulpit at Mass, in schools, and in the media. At the same time, it doubted that these things would be done because it believed that most Catholics would not be receptive to ideas calling for sacrifice in the interest of the environment.[13]

The NCRLC, along with leaders of all of the other major American religious denominations, expressed its concern for the environment in the Joint Appeal in Religion and Science. It helped plan a meeting of the organization in New York City in 1991 and signed its statement "Mission to Washington" that outlined its priorities in resolving the environmental crisis.[14]

Starting in the 1980s, some NCRLC leaders were influenced by the deep ecology movement. This movement, which originated in Europe in the 1970s, sought a new worldview that would replace a separation of people from nature and human attempts to manipulate nature with a philosophy of the "person-in-nature," in which individuals would see themselves as part of nature. Catholics such as Thomas Berry, C.P., Matthew

13. "Newly Elected President Redefines Our Mission for the '90s," *Common Ground* 10 (March 1991): 1; "NCRLC Board of Directors Makes Statement on Creation"; "Minutes of Board Meeting, National Catholic Rural Life Conference, January 22–23, 1991, Airport Sheraton, Bloomington, Minnesota," in "NCRLC: Board Mtg. (Minutes)," in Fitzgerald Files, Box 2, 1, 2, 4; "Renewing the Earth Study Guides Available Soon," *Common Ground* 11 (January 1992): 4; the three study guides on *Renewing the Earth* and brochure advertising them in box "NCRLC Pubs ca. 1990–1994, Rec'd 4/21/94," NCRLC; John E. Carroll, "Assessing the Document: *Renewing the Earth,*" *Common Ground* 11 (February 1992): 1–2.

14. "Religious Leaders Pledge Resolve on Environment," *Common Ground* 10 (June/July 1991): 1–2; "Joint Appeal Approves 'Mission to Washington,'" ibid. 11 (May/June 1992): 4.

Fox, Mary Daly, and Rosemary Radford Ruether (who spoke at one of the Theology of Land conferences) linked Christianity and environmentalism in ways—often quite radical—of the deep ecologists. NCRLC board member John Carroll, professor of environmental conservation at the University of New Hampshire, was the foremost exponent of deep ecology in the Conference. The central precepts of Christianity "are all fundamentally ecological," Carroll asserted in an article entitled "Christ the Ecologist." Conference board member Albert Fritsch, S.J., director of Appalachia—Science in the Public Interest; Keith Warner, O.F.M., who wrote for the Conference; and president William Wood were also affiliated with the deep ecology movement.[15]

The deep ecology movement seemed to have less influence on the Conference after Andrews became executive director in the mid-1990s. He did, however, hire the NCRLC's first environmental specialist, Tim Kautza, a scientist and educator, who symbolized the Conference's growing emphasis on those issues.[16]

The oldest environmental concern of the NCRLC was soil conservation. In a 1947 resolution, the Conference urged soil conservation in accordance with its ideals of stewardship and preserving the land for future generations. In this and later statements, it urged Catholic farmers and rural pastors to cooperate with the federal Soil Conservation Service and local soil conservation districts. The NCRLC supported all kinds of governmental action to help preserve the soil. It opposed a threatened dismantling of the Soil Conservation Service by the Eisenhower administration in 1955 and applauded the passage of the Soil and Water Resources Conservation Act in 1977. In the 1980s, 1990s, and 2000s, it supported the Conservation Reserve Program, Integrated Farm Management Program, Environmental Quality Incentives Program, and Conservation Security Program, all conservation-related components of the farm bills of those years.[17]

15. Carolyn Merchant, *The Columbia Guide to American Environmental History* (New York: Columbia University Press, 2002), 188; Marlett, *Saving the Heartland*, 164–66; John E. Carroll, "Christ the Ecologist," in *Embracing Earth: Catholic Approaches to Ecology*, ed. Albert J. LaChance and John E. Carroll (Maryknoll, N.Y.: Orbis Books, 1994), 30.

16. "Catholic Rural Life Appoints Science and Environmental Education Specialist," *Rural Landscapes* 8 (May 2001): 1.

17. "Serious Threat to S.C.S.," *Feet in the Furrow* 4 (June 1955): 15; Stephen Bossi, "How Law Will Help Slow Soil and Water Depletion," *Catholic Rural Life* 26 (September 1977): 5–7; "Diocesan Directors, Resolution on Soil Conservation, Silver Jubilee Convention, Lafayette, La., Nov. 21, 1947," NCRLC 8-6; "Citizen Protest and Action Helps to Implement Law," *Common Ground* 10 (May 1991): 3; "A Bird's Eye View," *Rural Landscapes* 3 (April 1996): 2; Dan Misleh, "A Bird's Eye View," ibid. 4 (December 1996): 2; "Responding to U.S. Department of Agriculture Farm Policy Questions," *Catholic Rural Life* (newsletter) 13 (October 2005): 4–5. See Hamlin and McGreevy, "Greening

Conference members participated in more direct ways in soil conservation efforts. Many rural pastors and diocesan directors cooperated in local soil conservation districts and in state and national soil conservation agencies. Particularly notable was the work of Monsignor George J. Hildner, whose work to prevent erosion on his Missouri parish's farms earned him the title "Master Conservationist." Beginning in the 1950s, the NCRLC had a representative on the National Association of Soil Conservation Districts, which by the 1960s included fifty state associations and nearly three thousand individual districts. Each year the NCRLC representative worked with other religious leaders to promote Soil (later Soil and Water) Stewardship Week (held in May), which included publishing a booklet and sponsoring activities encouraging responsible use of the land. From 1982 to 1984, the NCRLC sponsored the Land Stewardship Project, which conducted land-use seminars in ninety high-erosion counties in Minnesota, Iowa, Nebraska, and the Dakotas. After that, the project operated independently, although the Conference kept up a connection.[18]

Soil conservation was one of the motives behind the NCRLC's promotion of organic (or biological) farming. The interest in organic farming was linked to the back-to-the-land movement in the 1930s and 1940s, when it was called "biodynamic" farming. Beginning in the 1970s, it became associated with the new environmental movement. The Conference argued that organic farming would reduce dependence on energy-intensive technologies and help preserve the topsoil and the fertility of the soil. It would further the wider distribution of property and the family farm, because its technologies were most easily utilized on small farms. The NCRLC urged that the federal government initiate research in the methods of biological farming and helped get the Department of Agriculture to revise organic food standards to avoid adulterated products being termed "organic."[19]

By the late 1980s, the NCRLC, in referring to its goal, was using the term "sustainable" to describe agriculture that was not necessarily organic but included the ideas of conservation and the family farm in a system

---

of America," 464–99, for the origins of the NCRLC's environmentalism in the soil conservation movement.

18. Edward W. O'Rourke, "Soil Saving—A Plan," *Land and Home* 10 (March 1947): 22–23; "Soil Stewardship," *Rural Life Conference* 7 (May 1958): 3; "Clergy Promote Conservation," *Catholic Rural Life* 17 (May 1968): 5; "The Land Stewardship Project," ibid. 37 (February 1987): 9; Weber and O'Rourke, "Coalitions and Change," 19; "Soil and Water Stewardship Week," *Rural Landscapes* 9 (March 2002): inserted page; Witte, *Twenty-five Years*, 38–41.

19. Special issue on biological farming, *Catholic Rural Life* 25 (November 1976); "Fair Return to Producers Urged in NCRLC Testimony," ibid. 26 (April 1977): 16; David Andrews, "The Catholic Rural Ethic Alive and Well," ibid. 40 (Spring 1998): 39.

that would successfully cope with the challenges of the future. Conference president Bishop Raymond Burke defined it as "agriculture that is economically viable, ecologically sound, and socially just." The NCRLC joined the Sustainable Agriculture Working Group as its main conduit for influencing federal farm legislation in the 1990s and 2000s.[20]

The Conference's interest in soil conservation led to continuing calls for a national land policy. These began in 1947. A typical statement of the thrust of the NCRLC's proposed policy was issued in 1971: "Our goal must be a rural-urban balance which safeguards our prime agricultural land and at the same time develops a healthy relationship of people to land, water, air and resources." In the 1970s, the NCRLC supported a proposed federal Land Use Policy and Planning Assistance Act, which would have made funds available to states that engaged in comprehensive land-use planning. The Conference was especially concerned about the loss of agricultural land because of urban sprawl; recreational, commercial, and industrial developments; speculation by urban owners; pollution; and use for power lines. To prevent these harmful uses of agricultural land, the NCRLC recommended differential tax rates based on land use, zoning laws, and, especially, the formation of community land trusts, in which the community would hold the rights to the development of the land in its neighborhood. In 1981, NCRLC director Leonard Kayser called for the resignation of Interior Secretary James Watt, whose land-use policies were viewed unfavorably by environmentalists. In 2000, Andrews supported President Clinton's action protecting additional National Forest lands from road construction and logging. On the global level, the Conference was concerned about the destruction of tropical rainforests.[21]

Starting in the 1980s, the NCRLC developed an interest in promoting the proper use of Church-owned agricultural land. Throughout the United States, dioceses, parishes, monasteries, and other Church institutions owned much farmland—58,000 acres worth $38 million in Iowa alone. The

20. Raymond L. Burke, "Call to be Church: For Sustainable Communities" (July 24, 1997), in "Current Mailings, 1994–," NCRLC, 4; untitled article, *Earth Matters* 38 (Winter 1989): 3.

21. "Diocesan Directors, Resolution on Soil Conservation, Silver Jubilee Convention, Lafayette, La., Nov. 21, 1947," NCRLC 8-6; John George Weber, "Chaff and Wheat," *Catholic Rural Life* 20 (December 1971): 6–7; Stephen E. Bossi, "Washington Farm Front," ibid. 23 (February 1974): 16; special issue on land use, ibid. 25 (March 1976); Daniel Taufen, "Angry High Line Opponents Challenge Eminent Domain," ibid. 26 (March 1977): 11–14; special issue on farmland preservation, ibid. 28 (June 1979); "NCRLC Director Calls for Ouster of Watt," ibid. 31 (August 1981): 42–43; Mike Gable, "Is There 'Global Life Insurance?' Check with Your Rainforest 'Agents,'" ibid. 37 (April 1987): 8–11; NCRLC, *Land Use* (Des Moines, Iowa: NCRLC, 1975) and *Fact Sheet on Land Use* (Des Moines, Iowa: NCRLC, 1975), both in "Gen. Pubs., 1970–76," NCRLC 5-5; "We Want This for Our Children Forever," *Washington Post*, November 30, 2000, copy in unprocessed mailings, NCRLC.

Conference thought that it was uniquely suited to provide guidance regarding the use of this land. While he was director of the O'Hara Rural Ministry Institute in the 1980s, David Andrews developed a program that gave advice to various Catholic institutions throughout the country on land use. In 1990, the NCRLC, in cooperation with the Iowa pro-family farm nonprofit organization Prairie Fire and assisted by outside grants, started the similar Church Land Project. After five years, the grants and the Prairie Fire connections ceased, and the project was run by the Conference on a gradually decreasing scale. The project published a survey of Church-held farmland in Iowa, guides to Church use of land, an estate-planning guide, and a newsletter. In the first five years, the project advised over a dozen parishes, dioceses, and monasteries, mostly in Iowa and surrounding states, on their land-use policies. They were urged to use "sustainable" agricultural practices, to develop community-supported agriculture networks, and to lease or sell the land they did not farm themselves to family farmers. Eventually, the Conference came to doubt whether extensive involvement in land-management issues for particular institutions was a good use of time for its personnel, but they did continue to give such advice into the 2000s. When the NCRLC itself was willed the Joyce farm in Minnesota, it considered using it as a model for proper land-use practices but finally decided to sell it. The NCRLC held up for emulation church groups that practiced sustainable agriculture, in particular the Sisters of the Earth, a loose alliance of religious orders of women who managed their land in an ecologically sensitive way, practiced recycling, educated others about ecology, and used wind, solar, and other renewable energy sources.[22]

The Conference was concerned that much good agricultural land was being ruined by strip mining. Beginning in 1950, the NCRLC supported zoning regulations issued by Knox County, Illinois, that limited the areas

---

22. [David Andrews], "A Message from the Executive Director of NCRLC," *Church Farmland News* 4 (October 1995): 1, in "Current Mailings, 1994–," NCRLC; "Church Supported Agriculture," ibid., 2; "Pew Charitable Trust Funds Church Land Project," *Common Ground* 10 (Summer 1990): 2; Church Land Project documents in envelope "Bob Douglas," in "Fitzgerald Files: Board Related, ca. 1986–89," Box 1, NCRLC; "Minutes, Board of Directors Meeting, National Catholic Rural Life Conference, Airport Sheraton, Bloomington, Minnesota, November 9–10, 1992," in "NCRLC: Board Mtg. (Minutes)," in Fitzgerald Files, Box 2, NCRLC, 2; Board of Directors Meeting Minutes, May, 1992, in ibid.; "Some NCRLC Current Projects" (October 2000), in unprocessed mailings, NCRLC; "Report of the Science and Environmental Education Specialist, Tim Kautza, November 2005," in ibid.; John E. Carroll, "Catholicism and Deep Ecology," in *Deep Ecology and World Religions: New Essays on Sacred Grounds*, ed. David L. Barnhill and Roger S. Gottlieb (Albany: State University of New York Press, 2001), 183–85.

Stewardship of the Planet 347

of land that could be strip mined. Although in 1961 the Illinois Supreme Court, after a long battle, declared the Knox County laws unconstitutional, the Conference noted that some good came of the controversy because the mining companies were now aware of public opinion and were making some efforts to restore the strip-mined land. Throughout the 1970s, the NCRLC supported federal legislation to ban or closely regulate strip mining and urged that the federal government provide incentives for developing deep coal reserves as a viable alternative. Finally, in 1977, over strong coal-industry opposition, the Federal Surface Mining Control and Reclamation Act was enacted, which imposed controls on the environmental impact of strip mining.[23]

As with the land, the proper stewardship of water resources was also a concern. In a resolution of 1957, the NCRLC held that "recurrent disastrous floods, the drastic lowering of groundwater tables, the continuing pollution of streams by industrial wastes, the persistent and at times unprincipled battles between conflicting interests for available water supplies" all indicated the need for "a unified water policy and program on a national basis." It favored limiting irrigated land to use by family-sized farms as required by the Reclamation Act of 1902, and charged that irrigation by large farms depleted the water supplies in closed aquifers and caused land subsidence. Big farms also polluted streams by the use of chemical fertilizers, herbicides, pesticides, and large farm machinery. Strip miners, too, polluted streams, the NCRLC alleged. The Conference urged "comprehensive land use planning" with respect to water projects, which often inundated valuable land that was used for agriculture or other needs. It called for individual and social measures to conserve valuable water, such as cutting down on home consumption, reducing leakage, and recycling waste in municipal water systems. It praised the Carter administration for its comprehensive water policy statement, and endorsed the statement's endeavor to integrate concerns for conservation, state participation, water project planning objectives, and environmental protection. However, it regretted that the statement failed to give attention to water conservation in agriculture and the possible ecological costs of water navigation projects.[24]

23. Edward W. O'Rourke, "Coal and Profits vs. Soil and People," *Christian Farmer* 4 (December 1950): 2; "UPSETTING Soils and Communities," *Catholic Rural Life* 10 (July 1961): 20; Stephen E. Bossi, "Washington Farm Front," ibid. 21 (August 1972): 16; "Subcommittee Is Urged to Adopt Tough Strip Mining Regulations," ibid. 26 (April 1977): 19; David Ostendorf, "Strip Mine Law Survives Strong Industry Attacks," ibid. 29 (January 1980): 3–5.

24. "Resolutions Adopted at the 22nd Annual Convention, Cincinnati, Ohio, November 10–13, 1944," *Land and Home* 7 (December 1944): 92; "Resolution Adopted by the N.C.R.L.C. at the Ex-

In the 1980s, 1990s, and 2000s, the NCRLC continued to express anxiety about the cleanliness and availability of water. In 2002, on the thirtieth anniversary of the Clean Water Act, it acknowledged that the act had "turned the tide on water pollution," but it noted that "water management injustices are expected to become increasingly severe by changes in global climate." One concern was that the trend toward corporate ownership of municipal water systems, both in the United States and abroad, might result in higher prices and poor service to people on the margins of society. In 2006, Andrews cosigned the statement "Water: Essential for Justice and Peace" at a Mexico City meeting. The statement noted that 1.1 billion people (17 percent of the world's population) were without access to improved sources of water, and 2.2 million people died every year from diseases associated with lack of safe water. It asserted that access to water was a basic human right and that poor and marginalized people should not be deprived of it for economic or political reasons. The Conference supported a Congressional resolution on water as a human right that included language similar to this statement.[25]

The Conference responded to floods and droughts in various ways. In the 1980s, it published prayer brochures for use during these natural disasters and called for national days of prayer when they occurred. Sister Christine Pratt, Toledo diocesan rural life director, coordinated a relief effort by Ohio and Illinois parishes and schools for aid to the victims of the great flood of 1993. The NCRLC met with an official of Catholic Charities to make sure rural areas got their share of flood relief. According to the Conference, the official "admitted that this was the first time Catholic Charities assisted 'rural' people and that ministry and outreach to rural people differs from urban."[26]

The Conference propagandized for many of the popular individual environmental actions, such as recycling; use of low-phosphate detergents;

---

ecutive Committee Meeting in Milwaukee," *Rural Life Conference* 6 (February 1957): 3, 14; Gerard McMahon, "Carter Water Plan Would Remedy Some Deficiencies," *Catholic Rural Life* 27 (June 1978): 9–10; NCRLC, *Water* (Des Moines, Iowa: NCRLC, 1977), in "Genl. Pubs., 1977, 78," NCRLC 5-5.

25. "Community of Waters," *Rural Landscapes* 10 (September 2002): 1; "WATER: A Growing Concern in the Web of Life," ibid. 11 (May 2004): 7; "Water: Essential for Justice and Peace," *Catholic Rural Life* (newsletter) 14 (April 2007): 4–5; "Report of the Science and Environmental Education Specialist, Tim Kautza, May 20, 2004," in unprocessed mailings, NCRLC, 3.

26. "Drought Spurs NCRLC Call for Day of Prayer," *Courier*, August, 1988, clipping in "Drought/Liturgy Mailing," La Blanc Subject File, Box 4, NCRLC; "NCRLC Calls for Christians to Join in Prayer and Community for Communities Effected [sic] by Floods and Drought," NCRLC news release, July 22, 1989, in "Drought/Flood Materials 1989," in ibid.; "Flood Relief Means People Helping People," *Common Ground* 13 (Fall 1993): 2; "I Set My Bow in the Clouds," ibid. (Winter 1994): 2.

avoiding littering; bicycling or driving less, with a more fuel efficient automobile using lead-free gasoline; and starting neighborhood clean-up campaigns. By 1989, the NCRLC's newsletter *Common Ground* was being printed on recycled paper.[27]

The NCRLC joined in the antipollution movement of the 1970s. In *Population and Pollution in the United States* (1970), it stated its view that "the ideal role for mankind in this intricate 'web of life' is not to abstain from using plants, animals and natural resources; it is to use them intelligently and responsibly." At that time, the NCRLC thought that President Nixon was not doing enough to control pollution—it called him a "Johnny-come-lately" on the issue. The Conference appealed for "more attention to enforcing existing legislation which would speed antipollution practices by industries and municipalities," and asked for "new laws against pollution, with adequate sanctions . . . It is imperative that pollution and waste be made unprofitable to offenders." The NCRLC particularly stressed the need to prevent agriculture-caused pollution by eroded sediment, animal waste, fertilizers, herbicides, and insecticides.[28]

By the 1990s, rural areas were being increasingly targeted for solid and hazardous waste disposal because the cost of landfills there could be one-tenth or less that of landfills in cities and suburbs. Nearly half of the nation's trash was handled by two companies—Waste Management, Inc., and Browning-Ferris Industries—which were fined for numerous environmental violations. The NCRLC offered no solution to the national waste disposal problem but did advise local advocacy to prevent trash sites from being established in rural areas and to encourage the individual practice of less waste creation and more recycling.[29]

By 2000, it was clear to many that air pollution was causing global warming, or what was sometimes more generally called climate change. The NCRLC cited scientists who predicted that during the twenty-first century, the Earth's average temperature would rise by as much as six degrees Fahrenheit, causing food and water supplies to diminish, infectious diseases to spread, agricultural systems to collapse, species to become ex-

27. NCRLC, *Saving Our Environment* (Des Moines, Iowa: NCRLC, 1971), in "General Publications, 1970–76," NCRLC 5-5; "Taking Steps to Save Creation," *Common Ground* 8 (Fall 1989): 3.
28. Edward W. O'Rourke, "Washington Farm Front," *Catholic Rural Life* 19 (March 1970): 8; O'Rourke, *Population and Pollution in the United States* (Des Moines, Iowa: NCRLC, 1970), in "General Publications, 1970–76," NCRLC 5-5; NCRLC, *Saving Our Environment*; Executive Committee resolution "Agricultural Pollution," in "Executive Committee Mtg., Colfax, Iowa, June 23–24, 1970," NCRLC 8-23.
29. "Rural Areas Bombarded with Nation's Waste," *Common Ground* 11 (November 1991): 1–2; "Responding to the Waste Disposal Crisis," ibid. 11 (January 1992): 1–2.

tinct, and millions to die. In 2007, the Conference noted that global climate change already resulted in warmer, wetter weather in the Midwest—probably leading to increased agricultural productivity. But at the same time, the poorer tropical nations of South America, Africa, and South Asia would probably suffer.[30]

In 2001, the United States Catholic bishops issued "Global Climate Change: A Plea for Dialogue, Prudence and the Common Good," which called for action to prevent the harmful effects of global warming, especially on poorer nations. The NCRLC responded by joining the National Religious Partners for the Environment (NRPE), an organization founded in 1997 to respond to global climate change. The NRPE was concerned that the George W. Bush administration was isolating itself from the rest of the world in not doing enough on the issue. In 2002, Andrews and six other Catholic leaders met with members of Bush's staff and in a follow-up letter used religious arguments to urge the president to protect the environment. The NCRLC held a conference on climate change to educate Catholic social ministers from across the country, and it helped the United States Conference of Catholic Bishops develop an education program on the issue for Catholic schools and parishes. It coordinated the Iowa Interfaith Climate and Energy Campaign, which educated the public and urged Iowa's Congressional delegation to adopt legislation dealing with the problem. Iowa Interfaith Power and Light, an organization coordinated by the Conference, educated congregations and their members to improve energy efficiency in an effort to mitigate global warming effects.[31]

In light of their possible environmental effects, the NCRLC questioned the use of production-enhancing substances such as fertilizers and insecticides. As early as 1947, Ligutti warned that, although fertilizers may give some mineral-depleted soils a temporary "shot in the arm," in the long run they would injure the soil. He believed that soil fertility could be maintained without "artificial" fertilizers. By the 1970s, the Conference was

---

30. "April 22nd, Earth Day," *Rural Landscapes* 8 (March 2001): inserted page; "Climate Change and Agriculture: Food Security and the Future," *Catholic Rural Life* 49 (Spring 2007): 23.

31. "Catholic Bishops Call for Action on Global Climate," *Rural Landscapes* 8 (July 2001): 4; "National Religious Partners for the Environment," ibid. 9 (January 2002): 7; David Andrews et al., to President [George W. Bush], [ca. May 20, 2002], in unprocessed mailings, NCRLC; special issue on global climate change, *Catholic Rural Life* 47 (Spring 2005); "NCRLC Leads Interfaith Climate Change Initiative," *Catholic Rural Life* (newsletter) 12 (June 2005): 4; Tim Kautza, "Care of Creation," *National Catholic Rural Life Conference Annual Report, Fiscal Year 2005–2006*, 14–15; "Report of the Science and Environmental Education Specialist, Tim Kautza, November 2006," in unprocessed mailings, NCRLC, 1.

questioning not only the effects of fertilizers on the soil but also on health and nutrition.[32]

Similar dangers to human health were posed by the widespread use of insecticides. In 1986, the Conference reported that 350,000 to 700,000 people were poisoned worldwide by pesticides every year, fourteen thousand of whom died. Rather than using harmful chemical sprays to eliminate pests, the Conference urged that it be done by means of crop rotation and "natural insecticides" such as other insects and insect-specific viruses. In a special report issued in 1981, it charged that the United States was shipping pesticides banned at home (such as DDT) to foreign countries. To compound the folly, the Conference claimed, some of the contaminated food was imported back into the U.S.[33]

The Conference campaigned for reform of the federal pesticide law, and changes were made by 1990 that required longer testing periods and that farmers keep better records of their pesticide use. However, in the late 1990s and 2000s, the NCRLC reported that the "circle of poison" in which pesticides banned in the United States reappeared in imported food still existed and that many American children and women, and Mexican Americans of all ages and both genders, had unacceptable levels of toxic pesticides in their bodies.[34]

The NCRLC joined groups trying to stop the giving of antibiotics to livestock; intended to promote livestock growth, such application led to antibiotic-resistant bacteria spreading to humans via the products of the livestock. In 2000, the Conference noted that giving antibiotics to livestock was banned in Sweden and Denmark and that the Food and Drug Administration was testing antibiotics and considering prohibiting some of them in the United States. The next year, NCRLC science specialist Tim Kautza joined the steering committee of Keep Antibiotics Working (KAW), a

32. "You Said It!" *Christian Farmer* 1 (December 1947): 2; John George Weber, "Fertilizers," *Catholic Rural Life* 21 (January 1972): 2.

33. Edward W. O'Rourke, "Sanity and Insecticides," *Catholic Rural Life* 12 (January 1964): 2; Dana C. Jennings, "Foreseen: An End to the Poison Race," ibid. 14 (February 1965): 6; Edith Kermit Roosevelt, "The Pesticide Boomerang," ibid. 31 (September 1981): 31–37; Angus Wright, "Pesticides in Mexico: The Culiacan Valley Farmers," ibid. 36 (February 1986): 15–18.

34. Walt Grazer, "The Time for Pesticide Reform Is NOW!" *Catholic Rural Life* 38 (June 1988): 28; "More Legislative Items of Interest," *Common Ground* 7 (January 1989): 6; "Farm Bill Debate Reaches Final Stages," ibid. 10 (September 1990): 1; Joan Allsup, "Building Face-to-Face Relationships with Agriculture as the Basis: Local Food Systems and Food Security," in National Catholic Rural Life Conference, *Justice in the Global Food System: A Faith Perspective on Food Security* (Des Moines, Iowa: National Catholic Rural Life Conference, 1997), copy in "Current Mailings, 94–," NCRLC 3; "Report Shows 'Pesticide Body Burden' among Vulnerable Groups in U.S.," *Rural Landscapes* 11 (June 2004): 3.

group of nongovernmental organizations dedicated to ending overuse of antibiotics. KAW worked for federal legislation to phase out the use of antibiotics as feed additives for livestock. The NCRLC urged Catholic institutions to purchase locally grown food without antibiotics. Kautza and KAW had some success when McDonald's, Wendy's, Popeye's, Tyson, Perdue, and Foster Farms reduced or eliminated antibiotics in their chicken.[35]

Efforts to improve crops and livestock through biotechnology had side effects that concerned the NCRLC. Genetics was used to increase production, improve nutritional value, and make crops resistant to pests and diseases, but sometimes the resultant food was thought to have harmful effects on consumers' health. In the late 1980s, the Conference began to call for developing an "ethical construct" for biotechnology and requiring "social impact studies" (similar to environmental impact studies) of new agricultural technologies. When bovine growth hormone (BGH), which could increase milk production up to 25 percent, was introduced in 1990, the NCRLC feared that it would increase milk surpluses and the number of corporate farms and said its health effects on humans should be studied before it was approved for use. The Conference opposed "terminator technology" in genetically altered seeds, which prevented them from producing crops on replanting to ensure that farmers would have to buy new seeds from the biotechnology company every season. Andrews said this would hurt small farmers and accelerate the trend toward a few companies controlling seeds and agriculture in general. He also denounced the United States' blocking of a treaty that would have limited the market for genetically modified agricultural products. Conference president Bishop Raymond Burke sympathized with a European Union boycott of American food because much of it was genetically altered.[36]

In a series of statements culminating in 2002, the NCRLC set out a num-

---

35. "Antibiotic Resistance Campaign" [October, 2000], in unprocessed mailings, NCRLC; "Report of the Science and Environmental Education Specialist, Tim Kautza, NCRLC Board Meeting, November 9, 2001," in unprocessed mailings, NCRLC, 1; "Report of the Science and Environmental Education Specialist, Tim Kautza, NCRLC Board Meeting, May 31, 2002," in ibid., 1; Tim Kautza, "Care of Creation," *National Catholic Rural Life Conference Annual Report, Fiscal Year 2005–2006*, 15.

36. Hurt, *Problems of Plenty*, 159–63; whole issue on biotechnology, *Catholic Rural Life* 37 (November 1987); "National Office Releases Biotechnology Report," *Common Ground* 5 (December 1986): 2; Joseph K. Fitzgerald, "Tensions Disrupt World Food Conference," ibid. 7 (July 1988): 1; "Milk, Nature's Perfect Food, Produced Thanks to Chemicals?" ibid. 8 (April 1990): 2; "Nature's Perfect Food and rBGH," *Rural Landscapes* 1 (January 1994): 1; John L. Allen Jr., "Activists See Threat to Food Supply in Form of New 'Terminator Technology,'" *National Catholic Reporter*, May 15, 1998, copy in "Current Mailings, 1994–," NCRLC; David G. Andrews, "Joining the Struggle for Rural America," *Word and World* 20 (Spring 2000): 135–36, copy in ibid.; Thomas A. Szyszkiewicz, "A Bishop for Farmers," *Inside the Vatican* (December 2000): 27, copy in unprocessed mailings, NCRLC.

ber of ethical guidelines for agricultural biotechnology: although genetic engineering on plants and animals (though not on humans) was ethical, it "must respect the sacredness of created life." There should be a moratorium on the commercial introduction of genetically engineered crops until "a principled food policy is developed through public debate." As proclaimed by Pope John Paul II, the health and environmental effects of biotechnologies should be examined before they could be introduced to farmers; if approved, genetically altered food should be labeled. Technical processes could be patented, but not genes, gene sequences, or genetically engineered species. One NCRLC writer suggested that genetic companies be required to have "GMO [genetically modified organism] liability bonds" to cover their potential adverse effects. The concerns of the NCRLC and other consumer and environmental groups had considerable effect in reducing the marketing of genetically modified foods.[37]

Concern for the environment naturally led to an interest in the energy resources derived from and affecting that environment. Before the 1970s, when the Conference thought of "energy" at all, it was in a rural or farming context; thus, in 1958, NCRLC president Bishop Stephen S. Woznicki gave tributes to oil as "the key to world power today" and atomic energy as "the key in the near future," but claimed that the soil—often overlooked, but the one renewable energy source—was "the greatest of them all!"[38]

But in the wake of the environmental movement that began in the late 1960s, the New York City power blackouts of 1972, and the Arab oil embargo of 1973, the Conference began to view the rural aspect of energy in a wider context, and with the rest of the United States became aware of the urgent need to address the problem of the nation's future energy sources. The NCRLC believed that three measures were essential in the country's attempt to deal with the energy crisis: national planning to coordinate the use of energy resources, research and development of new energy sources, and energy conservation. No federal body fulfilled the Conference's desire for national energy planning until President Carter unveiled his plans to develop a national energy policy in 1977. Carter's proposals

---

37. "Farmers' Declaration on Genetic Engineering in Agriculture," *Rural Landscapes* 7 (January 2000): 8; Keith Douglas Warner, *Questioning the Promise: Critical Reflections on Agricultural Biotechnology from the Perspective of Catholic Teaching* (Des Moines, Iowa: National Catholic Rural Life Conference, 2000), copy in "Current Mailings, 1994–," NCRLC, 11, 28–32; "Agricultural Biotechnology, A Catholic Perspective, April 2002," NCRLC statement, in unprocessed mailings, NCRLC; Hurt, *Problems of Plenty*, 162–63, 166.

38. "Bishop Woznicki Gives Key Address," *Catholic Rural Life* 7 (November 1958): 4.

drew support from the NCRLC, which hoped the resulting policy would emphasize conservation and the development of new energy sources, but the various components did not survive intact through Congress.[39]

The NCRLC stated flatly that "energy conservation is a moral imperative." It believed that this was so not only because of the strictly limited reserves of energy supplies on earth, but more especially because of the need for a more just distribution of energy resources across the world. It noted that the United States, with its affluent lifestyle, consumed one-half of the world's energy, and it called for Americans to cut down on energy use to make more of it available to the rest of the world.[40]

The NCRLC advocated developing energy sources that were "safe, renewable and accessible to all people," not those that were "finite, exploitative of our natural resources, unsafe, and/or in violation of the human rights of people." It was against substantial reliance on coal in the future because of the damage from strip mining and the air pollution from coal-burning power plants. In the context of the frequent oil crises starting in the 1970s, the rural life directors resolved to promote reduced use of petrochemicals. The Conference noted that agriculture was among the sectors of the American economy overdependent on oil. Seventeen percent of America's oil was used in agricultural production—for running farm machinery, making pesticides and fertilizers, irrigation pumping, grain drying, and transportation of goods. Smaller, appropriate technologies would make American agriculture more sustainable, the NCRLC believed. During a debate on a Senate energy bill in 2002, the NCRLC was part of an ecumenical campaign urging a conservation-based energy policy. It advocated for stricter fuel economy in vehicles, greater renewable energy standards, and less dependency on foreign oil supplies.[41]

Many Americans were enthusiastic about the prospects of using ethanol produced from corn and soybeans as a fuel, because it would lessen dependence on foreign-bought oil and add to farmers' income. The NCRLC expressed lukewarm support for ethanol, warning that too much use

---

39. Stephen E. Bossi, "Washington Farm Front," *Catholic Rural Life* 21 (September 1972): 8; The Editors, "Why We're All Obligated to Do More Than Conserve," ibid. 25 (January 1976): 2; Helen Vinton, "National Energy Policy Direction Badly Needed," ibid. 26 (April 1977): 8–10; John J. McRaith, "Five Tests to Apply to National Energy Policy," ibid. 26 (September 1977): 3–4.

40. Bossi, "Washington Farm Front," *Catholic Rural Life* 21 (September 1972): 8; NCRLC, *Energy* (Des Moines, Iowa: NCRLC, 1976), in "Gen. Pubs., 1970–76," NCRLC 5-5.

41. NCRLC, *Energy*; "Rural Life Directors Business Meeting," *Common Ground* 5 (March 1987): 3; "America's Agriculture: Too Oil Dependent?" ibid. 10 (October 1990): 1; Robert Gronski, "Capitol Update," *Rural Landscapes* 9 (April 2002): 2.

of food crops as fuel could raise food prices and increase world hunger. Nonfood biomass should be used as fuel, it suggested.[42]

Nonpolluting energy sources like solar, wind, and geothermal alternatives were viewed most positively by the Conference. The NCRLC called attention to the potential of solar power at the relatively early date of 1972. A few years later, it stated: "Solar energy is here and now and anybody can do it . . . It is in the nation's interest to develop this free, non-polluting, inexhaustible, environmentally sound energy source as fast as possible." In 2003, the NCRLC coauthored with a coalition of Iowa labor, environmental, and farm groups a letter to presidential candidates calling for a $300 billion, ten-year "New Apollo Project for energy freedom," which would emphasize clean, renewable energy such as solar and wind power and would result in 3 million new jobs and retraining for laid-off factory workers.[43]

Like most Americans, the NCRLC at first was excited about the promise of nuclear power, without yet realizing many of the drawbacks. In 1955, it affirmed that nuclear power had great potential, especially for developing countries. It recommended "a bold and imaginative use of our atomic energy know-how by establishing reactors for the generation of power in remote areas where lack of power means very low standards of living. Such sharing of our technology will enable people in underdeveloped areas to leap the steam and hydro-electric age and catch up with the rest of the world, both industrially and agriculturally." However, starting in the 1970s, and particularly after the Three Mile Island and Chernobyl accidents in 1979 and 1986, the NCRLC raised doubts about nuclear power because of cost, possibilities of meltdowns and other accidents, problems of disposing of hazardous wastes, and possible weapons proliferation. It opposed proposals to store nuclear waste in the Texas panhandle where it could drain into the Ogallala Aquifer, source of much of the Great Plains' agricultural water. In 1990, the board of directors ordered that the Conference not invest in companies constructing or operating nuclear power plants.[44]

---

42. Robert Gronski, "Food Production and Renewable Energy: An Agricultural Crossroads or Collision?" *Catholic Rural Life* 48 (Spring 2006): 21–22.

43. John George Weber, "August 7, 1972—One Hour," *Catholic Rural Life* 21 (October 1972): 2; "How Sun Day Celebration Focused on Solar Energy," ibid. 27 (April 1978): 2; Rekha Basu, "Use Wind, Sun to Propel America Forward," Des Moines *Register*, October 22, 2003, 17A, clipping in unprocessed mailings, NCRLC.

44. NCRLC, *Program for Shared Abundance*, 8; NCRLC, *Energy*; special energy issue, *Catholic Rural Life* 25 (January 1976); Helen Vinton, "Why Nuclear Power Plants Are Getting into Trouble," ibid. (September 1976): 21–23; "Nuclear Accident Raises Accountability Question," ibid. 28 (April

There were cautions that applied to nuclear power as well as other sources of energy—that the industry possessed a "lack of accountability to the American people" and that the concentration of power in a few centralized units ran the risk of sudden widespread failure of services. To remedy these objections, the Conference urged that public regulatory authorities, rather than private companies, assume overall supervision of energy policy, that Christians as citizens take an active part in the formation of energy policy, and that energy be generated in smaller, decentralized plants.[45]

The ultimate threat that nuclear power posed to the environment—including the rural environment—was total destruction, including that of all human and other life on Earth. Thus, the NCRLC argued, the greatest challenge for responsible stewardship of the Earth was the prevention of nuclear war. The earliest NCRLC statement on nuclear war came in 1950, when Monsignor Ligutti rather curiously urged that the heavily urbanized Catholic population disperse to the countryside to decrease its vulnerability to a nuclear attack: "Approximately 66% of the Catholics in the United States live east of the Ohio-Pennsylvania state line and north of the Mason-Dixon line. It is estimated that 24 well placed atomic bombs could destroy well over 60% of the Catholic institutions and obliterate about the same percentage of Catholic people." By the time of the antinuclear movement of the 1970s and 1980s, the Conference shifted to more conventional concerns about the possibility of the destruction of the biosphere by a nuclear exchange, opposition to nuclear weapons systems, and arms control. In 1982, it endorsed the "nuclear freeze," proposing that instead the United States and the Soviet Union alleviate world hunger through the establishment of a food bank and by helping Third World countries develop nonexploitative, self-sustaining agriculture. It urged that Catholics give attention to the NCCB's 1983 statement on nuclear warfare and lined up on the side of liberal groups such as Mobilization for Survival in opposing large military expenditures, especially for nuclear weapons, and favoring more spending for social needs.[46]

1979): 2; Greg Cusack, "Chernobyl: Symbol of Our Separation from the Land," ibid. 36 (July 1986): 3; "Rural Life Directors Business Meeting," *Common Ground* 5 (March 1987): 3; "Fighting the Good Fight for Future Generations," *Rural Landscapes* 2 (November 1994): 4; "NCRLC Investment Policy Statement" (September 5, 1990), in Fitzgerald Files, Box 1, NCRLC.

45. Helen Vinton, "Blackouts Show Weakness of Huge Utility Systems," *Catholic Rural Life* 26 (September 1977): 21–23; NCRLC, *Energy*.

46. Luigi G. Ligutti, "National Catholic Rural Life Conference," in "Belleville Convention, A Review of the Past, 1950," NCRLC 8-7, 11; Gerard McMahon, "Why 'National Security' Concept Is Out of Date," *Catholic Rural Life* 27 (October 1978): 17–18; special issue on nuclear warfare, ibid. 33

The Conference gave some attention to other military and peace issues, especially when they were related to rural concerns. Executive Director Cusack was "impressed with the connections these good people [at a Pax Christi meeting he addressed in 1986] were making between the economic devastation facing our food producers and our rural communities and the serious entrenchment of the military-industrial complex in the U.S." A few years later, the NCRLC decided to avoid investment in any companies that produced nuclear or conventional weapons or that were substantially involved as a supplier to the military. In the wake of the September 11, 2001, terrorist attacks, Robert Gronski of the NCRLC argued for greater biodiversity and against large confined animal feeding farms to prevent the spread of viruses and diseases and protect the nation's food supply.[47]

The NCRLC's concern for the peace and survival of the Earth constituted a fitting culmination to its growing involvement in rural social action from 1960 to the end of the century. Its interest in rural society during this period grew naturally from its struggle to save the family farm and its work for the rural poor and minorities to continued involvement in international rural life, stewardship of the environment, and a concern to save the planet itself. By the end of the millennium, the Conference's increasing preoccupation with rural social action had expanded to the broadest possible limits. The Conference that had begun with a narrow focus on the Catholic rural population problem was now concerned with rural life in the widest sense.

(April 1983); "Minutes, NCRLC Board of Directors, May 26–28, 1982, St. Joseph's Retreat Center, Des Plaines, IL 60016," in "Board Communications," Cusack Subject File, Box 19, NCRLC, 8.

47. "News from the Director," *Common Ground* 5 (October 1986): 2–3; "National Catholic Rural Life Conference Investment Policy Statement" (September 5, 1990), unfoldered in "Fitzgerald Files," Box 1, NCRLC; "After Attacks, Food Supply Comes under Policy Review," *National Catholic Reporter*, October 12, 2001, copy in unprocessed mailings, NCRLC.

Chapter 15 Catholic and American

The NCRLC over Eight Decades

It remains to assess the important effects of the National Catholic Rural Life Conference—both intended and unintended—and the main themes of its development. Three important areas of the Conference's effects were the Catholic rural population problem, the NCRLC's role in the Catholic social action movement, and the Conference as an "identity group" for rural Catholics. The effects in all three areas involved the "Catholic" in the NCRLC assimilating itself to the "American."

The original purpose behind the founding of the NCRLC was to strengthen the American Catholic Church numerically in the countryside. Although this was hardly mentioned as a goal of the Conference by the end of the twentieth century, it was still important for a long enough portion of its history (at least through the 1950s) that it will be worthwhile to see how far the NCRLC was successful. For the NCRLC, solving the Catholic rural population problem involved first increasing the proportion of Catholics in the total American rural population, and second (through the high birthrates of rural people), increasing the proportion of Catholics in the total American population.

Although the Conference knew it was facing an uphill battle, it thought it was making at least some progress. In 1950, Monsignor Ligutti wrote: "If the NCRLC by its education and propaganda could retard the cityward movement it might be said to have accomplished the unexpected. While no scientifically accurate studies have been made it is the firm conviction of its leaders that the cityward trend of Catholics has been retarded through the persistent educational campaign of the NCRLC." Population statistics confirm that the goals of the NCRLC in this area were attained, at least relatively. While in 1900 the American Catholic population was 20.4 percent rural (2.9 million out of 14.2 million), and in 1920 Father O'Hara

Catholic and American 359

estimated that it was 19 percent rural, in 1974 (the last date for which rural Catholic data is available), the American Catholic population was still 17.7 percent rural (8.5 million out of 48 million). When one compares that to the fact that from 1900 to 1980 the rural percentage in the total American population dropped from about 60 percent to 26.3 percent, the Catholic population appears to have done remarkably well in preserving its rural component.[1]

During the NCRLC's existence, Catholics as a whole also more than maintained their proportion of the total American population. Studies using different methodologies resulted in varying numbers, but they revealed the same overall trend. Will Herberg's *Protestant—Catholic—Jew* (1960) showed that from the 1920s to the 1950s, when the NCRLC was most concerned about the Catholic rural population problem, Catholics in the United States actually increased relative to Protestants, as demonstrated in table 4. Over this period, Americans increasingly affiliated with both Protestant and Catholic churches: the Protestant gain was 32 percent, the Catholic gain 42 percent. In their well-known study of American religious population, *The Churching of America* (1992), Roger Finke and Rodney Stark calculated that from 1940 to 1985, Catholics increased from 33 percent of all American church members (not all of the American population) to 36.8 percent, a gain of 12 percent in "market share." A survey cited by the Pew Forum found that from 1974 to 2004, the Catholic share of the American population remained steady at about 25 percent while the Protestant share declined from 64.3 percent to 50.4 percent. Thus the religious/demographic goals of the NCRLC appeared to be met.[2]

How much the NCRLC itself was responsible for the vitality of the American Catholic population is debatable. It may indeed have had a substantial impact, as Ligutti claimed, on keeping Catholics in the countryside. But there are many other possible reasons for the increase in the proportion of the overall Catholic population, such as immigration from abroad, the

---

1. Luigi G. Ligutti, "National Catholic Rural Life Conference," in "Belleville Convention, A Review of the Past, 1950," NCRLC 8-7, 6; David Steven Bovée, "The Church and the Land: The National Catholic Rural Life Conference and American Society, 1923–1985," (PhD diss., University of Chicago, 1986), 25–27, 85; *U.S. Department of Commerce, Bureau of the Census, Statistical Abstract of the United States: 1985*, 105th ed. (Washington, D.C. Government Printing Office, 1984), 22; "National Catholic Rural Life Conference, Paid Memberships in Each Diocese, 1974," in "Diocesan Directors Meeting, Columbia, Missouri, October 22, 1974," NCRLC 8-24.

2. Will Herberg, *Protestant—Catholic—Jew: An Essay in American Religious Sociology*, 2d rev. ed. (Garden City, N.Y.: Anchor Books, 1960), 160; Finke and Stark, *Churching of America*, 248; "Religious Demographic Profile, United States," http://pewforum.org/world-affairs/countries/?countryID=222, accessed August 8, 2007.

Table 4. Protestants and Catholics in the U.S. Population, 1920s to 1950s

	Percentage of total population	
Year	Protestants	Catholics
1926	27.0	16.0
1940	28.7	16.1
1950	33.8	18.9
1955	35.5	20.3
1958	35.5	22.8

Source: Will Herberg, *Protestant—Catholic—Jew. An Essay in American Religious Sociology*, rev. 2d ed. (Garden City, N.Y.: Anchor Books, 1960), 160.

Catholic valuing of large families, and the Church's campaign against birth control. It is clear now that the predictions by NCRLC statisticians such as O. E. Baker of wide differentials between urban and rural birthrates did not hold up. The post–World War II baby boom—which was neither rural nor urban, but suburban—temporarily boosted the American population despite the rural exodus. At the same time, rural birthrates began to decline, and by 1990 they became practically equal to urban ones. Therefore, despite the theory of the Catholic rural population problem, the Catholic Church in America held its own numerically while remaining concentrated in the cities.[3]

At first, the NCRLC's role as the rural arm of the American Church's social action movement was not emphasized as much as its concern for the rural population problem. But from its beginnings as the Rural Life Bureau of the NCWC's Social Action Department, formed by a priest with a social action background—Father O'Hara—the social action function was a part of the NCRLC. Beginning in the 1930s, when the Conference began to speak out on economic affairs in response to the Depression, social action took precedence over the population issue. From that time on, the social action function was the primary focus of the NCRLC. The Conference formed the rural component of the Church's social action movement throughout the twentieth century, as outlined in Aaron Abell's *American Catholicism and Social Action: A Search for Social Justice*.

Although the NCRLC always tried to be and made claims to be a grass-

---

3. Carlson, *New Agrarian Mind*, 46–48, 52; Danbom, *Born in the Country*, 244.

roots membership organization of rural Catholics, it was actually more successful as an advocacy group for rural Christian and liberal causes. In fact, at times—notably during the 1960s under O'Rourke, and after 1980, when little attention was paid to membership—the Conference ran the danger of losing touch with the grass roots entirely and becoming a purely social action advocacy group of a small number of liberal rural Catholic activists.

The NCRLC's success in achieving its goals in the area of social action was mixed. In the areas where it seemed to fail, the odds against success were great. The Conference could not overcome the trend toward bigness and efficiency in agriculture and preserve a large middle class of family farmers or the ethos of farming as a way of life rather than as a business. On a larger scale, it also had difficulties in preserving rural and Christian values in society as a whole, in light of the modern trends toward urbanization and secularization. The Conference was perhaps most successful in its efforts for the rural poor. It became one of the very few spokespeople for this group. Moreover, under leaders such as Ligutti, Vizzard, and O'Rourke, it frequently affected national policies. It helped found subsistence homesteads and the Farm Security Administration, helped end the bracero program and legitimize migrant farm workers' unions, and assisted farmers in forming rural self-help projects in the United States and abroad. Together with other liberal individuals and groups, the tiny NCRLC did relatively much to mitigate the conditions of the rural poor.

To use the language of sociology, the purposes of solving the Catholic rural population problem and of forming the rural arm of the American Catholic social action movement were "manifest functions" of the NCRLC. But from the beginning, the Conference also had the hidden or "latent" function of forming an "identity group" for rural Catholics, who were unrepresented by any formal organization until 1923. As O'Hara found through his rural religious survey of 1920, the morale of rural Catholicism at that time was very low. It truly felt itself to be the backwater of the urban Church. By 1950, president Bishop Vincent Ryan said, "the NCRLC has done away with the inferiority complex of the rural pastor." The same could be said of the rural Catholic Church as a whole. Through its organization, programs, and philosophy, the NCRLC gave the rural Catholic religious and laity a positive direction—a confidence in their own special value in the scheme of Church and society. While other similar organizations died out, the NCRLC, despite its small size, continued to remain viable into the twenty-first century because, through its efforts, rural Catholics found they were a social group with a unique value and a special message to give to the rest of society.[4]

The idea of identity was also at the heart of the development process of the NCRLC. The Conference always identified itself as both "Catholic" and "American." In 1987, it affirmed: "The NCRLC is working to ensure that we engage in the current struggle for justice on the land in a manner which is consistent with our heritage of Judeo-Christian values and with our democratic legacy as Americans." But over the course of its history, these two elements shifted and rearranged themselves in a way that historian Philip Gleason, describing the process undergone by many American Catholic institutions, likened to the assimilation or "Americanization" of immigrants. The NCRLC, in fact, offers a perfect case study of Gleason's Catholic assimilation process.[5]

Just as the Catholic Church was still essentially an immigrant church in the United States in the 1920s, so the NCRLC, founded in that decade, was an "immigrant" institution in rural America. In the 1920s, the Catholic Church was still "defensive" and fighting to establish itself as equal to the Protestant churches in America. In the same way, the NCRLC fought to strengthen the Church numerically in rural areas. The religious or "Catholic" element in the NCRLC was predominant in the 1920s, because it considered the strengthening of the Catholic religion in rural areas to be more important than any other contribution it could make. Father Schmiedeler expressed this early emphasis on the "Catholic" over the "American" in the Conference in a statement he wrote in 1931:

Primarily, of course, the aim of the Rural Life work is to further the ends of the Church in the country, to help the Church in her great work of saving souls. The dominant *motif*, therefore, is undoubtedly a religious one, else, indeed, there would be little need for the existence of a special *Catholic* Rural Life Movement since a very progressive secular organization, the American Country Life Association, is already in the field.

---

4. Ligutti, "National Catholic Rural Life Conference," 6. For more on the NCRLC as an identity group for American rural Catholics, see Marlett, *Saving the Heartland*, 117–20, 124–28. For an example of a Catholic organization that failed to remain viable in response to changes in American society, see Philip Gleason's history of the German Catholic Central Verein, *The Conservative Reformers*.

5. "Theology of Land," *Catholic Rural Life* 37 (February 1987): 3; Philip Gleason, "The Crisis of Americanization," in *Catholicism in America* (New York: Harper and Row, 1970), 133–53. Gleason's *Contending with Modernity: Catholic Higher Education in the Twentieth Century* (New York: Oxford University Press, 1995), describes a similar example of assimilation in the case of Catholic higher education.

Catholic and American

For Schmiedeler and the Conference at this time, the religious and otherworldly goal of "saving souls" took precedence over improving the temporal state of rural society.[6]

The process of the NCRLC's assimilation began in the 1930s, when the Conference responded to the nation's Depression crisis by speaking out on the rural economy. The process continued in the 1940s and 1950s, when the United States became a world power following World War II, and the NCRLC followed suit by expanding its activities into international affairs under Monsignor Ligutti. The Conference reacted to the liberal climate of the 1960s by shifting its focus to antipoverty activities. In the 1970s, 1980s, 1990s, and 2000s, when a more urban and consumer-oriented United States became concerned about environmental, energy and food-quality issues, the NCRLC widened its conception of "rural" to include these matters as well. Thus, over the eight decades of its existence, the Conference evolved from a primarily evangelistic-oriented organization to one that came into close contact with American society in a multitude of ways. The primary purpose of the NCRLC was no longer, as it had been in Schmiedeler's day, to spread the Catholic religion in rural areas, but to provide judgment and influence from the Catholic perspective on American rural life. Stephen Bossi's statement on the purpose of the Conference organ *Catholic Rural Life,* written in 1977, provides an appropriate counterpart to Schmiedeler's 1931 statement: "This is not the only publication dealing with rural and natural resource issues. But it is the only one interpreting these issues from the point of view of Catholic social teaching."[7]

In many ways, the development of the NCRLC illustrated the process called the "De-Romanization" of the American Catholic Church by Edward Wakin and the Reverend Joseph F. Scheuer. According to Wakin and Scheuer, this process—really just another name for "Americanization"—involved the American Church's drifting away from Rome in the twentieth century through changes from "authority to freedom," "privilege to egalitarianism," "corporate to personal responsibility," and "other-worldly to this-worldly orientation." The change in mission of the NCRLC from bringing salvation to promoting social justice demonstrates the change from "other-worldly" to "this-worldly." The other three changes described by Wakin and Scheuer apply more to the internal structure of the NCRLC,

---

6. [Edgar Schmiedeler], "The National Catholic Rural Life Conference," in "Ntn'l Catholic Rural Life Conference, Purpose and Policy, 1931, 1933, 1958," NCRLC 8A-1, 1.

7. "Retiring Editor Steve Bossi Reviews Magazine's Role in Promoting Justice," *Catholic Rural Life* 26 (December 1977): 23.

which over the years experienced increased participation by the laity and women in its leadership, and maintained its quasi-independence of the bishops' conference and other authorities of the Church.[8]

However, the susceptibility of the NCRLC to assimilate to its American environment should not be exaggerated. Although the Conference was influenced successively by the immediate climates of opinion of religious divisions in the 1920s, the Depression in the 1930s, the rise of the United States to world power in the 1940s and 1950s, Vatican II and the antipoverty movement in the 1960s, and the environmental and energy crises in the 1970s, 1980s, 1990s, and 2000s, it also stayed within a number of important longer-term traditions. Most importantly, in its approach to rural issues, the NCRLC, despite the outside pressures of some contrary trends of American society, stayed faithful to the official teachings of the Church. The Conference took on the evangelizing mission of the Church—at first by trying to increase the number of rural Catholics, and later by trying to spread a more social gospel. It also kept a consistent Christian regard for the poorest of society. Finally, it carried on some very old American traditions, such as the Jeffersonian agrarian myth and the mission of spreading the best of American culture to foreign lands.

In fact, some critics have charged the NCRLC with holding on too tightly to the past. The Catholic writer John Cogley used the NCRLC as an example of what he said was the persistent tendency of Catholics to cling to the past and reject modernity, stating: "A return to the family farm was pushed by the leaders of the . . . Catholic Rural Life Movement long after subsistence farming ceased to be economically feasible." Historian Jeffrey Marlett made the related point that most Catholic farmers eventually disregarded the old-fashioned ethic of agrarian self-denial preached by Ligutti and other NCRLC leaders and embraced the abundant lifestyle offered by modern commercial agriculture.[9]

The NCRLC, perhaps protesting too much, always vehemently denied that it was backward-looking or trying to revive an irretrievable past. In a 1949 statement, "Industrialism and Agrarianism," the Conference decried in typical fashion the abuses of the industrial system—degradation of human dignity, exploitation of natural resources, oppression of labor, and the proletarianization of workers. However, it made sure to deny that it

---

8. Edward Wakin and Joseph F. Scheuer, *The De-Romanization of the American Catholic Church* (Westport, Conn.: Greenwood Press, 1979; reprint of New York: Macmillan, 1966), 284–88.

9. John Cogley, *Catholic America* (Garden City, N.Y.: Image Books, 1973), 153; Marlett, *Saving the Heartland*, 130.

opposed such modern developments as the mass-production system, corporate enterprise, wage contracts, or the social ownership of the means of production and that the Conference believed that rural life was "a panacea for social ills." In 1984, Executive Director Gregory Cusack wrote an extended defense of NCRLC opposition to many so-called inevitable modern rural trends:

> One of the most difficult myths to successfully confront is that our present situation represents "the inevitable wave of the future." The only thing "inevitable" about the future is that we will either responsibly act to take a hand in creating it or, by failing to act, we will passively capitulate to others who are acting to create it. Decisions about credit allocations, tax laws, machinery inputs, and who markets American grain are all human decisions. If we are serious about putting our food system aright we must act to bring all in accordance with our vision of a more just future. Such will not be easy, but that is no excuse to argue that our present course is inevitable.
>
> Opponents of the position of the NCRLC (which has, since its inception, strongly favored the family farming system) often argue that we are engaged in "historical nostalgia," that the time of the family farming system is passed. We must now prepare for the "new wave of the future." Either they misunderstand our position, or they understand it only too well and seek to discredit it by such misrepresentation. The NCRLC does not automatically oppose labor-saving or more "efficient" devices—what we do challenge is the automatic assumption that every new piece of machinery, or every new costly chemical input, is a forward step which will support a sound food production system. We observe that the effect of many allegedly progressive steps implemented since the 1950s has seriously eroded the position of the family farmer. Is this necessarily bad, some might ask? When you see that the consequences are ever-larger concentrations of land ownership into a shrinking number of owners, that control by near or actual monopolies in both the input and the processing categories have grown immensely, and that the quality of food consumed by Americans has declined, we conclude that the net effect is not what we'd like.[10]

A decade later, Executive Director David Andrews made a similar point:

> The message of the NCRLC has been the same for almost 75 years now. It has not been heeded. Farmers have not heeded it. In many instances, NCRLC has not left them, they have left NCRLC. Cooperatives have not heeded it. Some of them have become investment enterprises for a globalized economy, ignoring their past honor as stalwarts of local community control. If you're not heeded,

---

10. "Industrialism and Agrarianism," *Christian Farmer* 2 (February 1949): 1, 3; Greg Cusack, "Food!" *Catholic Rural Life* 34 (February 1984): 10.

should you give up on your message? Not if your principles are correct. We do need to read the signs of the times and review the Gospel in the light of current exigencies. But the reading of the signs of the times does not call for an easy accommodation with the prevailing trends.[11]

Throughout its history, the NCRLC believed that there was a disjuncture between the Christian profession of most Americans and the social values applied to rural issues. As the United States urbanized and secularized in the twentieth century, rural and Christian values were replaced by urban and "scientific" or "humanistic" values as dominant in American society. The NCRLC tried to call Americans back to their Christian profession by providing a Christian perspective on rural issues. In this way, by holding to its principles while striving to be relevant to the needs of American society, it attempted to reconcile the "Catholic" and the "American" elements in its character.

---

11. David Andrews, "Building Community," *Rural Landscapes* 4 (October 1996): 3. For similar statements, see Raymond L. Burke, "Call to be Church: For Sustainable Communities" (July 24, 1997), in "Current Mailings, 1994–," 3; Sandra A. La Blanc, "I Will Sing of Loyalty and of Justice" *Catholic Rural Life* 41 (Fall 1998): 3.

Bibliography

Unpublished Primary Sources

Archbishop Edwin V. O'Hara Papers. Catholic Archdiocesan Chancery. Kansas City, Missouri. Papers are filed in looseleaf binders. Cited in notes as OH, followed by the binder number.

Central Bureau of the Catholic Central Union of America Archives. St. Louis, Missouri. Microfilmed records were used. Cited in notes by roll title, followed by CU.

Confraternity of Christian Doctrine Archives. The Catholic University of America Archives. Washington, D.C. Archives are filed in transfiles. Cited in notes by folder title, followed by CCD, followed by transfile number.

Monsignor Luigi G. Ligutti Papers. Marquette University Archives and Special Collections. Milwaukee, Wisconsin. Papers are filed in lettered drawers in file cabinets and miscellaneous boxes. Cited in notes by folder title, followed by LGL, followd by file drawer letter or box title.

Msgr. Leon A. McNeill Papers. Newman University Archives. Wichita. Papers are filed in folders. Cited in notes by folder title, followed by McN.

National Catholic Rural Life Conference Archives. Marquette University Archives and Special Collections. Milwaukee. Archives are filed mainly in archival boxes, and are divided into twenty-one series. Processed records are cited by folder title, followed by NCRLC, followed by series number and box number. There are also a number of unprocessed records, which are cited by a description of the item followed by NCRLC.

National Catholic Welfare Conference Archives. The Catholic University of America Archives. Washington, D.C. Archives are filed in drawers and transfiles. Cited in notes by folder title, followed by NCWC, followed by drawer or transfile number.

United States Catholic Conference Archives. Washington, D.C. Several folders of Social Action Department records were used. Cited in notes by folder title, followed by USCC.

Printed Primary Sources

Abell, Aaron I., ed. *American Catholic Thought on Social Questions*. Indianapolis: Bobbs-Merrill, 1968.

America. 1909–.
American Country Life Association. *Proceedings of the Conference*. 1919–.
American Ecclesiastical Review. 1889–1975.
Baer, Urban. *Farmers of Tomorrow*. Sparta, Wisc.: Monroe Publishing, 1939.
Barnhill, David Landis, and Roger S. Gottlieb, eds. *Deep Ecology and World Religions: New Essays on Sacred Grounds*. Albany: State University of New York Press, 2001.
Bertels, Thomas More. *In Pursuit of Agri-power: The One Thing North American Farmers and Ranchers Can't Produce*. Manitowoc, Wisc.: Silver Lake College Press, 1988.
Boston *Pilot*. 1829–.
Catholic Action. 1932–53.
The Catholic Charities Review. 1917–74.
The Catholic Encyclopedia. 10 vols. New York: Encyclopedia Press, 1913–14.
Catholic Mind. 1903–82.
Catholic Rural Life Conference. Proceedings of the Eleventh Annual Convention, October 16-19, 1933, Milwaukee, Wisconsin. N.p.: n.p., n.d.
Catholic Rural Life Objectives: A Second Series of Discussions on Some Elements of Major Importance in the Philosophy of Agrarianism. St. Paul, Minn.: National Catholic Rural Life Conference, [1936].
Catholic Rural Life Objectives: A Series of Discussions on Some Elements of Major Importance in the Philosophy of Agrarianism. St. Paul, Minn.: National Catholic Rural Life Conference, 1935.
Catholic Rural Life Objectives: A Third Series of Papers Dealing with Some of the Economic, Social, and Spiritual Interests of the American Farmer. N.p.: National Catholic Rural Life Conference, 1937.
Catholic School Journal. 1901–70.
The Catholic World. 1865–1971.
Central-Blatt and Social Justice. 1909–40.
The Commonweal. 1924–.
Country Life Bulletin. 1923–24.
Elder, Mary Theresa. "Pauperism: The Cause and the Remedy." In *Progress of the Catholic Church in America and the Great Columbian Catholic Congress of 1893*, 4th ed., compiled by J. S. Hyland, 2:179–83. Chicago: J. S. Hyland, 1897.
Ellis, John Tracy, ed. *Documents of American Catholic History*. Milwaukee: Bruce Publishing, 1956.
Free America. 1937–47.
Gilson, Etienne, ed. *The Church Speaks to the Modern World: The Social Teachings of Leo XIII*. Garden City, N.Y.: Image Books, 1954.
Gremillion, Joseph, ed. *The Gospel of Peace and Justice: Catholic Social Teaching since Pope John*. Maryknoll, N.Y.: Orbis Books, 1976.
Harrington, Jeremiah C. *Catholicism, Capitalism, or Communism*. St. Paul, Minn.: E. M. Lohmann, 1925.
Heyde, Joseph. "The Country Church and Community Life." In *Second Wisconsin Country Life Conference, February, 1912*, 25–28. Bulletin of the University of

Bibliography

Wisconsin, serial no. 509; General Series no. 342. Madison, Wisc.: College of Agriculture, [1912].

Homiletic and Pastoral Review. 1900–.

Huber, Raphael M., ed. *Our Bishops Speak. National Pastorals and Annual Statements of the Hierarchy of the United States. Resolutions of Episcopal Committees and Communications of the Administrative Board of the National Catholic Welfare Conference.* Milwaukee: Bruce Publishing, 1952.

Husslein, Joseph. *The World Problem: Capital, Labor, and the Church.* New York: P. J. Kenedy & Sons, 1918.

———, ed. *Social Wellsprings.* Vol. 2: *Eighteen Encyclicals of Social Reconstruction by Pope Pius XI.* Milwaukee: Bruce Publishing, 1942.

Ireland, John. *The Church and Modern Society: Lectures and Addresses*, 2 vols. New York: D. H. McBride, 1903.

Kelley, Francis Clement. *Blood-Drenched Altars.* Milwaukee: Bruce Publishing, 1935.

———. *The Story of Extension.* Chicago: Extension Press, 1922.

———, ed. *The First American Catholic Missionary Congress.* Chicago: J. S. Hyland, 1909.

Kramer, A. Ph. "The Genoa Parish, Walworth County." In *Rural Social Development: Being the Third Annual Report of the Wisconsin Country Life Conference, January, 1913,* edited by Joseph Galpin, 46–48. Bulletin of the University of Wisconsin, serial no. 591; General Series no. 413. Madison, Wisc.: College of Agriculture, [1913].

La Farge, John. *The Manner Is Ordinary.* New York: Harcourt, Brace, 1954.

Ligutti, Luigi G., and Rawe, John C. *Rural Roads to Security: America's Third Struggle for Freedom.* Milwaukee: Bruce Publishing, 1940.

Lindstrom, David Edgar. *Rural Life and the Church.* Champaign, Ill.: Garrard Press, 1946.

Messmer, Sebastian G. "Some Moral Aspects of Country Life." In *Rural Social Development: Being the Third Annual Report of the Wisconsin Country Life Conference, January, 1913,* edited by Joseph Galpin, 38–46. Bulletin of the University of Wiscosnsin, serial no. 591; General Series no. 413. Madison, Wisc.: College of Agriculture, [1913].

Michel, Virgil. *Christian Reconstruction: Some Fundamentals of the Quadragesimo Anno.* Milwaukee: Bruce Publishing, 1937.

Michigan Catholic. 1883–.

Milwaukee *Catholic Herald Citizen.* 1869–.

The Modern Schoolman. 1925–.

[National Catholic Rural Life Conference]. *Justice in the Global Food System: A Faith Perspective on Food Security.* Des Moines, Iowa: National Catholic Rural Life Conference, 1997.

———. *Manifesto on Rural Life.* Milwaukee: Bruce Publishing, 1939.

———. *Proceedings of the Twelfth Annual Convention.* St. Paul, Minn.: National Catholic Rural Life Conference, 1934.

National Catholic War Council. Committee on Special War Activities. *Reconstruction Pamphlets,* nos. 1–13. Washington, D.C.: National Catholic War Council,

[1919–20]. Particularly no. 1, *Bishops' Program of Reconstruction;* no. 2, *Land Colonization;* and no. 12, *Cooperation among Farmers and Consumers.*

National Catholic War Council Bulletin. 1919–20.

National Catholic Welfare Conference. *Annual Reports, 1940, Department of Social Action.* Washington, D.C.: Administrative Board, n.d.

———. *Annual Reports, 1941, Department of Social Action.* Washington, D.C.: Administrative Board, n.d.

National Catholic Welfare Council Bulletin. 1920–1922.

National Conference of Catholic Bishops. *Economic Justice for All: Pastoral Letter on Catholic Social Teaching and the U.S. Economy.* Washington, D.C.: National Conference of Catholic Bishops, 1986.

N.C.W.C. Bulletin. 1922–29.

NCWC News Service. 1920–. Microfilm edition. Includes *NCWC News Sheet* and *NCWC Editorial Sheet.*

N.C.W.C. Review. 1930–31.

Nelson, Jack A. *Hunger for Justice: The Politics of Food and Faith.* Maryknoll, N.Y.: Orbis Books, 1980.

The Official Catholic Directory. New York: P. J. Kenedy & Sons, 1886–.

O'Hara, Edwin V. "Catholic Rural Extension Education." *Report of the Proceedings and Addresses of the Eighteenth Annual Meeting. The Catholic Educational Association Bulletin* 18 (November 1921): 273–75.

———. *The Church and the Country Community.* New York: Macmillan, 1927.

———. "The Family and Private Ownership." In *Needed Readjustments in Rural Life, Proceedings of the Eighth National Country Life Conference, Richmond, Virginia, 1925,* 132–35. Chicago: Published by the University of Chicago Press for the American Country Life Association, 1926.

———. *A Program of Catholic Rural Action.* N.p.: Rural Life Bureau, Social Action Department, National Catholic Welfare Conference, 1922.

———. "The Rural Problem in Its Bearing on Catholic Education." *The Catholic Educational Association Bulletin* 17 (February 1921): 176, 232–45.

———. "A Rural Religious Program as Viewed by a Catholic." In *Religion in Country Life, Proceedings of the Seventh National Country Life Conference, Columbus, Ohio, 1924,* 49–53. Chicago: Published by the University of Chicago Press for the American Country Life Association, 1925.

O'Rourke, Edward W. *Self-help Works.* New York: Paulist Press, 1978.

Preuss, Arthur. *The Fundamental Fallacy of Socialism: An Exposition of the Question of Land Ownership, Comprising an Authentic Account of the Famous McGlynn Case.* St. Louis, Mo.: B. Herder, 1908.

The Queen's Work. 1914–.

Ross, J. Elliot. *Cooperative Plenty.* St. Louis, Mo.: B. Herder, 1941.

Rural America. 1924–41.

Ryan, John A. *Distributive Justice: The Right and Wrong of Our Present Distribution of Wealth,* new rev. ed. New York: Macmillan, 1927.

———. *A Living Wage.* New York: Macmillan, 1906.

———. *Social Doctrine in Action: A Personal History.* New York: Harper & Bros., 1941.

Bibliography

Schlarman, Joseph H. *Mexico—A Land of Volcanoes*. Milwaukee: Bruce Publishing, 1950.

Schmiedeler, Edgar. *A Better Rural Life*. New York: J. F. Wagner, 1938.

———. *Cooperation: A Christian Mode of Industry*. Ozone Park, N.Y.: Catholic Literary Guild, 1941.

Shaughnessy, Gerald. *Has the Immigrant Kept the Faith? A Study of Immigration and Catholic Growth in the United States, 1790–1920*. New York: Macmillan, 1925.

Spalding, John Lancaster. *Essays and Reviews*. New York: Catholic Publication Society, 1877.

———. *The Religious Mission of the Irish People and Catholic Colonization*. New York: Catholic Colonization Society, 1880.

Speltz, George H. *The Importance of Rural Life According to the Philosophy of St. Thomas Aquinas: A Study in Economic Philosophy*. Washington, D.C.: The Catholic University of America Press, 1945.

Thebaud, Augustus J. *Forty Years in the United States of America (1839–1885)*. 2 vols. U.S.C.H.S. Monograph Series 2. New York: United States Catholic Historical Society, 1904.

U.S. Bureau of the Census. *Historical Statistics of the United States to 1970*. Washington, D.C.: Government Printing Office, 1975.

U.S. Commission on Country Life. *Report of the Commission on Country Life*. S. Doc. 705, 60th Cong., 2nd Sess., 1909. Washington, D.C.: Government Printing Office, 1909; reprint ed., Chapel Hill: University of North Carolina Press, 1944.

U.S. Congress. House. Hearings before the Select Committee of the House Committee on Agriculture to Investigate the Activities of the Farm Security Administration. 78th Cong., 1st Sess., Part II, 1943.

———. Hearings before the Subcommittee of the Committee on Appropriations on the Agriculture Department Appropriation Bill for 1943. 77th Cong., 2nd Sess., Part II, 1942.

U.S. Congress. Senate. Hearings before the Subcommittee of the Committee on Appropriations, Agricultural Appropriations Bill for 1943. 77th Cong., 2nd Sess., 1942.

U.S. Department of Commerce. Bureau of the Census. *Abstract of the Fourteenth Census of the United States: 1920*. Washington, D.C.: Government Printing Office, 1923.

———. *Fourteenth Census of the United States Taken in the Year 1920*. Vol. 2: *Population, 1920*. Washington, D.C.: Government Printing Office, 1922.

———. *Religious Bodies: 1906*. 2 vols. Washington, D.C.: Government Printing Office, 1909.

———. *Religious Bodies: 1916*. 2 vols. Washington, D.C.: Government Printing Office, 1919.

———. *Religious Bodies: 1926*. 2 vols. Washington, D.C.: Government Printing Office, 1930.

———. *Religious Bodies: 1936*. 2 vols. (2nd vol. in 2 parts). Washington, D.C.: Government Printing Office, 1941.

———. *Statistical Abstract of the United States: 1985.* 105th ed. Washington, D.C.: Government Printing Office, 1984.

U.S. Immigration Commission, 1907–10. William P. Dillingham, Chairman. *Reports of the Immigration Commission.* Senate documents of the 61st Cong., 2nd and 3rd Sess., 1911. 41 vols. Washington, D.C.: Government Printing Office, 1911.

Vizzard, James L. "The Extraordinary Cesar Chavez." *Progressive* 30 (July 1966): 16–20.

———. "The Long March of the Migrants." *Jubilee* 15 (May 1967): 36–40.

Ward, Leo R. *Ourselves, Inc.: The Story of Consumer Free Enterprise.* New York: Harper & Bros., 1945.

———, ed. *United for Freedom: Co-Operatives and Christian Democracy.* Milwaukee: Bruce Publishing, 1945.

Witte, Raymond Philip. *Twenty-five Years of Crusading: A History of the National Catholic Rural Life Conference.* Des Moines, Iowa: National Catholic Rural Life Conference, 1948.

Secondary Sources

Abel, Theodore B. *Protestant Home Missions to Catholic Immigrants.* New York: Institute of Social and Religious Research, 1933.

Abell, Aaron I. *American Catholicism and Social Action: A Search for Social Justice, 1865–1950.* Garden City, N.Y.: Hanover House, 1960.

———. "The Reception of Leo XIII's Labor Encyclical in America, 1891–1919." *Review of Politics* 7 (October 1945): 464–95.

Adams, William Forbes. *Ireland and the Irish Emigration to the New World from 1815 to the Famine.* New Haven, Conn.: Yale University Press, 1932.

Allitt, Patrick. "American Catholics and the Environment, 1960–1995." *Catholic Historical Review* 84 (April 1998): 263–81.

Anderson, Clifford B. "The Metamorphosis of American Agrarian Idealism in the 1920's and 1930's." *Agricultural History* 35 (October 1961): 182–88.

Baldwin, Sidney. *Poverty and Politics: The Rise and Decline of the Farm Security Administration.* Chapel Hill: University of North Carolina Press, 1968.

Barry, Colman J. *The Catholic Church and German Americans.* Milwaukee: Bruce Publishing, 1953.

Barton, Josef J. "Land, Labor, and Community in Nueces: Czech Farmers and Mexican Laborers in South Texas, 1880–1930." In *European Immigrants in the American West: Community Histories,* edited by Frederick C. Luebke, 147–60. Albuquerque: University of New Mexico Press, 1998.

Baudier, Roger. *The Catholic Church in Louisiana.* New Orleans: Roger Baudier, 1939.

Becker, Martin Joseph. *A History of Catholic Life in the Diocese of Albany, 1609–1864.* U.S.C.H.S. Monograph Series 31. New York: United States Catholic Historical Society, 1975.

Bell, Stephen. *Rebel, Priest, and Prophet: A Biography of Dr. Edward McGlynn.* New York: Devin-Adair, 1937.

Benedict, Murray R. *Farm Policies of the United States, 1790–1950: A Study of Their Origins and Development.* New York: Twentieth Century Fund, 1953.

Bibliography

Bennett, David H. *Demagogues in the Depression: American Radicals and the Union Party.* New Brunswick, N.J.: Rutgers University Press, 1969.

Berthoff, Rowland T. "Southern Attitudes toward Immigration, 1865–1914." *Journal of Southern History* 17 (August 1951): 328–60.

Billington, Ray Allen. *The Protestant Crusade, 1800–1860: A Study in the Origins of American Nativism.* New York: Macmillan, 1938.

Bovée, David Steven. "The Church and the Land: The National Catholic Rural Life Conference and American Society, 1923–1985." PhD diss., University of Chicago, 1986.

Bowers, William L. *The Country-Life Movement in America, 1900–1920.* Port Washington, N.Y.: Kennikat Press, 1974.

Boyer, Paul. *Urban Masses and Moral Order in America, 1820–1920.* Cambridge, Mass.: Harvard University Press, 1978.

Bradley, Cyprian, and Edward J. Kelly. *History of the Diocese of Boise, 1863–1952.* 2 vols. Boise, Idaho: Diocese of Boise, 1953.

Broderick, Francis L. *Right Reverend New Dealer, John A. Ryan.* New York: Macmillan, 1963.

Brown, Alden V. *The Grail Movement and American Catholicism, 1940–1975.* Notre Dame, Ind.: University of Notre Dame Press, 1989.

Browne, Henry J. "Archbishop Hughes and Western Colonization." *Catholic Historical Review* 26 (October 1950): 257–85.

———. *The Catholic Church and the Knights of Labor.* Washington, D.C.: The Catholic University of America Press, 1949.

Browne, William P. *The Failure of National Rural Policy: Institutions and Interests.* Washington, D.C.: Georgetown University Press, 2001.

Brunner, Edmund de S. *Immigrant Farmers and Their Children.* Garden City, N.Y.: Doubleday, Doran, 1929.

Burns, J. A. *The Growth and Development of the Catholic School System in the United States.* New York: Benziger Brothers, 1911.

Butler, Anne M., Michael E. Engh, and Thomas W. Spalding, eds. *The Frontiers and Catholic Identities.* Maryknoll, N.Y.: Orbis Books, 1999.

Čapek, Thomas. *The Čechs (Bohemians) in America.* Boston: Houghton Mifflin, 1920.

Carlson, Allan. *The New Agrarian Mind: The Movement toward Decentralist Thought in Twentieth-Century America.* New Brunswick, N.J.: Transaction Publishers, 2000.

Casper, Henry W. *History of the Catholic Church in Nebraska.* Vol. 1: *The Church on the Northern Plains, 1838–1874.* Vol. 2: *The Church on the Fading Frontier, 1864–1910.* Vol. 3: *Catholic Chapters in Nebraska Immigration, 1870–1900.* Milwaukee: Catholic Life Publications, Bruce Publishing, 1960, 1966, 1966.

Clark, Dennis. *Hibernia America: The Irish and Regional Cultures.* Contributions in Ethnic Studies 14. Westport, Conn.: Greenwood Press, 1986.

The Confraternity Comes of Age: A Historical Symposium. Paterson, N.J.: Confraternity Publications, 1956.

Conkin, Paul K. *Tomorrow a New World: The New Deal Community Program.* Ithaca, N.Y.: Cornell University Press, 1959.

Conmy, Peter Thomas. "Catholicism along the Gold Dust Trails." In *Some California Catholic Reminiscences for the United States Bicentennial,* edited by Francis J. Weber, 107–15. [Los Angeles?]: Published for the California Catholic Conference by the Knights of Columbus, 1976.

Conzen, Kathleen Neils. "Peasant Pioneers. Generational Succession among German Farmers in Frontier Minnesota." In *The Countryside in the Age of Capitalist Transformations: Essays in the Social History of Rural America,* edited by Steven Hahn and Jonathan Prude. Chapel Hill: University of North Carolina Press, 1985.

Corrin, Jay P. *G. K. Chesterton and Hilaire Belloc: The Battle against Modernity.* Athens: Ohio University Press, 1981.

Cox, Gerald F. *The Radical Peasant.* Victoria, B.C.: Trafford Publishing, 2006.

Crisler, Shirley, and Mira Mosle. *In the Midst of His People: The Authorized Biography of Bishop Maurice J. Dingman.* Iowa City: Rudi Publishing, 1995.

Cross, Robert D. "The Changing Image of the City among American Catholics." *Catholic Historical Review* 48 (April 1962): 33–52.

———. *The Emergence of Liberal Catholicism in America.* Cambridge, Mass.: Harvard University Press, 1958.

Curti, Merle E., et al. *The Making of an American Community: A Case Study of Democracy in a Frontier County.* Stanford, Calif.: Stanford University Press, 1959.

Danbom, David. *Born in the Country: A History of Rural America.* Baltimore: Johns Hopkins University Press, 1995.

———. *The Resisted Revolution: Urban America and the Industrialization of Agriculture, 1900–1930.* Ames: Iowa State University Press, 1979.

Davidson, Osha Gray. *Broken Heartland: The Rise of America's Rural Ghetto.* Iowa City: University of Iowa Press, 1996.

Davis, Lawrence B. *Immigrants, Baptists, and the Protestant Mind in America.* Urbana: University of Illinois Press, [1973].

Desmond, Humphrey J. *The A.P.A. Movement.* Washington, D.C.: New Century Press, 1912; reprint ed., New York: Arno Press and *New York Times,* 1969.

Dolan, Jay P. *In Search of an American Catholicism: A History of Religion and Culture in Tension.* Oxford: Oxford University Press, 2002.

Dolan, Jay P., and Gilberto M. Hinojosa, eds. *Mexican Americans and the Catholic Church, 1900–1965.* Notre Dame, Ind.: University of Notre Dame Press, 1994.

Dolan, Timothy Michael. *"Some Seed Fell on Good Ground": The Life of Edwin V. O'Hara.* Washington, D.C.: The Catholic University of America Press, 1992.

Donohoe, Joan Marie. *The Irish Catholic Benevolent Union.* Washington, D.C.: The Catholic University of America Press, 1953.

Douglas, Louis H., ed. *Agrarianism in American History.* Lexington, Mass.: D.C. Heath, 1969.

Doyle, Don Harrison. *The Social Order of a Frontier Community: Jacksonville, Illinois, 1825–70.* Urbana: University of Illinois Press, 1978.

Dudley, Kathryn Marie. *Debt and Dispossession: Farm Loss in America's Heartland.* Chicago: University of Chicago Press, 2000.

Bibliography

Dumenil, Lynn. "The Tribal Twenties: 'Assimilated' Catholics' Response to Anti-Catholicism in the 1920s." *Journal of American Ethnic History* 11 (Fall 1991): 21–49.

Duratschek, M. Claudia. *The Beginnings of Catholicism in South Dakota.* Washington, D.C.: The Catholic University of America Press, 1943.

Dyrud, Keith P., Michael Novak, and Rudolph J. Vecoli selected and introduced by. *The Other Catholics.* New York: Arno Press, 1978.

Ellis, John Tracy. *American Catholicism.* 2nd ed. Chicago: University of Chicago Press, 1969.

———. *The Life of James Cardinal Gibbons, 1834–1921.* 2 vols. Milwaukee: Bruce Publishing, 1952.

Faragher, John Mack. *Sugar Creek: Life on the Illinois Prairie.* New Haven, Conn.: Yale University Press, 1986.

Finke, Roger, and Rodney Stark. *The Churching of America, 1776–1990: Winners and Losers in Our Religious Economy.* New Brunswick, N.J.: Rutgers University Press, 1992.

Fite, Gilbert C. *American Farmers: The New Minority.* Bloomington: Indiana University Press, 1981.

———. *George N. Peek and the Fight for Farm Parity.* Norman: University of Oklahoma Press, 1954.

Flynn, George Q. *American Catholics and the Roosevelt Presidency, 1932–1936.* Lexington: University of Kentucky Press, 1968.

Foerster, Robert F. *The Italian Immigration of Our Times.* Cambridge, Mass.: Harvard University Press, 1924.

Folsom, Paul. "Rural Ministry—A Response to Change. What Has Happened to the Church on Main Street, U.S.A.?" 2 vols. Doctorate of Ministry Pastoral Project, Aquinas Institute of Theology, Dubuque, Iowa, May, 1976.

Friedberger, Mark. *Farm Families and Change in 20th Century America.* Lexington: University Press of Kentucky, 1988.

———. *Shake-out: Iowa Farm Families in the 1980s.* Lexington: University Press of Kentucky, 1989.

Gaffey, James P. *Francis Clement Kelley and the American Catholic Dream.* 2 vols. Bensenville, Ill.: Heritage Foundation, 1980.

Gardner, Bruce. Review of *Problems of Plenty: The American Farmer in the Twentieth Century* by R. Douglas Hurt. *American Historical Review* 108 (June 2003): 856.

Gillard, John T. *The Catholic Church and the American Negro.* Baltimore: St. Joseph's Society Press, 1929; reprint ed., New York: Johnson Reprint Corp., 1968.

———. *Colored Catholics in the United States.* Baltimore: Josephite Press, 1941.

Gjerde, Jon. *The Minds of the West: Ethnocultural Evolution in the Rural Middle West, 1830–1917.* Chapel Hill: University of North Carolina Press, 1997.

Gleason, Philip. *The Conservative Reformers: German-American Catholics and the Social Order.* Notre Dame, Ind.: University of Notre Dame Press, 1968.

———. *Contending with Modernity: Catholic Higher Education in the Twentieth Century.* New York: Oxford University Press, 1995.

———, ed. *Catholicism in America*. New York: Harper & Row, 1970.

———, ed. *Contemporary Catholicism in the United States*. Notre Dame, Ind.: University of Notre Dame Press, 1969.

Gleeson, David T. *The Irish in the South, 1815–1877*. Chapel Hill: University of North Carolina Press, 2001.

Goldman, Eric F. *Rendezvous with Destiny: A History of Modern American Reform*. New York: Vintage Books, Random House, 1952.

Grebler, Leo, et al. *The Mexican-American People: The Nation's Second Largest Minority*. New York: Free Press, 1970.

Greeley, Andrew M. *The Catholic Experience*. Garden City, N.Y.: Doubleday, 1967.

Griswold, A. Whitney. *Farming and Democracy*. New York: Harcourt, Brace, 1948.

Grueningen, John Paul von. *The Swiss in the United States*. Madison, Wisc.: Swiss-American Historical Society, 1940.

Guither, Harold D. *The Food Lobbyists: Behind the Scenes of Food and Agri-politics*. Lexington, Mass.: Lexington Books, 1980.

Hales, Edward E. Y. *Pope John and His Revolution*. Garden City, N.Y.: Doubleday, 1965.

Halsey, William M. *The Survival of American Innocence: American Catholicism in an Era of Disillusionment, 1920–1940*. Notre Dame, Ind.: University of Notre Dame Press, 1980.

Hamilton, David E. "Herbert Hoover and the Great Drought of 1930." *Journal of American History* 68 (March 1982): 850–75.

Hamlin, Christopher, and John T. McGreevy. "The Greening of America, Catholic Style, 1930–1950." *Environmental History* 11 (July 2006): 464–99.

Handlin, Oscar. *Al Smith and His America*. Boston: Little, Brown, 1958.

———. *Race and Nationality in American Life*. Garden City, N.Y.: Doubleday Anchor Books, 1957.

———. *The Uprooted: The Epic Story of the Great Migration That Made the American People*. New York: Grosset & Dunlap, 1951.

Harl, Neil E. *The Farm Debt Crisis of the 1980s*. Ames: Iowa State University Press, 1990.

Hassard, John R. G. *Life of the Most Reverend John Hughes, D.D., First Archbishop of New York*. New York: D. Appleton, 1866; reprint ed., New York: Arno Press and *New York Times*, 1969.

Hawgood, John A. *The Tragedy of German-America: The Germans in the United States of America during the Nineteenth Century—and After*. New York: G. P. Putnam's Sons, 1940.

Hays, Samuel P. *The Response to Industrialism, 1885–1914*. Chicago: University of Chicago Press, 1957.

Henthorne, Mary Evangela. *The Irish Catholic Colonization Association of the United States*. Champaign, Ill.: Twin City Printing, 1932.

Herberg, Will. *Protestant, Catholic, Jew: An Essay in American Religious Sociology*, rev. 2nd ed., Garden City, N.Y.: Anchor Books, 1960.

Hicks, John D. *The Populist Revolt: A History of the Farmers' Alliance and the People's Party*. Minneapolis: University of Minnesota Press, 1931.

Bibliography

Higham, John. *Strangers in the Land: Patterns of American Nativism, 1860–1925.* New Brunswick, N.J.: Rutgers University Press, 1955.

Hoffmann, M. M. *The Church Founders of the Northwest: Loras and Cretin and Other Captains of Christ.* Milwaukee: Bruce Publishing, 1937.

Hofstadter, Richard. *The Age of Reform: From Bryan to F.D.R.* New York: Vintage Books, Random House, 1955.

Hoglund, A. William. "Wisconsin Dairy Farmers on Strike." *Agricultural History* 35 (January 1961): 24–34.

Horgan, Paul. *Lamy of Santa Fe: His Life and Times.* New York: Farrar, Straus & Giroux, 1975.

Hurt, R. Douglas. *Problems of Plenty: The American Farmer in the Twentieth Century.* The American Ways Series. Chicago: Ivan R. Dee, 2002.

Issel, William H. "Ralph Borsodi and the Agrarian Response to Modern America." *Agricultural History* 41 (April 1967): 155–66.

Jensen, Richard J. *The Winning of the Midwest: Social and Political Conflict, 1888–1896.* Chicago: University of Chicago Press, 1971.

Jones, Maldwyn Allen. *American Immigration.* Chicago: University of Chicago Press, 1960.

Jordan, Terry G. *German Seed in Texas Soil: Immigrant Farmers in Nineteenth-century Texas.* Austin: University of Texas Press, 1966.

Kauffman, Christopher J. *Mission to Rural America: The Story of W. Howard Bishop, Founder of Glenmary.* New York: Paulist Press, 1991.

Keely, Charles B. "Current Status of U.S. Immigration and Refugee Policy." In *U.S. Immigration and Refugee Policy: Global and Domestic Issues,* edited by Mary M. Kritz. Lexington, Mass.: Lexington Books, 1983.

Keenan, Marjorie. *From Stockholm to Johannesburg: An Historical Overview of the Concern of the Holy See for the Environment, 1972–2002.* Vatican City: Pontifical Council for Justice and Peace, 2002.

Kelly, Mary Gilbert. *Catholic Immigrant Colonization Projects in the United States, 1815–1860.* New York: United States Catholic Historical Society, 1939.

Kinzer, Donald L. *An Episode in Anti-Catholicism: The American Protective Association.* Seattle: University of Washington Press, 1964.

Kirschner, Don S. *City and Country: Rural Responses to Urbanization in the 1920s.* Westport, Conn.: Greenwood, 1970.

Kleppner, Paul. *The Cross of Culture: A Social Analysis of Midwestern Politics, 1850–1900,* 2nd ed. New York: Free Press, 1970.

Knapp, Joseph G. *The Advance of American Cooperative Enterprise, 1920–1945.* Danville, Ill.: Interstate Printers and Publishers, 1973.

———. *The Rise of American Cooperative Enterprise, 1620–1920.* Danville, Ill.: Interstate Printers and Publishers, 1969.

The Knights of Columbus of Texas. *Our Catholic Heritage in Texas, 1519–1936.* Vol. 7: *The Church in Texas Since Independence, 1958; Supplement, 1936–1950,* by Carlos E. Castaneda, edited by James P. Gibbons and William H. Oberste. Austin, Tex.: Von Boeckman-Jones, 1936–58.

Lernoux, Penny. *Cry of the People: United States Involvement in the Rise of Fascism,*

Torture, and Murder and the Persecution of the Catholic Church in Latin America. Garden City, N.Y.: Doubleday, 1980.

Leuchtenberg, William E. *Franklin D. Roosevelt and the New Deal.* New York: Harper & Bros., 1963.

Levine, Herman J., and Benjamin Miller. *The American Jewish Farmer in Changing Times.* New York: Jewish Agricultural Society, 1966.

Levy, Jacques E. *Cesar Chavez: Autobiography of La Causa.* New York: W. W. Norton, 1975.

Lindert, Peter H. *Fertility and Scarcity in America.* Princeton, N.J.: Princeton University Press, 1978.

Linkh, Richard M. *American Catholicism and European Immigrants, 1900–1924.* Staten Island, N.Y.: Center for Migration Studies, 1975.

Lord, Robert H., John E. Sexton, and Edward T. Harrington. *History of the Archdiocese of Boston in the Various Stages of Its Development, 1604 to 1943.* 3 vols. New York: Sheed & Ward, 1944.

Lord, Russell, and Paul H. Johnstone, eds. *A Place on Earth: A Critical Appraisal of Subsistence Homesteads.* Washington, D.C.: U.S. Bureau of Agricultural Economics, 1942.

Lubell, Samuel. *The Future of American Politics,* rev. 2nd ed., Garden City, N.Y.: Doubleday, 1956.

Luebke, Frederick C. "Ethnic Group Settlement on the Great Plains." In *The American West: Interactions, Intersections, and Injunctions.* Vol. 5: *The Urban West,* edited by Gordon Morris Bakken and Brenda Farrington, 149–74. New York: Garland Publishing, 2000.

———. *Immigrants and Politics: The Germans of Nebraska, 1880–1900.* Lincoln: University of Nebraska Press, 1969.

———, ed. *Ethnicity on the Great Plains.* Lincoln: Published by the University of Nebraska Press for the Center for Great Plains Studies, University of Nebraska—Lincoln, 1980.

Macdonald, Fergus. *The Catholic Church and the Secret Societies in the United States.* New York: United States Catholic Historical Society, 1946.

Madison, James H. "Reformers and the Rural Church, 1900–1950." *Journal of American History* 73 (December 1986): 645–68.

Marlett, Jeffrey D. *Saving the Heartland: Catholic Missionaries in Rural America, 1920–1960.* DeKalb: Northern Illinois University Press, 2002.

Marx, Paul B. *Virgil Michel and the Liturgical Movement.* Collegeville, Minn.: Liturgical Press, 1957.

Maynard, Theodore. *The Story of American Catholicism.* New York: Macmillan, 1941.

McAvoy, Thomas T. *A History of the Catholic Church in the United States.* Notre Dame, Ind.: University of Notre Dame Press, 1969.

McConnell, Grant. *The Decline of Agrarian Democracy.* Berkeley: University of California Press, 1953.

McDonough, Peter. *Men Astutely Trained: A History of the Jesuits in the American Century.* New York: The Free Press, 1992.

Bibliography

McElvaine, Robert S. *The Great Depression: America, 1929–1941*. New York: Times Books, 1993.

McKeown, Elizabeth. "War and Welfare: A Study of American Catholic Leadership." Ph.D. diss., University of Chicago, 1972.

McShane, Joseph M. *"Sufficiently Radical": Catholicism, Progressivism, and the Bishops' Program of 1919*. Washington, D.C.: The Catholic University of America Press, 1986.

Merchant, Carolyn. *The Columbia Guide to American Environmental History*. New York: Columbia University Press, 2002.

Miller, Randall M., and Jon L. Wakelyn, eds. *Catholics in the Old South: Essays on Church and Culture*. Macon, Ga.: Mercer University Press, 1983.

Miller, Raymond W. *Monsignor Ligutti: The Pope's County Agent*. Washington, D.C.: University Press of America, 1981.

Miller, William D. *A Harsh and Dreadful Love: Dorothy Day and the Catholic Worker Movement*. New York: Liveright, 1973.

Moloney, Deirdre M. *American Catholic Lay Groups and Transatlantic Social Reform in the Progressive Era*. Chapel Hill: University of North Carolina Press, 2002.

Moody, Joseph N., ed. *Church and Society: Catholic Social and Political Thought and Movements, 1789–1950*. New York: Arts, Inc., 1953.

Moody, Joseph N., and Justus George Lawler, eds. *The Challenge of Mater et Magistra*. New York: Herder & Herder, 1963.

Moore, Edmund A. *A Catholic Runs for President: The Campaign of 1928*. New York: Ronald Press, 1956.

Moore, R. Laurence. *Religious Outsiders and the Making of Americans*. New York: Oxford University Press, 1986.

Moynihan, James H. *The Life of Archbishop John Ireland*. New York: Harper & Brothers, 1953.

Nelson, Paula M. *After the West Was Won: Homesteaders and Town-builders in Western South Dakota, 1900–1917*. Iowa City: University of Iowa Press, 1986.

Nolan, Hugh J. *The Most Reverend Francis Patrick Kenrick, Third Bishop of Philadelphia, 1830–1851*. Philadelphia: American Catholic Historical Society of Philadelphia, 1948.

New Catholic Encyclopedia. 15 vols. New York: McGraw-Hill, 1967.

Nuesse, Celestine J. *The Social Thought of American Catholics, 1634–1829*. Washington, D.C.: The Catholic University of America Press, 1945.

O'Brien, David J. *American Catholics and Social Reform: The New Deal Years*. New York: Oxford University Press, 1968.

———. *The Renewal of American Catholicism*. New York: Oxford University Press, 1972.

O'Connor, Dominic. *A Brief History of the Diocese of Baker City*. Baker, Ore.: Diocesan Chancery, 1930.

O'Hara, Joseph M. *Chester's Century of Catholicism, 1842–1942*. Philadelphia: Peter Reilly, 1942.

Osborne, William A. *The Segregated Covenant: Race Relations and American Catholics*. New York: Herder & Herder, 1967.

Owens, Meroe J. "John Barzynski, Land Agent." *Nebraska History* 36 (June 1955): 81–91.

Putz, L. J., ed. *Catholic Church, U.S.A.* Chicago: Fides Publishers, 1956.

Rich, Mark. *The Rural Church Movement.* Columbia, Mo.: Juniper Knoll Press, 1957.

Rolle, Andrew F. *The Immigrant Upraised: Italian Adventures and Colonists in an Expanding America.* Norman: University of Oklahoma Press, 1968.

Rothsteiner, John. *History of the Archdiocese of St. Louis in Its Various Stages of Development from A.D. 1673 to A.D. 1928.* 2 vols. St. Louis, Mo.: Blackwell Weilandy, 1928.

Salamon, Sonya. *Prairie Patrimony: Family, Farming and Community in the Midwest.* Chapel Hill: University of North Carolina Press, 1992.

Saloutos, Theodore, and John D. Hicks. *Agricultural Discontent in the Middle West, 1900–1939.* Madison: University of Wisconsin Press, 1951.

Santen, Herman W. *Father Bishop, Founder of the Glenmary Home Missioners.* Milwaukee: Bruce Publishing, 1961.

Savage, Robert. "Irish Colonists on the Plains." In *The American Irish Revival: A Decade of The Recorder—1974–1983,* edited by Kevin M. Cahill, 371–81. Port Washington, N.Y.: Associated Faculty Press, 1984.

Scarpaci, Jean Anne. "Immigrants in the New South: Italians in Louisiana's Sugar Parishes, 1880–1910." In *Studies in Italian-American Social History: Essays in Honor of Leonard Covello,* edited by Francesco Cordasco, 132–52. Totowa, N.J.: Rowman and Littlefield, 1975.

Schafer, Joseph. *The Social History of American Agriculture.* New York: Macmillan, 1936.

Schlereth, Thomas J. *The University of Notre Dame: A Portrait of Its History and Campus.* Notre Dame, Ind.: University of Notre Dame Press, 1976.

Schlesinger, Arthur M. *The Age of Roosevelt.* Vol. 1: *The Crisis of the Old Order.* Vol. 2: *The Coming of the New Deal.* Boston: Houghton Mifflin, 1957, 1959.

Schneider, Mary L. "Visions of Land and Farmer: American Civil Religion and the National Catholic Rural Life Conference." In *An American Church: Essays in the Americanization of the Catholic Church,* edited by David J. Alvarez, 99–112. Moraga, Calif.: Saint Mary's College of California, 1979.

Schuck, Michael J. *That They Be One: The Social Teaching of the Papal Encyclicals, 1740–1989.* Washington, D.C.: Georgetown University Press, 1991.

Shannon, James P. *Catholic Colonization on the Western Frontier.* Yale Publications in American Studies, vol. 1. New Haven, Conn.: Yale University Press, 1957.

Shapiro, Edward S. "Catholic Agrarian Thought and the New Deal." *Catholic Historical Review* 65 (October 1979): 583–99.

———. "The Catholic Rural Life Movement and the New Deal Farm Program." *American Benedictine Review* 28 (September 1977): 307–32.

———. "Decentralist Intellectuals and the New Deal." *Journal of American History* 58 (March 1972): 938–57.

Shaw, James Gerard. *Edwin Vincent O'Hara, American Prelate.* New York: Farrar, Straus, & Cudahy, 1957.

Shi, David. *The Simple Life: Plain Living and High Thinking in American Culture.* New York: Oxford University Press, 1985.

Shidler, James. *Farm Crisis, 1919–1923.* Berkeley: University of California Press, 1957.

———. "*Flappers and Philosophers* and Farmers: Rural-Urban Tensions of the Twenties." *Agricultural History* 47 (October 1973): 283–99.

Shover, John L. *Cornbelt Rebellion: The Farmers' Holiday Association.* Urbana: University of Illinois Press, 1965.

Slawson, Douglas J. *The Foundation and First Decade of the National Catholic Welfare Council.* Washington, D.C.: The Catholic University of America Press, 1992.

Smith, T. Lynn, and Paul E. Zopf. *Principles of Inductive Rural Sociology.* Philadelphia: F. A. Davis, 1970.

Soderini, Eduardo. *The Pontificate of Leo XIII.* Translated by Barbara Barclay Carter. 2 vols. London: Burns, Oates & Washbourne, 1934.

Southern, David W. *John La Farge and the Limits of Catholic Interracialism, 1911–1963.* Baton Rouge: Louisiana State University Press, 1996.

Speek, Peter A. *A Stake in the Land.* Americanization Studies. New York: Harper & Bros., 1921.

Swanson, Merwin. "The 'Country Life Movement' and the American Churches." *Church History* 45 (September 1977): 358–73.

Swierenga, Robert P. "Ethnicity and American Agriculture." *Ohio History* 89 (Summer 1980): 323–44.

Taylor, Mary Christine. *A History of the Foundations of Catholicism in Northern New York.* U.S.C.H.S. Monograph Series 32. New York: United States Catholic Historical Society, 1976.

Tentler, Leslie Woodcock. "'A Model Rural Parish': Priests and People in the Michigan 'Thumb,' 1923–1928." *Catholic Historical Review* 78 (1992): 413–29.

———. *Seasons of Grace: A History of the Catholic Archdiocese of Detroit.* Detroit: Wayne State University Press, 1990.

Tull, Charles J. *Father Coughlin and the New Deal.* Syracuse, N.Y.: Syracuse University Press, 1965.

Van Ravenswaay, Charles. *The Arts and Architecture of German Settlements in Missouri: A Survey of a Vanishing Culture.* Columbia, Mo.: University of Missouri Press, 1977.

Wakin, Edward, and Joseph F. Scheuer. *The De-Romanization of the American Catholic Church.* New York: Macmillan, 1966.

Walsh, James P. "The Irish in the New America: 'Way Out West.'" In *America and Ireland, 1776–1976: The American Identity and the Irish Connection,* edited by David Noel Doyle and Owen Dudley Edwards, 165–76. The Proceedings of the United States Bicentennial Conference of Cumann Merriman Ennis, August 1976. Westport, Conn.: Greenwood Press, 1980.

Ward, Leo R., ed. *The American Apostolate: American Catholics in the Twentieth Century.* Westminster, Md.: Newman Press, 1952.

Williams, Michael. *The Shadow of the Pope.* New York: Whittlesey House, 1932.

Wittke, Carl. *The Irish in America.* Baton Rouge: Louisiana State University Press, 1956.

Wolfe, Burton H. "Father Vizzard: Enemy of Exploiters." *Sign* 45 (May 1966): 16–18.
Wyman, Mark. *Immigrants in the Valley: Irish, Germans and Americans in the Upper Mississippi Country, 1830–1860.* Chicago: Nelson-Hall Publishers, 1984.
Yzermans, Vincent A. *The People I Love: A Biography of Luigi G. Ligutti.* Collegeville, Minn.: Liturgical Press, 1976.
Zwierlein, Frederick J. *The Life and Letters of Bishop McQuaid.* 3 vols. Rochester, N.Y.: Art Print Shop, 1926.

Index

Abell, Aaron I., 360
Abourezk, James, 288
"Adaptive Program for Agriculture"(Committee for Economic Development), 306–307
Ad Hoc Committee on Agricultural Issues, 296
Adrian, Minn., 12
AFL-CIO. *See* National Agricultural Workers Union
African Americans, 3, 62, 112, 127, 266, 282, 290, 313, 326, 329–34
Agar, Herbert, 103–4, 172
Agency for International Development (AID), 207
Ag-Land Fund I, 288
Agribusiness Accountability Initiative (AAI), 221, 288
Agribusiness Accountability Project, 305
Agricultural Adjustment Act (AAA): 94–97, 116, 123, 125, 127, 275; second AAA, 123–24
Agricultural Credit Improvement Act, 283
Agricultural Fair Practices Act, 290, 300
Agricultural Job Opportunity, Benefits and Security Act, 324
Agricultural Marketing Agreement Act, 300
Agricultural Missions, 223, 269
Agricultural Profession, The (Edwin O'Hara), 61
"Agriculture in California" (California diocesan directors), 322
Agriculture, Iowa Department of, 254
Agriculture, U.S. Department of (USDA), 81, 150, 192, 258, 281, 283, 326, 333, 344
Agrimissio, 211–12, 243, 255
Aiken, George, 298
Allitt, Patrick, 341

America, 47, 52, 83, 94, 233, 277, 330
American Agriculture Movement (AAM), 279
American Board of Catholic Missions (ABCM), 8, 57, 144, 145, 170, 171, 174, 242, 252, 253, 255
American Catholicism and Social Action: A Search for Social Justice (Aaron Abell), 360
American Committee on Italian Immigration, 191
American Country Life Association (ACLA), 45–46, 48, 54, 103, 362. *See also* Country Life Movement
American Immigration Conference, 191
Ames, Iowa, 43, 136, 293
Amos Award, 292
Ancient Order of Hibernians, 21, 34
Andrews, Brother David, C.S.C.: background, 260; and biotechnology, 352; and conservation, 345; on cooperatives, 291; director of Edwin V. O'Hara Institute, 241; and "eating as a moral act," 310–12, 311f23; and ecumenism, 269–70; executive director of NCRLC, 260–65; on family farm, 274; and Farm Aid, 306; and Fund for Rural America, 285; and globalization, 220–21; and International Catholic Rural Association, 179; and international rural life, 223; and land use, 346; and NCRLC concern for the environment, 343, 350; on National Commission on Industrial Farm Animal Production, 289; on NAFTA, 281; on Notre Dame Study of Catholic Parish Life, 338; on principles and lack of success of NCRLC, 365–66; on rural living environment, 337; on subsidiarity, 339; on water, 348

383

Anglo-Catholics, 1–3
Antigonish, Nova Scotia, 46, 119, 149, 290
Appalachia, 79, 248, 266, 313, 328–29
Appalachian Development Program, 328–29
Appalachian Regional School for Church Leaders, 240
Appalachia—Science in the Public Interest, 343
Apostolate Library Service, 156, 172
Aquinas, St. Thomas, 25
Aquino, Corazon, 219
Arab oil embargo, 353
Arizona Highways, 228
Arnold, Cecilia, 339
Asian farmers (ethnics in U.S.), 282
Association of Belgian and Holland Priests, 12
Assumption, Ohio, 290
Assumption Parish (Granger, Iowa), 138
Atchison, Kan., 54. *See also* St. Benedict's College
At Home in the Web of Life (Catholic bishops of Appalachia), 248
Audubon, Iowa, 295n22
Aurora, Kan., 232
Australia, 46, 212
Austrians: ethnics in United States, 15, 16t2

Baer, Rev. Urban, 148
Baker, O. E., 81–82, 360
Baltimore, archdiocese of, 54, 55
Bankhead, John H.: 107; Bankhead farm tenancy bill, 132
Bartholome, Bp. Peter W., 336
Barzynski, John, 12
Basilians, 49
Bay St. Louis, Miss., 162
Beland, Mr., 111
Beldon Foundation, 261
Belgians: ethnics in United States, 3, 15, 16t2
Belgium, 26, 46, 62, 108
Belize, 223
Belloc, Hilaire, 103, 120
Belleville, Ill., 163
Benedict XVI, Pope, 275
Benedictines (religious order), 48, 49, 105, 112. *See also* Schmiedeler, Rev. Edgar, O.S.B.
Bennett Law, 22
Benson, Ezra T., 306, 318

Berdyaeff, Nicholas, 105
Bergengren, Roy, 88
Bergland, Robert, 198, 298
Berrigan, Daniel, S.J., 265
Berrigan, Philip, S.J., 265
Berry, Thomas, C.P., 342
Berry, Wendell, 339
Bertels, Sister Thomas More, O.S.F., 304, 323
Better Rural Life, A (Edgar Schmiedeler), 148
Bishop, Rev. William Howard, 60, 62, 80f3, 142; on Agricultural Adjustment Act, 95; and anti-bigotry campaign, 74–75; and back-to-the-land movement, 93, 106–11; on cooperatives, 118; on Depression, 85, 91, 92–93, 99, 102; and Glenmary Missioners, 79; as NCRLC president in 1930s, 130–31, 136, 144; prospectus for diocesan directors, 146
Bishops' Committee for Catholic Migrants, 318
Bishops' Committee for Migrant Workers, 325
Bishops' Committee for the Spanish Speaking, 318, 325
Bishops' Program of Reconstruction, 29–30, 87
Bismarck, N.D.: 140; diocese of, 140, 255
Blacks. *See* African Americans
Blobaum, Roger, 245
Blue Ridge Summit, Pa., 178
Boerenbond, 46, 108, 116
Bolivia, 196
Bolling, Ala., 112, 120
Bolton, Mary V., 48
Borsodi, Ralph, 103–104, 122
Bossi, Stephen E., 207, 235, 248, 363
Boston, Mass.: 7, 88; archdiocese of, 156
bovine growth hormone (BGH), 352
Brannan, Charles F.; Brannan Plan, 276
Brazil, 212
Bread for the World, 202, 257
Briefs, Goetz, 99
Britain. *See* Great Britain
British Guiana, 215
Brockland, August, 43. *See also* German Catholic Central Verein
Brossard, Rev. J. G., O.M.I., 211
Brothers of Mary, 49
Browning-Ferris Industries, 349
Bryan, William Jennings, 34, 260

Index

Buddy, Bp. Charles F., 320
Bureau of Catholic Indian Missions. *See* Catholic Indian Missions, Bureau of
Bureau of Immigration (NCWC). *See* Immigration, Bureau of (NCWC)
Burke, Edmund, 339
Burke, Rev. John J., 107
Burke, Abp. Raymond L., 262–63, 296, 345, 352
Burlington and Missouri Railroad, 12
Bush, George H. W., 222, 280
Bush, George W., 272, 282, 350
Butler City, Kan., 12
Byers, David, 235
Byrnes, Rev. James A., 101, 130–37, 143, 144, 145, 148, 152, 157

California Agriculture Labor Relations Board, 322
"Call to Justice and Action by the People of the Land" (ecumenical statement), 269
Calverts (family), 1
Camara, Abp. Dom Helder, 250
Campaign for Human Development, 258, 261, 326
Campbell, Rev. Joseph M., 43, 94, 96, 132, 136–38
Campbell's (company), 323
Canada, 67, 68, 76, 108, 154, 177, 280, 289, 295
Canadian National Railways, 150
Canadians, 211; ethnics in United States, 16t2. *See also* French Canadians
Cancun, Mexico, 221
Caracas, Venezuela, 178, 214
Cardinal Gibbons Institute, 62, 330–31
CARE, 194
Carey, Rev. Thomas R., 51, 60, 70
Cariacou, 206
Carroll, John E., 343
Carroll, Bp. John P., 67
Carter, James E. (Jimmy), 222, 279, 297, 347, 353–54
Casagrande, Emma, 67
Catholic Association for International Peace, 44
Catholic Charities, 258, 348. *See also* National Conference of Catholic Charities
Catholic Charities Review, 47, 52, 71
Catholic Church Extension Society, 7, 37, 39, 44, 49, 51, 60, 70

Catholic Citizen (Milwaukee), 52
Catholic Colonization Society of the United States, 13
Catholic Committee of Appalachia (CCA), 248, 328–29
Catholic Conference on Industrial Problems, 53, 91
Catholic Daughters of America, 237
Catholic Engaged Encounter, 246
Catholic Farmer, The, 148
Catholic Herald (Milwaukee), 148
Catholic Indian Missions, Bureau of, 23
Catholic Institutional Cooperative Association, 290
Catholic Layman's Union, 330
Catholic Missionary Union, 7, 71
Catholic Relief Services, 171, 181, 189–90, 192, 194, 196, 208, 223. *See also* War Relief Services—NCWC
Catholic Rural Life: 55, 56, 57, 63, 64, 66, 71, 74, 144, 148, 160, 228, 232, 235, 240, 245, 253, 256, 264, 363; newsletter, 264
Catholic Rural Life Bulletin, 135, 143, 148, 157
Catholic Rural Life Objectives, 135, 148
Catholic Rural Life Page, 159, 232
Catholic Students Mission Crusade (CSMC), 61, 70
Catholic Truth Society (Britain), 46
Catholic Union of Missouri, 45, 49
Catholic University of America, the, 138
Catholic Worker, xiv, 112–14, 183
Catholic World, 47
Catholic Youth Organization, 166
Center for Concern, 221
Center for Social Research and Action (CESTA), 211
Central American Free Trade Agreement (CAFTA), 281
Central-Blatt and Social Justice, 45, 94, 124
Chapman family, 111
Charleston, S.C., 7, 11
Chavez, Cesar, 320–21
Chernobyl, Russia, 355
Chesterton, G. K., 103, 120
Chicago, Ill.: 7, 12, 30, 49, 288; archdiocese of, 339
Chicago, University of, 138
Children's Aid Society, 9
Chile, 178, 214, 215
Chilton, Wis., 163

China, 220, 222
Choynice, Neb., 12
Christian Brothers Investment Services, 262
Christian Farmer, Christian Farmer News Letter, 157–60, 163, 170
Christian Rural Overseas Program (CROP), 193–94, 302
Church and the Country Community, The (Edwin O'Hara), 47, 61, 66
Churching of America, The (Roger Finke and Rodney Stark), 359
Church in the Modern World, The. *See Gaudium et Spes*
Church Land Project, 346
Church of the Brethren, 193
Church World Services, 193
Cicognani, Ameleto Giovanni, 100
Cincinnati, Ohio, 54; province of, 98
Civil Rights Act, 328, 332
Clarksville, Md., 131. *See also* Bishop, Rev. William Howard
Claryville, Mo., 22, 57
Clean Water Act, 348
Clean Water Network, 261
Clement XIII, Pope, 25
Clergy Conference on Negro Welfare, 330
Cleveland, Ohio, 302
Clinton, William J. (Bill), 281, 297, 315, 324, 345
Club of Rome, 341
Coady, Rev. M. M.: 149; Coady Institute, 290
Coalition for Land Reform, 307
Coalition for Rural America, 291
Coalition of 22, 304
CODEL ("Coordination [sometimes "Co-operation"] in Development"), 207
Coffee Farms, Ala., 126
Cogley, John, 364
Collegeville, Minn., 149. *See also* St. John's Abbey, St. John's University
Collins, Joseph, 202
colonies, colonization (Catholic rural), 1, 3, 8–14, 17, 24, 29–30, 35, 37, 42, 49, 71–72, 89, 93, 108, 111–12, 145, 146, 173, 189–90, 212, 285
Columbia, 178, 206, 209
Columbia County, Wis., 139
Columbia University, 138
Columbian Institute for Agrarian Reform, 206

Columbus, Ohio, 165
Commission on Country Life, 28; call for new, 284
Commission on Religion in Appalachia (CORA), 328–29
Committee against the Extension of Race Prejudice in the Church, 330
Committee for Economic Development (CED), 306
Common Ground, 245, 255, 256, 349
Commonweal, 96, 102
Community Food Security, 261
Community Service Organization, 321
Company of St. Isidore, 168, 226
Conception Abbey, 49
Confraternity of Christian Doctrine (CCD), 38, 62, 66, 68, 166
Congregation of the Holy Cross, 260. *See also* Andrews, Brother David, C.S.C.
Conservation Reserve Program, 343
Conservation Security Program, 343
Consumer Product Safety Commission, 337
Cooking for Christ (NCRLC), 259
Co-operative Creameries of Minnesota, 87
Cooperative for American Remittances to Europe (later Everywhere). *See* CARE
Cork, County (Ireland), 23
Corning, Iowa, 300
Coronado, Francisco, 4
Corpus Christi, 19
Corvallis, Ore., 43
Cottage Grove, Ore., 63
Coughlin, Rev. Charles E., 142, 143
Country Beautiful, 227–28
Country Beautiful Foundation, 228
Country Life Movement, 28, 42, 63. *See also* American Country Life Association
Covington, Ky., 138. *See also* Mulloy, Bp. William T.
Cram, Ralph Adams, 102, 105
Credit Union National Association, 290
Credit Union National Extension Bureau, 88
Cretin, Bp. Joseph, 11
Crookston, Minn., diocese of, 246
Crown-Zellerbach Foundation, 173
Crusade Against Poverty, 314
Cuba, 215, 218
Curley, Abp. Michael, 54
Cusack, Gregory D.: background, 249; and

Index

ecumenism, 269; and the environment, 341; and "just food system," 309–10; on liberation theology, 219; on NCRLC and modern trends, 365; as NCRLC executive director, 249–56, 258–59, 262; and NCRLC focus on Iowa, 264; and the peace movement, 357; and rural advocacy groups, 305–6
Czechs: ethnics in United States, 3, 15, 17, 19, 21

Dachauer, Rev. Alban, S.J., 167
Daly, Bp. Edward, 227, 229
Daly, Mary, 343
Danbom, David B., 273
Daniel, Victor, 331
Daughters of Isabella, 237
Davenport, Iowa, diocese of, 189, 244
Davidson, Gabriel, 108
Davis, Chester, 183
Day, Dorothy, 112, 114
Day, Msgr. Victor, 43, 48, 67–68, 71, 111
Delano, Calif., 321–22
Democratic Party, Democrats, 22, 28, 94, 249, 281, 287, 297–98
Denmark, 30, 46, 351
Denver, Colo., diocese of, 279
Department of Agriculture, U.S. *See* Agriculture, U.S. Department of
Des Moines, Iowa: 54, 55, 136, 138, 219, 247, 257, 263, 305; diocese of, 152; NCRLC headquarters in, 133, 139, 152, 157, 168, 177, 232, 236, 252, 262, 285
Des Moines *Register*, 139
Des Moines *Tribune*, 139
Dineen, Rev. Michael P., 153, 156, 160, 169, 171, 175, 224–30, 232, 237, 243, 245
Dingman, Bp. Maurice J., 244–45, 249, 253, 267, 293–94
Displaced Persons Act, 187–88
Distributism (Distributists), 46, 103, 108, 120, 172, 182
Divine Word Fathers, 330
Dolan, Jay P., xiii, 338
Donnelly, Ignatius, 34
Donohue, Bp. Hugh, 320
Douglas, Louis H., 272
Douglas, Paul H., 298
Downs, Ill., 231
Drumm, Bp. T. W., 48

Du Bois, W. E. B., 331
Dubuque, Iowa, 11, 92, 93, 131, 259
Dunn, Rev. Daniel F., 156, 160, 224, 225
Duren, Rev. Hubert, 120, 290
Dutch: ethnics in United States, 3, 12, 15, 16t2

Earth Day, 341
Earth Matters, 256
Easton, Pa., 114
"Eating as a Moral Act," 310–12
Economic Justice for All (NCCB), 202, 249, 275, 294, 309, 313, 323
Economic Opportunity Act, 327–28
education: adult, 146; Catholic rural, 11, 13, 20–21, 23, 32, 34, 35–39, 62–69, 110, 146, 147, 331–32; compulsory public school attendance laws, 22, 58; correspondence courses, 46, 61, 66–68, 75, 83; in developing countries, 209, 210, 214; for Hispanics, 319, 322, 324, 325; parent-educator movement, 77–78; parochial schools, 5, 8, 22, 32, 36, 63, 139, 311, 339, 348, 350; religious vacation schools, 32, 44, 49, 56, 57, 61, 62, 63–66, 70, 71, 75, 76, 83, 144, 146, 147, 161, 331, 332, 334; rural-oriented, 68–69, 77, 123, 146; rural summer schools, 155, 161–62; weakens family, 336
Education Department (of NCWC), 39
Edwards Law, 22
Edwin V. O'Hara Institute for Rural Ministry Education, 241, 260, 346
Eisele, Susan Frawley, 158
Eisenhower, Dwight D., 173, 272, 277, 297, 343
Elder, Mary Theresa, 7, 30, 35
Elkhorn, Neb., 166
El Salvador, 218
Emanuel, Victor, 173
England, 19, 30, 295. *See also* Great Britain
England, Bp. John, 7, 11
English: rural Catholics in United States, 1, 16t2
Ennis, James F., 260
Environmental Quality Incentives Program, 343
Eugene, Ore., 40–41, 63
European Union, 220, 221, 352
Evansville, Ind., diocese of, 186
Everywhere Iowa, 340
Extension Service (U.S. Department of Agriculture), 146, 183, 296, 299, 316, 333

Extension Society. *See* Catholic Church Extension Society

Fair Labor Standards Act, 318
Family Farm Antitrust Act, 287
Family Farm Coalition. *See* National Family Farm Coalition
Family Farm Development Act, 285
Family Life Bureau (NCWC), 134
Fargo, N.D.: 139–40, 155, 186; "Fargo Trio," 140, 148
Farm Aid, 306
Farm Bureau, 22, 45, 116, 271, 272, 276, 278, 296, 298–99, 302–5, 307, 316
Farm Credit Act, 94–95
Farm Credit System, 294
Farmer-Labor Co-operative Congress, 30
Farmers' Holiday Association, 90
Farmers Home Administration (FmHA), 282–83, 294, 333
Farmers' Legal Action Group, 267
Farmers of Tomorrow (Urban Baer), 148
Farmers' Union, Farmers Union, 161, 272, 276, 298–99, 302–3, 305
Farm Labor Organizing Committee (FLOC), 323
Farm Organization Unity Program, 303
Farm Security Administration (FSA), 107–8, 122, 123, 126–27, 157, 161, 299, 316–17, 361
Federal Emergency Relief Administration (FERA), 107–8
Federal Farm Board, 90, 91
Federal Reserve system, 287
Federal Surface Mining Control and Reclamation Act, 347
Federated Colored Catholics of the United States, 330
Federation of Communities in Service (FOCIS), 266
Federation of Southern Cooperatives, 326
Feet in the Furrow, 160, 177
Fenwick, Bp. Benedict, 9
Fernholz, Sister Annette, 240
Finke, Roger, 359
Fite, Gilbert C., 272–73
Fitzgerald, Joseph K., 255–59, 262, 338
Flemish: ethnics in United States, 12
Foley, Rev. Gerald, 246–47, 319
Food Action Campaign, 288
Food Alliance Midwest, 260

Food and Agriculture Organization (FAO) (of United Nations): 209, 210, 213, 214, 223, 268; formation of, 196; Freedom from Hunger Campaign, 199; Ligutti as Vatican observer to, 173, 178, 180, 196–97, 199n14; World Food Program of, 198, 202
Food and Drug Administration, 351
Food First, 257
Food First (Frances Moore Lappe and Joseph Collins), 202
Food for Peace, 197–99, 201, 208, 299
Ford Foundation, 173, 211
Ford, Gerald, administration, 315
Forest Grove, Ore., 65f2
Fortier, Msgr. Charles, 241
Fort Wayne, Ind., 227, 229
Foster Farms, 352
4-H Clubs, 146, 161, 166
Fox, Matthew, 342–43
France: hybrid corn in, 194; rural activities in, 46
Francis, Sister Millicent, R.S.C.J., 211–12
Franklin Research and Development, 255
Free America, 103, 150, 172
Freedom from Hunger Campaign. *See* Food and Agriculture Organization (FAO) (of United Nations)
Freedom to Farm Act, 281, 295
Freeman, Orville, 200, 278
French Canadians: in United States, 2, 3, 15, 16t2
French: Catholics in United States, 1, 3, 15, 16t2, 18, 23; Young Christian Agriculturists, 166
Friedberger, Mark, 296
Fritsch, Rev. Albert, S.J., 343
Frommherz, Rev. J. Fridolin, 290
Fund for Rural America, 285

Garcia, Bp. Richard, 289
Garryowen, Iowa, 23
Gaudium et Spes (The Church in the Modern World) (Vatican II), 181, 341
Genoa, Wis., 17
George, Card. Francis, 288
George, Henry, 25, 27
Georgia, University of, 43
German Catholic Central Verein, 21, 43, 45, 47, 48, 49, 53n45, 56, 57, 91, 92, 115, 127, 362n4

Index

Germans, 195; ethnics in United States, 2, 3, 6, 9, 11, 12, 14, 15, 16, 17, 18, 19, 20, 21, 23, 72
Germany, 26, 46, 101, 108, 188, 194
Ghana, 211
Gibbons, Card. James, 27
Gibbons, Rev. William J., S.J., 157, 190
G.I. Bill, 185
"Gifts . . . Returning . . . One World." *See* GROW
Gigot, Paul, 258
Gilmore, Bp. Ronald M., 263, 264
Gleason, Philip, xiii, 53n45, 362
Glendale, Ohio, 79
Glendon, Mary Anne, 258
Glenmary Home Mission Society: 60, 79, 83, 131, 161, 240, 241; ex-Glenmary sisters, 266
Glenmary Research Center, 240
Glennon, Abp. John J., 48, 49, 86n4
Glennonville, Mo., 48
Glickman, Dan, 282, 298
"Global Climate Change: A Plea for Dialogue, Prudence and the Common Good" (U.S. Catholic bishops), 350
God's Bounty and Human Hunger (ecumenical statement), 269
Gottschalk, Rev. Andrew, 279
Graber, L. F., 56
Grafton, N.D., 137
Grail, the, 162
Grailville, Ohio, 162
Grange, Grangers, 21, 271, 272, 299, 303, 305
Granger, Iowa, 111–13; 120, 125, 134, 138, 139, 161, 172
Grapes of Wrath, The (John Steinbeck), 124, 233
Grassroots Rural Ministry Program (GRMP), 257
Grazer, Walt, 235, 280
Great Britain, Britain, 30, 46, 103, 108. *See also* England
Great Falls, Mont., 129, 130
Great Plains Church Leadership School, 240
Greeley, Rev. Andrew M., 338
Green Bay, Wis.: 165; diocese of, 186
Green Party, 297
"Green Revolution," 200, 203
Green Ribbon Campaign, 295–96, 303
Gremillion, Rev. Joseph, 181
Grenada, 206
Griswold, A. Whitney, 273
Gronski, Robert, 179, 220–21, 287, 357
Gross, Rev. Francis, 111
GROW, 194
Growing Food and Profit program, 340
Guatemala, 215

Halsey, William M, 53
Hamilton, Stanley, 269
Hard Tomatoes, Hard Times (Jim Hightower), 283
Harkin, Tom, 279, 298
Has the Immigrant Lost the Faith? (Gerald Shaughnessy), 8
Hayes, Bp. Ralph, 225
Heartland Project, 245, 253
Hehir, Rev. J. Bryan, 294
Heifer Project (Heifer International), 193–94, 223
Helena, Mont.: 43; diocese of, 67
Henderson, Minn., 261
Herberg, Will, 359, 360t4
Heron Lake, N.Dak., 23
Hildner, Msgr. George J., 22, 57, 344
Higher Plain, 261
Hightower, Jim, 283
Hill Country, Tex., 21
Hilton Head, S.C., 333
Hispanics, 1, 3, 4, 7, 15, 16t2, 21, 257, 266, 281, 282, 316–25, 333, 338, 351
Holland. *See* Netherlands
Holy Names of Jesus and Mary, sisters of the, 63
Homeland Foundation, 172–73, 217, 243
Home Mission Confraternity of Catholic Rural Life (Rural Life Confraternity), 75–76
Hong Kong, 221
Hoover, Herbert, 29, 90, 91, 92, 106
Hoxie, Kan., 232
Hughes, Abp. John, 10
Human Economic Appalachian Development (HEAD) Corporation, 329
Humphrey, Hubert H., 199, 298
Hungarians: ethnics in United States, 3, 6, 15, 16t2
Hunger and Global Security Bill, 202
Hunger Prevention Act, 315
Hynes, Emerson, 336

Idea Book for Small Town Churches (NCRLC), 239
Illinois Supreme Court, 347
Illinois, University of, 231
I'll Take My Stand (Nashville Agrarians), 103
Immigration and Naturalization Service, 324
Immigration, Bureau of (NCWC), 13, 72, 111n21
Imokolee Farmworkers, 324
Index of Forbidden Books, 27
India, 200, 207, 208
Indians. *See* Native Americans
"Industrialism and Agrarianism" (NCRLC), 364–65
Integrated Farm Management Program, 343
Interfaith Center on Corporate Responsibility, 288
Interior Department (U.S.), 284
Intermediate Technology Development Group, 209
International Caribbean Cooperative Union, 206
International Catholic Migration Commission (ICMC), 190
International Catholic Rural Association (ICRA), 178–79, 212, 223
International Catholic Rural Life Conference, 178, 211
International Country Life Association, 46
International Federation of Catholic Institutes for Social and Socio-Religious Research (FERES), 211, 217
International Federation of Rural Adult Catholic Movements (FIMARC), 179
International Food Aid Convention, 198
International Institute of Agriculture, 46
International Monetary Fund (IMF), 222
International Voluntary Services (IVS), 198, 207–209
Iowa Farm and Commodity Organizations (IFCO), 304
Iowa Farm Unity Coalition, 294–95
Iowa Foundation for the Environment, 261
Iowa Interfaith Climate and Energy Campaign, 264, 350
Iowa Interfaith Power and Light, 264, 350
Iowa Partners of the Alliance Committee, 196
Iowa Supreme Court, 339
Iowa-Yucatan Partners of the Alliance, 206
Iran, 200, 212
Ireland, 46
Ireland, Abp. John, 9, 12, 23
Irish: ethnics in United States, 2, 3, 5, 9, 10, 11, 12, 15, 16t2, 17, 18, 19, 23, 28
Irish Catholic Benevolent Union, 12
Irish Catholic Colonization Association of the United States, 12
Isidore, St.: 47, 167–68, 170, 180; fund, 255. *See also* Company of St. Isidore; Project Isidore
Israel, Henry, 46
Italians: ethnics in United States, 2, 3, 5, 15, 16t2, 17, 18, 19, 28, 36, 189, 191, 229
Italy, 26, 46, 101, 138, 139, 188, 189, 194, 204

Jackson, Ron, 235
Japan, 200, 212, 213
Jefferson City, Mo., 140, 154f7
Jefferson, Thomas: Jeffersonian, 8, 103, 273, 339, 364
Jesuits, 49, 116, 265, 330. *See also* Berrigan, Daniel, S.J.; Berrigan, Philip, S.J. Dachauer, Rev. Alban, S.J.; Fritsch, Rev. Albert, S.J.; Gibbons, Rev. William J., S.J.; La Farge, John, S.J.; Rawe, John C., S.J.; Vizzard, James, S.J.; Wood, Rev. William J., S.J.
Jewish Agricultural Society, 108
Jews (Jewish agencies), 45, 81, 268, 270
John XXIII, Pope, 180–81, 197, 201, 313
John Paul II, Pope, 25, 220, 222, 245, 247–48, 263, 341, 353
Johnson, Lyndon B., 278, 313, 332
Joint Appeal in Religion and Science, 342
Joint Venture Services (JVS), 206–207
Josephinum Seminary, 232
Josephites, 330
Joyce, Edith, and farm, 261–62, 346
Joyce, Rev. John, and farm, 261–62, 346
Junction City, Ore., 63
"just food system," 275, 309–10
Justice Department (U.S.), 301

Kansas Supreme Court, 123
Kautza, Tim, 260, 270, 325, 343, 351–52
Kayser, Rev. Leonard, 218, 247, 252, 345
Keep Antibiotics Working (KAW), 351–52
Keileyville, Va., 12

Index

Kelley, Bp. Francis C., 49, 51, 60, 216
Kellogg Foundation, 261
Kelly, Rev. Michael V., 49, 59
Kelso, Louis, 291
Kenkel, Frederick P., 43, 45, 48, 56, 115. *See also* German Catholic Central Verein
Kennedy, John F., 222, 228, 272, 277, 297, 307, 313, 318, 328
Kenrick Seminary, 48, 69
Kerens, Richard C., 23
KFH (radio station), 142
Knights of Columbus, 21, 34, 44, 49, 56, 65, 261
Knox County, Ill., 346–47
Kucera, Patricia Prijatel, 245
Ku Klux Klan, 44, 58, 73–74

La Blanc, Sandra A., 245, 259, 260f20, 267, 270
Labor-Contractor Crew Leader Registration Act, 318
La Crosse, Wis.: 165, 169, 262; diocese of, 196
La Farge, Rev. John, S.J., 62, 100, 104, 108, 118, 127, 330, 332
Lafayette, La.: 165, 326; diocese of, 241
Land and Home, 157, 158, 177
Land Stewardship Project, 245, 344
Land Use Policy and Planning Assistance Act, 345
Landward, 109, 131, 136, 144, 148
Lane County, Ore., 41, 44, 63, 64, 67
Lanesboro, Minn., 32
Lansing, Mich., 46
Laos, 208
Lapeer, Mich., 49, 51, 60, 70
Lapp, John, 58
Lappe, Frances Moore, 202
Lawrence, Rev. Andrew, 157
League for Family Education (Belgium), 46, 62
Leipzig, Rev. Francis P., 43
Leo XIII, Pope, 7, 23, 25–26, 31, 89, 102, 139
Leopold Center, 261
Leopoldine Stiftung (Society) of Vienna, 7, 11
Libby's (company), 323
Libertyville, Ill., 162
Ligutti, Msgr. Luigi G.: 150, 234, 244, 245, 257, 364; background, 138–39; and Catholic rural population, 358, 359;

and Catholic Worker movement, 114; and cooperatives, 120; on corporatism, 116; and displaced persons, 187–88; and ecumenism, 268; as executive secretary of NCRLC, 129, 151–63, 224–32, 241; and farm parity, 276; and Farm Security Administration, 126–27; on fertilizers, 350; on food stamps, 314; and Granger homesteads project, 111–12, 113f4, 136; and hunger, 192–201; and immigration laws, 190–91; and International Catholic Migration Commission, 190; and Iowa farm tenancy committee, 125; on James Byrnes, 134–35; and land reform, 212–23; "Ligutti-isms," 155; on migrant workers, 319; as NCRLC director of international affairs, 177, 230; and NCRLC finances, 144, 169–75, 243; and NCRLC internal conflicts of 1930s, 137–39; and NCRLC international affairs, 176–23, 234, 363; and NCRLC memberships, 169; on nuclear war, 356; personality, 153–55, 260; relations with popes and Vatican, 153, 179–81, 260; and rural poor, 361; and rural retreats, 167; and *Rural Roads to Security*, 148, 307; and self-help projects, 204–11; and shrine of St. Isidore, 168; and York County project, 189
Ligutti Rural Community Support Program. *See* Luigi Ligutti Rural Community Support Program
Limerick, County (Ireland), 23
Limits to Growth, The (Club of Rome), 341
Lincoln Township, Mo., 288
Lithuanians: ethnics in United States, 3
Living History Farms, 247
Living Wage, A (John A. Ryan), 34
Long, Huey, 143
Loras, Bp. Mathias, 10, 11
Louisville, Ky., archdiocese of, 255
Loveland, Ohio, 162
Lubbock, Tex., diocese of, 255
Lucerne Memorial, 7
Luckey, Rev. Arthur J., 43, 60
Ludwig-Missionsverein (Mission Society) (Bavaria), 7, 11
Luigi Ligutti Rural Community Support Program, 262, 264, 339–40
Lutheran(s): 259, 270; religious vacation schools, 32, 38

Lutheran World Relief, 193
Lynch, Margaret, 56, 64

McCarren-Walter Act, 190
McCarthy, Eugene J., 298
McCullough, Rev. Thomas, 320
McDonald's (company), 352
McDonnell, Rev. Donald, 320–21
McGee, Thomas D'Arcy, 9
McGlynn, Rev. Edward, 25, 27
McGovern, George S., 298
McGuire, A. J., 43, 87
McKnight, Rev. Albert, 326
McLean County, Ill., 231
McNamara, Bp. Lawrence, 222, 253
McNicholas, Abp. John T., 79
McRae, Hugh, 108
McRaith, Bp. John J., 232, 237–42, 246, 279, 304, 307
Madison, Wis., diocese of, 186
Madrid, Spain, 168
Malone, Bp. James, 256
Malta, 153
Manhattan, Kan., 43, 60
Manifesto on Rural Life (NCRLC), 134, 135, 140, 148, 178
Manizales, Columbia, 178, 214
Man's Relation to the Land (ecumenical statement), 268–69
Manual of Religious Vacation Schools (NCRLC), 66
Marcos, Ferdinand, 219
Marlett, Jeffrey D., xiv, 17, 103, 364
Marty, Bp. Martin, 23
Mary Welsh Fund, 172
Masons, 21
Mater et Magistra (John XXIII), 181, 201, 265, 341
Maurin, Peter, 112–14
Meisner, Joseph C., 171
Menominee Enterprises, Inc., 334
Merrill Trust, 173, 325
Messmer, Abp. Sebastian G., 12, 28
Mexican Americans. *See* Hispanics
Mexican War, 4
Mexico, 177, 187, 200, 206, 213–14, 216, 223, 280–81
Mexico City, 348
Meyer, Abp. Albert, 225
Michel, Dom Virgil, O.S.B., 105, 118, 166

Midwest Sustainable Agriculture Coalition, 261
Migrant Health Act, 318
Miller, Rev. H. J., 193
Milwaukee Council of Catholic Women, 64
Milwaukee, Wis.: 54, 64, 72, 94, 110, 142, 160; archdiocese of, 64, 156, 292
Misleh, Dan, 235, 297
Missionary, 71
"Mission to Washington" (Joint Appeal in Religion and Science), 342
Mitchell, James P., 318
Mobilization for Survival, 356
Mondale, Walter, 300
Montezuma, N.M., 216
Morocco, 208
Morse, Wayne, 298
motor missions, 78–79
Muench, Card. Aloisius J., 102, 116, 119, 134, 140, 148, 160, 181, 183, 275
Muldoon, Bp. Peter, 39, 41, 47, 48, 51, 59, 67
Mulloy, Bp. William T., 130, 137–38, 140, 148, 181, 187, 225
Murray, Abp., John G., 145
Muslims, 270
Mutual Security program, 234, 299
Myricks, Mass., 260

Nashville Agrarians, 103–104
Nathan Cummings Foundation, 261
National Advisory Committee on Rural Areas Development, 326–27
National Advisory Committee on Subsistence Homesteads, 107
National Agricultural Workers Union (AFL-CIO), 320
National Association of Manufacturers (NAM), 314–15
National Association of Soil Conservation Districts, 344
National Broadcasting Company, 142
National Catholic Agrarian Confederation (Spain), 46
National Catholic Coalition for Responsible Investment, 288
National Catholic Educational Association (NCEA), 34, 39
National Catholic Resettlement Council, 188–89

Index

National Catholic War Council (NCWC), 29–30
National Catholic Welfare Conference (NCWC), 13, 48, 51, 53, 58, 59, 60, 72, 86, 88, 94, 107, 109, 111, 129, 130, 132–34, 139, 147, 148, 149, 152, 188, 207, 234, 236, 240, 265, 318, 360
National Catholic Welfare Council (NCWC), 39–40, 44
National Center for Appropriate Technology, 305
National Citizens Committee for Community Relations, 332
National Commission on Industrial Farm Animal Production, 289
National Committee on Religion and Rural Life, 269
National Conference of Catholic Bishops (NCCB), 202, 236, 256–57, 316, 356. *See also* United States Catholic Conference (USCC); United States Conference of Catholic Bishops (USCCB)
National Conference of Catholic Charities, 157, 187. *See also* Catholic Charities
National Conference of Catholic Women, 237
National Consumer Cooperative Bank Act, 290
National Cooperative Service Bureau, 137
National Council of Catholic Men, 56
National Council of Catholic Women (NCCW), 43, 49, 56, 64–66, 77
National Council of the Churches of Christ (National Council of Churches), 193, 270
National Council on Agricultural Life and Labor, 318
National Family Farm Coalition, 285, 305
National Farmers Organization (NFO), 299, 300–303, 305
National Farmers Union. *See* Farmers' Union
National Farm Workers Association, 321
National Federation of Priests Councils, 240
National Labor Relations Act, 322
National Land for People, 305
National Poultry Justice Alliance, 289
National Recovery Administration (NRA), 97
National Religious Partnership (Partners) for the Environment (NRPE), 270, 350

National Religious Vocation Conference, 268
Native Americans: 4, 240, 313, 329; farmers, 282; missions among, 1, 4; on NCRLC board of directors, 266; NCRLC concern for, 334–35; perspective on life, 251; reservations, 305, 314
NCWC Bulletin, 62
NCWC News Service, 44, 52
Nelson, Gaylord, 287–88, 298
Netherlands (Holland), 26, 46, 150, 162
New Deal, 95–96, 97–98, 100, 107–8, 112, 118, 124, 281. *See also* Roosevelt, Franklin D.
New Guinea, 216
New Hampshire, University of, 311, 343
New Melleray Abbey, 259
New Posen, Neb., 12
New Subiaco Abbey, 49
New Ulm, Minn., diocese of, 237–38, 261
New York, N.Y.: 27, 39, 112, 172, 173, 207, 342, 353; archdiocese of, 54
New York Times, The, 150
Nicaragua, 218
Nira, Teresa, 248
Nixon, Richard M., 278, 297, 314, 327, 349
Nollette, Rev. Neal P., 288
Nonpartisan League, 30–31
North American Free Trade Agreement (NAFTA), 223, 280–81
Norwegian: ethnics in United States, 19
Notre Dame, University of: 69, 112; Study of Catholic Parish Life, 338
Nueces County, Tex., 21
Nutting, Willis, 105, 307
Nyasaland, 212

Oblate Sisters of Providence, 330
Oblates of Mary Immaculate, 49
O'Brien, David J., 91, 128
O'Connor, Neb., 12
Octogesima Adveniens (Pope Paul VI), 341
Odd Fellows, 21
Office of Economic Opportunity (OEO), 327–28, 334
O'Grady, Msgr. John, 126–27, 157, 187
O'Hara, Abp. Edwin V.: 159f8; and antibigotry, 74–75; appointment as bishop of Great Falls, 129; background, 32–34; and back-to-the-land movement, 114;

O'Hara, Abp. Edwin V.: *(cont.)* and birthrate theory of rural Catholic weakness, 80, 84; and Confraternity of Christian Doctrine, 75; as director of Rural Life Bureau, 39–47; and educational remedies for Catholic rural population problem, 62–69; and establishment of NCRLC, 47–52; as executive secretary of NCRLC, 51, 54–57; and goal of ten thousand strong rural parishes, 185; and home missionary work, 69–71; and intemperance, 73; and Mexico, 216; and NCRLC internal conflicts of 1930s, 129–34; and parent-educator movement, 77; publicizing Catholic rural population problem, 58–62; and rural colonization, 71–72; and rural economics in the 1920s, 86–88; and St. Isidore, 167–68; social action background, 360; studied rural life in Europe, 176; study for NCEA of Catholic rural education, 34–39, 338, 358–59, 361; and voluntary domestic allotment plan, 93

O'Hara, Frank, 40
O'Hara, John, 40
O'Hara, Margaret, 32
O'Hara, Owen, 32
Omaha, Neb., diocese of, 90, 255
Omar Research Farm, 166
Omnibus Housing Act for farm workers, 318
100–League of St. Isidore, 236
Operation MATCH (Marketing Appalachia through the Church), 329
Oregon Agricultural College, 43
Oregon City, diocese of, 54
Oregon Minimum Wage Law, 34
Oregon, University of, 40
Organization for Competitive Markets (OCM), 282
Organized Social Justice, 116, 150
O'Rourke, Bp. Edward W.: 224, 361; and Agricultural Fair Practices Act, 300; on agricultural revolution, 200; and antipoverty programs, 313–16; background, 231; on communism, 216–17; on cooperatives, 289–90; on corporate farms, 286–87; and *Economic Justice for All*, 249; and ecumenism, 269; and environment, 341; and family farms, 307–8; and farm organizations, 303–4; on federal farm programs, 277–78; and the laity, 266; and the liturgy, 268; and migrant farm workers, 320–25; as NCRLC executive director, 230–39, 241, 246; and National Farmers Organization, 301–302; and partisan politics, 297; on "population explosion," 200–201; on profit-sharing plans, 291; and rural minorities, 332–34; and self-help, 204–10, 325–29; on superior rural culture, 337; on U.S. interventions in developing countries, 218; and world hunger programs, 198–99

Ostendorf, David, 305
Our Sunday Visitor, 229, 235
Owensboro, Ky., diocese of, 238, 255
Oxfam—Holland, 261

Pacem in Terris (John XXIII), 197
Palewski, Gaston, 200
Panama, 178, 206
Panama City, Panama, 178
Papal Volunteers for Latin America (PAVLA), 207
Parent Educator, The, 77
Parish Credit Union Institute, 88
Parish Credit Union National Committee, 88, 119
Park, Kan., 232
Patton, James, 276
Paul VI, Pope, 180, 197, 206, 209, 321, 341
Paulists, 7
Pax Christi, 357
Payment in Kind (PIK) program, 272, 279–80
Peace Corps, 207
Peasants League (Netherlands), 46
Peoria, Ill.: 140, 160, 268; diocese of, 231–32
Perdue (company), 352
Peru, 196
Pew Charitable Trusts, 289
Pew Forum, 359
Phelan, Betsy, 163
Philippines, 178, 200, 206, 211, 219
Philipps, Rev. Charles, 283, 316, 320
Piedmont (Italy), 17
Pierz, Rev. Francis, 11
Pittsburgh Diocesan Confraternity of Christian Doctrine, 38
Pius XI, Pope, 25, 91, 97, 98, 102, 104, 115, 116, 120, 124, 139

Index

Pius XII, Pope, 155, 167, 180–81, 184, 194
Point IV program, 198
Pojda, Judith, 221
Poland, 196, 222
Poles: ethnics in United States, 2, 3, 6, 11, 12, 15, 17, 28, 187
"Policy Statement on Family Farms" (USCC), 275
Polish Roman Catholic Union of America, 12
Pontifical Commission on (Council for) Justice and Peace, 181, 223
Popeye's (company), 352
population: attempts to restrict, 341; Catholic rural, in United States, 1, 4, 14–15, 90, 160; Catholic rural population problem, 34–39, 49, 52, 53, 58–84, 85, 109, 129, 150, 176, 357, 358–61; explosion, 200–201; rural, in United States, 106, 273, 309, 337; rural nonfarm, 337 world, 200–201
Population and Pollution in the United States (NCRLC), 349
Populist Party, Populism, Populists, 28, 34
Populorum Progressio (Paul VI): 197, 219, 341; *Populorum Progressio* Fund, 206
Portland, Ore., 34, 40; diocese of, 40, 67
Portland Unemployment Commission, 34
Portland, University of, 339
Portugal, 194
Portuguese: ethnics in United States, 16t2, 17, 36
Prairiefire (Prairie Fire), 305, 346
Pratt, Sister Christine, 258, 267, 348
Premium Standard Farms, 288
Presbyterian Church, 261
Presidential Committee on Farm Tenancy, 126
President's Commission on Immigration and Naturalization, 190
Prince Edward Island, 37
Proceedings (of NCRLC conventions), 148
Program for Migratory Farm Labor, A (NCRLC), 319
Program for Shared Abundance, A (NCRLC), 197, 299
Program of Catholic Rural Action, A (Edwin O'Hara), 41–42, 60, 87
Progress and Poverty (Henry George), 27
Progressive Era, 28
Prohibition, 58, 73–74

Project Isidore, 292
Protestant—Catholic—Jew (Will Herberg), 359
Protestants, Protestantism: and African Americans, 330; and capitalism, 102; Catholic attempts to convert, 69, 78–79; and Country Life Movement, 28, 42, 45, 63, 103; influence on or conversion of rural Catholics, 5, 8, 18, 24, 35, 37, 59, 80, 362; NCRLC cooperation with, 45, 81, 197, 211, 223, 268–70, 293, 295, 328, 329, and religious bigotry, 73–74; in rural America, 6, 7, 8, 18–23, 58, 82, 84, 359; in U.S. population, 360t4
Protestant Institute of Social Studies, 211
Public Law 78, 316
Public Law 480. *See* Food for Peace

Quadragesimo Anno (Pius XI), 91, 92, 93, 97, 98, 104, 109, 115–16, 118, 124
Queen's Work, The, 49
Quinlan, Rev. Patrick, 160
Quinn, Rev. Bernard, 240

Racine, Wis., 55
"Raiffeisen" banks, 46
Ramacher, Rev. Edward, 224, 228–29
Rawe, Rev. John C., S.J., 122, 148, 166, 307
Reagan, Ronald, 218, 272, 279–80, 294, 297, 315, 324
Reclamation, Bureau of, 284
Reclamation Law of 1902, 283–84, 347
Reclamation of Independence (Willis Nutting), 307
Reclamation Reform Act of 1979, 284
Reconstruction Finance Corporation (RFC), 90, 117
Red River Valley, 286
Reform Party, 297
Refugee Relief Act, 188
Reisner, John, 197
Religion and Rural Life Council (of Rural America), 305
Renewing the Earth: An Invitation to Reflection and Action on the Environment and Catholic Social Teaching (USCC), 342
Republican Party, Republicans, 22–23, 28, 124, 282, 287, 297–98
Rerum Novarum (Leo XIII), 25–27, 31, 109
Resettlement Administration, 107–108, 112

Reynolds, Lucille, 43
Richmond, Ind., 269
Richmond, Va., 100, 140, 141
Ricken, Bp. David, 263
Rivas, Andrew, 235
Roach, Abp. John R., 256–57
Rochester, N.Y., 141
Rochdale model of cooperatives, 30
Rockefeller Foundation, 173
Rogation Days, 19, 62, 166, 167
Romans, Italy, 138
Rome, Italy, 178, 196, 197, 211, 220, 223, 230, 263
Roosevelt, Eleanor, 112, 113f4
Roosevelt, Franklin D., 91, 93, 94, 97, 124, 141
Roosevelt, Theodore, 28, 284
Rose Creek, Minn., 167
Ruether, Rosemary Radford, 251, 254, 343
Rural Advocacy, 264
Rural America (organization), 304–305
Rural Area(s) Development (RAD) Act: 326–27, 333; Committees, 266
Rural Bureau Notes, 132, 147, 148
Rural Church Network, 269
Rural Coalition, 305
Rural Development Act (1972), 284, 292
R.U.R.A.L. Education Service, 240
Rural Electrification Administration, 117, 161
Rural Faith and Justice, 251. *See also* Theology of Land conferences (project)
Rural Landscapes, 256
Rural Life Association, 269
Rural Life Bureau (of NCWC): 49, 50; and colonization, 71–72; and correspondence courses, 67; director of, 51; early activities of, 41–47; end of, 134, 153; and finances of NCRLC, 57; formation of, 39–40; and NCRLC internal conflicts of 1930s, 129–34, 138, 139; organization of, 40–41; publication of, 55; preoccupation with Catholic rural population problem, 58–59, 80; and Prohibition amendment, 73; and religious vacation schools, 63–66, 76; as representing rural Catholic interests, 53; and rural economics in the 1920s, 86–87; and rural religious communities, 70; social action function of, 360; state advisory committees (councils) of, 43–44, 50, 55, 56. *See also* O'Hara, Abp. Edwin V.
Rural Life Conference, 160

Rural Life Conference—Feet in the Furrow, 160
Rural Life Confraternity. *See* Home Mission Confraternity of Catholic Rural Life
Rural Life Page. *See Catholic Rural Life Life*
Rural Life Prayerbook, The (NCRLC), 167
Rural Life Prayers, Blessings and Liturgies (Victoria M. Tufano), 259
Rural Parish Service, 239–40, 259
Rural Pastor News Service, 159
Rural Roads to Security (Luigi Ligutti and John C. Rawe, S.J.), 148, 307
Rural Sociology Society, 340
Russia (Soviet Union, USSR), 87, 178, 215, 218, 222, 286, 298, 356
Russians: ethnics in United States, 16t2, 18
Ryan, Msgr. John A., 26, 34, 59, 71, 86, 96, 107, 138, 149
Ryan, Bp. Vincent J., 85, 138, 139–40, 144, 148, 154, 181, 185, 361

Sacco, Paul, 163, 166, 189, 290
Sacramento, Calif., 321
Sacred Foods Project, 270
St. Ambrose College, 166, 244
St. Benedict's College, 69, 130, 149, 161
St. Cloud, Minn., 140, 141f6, 142, 150, 163, 164, 237
St. Francis Xavier University, 46, 119, 149. *See also* Antigonish, Nova Scotia
St. Isidore: 167–68, 170, 180; fund, 255. *See also* Company of St. Isidore; 100–League of St. Isidore
St. Isidore's Plow, 47, 50, 55, 167
St. John (New Brunswick, Canada), 2
St. John's Abbey, 112
St. John's University (Collegeville, Minn.), 149, 161, 166, 250
St. Jude, devotions to, 166
St. Louis *Catholic Herald*, 110
St. Louis, Mo., 43, 45, 47–48, 52, 54, 69, 303; archdiocese of, 110
St. Louis Rural Life Conference, 110, 147
St. Louis University, 161
St. Maria della Cabeza, 168
St. Mary's Parish (Eugene, Ore.), 41
St. Paul, Iowa, 244
St. Paul, Minn.: 32, 34, 43, 54, 69, 133, 152; archdiocese of, 134; diocese of, 11
St. Paul/Minneapolis, archdiocese of, 255, 261

Index

St. Paul Seminary, 34, 69
St. Stanislaus College, 161–62
St. Teresa's Village, 112. *See also* Bolling, Ala.
St. Thomas College, 32
Salina, Kan., diocese of, 232
Salm, Martin, 163
Sandinistas, 218
San Francisco, Calif.: 233; archdiocese of, 283, 316, 320
Santa Clara University, 173, 233, 235
Santiago, Chile, 178, 215
Scandinavians: ethnics in United States, 19
Schaefer, William J., 246–47
Schaeffer, Rev. Peter, 111
Scheuer, Rev. Joseph F., 363–64
Schiltz, Rev. Michael, 50
Schimek, Rev. William, 167
Schlarman, Bp. Joseph H., 167, 216, 231
Schmiedeler, Rev. Edgar, O.S.B.: on Agricultural Adjustment Act, 94, 116; and back-to-the-land movement, 106, 107, 111, 115; on "Catholic" and "American" in NCRLC, 362–63; and credit unions, 119; on Depression and Catholic rural life movement, 102; edits *Rural Bureau Notes*, 147; and NCRLC finances, 144; and NCRLC internal conflicts of 1930s, 130–39, 149, 152–53; and NCRLC propaganda, 148; on 1932 election, 92; and parent educator movement, 78; radio broadcasts, 142
"School for Living," 103, 122
Schools. *See* education
Schumacher, E. F., 209
Scopes trial, 73
Scots: ethnics in United States, 16t2, 19
Sears Foundation, Sears-Roebuck Foundation 173, 327
Seattle, Wash., 221
SEDOS, 211
Seedskadee Project, 283
Servites, 49
Shapiro, Edward S., 95, 97, 98
Shaughnessy, Bp. Gerald, 8, 80
Sheen, Bp. Fulton, 141
Sherman Anti-Trust Act, 302
Shields, Mark, 258
Singapore, 217
Sinsinawa Mound, Wis., 23
Sioux Falls, S.D., diocese of, 247, 252
Sisters of the Blessed Sacrament, 330

Sisters of the Earth, 346
Sisters of the Holy Family, 330
Sisters of St. Joseph, 339
Skylstad, Bp. William S., 257, 296, 324
Small Is Beautiful (E. F. Schumacher), 209
Smith, Al, 73–74
Smith, Carol Richardson, 339–40
Smithfield Foods, 222
Social Action Department (of NCWC): cooperation with NCRLC on migrant workers, 318; organizational link with NCRLC, 51; as organizational superior of Rural Life Bureau, 39–41, 53; and Parish Credit Union National Committee, 88; relations with NCRLC, 149; represented at formation of NCRLC, 49; spearhead in development of Catholic "social gospel," 86; view on Catholic rural population problem, 59. *See also* Rural Life Bureau (of NCWC); Ryan, Msgr. John A.
Social Development and World Peace, Department of (USCC), 294
"Social Reconstruction: A General Review of the Problems and Survey of Remedies." *See* Bishops' Program of Reconstruction
Social Security Act: 146, 276; Social Security benefits, 318; social security programs, 97
Society of Missionary Catechists of Our Blessed Lady of Victory, 7
Society for the Propagation of the Faith of Lyons and Paris, 7
Soil and Water Resources Conservation Act, 343
Soil Conservation Act, 124, 127
Soil Conservation Service, 343
Soil (Soil and Water) Stewardship Week, 341, 344
Solutions to Employment Problems. *See* STEP program
Somoza, Anastasio, 218
South Africa, 211
South Bend, Ind., 112
Southern Consumers' Cooperative, 326
Southern Tenant Farmers Union, 125
Southwest Indian Foundation, 334
Soviet Union. *See* Russia
Spain, 46, 155, 194, 204
Spalding, Bp. John Lancaster, 9–10
Spalding, Neb., 12

398   Index

Spanish. *See* Hispanics
Spanish Mission Band, 320
Speltz, Bp. George H., 249, 274
Spokane, Wash., 140
Springfield, Ill., 76, 77, 88: diocese of, 186, 292
Springfield, Ore., 63
Staley, Oren Lee, 301–302
Stark, Rodney, 359
Statement on the Present Crisis (U.S. Catholic hierarchy), 150
Stearns County, Minn., 11, 17, 166, 323
Stephan, Msgr. Joseph, 23
STEP (Solutions to Employment Problems) program, 314
Stillman, Chauncey, 172–73, 189, 229, 243
Stockton, Calif., 320
Strangers and Guests (Midwest rural Catholic bishops), 245, 248, 291, 334
Stratton Bill, 187
Strecker, Abp. Ignatius J., 241–44, 249, 251, 253–54, 256
Subsistence Homesteads Division, 107–8, 110, 111
Survey of Catholic Weakness (NCRLC), 82–83
Sustainable Agriculture and Rural Development Initiative (SARD), 209
Sustainable Agriculture Working Group (SAWG), 306, 345
Sweden, 351
Swiss: ethnics in United States, 3, 15, 16t2, 17

Taff, Paul C., 43, 165
Taylor, Jay, 183
Technical Cooperation Administration (TCA), 210
Terminiello, Rev. A. W., 112, 120
Terrebone, La., 126
Theology of Land conferences (project), 250–51, 254, 267, 309, 341–43
This Land Is Home to Me (Catholic bishops of Appalachia), 248, 328
Three Mile Island, Pa., 355
Time to Act, A (U.S. Department of Agriculture), 282
Timpe, Rev. George, 110–11
Tishomingo, Okla., 111
Tobacco Road (Erskine Caldwell), 124
Tocqueville, Alexis de, 339
Toledo, Ohio, diocese of, 258, 323, 348

"Tools for Freedom," 196
Truman, Harry S, 190, 192, 198
Tufano, Victoria M., 259
Turkey, 212
Tyson (company), 352

Udall, Stewart, 284
Uncommon Network, 340
United Farm Workers (UFW), 235, 321–24
United Nations: 197, 198, 207, 218; Declarations on a New International Economic Order (NIEO), 220. *See also* Food and Agriculture Organization (FAO) (of United Nations)
United States Catholic Conference (USCC): 265; becomes United States Conference of Catholic Bishops, 258; coordinator for rural issues, 235; division of responsibilities between NCRLC and, 256; financial aid to NCRLC, 236, 242, 252, 255; on minority farm ownership, 333; NCRLC as a division of, 172, 236, 242; NCRLC participation in social ministry gathering of, 258, 263; "Policy Statement on the Family Farm," 275; statement on Central America, 218; statement *Renewing the Earth*, 342; statement on Indians, 334; statement on reclamation law, 284. *See also* Social Development and World Peace, Department of (USCC)
United States Catholic Miscellany, 11
United States Census, 14, 34, 58, 73
United States Conference of Catholic Bishops (USCCB), 258, 261, 297, 350. *See also* National Conference of Catholic Bishops (NCCB); United States Catholic Conference (USCC)
Upper Midwest Sustainable Campus Association, 339

Vanishing Homesteads (Edgar Schmiedeler), 115
Vatican II (council), 79, 153, 167, 169, 181, 205, 214, 231, 265–70, 341, 364
Vietnam, Vietnam War, 208–9, 218, 315
Venezuela, 178
Vincennes, Ind., 114, 140
VISTA (Volunteers in Service to America), 314
Vizzard, Rev. James L., S.J.: 265, 361; back-

ground, 233; on cooperatives, 290; criticism of Farm Bureau, 299; and Democratic Party, 297–98; on family farm, 274; and National Association of Manufacturers, 314; and NCRLC financial and organizational crisis of late 1950s, 224, 228–30; NCRLC Washington representative, 157, 173, 233–35; and National Council of Agricultural Life and Labor, 318; for new Country Life Commission, 284; on reclamation law acreage limitation, 283–84; and STEP program, 314; on "too many farmers" issue, 306–8; on VISTA, 314; work for migrant farm workers, 233–34, 318–22, 327
Volunteers in Service to America. *See* VISTA

Wakin, Edward, 363–64
Wallace, Henry, 124
Walloons: ethnics in United States, 12
Ward, Rev. Leo L., C.S.C., 121
Warner, Keith, O.F.M., 343
War on Poverty, 313–15, 325, 327–28, 333, 334
War Relief Services—NCWC, 188–89, 192–94. *See also* Catholic Relief Services
Warren, Louis, 172
Warsaw, Neb., 12
Washington, D.C.: 55, 64, 196, 236, 241, 253, 258, 263, 279, 290, 304, 305; NCRLC representative (office) in, 156, 157, 173, 233–35, 242, 297; Rural Life Bureau office in, 131, 133
"Washington Farm Front" (column in NCRLC periodicals), 157
Washington Grove, Md., 29
Washington Memorandum, 235
Washington Theological Union, 241
Washita Farms. *See* Tishomingo, Okla.
Waste Management, Inc., 349
"Water: Essential for Justice and Peace" (joint statement), 348
Watson, Tom, 43
Watt, James, 345
Weber, Msgr. John George: 206, 224; background, 232; and farm organizations, 302–304; as NCRLC executive secretary, 230, 232–33, 235–37, 242; and NCRLC international fund, 243

Weber, Leonard, 222
Wehrle, Bp. Vincent, 48, 49, 72
Wellmark Foundation, 261
Welsh: ethnics in United States, 16t2
Welsh, Mary. *See* Mary Welsh Fund
Wendy's (company), 352
Westlands Project, 284
Westphalia, Iowa, 120, 290
Wheat Farming Corporation, 123
Where Shall the People Live? (USCC), 307
White House Office of Faith-Based and Community Initiatives, 270
White, Kathleen, 235
White, Rev., Norm, 292
"Who Is My Neighbor?" (NCRLC), 289
Wichita, Kan., 142
Wickard, Claude, 183
Williams, Katherine, 64
Willie, Louis J., 137
Willinger, Bp. Aloysius, 321
Wilson, M. L., 107, 141, 183
Wilson, Woodrow, 28
"Women, Land, and Legacy," 340
Wood, Rev. William J., S.J., 257, 335, 341–42, 343
Woodbine, Iowa, 138
"Work of Our Hands" (NCRLC), 340
World Food Conference, 197–98
World Food Program. *See* Food and Agriculture Organization (FAO) (of United Nations)
World Food Summit: 223; World Food Summit +5, 220–21
World Trade Organization (WTO), 220–22
World Vision, 196
World War I, 13, 28, 34, 330
World War II, 83, 143, 153, 176, 182–91, 192–95, 271–72, 275, 363
Woznicki, Bp. Stephen S., 229, 234, 353

Yakima, Wash.: 325; Yakima Valley, 257
York County, S.C., 173, 189–90
York County Produce Company, 189–90
Young Christian Agriculturists (France and Belgium), 166
Yzermans, Msgr. Vincent A., 153, 224–27

Zeitler, Rev. John, 196, 218

The Church & the Land: The National Catholic Rural Life Conference and American Society, 1923–2007, was designed and typeset in Dante by Kachergis Book Design of Pittsboro, North Carolina. It was printed on 60-pound House Natural Smooth and bound by Sheridan Books of Ann Arbor, Michigan.